Norman Podhoretz

A Biography

This is the first biography of the Jewish-American intellectual Norman Podhoretz, longtime editor of the influential magazine *Commentary*. As both an editor and a writer, he spearheaded the countercultural revolution of the 1960s and – after he "broke ranks" – the neoconservative response. For years he defined what was at stake in the struggle against communism; recently he has nerved America for a new struggle against jihadist Islam; and always he has given substance to debates over the function of religion, ethics, and the arts in our society.

The turning point of his life occurred at the age of forty, near a farm-house in upstate New York, in a mystic clarification. It compelled him to "unlearn" much that he had earlier been taught to value, and it also made him enemies.

Revealing the private as well as the public Podhoretz, Thomas L. Jeffers chronicles a heroically coherent life.

Thomas L. Jeffers, a Yale Ph.D. and a professor of literature at Marquette University, earlier taught at Cornell and Harvard, where he was a Mellon Fellow. Author of *Samuel Butler Revalued* (1981) and *Apprenticeships: The Bildungsroman from Goethe to Santayana* (2005), he has also published pieces in numerous journals, including the *Yale Review*, the *Hudson Review*, *Raritan*, and *Commentary*. In 2004 he edited *The Norman Podhoretz Reader*, which provided the inspiration for this book.

This book is dedicated to my mother,
Viberta Lorraine Jeffers,
and to the memory of my father-in-law,
Norman B. Livermore, Jr. (1911–2006)

Norman Podhoretz

A Biography

THOMAS L. JEFFERS

CAMBRIDGE UNIVERSITY PRESS
Cambridge, New York, Melbourne, Madrid, Cape Town, Singapore,
São Paulo, Delhi, Dubai, Tokyo, Mexico City

Cambridge University Press
32 Avenue of the Americas, New York, NY 10013-2473, USA

www.cambridge.org
Information on this title: www.cambridge.org/9780521198141

First published 2010

Printed in the United States of America

A catalog record for this publication is available from the British Library.

Library of Congress Cataloging in Publication data

Jeffers, Thomas L., 1946–
Norman Podhoretz : a biography / Thomas L. Jeffers.
    p.   cm.
Includes bibliographical references and index.
ISBN 978-0-521-19814-1 (hbk.)
1. Podhoretz, Norman.   2. Intellectuals – United States – Biography.
3. Jews – United States – Biography.   4. Editors – United States – Biography.
5. Authors, American – Biography.   6. Conservatism – United States – History.
7. Liberalism – United States – History.   8. United States – Intellectual life.   9. United States –
Politics and government – 1945–1989.   10. United States – Politics and government – 1989–
I. Title.
CT275.P66824J44   2010
973.931092 – dc22   [B]

2010014791

ISBN 978-0-521-19814-1 Hardback

Excerpts from the letters of Lionel Trilling, part of the Lionel Trilling Papers housed
at the Butler Rare Books and Manuscripts Library, Columbia University,
Copyright © by Lionel Trilling, reprinted with permission of The Wylie Agency LLC.

Contents

Illustrations

Acknowledgments

I wish to acknowledge the assistance of Norman Podhoretz himself, who granted me permission to quote from his letters and papers, gave me hours of interviews, and, crucially, left me free to make of everything what I would; of his wife, Midge Decter, who not only offered me interviews but read through an early draft of this book; and of Neal Kozodoy, Podhoretz's second-in-command at *Commentary* for nearly thirty years and editor-in-chief for thirteen years thereafter. Having let me loose in the magazine's archive, Kozodoy also read this book in draft, helping me condense and sharpen the narrative. Three foundations – the Bradley, the Achelis & Bodman, and one wishing to remain anonymous – either paid my travel expenses or bought me out of some teaching assignments, which gave me time to read and write. Finally, a pair of Marquette University deans paid my permissions fees. I am deeply grateful to them and, finally, to my wife, Pauli, who, vetting these pages, often put her finger on what an "outsider" would need to know.

Prologue

It has been difficult for many people to get a handle on the Jewish-American intellectual Norman Podhoretz. When he started out as a writer in New York in the fifties, his friend, the novelist Norman Mailer, admiringly called him the "hanging judge" of literary criticism, while others – the novelist Saul Bellow and the poet John Berryman – thought him much too big for his britches. Fifty years on, neoconservatives – intellectuals who began as liberals but then changed their minds – regard him as an icon speaking truth, whether about democracy's struggle against totalitarians, the promise of America, the condition of Western culture, or the essence of Judaism. Liberal intellectuals, for their part, remain wedded to their idea of him as a warmonger – a "zany" hysteric, as one put it recently, with a "toughness problem."[1]

In most academic neighborhoods, "neoconservative" is a sort of swear word. Intellectuals in general, especially Jewish-American ones, are nearly always liberals, and liberals are supposed to be the children of light – tolerant, fair, charitable people whose bumper stickers declare that "war is not the answer." How can an enlightened American intellectual, Jewish or otherwise, call himself a conservative, with or without a prefix?

Much of the interest in Podhoretz's career lies in this apparent incongruity. He started out as a liberal but then "broke ranks." Why? That is one of the questions this biography seeks to answer. It is the story of how Podhoretz's experience of life, and the endless thought he has devoted to understanding that experience, led to a great "unlearning." His relentlessly honest articulation of that process over the decades, while making him the figure liberals love to hate, has more tellingly made him a uniquely valuable witness, surely one of the most important in our cultural history.

Podhoretz is important for four reasons. The first is that from 1960 to 1995 he edited *Commentary*. In the late seventies the *Economist* called it, "with just the prudent hedging of a question mark," the "world's best magazine?"[2] By the early nineties it was, for the *Washington Post*, "America's most consequential journal of ideas." Podhoretz had raised it to that eminence initially by getting out in front of the countercultural and New Left revolutions of the sixties – promoting the social critic Paul Goodman, Mailer, and others – and then in "breaking ranks" by helping to instigate the *counter*-countercultural and anti-leftist revolutions of the seventies and beyond, when contributors like Daniel Patrick Moynihan, Jeane Kirkpatrick, Milton Himmelfarb, Robert Alter, and others registered their principled, reasoned dissent from what was being touted as politically, aesthetically, or morally correct. Whether the subject was the nature of class in America, the question of America's role in the world, the job of the intellectual in public life, the struggle between the liberal and conservative visions of the world, the proper ends of education, the stance of the artist versus the interests of society, the war between the sexes or the generations, the interests of the Jews, or the place of Judaism – no particular reason to stop here – month after month, Podhoretz's *Commentary* had something urgent and original to say that no thinking person could ignore.

That is the second reason Podhoretz is important: what he published in *Commentary* and what he wrote under his own name helped significantly shape the form and often the substance of American public discourse. If this was true when it came to defining, with consummate clarity, what was at stake in the Cold War against Soviet totalitarianism and, more recently, in the hot war against jihadist Islam, it was no less so when it came to the boiling-hot quarrels among intellectuals over the place and function of religion, ethics, culture, and the arts.

The third reason for Podhoretz's distinction is that he has been so strong a *literary* voice. He came to public notice in the fifties as a book reviewer – Mailer's "hanging judge" – his acumen raising him to the editorship of *Commentary* at age thirty. At later periods of his career, he has shown an undiminished ability to "crack" a novelist's, a historian's, or a fellow critic's work, revealing not just its qualities but its meaning and its status. But beyond that he has *created* literature, primarily in the mode of autobiography. His reminiscences – *Making It, Breaking Ranks, Ex-Friends*, and *My Love Affair with America* – stirred controversy in their day, in part because they refought the battles of a fascinating coterie, the New York Intellectuals. Those battles were entertaining, at least in the retelling, for they were waged not just in print but in the apartments and restaurants where, from the fifties through the early seventies, these intellectuals, many if not most of them Jewish, spent so much time talking "about people who weren't there." So quipped the sociologist James Q. Wilson, who, living in Southern California, added: "Of course we spend a lot of time doing that out here, but we just call it gossip, not literature. The New York Intellectuals *made* it literature."[3]

It would, however, be a mistake to suppose that Podhoretz's writerly achievement was the mere elevation of gossip into literature. As George Weigel, the Catholic thinker, remarked: "Norman's importance as an American intellectual and cultural figure far transcends the question of whether people thought *Making It* was pissing in their soup, or what scores were being settled in *Ex-Friends* – the proper subtitle of which, if one wanted to be cruel, might have been 'I spit on your grave!'" What mattered, Weigel believed, was Podhoretz's work "in a prophetic rather than a political mode." His "rabbinic determination to be a truth-teller, the most enduring thing about him, accounts for what others take to be his inconsistencies."[4]

That is the fourth reason for studying Podhoretz's career. He has been a kind of prophet, putting his finger on the underlying issues that have agitated his times and insisting on locating and arguing for the truth about them as he sees it. As with the truth-telling Hebrew prophets whom he studied in his teens, and about whom he would write a book in his seventies, his mature ideas about politics, society, and culture were wrapped in a larger, overarching vision of the nature and purpose of human existence. In his case, that vision came into full focus, at the age of forty near a farmhouse in upstate New York, in a kind of mystic clarification that proved to be the hinge event of his personal and intellectual life, compelling him to "unlearn" much that he had been taught to value while apprehending afresh, now as an urgent and integrated whole, much that he had turned his back on. From that point forward he would remain faithful to what had been revealed to him, and to its demands.

Is it any wonder that, again like those Hebrew prophets of old, he made enemies? The novelist and critic Cynthia Ozick remembered walking with him down a mall in Copenhagen:

[T]he sun was low in the sky, the glare was so intense as we walked into it. I have no idea what we were talking about, but I remember Norman said – it hit me very hard and stayed with me – "It's important to have enemies, because everything depends on the *kind* of enemies you have." It was perhaps late in my life, never to have encountered that idea before, but he said it with such passion and precision, with a kind of prophetic clarity, that I've never forgotten.[5]

It needs only to be added that, in emphatic contrast with the biblical prophets, this one never did manage to shed his sense of irony, his sardonic wit, or his quintessentially American boyishness. To the British man of letters John Gross, who recalled meeting him in the fifties, he was like nothing so much as "a character I'd expect to see in the sort of Hollywood movies I really like, the kid from around the block with all that intellectual energy, immensely likable, almost in the Mickey Rooney style, which suited me down to the ground."[6] In this sense he never changed at all.

My own acquaintance with Podhoretz began about twenty years ago with a belated reading of *Making It*, the memoir he published in 1968. I thought it not just beautifully written – evocative of episodes and characters typical of my own, and many people's, growing-up years, and often very funny – but also astute in its judgments about my own specialty, literature. He had begun as a literary critic but, as I soon discovered while following his writings in *Commentary*, he was also a sharp polemicist in debates about our culture and our politics. Again I found him astute, even if I wasn't always prepared to embrace his conclusions. I kept an open mind, however, for I knew there were subjects, especially those having to do with American foreign policy and the wars Israel had been constrained to fight in the Middle East, about which I understood only, as they say, what I read in the newspapers. And the newspapers were so absorbed in the sensational – terrorist attacks and police responses, the threat of a great-power shoot-out and the demonstrations against nuclear weapons – that like most citizens I wasn't confident about the underlying principles.

As I went on reading Podhoretz, however – *Breaking Ranks*, *The Present Danger*, *Why We Were in Vietnam*, *The Bloody Crossroads*, *Ex-Friends*, all published between 1979 and 2000 – I felt my comprehension of those principles deepen. Certainly my admiration for his lucidity in exposition, and his fearlessness in argument, continued to grow, and when, using *My Love Affair with America* as a point of departure, I did a long essay on him for the *Hudson Review*,[7] I felt the satisfaction of having tried to present an embattled writer in terms as critically dispassionate as I could.

But it was a mere outline. I did not know the man, wasn't sure how to pronounce his name, and had never met any of the friends and ex-friends he wrote about. I was beginning to grasp his motives as a writer, however, and often to feel instructed – even convinced. After editing *The Norman Podhoretz Reader* (2004), I thought myself equipped to attempt what you have here – a critical biography. My being neither a Jew nor a political thinker would be an advantage: I could explain to a mixed audience the sometimes arcane material I myself had needed to learn. In any case, I would try to put all of Podhoretz's activities – the many sides of his mental, emotional, and spiritual life – together.

Through interviews, I came to know the man, his family, and many of his enduring friends. His ex-friends had either died or didn't return phone calls, but they had published a great deal about him, and by the time I had gone through the voluminous cache of papers he gave to the Library of Congress and the correspondence in the archives at *Commentary* and elsewhere, I had material for a book many times larger than this. The man at the center of it was neither a monster nor an icon, but a human being engaged with the world. Not an abstract thinker standing above the mire, Podhoretz has been a son, friend, enemy, husband, father, grandfather, doubter, and believer who has known the full range of human emotions – and who, through stresses that would have broken a merely ordinary person, has achieved a heroical integrity.

I

Brownsville

Norman Podhoretz was born on January 16, 1930, in the Brownsville section of Brooklyn, New York. His father, Julius Podhoretz, had come to America in 1912 at age sixteen, his mother Helen in 1920 at age seventeen. They were distant cousins, introduced by relatives in America. Nearly everyone in the extended family entered into traditionally brokered wedlock with some cousin or other,[1] but the Julius–Helen marriage in 1923 was a newfangled love-match. The family came from Galicia, which during World War I had been conquered by Cossacks and occupied by Russians. Helen, the oldest of five children, had to take care of everyone, including her mother, "a useless woman" who, Podhoretz has written, "made a habit of passing out every Friday night before the onset of the Sabbath, thereby leaving my humiliated but brassy preteen mother to run shouting through the village, 'Mama just fainted again, please come help.'" The anecdote gives a glimpse of the travails undergone by a girl whose father ("a mean prick," according to his grandson) had emigrated to America just before the war broke out.[2]

The "prick" was M'shitzik Woliner, "a *bayzer Yid*, an angry Jew," a Hasid who never smiled. He grew more devout with age, and Norman would later joke that "since the 613 commandments binding upon a pious Jew were not enough for him, he had invented new ones, like a prohibition against whistling, which he was firmly convinced had been ordained by God." Reunited in America, M'shitzik and his wife Esther (née Malkah) lived together in "a loathing so intense that [they] literally ceased speaking to each other until death did them part."

When Norman's paternal grandfather, Yidl Podhoretz, came to America, he didn't change his family name, though it is difficult for most people to pronounce. (The right way is Pod-hór-etz, aspirating the "h."[3]) In Europe he had married a girl named Runyeh, who bore him five sons, including Julius. In America, however, Yidl and Runyeh separated, mainly because of the suicide of her sister, for which Runyeh held Yidl responsible. So she walked out with her youngest son and all her pots and pans, and moved without invitation into

1

FIGURE 1. Julius and Helen Podhoretz at their wedding, 1923.

Norman's parents' small apartment. The guilt-laden, abandoned Yidl would take the trolley from lower Manhattan to Brooklyn and, according to Norman, would lurk "across the street from our apartment building in order to catch a glimpse of the infant grandson (me) he adored but could never again embrace." He died in 1934 of a bronchial infection he was too dispirited to fight. Runyeh died of cancer in 1938.

One mustn't forget how alien such older folk would look in "native" American eyes. Podhoretz's grandfathers were like many of their generation, "with their full beards and sidecurls, dressed in long black coats and hats to match," while his grandmothers wore "unadorned ankle-length dresses and *shaytlach* (the wigs – cheap, rarely washed, and often smelling unpleasant – that married women were required to wear)."[4] None learned to speak much English, and they were largely ignorant of America's role in the larger world – including the

Europe they had all left. Thus, when her youngest son, Maxie, was drafted in World War II, Esther Malkah turned to her grandson Norman and cried: *"Ver iz er, der Uncle Sam? Im hob ikh extra in dr'erd!"* ("Who is he, this Uncle Sam? Him I would especially like to send six feet under.") Beyond her comprehension was that Uncle Sam was calling Maxie to fight against Hitler, Nazism, and the "final solution." She only knew she had to defend her cubs, and to the death. And so, some years after Maxie was drafted, she "got herself killed by not hesitating an instant in chasing her two-year-old granddaughter [Norman's cousin Sharon] . . . into the street and throwing her own body between the child and an approaching automobile."[5]

Maxie was but one of a dozen or more relations who went into the army. Not one was killed or wounded, and this, Podhoretz would later write, only "helped bolster the romantic fantasies I entertained about going to war and giving my all for 'the land of the brave and the free.'" Like the other underage kids in the neighborhood, he recycled "silver foil from cigarette packs" and saved "dimes for stamps that slowly grew into $25 war bonds." For Podhoretz, as for his wife-to-be, Midge Rosenthal, it was "Oh, What a Lovely War," a time of uncomplicated patriotism. With the war's end came "a touch of regret. Now I would never get a chance to find out what it was like to be a soldier fighting for my country and whether I was man enough to take it."[6]

The Yiddish spoken by parents and grandparents was the language of the *shtetlakh*, the towns and villages of Russian and East European territories, including the Podhoretzes' Galicia. Small wonder, therefore, that with his peculiar Yiddish-inflected accent, young Norman was often mistaken for a "greenhorn" just off the boat. The "embarrassment and indignation" he felt was relieved directly after he enrolled at Public School 28. The kindergartener had somehow gotten lost and was climbing a staircase alone, looking for his classmates, when a teacher spotted him and asked where he was going. "I goink op de stez," he replied, and was directly marched to the principal's office and "placed in a remedial-speech class." It was universally agreed in that era of the "melting pot" that, besides inculcating habits of personal hygiene, the school's job was "to burn out our foreign impurities and turn us into real Americans" – that is, to sound "more like an announcer on one of the 'coast-to-coast' radio programs of the thirties than like a kid from a Brooklyn slum."[7]

The Brooklyn slum was one-third Jewish immigrants, one-third Italian immigrants, and one-third blacks, who had only recently come up from the South. The Podhoretzes lived at 2027 Pacific Street. Nearby were many of their aunts, uncles, and cousins. The Podhoretzes' small apartment was a lodestone because, though everyone was poor during the Depression, Julius, unlike a third of the country's working-age men, had a steady job. He was a milkman for Sheffield Farms, sleeping during the day and at night driving a horse and wagon to deliver bottles of milk and pick up the empty ones.

Because Julius earned between $2,000 and $3,000 a year, the immediate family was spared the shame of being "on relief" like many of their neighbors. Even a milkman's salary "could buy a lot of groceries": hence the frequent lodgers and, on holidays and weekends, hungry visitors converging from the Bronx or from other neighborhoods in Brooklyn.

Quizzing, cajoling, charming, and cooking for them all was Norman's mother, who would later recall how "In those days, I was a queen! A queen!"[8] – a "very pretty" queen, according to Midge Decter, "lively like anything, and extremely clever."[9] She was "a great raconteuse, maybe the best that I've ever known," Norman remembered, "and she would hold the audience spell-bound." The men would let her into their card games, where she more than held her own. That would be in the kitchen, and while she was cooking for upward of a dozen people. There was noise everywhere, and "she was at the center of this, managing it."[10]

Julius Podhoretz's grandchildren would remember him as "a true intel-lectual," forever curious about the world. He read the Yiddish *Der Tog* ("The Day"), which was more elevated than the imperatively titled *Forvertz* ("Forward") with its "pidgin-Yiddish" and leftist politics. A Zionist, he never went in for the socialism or communism that dominated the thinking of most immigrant Jews in New York. When Norman's sister, Millie, enrolled in the American Youth for Democracy, a Stalinist front, her father "constantly berated her for caring more about the fate of the Negroes in America than for her own people, which were, he kept telling her, just then being persecuted to a greater extent in Europe."

Norman's father had some understanding of, as well as pride in, what his son became. His mother, however, would never understand what her adult son actually *did*, and since her husband didn't "deign to explain," she was handicapped in the bragging game mothers played. "So what is he? A joinalist?" her friends would ask. Looking at the semiexotic literati around Norman, she would murmur, "I should have made him for a dentist," since dentists tended to remain in the neighborhoods where they grew up, only with a lot more money. When in the mid-fifties Norman wavered between taking a Ph.D. in English or going directly into the higher "joinalism," his mother urged him to take the Ph.D. It would be "something to fall back on" and, more importantly, people would call him "Doctor."[11]

"Queen" Helen had a true "prince" in Norman, who was quite as good-looking as his "extremely handsome" father[12] and was accordingly coddled and praised by all the women at home as well as by the female teachers at school. But if the boy was made to feel like a conqueror, his father, despite his Depression-era good fortune, became ultimately a defeated man. What happened was that Sheffield Farms abandoned the horse and wagon and began using trucks. Julius, who had never learned to drive, was too vain to take the necessary lessons; failing the driver's tests led to the humiliation of being fired, despite his being a member of the Teamsters Union. (Podhoretz remembers feeling "enormous indignation" at the union for "failing to protect him."[13])

Even when he was working for Sheffield Farms, Julius had slept most of the day, and therefore must have seemed an absent presence in Millie and Norman's lives. Still, his influence – dark and underground – is palpable in Norman's

FIGURE 2. Norman Podhoretz at age two, with his sister, Millie, 1932.

fulfillment of the intellectual aspirations he vaguely harbored. Decter indeed would declare, looking back, that unlike most of his fellow intellectual "young men from the provinces" who moved to metropolitan centers, Norman never "discarded or patronized" his father, particularly his father's Jewishness.[14] Though Julius went to synagogue only on the high holy days, he took his people's culture very seriously. When he had a heart attack at age forty-nine and seemed to be dying in the hospital, he got his son to promise to attend the Jewish Theological Seminary (JTS). The idea wasn't to qualify as a rabbi but to become knowledgeable about Hebrew, the Bible, Talmudic law and commentary, and Jewish history, philosophy, and literature. A Jew with brains should master the intellectual tradition of his people.

His father's presence is seen also during the commencement ceremonies at Norman's graduation from Boys High. As we will shortly see, he had already won a tuition-only scholarship to Harvard that he couldn't afford to accept, and he had lost hope of winning a Pulitzer Scholarship to Columbia. It looked as though his destination would be his third choice, New York University. Then, as he remembered, "at the graduation itself, the principal said he had an

FIGURE 3. Norman Podhoretz's Bar Mitzvah portrait, 1943.

announcement to make and he read this letter" announcing that Norman had been awarded a Pulitzer Scholarship after all. Very dramatic, "and you know, it was just – my father just was hysterical."[15]

But in reality Norman's father was in a bad way. In 1947 he and Helen owned a commission bakery in Brooklyn, an outlet for the rolls, cakes, and fresh loaves baked at a larger facility nearby. Working fourteen hours a day, they barely scraped by. Julius would fall asleep behind the counter, while Helen – all the customers loved her – ran the shop. She began, for the first time, to lose respect for him. When the business failed, he lapsed into a depression that lasted nearly twenty-five years until his death, at seventy-five, in 1971. With the heart attack, serious prostate trouble, and emphysema, he had little to offer any employer. His last job, in his sixties, was humiliatingly that of a messenger boy.

Whatever their troubles, Norman's parents made a cohesive pair, giving him and his sister a lovingly supportive home in which to grow up. So what if Norman had to share his bed with an uncle or a cousin, or do his homework at the kitchen table while his mother and her cronies gossiped away? Home was still a haven, and the schools assigning the homework were safe and nurturing. The only dangerous turf lay in the streets, where Jews, Italians, and blacks unpeacefully coexisted.

As Podhoretz would record in his much-reprinted essay "My Negro Problem – and Ours" (1963), the turf wasn't contested according to liberal stereotypes. For one thing, it wasn't rich whites oppressing poor blacks: *everyone* was poor. For another, to a Jewish kid it was the blacks who had the upper hand on the street, where Podhoretz was on several occasions mugged. Hostilities began in third grade, when a black boy, formerly his best friend, hit him after school "and announced that he wouldn't play with me any more because I had killed Jesus." Then there was the playground. The black kids would win a fight and the white kids would "retreat, half whimpering, half with bravado. My first nauseating experience of cowardice," Norman recalled.

Interethnic or inter-racial scuffles are a common feature of Jewish memoirs from the early decades of the twentieth century.[16] A little guy, Podhoretz was nearly always afraid, but he quickly understood that the pain would be much worse if he ran away. As the sportswriter Frank Deford said in a piece about Hall of Fame boxer Billy Conn and his wife, "Big guys grow up figuring nobody will challenge them, so they don't learn how to fight. . . . Little guys are the ones who learn to fight because they figure they had better."[17] In the Brooklyn streets, "I got beaten up a couple of times, and I don't think I ever really won a fight," Podhoretz confessed, "but I was good or staunch enough to hold my own and not be totally humiliated. It was okay to be beaten, as long as you didn't run away." Besides, he added, "It was good training for the life I was to lead."[18]

If giving ground was unthinkable, so was winning – at least on the streets. In the classroom it was different. What counted were intellectual credentials, and Podhoretz's were evident early on. He had an excellent ear. In elementary and middle school he memorized the heavily accented, masculinely rhymed works of Joyce Kilmer and Rudyard Kipling; his own poetic juvenilia, "fortunately" (as he said) lost, imitated them. Later came the subtler verse of Thomas Gray's "Elegy Written in a Country Churchyard," a 1750 classic lamenting the unrealized promise of the poor folk buried beneath simple gravestones – this "flower . . . born to blush unseen." Like many young readers of that elegy, Podhoretz wanted to "blush" – to blossom – in a way that people would notice.

The strength of his ambition was plain in the weeks after his parents bought, on installment, a Smith-Corona typewriter for Millie. She had been persuaded to take the "commercial" curriculum in high school since after all she would be getting married and, before that, would probably work as a secretary.[19] The Smith-Corona was supposed to help her learn to type, and it did. But her kid brother claimed the typewriter for himself, Millie teaching him to use the expensive machine properly and "hat[ing] having to do so," Podhoretz has admitted, "especially as to her it seemed yet another mark of the greater favor in which our parents held me."[20] He soon became adept, first copying pieces from the newspaper and then composing his own poems and stories.

The books he most liked to read, in and out of school, were the ones that boys in the late thirties and early forties often liked: Andrew Lang's fairy books (his "euphonious style...was as mesmerizing as the stories"), Norse myths, the baseball novels of John R. Tunis, the adventure novels of Rafael Sabatini, "and countless others by authors whose names I have ungratefully forgotten," he added. Then there was a complete set of the works of Mark Twain, among the very few books (apart from a handful of Yiddish and Hebrew volumes) the family owned, no doubt purchased from a door-to-door salesman. Some of Twain was too difficult, but Podhoretz at once adored *The Adventures of Tom Sawyer*, despite its often adult vocabulary, and he would later be "proud to say that as a kid I was already a good enough literary critic to like *Adventures of Huckleberry Finn*, a much greater work, even more."[21]

Podhoretz was indeed precocious, and the educational establishment twice had him skip a grade, which meant he started junior high at age eleven. By then he had begun, on his own, to read, reread, and in many cases memorize poems in a paperback anthology, possibly given him by Millie or her fiancé, which was filled with uplifting works like Oliver Wendell Holmes's "Old Ironsides" and satirical, down-to-earth ones like Edwin Arlington Robinson's "Miniver Cheevy." In school, in the ninth grade, Podhoretz was, like millions of American students, required to read Shakespeare's *Julius Caesar* and found it very hard going. Not so, however, the sea-swells of Whitman's *Leaves of Grass*. He was "intoxicated...from the first" and was astonished when his most important teacher at Boys High, Mrs. Haft, informed him that it was time for him to drop Whitman and pick up the then cutting-edge T. S. Eliot, the slightly risqué Robinson Jeffers (*Roan Stallion*) and Djuna Barnes (*Nightwood*, which is about lesbianism), and finally the gold standard John Keats, a volume of whose poems she gave him on his fifteenth birthday.[22]

Mrs. Haft, memorialized as Mrs. K. in *Making It* (1968), was that indispensable teacher with whom many successful people have had the good fortune to study in high school. Boys High, where she worked, was once among the most celebrated of New York's public schools.[23] Her influence on Podhoretz is manifest in his devoting quite as many pages to her as to Lionel Trilling or F. R. Leavis, his principal teachers at Columbia and Cambridge, respectively. Those renowned critics recognized in him a tyro who might become like themselves, but they would never have been so impressed if he hadn't first been brought along by Harriet Cashmore Haft.

The Cashmores were an "old Brooklyn" WASP family. After an education at Vassar, Harriet had married an elderly, wealthy, well-assimilated German-Jewish businessman. They lived in Brooklyn Heights, the one section of Brooklyn "fashionable enough to be intimidating," and she occasionally invited her star pupil for visits that may well have been against school rules. Childless, she was in her early forties at the time. While Podhoretz would read her his poems and hear about her own education or "about writers she had met," old

Haft would sit reading a newspaper. He wore "the first *pince-nez* I had ever seen outside the movies," and, in response to Podhoretz's "tearful editorial for the school newspaper on the death of Roosevelt" – the "happy warrior" was the boy's hero – he delivered a "blasphemous" harangue against that betrayer of the American plutocracy.

If Mr. Haft could have seen his wife's pet student out on the streets, he might have reached for his whip. Though the boy never expressed anything like disrespect toward his parents or teachers, he did have a naughty side. As Decter puts it, "he was always doing things that his mother would have died had she known,"[24] such as jumping off the roof of the one-story laundry behind their building or, in that rougher version of River City, hanging out at a pool hall where the tables were a front for "professional gamblers, hustlers, and bookies." The legal age for pool-hall admission was sixteen, but Podhoretz at fourteen would sneak in just to look big.[25]

An alpha student in all subjects but physics, Podhoretz did what was expected, and then he had fun. Even in prepubescence, he and his best friend, "Mutt," formed a Casanova Club, the chief activity being necking with girlfriends. These initiatory gropings sound innocuous enough in *Making It*, where Podhoretz elaborately thanks "a series of quietly smoldering rabbis' daughters ... who (blessings upon them all) made my adolescent sex life far more abundant than the fiercely pragmatic chastity of the girls in my own neighborhood would otherwise have permitted."[26] In truth, however, he had by age seventeen made one of those neighborhood girls pregnant. When she told her "very religious" Jewish parents of her predicament, they insisted that she have an abortion, which required Podhoretz to take her to a back-street doctor in New Jersey. This was during his freshman year at Columbia, and he confided in his classics professor, Moses Hadas, who gave him the necessary money. It took the frightened couple two trips, for on the first try they were waylaid in the train station by an apparently friendly con man who, for a small fee, gave them a bum steer to a nonexistent doctor at a nonexistent address.[27]

There would be no unwanted baby or shotgun wedding. The academic star of Boys High and the Pulitzer Scholar of Columbia wasn't deliberately going to do anything that would bring ruin upon himself, his family, or a neighborhood girl who "thought I was a poet." But he was extremely fortunate to have been noticed by grown-ups who, if they couldn't exactly mandate responsible sexual practices, could at least sympathize, as Hadas did, and help out.

Back during Podhoretz's junior year in high school, Mrs. Haft's great inspiration was that he should do his senior year at Phillips Exeter Academy in New Hampshire, one of the most prestigious schools in the country. "They want to send me to boarding school," he told his mother. "What! Leave home? You're crazy!" she said. In later years he thought it was probably a lucky escape from the humiliations a scholarship boy would have had to endure. But it was just such humiliations that Mrs. Haft anticipated and wanted to minimize, all the more so when, as a senior, he began applying for scholarships to the best colleges.

Hoping to give him a bit of polish, she would take him to the Frick and Metropolitan museums to look at paintings, or to the theater to see *The Late George Apley*. She was determined that he should win a scholarship to Harvard, which is why, on one such excursion into New York, she sprang a change of plan on him, turning away from the Museum of Modern Art and taking him to the "college department" of a then famous preppie clothing shop. He would have to choose which set of externalities, as it were, he wanted to be associated with – the red satin jacket emblazoned with "Cherokee, S.A.C." (social athletic club) that was his habitual tough-guy outerwear or a blue blazer. It was a crisis that brought all his divided loyalties into archetypal collision:

I had never been inside such a store; it was not a store, it was enemy territory, every inch of it mined with humiliations. "I am," Mrs. K. declared in the coldest human voice I hope I shall ever hear, "going to buy you a suit that you will be able to wear at your Harvard interview." ... Oh no, I said in a panic (suddenly realizing that I *wanted* her to buy me that suit), I can't, my mother wouldn't like it. "You can tell her it's a birthday present. Or else I will tell her. If I tell her, I'm sure she won't object." The idea of Mrs. K. meeting my mother was more than I could bear: my mother, who spoke with a Yiddish accent and of whom, until that sickening moment, I had never known I was ashamed and so ready to betray.[28]

Somehow they left without buying anything.

From ages thirteen to sixteen, Podhoretz was the "pet" Mrs. Haft endeavored to civilize. "She flirted with me and flattered me, she scolded me and insulted me. Slum child, filthy little slum child, so beautiful a mind and so vulgar in manner."[29] If this were a nineteenth-century French novel, we might have a teacher trying to seduce her student. But his and Mrs. Haft's relation involved nothing sexual.[30] She was simply hoping to acculturate a promising boy. He liked to read, but had latched onto inferior authors. She gave him some hints about better ones. He seemed ambitious to learn about the world across the Brooklyn Bridge – the people of New York, their work, their talk, their habits – but he dressed like a "*konnabum*" (to use his father's Yiddishization of "corner bum"). If he would only listen to her, he might go to Harvard and enter "a life of elegance and refinement and taste."

The top students at Boys High took their gifts and achievements seriously. Podhoretz graduated third in his class (his so-so performance in physics cost him). The valedictorian was a refugee from Nazi Germany named Wolfgang Hallowitz, who later became William W. Hallo, "a big-league" professor of Assyriology and Sumerology at Yale. The salutatorian, whose name Podhoretz could not recall, eventually went to Harvard Medical School and became a psychiatrist. Just below Podhoretz on the slippery but finely calibrated pole was Carl Spielvogel, who graduated from Baruch College in 1952, went on to an extraordinarily successful career in advertising, and became Bill Clinton's

FIGURE 4. Cherokees, the "social athletic club," circa 1943 (Norman Podhoretz in upper right).

ambassador to Slovakia. Half a century on, this high achiever would still remember having been edged out of the number-three slot at Boys High. "I've hated you ever since," he more-than-half-seriously told Podhoretz during a chance meeting in a restaurant.[31]

In 1945, with no preppie clothes, all Podhoretz had for his college and scholarship interviews was a suit that had been handed down from an uncle, and it didn't fit. Still, his Harvard interview, and another at NYU, had gone well, and by commencement he had been offered tuition scholarships to both. But all his hopes were on the Pulitzer that would send him to Columbia. He had been nervous about the interview, where he confronted "three very dour looking men" who remained icy throughout.[32]

Icy but impressed. The Pulitzer gave him full tuition to Columbia plus a small stipend, which meant that, living at home, he would have money for books, the subway, and occasional meals on campus. "Everyone was consoled, even Mrs. K.: Columbia was at least in the Ivy League." And when he saw her again four years later, after she had read in the *Times* of the Kellett Fellowship that would take him to the older and "even better" Cambridge, she was very consoled indeed.[33]

Bright kids know that they ought "not to forget where they came from" –
a formula invariably applied to down-market origins. The up-market people
seem to have no difficulty remembering where *they* came from. Mrs. Haft
certainly remembered: she was forever reminding the students at Boys High
of her origins, and was implicitly inviting Podhoretz to forget – by rising
above them – his own. This he stubbornly resisted doing. Weren't manners and
clothes simply "a highly stylized set of surface habits and fashions" belonging to
WASPs? Didn't his own Galician-Jewish parents have greater tact and delicacy
(and more comfortable clothes)? Mrs. Haft would quote Cardinal Newman's
definition of a gentleman as a person who could be at ease in any company,
but "the gentleman" was in practice identical to "the genteel" – something
far removed from the lower depths of Brownsville, the Cherokees, and his
family.

The social terms of *that* "brutal bargain" Podhoretz consciously rejected.
At Columbia he continued to wear, if not the red satin jacket, then some
facsimile thereof. And, necessarily, he continued to live at home. "But the
joke was on me," as he later realized. While seeming not to care a fig about
clothes and devoting himself entirely to the life of the mind, he found that
his manners and his speech insensibly changed. He developed an even more
"neutrally American" accent than the Brooklyn public schools had promoted,
and his manners, while never preppie, were palpably more Ivy League than
Cherokee.[34] In his Boys High days, neighborhood women had told him that
"Ten years from now, you won't even want to talk to me, you won't even
recognize me if you pass me on the street." "'That's crazy, you must be kidding,'
I would answer. They were not crazy and they were not kidding. They were
simply better sociologists than I."[35]

And so, in the end, was Mrs. Haft. She insisted that taste in art was indistinguishable from taste in clothing or manners. He insisted, much less realistically,
that art and artists belonged to "some mystical country of the spirit and not
a place in the upper reaches of the American class structure." The mystical
country was supposed to be like the apostle Paul's Christian paradise, where
one was neither Jew nor Greek, neither rich nor poor. Podhoretz accordingly
wanted "not to be Jewish, but not to be Christian either; not to be a worker, but
not to be a boss either; not . . . to be a slum child but not to be a snob either."
What the Brownsville women and Mrs. Haft would not or could not explain he
gradually and painfully learned for himself: "that there was no socially neutral
ground to be found in the United States of America, and that a distaste for
the surroundings in which I was bred, and ultimately (God forgive me) even
for many of the people I loved," went along with "a taste for the poetry of
Keats and the painting of Cézanne and the music of Mozart," and therefore,
by an inexorable "logic," with a taste for the "kinds of people" who liked such
poetry, painting, and music.[36] Brutal bargain enough.

2

Columbia

Commuting from Brownsville to Columbia and the Jewish Theological Seminary, Podhoretz embodied, between 1946 and 1950, the cultural contradictions among them. Brownsville remained home, for he couldn't afford to live in a dorm or fraternity house. This was no cause for tears. The subway journey, ninety minutes each way, was a time for study, and he developed what he later called "the apparently imperishable faculty of reading with greater concentration and attention on moving vehicles than in such prosaic and conventional locations as arm-chairs, desks, beds, and the like."[1] He got along with his parents, went dutifully to visit relatives, and, whenever he could, still mixed with his Cherokee pals at the pool hall or on the street corner, even as they began working menial jobs or, in a few cases, taking night classes in accounting or engineering.

Between family and Cherokees there was always a separation, but not the kind that caused anguish. They stayed out of each other's way, and Podhoretz loved them both. As for the Jewish Theological Seminary, lots of bright Brooklyn boys went there, mostly but not invariably to study for the rabbinate.[2] That wasn't Podhoretz's goal. His maternal grandfather M'shitzik, the Hasid, had wanted him to go to a more traditional *yeshiva*, but his father would have none of it: "Had he cut off his own earlocks in order that his American son should grow a pair?" Julius Podhoretz was a leftist without being a socialist, a Yiddish speaker without being a Yiddishist, and a Zionist but of the dispassionate kind, and he wanted his son to be like himself: a nonobservant New World Jew who at the same time treasured the Hebraic tradition – "in short," as that son would write, "a Jewish survivalist, unclassifiable and eclectic."[3] Hence an after-hours Hebrew high school in Brooklyn starting at age twelve and his father's demand in 1945 that, whatever university his son might go to, he would at the same time attend JTS. Not one to procrastinate, Norman enrolled in the Seminary College while still a second-semester senior at Boys High.

At JTS, located six short blocks north of Columbia – for Podhoretz the walk was "like the journey from Paris to the provinces" – classes were held every

FIGURE 5. Norman Podhoretz with his mother at his Uncle Max's wedding, June 1946.

Tuesday and Thursday night from 6:00 to 10:00 and every Sunday afternoon from 1:00 to 6:00. H. L. Ginsberg's class in Bible and Abraham S. Halkin's in Jewish history were rigorous – both men were world-class scholars – but other classes consisted of "endless pep talks disguised as scholarship." As Podhoretz would later declare, "They were not training minds or sensibilities; they were training Jews."[4]

In his way the ultimately most famous figure at JTS was Abraham Joshua Heschel (1907–1972), whose book *The Prophets* (1962) would be one provocation for Podhoretz's own book of that title forty years later. Heschel was named after his grandfather, a Hasidic rebbe with a lively following in Poland. On discovering that Podhoretz's grandfather M'shitzik was also a Hasid, Heschel hoped his pupil might have some colorful tales to add to his collection of lore. But the pupil couldn't square what he knew of his grandfather with what Heschel said about Hasidim joyfully worshipping God through song and dance. "I thought 'What?!' I had never seen my grandfather *smile*, let alone sing or dance," Podhoretz would say. "So I wondered, 'What the hell is Heschel talking about? Maybe there's some Hasidic world out there that I don't know.'" In fact there had been, but for Podhoretz that wasn't the point. He was facing an early example of contradiction between his own experience and the authoritative line – in this case Heschel's "sentimentalized, romanticized" vision of an aspect of Jewish culture. He caught a whiff of "fraudulence" in the older man and, at JTS generally, of parochialism.

Between that and the cosmopolitan allure of Columbia, which he entered in the fall of 1946 at sixteen, it was no contest. Compared with the JTS curriculum, Columbia's seemed like a new-found land, and without any "No Jews Need Apply" signs. On the contrary, he was being invited to come all the way in. First, because he was an American, and American civilization was demonstrably an extension of Europe's and therefore an essential part of the West. Second, because as his soon-to-be mentor Lionel Trilling had learned from the Victorian Matthew Arnold, the West was a product of two traditions, the Hellenic and the Hebraic. The philosophical, political, and mathematical genius of the one had been coupled, in part through Christianity, with the theological and ethical genius of the other. Christianity's anti-Semitism, undeniably part of the record, was understood to be aberrant as well as abhorrent. Altogether, the message was not only that Jews had been contributors to and sustainers of Western culture but also that they could continue to play those roles.

The faculty included men such as Hadas, Irwin Edman, Mark Van Doren, Andrew Chiappe, F. W. "Fred" Dupee, and Trilling. One could find their counterparts at Harvard, Yale, Penn, or Princeton, but at those places one usually needed to be a graduate student to come anywhere near them, while at Columbia the distinguished professors taught both graduate and undergraduate students, and in small seminars. Not everyone at Columbia was philo-Semitic, of course, but the only manifestations of anti-Semitism Podhoretz noted came, in a self-hating genteel form, from his fellow Jewish undergraduates, and once from Raymond Weaver, who directed a question about anti-Semitism in a Chaucer work to Podhoretz because, obviously, Podhoretz was a Jew.[5]

It is important to get a feel for what the Columbia curriculum meant to students like Podhoretz in the late forties. Writing about it in 1966 – before the devastating campus uprisings of the New Left – Daniel Bell described it as a "conversion" experience for students, meaning a conversion to "culture" in a Western civilizational sense. That culture seemed, between the classroom, the library, and the kitchen table on which Podhoretz wrote his papers, to be of no specified time and place. It seemed, and was made by the faculty to seem, "universal." Of course there were national, ethnic, and religious particularities, which Podhoretz would become more conscious of at Cambridge, but that was a commonplace pedagogical problem, and Columbia faculty already knew how to deal with it. Otherwise they wouldn't have been able, as they illustriously were, to make the *Iliad* or *Paradise Lost* intelligible to mid-twentieth-century American students.

Universal themes aside, the students' daily intellectual task in literature courses was the so-called New Critical one of identifying, analyzing, and assessing the technical ways in which an author conveyed his or her themes. A Shakespeare course that had once been the property of Van Doren had in the immediate postwar years been turned over to Chiappe. As a sophomore, Podhoretz's participation in it was a special dispensation – and an opportunity to learn how poetry really worked. Over two semesters, the students read chronologically through the entire Shakespearean corpus. Chiappe would never publish anything – at all truly good colleges, it was then understood that tenure ought to depend primarily on teaching ability – but he had absorbed the superb writings of critics like G. Wilson Knight, Eliot, Leavis, and L. C. Knights, who together formulated the view that Shakespeare's plays, like his sonnets, were *poems* – "dramatic poems." "Get outta the way!" Hadas would mutter to the actors when he had to sit through a performance. The ideal was to "close-read" the lines, asking basic, and difficult, questions: What *is* imagery? What is a metaphor? What is a symbol? And how does this particular play build on those that came before? Chiappe had no objection to a student's using his own eyes and ears and drawing his own conclusions; if Podhoretz needed further information or a how-to demonstration, there were the critics, whom he would devour outside of class.[6]

The brighter literary students, Podhoretz felt, were acquiring "a veritably gnostic sense of power" – a grip on precious, almost secret knowledge. He had come to Columbia determined to be a great poet, theatrically telling girls that he would commit suicide if he hadn't become such a figure by age twenty-five. But did he really have the makings? He had to admit that the poetic talent in his Columbia generation resided not in him but in Allen Ginsberg, John Hollander, and a half-dozen others now forgotten. And even the Ginsbergs and Hollanders were up against an unpropitious historical moment. The high modernist breakthroughs of the early twentieth century were accomplished, and the thirties and forties had finished the important task of consolidating those gains. What came after was too often little more than repetition, parody, or (among Ginsberg and the Beats) adolescent outrage, hysteria, and exhibitionism.

If literary criticism was indeed his calling, Podhoretz had to prove it to his professors. Hollander could recall meeting Podhoretz in his first year, when the subject of the Kellett Fellowship came up. "I'm going to get me one of those!" the freshman said.[7] A student couldn't apply for a Kellett; it had to descend upon him, like grace, which it would never do unless he was spectacular over a full four-year span. Therefore, Podhoretz did in seminars what he had done at Boys High, participating eagerly in discussions (front row, hand up) and writing exams with a degree of quickness and concentration that suggested both the journalist working under a deadline and the thinker with something on his mind. He would later depict himself, with bemusement, as half *tabula rasa*, half foil: "Utterly open, limitlessly impressionable, possessed of something like total recall and a great gift for intellectual mimicry, I also succeeded, and without conscious intent, in writing papers for each of my professors in a different style – one which invariably resembled his own." Not deliberate flattery, just a remarkable ear and a flair for verbal imitation. Plus, of course, he did the reading.

Meanwhile, other sets at Columbia – the preppy "snobs," the classily dressed homosexuals, and the prissy middle-class Jews – hated him for being so "insufferably crude," and some were sufficiently Anglophile to hiss at the idea of his winding up with a Kellett: "Can you imagine *him* at Oxford or Cambridge? Sammy Glick in the *Agora*!" (Sammy Glick was the hustler, operator, and plagiarist in Budd Shulberg's 1941 novel *What Makes Sammy Run?*) Podhoretz had his own set, however, the handful of literary intellectuals that included Steven Marcus, whose wide study told him Podhoretz was neither Shulberg's Sammy Glick nor Faulkner's Flem Snopes. He was rather Stendhal's Julien Sorel or Balzac's Rastignac, a young man from the provinces who hoped to "make it" in the big city.[8] Furthermore, he was a young man strongly loyal to, if also a bit ambivalent about, his province and his family.

That loyalty and ambivalence would give him what his Columbia professors soon recognized as a distinctive point of view. Here was a Brownsville boy – he didn't turn twenty until his senior year – who already had not just a remarkable verbal facility but something to say. This was good because Columbia classes demanded a lot of writing. Students in Trilling's year-long seminar in Romantic and Victorian poetry, which Podhoretz took as a senior, besides having the usual term papers and exams, kept a running notebook of responses to the reading, which Trilling periodically perused and annotated.

Podhoretz's talents stood in such promising combination that Trilling backed him for three of the best available prizes. First was a junior fellowship with the Society of Fellows at Harvard, a three-year position that was said, somewhat misleadingly, to be equivalent to taking a Ph.D. One of the interviewers was Harry Levin. As the first Jew to have a tenured position on the Harvard literature faculty, he was in a way Trilling's double, but unlike Trilling at Columbia, he was (it was commonly said) determined to remain the *only* Jew in a tenured position at Harvard. In any event, he "was nasty beyond belief," as Podhoretz recalled. Levin also happened to be a committed leftist – not a Communist Party member but a close fellow traveler – and Podhoretz later wondered whether his political sensibility was venting itself in hostility toward the more conservative Trilling's protégé. In any case, like not going to Phillips Exeter, this was a lucky miss: Podhoretz was spared the constraints of the Genteel Tradition that still dominated Harvard.

For a student of literature at mid-century, the places to be were his own Columbia; Yale, the home of the New Critics; or Cambridge University, the home of the critic Leavis, his wife Queenie, and their disciples. Cambridge is where the other two prizes Trilling recommended him for would send him. Podhoretz applied for and won a Fulbright Fellowship, a program in only its second year. Then the longed-for Kellett did indeed descend upon him: it would dispatch him specifically to Clare College at Cambridge, where, among literary Columbians, Chiappe and the poet John Berryman had gone before.

Technically, one wasn't supposed to hold any fellowship concurrently with a Fulbright, but the program directors, too new to the game to have grown rigid, told him to forget about the technicality. Podhoretz would thus have plenty of money with which to travel during vacations, buy books, and, when his Fulbright was renewed, stay for a total of three years altogether.

Podhoretz's going to Cambridge, England, might have seemed a vicarious triumph for Trilling himself, who was to be a centrally important figure in his adult life as well. To generations of Columbia students from the late thirties into the seventies, Trilling seemed the model man of letters: soft-spoken, natty, handsome, and engaged with the world. Hollander remembered how he and his fellow undergraduates "saw in Lionel a complete reversal of the American stereotype of the English professor: instead of a rather clerical, scholarly sort of person here was somebody implicitly and consistently arguing by his concerns, and by the unique quality of his seriousness, that being a professor of literature might amount to one of the few remaining pursuits worth following."[9] Above all, he was an Anglophile. Though he never earned the Oxford Ph.D. for which his mother had told him, at age five, he was destined, he became a natural choice as Eastman Professor at Oxford in 1964, when he was nearly sixty. Until then, largely because his wife, Diana, was terrified of flying (as she was of many other things), he had never been to England; hence the pleasure of sending Podhoretz over.

Plus, Podhoretz was Jewish, and back during the Depression, Trilling's routine rough start as an academic had been exacerbated by his own Jewishness. Made an instructor at Columbia in 1932, he ground out a couple of courses a semester, taught for nickels and dimes at Hunter College in the evenings, and mostly failed to get on with his doctoral thesis; worse, he was trying to support his parents, who had been ruined in the stock market crash. Then, in 1936, the English department gave him a pink slip. He was going nowhere with his thesis on Matthew Arnold. Moreover, the combination of being theoretically Marxian, practically Freudian, and nominally Jewish rendered him a discomfiting presence in the eyes of the guardians of the Anglo-Saxon tradition who in the thirties were still the regular English faculty.

Trilling fought back, however, and with more resolution than he would ever show again. His instructorship was renewed, his spirits rose, and he directly wrote what remains the best book on Arnold, which Norton published in 1939. He sent a copy to Columbia's president, Nicholas Murray Butler, who was so impressed that he ordered the English department to promote the instructor to an assistant professorship. This made Trilling the first Jew to have a regular faculty position in English at Columbia – and some people, including his thesis adviser and now colleague Emery Neff, hoped he wouldn't use the appointment "as a wedge to open the . . . department to more Jews." It was against such polite anti-Semitism that Butler had set his face.[10]

What Columbia had done for, and to, Trilling was representative of its self-appointed mission toward Jewish students as well – the sons of those Jewish immigrants who, earlier in the twentieth century, had so unsettled patrician writers like Henry Adams and Henry James. As "the college of Old New York society," Columbia would acculturate these second-generation Jews in a way that would transform them, as Dean Frederick P. Keppel put it in 1914, into "entirely satisfactory companions." By Podhoretz's time, when the student body contained not only many more Jews but also a huge influx of World War II veterans, the *mission civilisatrice* of the college hadn't really changed.

Painfully but surely, Mrs. Haft's "slum child" was learning the manners that would help him fit in "with the oppressively genteel atmosphere of the Columbia Faculty Club" and become, as Trilling was, "a reasonable facsimile of an upper-class WASP." Sociologists in the fifties would reveal that WASPs were "an ethnic group like any other," whose "characteristic qualities ... are by no means self-evidently superior" to those of any other group. But that sort of historical insight, with its dubious leveling of distinctions, was theory. On the ground in the forties, a non-WASP like Podhoretz still faced some hard choices: what to embrace and what to reject among the three worlds that had a claim on him. He might love Brownsville, wearing its clothes and using its salty language, but literally going back to stay was becoming less and less thinkable. Obeying the JTS commandment to "Become a good Jew!" was perfectly thinkable, and ancestral voices told him it was indeed obligatory. Yet the Columbia imperative to "become a gentleman" seemed to imply the suppression of its JTS as well as its Brownsville contrary.[11]

Podhoretz would not in the end transcend these dilemmas through some higher synthesis, but he could try. After all, this or that modality of manners, clothes, food, and accent was only culture in the diluted sense. Many people, including his parents, might take them very seriously. But the richer culture he was learning to care about, the music, art, philosophy, and above all literature constituting what Arnold called the "best that has been thought and said," didn't demand the sacrifice of the higher Jewish tradition – its literature, certainly its law. Quite the opposite: the great-books syllabus folded the Hebraic strand of Western culture into the Hellenic and later Christian strands, and in principle honored the Hebraic as the oldest and morally most profound of them all.

In principle, indeed. In the classroom, once again, texts by Jews were superseded – their ideas subsumed – by pagan, Christian, or generally Gentile writers. Trilling didn't teach the Prophets; he taught Keats, Jane Austen, James, Joseph Conrad, and so on. It would be something of an event when, in 1950, he came out with an essay entitled "Wordsworth and the Rabbis." It is simplistic to argue that Trilling's "taste" for the Gentile canon of English and American literature was the upshot of any Jewish self-hatred – though he certainly felt something like it. Except for the Bible and the Talmud, there wasn't, in Trilling's view, any powerful Jewish literature prior to the early twentieth century *to* study – just stereotypes of Jewish ogres by Christian writers (Shakespeare's Shylock or Dickens's Fagin, for instance).

Trilling believed that he was stepping beyond the ghetto walls, his own "provinces," to encounter the riches of Anglophonic literature. His best pupil, going off in the fall of 1950 to Cambridge, felt the same. Podhoretz thought he knew Jewish literature pretty well, and for the time he'd had enough of it. He was keen on studying Trilling's favorite authors, and others whom he would discover at Cambridge. After all, as he would say half a century on: "If Hebrew . . . is God's first language, then English . . . must be His second."[12]

One day, in the summer of 1946, Podhoretz quoted a specimen of God's second language – lines from Eliot's "Love Song of J. Alfred Prufrock" – to Pearl, secretary in the office of the JTS College of Jewish Studies. All the male students, including the rabbis-to-be, were hot for Pearl, who was well into her twenties and a beauty.

Midge Decter – Rosenthal she then was, at age nineteen – would later remember the moment: "I'd come into the office to ask Pearl something, and there was this kid showing off – actually telling her about having been interviewed by the Pulitzer Committee for a scholarship to Columbia, telling her what they'd asked him and what he'd said. None of which was the point, that was very clear." The lines from "Prufrock" – probably, though Decter isn't sure, "I should have been a pair of ragged claws / Scuttling across the floors of silent seas," that cry of the overly analytical for the life of sheer instinct – he got slightly wrong. "I corrected him and he *spun around* on his heel to see who was this interloper."

This was Midge's first summer in New York, and she was studying Hebrew grammar, Bible, and literature for eight hours a day. That autumn she and Podhoretz would occasionally run into each other on Sundays, she to "tease" and joke with him, he to tell her about his girlfriends, cry on her shoulder "once or twice," and get that combination of jesting and sympathizing a boy often needs from a comparatively "mature" woman.[13]

This meeting with Midge Rosenthal was more important than either party could then realize. Born in St. Paul in 1927 – there were obviously young women from the provinces as well as young men – she had come to New York, after a year at the University of Minnesota, for the sake of the intellectual and social adventure. It was the more serious of her two adolescent ambitions, the other being to go to "Palestine and die on the barricades." She enrolled in the Teachers Institute not because she wanted to become a teacher "but because classes were in the daytime" and she wanted to be free at night. She was drawn into a slightly mad circle of Hebraists, students who forced themselves to speak of "*everything*, from tying one's shoe to eating ice cream, in Hebrew," and she met a terrifyingly learned fellow named Moshe Decter.[14]

Within two years, she married him, and they had two daughters: Rachel, born in January 1951, and Naomi, a year later.[15] Moshe Decter (1921–2007) had been wounded in the fighting at Anzio, Italy, and was now, on the GI Bill, doing graduate study in sociology at the New School.[16] Midge was meanwhile going through a number of clerical and retail jobs before ending up at *Commentary* as the editor Elliot Cohen's secretary. The Decters' walk-up apartment in Greenwich Village was usually empty during the day, and Midge had given Podhoretz a key "just in case he needed a place to take a girlfriend. There were two or three other people who used the apartment in the same way."[17] It sounds fairly louche, but the experienced woman's understanding of her young friend's needs – plainly he couldn't take girls home to Brownsville for sexual purposes, and he had no digs of his own – was based on the down-to-earth assumptions that anyone going up those stairs with him was a consenting adult and that boys will be boys.

A number of the "boys" at Columbia were going upstairs not with girls but with other boys. Growing up in Brooklyn, Podhoretz had been casually homophobic like his Cherokee pals, employing slurs like "fag" and "fairy," and making sure nobody ever suspected *him* of being one. At Columbia, though, he had to begin *thinking* about homosexuality – along with other alien phenomena. In his freshman year, his closest friend was Bill Clark, an army veteran from upstate New York and "one of the first real WASPs I ever got to know." That December, Clark asked him "to go do some Christmas shopping with him, a totally alien concept to me." At Rockefeller Center, he was "absolutely entranced" by the stores, the displays, the lights. "And really for the first time in my life I felt the sense of exclusion as a Jew." What came into Podhoretz's mind, thinking back on this episode, was Ira Gershwin's "They're writing songs of love, but not for me" – the "not for me" meaning both Christmas and what Clark soon after sprang on him: the "astonishing" announcement "that he was a homosexual."

Taken aback by this disclosure from Clark, who soon drifted away, Podhoretz began noticing that other Columbia students he admired were homosexuals, too. So were some of the professors. After the Shakespeare course was over, Podhoretz learned – another surprise – that Chiappe was one. There was also Fred Dupee, married and "very much in the closet," whose same-sex preferences were no secret among the students. And there was one of Chiappe's disciples, a young instructor from England who offered Podhoretz an oblique invitation that the latter failed to recognize. Later, at Cambridge, "a real hotbed" of homosexuality, he was able to recognize such invitations and, being "heterosexual to a fault," as one friend said, to reject them.

Podhoretz graduated from Columbia in June 1950, and his reputation would linger on there for at least a decade. Herb London, who later became a dean at NYU, a sometime politician, a foundation director, and a social commentator, was in 1960 "a twenty-one-year-old student in the [Jacques] Barzun-Trilling seminar, and it was 'Norman Podhoretz said this, Norman Podhoretz said that.' He was a legendary figure – bright, resourceful, remarkably quick, one of a kind."[18] Apparently Trilling was still holding Podhoretz up as an exemplar to other students, even as he had in 1950. In that year, the bright Paul H. Stacy had submitted "a surgical analysis of a Tennyson poem" that Trilling dismissed as a "ganglionectomy." "Though I knew in my heart that my paper was twitched, huffed and puffed, straining too proudly and visibly," Stacy would later tell Podhoretz, "I didn't know exactly what his objection was. I went to see him. And here is what he said: 'You mustn't try to Podhoretz it up.' He admired you greatly. So did I. But there I was: Salieri to your Mozart."[19]

Stacy and London were on the whole content to admire what the latter called "a force of nature," but many of Podhoretz's contemporaries at Columbia had different ideas. True, the most sympathetic of them, especially Steven Marcus, relished the light that was generated by his heated brain – the two were friends as well as rivals – but others must have groused. The Kellett and Fulbright fellowships meant that their particular Sammy Glick really *was* running to the agora, and Podhoretz discovered, for the first time, the subtle difference between jealousy and envy. He had known the former plenty of times in Brooklyn, when other kids wished they could be as smart or as sexually exploratory as he was – but never resented *his* being so. At the end of his Columbia career, jealousy was supplanted by envy, with many whom he had imagined to be his friends effectually wishing that *they* were going off on a Kellett and Fulbright and that he would have nothing.

Podhoretz had been "incredibly" dull not to have seen it coming. Coddled all his life, he'd had a youngster's version of King Lear's "They told me I was everything" syndrome. Better to unlearn this soon (if age twenty is soon) rather than, like Lear, late. Were these the wages of triumph? If so, they might make him so miserable that his friends "would finally have nothing to envy me for. Theirs the virtue of failure, mine the corruption of success: who then was the enviable one?"[20]

Podhoretz would have more success, corrupting or not, at Cambridge, and some measure of failure, too. But the "who's to be envied?" question wouldn't become any easier to answer.

3

Cambridge

During the summers of 1949 and 1950, Podhoretz worked at the Hebrew-speaking Camp Ramah in northern Wisconsin. His particular role, besides teaching the prophet Jeremiah to teenagers,[1] was to be the drama coach: he would write up skits of biblical stories in Hebrew, which the campers, after swimming or archery, would act out. Other counselors included Gerson Cohen and Moshe Greenberg, both of whom went on to become notable Jewish scholars. Cohen then and forevermore called Norman "Nifty" (from his Hebrew name Naphtali), and Nifty, for his part, would always remember Greenberg with "a copy of the Kittel edition of the Masoretic text under his arm. I think he even went swimming with it."[2] They were comrades.

At the end of the second summer, Podhoretz was invited by another counselor to his family's cottage in Glencoe, Illinois. It was a nice place. The mother showed him to his room and, when the door latch clicked firmly behind him, he burst into tears. At first confused by this meltdown, he quickly realized what had caused it: the doors in his family's Brownsville apartment had been painted over so many times that they never clicked shut. What he felt, besides a trace of self-pity, was – to pursue the distinction marked at the end of the previous chapter – not envy but jealousy. He didn't resent his friend's family having their bit of luxury; he simply wanted some for himself. Moreover, he felt overwhelmed by "vistas of previously undreamed of possibility" not exactly for money, which might buy him a cottage like that, but for the opportunities America offered people like himself to pursue happiness. If he could become "great" or "famous" as a writer of some kind, then surely – the details would be unimportant – he would be happy.[3]

Podhoretz heard another firm click when he moved into three rooms, "all paneled in wood and furnished in leather," at Clare College, Cambridge. Again he shed sudden tears, only now for his amazingly good "luck." Luck generally to have grown up in a meritocracy where one could earn prizes like the Fulbright and the Kellett, and luck specifically to have landed in England, where few if any could detect his class origins, which were as lowly as those of Aubrey, his servant or "gyp." As far as "Aub" or all England was concerned, Podhoretz was simply a Clare man and therefore a "young gentleman" who was owed a combination of amenities and deference.

Even before World War II, the ancient English universities, Oxford and Cambridge, had begun to admit lower-middle-class and working-class students. Podhoretz's supervisor at Clare, John Northam, had grown up in the parish of Wollwich, outside of London, where his father worked in the arsenal at Pubstone. The house had one tap, and no hot water. Northam went to a ghastly Dickensian school but did so well on an exam that he won a scholarship, the first in the school's history. What followed was a preparatory school, a year at Clare, five years in the Royal Air Force, and Clare again, where in 1948 he earned a first on the English exams (called "tripos," from the archaic association with the examiner's three-legged stool). He would always remember his prewar arrival, unsuitably dressed, dragging some clunky luggage, and greeted by "a very fine gyp, an ex-army man," who put him directly at ease: "Your room is H10, sir, right up those stairs." "It was a place," he said, "where you were taken in."

Not that Northam, only eight years older than his supervisee Podhoretz, would have openly acknowledged the affinities between their backgrounds had he been aware of them. In fact he wasn't aware, which is a sign of how far Columbia had gone in turning its newest Kellett into "a facsimile WASP." Nor was Podhoretz aware of Northam's origins. They were gentlemen alike, and their business was to prepare for the tripos that, if passed, would give Podhoretz his second B.A. in English literature. Northam's task was to coach him and a half-dozen other charges in weekly meetings focused on essays they had written. He would recall that Norman was a "toughie," a student who "never took anything for granted," and "was so gifted you could feel you weren't good enough for him. Not that he ever *made* you feel that way." There was "no spoon-feeding with him, just a gesture toward the landscape and asking whether he'd thought of climbing up this or that hill."[4]

Podhoretz soon understood that this Englishman's hardheaded empiricism was the precise corrective needed for the habits of metaphysical "brilliance" he had acquired at Columbia. He would submit an essay heavy with "Eliotic pomposities" or "Blackmurian obscurities," and Northam, between puffs on his pipe, "quietly challenged [me] to tell him what it meant." When, for instance, Podhoretz claimed that D. H. Lawrence's analysis of civilization's sickness ranks with "Plato's great analysis of the pathology of governments," Northam tersely commented, "You don't convince me" – adding in summary that "All this is fascinating but confused as hell. . . . Your point is lost, buried, dead."[5] This was the way to make the toughie tougher.

The tripos required students to cover large tracts. Hence Northam's insistence that Podhoretz take on big subjects – "the idea of progress" among the English moralists, the idea of justice in Plato's *Republic*, Edmund Burke's "hatred of abstraction in his attack on mathematical democracy," or "the curse of liberalism in politics and literature." Podhoretz was attending a dialogue among "greats," as they are called at Oxford, and he came to it with a certain predisposition. Years of Jewish studies had inclined him to favor law and tradition over anarchy and revolution; Columbia, and particularly Trilling, had shown him the value of an "organic" development of liberty and the disasters of start-from-scratch social engineering; and Brownsville had given him, at the very least, what Hemingway called an internal "bullshit detector."

Podhoretz's essay on Edmund Burke, the most powerful opponent of the French Revolutionists, was thus more than an academic exercise. The Revolutionists, Podhoretz wrote, made the mistake of thinking they could imitate the seventeenth-century scientists' rebellion against authority: first throw over the king and the whole apparatus of the old regime, then build a new society on the basis of rational laws. Burke understood that society wasn't susceptible to being manipulated by that kind of analysis and reconstruction. Society was a "relationship between past and present... a continuity to be explored, a partnership to be developed, and [Burke] was naturally repelled by the sort of mind (eminently typified by [Jeremy] Bentham) which presumed to begin every enquiry *de novo*."[6]

Of course this is only student scribbling, however savvy. But it does reveal a sensibility gelling on the threshold of adulthood. More Burke than Bentham, Podhoretz thought about the world not like a geometrician but like a historian.

Podhoretz was finding himself socially as well as intellectually. As he wrote Trilling two months after arriving in England, he had walked all over London in "a veritable ecstasy," seen Shakespeare performed at Stratford, and driven "through the Wye Valley, and as far as Tintern Abbey (which, I assert dogmatically, is by far the most beautiful spot on earth)" — all prior to settling into "the three-room apartment which they had given me (and a *servant* to boot!!)."

He told Trilling that while he was actually reading and writing more than he had at Columbia, the fact that the essays were ungraded meant, wonderfully, "that there is no one to impress." Nor did the Clare men talk about literature: "it would be most improper to get excited about a book." They took it easy during term and crammed for the tripos during vacations.

The irony was that Cambridge seemed untroubled. A member of the upper class – that is, any member of the university – could do what he damn well pleased. This at any rate was what Podhoretz inferred from the example of his best friend at Cambridge, the Australian Maxwell Newton, a self-dramatizing "wild man from the bush" and a sort of "premature Thatcherite" who had come there to study economics. Newton would outrage the stodgy Brits, as Podhoretz would recall, by "loudly imitating the sounds of a woman having sexual intercourse as we walked together through the densely packed narrow streets of Cambridge." He not only reminded Podhoretz of some of the raunchier wits in Brownsville but also showed the breadth of the privileges of eccentricity the British upper class permitted a rebellious cousin from down under simply because he was a gentleman like themselves.[7]

Still, if the majority of students didn't care much about "mind," Podhoretz certainly did, and so, plainly, did Northam, Newton, and the man whose seminars at Downing College he was soon attending – F. R. Leavis. Trilling had urged Podhoretz to get in touch with this difficult but great critic who, against immense opposition, had turned the study of English at Cambridge away from the merely philological and textual toward the historical and critical, and whose famous quarterly, which ran from 1932 to 1953, was aptly named *Scrutiny*. Running aesthetic and moral criteria together, Leavis had among the poets argued for the superiority of Alexander Pope over John Dryden, Shakespeare over Milton, and Keats over Shelley, and among the novelists for the "great tradition" of George Eliot, James, and Conrad, abetted by Jane Austen, Emily Brontë, and eventually Dickens and Lawrence over Samuel Richardson, Walter Scott, William Thackeray, George Meredith, Anthony Trollope, Thomas Hardy, and the rest.

Leavis was an evaluative critic, which was bracing. But Podhoretz was a little downcast at how, with "by far the best mind in the English school," the man would "dissipate his energies attacking Bloomsbury and the Georgians all the time" and complaining of "his persecutions at the hands of his colleagues."[8] His wife, the formidable Queenie Leavis, was Jewish, but never mentioned the fact.[9] The Leavisites – the Leavises and their students – had persuaded themselves that they had been marginalized by the Bloomsbury clique then in control of quality metropolitan newspapers like the *Times Literary Supplement*. They felt rather like a band of guerrillas, self-identified defenders of "minority culture" against the corruptions of a "mass civilisation." These embattled "Scrutineers" inhabited a world half a galaxy away from that of the Family of New York Intellectuals ("Family" was Murray Kempton's term, given currency in Podhoretz's *Making It*), but it was quite as sanguinary and in the person of Leavis as uncompromisingly intelligent.[10]

In June 1951, Leavis invited Podhoretz to contribute to *Scrutiny*. It was like a call to a secular priesthood, a feeling he had never gotten from Trilling, who, although an earnest man of letters, once startled Podhoretz and his classmates by admitting "that there were times when he felt that he would rather do almost anything than read a book." Leavis would never have said that, and probably never felt it. What the Bible had been to his Huguenot forebears, great imaginative literature was to him – a key to knowledge, a guide to life – and he brought a "religious" intensity to the task of criticizing it. Not unlike the rabbis who once had to decide which texts were canonical, Leavis endeavored to establish *the* great tradition, and to cherish it as "a substitute for devotional meditation and scriptural exegesis."[11] By the same token, to favor the wrong poem or novel was to whore after strange gods. The critic's job was to rebuke you, and if you seemed worthwhile, as well as contrite, to shepherd you back into the fold.

Podhoretz certainly wanted to be thought worthwhile. "I became a Leavisian," he would write, "not, perhaps, the most ardent of his young epigoni at Cambridge, but, in all truth, the others being a singularly dreary and humorless lot, the most adept."[12] This is true, if only because he was lively and humorous, not merely knowledgeable and intense.

Leavis wanted his young American devotee to review Trilling's new collection of essays, *The Liberal Imagination*. Although claiming to admire Trilling's book on Arnold, Leavis didn't really like the tenor of his work. On the other hand, he didn't "wish to run an attack on it."[13] As for young Podhoretz, he wanted to project an alliance between his two formidable masters. He would praise Trilling's ability to read as "closely" (i.e., with attention to literary devices) as the best New Critics, to marshal facts as well as the old German historians, and to understand the relations between literature and society better than the Marxists.[14] Trilling, that is, was like Leavis, only in an American context. It was a characterization Leavis didn't agree with, but to show his broad-mindedness and to retain an influential "agnostic" American ally, he printed the piece anyway.

This was Podhoretz's first professional publication. One diverting consequence was a rumor immediately "circulating around Cambridge that," as he wrote Trilling, "you are, quite literally, my foster-father."[15] Another was the usual authorial letdown once the review was out of his hands: "The only important things I managed to say," he gently wailed to Trilling, "were paraphrases of your ideas or observations about them that looked so hopelessly obvious on the galleys that I felt pretty completely humbled and chastened."

And another thing, for all the Leavis tea parties and the noble life in the eating hall and along the Backs (the lovely college gardens by the river Cam), Podhoretz wasn't an Englishman. He was an American. It was true, as he would later say to Gore Vidal, who didn't get the joke, that great national events like the Civil War or the War of Independence meant no more to him than the War of the Roses. The only national watershed that meant anything to him "was, ridiculously, the Depression of the thirties. Nor," as he would confess, "had I ever thought of myself as an American. I came from Brooklyn, and in Brooklyn there were no Americans; there were Jews and Negroes and Italians and Poles and Irishmen. Americans lived in New England, in the South, in the Midwest: alien people in alien places." That, however, was merely what he had felt back home. Abroad, he was finding out that he was quite as American as he was Jewish.

Whether the habits and tastes inculcated by Brownsville, Boys High, JTS, and Columbia were inferior, superior, or simply equivalent to the habits and tastes of England or Europe, they were indelible.[16] Michelangelo and Chartres might share mental space with the "lyrics of long-forgotten [American] popular songs, advertising slogans, and movie plots" but could never drive them out. Were the songs, slogans, and plots vulgar? Sometimes, no doubt. The "sheer vulgarity" of anti-Americanism in Europe, on the other hand, was far worse.

Indeed, it pushed Podhoretz into feeling patriotic. He would explain, even to exaggeration, that Americans lived for something besides money, that Europe wasn't about to be drowned in Coca-Cola or poisoned by hamburgers, that Alger Hiss was a communist, that civil liberties would survive Joseph

McCarthy, that the military wasn't using germ warfare in Korea, and that the commander-in-chief didn't intend to drag the world into a nuclear holocaust.[17] All these protestations seemed especially needful in the face of the French intellectuals around Jean-Paul Sartre, whom Podhoretz met in Paris and whose apologies for Stalin's crimes simply dumbfounded a young man who had cut his ideological teeth on the anti-Stalinism-cum-modernism of the circle around the New York quarterly *Partisan Review*.

The stop in Paris was the beginning of the long summer vacation of 1951, the high points of which would be Greece and Israel. The visit to Greece sounds, in Podhoretz's offhand remarks to Trilling several months later, like a lark, but actually he was seeing Athens in the company of a remarkable woman whom he had met on the airplane from London. Her name was Jacqueline Clarke, and she would be the most important person in his life for the next few years. Born in 1924, Jacquie (or Jay) was twenty-seven years old, and experienced: she had been a Communist Party member at age sixteen and had an affair with a cartoonist for the *Daily Worker*.[18] Podhoretz was twenty-one, and in his own fashion tolerably experienced, too. "More than just interesting," as he later said, Jacqueline "had a certain genius," which turned out to be literary. In 1966 she would publish a 600-page novel, somewhat primly titled *Mrs. Bratbe's August Picnic*, and for years afterward worked on a Proust-length, multivolume work that was psychologically astute, stylistically brilliant, but in the end unfinished and too unwieldy for any publisher to take a chance on it. Back in 1951, however, she was studying at the London School of Economics (LSE).

Her father, a Hammersmith-Irish toolmaker, had died when she was six. Her mother was a Cockney – as Podhoretz recalled, "the kind you'd see in a British comedy, sort of stout, who'd actually played the trumpet in a band, very plainspoken and forthright." After the war, living with her mother in Ealing, Jacqueline became active in, and ultimately chaired, the local Labour Party League of Youth. She invited Harold Laski, the prominent Labour intellectual and organizer who taught at LSE, to speak to the League, and her questions afterward so impressed him that he urged her to prepare for the LSE entrance exams. Entering the school in 1948, she began studying under Kingsley Bryce Smellie but, in 1951, gravitated toward Michael Oakeshott, the by then deceased Laski's conservative replacement. She finished her bachelor's degree and started a dissertation on comparative method and the London county councils.[19]

On the flight to Athens in May 1951, Podhoretz had seen "this older woman sitting absorbed in thought" and was instantly attracted. He began a conversation, "showing off, dropping names, quoting things." She was, as he would reminisce, "slightly puzzled by, disapproving of," yet "clearly taken by this young American, a new phenomenon to her." They toured Athens together, he "talking a mile a minute" until she finally said, "Do you ever *look* at anything?

Why don't you stop talking and *look*? There are beautiful things all around you but have you *seen* any of them?" She was right, and he was forever grateful.

They spent a good deal of time together back in London and soon became most affectionate friends. She was struck by how he, too, had discovered Oakeshott's writing, and by the range of his intellectual interests altogether. He did what he could – a nudge was all that was needed – to steer her toward literature. "In the end," he has said, "she became obsessed" by literature, and the germ of that obsession must have been one reason she so fancied this student of Trilling and Leavis. We will return to Jacqueline Clarke.

From Athens, during that summer of 1951, Podhoretz flew to Tel Aviv. He had never been an active Zionist during his years at JTS, not in the morally determined way that Midge Rosenthal had been, and certainly not in the culturally saturated way of certain left-wing students, particularly some of "the least attractive girls at the Seminary." Even on the day the Jewish state was proclaimed, May 14, 1948, when "a *huge* celebration" took place at JTS, he felt detached. Preoccupied as he was with the mostly supra-Jewish curriculum at Columbia, the hora-dancing Zionists reminded him too much of the provinces he was journeying *from*.

All the same, he did choose to cap that "damn Long Vac" in 1951 by going to Israel and not, say, Spain. Staying for six weeks, his Hebrew becoming ever more fluent, he gathered reflections for a remarkable letter to Trilling:

I covered almost every inch of Israel, spent lots of time in kibbutzim, fell in love with the Yemenites, argued endlessly about What is Judaism, Who is a Jew, and Why Not, explored Tel Aviv (which is vile), Jerusalem (which Jehovah did well to choose as his city), Haifa (which is lovely, but loaded with anti Semitic Germans [i.e., German Jews] who refuse to learn Hebrew), attended election meetings, became very depressed over a demoralized population, and finally went away a sadder and wiser man, with a slightly bitter taste in my mouth and a sense of having been strangely dispossessed. I felt more at home in Athens! They are, despite their really extraordinary achievements, a very unattractive people, the Israelis.... On the one hand, they realize that their only claim to status as a civilization rests on the past and that only the most intensive of efforts to establishing a living continuity with the past can overcome the artificial process by which the country was contrived. And on the other hand, they are too arrogant and too anxious to become a real honest-to-goodness New York of the East. But I'm being uncharitable, unhistorical if you like. So many of these things can be explained away – in fact they are [explained] by the more conscious and intelligent people you meet here and there. And though I wouldn't claim that this is a *fair* account of Israel, it's certainly an honest account of my reactions to it. Some day I'd like to discuss the whole business with you. It's a very fascinating country.[20]

Trilling must have liked the critical disinterestedness of these remarks – to say nothing of the young man's cultural preference for Athens over Jerusalem and the implicit affirmation of his own Americanness.

FIGURE 6. Norman Podhoretz in Florence, Italy, en route to
Greece and Israel during the long vacation, spring 1951.

Trilling wrote his friend Elliot Cohen, editor of *Commentary* since its inception in 1945, recommending "that remarkable undergraduate of mine who
went to Cambridge and who reviewed my book for *Scrutiny*. He's a first class
Hebraist (ancient and modern), a good writer, and a brilliant scholar, now
involved in history and philosophy as well as in literature." Typing out, in
full, the just-quoted paragraph, Trilling suggested that Cohen ask Podhoretz
to write on Israel.[21] Cohen wasn't just then keen on such a piece, but he did
enthusiastically pass Trilling's letter on to his associate editor, Irving Kristol,
who wrote Podhoretz in England: "Naturally, we are more than a little
interested. Are you interested in writing for us? If so, what subject most engages
you at the moment?"[22]

Podhoretz would pursue that inquiry the following summer. Meanwhile he
had to prepare for the tripos in the spring of 1952. He would be asked to
give reasons for identifying the authorship and date of passages (a matter of
responding to diction, imagery, theme, and ethos); to do close readings of

FIGURE 7. Norman Podhoretz at work in a London flat while on break from Cambridge, 1951.

passages comparing "the character and value of the thought, feeling and sense-perception"; to treat the political and moral theories of Plato, Augustine, and Hobbes; to discuss Lawrence's "indictment of modern civilization"; to do a paper on "Tragedy" ("How far does the effect of Greek tragedy depend upon attitudes and beliefs which are no longer current in the modern world?"); and finally to translate and comment on an unseen French text.

So comprehensive an exam exceeded anything Podhoretz had been asked to do at Columbia, but he had read widely, and as always he could write well while the clock ticked. He got a "first," a then very hard-to-achieve highest mark. Should he now pursue a Ph.D. in English at Cambridge? Fulbright money would pay for a third year, and no doubt the university would help beyond that. Or should he do a Ph.D. at home? Harvard had made him an offer (with stipends).

He could decide later. With the tripos done, he returned to Brownsville for a well earned break. Obligingly, the Trillings invited him up to their summer place in Westport, Connecticut. There he aired his doubts about whether the academic life would be right for him. The "witchlike" Trilling put his finger on the central question: "What kind of power was I after?" Podhoretz had never thought about the matter, but Trilling told him not to "be silly... everyone wants power. The only question is what kind." If the choices included money, fame, or eminence in a profession, then the answer was easy: Podhoretz wanted "fame, no doubt about it; I wanted to be a famous critic." Diana, whom he was meeting for the first time, said that if he wanted to write criticism but wasn't so sure about academia, maybe he should find another way to support himself, like going to law school and becoming a lawyer. At first "outraged and humiliated" by the suggestion, which seemed to imply "selling out" to the workaday world, he later found her remarks liberating: "*There were other things in the world to do*" besides teaching literature in college. He just had never given them a thought.[23]

Hence, following that query from Kristol, the significance of Podhoretz's going into New York to meet Elliot Cohen. They didn't talk about money, and Cohen never intimated that he could make a living as a freelance critic. But he did explain the character of *Commentary* as both a Jewish magazine and one focused on the "'general' worlds of culture," like *Partisan Review*. "The main difference between *Partisan Review* and *Commentary*," Cohen mischievously said, "is that we admit to being a Jewish magazine and they don't." Then, with "his famous smile," he asked whether Casey Stengel, the colorful manager of the New York Yankees, was as worthy a subject "for the critical intelligence" as Henry James, or had Podhoretz's highbrow education taught him to imagine a great gulf between them? Was he *kidding*? Podhoretz asked. What Cambridge especially had shown him was that America's popular culture – its sports, swing bands, radio jingles, and vernaculars – was in his blood. Fine, said Cohen: "You seem to know something about novels, you know something about symbolism, you know something about Jews, and you know something about baseball. Here's a symbolic novel by a Jewish writer about a baseball player. I guess you're qualified to review it." It was Bernard Malamud's first book, *The Natural*.

The people in the *Commentary* offices didn't look intimidatingly mature. They were just intimidatingly smart. The big guns were the bald Clement Greenberg, America's "most influential art critic" at forty-three, and Robert Warshow, thirty-four, product of the University of Michigan (not City College like most of the others) and author of luminous essays on Clifford Odets, Arthur Miller, and gangster movies. They were ably assisted by Nathan "Nat" Glazer, twenty-eight but looking sixteen, who was David Riesman's acknowledged assistant in the sociological classic *The Lonely Crowd* (1950), and by Irving Kristol, about thirty-two and looking twenty, who was already known for his clear analyses of liberal-democratic politics. As Podhoretz's tripos papers had made evident, these were just the sorts of intellectuals he identified with. And behold, no sooner did he get back to his parents' apartment with *The Natural* under his arm than Warshow phoned to ask him to lunch: "I felt as a girl with a secret infatuation must feel when the boy she has been mooning over asks her for a date." An important date. Bob Warshow would become his friend, "a guide on my first brief safari into the wilds of New York literary society," writing both for *Commentary* and for *Partisan Review*.[24]

Since he couldn't make up his mind about academia, in late August 1952 Podhoretz sent his regrets to Harvard and, with his Fulbright funds still in hand, returned to Cambridge. Yes, it was a Ph.D. program, but it felt like a moratorium – an extension of the gentlemanly, contemplative strolls about the "agora" that for two years he had become fond of. As a third-year, needing to live away from Clare, he found some lovely digs right on King's Parade, shared, as he would recollect, "with a most unlikely roommate named Willie Carruthers, an *echt* gentleman" whose father was "a landowner or banker."

Podhoretz was sketching out a dissertation prospectus. His initial thought, as he told Trilling, had been "Burke and early English romanticism," but to the English faculty this seemed only marginally literary. With help from Marcus, who had earlier entered Cambridge's Ph.D. program, he then "hit upon" the novels of Benjamin Disraeli, the most pertinent of which were the 1840s works whose subtitles indicate their sociopolitical edge: *Coningsby, or The New Generation; Sybil, or The Two Nations;* and *Tancred, or The New Crusade.*

Disraeli is now famous as *the* Tory prime minister of the Victorian period. His Jewish father had him baptized into the Church of England at age twelve for the same reason that Heinrich Heine's father had him baptized a Lutheran – namely, to remove a barrier to his career. Looking back, Podhoretz could see very clearly that in his fiction Disraeli invented "a lot of stuff about the ancient 'oriental' civilization of the Jews, all to persuade the upper classes that they should not look down on him as a Jew." In fact, however, Disraeli had no special "feeling about being Jewish," and though "down deep" probably skeptical about religion of any sort, he always remained "a perfectly loyal member of the Church of England."[25]

Podhoretz's prospectus began with Disraeli's view of Judaism, the deep well from which the other great monotheistic religions, Christianity and Islam, had risen. Disraeli thought that the Church of England would be revivified if it recalled "its Semitic origins," quite as the aristocracy would be revivified if, in what he termed the Young England movement, it allied itself with the working class against the philistine, commerce-driven middle class. Podhoretz's thesis would be that Disraeli's program called for transmuting "Byronism," the glamorous, passionate, but finally feckless egoism of the poet, into "Victorianism," the forceful, intelligent public spirit of the novelist, the citizen, and the politician.

The high rhetoric surrounding Disraeli's fictional man-of-action heroes reads like the paeans that in 1960 would surround John F. Kennedy's election to the presidency. Something like this Disraelian excitement, Podhoretz would later feel, was what the comparatively quiescent fifties actually needed – and what the sixties got in unwholesome measure. The 1840s, at any rate, were a time of tremendous political ferment in England and on the Continent, and while some novelists – the aesthete Flaubert, for instance – preferred to withdraw into an "unconditioned life" devoted to the pursuit of amours and the contemplation of art, others, like Stendhal and Disraeli, found the upheavals fascinating. Their belief was "that the unpolitical life is not worth living." As in Stendhal's *The Red and the Black*, "the main characteristic of Disraeli's early novels is to see

the problem of youth as the problem of finding a career, and of his mature
novels – once politics has been settled on as *the* career – as that of finding a
creed. To find a creed is to find oneself."[26]

Find a career, find a creed, find a self: that is the plot of Podhoretz's own
early life.

Getting a Ph.D. at Cambridge was a pretty free-form affair: one put in a certain
period of residency, wrote a dissertation, and defended it orally. The affair was
also ruthless. As Podhoretz wrote Trilling, "around 50%" of the candidates
were failed – "some of them very bright people too" – as Marcus's dissertation
on Dickens would shortly be failed.[27] But Podhoretz could cross that bridge
later. Meanwhile he hunkered down to pore over the documentary material
and (once more) Disraeli's three political novels.[28]

Occasionally he would chat with his supervisor, the historian Noel Annan,
who in 1935, as a student at King's College, had been recruited into the Apos-
tles, the secret Cambridge debating society whose members in the late thirties
included Kim Philby, Guy Burgess, Anthony Blunt, and Michael Straight. The
sympathies of those four leaned so far to the Left that they became spies for
the Soviet Union. In 1952–53, Podhoretz understood, Annan was recruiting
him to become a fellow at King's, which would have meant not only teaching
undergraduates but also entering into that college's homosexual culture (from
which a heterosexual like Podhoretz would presumably be exempted).[29] As
events unfolded, however, Podhoretz never became a King's man.

Two episodes underscored his suspicions that he was after all "too American" for Cambridge. The first was superficially trivial. Queen Elizabeth II was
crowned on June 2, 1953, and three days later Podhoretz wrote to Trilling:

We're all exhausted by the Coronation, which has been the occasion for me of a
swarming mess of uncomfortable emotions. Admiration, repulsion, jealousy, worry
about being left out, an impulse to lock the door and hide from it. A group of us . . . sat
and listened to the radio report and the Abbey service for about seven hours, at the end
of which the gloom in our souls was even deeper than the gloom in the atmosphere. But
how wonderful it all was. I wish I were enough in command to write more coherently
about it.[30]

The jealousy, the gloom, and the worry about being left out are affecting – a
sort of reprise of Henry James's feelings of alienation from European culture.
Trilling certainly shared the regret, replying that "The Coronation must have
been extraordinary – not merely from its effect on you. A nation says, What
joy to be a nation. How terrible not to be. How can that not be moving?"[31]

"How terrible not to be"? This was to suggest that America's status as "a
nation" was still in question. In the absence of royal and religious ceremony,
what gave our culture coherence? Podhoretz could find out only by repatriating.

The second episode, not at all trivial, came on the heels of the first. Podhoretz had submitted a thirty-some-page essay on Disraeli's political novels,

an epitome of the dissertation, to *Scrutiny*. The typescript of the essay is informative, pithy, and luminous, and would surely have been welcome to readers both familiar and unfamiliar with Disraeli's fiction. Only, Leavis didn't think so. "My dear Podhoretz," he wrote by hand,

> It seems to us... that you haven't got beyond the first rough-jottings stage in respect to Disraeli. It's not only that the whole essay would have to be re-written – or written (for you can't really correct unthought sentences in the way you've attempted) – before it could be published anywhere: from the *Scrutiny* point of view, the *theme* hasn't been thought enough (or that's the impression you convey). We couldn't print anything that did so little more than a hundred or two readers of *Scrutiny* could do impromptu.[32]

Leavis was telling Podhoretz what others were telling Marcus: go back to your own country and, if you must be a critic, focus on *its* literature, not ours. There was, as Q. D. Leavis would argue in an extraordinary essay, an "Englishness" about "English literature" that in the end non-English people couldn't understand. And this was in spite of the authoritativeness of tone with which both Leavises wrote about such American figures as Melville, Twain, Hawthorne, and James.

It is impossible to say precisely where Podhoretz had diverged from the *Scrutiny* line. In any event, "My dear Podhoretz," who couldn't help showing a strong mind, had begun rubbing the strongest mind in Cambridge the wrong way,[33] and he drew the proper conclusion from this comeuppance. The truth is that we Americans often don't "get" English literature, nor do the English get ours, and, as Podhoretz would write in *Making It,* he was finding each nation's literature "carefully fenced around by its own inherent limitations – that is, its own untranscended parochialism and provinciality – against trespassers from outside the family."[34] He wouldn't in the end yield to the thoroughgoing particularism – and moral relativism – that this statement might suggest. But after three years in England, it seemed time to go home.

Podhoretz wasn't eager to leave Jacqueline Clarke exactly, but it was increasingly obvious that they would never be more than loving friends. She was working on her LSE degree, and he would often visit her and her mother during vacations or on weekends.[35] He would tell his own parents about Jacqueline in due course, but his mother, as he later said, could only liken her to "the archetypical blond *shiksa* who once troubled the sleep of all Jewish mothers: the beautiful young siren luring innocent Jewish boys into her embraces with secret sexual wiles known only to the Gentile world."[36]

Actually, Podhoretz's relationship with Jacqueline was based more on spiritual affinities and psychological needs than on anything merely sexual. He twice took her to the May Ball, the annual black-tie festival. It was a chance to show her how, for all his intellectualism, he could dance to those big-band sounds that were in his blood. Should they ever have gone from dancing to marrying, she would, however unreligious she then was, have been willing to convert to Judaism. But they never did go beyond dancing.[37]

FIGURE 8. Jacqueline Clarke rowing on the Serpentine in Hyde Park, London, in the late 1940s or early 1950s. (By permission of Wynn Wheldon.)

Jacqueline remained at the center of his personal life for at least another year, and she would never be apart from it – or eventually from Decter's – in all the years until her death in 1993. In summer 1953, though, Podhoretz's face was turned back to America, and specifically to the army. The Selective Service would be calling him, and he had deferred the moment long enough. Besides, he wanted to be drafted. As most American men understood for at least two decades after Pearl Harbor, it was a rite of passage, a test of manhood. He was eager to see how he would do.

4

The Family and the Army

Podhoretz had to wait a full five months before being drafted. Like Saul Bellow's "dangling man," he slept late and goofed off a bit, yet, given "a superego like a horse," he also wrote six articles for *Commentary*. Cohen and the other editors had liked the piece on Malamud, which came out in March 1953, and the "paternally proud" Warshow, "like a broker ticking off the latest stock-market reports," kept tabs on what people were saying about him. Forget about Malamud's hero Roy Hobbs; Clem Greenberg declared Podhoretz "the natural."

This was welcome after his somewhat frosty good-bye to Cambridge. There was nothing wrong with being too American in America, especially at *Commentary*, where knowing about baseball was a plus and essays on big-band music, television, or Western and gangster movies were comfortably juxtaposed with essays about the Lodz Ghetto, the Cold War, or Martin Buber. By the early fifties, *Commentary*, sponsored by but editorially independent of the American Jewish Committee (AJC), could claim partial ownership of American culture in a way that its spiritual predecessors, the *Menorah Journal* (1915–62) and the *Contemporary Jewish Record* (1938–45), never could. Back in the mid-forties, when Alfred Kazin, in a *Partisan Review* piece on Francis Parkman's *Oregon Trail*, had waxed eloquent about "our" American forests, Philip Rahv had teasingly asked, "*Our* forests, Alfred?" *Commentary* was implicitly answering: yes, "why *not* 'our' this time?"[1]

That assertive question prompted *Partisan Review*'s 1952 symposium titled "Our Country and Our Culture." It wasn't just the forests that were grand: so were the achievements of writers on what Kazin called our "native grounds" and of the American people in general during World War II. The Family of New York Intellectuals (Murray Kempton's term again, which I will deploy throughout) had been an elite living in exile from the rest of America – their bodies in New York and their souls in Paris. That is why an editor at the *New Yorker* would once jokingly ask Podhoretz whether the typewriters at *Partisan Review* had a special key with "alienation" embossed upon it in full. The "Our

Country and Our Culture" symposium marked the Family's determination to get "beyond alienation," and by 1958 Delmore Schwartz, the poet, critic, and storywriter, could affirm that "America, not Europe, is now the sanctuary of culture; civilization's very existence depends upon America, upon the actuality of American life, and not the ideas of the American Dream. To criticize the actuality upon which all hope depends thus becomes a criticism of hope itself."[2]

Not that Schwartz or anyone else in the Family wanted to stifle criticism of the way things really were in America – on the subject of race relations, for instance. Quite the contrary, especially at *Partisan Review*. Cohen's *Commentary*, however, was particularly careful to ally its focused criticism with the spirit of liberal anticommunism. Cohen knew very well that discrimination against blacks and Jews was still prevalent in America, but he was also persuaded that the country had the constitutional mechanisms for eliminating it and that, as Podhoretz later remarked, one mustn't meanwhile "give aid and comfort to the totalitarian enemy whose main ideological purpose was to demonstrate that American capitalism was both unjust and unviable, that American democracy was a sham," or that "outright fascists" were bent on taking over the government and sparking "a nuclear war."[3]

Internal disagreements within the Family weren't long in coming, however. We can see hints of them in a letter Podhoretz wrote Jacqueline about Whittaker Chambers's *Witness*, the then sensational account of an intellectual's deconversion from communism:

A marvellous book, Clarke, even where it's bad, because it's bad in the right way. I don't mean to be cryptic. The best things in the book are about the Communist party and the Hiss case; the worst stuff is Chambers' gaffing about his new-found Christianity. But in both sections the man comes through as a fascinating character (Rahv calls him Dostoevskyan, which he is).

Podhoretz was also watching Senator McCarthy responding on television to President Truman's attacks:

It was sickening, especially the parts in which McCarthy was right. How much we would love for people like him to be absolutely vicious, to have absolutely nothing to say, and what a beastly disappointment when they turn out to be ordinarily vicious, not ogres at all. It would be so much easier to deal with a monster.[4]

These were justified ambivalences. But for the most part the atmosphere in 1953 was one of "exhilaration" – what, several years before, the novelist and critic Mary McCarthy had identified as a feeling of possibility: our uncouth frontier nation was becoming a civilization after all.[5] Cohen's *Commentary* was the voice of such sophisticated patriotism, the audience for which had been augmented by the large number of postwar college graduates, many of them on the GI Bill, who knew something about literature, could follow debates about the differences between totalitarianism right and left, and grasped the importance of democracy's opposition to both. *Partisan Review* might still be a magazine for "producers," the writers who conceived ideas, but *Commentary* was for the "consumers," who needed and wanted help surveying those ideas. And unlike the editors of *Menorah Journal* and the *Contemporary Jewish Record*, Cohen wanted to reach educated Gentile readers as well as Jews.[6]

Family writers had shown themselves capable of extraordinary "verve, vitality, wit, texture, and above all brilliance," but they could also be "overly assertive" (Rahv), "overly lyrical" (Kazin), "overly refined" (Trilling), or "overly clever" (Schwartz), "and even on an amazing occasion or two overly diffident."[7] The strain and the diffidence came from the feeling that those forests, literal and literary, still belonged to WASPs like Edmund Wilson. Columbia and Cambridge had given Podhoretz a slightly stronger sense of belonging, however, which meant that his prose was confident without being bumptious. He also had a knack for keeping his words flowing, not eddying back on themselves. That enabled readers to see bottom – to see what Arnold called "the object as it really is," or what Warshow called "the immediate experience."

One "immediate experience" Podhoretz could be clear and candid about was the new genre of television drama. In the fall of 1953 he wrote and, under Warshow's tutelage, revised and re-revised "Our Changing Ideals, as Seen on TV," which anticipated some of the insights Marshall McLuhan would soon purvey.[8] The plan at *Commentary*, he wrote Jacqueline, was for him to "build up a real backlog of articles, so that they can continue to publish my stuff while I go through basic training in the army," after which he might have time to write fresh material. Building up a backlog was fine by him: "I have literally nothing else to do. Waiting around to be drafted, with no regular occupation, no income (except what I get from writing), no social life, left out of everything – it would be enough to drive me round a bend."[9]

Warshow was just the sort of coach a young critic should pray for, advising Podhoretz to "thicken" his television article, and admonishing him "for saying that I considered this article a kind of hack-job."[10] By the third draft, Warshow was *really* pleased, and so was Podhoretz. "I keep concentrating on the *qualities* of things instead of on their meaning," he told Jacqueline, "and it seems to have wrought a revolution in my style." Thus in the essay he summarizes a television drama "about a young man of twenty who discovers his mother committing adultery while his father is away on a business trip." The father responds "patiently and sympathetically" by "trying to convince his son that their family is too important to be destroyed by a mistake." The boy goes "upstairs to comfort his mother," and Podhoretz concludes that "This is an atmosphere in which adultery and betrayal breed not hatred, but new responsibility."[11]

It was gratifying to write and rewrite his way into such insights, but he needed to keep his mind on his job: "A voice just came into my head," he told Jacqueline, referring of course to *her* voice, "saying ... 'Keep calm, and above all, NOT to get infatuated with your literary image of yourself.'" He also had to consider his ongoing relations with his parents. His mother felt no happiness about his literary productivity:

While I'm writing, she peeks in at me, shakes her head, and says pityingly, "It's not going, huh? Oy, why do you have to suffer so much? What good is having such a brilliant mind if you have to work so hard and get such a little bit of money for it?" I suppose she's got a point. But the peculiar thing is that she means it. She never boasts about me anymore to her friends . . . and when they ask her on the telephone what I'm doing these days, she kind of shrugs and sighs deprecatingly, "Nothing much. He writes. Yeah, for a magazine. You wouldn't know it even if I told you the name: Commentary. No, not much, just expenses. Aaah, the damn draft board killed a whole year of schooling. Sure, he just waits and goes crazy. Most of the time he doesn't even know what you're saying to him. What's the use of talking? There's nothing I can do. So what's by you?"

His father's ill health, meanwhile, was a torture for everyone: "It breaks my heart, keeps me from sleeping."[12]

Podhoretz's most important assignment that fall was to review Bellow's *Adventures of Augie March*. The novelist had shown the manuscript to most of the Family elders, who, knowing his sensitivities to criticism, told him it was wonderful – even if they hadn't read it. Since Podhoretz didn't know Bellow and hadn't seen the manuscript, the *Commentary* editors thought he would be "a disinterested party." Naturally he had heard the buzz and looked forward to reading the ever elusive "great American novel," but alas he found *Augie* wasn't it. Despite its commendable declarations about belonging to America, its "effervescent" mingling of mandarin and demotic speech, its tumbling of modes ("from farce to melodrama") – all attempts "to put blood into contemporary fiction and break through the hidebound conventions of the well-made novel" – *Augie* fell short of greatness. Podhoretz could tell by the "forced spontaneity" in many passages, which betrayed something "willed" and therefore "empty" in the book's beyond-alienation "affirmation." Bellow could sometimes sound "larky" in his optimism – an optimism that seemed unearned by a protagonist who "goes through everything and undergoes nothing."[13]

Could a novice critic dare come out with such a contrarian judgment? What if he was wrong? Dwight Macdonald, Podhoretz knew, "was still being laughed at for a youthful attack on T. S. Eliot thirty years earlier." Worse than being wrong, however, was being gutless. Warshow himself would withdraw his "respect if I played false with my response to the book – the one unforgivable sin in his otherwise absolutely tolerant eyes." So in good conscience, and with justifiable trepidation, Podhoretz went forward.

By the time the review appeared in October 1953, Bellow was moving his batteries into position. Warshow happened to admire *Augie*, thought Podhoretz's criticism "too harsh," and "with a dissenting and mollifying covering letter" sent Bellow an advance copy. But Bellow thought he smelled a rat. His "reply to Warshow," Podhoretz recalled, "with carbon copies sent to a dozen or more people, ran to two single-spaced typewritten pages. 'Your young Mr. P,' he called me throughout, understandably not being able to bring himself to utter my despicable name."[14] Although Trilling himself had written a "glow-ing review" of the book, Bellow imagined that for "dark" reasons of his own he had colluded with the editors at *Commentary* to get Podhoretz to reveal "what they all really thought... but were afraid to come out and say."[15]

Fifteen years later, Podhoretz would remark that such paranoia wasn't pecu-liar to Bellow. It was an occupational hazard for serious writers, especially in an age of no secure faith.[16] Still, our "young Mr. P" could count on the friendship of Warshow and Trilling, and even the Family members who were dismayed by his dissent on *Augie* seemed ready to take their hats off. He had done what they respected: set forth a cogent case that got people talking. Accordingly, Philip Rahv, co-editor of *Partisan Review*, invited him to a party at his and his wife Nathalie's apartment in Greenwich Village. It was like a second bar mitzvah – but as Podhoretz realized even then, he wasn't necessarily among well-wishers.

As William Phillips, Rahv's fellow editor at *Partisan Review*, once noted, the difference between the Family and the WASPy New Critics prominent in quarterlies like the *Kenyon* and the *Sewanee Review* was simple: "All they ever do is praise and promote one another, and all we ever do is attack one another." It seemed an honor "to be adopted into the family" – "you *existed* as a writer and an intellectual" – but from there on "you could expect to be spoken of by many (not all) of your relatives in the most terrifyingly cruel terms."[17] At least Podhoretz was not alone. When in the course of the evening at the Rahvs he heard Clement Greenberg "called stupid" and Diana Trilling, Phillips, Mary McCarthy, and others traduced, he figured no one was safe. Besides, if Greenberg was stupid and Warshow an "educated fool," then he didn't "mind being an upstart, or whatever it is I'm supposed to be."[18]

One very positive thing happened at that party: Rahv asked him to write for *Partisan Review*. Then, later the next week, William Shawn asked him to write for the *New Yorker*. "You lucky bastard... I wish they would ask me," Warshow jealously confessed, the next moment heaping praise upon his protégé. Shawn's invitation came upon the recommendation of Dwight Mac-donald, who agreed with Podhoretz's reservations about *Augie* and thought the young man might complement the handful of older highbrow critics – himself, Kazin, Wilson – then writing for the middlebrow sophisticates' weekly bible.

Podhoretz was euphoric. The *New Yorker* people "treated me as if I were royalty," he wrote Jacqueline; they "wanted to know how come they hadn't heard of me before, where I've been hiding all these years, etc." Perhaps he could do reviews while he was in the army, after which there was the possibility of a staff position: "I'd be paid something like $5,000 for ten pieces a year." And all this was "on the strength of that one review" of Bellow, which, they told him, was "the best piece of literary criticism we've come across in years." Not that, compared with Rahv, Phillips, Cohen, or Warshow, someone like Shawn would really know. But who could not be drawn by the promise of "money and fame"? The one would "make it possible for me to earn a living without teaching," while the other would come down to having a great number of readers.

All such prospects would in any event have to wait for two years since Podhoretz's draft notice had at last arrived. Ten days before reporting to the induction center, he had lunch with Trilling, who quite rightly told him that it was a good thing he was going into the army. His "success has been too rapid," and staying around "literary New York," especially unmarried, could be dangerous.

That is, I have (as he does, or so he told me) a "charismatic quality" that is my most important asset. I'll have to protect it, guard it, make sure I don't betray it, but at the same time, I'm not supposed to think about it too much! People will try to kill it in me, and I may even be persuaded to betray it; but it's my duty to see that it remains intact.

Army service would postpone that particular test of his character, and in the meantime, he told Jacqueline, "as wot *you'll* protect me from getting corrupted."[19]

He wasn't in uniform or out of town yet, however. Warshow ran into Bellow and John Berryman at a *Partisan Review* fund-raiser. Bellow had softened, but Berryman, then a rising poet, told Warshow, as Podhoretz related to Jacqueline, that "I was contemptible. *He* knows what my motives were in attacking a great book like Augie March; I was just trying to get a little attention for myself.... He also said that no matter how good I become, I won't be allowed to forget this review 'for 20 years.'"[20] How right Trilling had been to say "that I was too young to be forced to cope with such things; he knew of people who were driven out of writing from sheer panic, once they started to make their mark."

Before Podhoretz reported for induction on December 15, the *Commentary* staff threw him a going-away party – yet another bar mitzvah. As he wrote Jacqueline, Clem Greenberg first presented him "the most traditional of bar mitzvah gifts: a [Parker '51'] fountain pen," and "then proposed a toast to me as 'the nicest writer we've ever had up here and one of the nicest people I've ever met.' Proomph. I'd better put such things out of my mind for the time being and concentrate on being a soldier and staying out of trouble."[21] Indeed.

Basic training (at Fort Dix, New Jersey) was the first school, so to speak, that Podhoretz had gone into and not ended up at the top of the class. His letters to Jacqueline are replete with statements such as "the most horrible experience I've ever gone through" and "more of a challenge to my power of 'taking it' than I expected." But there was no way out. He relieved himself by describing the military system and the men who ran it, including his first sergeant, a Hawaiian and "easily the toughest character I've ever run into," and his company commander, a black who "carries himself with such assurance and such dignity and power that his color strikes you as merely another element of his attractiveness." Since Truman's desegregation order in 1948, the armed services had become what they have remained – a laboratory for meritocracy. The merit of these two men was that they could run forever, do pushups, or take a rifle apart and put it back together in lightning time. Podhoretz couldn't. As a result, the army seemed to him "a calculated conspiracy to bring out all my limitations.... All that matters is that I'm running in a mob, panting and

FIGURE 9. Norman Podhoretz as a private in the U.S. Army, 1954

aching, and I want to stop; and there's a sergeant alongside me who won't let me stop, screaming at me, calling me weak."

When Podhoretz was inducted, the personnel interviewer, hearing him say he had taught English – i.e., done some supervisions during his third year at Clare – listed him as a "language teacher," which meant automatic assignment to communications intelligence. The more glamorous communications intelligence track was the language school at Monterey, California. Podhoretz got the unglamorous track – beginning in the Army Security Agency School at Fort Devens, Massachusetts. Unglamorous but important, for it decoded military traffic all over the world. In 1954, one would have seen a pool of men like Podhoretz listening through earphones to Morse code transmissions, typing out, very quickly, the dots and dashes, then sending the sequence up to the cryptanalysts.

The training at Devens lasted four months, into June 1954, and compared with Dix the life was grand – "a great leap," Podhoretz said to Trilling, from hell "right over Purgatorio" and directly into paradise.[22] He routinely got three-day weekend passes, plus most weeknights free, and with a new Chevy, which cost $1,800 (now about $13,700), he was off base frequently – driving to Brooklyn to visit his parents or to nearby Lowell, Fitchburg, or Worcester, where, with his pals, he went "hunting for girls." Other weekends were spent driving around New England, a Puritan America he had never seen before.

One day he paid a call on Irving Howe, then teaching at Brandeis, and wrote Trilling an account:

We spent a few hours together, fencing cautiously with one another, both of us bored by our mutual dishonesty, and all the while Mrs. Howe sat silently by, knitting inexorably, like Madame Defarge. He "casually" introduced mention of his article ["The Age of Conformity" had appeared that winter in *Partisan Review*], and within two minutes I found him asking why "Lionel was so violent in his reaction." I told him that as far as I knew, you weren't violent at all; merely sad.[23]

"The Age of Conformity" bemoaned the sort of optimism Trilling himself expressed to Podhoretz when, in 1953, the *New Yorker* had asked the younger man to write reviews: why should high- and middlebrow people be forever at odds the way they were in 1923 or 1933? Wasn't it a good sign that in America "wealth" and "intellect" were in rapprochement, not only in the pages of the *New Yorker* but in business and government offices, where highbrows were increasingly being hired? Howe, a socialist, thought it a bad sign. Intellectuals weren't supposed to work for the wealthy and the powerful; they were supposed to unmask and castigate them.

On this occasion, too, Podhoretz told Howe that army service was making intellectual concerns seem less important than they had seemed before – to which the older man dampeningly replied: "maybe you should consider going into another line of work." Howe himself had served in the army during the war, but since he was stationed in the Aleutian Islands, where the enemy was not troubling, he passed nearly all his time reading literature. He hadn't, during his army hitch, learned much about ordinary Americans and their unliterary concerns, as Norman Mailer had learned and as Podhoretz was learning, and he continued all his life to regard patriotism as a scoundrel's lapse from "the internationalist perspective" of the revolutionary.[24]

Podhoretz sorely missed Jacqueline back in England. "*I won't* have you sitting around by yourself moaning because the Dreaded Day [her thirtieth birthday] has finally come." She represented those blessed Cambridge years, and their visits together in *noir* London. He had, he wrote her, all day been

enclosed in an inviolably private trance, remembering you. . . . We were sitting in a café somewhere one night a long time ago, discussing something or other. We were on high stools at a bar (as a matter of fact, I think we were eating sandwiches at a pub not far from LSE). You were dressed in blue (it was the first time I saw your coat after you had it dyed), and your make-up looked very beautiful in the light of the room. You had a cigarette in your hand (and the tip was red from lipstick), your legs were crossed, and you were turned toward me, but not looking at me, holding your arm out, and there was that miraculous smile of incipient discovery (I think we were groping toward some new idea) that transfigured your face and made you look beautiful and more than beautiful. I remember my main feeling at that moment. It wasn't tenderness or anything like that. It was pride.

That would be pride in having such a woman as his friend.

Another sort of pride comes out in Podhoretz's evocation of an Armed Forces Day parade at Devens, which reveals a great deal about the mood of American soldiers right after the Korean War:

I even experienced for the first time something of the uplift you're supposed to feel when you're in uniform and part of a great militant organization. When we snapped smartly to attention and saluted en masse as the band played the national anthem I actually got one of those chills down my spine. And marching to a very good army band helped a great deal. It would have amused you to hear the different marches.

It was fitting that, in uniform and trying to read again, he chose the classic military novel: "I bought me a cheap edition of *War and Peace* (which made no impression on me at sixteen), and I've succeeded in finding enough time and energy to read the first 100 pages. It's colossal, Clarke – I can finally understand why they say Tolstoy is as great as Dostoyevsky."[25]

One weekend, Podhoretz and a couple of pals from Devens, all in uniform, were driving through southern Vermont and saw a sign for the Marlboro Festival, which, knowing nothing about classical music, he had never heard of. "The campus was utterly charming," he would remember, "and you could hear music coming out of the buildings. I looked up in the parking lot and suddenly there was Midge." He hadn't seen her in four years. She was sharing a summer cottage with Lloyd Tannenbaum and his wife, Sylvia, who was the stepdaughter of conductor William Steinberg of the Pittsburgh Symphony. Moshe was working in the city. "Midge and I greeted each other very warmly," she urging him to "'come visit us: I have two little girls.' Little did I know! These two little girls."[26] The girls, three and a half and two-and-a-half years old, were Rachel and Naomi Decter, who would later be central to Podhoretz's life. But at the moment he thought only of how lucky people like Midge were – free to vacation in Vermont and go to music festivals – and how unlucky he was most of the time, confined to base.

His Devens training over, Podhoretz was in September transferred to Germany, first to Giessen and then to Kassel, where he and three other soldiers shared quarters that once housed a single German air force officer. Code recorders like himself worked in three shifts around the clock, a routine "challenging enough," he wrote Trilling, "but – as D. H. Lawrence once said – this place is no good." The reference was to Giessen, but it encompassed Frankfurt, too: "I've never seen a city so depressing. It's rather like the Germans, in fact – industrious, cold, utterly devoid of grace or charm." He also felt cut off: "Europe is behind a thick wall of glass – you can see it but you can't reach out to touch it."[27] A specialist third-class, Podhoretz was in an outfit made up of men from all over. "Talk about *diversity*!" he would later say. And they respected the "scrap of pidgin-German" he had acquired, mostly by "subtracting my Hebrew from my Yiddish and changing my accent." The German was tapped when the guys would go into town hunting *Schatzies* (from *Schatz*, "sweet-heart") at the *Gasthausen*. Podhoretz would be their designated schmoozer. Drinking, the American soldiers got into conversations with German men, too. "It was a common joke," Podhoretz recollected, "you never met anybody who'd served [in World War II] anywhere other than the Russian front. You never really knew to whom you were talking, and as a Jew I was extremely uncomfortable."

Once he got into an altercation with a German who had either praised the *Waffen* SS or dismissed the stories about persecution of the Jews as British propaganda. Podhoretz angrily retorted that "the SS were murderers," and they were on the verge of a fight when a Southerner named Warren, "a real redneck, almost a hillbilly, seeing trouble coming – it was like in a Western movie – grabbed this beer bottle, smashed it on the counter, and went at this guy. He never cut him, but he sprang to my defense. Without knowing what the argument was about, he was a brother."[28]

If he couldn't educate the Germans during his tour of duty, he could do something to educate his fellow soldiers. On one occasion, an Information Education officer tried to conduct a course for the troops explaining why they were in Europe – the Pentagon had decided that a primer on the Cold War would be useful – but he was soon "completely at sea":

"There was this guy Marx," he would say, "and this other guy...." I called out "Engels" and so on, helping him out at various junctures. And instead of being annoyed, he was grateful. Next day I was summoned to the company commander's office. "I've been studying your jacket and see that you have a whole shitload of college degrees." "Yes sir." "I hear you were helping out Lieutenant Blah-blah the other day. How would you like to take over this job? Let me explain it's not legal because you're not an officer. But if you won't tell anybody I won't tell anybody, and I'll relieve you of your other duties." So I said I'd love to.[29]

He discarded the Information Education pamphlets and outlined his own course. "I think it was the most successful thing I've done in my entire life," he later declared. "They *adored* it, these guys, they simply adored it." He didn't talk over their heads but simplified ideas without distorting them. Many of the soldiers, who had "never encountered an idea before," ended up going to college. He had shown them that ideas were in fact "something they cared about." From Marx to Stalin, from the *Federalist Papers* to the Truman Doctrine, he spoke on "what the country was about, why we were all here, why we'd fought a war in Korea. I've drawn on this all my life, having gotten it straight in my own head during those lectures."[30]

Shipped back to America in the fall of 1955, for three months Podhoretz interviewed new recruits to determine their "military occupational specialty." Fortunately, he had frequent weekend passes, and it was then that he began to see Midge Decter, now divorced and mothering those "two little girls," on a serious basis. She happened to be working as Cohen's secretary at *Commentary*.

5

The Practicing Critic

In January 1955, on a two-week leave, Podhoretz visited Jacqueline. She had fallen in love with Huw Wheldon, whom she had known since 1951, when, as head of the Welsh Arts Council, he had helped organize the Festival of Britain, for which he was named an Officer of the Order of the British Empire. He was six years older than Jacqueline – her vanished father's name had also been Huw – just as she was seven years older than Podhoretz. Wheldon was therefore thirteen years older than Podhoretz, which initially made the younger man feel awkward, but they soon got on exceedingly well and eventually became each other's best friend.

Huw and Jacqueline were to marry in the fall of 1956, and Norman and Midge Decter directly followed suit. They would comprise a fascinating four-some, the men fraternally bonded and the women intimate, too. The ocean between the couples was in one way a blessing, for it required a correspondence, the women writing especially splendid letters. They would see each other in London or New York and would take adoptive interest in each other's children – just as those children, "mad for each other," would share a kind of cousinly bond.

Wheldon's father was a prominent Welsh educator, and the family had led a very chapel-centered life. Deeply Presbyterian, Huw seemed to Podhoretz to "know the Bible by heart. It was from him," he said, "that I learned the phrase 'spiritual illiteracy' – meaning those who don't understand that there are things of the spirit, as opposed to the emotions or the mind." Shortly after graduating from LSE, Wheldon entered the army, where he saw action in France and served after the war with British forces in Palestine. In 1954, he was just starting to become a familiar face on BBC television. At first, he hosted a program for children called *All Your Own* that capitalized on his tall stature and friendly face persona. Later, he was in charge of cultural programing, which meant producing *Monitor* and bringing out controversial films like Peter Watkins's *The War Game* or celebratory series like Kenneth Clark's *Civilisation* or J. H. Plumb's *Royal Heritage*, which he co-authored. Ultimately he "got his 'K'" – that is, like his father, he was knighted for his services to the British public. "Sir Huge," as he was affectionately called, died in 1986.

Podhoretz's friendships with other men in England – for example, Aaron Klug (a biochemist who eventually won a Nobel Prize) and Dan Jacobson (a writer), both South African Jews whom, as we have seen, he knew at Cambridge – had their personal ups and political downs as the years passed, but "Huw became the closest friend I ever had," one who "stuck till the day he died." Podhoretz has never known – "I've been embarrassed to inquire" – whether the Wheldon children (a son, Wynn, and two daughters, Sian and Megan) have understood how close he and their mother once were. He and she did indulge in some impossible talk about marriage, as alluded to in *Making It*, and from that book one might suppose the Wheldon children long ago drew the obvious conclusion.

In any case, Podhoretz remarked, Jacqueline came over the years to feel "that I stole Huw from her," spiritually speaking, and "she became more and more difficult for me to reach." On the one hand, she focused on her three children, her husband's career, and social events like the annual Christmas party they would give in Richmond, for which she did all the decorating and all the baking. On the other hand, she was spending much of her time reading and writing, and therefore becoming less sociable. Meanwhile the husbands and the children got on gloriously. Wynn would remember the first Seder the families shared, his father reading a Psalm in Welsh and he an English poem, after which "Midge and Norman began singing advertising jingles from the forties and fifties. How blithely they could move from the serious to the light within a sentence, and with perfect timing."[1]

That of course would be much later. In the late forties, as we have seen, Midge had been Norman's older and soon-married woman friend while he was at JTS and Columbia, and in the summer of 1954, when she was the mother of two little girls, she had seen him by chance at the Marlboro Festival. Upon the birth of their first daughter, Rachel, she and Moshe Decter had, at Midge's mother's insistence, moved out to the suburb of Glen Oaks Village – supposedly a more suitable place to raise a family. Though "to the naked eye there seem[ed] to be no drastic difficulty," Decter looked in the mirror and wondered "Is *this* all there is going to be forever?" She told her husband she needed a divorce. "Doesn't anyone want to lead the life of quiet desperation any more?" a friend asked. Not Decter, anyway: she wanted the life of *un*quiet desperation – in the city. Yes, she felt guilty "for the hurt I caused," but at the same time she was sure (and remained sure) that the divorce "saved my own life."[2]

She had earlier been Warshow's secretary at *Commentary*, and in 1955, entrusting the girls to an incompetent but faithful governess, she returned to work as Cohen's. She couldn't take shorthand, so while he dictated she would "scribble down the gist" and then write his letters for him – thereby preventing the occasional "folly, such as insulting an old friend, or being brutal to one of the authors on whom he particularly depended." Glazer and Kristol had

FIGURE 10. Norman Podhoretz with Irving Kristol (left) in the office of *Encounter* magazine, London, 1954.

departed – the first to work for a time at Anchor Books, the second to edit (with Stephen Spender) a new magazine, *Encounter*, in London – but Sherry Abel (then married to the writer Lionel Abel) and, for a while, Warshow were still on staff.

By the time Podhoretz came on board as an editor, after his discharge from the army in mid-December 1955, he and Decter had been seeing each other for three months and had become "*very* good friends." To keep their burgeoning relationship out of the office, she left *Commentary* to join the Zionist magazine *Midstream*. She would bring him home to the girls and, she has written, "I tried as subtly as I knew how to convince them that their daddy would not consider them disloyal if they made friends with my new friend (which was a lie, and not, I am humiliated to say, the last one of its kind I ever tried to palm off on them)." More than friends, she and Norman were lovers and wanted to marry. His mother, "to understate the matter by a mile, [was] far from pleased by the idea that her son was marrying a divorced woman with two children." Nor were Midge's own parents ecstatic about her affair.[3]

When Podhoretz began working at *Commentary* (Cohen had held a post open for him), Warshow was no longer there. He had died of a heart attack, a bolt from the blue, at age thirty-eight. In mid-March 1955, Podhoretz, still in Germany, read the news in a telegram from Decter. "I'm going to miss him terribly," he told Jacqueline. "I've even thought, almost resentfully, that

I knew him such a short time, and that I still need him. I'm afraid that I feel sorrier for myself than for him."[4] For Trilling also the death of Warshow was "shattering"; he was sure it had given pause "to everyone" in the Family. "It seemed to me that many of us – for suddenly there was an 'us' – had realized the fact of death almost for the first time," he wrote to Podhoretz.

Trilling himself was only fifty, but the intimations of mortality occasioned by Warshow's demise were obvious. Had the heart attack been connected with tensions at *Commentary*? Trilling didn't know, but Warshow had told him enough to make him worry about Podhoretz's plan to work there. "I do think that you should conceive again the possibility of an academic career, but if not that, then you must not be simple about what will face you at *Commentary*, especially with Bob gone."[5] Podhoretz's reply does sound a little frightened, admitting that Warshow had "expressed misgivings about having influenced me to take" Cohen's offer. As for "the academic career I seem to have forsworn," he told Trilling about the hit he was making with his army lectures. "[E]very time one of them succeeds in reaching the men, I begin wondering all over again whether I'm right to give up teaching." But, feeling old at twenty-five, he worried that "the endless process of getting the PhD would do more damage to whatever it is about me that's vulnerable than a few years of working under Elliot Cohen."

No, convinced "that writing is going to be my life," he wanted "to get on with it right away." He had "35,000 words of a novel down on paper, and a few short stories. At the moment the novel seems hopeless, but working on it has at least convinced me that I *can* write respectable fiction,"[6] and he strongly encouraged Trilling, who had already published a novel (*The Middle of the Journey*, 1947) and a number of short stories, to do more of the same: "I wish you'd forget about whatever it is that's been holding you back, and really let loose. You've done your duty by the discursive essay."[7]

Podhoretz's aborted novel is lost, but his three attempts at short stories survive in typescript. They are competent, but in this vein he wasn't going to give Bellow et al. any headaches.

Getting started at *Commentary* was hard. When Decter left to work for *Midstream*, the only person on staff whom Podhoretz could call friendly was Sherry Abel. Having been with the magazine as an editorial assistant since 1950, she had transferred any literary ambitions she may have had "to the men she admired" and thus, as Podhoretz later wrote, robbed the world "of one of the potentially great minor novelists of all time." She was a marvelous and "compulsive *raconteuse*."[8]

Beyond the ebullient Sherry, however, lay gloom. Cohen was in the Payne Whitney Clinic with bipolar disorder and, as Podhoretz wrote Jacqueline, "nobody quite knows when or whether he'll ever be back. That leaves the Greenberg brothers – Marty and Clem – who are difficult to work with and even more difficult to like after you get to know them well." Clem was associate editor, and Marty (his brother Martin) managing editor. Together they constituted "the Boss," though in fact Clem outranked and led Marty.[9] "My main complaint," Podhoretz continued, "is that I have virtually no autonomy, no authority to move on my own. . . . Things are amicable enough on the surface, but we all hate one another, deep down."[10]

In fact, with Cohen incapacitated, the Greenbergs appeared to want *him* to leave, too. Clem thought an assistant editorship, on a six-month trial basis at $5,500 per annum, appropriate for a whippersnapper like Podhoretz. Cohen, however, had promised him an associate editorship at $7,000. The whippersnapper asked himself if "*this* [was] what the glorious life of intellectual New York was going to be – army-style chicken-shit, trial periods, hostile and suspicious superiors, and a lousy hundred bucks a week?" His mother wasn't surprised. Hearing his account of office politics, she put the round peg in the round hole: "Of course. He [Clem] wants everything for himself, so he's trying to cut you out."[11]

Despite all the hazing, Podhoretz knew he was a good editor. Sherry had thus assured him, as had contributors. He had an instinct for knowing what to do with manuscripts, especially those by the "recently arrived German Jews whose ignorance of English was matched only by their blandly arrogant assurance that they had already mastered what was, in their eyes, the language of an inferior culture." The crystallizing moment came with the first manuscript given him, a total mess on Spinoza and the Jews. Working quickly, he reorganized the essay's parts and, without putting words in the author's mouth, got inside his mind and said what, if the man had known the rules of the language and had been able to order his ideas so that readers might grasp them, he *would* have said. Call it less editorial dictation than editorial ventriloquism.[12]

In the meantime, Podhoretz was also busy writing, assessing the would-be classics of the moment – as he had done with Bellow's *Augie*. The assignments that the *New Yorker* had promised now came regularly. Between the fall of 1956 and the fall of 1958, the magazine ran his reviews of Nelson Algren's *A Walk on the Wild Side*, Simone de Beauvoir's *The Mandarins*, Alan Moorehead's *Gallipoli*, Faulkner's *The Town*, P. H. Newby's *Revolution and Roses*, William Golding's *The Two Deaths of Christopher Martin*, Vladimir Dudintsev's *Not By Bread Alone*, Albert Camus's *Exile and the Kingdom*, and C. P. Snow's *The Conscience of the Rich*. In that same two-year period, he was also contributing to *Midstream*, the *New Leader*, the *New Republic*, *Esquire*, *Partisan Review*, the *New York Times Book Review*, the *New Statesman*, and, toward the end, Kristol's new magazine, the *Reporter*.

This wasn't churning out copy for a daily newspaper, or for the Luce consortium. It was the journalistic side of what the novelist Terry Southern, in a phrase that always piqued Podhoretz, called "the quality lit. biz." And it *was* a business, not least in the matter of fees. What Podhoretz made on a review varied – the *New Yorker* paid a "gigantic fee" of $250 (about $1,900 now), *Commentary* between $25 and $50 ($190 and $380, respectively), depending on the length. He was calculating that if worse came to worst under the Greenbergs and he launched out on his own, he would have to earn around

$7,500 (by 1958 his salary at *Commentary*) beyond the $2,000 he was already getting as a writer. That would mean tripling his output. He needed that much because he and Midge had married and were paying $165 a month ($1,250 currently) for their huge – seven rooms, two and a half baths – Upper West Side apartment.[13]

"Most women want to be married," Midge Decter would later say, "and most men are scared to death of it. So usually, when there's a marriage, it's the result of a woman reassuring a frightened man that it's going to be OK."[14] In her own second marriage, this included reassuring the frightened man's frightened mother. Helen Podhoretz threatened everything up to and including self-defenestration if her darling son should marry an older woman with two children. True, Decter was at least Jewish, but St. Paul, Minnesota, where she was from, was so far beyond Brooklyn as to be unlocatable. The couple was nevertheless insistent, not just about getting married but about having Rachel and Naomi in attendance, thus confessing to Podhoretzes far and wide that "Normie" was marrying a divorcée. The moment of truth came when they brought the girls to Brownsville to meet the adoptive grandparents – Norman's father already acquiescent, his mother still opposed. The door opened, the girls looked up at the still very handsome Helen, and Rachel blurted out: "You're *so beautiful!*" That did the trick. She took the girls to her heart on the spot, and Midge quickly won a place there, too. The wedding took place on October 21, 1956, Midge being twenty-nine, Norman twenty-six.

Just weeks before, when Jacqueline and Huw were married in England, Podhoretz had written to offer his congratulations and to tell Jacqueline of his own impending wedding: "I'm very much in love with Midge, and have been for some time, but the prospect of becoming a stepfather to two robust and clamorous little girls was frightening." Mainly he felt "bewildered and scared, but also very pleased and even a bit proud of myself."[15]

"Don't come to New York unless you plan to be lucky," Gay Talese once said.[16] Podhoretz had so far been very lucky, first as a writer and now as a husband and stepfather. The "position" at *Commentary*, however, hadn't grown more comfortable. Since Cohen was still expected to return, Clem wouldn't lead, so the magazine drifted and its assistant editor stewed. Finally, after an unremembered but "particularly nasty piece of provocation" from the Greenbergs, the assistant editor "exploded in a voluptuous emission of obscene expletives" and walked out. All bravado, Podhoretz was going to choose the life of a freelancer.

But first he had to resign, which entailed an interview with the AJC to explain his reasons. Without prior thought, he let loose his complaints against the Greenbergs, who weren't working in Cohen's spirit and who, if Cohen ever did come back, were surely "planning to make life so miserable for him that the return would last only long enough to induce a relapse and set the stage for a coup." There followed six weeks of AJC meetings, hearings, and "enough intrigue to have launched the Russian Revolution itself." They arrived at an impossible plan: Clem was fired while Marty was retained and yoked to Podhoretz and George Lichtheim, a brilliant German-English intellectual who was an important contributor to the magazine and was then living in New York. This troika would run the magazine until Cohen came back.[17]

The troika muddled through 1957–58. Podhoretz was professional. He and Lichtheim, "a real polymath who knew everything and read eight languages," got on swimmingly, outvoting the seething Marty time and again. Incidentally, Al Pacino, then in an acting studio, "was a very good office boy for part of this time,"[18] and the young Susan Sontag, whom Sherry Abel called "a fishnet bluestocking," served for a while as editorial assistant.

The Cohen who returned to *Commentary* in late 1958 after two years in the hospital wasn't the leader Podhoretz had been waiting for. Neither psychotherapy (including shock treatment) nor psychoanalysis had helped. He was "a shrunken, shaken man," who would timidly take Marty's side in disputes – for example, rejecting pieces by Robert Graves or Hannah Arendt "on the basis of various high-sounding pretexts but actually because they were too controversial."[19] So Podhoretz resigned again, this time quietly, and regretting he hadn't held firm to his decision the year before.

He had an out. Jason Epstein, with help and advice from Podhoretz and other Columbia friends, had launched a publishing revolution with the Anchor Books series of quality paperbacks at Doubleday. Epstein was offering him half-time work at Anchor, with an annual salary $500 greater than *Commentary*'s and with "four days a week to write." After only three weeks, though, the scheme collapsed. Epstein had lost a power struggle of his own at Doubleday – which, ironically, now offered his job to Podhoretz. To turn on enemies like the Greenbergs was one thing, but he couldn't turn on a friend. So, in late 1958, with Midge and now three kids at home (Ruthie having been born in February), Podhoretz was jobless but happy. It was, after all, 1958, not 1938. The offer from Doubleday had convinced him "that there was money around in America – even for the likes of me."[20]

For much of 1958 and all of 1959, Podhoretz was a freelance reviewer, mostly of American books. He had chosen to construe Leavis's implicit "Yankee go home" as "remember where your home *is*." Thus the attention to *Augie March*, which in later reviews he extended to Bellow's subsequent fiction, including the near-masterpiece *Seize the Day* (1956), and the attention to other writers then attempting cultural breakthroughs. Like most of the fifties' younger intellectuals, Podhoretz was tantalized by the thematic and stylistic derring-do of Norman Mailer (1923–2007), but his best essay of the decade, "The Know-Nothing Bohemians," shows that his allegiance was not to the cultural Left but to the center – meaning, if we will, to Trilling and Leavis.

Appearing in *Partisan Review* in 1958, Podhoretz's essay contrasts the Bohemians of the twenties and thirties – Hemingway, Fitzgerald, Sinclair Lewis, Eliot, Pound, et al. – who fled the Midwest to New York or Paris in quest of a civilization marked by "intelligence, cultivation, spiritual refinement," with the Bohemians of the fifties, Ginsberg and especially Kerouac. The preferences of the latter were for "primitivism, instinct, energy, 'blood'" – a species of dumbed-down D. H. Lawrence. They held up Whitman's "spontaneity" as a cover for laziness: in their case not "the *right* words... but the first words, or at any rate the words that most obviously announce themselves as deriving from emotion rather than cerebration." The upshot was vagueness punctuated by bop ejaculations like "wild" or "crazy."

The Beats also wanted to be spontaneous about sex. Ginsberg in particular thrashed out against "repressive" laws banning hallucinogens and sex with underage boys – his thrashings-out often becoming physically violent. The history of fascism, to say nothing of the history of sadism, suggested to Podhoretz "that there is a close connection between ideologies of primitivistic vitalism and a willingness to look upon cruelty and blood-letting with complacency, if not downright enthusiasm."[21]

Philip Roth cheered the way Podhoretz had diagnosed the Beats' failings, although he also felt "that each word spoken about them is one more word than they deserve. I hope your word will be definitive, however."[22] Ginsberg himself was naturally dismayed by the aspersions from his fellow Columbian – and in *Partisan Review*, no less. As soon as the essay appeared, he wrote John Hollander, who had introduced him to Podhoretz in 1946, to complain about the latter's obtuseness: he mistakes "spontaneous bop prosody... [for] the use of hiptalk not realizing it refers to rhythmical construction of phrases & sentences." Ginsberg threw up his hands: Podhoretz was "stuck in his own hideous world," which objected to "juvenile delinquency, vulgarity, lack of basic education, bad taste, etc etc," and which was "so basically *wrong* (unscientific) so dependent on ridiculous provincial schoolboy ambitions & presuppositions." To Ginsberg, this was all "a sort of plot almost, a kind of organized mob stupidity.... I mean I give up, that's just too much fucking nasty brass."[23]

Podhoretz had opposed Ginsberg's inflation of homosexuality into a big deal. Yet how, Ginsberg asked an interviewer, could his daring proclamations of "being queer, homosexual all the time," which he admitted he "would not have wanted my father or my family to see," *not* be "interesting socially"? Especially when, as he believed, buggery and blow jobs were mystically linked with the "visions of Blake" he had had in 1948, and with Kerouac's preoccupations with "the Lamb of Jesus and spontaneous Buddhist mind."[24]

Ten years after "The Know-Nothing Bohemians," Podhoretz would look back and wonder whether he had been too severe: "Did I really care whether or not a bunch of idiot kids thought [Kerouac's] *On the Road* was a great novel?" But as the sixties wound down, the answer became clear: he *did* really care. The seductions of "bop prosody" had, with respect to drug abuse and sexual promiscuity, damagingly affected the lives of the idiot, and not-so-idiot, kids of what could seem an entire generation.

It was the kids that the Beats and their critics were fighting over. One Saturday evening in the fall of 1958, Ginsberg, Kerouac, and Podhoretz got together to talk over their differences. In the walk-up apartment to which they had invited him, Podhoretz was introduced to the so-called poet "Peter Orlovsky, to whom Ginsberg would remain married for all practical purposes other than sexual fidelity for the rest of his life." Kerouac's good looks in person exceeded even what his pictures in the glossy magazines had led Podhoretz to expect, and he had shaved off his signature stubble. "Had he perversely cleaned himself up for this meeting, just as I had done?" Podhoretz wondered.

At Columbia, Ginsberg "had been arrogant and brash and full of an in-your-face bravado," and capable of what he called "towering rages." (His famously "sweet and gentle persona" would come later.) The furious tirade that evening boiled down to a question the novelist Herbert Gold had also asked: Why wasn't Podhoretz *encouraging* young writers, the way Wilson or Pound had done during the twenties? The answer was that *they* had Fitzgerald, Hemingway, Eliot, Lawrence, Yeats, Eliot, and Joyce "to push and promote... whereas all poor Ginsberg had to work with were the likes of Jack Kerouac, Gary Snyder, and Lawrence Ferlinghetti."

Thus the conversation didn't go well. Ginsberg was so "seething" that Podhoretz seemed unable to make an impression on him. Kerouac was much nicer – as "disconcertingly... likable in the flesh as he was repellent in print" – and Podhoretz "could not help regretting the nastiness with which I had treated him and wishing I could say that I had been won over and now saw his novels in a new light." But *On the Road* was worse than a know-nothing exhibition. It was one of the seductions that made good on the threat Ginsberg hurled at Podhoretz as he was leaving the apartment: "We'll get you through your children!"

That threat – to look far ahead – wasn't carried out with Podhoretz's own children, who escaped the counterculture with "minimal damage." Many of their classmates, however, weren't so lucky. Their sufferings were emblematic of the "spiritual plague" of the sixties for which the antinomianism (*"nomos"* is Greek for "law") of Ginsberg, Kerouac, and their fellow Beats had been in no small part responsible.[25]

In 1958, Ginsberg looked to Mailer as an ally. The novelist's "The White Negro," an essay that appeared the year before in *Dissent*, seemed to the poet to have such "a great grasp of the Goof" as to stimulate the hope that he would drop fiction altogether and become "an angel poet."[26] Mailer's ideas about the "hipster" did have much in common with the Beats' obsession with "the Goof" – spontaneity, juvenile delinquency, and "going to eternity" by way of drugs or sex. It was an edgy, low-Bohemian position that Podhoretz and Mailer quarreled about from the start. What made Mailer different from Ginsberg, Podhoretz believed, was that he wasn't a complete Know-Nothing. Quarreling with him might pay off if it got him to articulate the something he did know.

Podhoretz's friendship with Mailer was the most important one in his life from the late fifties through the late sixties. They met at one of Lillian Hellman's dinner parties, possibly as early as the fall of 1957. Diana Trilling sat on

Mailer's left, admiring the polite attention he gave to Mrs. R. Kirk Askew, the "dowagerlike" wife of an art dealer and the kind of woman, Diana thought, most writers would have ignored. Then Mailer turned to Diana: "Now, what about you, smart cunt?" She laughed, tickled by the rough language – "so boldly flirtatious," she recalled, "so funny and outrageous applied to me."[27] Later in the evening Podhoretz told Mailer, "I'm working on an essay about you right now." "I'll bet you ten dollars I can tell you what you're going to say," Mailer replied, the message being: all you New York Intellectuals think alike. But this one shot back, "I'll bet you ten dollars you can't" – and won the bet.[28]

Midge wrote Jacqueline about this new friend, the "intellectual hipster" who had helped her husband rid himself of the anxiety "that his horror of becoming a professor was just a mark of some crucial inner inability to be 'serious.'"[29] To the contrary, if, as W. H. Auden had said, poetry makes nothing happen, then academic criticism operated at an even greater degree of irrelevance. That wasn't true, Podhoretz believed, of non-academic criticism, especially when it was devoted to living poets and novelists. Together, truly creative and critical writers *could* make something happen: they could affect a culture's sensibility, and therefore its behavior.

Though no hipster himself, Podhoretz saw both in Mailer's writings and in his flamboyant conduct an escape from "the dull round of aimless anxiety that has marked the Eisenhower years" – not so much by engineering "a more equitable world" as by inaugurating "a more exciting one" in which people would be larger, more heroic, more truthful.

Podhoretz was not without his doubts, however. His "ten-dollar" essay surveyed Mailer's career from *The Naked and the Dead* (1948), in which liberalism is at war with fascism; to *Barbary Shore* (1951), in which Trotskyite communism is offered as a system putting courage and imagination "into the service of freedom and equality rather than class and privilege"; to the more apolitical "White Negro," in which the hipster, following "the close call of his instinct as far as he dares," is trumpeted as "the herald of a revolution moving 'backward toward being and the secrets of human energy.'" But what was *that* supposed to mean? Nothing less than every infant's dream of "pursuing the immediate gratification of his strongest desires at every moment and by any means." Podhoretz understood that this was tantamount to the Beats' devolution into promiscuity and substance abuse. His essay's call was for Mailer to use his extraordinary genius to produce fiction in the service of more grown-up ideas.[30]

Such coaching was far friendlier than what the other Family members were offering – see, for instance, William Barrett's dismissive critique of *Barbary Shore* in *Partisan Review* – and Mailer responded gratefully. He kept his "craziness" in check whenever he and Podhoretz were together.[31] There was none of his trademark thumb-wrestling or boxing, marijuana appeared on only one occasion (a chain smoker, Podhoretz inhaled but didn't like it), and Podhoretz asked to be excused from an implied invitation to a three-way orgy. The two presented themselves as intellectuals. Thus, at a 1959 *Partisan Review* symposium on the thirties, they teamed up on behalf of radicalism, opposite Mary McCarthy and Arthur Schlesinger, Jr. on behalf of liberalism. The radicals didn't do so well, as Podhoretz would recall: "Mailer practically threw the debate by appearing in a work shirt and blue jeans" – "a childishly provocative act" given the audience – and "I spoke almost as bumblingly as Mailer." But they would have lost anyway for, as Schlesinger said, what mattered in the thirties was Roosevelt's liberal New Deal, and all the Stalinist or Trotskyist socialist chatter in America was "just that: chatter, none of it of any influence or significance."[32]

At the end of the fifties, Podhoretz and, to a lesser degree, the Trillings were Mailer's ambassadors to the Family. Because *The Naked and the Dead* had been a best-seller, Rahv and Phillips suspected its author of being middlebrow. By publishing "Norman Mailer, the Embattled Vision" in *Partisan Review*, Podhoretz put the bad-boy novelist onto the highbrow critics' register. Not without their demurring: Trilling, for one, wrote Podhoretz a letter amounting to a critique, praising the essay's "energy" and "perception" but nevertheless insisting "that our cultural situation couldn't be properly dealt with by a mind that had this much of Tom Sawyer in it, entrancing as Tom Sawyer can be." Besides, Mailer's "histrionic" sense of himself as an actor on the media stage was, for Trilling, too consonant with the self-regarding, role-playing culture he was attacking.

Part of this reaction, Trilling thought, was temperamental. He felt a Maileresque "disgust with the culture" but almost more disgust with artists and intellectuals who took every occasion to denounce it. In particular, he was disturbed by "the acceleration of anti-scientism" that the Ginsberg–Mailer romantic irrationalism seemed to entail. He, for one, wasn't giving up on literature and the humanities just because some late Romantics were committing the twin errors of aestheticism and irrationalism. In those errors, he concluded worriedly, "I smell a situation, the odor being of gunpowder."[33]

Podhoretz's hope was to keep Mailer's sparks from igniting that gunpowder – but not altogether to suppress the sparks, for they could be dazzlingly luminous. Their friendship in any event was professionally mutual: the novelist benefited from having the critic sponsor him inside "the so-called literary Establishment," while the critic finally had a "tiger" to ride. Mailer "was acting out in public the radical mode I believed in then," Podhoretz remembered. "Bored with my own sensibly moderate liberal ideas, but with Marxism and all its variants closed off as an alternative," he thought he had reached a kind of late-youth dead-end. Mailer represented a way out, "the possibility of a new kind of radicalism" – new insofar as it didn't "depend on Marx and . . . had no illusions about the Soviet Union." Mailer's "particular doctrines" were often balmy – for example, "constructing a theory of revolution with the psychopath playing the role Marx had assigned to the proletariat" – but the ambition to reach for "something very large," even if it risked "looking foolish," was something Podhoretz couldn't help admiring.[34]

Thus did the successor to Hemingway, Fitzgerald, and Lewis become the "drinking buddy" of the successor of Wilson and Trilling. Mailer and Podhoretz "confided in each other, and . . . read each other's writing."[35] Not that all of literary New York was charmed. "On the rare occasions when I was invited to one of [the Podhoretzes'] parties when they lived on the Upper West Side," the art critic Hilton Kramer recalled, "to see the look on Norman's face the moment that Norman Mailer arrived was to me a profound embarrassment. It was hero-worship of a kind that I didn't expect from a serious intellectual."[36] Even in 1959, though, the intellectual was as serious as a Kramer or a Trilling could wish. And in the sixties, the combat to maintain his spiritual independence would become mortal.

The kind of party Kramer referred to – whether hosted by the Podhoretzes, the Mailers, the Epsteins, the Rahvs, the Trillings, or Mary McCarthy – made Family relations both intimately affectionate and intimately hateful. Here was the person who had praised your essay – and there was the one who had damned or, worse, not even mentioned your novel. Married happily and writing prolifically, Podhoretz at the end of the fifties had gotten over most of the trepidation he had felt when invited to the Rahvs' dinner party in 1953, for he was now a recognized player, simultaneously a *Commentary* and *Partisan Review* insider, a *New Yorker* reviewer, and an occasional habitué of the in-between world represented by George Plimpton's *Paris Review*. For an enchanted while, everyone, he was almost young enough to believe, seemed to love him.

A similar rush would be put on Susan Sontag in the mid-sixties. And indeed a Podhoretz or a Sontag could make a startling first impression. The question was whether they could make a substantial second one. Podhoretz's plan, in 1958, was to make his bid with a book about twentieth-century American writing. An anxious business, as Midge described it to the Wheldons: Norman "sitting next to me alternately gnawing his knuckles and banging on the typewriter and cursing the first day he ever put pencil to paper." But also exhilarating: "The plain fact is that N. has not had such a good time since he was at Cambridge, 'cracking' Burke, and Disraeli, and all those other romantic gentlemen."[37] This was by day. By night, at least two or three times a week, he and she were mingling with the Family for cocktails or dinner.

For Jacqueline's benefit, Midge described the nocturnal "literary season," which at a given moment might mean

a cocktail party to meet Philip Toynbee (who looks like a ravaged nine-year-old), a gathering apparently sponsored for the purpose of bringing Diana Trilling together with some socialist so that they can fight about something he called her in print five years ago, etc., etc. In my October frame of mind, I hate all the bastards passionately; by June, I have to concede everyone else is much worse; and in August, I even miss one or two of them – and everyone else *is* much worse.

Still, inside the Family circle, Midge found herself longing for something else. What she and Norman missed were true "*friends*" like the Wheldons. In

FIGURE II. Huw and Jacqueline Wheldon in London, circa 1965. (By permission of Wynn Wheldon.)

the summer of 1958, the two families, each with brand new babies (Ruthie and Wynn Pierce, respectively), had spent the better part of six weeks together in England. Jealous of Huw's having a son, Podhoretz was illogically convinced such good fortune would never be his. But that would be a question for nature to settle.

By autumn 1959, he was still beavering away at the book on American writing. One of the icons he was writing about was Edmund Wilson, who, he noted, had made "the republic of letters" seem an actual place, and one that in the late fifties was more exciting than the republic defined by politicians. In politics, the large ideological debates appeared to have been settled; the remaining problems – how to tweak this or that part of the governmental machinery – were technical. In the culture, by contrast, tremendous things were happening, especially in music, painting, sports, movies, and literary nonfiction. Debate was lively, and as a critic Podhoretz took it up with force. He was mainly concerned with judgment and taste: Were Faulkner's *A Fable*, Kerouac's *On the Road*, or Nathanael West's *Day of the Locust* great novels? Could the playlets on TV tell us enough about ourselves to make them worth watching? Were the memoirs of Harry Truman deeply revealing of the American character and the inner workings of legislation and statesmanship? Those with sufficient taste to

admire the right book, the right symphony, the right abstract painting, or even
the right double-play combination were of the elect. The rest were damned to
philistinism.

What Podhoretz specifically contributed to these arguments was an insistence on quality. He saw how most other critics, again including highbrows,
ranked a work according to its "having something relevant to say" – about,
for example, "the Negro problem" or the threat of nuclear war – and the more
unmistakable the "say," the better. But how should one discriminate between
agitprop, which said the "right" thing and was accordingly cheered, and art,
which, whether intent on saying the right thing or not, was concerned with
much else besides?

Podhoretz's insistence on artistic quality didn't make him a believer in art's
autonomy. "Art for art's sake," as a style of living or as a theoretic doctrine,
was never for him. Rather, he had learned from Trilling and Leavis the principle
they learned from Eliot: the value of a work of art consists in its coherence and
consistency (Does the action make sense? Are the characters' thoughts and
deeds intelligible?) and in the intensity and idiomatic freshness of its phrasing
(Does this phrasing enable us to *feel* the presence of the action and the actors,
and their psychological, moral, and possibly political significance?). Literature
that is literature at all is about life, and great literature is about life greatly.

Podhoretz also knew what has since been widely forgotten, that "the serious literature of a country, *properly read*, carried significant clues to the true
state of affairs in the society of which it was inevitably, *though not solely*,
a reflection." Those italics – the words are from the retrospective *My Love
Affair with America* – are aimed at critics "who praised or damned novels and
poems and plays entirely for the political or ideological positions they took,
and not for how well or badly the writer's intentions – whatever they might
be – were realized."[38] That is, if Faulkner wanted to make demigods out of his
Yoknapatawpha characters, fine. The first question, aesthetic, was how well he
had done so, and in which of his books. The second question, moral, was how
much we agree with the sentiments and ideas he expresses through those characters. A third question can be how, and to what degree, the aesthetic and the
moral achievements of an artist are bound up with one another. Answering that
third question – which entails *demonstrating* the connection not just between
aesthetic form and moral content but also between the work and its social
context – is something very few critics can do. Podhoretz, a really extraordinary critic, could.

Still, although Leavis had given him a vocabulary for discriminating between
Pope and Dryden, or *Middlemarch* and *The Mill on the Floss*, bringing that sort
of artillery to bear on most current novels seemed like overkill. How wonderful
it would be to salute a genuine artistic achievement at the level of *Moby-Dick*
or *Huckleberry Finn*! And how melancholy it was to have to say things like "If
Eudora Welty is a good writer, so is Elizabeth Spencer," whose "competent
and inconsequential novel" he had been assigned to review.[39] He was more
and more tempted to beg off – to face the fact that, in the fifties, neither the

fiction nor the poetry (Lowell's *Life Studies* excepted) *did* really matter – not as they had mattered "in the great creative explosion of the teens and twenties."

The most valuable creative explosion of the postwar years, Podhoretz increasingly realized, had been in *non*-fiction: Trilling's *The Liberal Imagination,* Hannah Arendt's *The Origins of Totalitarianism,* and James Baldwin's *Notes of a Native Son,* for example. These books were "literature" – a claim less startling now than it was in the late fifties – precisely because they put the right words in the right order, had themes and sometimes even characters, and were possessed of a moral-political seriousness analogous to what we look for in the best novels, plays, and poems. Besides hailing such nonfiction masters, Podhoretz wanted to join their company, and essays like "The Know-Nothing Bohemians" showed he just might do it. He admired a Trilling or an Arendt because they were addressing "society" in ways that the American novel – with its "increasingly boring emphasis on love as the be-all and end-all of life, . . . its narcissism, its self-pitying tones, its constricted sense of human possibility, its unearned wisdoms, its trivial emotional dramas" – wasn't.[40]

It was in this frame of mind that he set out to write his book about postwar nonfiction. He got a $2,500 (now $17,725) advance from Farrar, Straus; it was "enough to pay the rent for a few months, and more than enough to give me nervous thoughts about the fix I would be in if I proved unable to write the book and had to return the money." Unfortunately, the project was too ambitious. He managed fifty pages on Wilson, the longest piece he had ever written, and directly got stuck. Plan B was to do a study, along the lines of Wilson's own *Axel's Castle,* of six postwar American novelists, capped by a "Whither Mankind?" conclusion. The point would be not to impugn the novelists (he had done enough of that in his *Partisan Review, Commentary,* and *New Yorker* pieces) but to show both how they were unmanned by their belatedness – i.e., doomed merely to consolidate the victories of the high modernists – and how they felt stymied by current social conditions, especially the Cold War.[41]

He expanded what he had already written on Bellow and Mailer, then got blocked again. These pieces and the long one on Wilson eventually found their way into the collection *Doings and Undoings.* Meanwhile, suddenly and inexplicably, the munificent *New Yorker* stopped phoning. He drew a little unexpected mileage from the "victim" status that being "fired" conferred on him, but in all earnestness he needed another job just to pay his family's rent.

Enter Jason Epstein once more. His setback at Doubleday hadn't scotched his conviction that an intelligent person should "go into business and get rich." America was after all a capitalist society, "rigged so that the only way to beat it was to join it," and join it only as a nominal employee, if that. He wanted to run something big, and his newest something was the Looking Glass Library, a young-parents project for reprinting some hard-to-find children's classics – from H. G. Wells's *War of the Worlds* or E. Nesbit's *The Enchanted Castle* to Richard Arthur Warren Hughes's *The Spider's Palace* or George MacDonald's

The Princess and Curdie. Many of the volumes would be illustrated by Edward Gorey, who also did covers for Anchor Books.

Epstein's notion was that Podhoretz and he would round up financial backers, claim fifty-percent ownership for themselves "in return for having conceived the idea and providing the talent," and make a killing within five years. Podhoretz was to be the editor, with star advisers like Wilson and Auden. Together they would bring about an "anti-progressive counter revolution" in children's publishing.

Norman was "quite looking forward to becoming thoroughly expert in juvenile literature," Midge told Jacqueline, adding that "Most of the stuff they begin with, of course, is English and Victorian. And did you ever stop to think how many creeps and lunatics were running around England about 75 years ago? It takes a near-psychotic, we have decided, to write a great children's book."[42] More prosaically, Podhoretz was putting in time in the Children's Room at the New York Public Library, where he got strange looks from parents and librarians, and where he found "that children's books, with very few exceptions, really are for children." Random House did manage in the first year to bring out twenty titles. But at that rate neither Epstein nor Podhoretz was going to get rich.[43]

The Children's Room became instantly irrelevant one day in the spring of 1959, when Elliot Cohen committed suicide by smothering himself in a plastic bag. The AJC had, as Clem Greenberg expressed it, "sent Elliot back to the trenches where he'd been mortally wounded anyhow."[44] Coming back to *Commentary* to replace Cohen was the farthest thing from Greenberg's mind. His main interest, apart from writing about abstract-expressionist paintings, had become alcohol: "Before I got fired from *Commentary* I drank at night, but then I discovered I liked drinking in the day too. So?"[45]

Replacing Cohen was also the farthest thing from Podhoretz's mind. He was simply a writer at work, sensing the approach of his thirtieth birthday and looking, Midge told Jacqueline, "much the same, thinner at the top and thicker at the middle, face more lined about the eyes from squinting, for yet another year, speculatively and judiciously at the world."[46]

6

Boss

Elliot Cohen had been so disabled throughout 1959 that Marty Greenberg was the one who got *Commentary* out each month, and now that Cohen was dead, Greenberg naturally expected to be named his successor. The AJC, however, wanted to consider a range of candidates. Kristol, Kazin, and Daniel Bell said they preferred not to apply, but Leslie Fiedler, teaching at Montana State, declared himself open to a "Visiting Editor-in-Chief" appointment. When the magazine's publication committee failed to confirm him as quickly as it might, he lost interest and recommended Podhoretz, whom it had approached independently.[1] It is significant that Fiedler, the *enfant terrible* of American Studies (his *Love and Death in the American Novel* would be a sensation in 1960), regarded Podhoretz as an ally. They were both firmly anticommunist, on the one hand, and, on the other, would turn out to be thoughtfully enthusiastic about three things: Mailer's talent as a novelist, Norman O. Brown's breakthrough as a psychoanalytic theorist, and Paul Goodman's insight as a critic of education and culture.

No credible intellectual in that year was looking for a revolution in the streets, but many were looking for a revolution in consciousness – which vaguely meant a change in the ways people thought and felt about sex, race relations, hallucinogens, juvenile delinquency, and the Cold War. As John Kenneth Galbraith later said, intellectuals ought to give "more credit to the Eisenhower administration," for not only had it put them all into "opposition," but opposition was also suddenly legit.[2] At the beginning of what everyone would soon be calling the New Frontier, critical opposition seemed, in fact, ready to come to a boil.

Podhoretz told the publication committee, first over a series of lunches and then in formal interviews, how he would turn up the heat. He would not only move the magazine to the Left but would make it more general – less parochially Jewish – both in its roster of contributors and in its range of topics. (In doing so, he would also be making the magazine more seriously Jewish, for Cohen's lack of grounding in the Judaic tradition caused him to favor what

Midge Decter later dubbed "the folksy crap."[3]) Podhoretz's friends thought him silly even to be thinking about taking the editorship. Epstein was sure that *Commentary* was "finished, played out"; Kristol said that a Jewish magazine would be too confining;[4] Diana Trilling was maternally concerned that he was too young for a position where, as he put it, "I would be constantly forced into a hasty overformulation of my ideas"; and Phillips also thought him too young.

Podhoretz was initially inclined to agree. If he was willing to interview for the position, it was for the sake of getting an offer and then vengefully letting Marty Greenberg know he had turned it down. But the more Podhoretz declared himself sincerely uninterested in the job, the more the committee wanted him. An offer was tendered. He could have a free hand to "shake things up" as he wished; his salary wouldn't be the $20,000 per year he asked for, but a still ("with my peasant's idea of wealth") handsome $17,000 ($118,500 now).[5]

So what was not to like? There was the prospect of his having to give up his career as a literary critic, notably the *Axel's Castle*-style book on postwar American writers. But he wasn't getting on with that book, and if he put it on the shelf, he would be able to pick it up with fresh energy a few years down the road. An opportunity like this, by contrast, would hardly present itself in a few years, at the onset of middle age. One reason the committee favored him was that, right now, he was so blessedly young. Call it the necessary illusion of a person still at the threshold of his career, but Podhoretz, with the AJC's offer in hand, lay awake thinking that as editor of *Commentary* he just might be able to shape and direct the freshened national interest in youth – not the youth who took after the crazy Beats but the youth who were as seriously concerned with social, political, and cultural issues as he was. He said yes.

Taking over in January 1960, the young editor began by cleaning house. He fired Greenberg and all the old staff save for Sherry Abel, whom he persuaded to remain as managing editor. He redesigned the cover and format ("badly, but at least it was different") and flushed the entire backlog of manuscripts. As before, *Commentary* would solicit pieces on non-Jewish as well as Jewish subjects, and by Gentile as well as Jewish writers. But all would have to meet the same high standards. Under Cohen, there had been a work of fiction in nearly every issue, whether it was good or not. Under Podhoretz, only first-rate stories would appear, and no poetry at all – "like Rabbi Plato," Abel said, he banished the poets from his republic, though mainly because it was so hard to find verse of high quality that would also fit the magazine's new "preoccupations." The biggest decision, and one affecting the tone of every piece in every issue, was to move away from academic contributors and toward Family writers and their kin abroad, mainly in England. This was because they were usually more adept at addressing the common reader, and more broadly learned.

What about moving the magazine to the Left? We have to remember it was a matter of degree. During the early Cold War years, when the Soviet leader was Joseph Stalin, the hard anticommunists, which included everyone in the Family, agreed that the Soviets' left-wing totalitarianism was as "unqualifiedly evil" as the Nazis' right-wing version, and that the Soviets were committed to a world revolution, by military force if necessary, which only American power could forestall. Stalin died in 1953. When, three years later, his successor, Nikita Khrushchev, made a speech denouncing his crimes and cult of personality, some hopeful Western observers regarded this as a "thaw" in the Cold War, and perhaps as the beginning of a socialism that would fulfill rather than travesty Marx's vision.

At Columbia and Cambridge, Podhoretz had been on the hard anticommunist side, which, he wrote, not only had "the better arguments" but was also "more thrillingly brilliant and moral" than any competing politics then on offer. But had Khrushchev's speech opened up the possibility of a *soft* anticommunism?[6] If the new Soviet leader himself could admit Stalin's crimes, perhaps the system he served was amenable to moral correction. The redoubtable hard anticommunist Bertram D. Wolfe, writing in *Commentary*, would have none of this: Khrushchev's de-Stalinization rhetoric was "an obvious tactical retreat" that had no relevance to the Soviet quest for world domination. But the young Podhoretz was as breathless as other newly soft anticommunists: "How could Wolfe possibly be so *sure* so quickly unless he had closed his mind to any evidence which might interfere with his comfortable theories?"[7] He expressed the same skepticism, if in the opposite direction, when it came to the old *Commentary*'s vision of the United States. What Elliot Cohen had argued, in Podhoretz's impressionistic version, was

that the United States of America, for all its imperfections (the persistence of discrimination against Jews and Negroes being the main one), was the best society a human nature beset and limited by its own built-in imperfections ... was likely to be able to build. American society was, therefore, Reality ... and any large dissatisfaction with it was to be attributed to the Human Condition itself, against which it was of course "childish" or "foolish" or "infantile leftist" or pathological to struggle.

This, in point of fact, is the vision of America that the experience of the late sixties would bring Podhoretz back to. But at the beginning of the decade he was keen on mounting a reformist struggle against the needless imperfections of American society.[8] The question for the liberal reformer in 1960, as in any era, was which imperfections were needless and which were not.

Enter Paul Goodman (1911–1972), "that prodigal genius," who had a particular fascination, not untinged by eros, with the troubled youths then known as juvenile delinquents. Were they, à la Stephen Sondheim's lyrics in *West Side Story*, depraved on accounta they were deprived, or deprived on accounta they were depraved? Writing about the Beats in 1957, Podhoretz himself had favored the second theory: these young people needed to pull themselves together and learn to act like responsible adults. Goodman favored the first theory: the kids *couldn't* pull themselves together, for the simple reason that the society wasn't "together."

Though Goodman, very "idiosyncratic in his ideological formation," had published in *Commentary* from the beginning, he hadn't contributed since 1958, by which time he had fallen out with much of the Family. As a new

editor, Podhoretz wanted to bring back such disaffected writers, inviting them
to his and Midge's parties and visiting with them over drinks or lunch. "Con-
descending to meet," Goodman gave him a manuscript he had been fruitlessly
circulating. It was *Growing Up Absurd*, which Podhoretz decided "was exactly
what I was looking for. I basically cut three big chunks out of it," he recalled,
"and ran it in my first three issues: they created a sensation."[9] He had also
phoned Epstein, whose skeptical reaction was "Goodman? . . . that has-been?"
Epstein nevertheless read it "that very night in my apartment," Podhoretz said,
and the next day Goodman had a contract from Random House, one of the
"nineteen publishers" that had earlier rejected him. *Growing Up Absurd* would
sell over 100,000 copies in paperback and become "one of the campus bibles
of the sixties." It also gave Epstein and Podhoretz "a reputation as partners in
the making of literary careers," though in fact only Goodman and, earlier in
1959, Norman O. Brown, of *Love Against Death* fame, were ever "made" by
the pair.[10]

With his Ph.D. in philosophy, anarchistic temperament, and married-but-
queer sexual orientation, Goodman was too complicated to "follow even his
own party line."[11] A belated Romantic, he defied the authoritarian pessimism
of the high modernists.[12] But neither did he accept, with Nietzsche and Marx,
the claim that "the Protestant-liberal-bourgeois synthesis," child of the Enlightenment and father to American democracy, was "finished." Rather, he called
for the fulfillment of the Enlightenment's "incomplete revolutions" – notably
on behalf of people "alienated" in their work and frustrated in their sex lives.[13]

The large sections of *Growing Up Absurd* featured in Podhoretz's first three
issues of *Commentary* (February to April, 1960) certainly caught people's attention. Here was what everyone had regarded as a tired Jewish magazine talking
about cultural, particularly sexual, revolution: small wonder that *Commentary*
soon became what *Esquire* would call "the red-hot center" of the literary world,
gaining in circulation and also quickly surpassing *Partisan Review* (whose circulation was always tiny) in influence among the Family and its followers. It
would have no serious competitor until the rise of the lefter-than-thou *New
York Review of Books*.

Commentary was hot because of Goodman, among others. But why, intellectually, was Podhoretz hot for him? Some people familiar with Podhoretz's
own writing in the late fifties weren't surprised. As he put it in "The Young
Generation" (1957), a piece in the *New Leader*, the "non-generation" born
between 1925 and 1935 hadn't swum "in the Plaza fountain in the middle of
the night" like the youth of the twenties, joined the Popular Front and dreamed
of socialist revolution like those of the thirties, or (for the most part) fought
against fascism in the early forties. Rather, they had gone to school in the late
forties and early fifties, studying under professors like Trilling, who, having
analyzed the methods and outcomes of the Soviet and Nazi attempts at total-
ist engineering, and having likewise rejected liberalism's naïve optimism, had
instructed them in a "more subtle, skeptical temper," which spoke less about
"the rights of man" than about his "duties and responsibilities."

Good students, the brightest postwar young were convinced that "the real adventure" lay neither in revolutionary politics nor in artsy, permissive Bohemia. It lay "in the 'moral life' of the individual." Podhoretz's sober generation married early, had children, and held steady jobs. And the novels and poems written by their artists were equally "well-bred" and "impeccable."

So far, so grown-up. Yet such etiolated people could not produce important literature, and might not even be said to be fully alive. Podhoretz's restlessness, implicit throughout "The Young Generation," was virtually explicit at the end: his generation, unhappy with its lack of identity, was "beginning to feel cheated of its youth." Having "willed itself from childhood directly into adulthood, it still has its adolescence to go through – for a man can never skip adolescence, he can only postpone it."[14]

He was in effect declaring that he was twenty-six, not thirty-six, years old and that his politics were going to be different from that of his older Family relatives (at Cambridge, he and Steve Marcus had joked about writing a piece to be called "So What If We Never Fought in the Spanish Civil War?"). Moreover, he was declaring that his older relatives' "sacred scriptures" – Faulkner, Fitzgerald, & Co. – weren't necessarily sacred to *his* generation.[15]

It was a matter of clearing space for his own maturation. "Middle-aged before my time," Podhoretz could see through the childish irrationalism of the Beats, but in his delayed adolescence he could feel drawn, powerfully, to the parties and strong sexual impulses that much of Mailer's writing tried to glorify. Also, he could sense in the sociology of Goodman a peculiar and attractive state of "innocence" – a mind that hadn't yet "crashed up against" the "limitations" of the human condition.[16]

Not everyone was pleased with the utopian socialist note struck by Podhoretz's early issues. The historian of America and France Denis W. Brogan, whom he had admired over in England, wondered why smart people were praising Goodman, who was saying nothing that the critic Herbert Read or A. S. Neill, of *Summerhill* celebrity, hadn't said a few years before.[17] The education writer Martin Mayer asked Podhoretz how Goodman's "ill-written refugee from the pages of *Dissent*" ever became the lead piece in his inaugural issue. Mayer quoted Kristol to the effect that, while Goodman was capable of scoring some intuitive "hits," he "doesn't *know* anything" – meaning he had done no serious sociological research.

While admiring Podhoretz's "loyalty" to the Goodman articles, Mayer offered some editorial advice:

[T]here is an infinite number of good reasons to run a piece, and only one bad reason – that you agree with it. The Goodman piece is demonstrably by a man who has not taken the trouble to *investigate* what he is writing about, and thus should not be run, whether one agrees with his conclusions or not.

...Finally, if I may echo the whining complaint of the writer since time immemorial – the world is a much more complicated place than anyone is likely to learn from sitting in a publishing office and chatting with fellow intellectuals.[18]

It is significant that Podhoretz saved this letter. Mayer was not just articulate; he was right about how an editor needs to evaluate a manuscript. One can appreciate the degree of Podhoretz's editorial intelligence in then asking Mayer to write for *Commentary*, which for the next fifteen years he did. *Commentary* would have a grand symphonic design, but many different instruments would contribute to it.

"I remember your saying once you 'were meant for' Commentary," Bernard Malamud wrote Podhoretz after the first issue. "Fate listened."[19] People in high places were listening, too. Thanks to *Commentary*, Paul Goodman had become well-known in Washington, and the two of them had been invited along with others "to address a group of young liberal congressmen ... on problems of American education and culture."

The meeting was a disappointment – "now that I was being asked to tell the politicians what they ought to be doing, I found that I had absolutely nothing to say"[20] – but this was not the only invitation to Washington Podhoretz would receive during the Kennedy years. On one occasion, when asked to offer his "'ideas' ... about the situation in Harlem," he held forth over lunch until he noticed the administration official getting restless. "I asked him whether he disagreed with what I was saying. 'No, no,' he answered, 'what you're saying is all very well, but what should we *do* about it?'"[21]

The Kennedy White House, outflanking the Republicans by shifting power away from the legislative and into the executive and judicial branches of government, was hoping to *force* liberal reforms on a stubbornly conservative country. But then the administration was blindsided by its own left wing – the New Left that (in its first incarnation) dogmatically opposed centralized concentrations of power.[22] What next? For the Kennedyites – as Oscar Gass, an economist as well as a peerless intellectual, noted – the default answer was to adopt "the tone of café society ... on the cobbled, shaded streets of Georgetown" while putting on "the demeanor of Churchill during the Battle of Britain."[23] If many intellectuals, especially from Harvard, idolized Kennedy, it was in part because they, too, had a predilection for café society and Churchillian posturing. But, like Podhoretz, they had "nothing" to offer in the way of doable policy.

Still the invitations continued. During the Johnson administration, Eric F. Goldman, the historian and presidential assistant, asked Podhoretz and a handful of other intellectuals to write "what then must be done" letters. Podhoretz's was a standard left-liberal call for "a more energetic attack on the related problems of racial discrimination and structural unemployment"; large cuts in defense spending and the conversion of arms factories to produce peaceful things and give poor people jobs; subsidies for "little magazines, local newspapers, experimental theaters, and small television stations": and, above all, the creation of a climate in which we could "hope to get beyond the acquisitive habits of soul that the past ages of scarcity have transmitted to us as their fitting legacy."[24] This sounded, even then, like an intellectual merely going through the motions.

In June 1964 came a summons to a state dinner at the White House for the Israeli Prime Minister, Levi Eshkol. Midge Decter wrote to Jacqueline Wheldon:

Norman still cannot make up his mind whether an invitation from Johnson to meet Levi Eskhol means more or less than an invitation from Kennedy to be among Jackie's writers. In a certain sense, an invitation from Johnson means more than one from Kennedy, who was after all even a friend of friends of ours. On the other hand, for the editor of *Commentary* to meet a Jewish prime minister – seems a little routine. As for me, all I can think about is will my gold shoes last the night.[25]

As it turned out, the gold shoes served her well. "The White House was absolutely marvelous," Podhoretz wrote to George Lichtheim in London, "and Midge even danced with Johnson (to the tune of *Never on Sunday*)."[26]

It was an election year, and Johnson marched unopposed to his party's nomination. As for the Republicans, Podhoretz told Hans J. Morgenthau how, watching the GOP convention on television, "I found myself growing alarmed by the ferocity of the Goldwater forces. Did you feel that way too? He will, of course, be nominated on the first ballot tonight and – God help us – by some miracle, he might even win [the general election]."[27] It didn't take long for that worry to dissipate, but, as Podhoretz wrote to Malcolm Muggeridge, "Whether or not [Goldwater] himself is a menace, the forces behind him are really vicious." Yet was Johnson much better? Podhoretz thought LBJ might well have "manufactured" "the recent crisis in the Gulf of Tonkin" precisely "to demonstrate the firmness of his resolve and to force Goldwater into a posture of bipartisan support."[28] A plague-on-both-your-houses mood was threatening to set in.

Starting in 1960 and for many summers thereafter, Midge and the children would spend July and August in a rented house on Fire Island that, Podhoretz told Lichtheim, was "very primitive, very deserted and very stark."[29] He would come out on the weekends, and while they would have occasional visitors from England – the Wheldons, Aaron and Liebe Klug, the Dan Jacobsons – Fire Island generally meant a break from their constant socializing in the city.

And "constant" is the right word. A look at their calendar gives one a feeling of vicarious exhaustion: Podhoretz's diary for winter 1962, for instance, recorded lunches, dinners, and cocktail parties with the Louis Kronenbergers, Mary McCarthy, the William Phillipses, the Epsteins, Irwin Ross, and a preview of a Lillian Hellman play; for spring, more of the same, plus Mailer, Edwin O'Conner, Robert Pickus, and dinner with Elie Wiesel, followed by a party for Shimon Peres; for fall, ditto, plus the Ted Solotaroffs, Herb Gans, Dan Bell, Richard Crosland, the Trillings, a *Show* magazine party at the Plaza – while, throughout the year, get-togethers with the John Hollanders, the Robert Lowells, the Jules Feiffers, and the John Marquands.

This flitting was part of an editor's function, keeping tuned to the hum and buzz of who was thinking, writing, publishing, courting, dropping what or whom. Fire Island weekends meant relaxation for the husband and father. But even in the city he wasn't always flitting. He had two particular friends, Jason Epstein, close since Columbia days, and the dozen years older John "Jack" Thompson, with whom he could relax man-to-man. The Epsteins and the Podhoretzes – Jason was a fabulous cook – had dinner together a remarkable two or three times a week, creating what might have seemed a blended family. Then, on Thursdays, Jason, Norman, and Jack would have a boys-night-out meeting of what Jason facetiously labeled the Newport Reading Club – "Newport" as in high-toned rich, "Reading" as in literary-intellectual. The purpose was to eat, drink, and be conversationally merry, usually at the best steak houses in the city.

It was expensive, like everything else they deemed necessary: good food, high-class recreation, the best private day schools for the children. Epstein's published view was that a salary of $50,000 a year (now $333,000), never mind what one might realize in the way of dividends, "will keep a family, if not in luxury, at least in reasonable comfort and safety." Yes, cheese-paring on the West Side might enable a family to live on half that sum, but beneath that level one became "not a citizen but a victim of New York." Epstein's lament – "To be without money in New York is usually to be without honor" – could apply to any decade in the last six.[30] Terrified of the abyss of honorless poverty, either in Manhattan or "in those miles of flats in Queens or Brooklyn," which is where Podhoretz had been born and raised, the members of the Newport Reading Club fell into the trap of making rich people's choices when they weren't really rich.

Not that Thompson had always been a near-penniless poet. As Midge Decter would recall, his first wife had been "an immensely rich woman" from his hometown of Grand Rapids ("Grand Rapture," he called it), Michigan: "He was the boy from the other side of the tracks, very beautiful, and she was the richest girl in town." He had gone to Kenyon College in the footsteps of Lowell, who had become a friend; studied and taught at Columbia when Jason and Norman were students; and later taught at Stony Brook. He and the heiress had three children and lived "in splendor on Fifth Avenue." After a divorce, he married someone without a nickel and lived the life of a far-from-wealthy academic.[31] He was perhaps the only Norwegian-American Podhoretz ever knew:

> Ten-thousand Swedes
> Ran through the weeds
> Chased by one Norwegian.

"That's something I learned from him," Podhoretz would remember. "One of the most brilliant people I've ever known, just a wasted talent, a serious alcoholic, very nihilistic," with a mordant sense of humor: "Jack used to play a wicked game about 'who would hide you in the Holocaust.'" Epstein, he said, would be kind enough to "put you in the closet, but he wouldn't be able to stand it because one day he'd look out the window and see an SS guard and shout, 'Hey, you'll never guess who I've got in my closet!'"[32]

We get a glimpse of Podhoretz's hectic life in a letter to Lichtheim in December 1960: "Midge is pregnant and will undoubtedly give birth to another girl come the spring. I have now definitely become a comic character and I am trying to behave with dignity under the circumstances."[33] That winter, Midge told Jacqueline how "my children are growing and growing – right through my hands. They have lives all their own, which I find a great relief and also resent." The older girls had "snatched Ruthie right out of infancy." She "fiercely" imitated "their speech and gestures," and while it was "comic," her mother found "it rather disconcerting in one so small to be so corrupt." Rachel was "promising to disappear in a puff of cheap, teen-age fantasy ... she is just everybody's longings rolled into one package." Naomi, for her part, "is a sharp little self-pitying Jewish intellectual of a kid, who sees through everything and plots great conspiracies against herself. She is also turning out to be an immensely gifted musician and a great beauty, and I am usually at a loss to understand the relation of her existence to mine."[34] When her fourth child was born, it was, as an astonished and elated Podhoretz told the Wheldons, "a BOY (repeat: BOY)," whom they named John Mordecai. John, he had to remind people "who ought to know without being told," was "a *Hebrew* name": "Yokhanan = John = the first Jewish President of the U.S."[35]

Apart from bearing and nurturing children, Midge kept busy writing the occasional essay and pondering a book on the eighteenth-century novelist Henry Fielding, which was never finished. Jacqueline was forever scribbling, too, but the women's letters were often less about their literary work or even about their husbands or their kids than about the tension of the times, especially, as Midge wrote, "the prospect of the nuclear war that our government seems intent on preparing us all for." Under that sort of cloud, she found herself "wondering why poor old Rachel, who is such a love, must undergo the pressure of extra drill in arithmetic, toward which she has turned a completely closed and blank mind."[36]

Mushroom clouds had been very much on Podhoretz's mind in 1961. "I still think of virtually nothing but *Commentary* and nuclear war (which for me have turned into the same subject)," he told Nat Glazer,[37] and in soft anticommunist mode he was entertaining the possibility that the Cold War was less the Soviets' fault than the Americans'. Voicing this argument explicitly was the Columbia historian Staughton Lynd, son of the pioneering sociologists Robert and Helen Lynd whose *Middletown* (1937) had been a Leavis favorite. By not allowing Stalin the traditional Russian sphere of influence in Eastern Europe, Lynd maintained, Truman had provoked the hostile standoff that was the Cold War.[38] The Trillings and other anticommunist elders had seen this stalking horse before. They warned Podhoretz that Lynd was "more benevolent" toward communism than he sometimes found it politic to declare.[39]

Did thinking like Lynd mean joining the movement for unilateral disarmament? Podhoretz wanted to work it through, which he did in a remarkable series of articles and symposia focusing on the implications of Herman Kahn's

On Thermonuclear War, a book that even pro-disarmament figures like the Harvard historian and social activist H. Stuart Hughes recognized as "one of the great works of our time." The arguments about nuclear war at the start of the sixties would remain central to Podhoretz's evolving attitude toward foreign policy over the following decades.

To simplify, Herman Kahn was all for *controlling* nuclear arms, but he was against unilaterally abandoning them. The best strategy was deterrence: the threat of our nuclear weapons would keep the enemy from using theirs.

People like Hughes regarded this policy of "mutually assured destruction" (MAD) as immoral. Why, Hughes rhetorically asked, had we armed ourselves with nuclear weapons in the first place? Were we sure that the contest between liberal democracy and the communist world was worth dying for? Admittedly, waiting for some world government to compel all nations to disarm seemed "vacuous and sentimental." Hughes's own proposal was unilateral disarmament – which may have been sentimental, too, but he tried to redeem it by appealing to the "theological requirement that 'good faith be kept with an enemy.'"[40]

Podhoretz moderated a discussion on "Western Values and Total War," in which Hughes's sharpest antagonist was Sidney Hook. To Hook, our choices, confronted by left-wing totalitarianism, were analogous to the ones we had faced with its right-wing cousin in the thirties. We could surrender, in which case "Communism, with all its evils, will take over the world." We could appease, in which case we would later have to face a stronger enemy whose defeat would be yet more costly. Or we could demonstrate that "we are prepared to fight," which because the Soviet leaders were rational would almost certainly mean that we would "not have to fight." To Hook, the foundational truth was this: "Our willingness to fight for our freedom may be the best way of preserving it."[41]

As Podhoretz would later recall, Hook's long experience as a debater was simply too much for Hughes. The debate's invited audience, however, shared Hughes's conviction that the balance of terror was morally unacceptable. Podhoretz felt the same way, but he couldn't endorse Hughes's call for unilateral disarmament either. His "intellectual" position was closer to the anticommunism of the tough-minded Hook, and within a decade his "moral" position would be, too.

Between geopolitical worries about nuclear weapons and local excitement about cultural revolution, Podhoretz needed ways to unwind. Booze was one way. His lunches, usually with writers, would include a martini or two, and later in the day, before and after supper, he would drink Jack Daniels – consuming "approximately three quarts ... a week."[42] Like the Family as a whole, he was playing the Jazz Age game, Fitzgerald or Hemingway being the model of the genius who couldn't get his "talent" to work without the inspiration of alcohol. Podhoretz had started drinking heavily when he "discovered, almost by accident" that it was "the only way to turn off" his racing editorial mind

FIGURE 12. *Commentary* symposium on "Western Values and Total War" (1961). Seated from left to right are Sidney Hook, Norman Podhoretz, Hans J. Morgenthau, and H. Stuart Hughes.

and get some sleep. "When I quit drinking," he remarked, "Pat Moynihan told me this was a wanton waste of a great gift: I was the most talented drinker he'd ever known, the only Jew who could drink an Irishman under the table."[43] Also, like many writers of his generation, he was smoking two or three packs a day.

Could pornography, or at least the cause of pornography, be far behind? That became a lively question in October 1960, when a British court granted Penguin the right to print Lawrence's *Lady Chatterley's Lover*. Everyone agreed that the novel was about sex, but was it pornography or literature?[44] At Cambridge, Podhoretz had judged *Lady Chatterley* to be "a great book."[45] Leavis didn't think so – hence his refusal to testify on Penguin's behalf – but he, Diana Trilling, Henry Miller, Mailer, and a host of writers who had little else in common did agree that Lawrence, in his *truly* great books, was an artist capable of saving a sick civilization. It was a conviction that, in Podhoretz's case, led to the promotion first of Goodman's *Growing Up Absurd* and then of an essay by Goodman on pornography.[46]

Podhoretz's own contribution came in a talk at Bard College entitled "Sex, Pornography, and Literature." Lawrence had advocated censorship of hardcore pornography because it "did dirt" not just on sex but on life itself. Critics like Kazin and Rahv didn't get into a flutter over this: the literary artist remained free, precisely because "hard-core pornography can never be literature." But why not? Podhoretz asked. Pornography, he averred, can sometimes rise to the level of literature "because it expresses a fundamental truth of human experience," namely, that people not only derive pleasure from what is forbidden but will protest "*any* restraint on sexual freedom of any kind whatever, including the biological." (His example was Molly Bloom's soliloquy in Joyce's *Ulysses*.) True, there is never going to be a society that doesn't impose restraints, and so pornography – whether at the level of literature or not – will be with us forever. But neither the writing nor the reading of pornography "is a crime or a sin."[47]

Podhoretz and his generation were (to repeat) entering their deferred adolescent rebellion, just as the generation after them was entering, on time, its own. The sixties were like a belated Jazz Age, and a sexual revolution – with two generations pouring their libidos into it – was *going* to play itself out. Pornography would be part of it. But if not a crime or sin, it was, as Midge Decter soon came to realize, in danger of becoming a source of cultural pollution. To jump just three years ahead, she wrote Jacqueline about "the sexually liberated's" idea of the good fight:

The same literary critics who were being called on to testify in court on behalf of *Lady Chatterley* and Henry Miller are now being called on to defend, one by one, every piece of pornography ever published by the Olympia Press. Not to defend pornography itself, mind you, but simply because publishers and radicals don't know the difference.[48]

Podhoretz would in due course take her point.

In the whirlwind of his first six months as editor, Podhoretz had noticed a piece by Theodore Solotaroff in the *Times Literary Supplement (TLS)*, and in the summer of 1960 an exchange of notes brought the former University of Chicago graduate student, a friend of Philip Roth, into the *Commentary* office for a meeting. In his memoir, Solotaroff (1928–2008) gives a hard-edged picture of the magazine's new editor. The Podhoretz who

came rapidly out of his office, [was] a man on the move, his hand already outstretched, a welcoming, one-of-the-guys' smile, followed by a measuring blue-eyed gaze. Heavyset, already balding at thirty, wearing a pale lemon short-sleeve shirt over a summer tan, he had a fresh, vigorous air, as though he had just emerged from a cold shower rather than a phone call.[49]

Over lunch, Podhoretz said to Solotaroff, "I could tell from the *TLS* piece that you didn't know what you were talking about but had guessed right about 90 percent of the time. So I figured you'd make a good editor. Are you interested in working for me?" He spoke frankly about the difficulties of moving wife and children from Seattle to New York, and about the career implications of taking an editing job: "If it didn't work out with me, you could go back to teaching. A year or two at *Commentary* would be a pretty good credential, particularly if you keep writing for the magazine." It was a comment, accompanied by "a genuinely appreciative look," that disclosed both "a manly guy" and "a careerist who was likely ruthless." The clincher was that the manly careerist gave him the "approval and candor" he never got from his own father. He took the job.[50]

Solotaroff enjoyed editing – it was like teaching composition at Chicago, only at a higher level – but he was bored, he recalled, by "the weekend dinners and parties at the apartment of one or another of the fabled New York intellectuals." He noticed what Podhoretz himself had noticed back when he started going to Family gatherings – the gossip, the rivalry "in gracious living" – but now some of the grumbling was also "about the latest leftist delinquency" of Podhoretz himself. And tedious grumbling it was. "Coming away from Hannah Arendt's prestigious annual New Year's Eve party," Solotaroff's wife, Lynn, remarked, "So this wake is what I gave up Seattle for?"[51]

There was discontent on the other side as well. In December 1962, Sherry Abel was going on leave because of eye problems, which meant, as Midge wrote to Jacqueline, that "Norman now faces the prospect of being alone with one T. Solotaroff, who is a great lumbering ox and functions as an editor by being very proud of all the things he is responsible for keeping *out* of the magazine." Podhoretz had undergone a "revolution in his spirit," she confided. Ever since Columbia he had felt "guilty toward all his friends" on account of his success, but now he had made the simple "discovery that he does what he does better than they do . . . and therefore the prizes and jobs" have properly come to him; they had been *earned*. Therefore, "his hiring policy does *not* have to be one of helping out the less fortunate or providing a warm berth for misunderstood talent."

This great clarification had occurred, Midge said, on "a small island 5 minutes off the coast of Nassau," a spot formerly called Hog Island but renamed Paradise Island.[52] Here Podhoretz had been brought by Huntington Hartford (1911–2008), heir to the Great Atlantic and Pacific Tea Co. (that is, A&P) fortune and founder of a glitzy magazine called *Show*, where Podhoretz had been given *carte blanche* to write monthly reviews on any books he wanted. And this at top-dollar rate: twenty pieces over twenty months brought him $15,000 (now $104,000). At a conference called by Hartford at his unimaginably luxurious island hotel, Podhoretz partied grandly in the company of a bunch of even more eminent North and South American writers – Max Lerner, Arthur Schlesinger, Edward Albee, et al. "Well," Midge wrote to Jacqueline, "when I went to Idlewild to fetch my wandering boy home, you can imagine what I saw: thirty drunken, suntanned men announcing in their very being what possibilities could be wrought for men on earth."

From New York, the party, now with Midge in tow, proceeded to Washington, where the highbrows were

treated to a 3-minute reception from JFK, and a ghastly, ghastly cocktail party at Bobby Kennedy's house, where Norman spilled a full glass of bourbon on the green rug, kept shouting "Don't arrest me, I'm innocent!" and lovely Ethel Kennedy's smile (which not only appears on her face, but is reflected from several spanking-new portraits of the Kennedy family hung from every wall in the house!) got smilier and smilier.[53]

Decter could be relied on both for enjoyment and for ironic detachment. She knew that the Washington establishment was out to flatter Jewish intellectuals. For Podhoretz, the five-star company's patent affection for him confirmed a sense of arrival – a step beyond his achieved status as a brilliant student and the leading third-generation Family critic and editor. He was now established enough to feel like a personage among personages. As he would write: "'From now on,' says a character in Clifford Odets' movie *The Sweet Smell of Success*, 'the best of everything is good enough for me.' I left Paradise Island with those words ringing in my head."[54]

Personages don't all have the same rank, however. Trilling had taught that, though the signs were often subtler, classes existed and mattered in the America of Fitzgerald and Bellow just as they had in the England of Jane Austen and Dickens. It was a difficult and discomfiting lesson for a scholarship boy from Brownsville to learn. He would discover, five years later when he published *Making It*, that it was also an anxiety-provoking lesson to pass along. Americans were almost constitutionally obliged to pretend that classes, and the social ladder connecting them, didn't exist. Therefore, as Podhoretz was starting to understand, class had become among us what Lawrence said sex had been among the Victorians: our "dirty little secret."

Partisan (and class) differences aside, Democrats and Republicans alike would soon feel threatened less by each other than by the emerging New Left. Podhoretz was never *of* the movement, but his sponsorship of Goodman, Mailer, and Brown, in addition to what he was saying in his editorial statements at the front of each issue of *Commentary*, made him an obvious figure of interest to young radicals like Tom Hayden.

One year out of the University of Michigan, where he had been editor of the student newspaper, Hayden offered *Commentary* the "Port Huron Statement," the founding document of Students for a Democratic Society. Podhoretz rejected it, thus either committing one of the decade's greatest publishing blunders, as Epstein thought, or signaling that even in its leftist period *Commentary* had strict intellectual standards. Goodman had a distinctive and learned voice, and Lynd was an exquisitely lucid expositor, but Hayden's prose read like what it was – a rough draft composed on a portable typewriter in the back of a Volkswagen bus between confrontations with state and local police in Mississippi, where he and other young radicals were working to register black voters.[55] However brave that activity might have been, his manifesto's theme of participatory democracy, derived from Marx's account of the Paris Commune of 1870, when an armed and politicized "people" met daily to decide policy, was "intellectually callow."[56]

Hayden's projection of a New Left was predicated on the belief that, in a world fraught with "international tensions [and] unresolved domestic troubles," the Old Left had run out of ideas. Who, he asked, was going to oppose the New Right, as represented by the Young Americans for Freedom, "a radically conservative youth group formed at William F. Buckley's Connecticut home last summer"?[57] Only a New Left could.

Hayden and other "student boat-rockers," as they were calling themselves,[58] were active not just in civil rights in the South but, across the country, in agitation on behalf of Fidel Castro. This troubled Podhoretz, who, writing to Hughes, saw the possibility that the young leftists would be corrupted by third world communists just as the old leftists of the thirties had been corrupted by the Party directed from Moscow. Would Hughes be willing to continue the lesson? It was vital, for "the only people from whom these young radicals would be willing to take instruction are people like yourself – people sympathetic to their concerns."[59]

Hughes was too busy mounting a quixotic independent challenge to Ted Kennedy in the Massachusetts Senate race. So Podhoretz turned to the formidable sociologist Dennis Wrong, who produced a masterful diagnosis of the peril that revolutionary developments in Cuba posed for American radicalism. The young radicals, he wrote, were sure that Cuba would be *their* cause, as the Spanish Civil War had been their elders'. Hence Mailer's hip hosannas to Castro and his post-Bay of Pigs lecture to Kennedy: "You will never understand that [Castro] is the country, revolutionary, tyrannical, hysterical, violent, passionate, brave as the best of animals, doomed perhaps to end in tragedy, but one of the great figures of the twentieth century, at the present moment a far greater figure than yourself." With the Left in that sort of mood – Nathan Glazer would later remember that along with thousands he wildly cheered Castro in New York, but he couldn't remember exactly why – it was difficult but all the more crucial to focus attention on the emerging evils of a secret police and arbitrary arrests, a cult of personality and no elections, and the suppression of labor unions and the press. Castro's New Left supporters had in an instant "traveled from a fresh rebellious idealism, sorely needed after the confusions and timidities of the 50's, to a fascination with populist totalitarianism that is scarcely distinguishable from that of the latter-day communist apologists of the late 30's and early 40's."[60]

A parallel but slightly more leisurely journey was taken from the "Port Huron Statement" and the founding of SDS in 1962 to the urban riots and violent demonstrations at the Democratic National Convention in Chicago in 1968. The source of 1968's intolerance and indiscipline could be traced directly back to Hayden's seraphic declarations of 1962 – that, for example, "We regard men as infinitely precious and possessed of unfilled capacities for reason, freedom, and love." From Calvin to Lenin, as Podhoretz would later note, the "inherently authoritarian" pattern of this kind of thinking was clear. The New Left leaders were asserting "that *they* knew what was best not only for themselves but for everyone else as well," and if others didn't come around, they would add coercion to persuasion. That was where the Weathermen and their imitators came in, "shouting down speakers with whom [they] disagreed on the ground that only the 'truth' had a right to be heard" or setting off explosives in government offices or defense-research labs.[61]

The New Left insisted that a society whose roots were fundamentally "poisoned" could be set right only by "something grand and apocalyptic," to wit, "a violent overthrow" that would be followed by the birth of a fresh and beautiful world.

Glazer's 1968 appraisal in *Commentary*, "The New Left and Its Limits," carrying Podhoretz's full endorsement, tried to introduce some complications. True, the country had serious problems, but radical diagnoses and prescriptions founded on the romantic notion of innate human purity and invariable institutional corruption, aside from being a most improbable anthropological premise, didn't address them. Besides, the metaphor of a poisoned social organism was inapt. America, as Glazer maintained, was basically healthy. Take the war in Vietnam that was agitating everyone: "The key point to me is this: *America would not have had to be very different from what it now is for some President to have gotten us out of Vietnam rather than deeper and deeper into it.*" That is, it was a question of leadership, not of national character. So, elect different leaders.[62]

Where had the students gotten their ideas about the poisoned roots of their country and their culture? One needed to look no further than the classrooms. That at least was Trilling's rueful conclusion: he had taught his Columbia students the works of "alienated" or demystifying writers, from Frazer, Nietzsche, and Freud to Conrad, Mann, and Pirandello, whose attitude toward middle-class culture and liberal democracy was variously discontented, subversive, and adversarial.[63] He had imagined that his students would imitate his own generation in its maturity by doing the work of necessary reform. Instead, they imitated his generation in its immaturity – the sixties repeating the thirties – by declaring that the society was irredeemable and that only a revolution, tearing everything down and starting over, could make it right.

At this point the *New York Review of Books* becomes especially relevant. It was founded, in the winter of 1962–63, when a newspaper strike in the city clarified something in the minds of several intellectuals – the critic (and wife of the poet Robert Lowell) Elizabeth Hardwick, Jason and Barbara Epstein, and Podhoretz. They realized that they didn't really miss the *New York Times Book Review* because it had for years been so "lousy" (Barbara Epstein's word). She and Jason figured that a new review could "get publishers to advertise because they've got no place else to go." Because Jason didn't want to assume a position that might conflict with his interests as editor at Random House, Barbara continued, "We first asked Norman Podhoretz to edit the magazine with me. . . . Thank God Norman turned us down. Said he couldn't afford it."[64] It wasn't just the money. He had stipulated that, if he were to be editor, Robert Silvers, who had been at the *Paris Review* and was then editor at *Harper's*, be brought in as his deputy. But Silvers, as Podhoretz recalled, "insisted on co-equal status and I wasn't going to do that. So in the end it became Silvers and

Barbara. No question that a lot of New York literary and intellectual history would have been different if I had made that move."[65]

Besides, Podhoretz had good reason to feel that *Commentary* was already truly *his*. The inevitable competition with the *New York Review* could only make it better, particularly if the two publications were to diverge politically – as they palpably did when radical student and black protesters started to take to the streets. Silvers lacked either the courage or the desire to criticize the campus rebellions – the courage that *Partisan Review* had shown in the thirties when it broke with the communists. Podhoretz pledged *Commentary* to perform now the intellectual duty that *Partisan Review* had performed then. And courage was needed. In the thirties, the young Mary McCarthy and Philip Rahv were penalized for their anti-Stalinism by fellow-traveling editors like Malcolm Cowley at the *New Republic* – no book reviewing assignments for stooges! Now, in the sixties, if one wrote an anti-SDS article, Podhoretz would recall, "one's reputation was besmirched, with unrestrained viciousness in conversation and, when the occasion arose, by means of innuendo in print."

Jason Epstein, who had also become increasingly radical, was the enforcer within his own circle of friends. When one of them happened to say he was anxious about a communist takeover if the United States withdrew from Vietnam, "Jason turned on him and snarled: *So you like to see little babies napalmed.*" Most of those present were stunned, but few protested. The "herd of independent minds," as Harold Rosenberg called them, was migrating sharp left, and though there were some prominent mavericks – from the poets Marianne Moore and W. H. Auden to the novelists James Michener and John Updike – they felt, especially in Cambridge or Manhattan, exposed and lonely.

Podhoretz personally had no fear of Epstein, never hesitating to call him on the "outrageous statements" that, not coincidentally, were starting to chime with the trumpery arguments of New Left spokesmen like Noam Chomsky:

[O]nce I even made a drunken public scene in a restaurant when [Epstein] compared the United States to Nazi Germany and Lyndon Johnson to Hitler. This comparison was later to become a commonplace of radical talk, but I had never heard it made before, and it so infuriated me that I literally roared in response. [Epstein] was taken aback and so was I, and when we both calmed down a bit, I told him that he had better be careful about saying such things because if he really meant them he ought to leave the country or join a revolutionary party.

Epstein didn't leave the country, nor of course did his wife or Silvers. But they did the equivalent of joining a revolutionary party in the pages of the *New York Review*. As revolutionary cant became the order of the day, Podhoretz began to feel that, as he wrote to Jacobson, "liberalism as an intellectual tradition and as an attitude of mind seems to me rather more in need of defense than of criticism."[66] The English novelist C. P. Snow, whom Podhoretz interviewed for radio in fall 1962, agreed. The New Left in England, Snow believed, was a symptom of life "in an affluent society": as "a lot of the major modest expectations of man [appear] to have been fulfilled . . . people look around and say 'So what? Is this good enough?'" That was why the show-off intelligentsia were engaged in "curious nihilistic kicking out at everything within sight."[67]

What could responsible intellectuals *say* to such anarchists? Podhoretz wrote that "William Phillips once told the New Left-minded English critic Kenneth Tynan that he could not argue with him about politics, because Tynan's arguments were so old that he, Phillips, could no longer remember the answers."[68] As the sixties unfolded – the inner cities burning, the war in Vietnam expanding – the pages of Silvers's *New York Review* and even of Phillips's own *Partisan Review* suggested that remembering the answers was indeed a problem. *Commentary* had to address it.

But that lay ahead. At the hopeful beginning of the decade – to go back – when Podhoretz felt "surprisingly elated over Kennedy's victory," he told George Lichtheim, facetiously, that "I myself will probably be running for Governor in 1964."[69] This jest had an edge: his friend Mailer was actually running for Mayor of New York. Kennedy had made politics seem fashionable – "Superman," Mailer wrote, "Comes to the Supermarket" – and if the superman from Hyannis Port could win elections, why not the potentially great novelist from Brooklyn Heights?

On Saturday, November 19, 1960, two weeks after Kennedy's victory, Mailer threw a party to "announce his candidacy on behalf of the underprivileged and the disenfranchised masses of the city." He was running "under the Existentialist . . . banner," and with Allen Ginsberg, Seymour Krim, and Noel Permental, Jr. as his press secretaries. This party was the occasion, Ginsberg later alleged, when Podhoretz told him that if he would only drop Kerouac, Burroughs, Snyder, and the other Beats, he could, with his considerable poetic gifts, become an important figure in "the New York literary scene." "I suddenly saw myself in a B movie out of Balzac," Ginsberg would tell Peter Manso, "with me as the distinguished provincial being tempted by the idiot worldly banker . . . [or by] Blake's devil who is ignorance, so I started screaming at him, 'You big dumb fuckhead! You idiot! You don't know anything about anything!'"

This, as Podhoretz later insisted, was but an example of Ginsberg's knack for "pure hallucination." What Podhoretz "actually may have been foolish enough to do . . . was repeat what I had already said several times in print – that I thought he was one of the few Beat writers who had genuine literary talent," as evidenced in *Kaddish and Other Poems* (1961), "and that his relentless evangelizing on behalf of the others was obscuring the difference between his work and theirs." Ginsberg did indeed scream abuse at him at Mailer's party, but if either of them went limp at the prospect of coming to blows, it wasn't Podhoretz: "The idea that I would be afraid of trading punches with Allen Ginsberg," he deadpanned, "reminds me of what James Cagney . . . once said about a similar possibility involving Humphrey Bogart . . . : 'When it comes to fighting, he's about as tough as Shirley Temple.'"[70]

If Ginsberg and Podhoretz weren't going to duke it out, Mailer, a few drinks later, became excited about taking someone on himself. He tried to get George Plimpton to box, and when that "Paper Lion" athlete declined and tried to edge away, Mailer kicked him in the leg. Meanwhile Mailer's wife, Adele Morales, rumored to be bisexual, was spending some "very cozy" time in the bathroom with a young woman. It was just the provocation Mailer needed to believe her to have been unfaithful – rejecting not just him but phallic power generally.[71]

By 4:30 in the morning, everyone had gone. Having been out on the street chasing people and getting into scuffles, Mailer returned to "his apartment with a black eye, a bloodied face, and a bloodstained bullfighter's shirt." Using language of which there is no exact record, Adele in effect told him that, in Carl E. Rollyson's account,

she did not recognize or accept him as her husband. He took out the two-and-a-half-inch penknife he usually carried with him. All Adele remembers of this moment is the funny look in his eyes before he stabbed her – once in the upper abdomen and once in the back.[72]

The upthrust stab in the abdomen had punctured her cardiac sac. An ambulance took her to the hospital, and before she went into surgery Mailer begged her not to talk to the police and to tell the hospital staff that she had fallen on a piece of glass. The hospital had already notified the police, however, and by Monday afternoon Adele charged that her husband had stabbed her and begged that he be kept away.

On Monday night, Mailer appeared on television for a Mike Wallace interview to elaborate his proposal for juvenile delinquents to let off steam in jousts in Central Park – they would wear full armor and charge one another on horseback. He didn't tell Wallace anything about his own letting-off-steam some thirty-six hours earlier – though at the hospital he had explained to his sister and brother-in-law that he had stabbed Adele to "relieve her of cancer."

In due course he was sent to Bellevue Psychiatric Hospital, where he stayed two weeks. Podhoretz, whom he had tried but failed to wake in those early-morning hours after the stabbing, didn't know all that had happened, and Mailer declared that "for his own protection" he ought to remain ignorant of the details. But he agreed with Mailer on the importance of staying out of psychiatric treatment and of not giving hostile critics reasons to damn his writing as the work of a lunatic. Pleading guilty to third-degree assault, Mailer was placed on probation. Therapy would have been wasted on him, for, in one doctor's words, his "defenses . . . had [been] built up . . . [with] such intricacy that there was no way to demolish them." He had stabbed his wife, he believed, in obedience to an inner demon – the crystallizing of "a decade's anger made me do it." This was his writerly version of what would later be jeered at as the Twinkie Defense. Privately but not publicly, he acknowledged that, demon or no demon, stabbing his wife was indefensible[73] – but life, his life anyway, had to go on.

We can gauge how completely Mailer managed to screen out any authentic consciousness of moral responsibility when we observe his preoccupation, twenty-two years later, with the quickness with which his friends rallied around him: "A week or two after I got out of the coop, Norman Podhoretz and Midge Decter took me to a party and everybody was shocked that they would take me there, but still they all closed ranks behind me." People's reaction was cooler than before, but not by much: "Five degrees less warmth than I was accustomed to. Not fifteen degrees less – five."[74]

Check. Trilling, the doyen of "the moral imagination," thought Mailer's "stabbing of Adele was, so to speak a Dostoyevskian ploy ... to see how far he could go."[75] Lichtheim lightheartedly wrote Podhoretz: "I see your namesake has got himself in trouble by stabbing his wife. I didn't know this was illegal in New York."[76] And the New England novelist John Marquand, a friend and occasional *Commentary* contributor, showed how even tertiary hangers-on could answer the call to the colors: "I am writing on the outside chance that you may be involved in some kind of action or 'group' on behalf of Norman Mailer." He and Mailer had only a "hectic acquaintance" and their "personalities were hopelessly incompatible," but the superior novelist's "gifts, his very powerful compassion and his courage, however purblind at times I have found it, would impel me to stand up for him any way I can in this cruel predicament."[77]

All this gaga irresponsibility makes Decter's response shine forth with singular clarity. She wrote Jacqueline:

I must tell you that the whole business with Mailer turned me so sick with literature, with "insight," with Columbia University, that I couldn't bear to do anything but go to the movies. Everyone in New York came alive with sex and titillation. And in this whole God-forsaken city of 8,000,000 there could not be found one healthy philistine to say – the man is a thug, or a criminal. It's all nothing but experience, experience, experience.

She may have been thinking of Trilling's implicit endorsement of the notion that the genius has some "Dostoevskyan" duty to push the moral envelope. But this exceptionalism made her, she added, recoil completely: "When I think of a world in which things really do operate by [such] categories" – one morality for geniuses, another for you and me – "I want to slit my throat, is all."[78]

7

"This Was Bigger than Both of Us"

The prestige of science had, through much of the twentieth century, imposed a dry objectivity onto humanistic discourse. Even in literary criticism – Trilling on Wordsworth's passionate Immortality Ode, for example – the voice of the writer endeavored to be as *dis*passionate as possible. On the other hand, there was Lawrence's *Studies in Classic American Literature,* where the critic made the "I" of Cooper, Poe, Hawthorne, and the rest seem to be addressing the "I" in each of their readers. What Podhoretz noticed in the fifties was a recrudescence among the best writers of Lawrence's kind of nonfiction prose. Call it impressionistic criticism, the familiar or autobiographical essay, or, in Podhoretz's own formulation, the auto-case history.

This last phrase, awkward as it is, best describes his own memoir writing: an attempt to get beyond the merely personal – the narcissism of the Beats – and to stress, in a social-scientific vein, the typicality of a given history, his own. This was also the discovery of Mailer and James Baldwin, whose nonfiction pieces in *Advertisements for Myself* and *Notes of a Native Son,* respectively, had a power lacking in the former's *The Deer Park* and the latter's *Giovanni's Room.* If, for whatever reasons, the investment in *imagining* lives – creating fiction – wasn't paying dividends, perhaps it was time to recur to the facts of one's actual experience, transmuted by the imagination for dramatic purposes but avowedly historical in substance.

Wouldn't it be a coup to bring Baldwin back to *Commentary,* where in the fifties he had published many of his early pieces in this nonfiction vein? Podhoretz had met him in Paris while on vacation from Cambridge in December 1950. Now, in 1961, he wrote commending his performance on a television show:

I was especially intrigued by the brief remark you made about the [Black] Muslims. I hope you're working on the piece, which seems to me more and more important for you to write – and for me to publish.... I've come to feel that *Commentary* has a real job to do in interpreting Negro militancy to the white liberal community, and particularly the Jewish liberal community.[1]

Meanwhile Podhoretz was turning to Dan Jacobson for a review of Baldwin's essay collection *Nobody Knows My Name*, asking for a full-scale article that would "confront Baldwin in his own terms – that is, you might write a personal essay in response to his 'psychic' reading of the race question in America." Baldwin's collection ended with a piece on Mailer called "The Black Boy Looks at the White Boy," and Podhoretz suggested that Jacobson turn it around by writing "something like 'The White Boy Looks at the Black Boy.'" Jacobson demurred on the grounds that it really "should be an *American* who tackles Baldwin." Podhoretz agreed in principle, asserting that perhaps he was the person who might do it right but lamenting that he was currently blocked.

Time would tell. But for now he encouraged Jacobson to proceed, noting that Baldwin was "involved in a transformation of possibly major proportions." No longer "forcing himself (if he has indeed been forcing himself) into the mold of highbrow respectability," he was "trying to let the Nigger in him come to the surface. That effort, of course, has resulted in a certain strain in his writing, but I suspect that after a while he'll achieve a new equilibrium on a higher level of authenticity."[2] The review of *Nobody Knows* that Jacobson submitted was, he regretted to say, both less "personal" or confrontational than Podhoretz had called for and less mollifying. He had to be "hard on Baldwin, hard about the situation, but I honestly don't know what else it could be, when he himself is so serious and the situation he describes is so bad."[3]

The racial situation was indeed bad in 1961, and the militancy of the Black Muslims threatened to make it worse. It was late that year or early the next that Podhoretz commissioned Baldwin to write about them for *Commentary*. No "white devil" writer could gain access to the Black Muslim leaders, but they would let themselves be interviewed by Baldwin, who seemed to appreciate that what Martin Luther King, Jr.'s nonviolent protests hadn't achieved in the South black armed resistance might. Yet Baldwin also believed that a policy of meeting violence with violence promised to become a débâcle, especially for blacks, a small minority. His own hope therefore lay with integration, a world made whole by cross-racial bonds of love.

A confrontation between Baldwin and the Muslims, who took a defiant "they segregate us, we segregate them" approach, even dreaming of a way for blacks to secede from the United States, was likely to make an impression as great as Goodman's antiestablishment fireworks, and Podhoretz waited impatiently for the promised article. Baldwin was never good about deadlines. Having taken an advance from William Shawn at the *New Yorker* for a piece on Africa, he traveled with his sister along "the west coast . . . from Senegal to Ghana" while working on the article for *Commentary* and his novel *Another Country*. Upon returning to New York, he had nothing to give Shawn, whose money he had spent. Owing him *something*, Baldwin directed his agent to offer the piece on the Black Muslims. When Podhoretz telephoned wondering how that essay was coming, Baldwin said it was finished. The delighted Podhoretz said he would send someone over to pick it up, whereupon Baldwin had to confess it was on Shawn's desk. "But not to worry," Podhoretz remembered him adding, "he was sure it would be unsuitable, and as soon as they rejected it he would pass it on to *Commentary*."

Shawn did not reject it. The *New Yorker* ran the 20,000-word "Letter from a Region in My Mind" on November 17, 1962. It became the chapter "Down at the Cross" in *The Fire Next Time*, one of the classics of the sixties. "I was thunderstruck," Podhoretz would recall. "No greater violation of the ethics of the trade could be imagined than Baldwin had committed in taking an article he had been invited to write by the editor of one magazine and giving it to the editor of another. I considered taking legal action but dropped the idea as unseemly." He also dropped the idea of protesting to the *New Yorker* itself when he found that Shawn was paying Baldwin $12,000 ($82,000 currently: Baldwin's biographers insist the sum was $6,500, but Podhoretz was including the $5,500 advance Baldwin had spent in Africa), which was twenty times what *Commentary* could afford.[4]

What truly incensed Podhoretz was that Baldwin had played his dirty trick knowing he could get away with it – and this because he was black. Blacks not only needed the money, the excuse went, but after centuries of slavery and segregation they also deserved it. Or black culture was different from white, and it was an honorable tradition to pull a fast one on "the Man" if you could. The point remained: *The Fire Next Time*, a masterpiece, "had been stolen from me."

Podhoretz invited Baldwin for lunch and spoke with a candor that, if it was unusual in 1962, has since become nearly extinct:

Not even the contrition he showed, nor his minimally honorable refusal to justify what he had done, could stop me. I said that he had dared to commit such a dastardly act because he was a Negro, and had been counting on the white-liberal guilt that he knew so much about . . . to enable him to get away with it. And he had gotten away with it – he who went around preaching the virtues of "paying one's dues." Even I had let him get away with it by my failure to sue, but . . . if he thought I felt guilty toward him or any other Negro, he was very much mistaken. Neither I nor my ancestors had ever wronged the Negroes; on the contrary, I had grown up in an "integrated" slum neighborhood where it was the Negroes who persecuted the whites and not the other way round. . . . "You ought," he whispered when I had finished, "to write all that down."

Baldwin's whispered suggestion was soon acted on. Since his exchange of notes with Jacobson, Podhoretz had been thinking about doing it anyway, exposing "all the sentimental nonsense that was being talked about integration by whites who knew nothing about Negroes, and by Negroes who thought that all their problems could be solved by living next-door to whites." Baldwin excitedly, earnestly insisted: "It was important, more important than I knew, for such things to be said; and they had to be said in public."[5]

Baldwin's *New Yorker* "Letter" disclosed a tension in his own consciousness and in the nation at large. On the one side, despite his young-adult deconversion from the black Christianity he had heard preached in Harlem pulpits, there was still a yearning for love between the races. On the other side, there was a fear that, absent this love, the Black Muslims' threat of violent racial strife would be carried out. If blacks picked up arms, Malcolm X had argued, they would gain instant respect. As for the Muslims' theological myth, which regarded the original paradise as a black Allah's arrangement for black people, tragically spoiled by the white Satan and his white people, that was merely an inversion of the orthodox Euro-Christian myth of paradise. Baldwin rejected both the black and the white theologies, telling Elijah Muhammad that "I love a few people and they love me and some of them are white, and isn't love more important than color?"[6] It was easier to entertain this quixotic hope at his country place in France than back in Harlem.

"Your piece in the *New Yorker* is superb," Podhoretz wrote him. "Maybe the best thing you've ever written. Apart from everything else, it provoked me into writing a kind of counter statement that I'm going to publish in the February [1963] issue of *Commentary* (which may, as a result, be the last issue of *Commentary* that the world will ever see)."[7] He wrote "My Negro Problem – and Ours," "or rather it wrote itself," during "three hot, blissful sessions at the typewriter."[8] Midge told Jacqueline that Baldwin's "blast" was "a fantastic document of the American Negro, maybe the most important thing published in this country in years," and that her husband's riposte was "the story of a New York white child's hatred and fear of the Negro." She understood his trepidations: "Somewhere along mid-winter, we shall be expecting rocks through the window. The only thing worse than telling a Negro he is responsible for anything, is telling a white liberal that he hates Negroes."[9]

"My Negro Problem" did at first seem to contain something to offend everyone: integrationists, black nationalists, Jews, and whites generally. Later it would be misread as suggesting that whites were incurably racist.[10] But the brilliance of the essay, the first one Podhoretz felt he was writing on his own hook, resides less in generalizations than in street-level particulars – his "problem" with blacks originating in encounters with them as a boy in Brownsville. What as an adult he read in the liberal, integrationist press didn't square with what he remembered from the thirties and forties: the Jews he knew weren't rich, they were poor; and the blacks, while hardly rich (who in Brownsville was?), weren't persecuted, they were persecuting. Baited, bullied, and beaten by blacks, the child Podhoretz feared and hated them – just as, noting their physical grace in sports or dance, or their ability to thumb a nose at authorities in school or on the streets, he envied them. For they were "*really* bad, bad in a way that beckoned to one, and made one feel inadequate."

If whites looked upon blacks in this faceless way, blacks returned the favor. Such reciprocal fear, hatred, and envy were no basis for living together, which is why Podhoretz believed the integrationist program was doomed. Doomed also were Baldwin's pleas for love, fine on the Sabbath but of little relevance to the weekday world of politics. Besides, the hatred on both sides was too strong for love to overcome. Hence Podhoretz's very American, and very desperate, assimilationist proposal – which in fact echoed Tocqueville's some 130 years before[11] – was to let the races blend together through mixed marriages. It often hadn't seemed to him worthwhile, over the centuries, to have maintained a pure and separate Jewish people only to provoke persecution. Why should blacks, whose history as a distinct race seemed to him less richly positive than other groups', want to insist on remaining distinct?[12]

Whenever he had a controversial piece coming out in the magazine, Podhoretz would circulate advance copies, hoping to bring in responses for the letters column. Occasionally, the buzz would reach a pitch justifying a full-blown item in itself, usually published three months later. That was the sequence following "My Negro Problem." Since the late forties, blacks like Baldwin and Ralph Ellison, building on the work of W. E. B. Dubois and Richard Wright, had made candor possible among their own people. Now Podhoretz made it possible among educated whites, too. Many of them, Baldwin remarked, no doubt felt the way Podhoretz did about blacks, but while "they lie about it," he had confessed the truth.[13]

Repression of hatred, fear, and envy, if sustained too long, could aggravate the sickness Podhoretz spoke of. Health depended on getting the emotions out into the open. That was certainly Trilling's Freudian view. How could he not "like" the essay, he wrote Podhoretz privately, "my exasperation with the clichés of liberal-progressive sentiment being what it is? Against the dreadful liberal-progressive no-feeling, which eventually establishes itself as no-thought and no-action, the only antidote is personal testimony of such honesty as yours has."[14]

The sociologist David Riesman also wrote privately, urging Podhoretz to make distinctions among underprivileged experiences in Brownsville based on race; Riesman's own overprivileged childhood experiences in Philadelphia based on class; and Baldwin's differently underprivileged experiences in Harlem based on the peculiarities of being both a preacher's son and a homosexual.[15] For his part, Paul Goodman didn't hesitate to recommend publicly that Podhoretz "consult psychotherapy and find out why it is so hard for him to be rational" about the "emotional turmoil" he felt when confronted by the imperative for racial justice.[16] Burton Raffel, later to become a noteworthy translator of literary texts, suggested that while everyone's childhood experiences were important, everyone needed to move on.[17]

Two retorts from Ralph Ellison addressed Podhoretz's suggestion of miscegenation. First, the children of white–black marriages would simply be looked on as black and would accordingly suffer from white prejudice; second, black culture had, in America as well as in Africa, produced music, literature, religion, and folklore worthy of respect. Rather than cast their culture off as a "stigma," blacks should continue to build on it.[18] Podhoretz took both points.

Lorraine Hansberry, then famous for her play *A Raisin in the Sun* (1959), had small interest in such essentially friendly dialogue. Didn't people see what "an ugly item" Podhoretz's essay was? Miscegenation had been widely practiced since the first slaves were brought from Africa, and the blacks, perhaps forty percent of whom were already "misceged" to some degree, were in their "pride" too "ferocious" to want any more of it.[19] If Hansberry didn't expressly call Podhoretz a racist, Stokely Carmichael, in a speech in Philadelphia, did. Thought of at the time as sweet, non-violent, and "responsible," the young Student Nonviolent Coordinating Committee leader was a portent of the "black rage" to come. His defamatory remark seemed to Podhoretz grounds for a libel suit: "Literally the last thing any racist would advocate was a wholesale merger of the two races. Since Carmichael had to have known this, he was clearly giving voice to a lie."[20]

Carmichael and Hansberry's Afrocentric defiance was echoed by some liberal whites, particularly Jews. The head of the AJC in Detroit wrote John Slawson, head of the national office in New York, damning Podhoretz as "reactionary because he is driving toward a monolithic" as opposed to a "pluralistic" society: "History is full of this kind of 'solution'" – a "Negro-free" world being like the Jew-free world the Nazis desired. Podhoretz couldn't fulfill his hope through gas chambers, firing squads, or ghettos, "So he says let's interbreed them away."[21] Having sent Podhoretz a carbon of his attack, the writer got a reply:

[I]f you knew how to read, you would have noticed that I used the word "despair" in expressing my skepticism over the possibility of integration as a solution. I chose that word carefully, for I meant to convey – and did convey, to people not afflicted with tone deafness where English prose is concerned – that I would be happy if I thought that integration *could* work. I gave reasons for my skepticism, and not all of them were personal. . . .

You accuse me of being "certain" about my position, but I am certain of nothing except that people like you are a menace to serious and truthful public discussion.[22]

Another day at the office. Between the blacks on one side and the liberal Jews and other whites on the other, Podhoretz had reason to feel he could please nobody.

It wasn't just him. Many Jewish writers were starting to notice once-sympathetic blacks (and whites) resenting their considered views. Irving Howe, for example, faced a barrage of negative comment when he published a critique of Wright and Baldwin, "Black Boys and Native Sons."[23] The most forceful came from Ellison. "I was a bit astonished at Ellison's violence," Howe told Podhoretz, who had gone to bat for him, "which finally seemed directed not at me but at the civil-rights movement 'behind' me." With the hullabaloo over "My Negro Problem" more or less over, Podhoretz replied: "I guess things have reached the point where it seems impossible for anyone to say anything about Negroes without falling into a poisoned well. But maybe that's one of the prices we'll all have to pay for America's oppression of the Negro."[24]

A tolerant attitude, looking perhaps for a reciprocal understanding. But not much would be forthcoming. The strains between blacks and Jews were growing tense enough for even Edmund Wilson, writing in his diary, to impute low motives to the Jewish side: "One does get the impression that the Jews regard themselves as having a monopoly on suffering, and do not want the Negroes to muscle in."[25] By contrast, noting that *Time* itself had taken alarm at the repercussions of "My Negro Problem," Daniel Patrick Moynihan offered Podhoretz some cheer: "One hears all too frequently of liberals gone mush or far out, but you are the first, to my knowledge, to be reported in a Luce publication as having gone sinister. My best congratulations to you."[26]

Podhoretz hadn't gone sinister, but he had gone under the weather – a price for having stuck his neck out in increasingly perilous times. He wrote Lichtheim: "I had been feeling pretty lousy, and the doctor discovered that my liver was bad, I was anemic, run-down, and suffering 'from complete physical and nervous exhaustion.' He ordered me to stop drinking and to take a long vacation, and I complied to the extent of going on the wagon and spending a week in Jamaica. I feel much better now, though still somewhat low in energy."[27] He needed to catch his breath. Publishing "My Negro Problem" and dealing with the aftermath had constituted, in effect, a strenuous, risky bid not only for truth-telling but also for major status as a writer. The risk, as he would later assess it, was "of being told that I simply was not good enough to merit the kind of fame I was after and that the best of everything was much too good for me." But he hadn't advanced this far to retreat. He was either going to follow "the holy inner light" of his personal feelings and ideas – the phrasing adumbrates the epiphany that would come to him in the spring of 1970 – or shut up shop as a writer.[28]

No sooner was "My Negro Problem" off his chest than Podhoretz was confronted with a take-no-prisoners conflict within the Family itself. The casus belli was another *New Yorker* scoop (February–March 1963): Hannah Arendt's dispatches from Israel on the trial of the Nazi war criminal Adolph Eichmann, subsequently enlarged as *Eichmann in Jerusalem: A Report on the Banality of Evil*. Listening to the court testimony, Arendt had been relieved to confirm that there had been some Jewish resistance fighters but depressed to hear, all over again, how "the actual work of killing in the extermination centers was usually in the hands of Jewish commandos . . . how they had worked in the gas chambers and the crematories, how they had pulled the gold teeth and cut the hair of the corpses, how they had dug the graves and, later, dug them up again to extinguish the traces of mass murder," and so on.

To Arendt, these were simple horrors. The moral mystery "lay in the amount of truth there was in Eichmann's description of Jewish cooperation, even under the conditions of the Final Solution" – the cooperation, that is, of Jewish leaders. Why had they gone along instead of rebelling? If the Jews had had no leaders, no community organizations whatsoever, she claimed, "there would have been chaos and plenty of misery but the total number of victims would hardly have been between four and a half and six million people."[29]

To say that this remark, and others similarly barbed, divided intellectual circles throughout the world would be an understatement. The Eichmann trial signaled a return of the repressed for Germans, Jews, and anyone who for all too human reasons had not been able to look, with steady concentration, on the greatest genocidal crime in history. Six million Jews had perished. Were their own leaders responsible – morally guilty – for a significant proportion of those dead? Did those leaders so hate their own Jewishness, and their fellow Jews, that they would in effect collaborate with the Nazis? Or was Arendt distorting? If so, what was one to make of her own disposition toward the Jewish people, of whom she was one?

Podhoretz regarded Arendt as a friend. Only five years before, he had written her of his "excitement" over her "superb" and "daring" book *The Human Condition*,[30] and her *Origins of Totalitarianism* had been central to his intellectual formation. The Arendt who wrote such books knew that, whenever a crucial moral problem was on the table, truth mattered more than friendship. Still, Podhoretz hesitated because, as he told Lichtheim, "the whole of the organized Jewish community is up in arms against her and I'd hate to join the pack. If I can think of a way of criticizing her and attacking her vulgar critics at the same time, I'll probably go ahead and write the piece" – referring to what would become "Arendt on Eichmann: A Study in the Perversity of Brilliance."

Lichtheim thought Arendt's handling of the actual trial and Eichmann's personality was acceptable, though marred by "the usual hysterical inaccuracies." He wasn't upset about her account of the collaborationist Jewish leaders because he believed it was more or less true. He had heard the initial protests from Family members but was disinclined to chime in: "knowing the assimilated . . . Jewish bourgeoisie at first hand, I am not prepared to let them off quite so easily. Their philistine cowardice and servility *was* a factor in the catastrophe."[31] This was precisely the impressionistic conclusion that Philip Rahv believed "the *goyim* will be delighted to discover": "The millions of Jews the Nazis murdered are at least partly responsible for their own deaths. It takes a brainy Germanic Jewess," he wrote Podhoretz, "to think up that one! I have always objected in principle to the demand upon the Jews that they show themselves to be braver – more heroic – than other people."[32]

Podhoretz's "Arendt on Eichmann" didn't appear in the *New Yorker*, but it would have a wide impact. How brilliant, he wrote, was Arendt's story not of the monstrous but of the banal Nazi, and not of the Jew as virtuous martyr but of the Jew as executioner's accomplice. Brilliant but perverse – by which he meant false.

The Final Solution was a monomaniacal means to an irrational end, namely the wholesale slaughter of European Jewry. Jewish cooperation didn't begin to account for six million dead – just how many deaths such cooperation occasioned was plainly indeterminable – and anyway, the attempt to cooperate merely replicated the attempts of appeasing Western politicians during the thirties to deal with Hitler as a "statesman." They all assumed, wrongly but humanly, "that the Nazis were rational beings and that their aims must therefore be limited and subject to negotiation." So relentless was Arendt's attack on the Jews that, whether going to their death, running a country (Israel), or prosecuting a trial, they seemed unable to do anything right. Podhoretz called for an end to recrimination and apology: the Jewish leaders did what they did, and were what they were. "None of it mattered in the slightest to the final result," he wrote. "Murderers with the power to murder descended upon a defenseless people and murdered a large part of it. What else is there to say?"

One more thing, actually: the utter inadequacy, in this instance, of Arendt's own theory of totalitarianism. Under that system, people are supposedly reduced to machines ("banal" functionaries). What we know about the nature of man, however, tells us that people make and are responsible for moral choices – for example, to run or not to run with murderers. Though it may be "uninteresting" – unbrilliant – "to say so, no person could have joined the Nazi party, let alone the SS, who was not at the very least a *vicious* anti-Semite; to believe otherwise is to learn nothing about the nature of anti-Semitism." As for the Jews, they are ordinary people, capable of evil and good like anyone else. They should therefore see that, under persecution, they behaved as any group has behaved "when they are set upon by murderers, no better and no worse: the Final Solution reveals nothing about the victims except that they were mortal beings and hopelessly vulnerable in their powerlessness." "The Nazis destroyed a third of the Jewish people. In the name of all that is humane, will the remnant never let up on itself?"[33]

Richard Ellmann, the biographer of Yeats and Joyce, extolled the essay but wondered what Podhoretz meant "about the Jews letting up on themselves." Nothing obscure, Podhoretz replied: "the Jews ought to stop picking on themselves from one side and the other. They *do* have a right to be 'like unto all the nations.' Or, as the joke puts it, let God choose somebody else for a change."[34] Finally, to Lichtheim, he admitted that "It was a painful thing to write, since I knew that [Arendt] would take it personally and I really value her friendship. However, as the popular song has it: 'This Was Bigger than Both of Us.'"[35]

Many of Arendt's critics wondered whether a species of Jewish self-hatred hadn't, unconsciously, guided her pen. Podhoretz himself suspected that she was inclined to presume that her European background, with all its cultural richness, made her superior to culturally impoverished Americans, who shouldn't carp about her writings but sit still and take notes. "Why did you do it?" she asked Podhoretz after his essay appeared, seeking a psychological explanation for *his* ideas. Hadn't she gotten her facts right, and wasn't her thesis, that concentration camps were the *ne plus ultra* of totalitarianism, airtight? Her haughty defiance led her, in a public debate at the University of Maryland in 1965, to dismiss Podhoretz's challenges by saying he had never lived "even 'in the neighborhood of a concentration camp,'" so how could he know anything about the subject? "Here," as Podhoretz later wrote, "I bit my tongue, hard, because I instinctively sensed that if I let fly with the sarcastic riposte that was on the tip of it, Hannah would never forgive me." What he wanted to say was "something like this: 'It is true that growing up in America, with its superficial culture, has deprived me of the great spiritual and intellectual advantages Miss Arendt derived from living in a society that produced concentration camps, but one does the best one can.'"[36]

When President Kennedy was assassinated in Dallas on November 22, 1963, reactions from Podhoretz's friends in England were eloquent. From John Gross: "One's got some sense of what the Elizabethans felt about the death of a king." And from Lichtheim: "There is all the business about having been struck down, like Lincoln, during an effort to get support for Negro rights.... Died as a soldier under fire, says de Gaulle, but it is the youth and the reckless exposure in a hostile city that evokes the sentiment. That and his wife and children."[37] Together when the news broke, Podhoretz and Mailer were both personally stunned and quick to look for larger meaning. Mailer would revert to the question of larger meaning for the rest of his life, the novel *Oswald's Tale* (1995) being his culminating attempt to find an answer. Podhoretz's immediate judgment was that Kennedy's most significant achievement might have been the negotiation of an atomic test ban, "perhaps ... the first notable move in the direction of a workable Soviet-American *rapprochement*" – which, it went without saying, was unrelated to the peace-activism of those calling for unilateral disarmament.[38]

But Podhoretz's thoughts about Kennedy would soon focus on his widow. Seeking to resume a life of her own, Jackie moved to New York and asked Richard Goodwin, adviser and speech-writer for both JFK and LBJ, to introduce her to the city's intelligentsia. On a Sunday in December 1964, he brought her, dressed in jeans, to the Podhoretzes' apartment for drinks, Norman telling him the next day that "We enjoyed it enormously – she's marvelous. I may recover, but I don't think the kids ever will."[39] Midge told the other Jacqueline in England that, with Jackie's "entrance ... into our lives," she felt she "no longer own[ed] my household, my husband, or myself." The most famous woman in the world

was charming, Norman was charming, and I, as I always am when the old master is preening his feathers before some delectable female, was oh so suitably demure, brow furrowed, eyes moist, and so on. Quickly thereafter we were informed by Mr. Goodwin that Mrs. K. was expecting (*expecting*, mind you, a grand upper-class American word!) a dinner invitation from us. The guests should be few in number and above all, amusing. And thereupon hangs the saga of the Verdurin-Podhoretzes. Whom, in our vast circle of acquaintances, could we possibly *not* invite to such an occasion? And who in the name of God is amusing?!

For a week, "day and night," the Podhoretzes agonized over the Proustian problem of "the 20 people we were about to mortally offend," principally Mailer, whose pieces on the Kennedys, and one in particular about Jackie, had more than mildly annoyed the clan. But at last "we found Swann, Odette,

Charlus (a piss-poor tacky little Charlus it was, too), and company. For Duc de Guermantes we had Edmund Wilson – whom Norman can't abide and whom I adore. The whole thing was – what shall I say – preposterous," since "in retrospect . . . it couldn't have made less difference whom we had or how many or anything."

Podhoretz's own account to Hellman indicates some of what, in the haze of the evening, transpired:

Mostly it was anti-climactic, by which I mean that it went off perfectly well, though not perfectly. Almost everyone there was a bit nervous, except Edmund and Bayard Rustin [the civil rights leader]. Jason said not a word all evening and fled the minute She left (on the stroke of 12). Lizzie [Hardwick], sitting two seats down from Mrs. Kennedy at the same table, announced aloud to John Marquand that she was planning to write a play about Oswald because he was such a fascinating character. Fortunately, Mrs. Kennedy was locked in intense conversation with me (I was nauseatingly charming) and didn't hear. . . . Philip Roth fell in love with Mrs. Kennedy, but I made sure that he had very few chances to get anywhere near her, so he couldn't beat my time. Barbara Epstein, on leaving, asked me when we were planning to have a party for Margaret Truman. Lizzie followed up that brilliant witticism with the remark that Jackie is just plain folks, whereupon (for reasons I'll leave to your imagination) I sweetly told her to go fuck herself. This shocked Rachel and Naomi, who managed to eavesdrop on every single conversation of the evening.[40]

As for the fairy queen who left at the stroke of midnight, Midge told the Wheldons that "The lady herself seems to be extremely nice, though not without her, to be sure, extremely refined edges. She is a good deal brighter, and a great deal livelier, than [anyone (?)] in the movies. Prettier, too. . . . What she really is, is the brightest and most innocently decent girl in the poshest boarding school."

Norman, Midge went on, had afterwards seen Jackie for lunch and for drinks, the ostensible purpose being to promote the career of Robert Kennedy. Apparently, the senator from New York had "been rather slow about discovering that hob-nobbing with the old Yankee aristocracy is not the way to men's hearts in this great city," so he had invited the Podhoretzes to lunch in Washington. Decter allowed that she was "far more curious to meet Bobby than ever I was to meet Jackie – 1) for the obvious reasons of sex, and 2) because I still have a schoolgirl thing about a United States Senator."[41] The trouble was that Bobby, like nearly everyone in the Democratic establishment in 1965, was hawkishly defending his brother's policy in Vietnam: the United States should not back down in the fight to contain communism.

Back in New York, Jackie soon reciprocated the Podhoretzes' dinner party. She would host a liberal-chic affair, and Podhoretz would help her draw up a guest list – again stipulating the omission of Mailer. He suggested, aside from Washington types, Richard Hofstadter, Arendt, Harold Rosenberg ("He writes about art, literature, society, politics, and the kitchen sink"), Rustin, Howe ("a very good literary critic"), Kristol, Bell, Lichtheim, Phillips ("Editor of *Partisan*

Review and erstwhile literary dictator of New York"), Rahv ("Same description as Phillips [except they hate each other and have remained together, as it were, for the sake of the child – the child being, of course, *Partisan Review*]"), Wrong, Michael Harrington, Silvers, Epstein ("Inventor of the quality paperback . . . and éminence grise of the *New York Review*"), Kazin, Kempton, James Wechsler et al., plus Schlesinger, Galbraith, and Richard Neustadt. And if Jackie wanted "more people in the arts, I would suggest the following possibilities: Lillian Hellman, Robert Penn Warren, Philip Roth, Arthur Penn, Bill Styron, etc." While there is no record of how Jackie's gathering went, what Podhoretz suggested was that a talk on civil rights from Nicholas Katzenbach, Johnson's attorney general, "would be a good start – some of the people I've listed would probably have hard questions to put to him and we might get a lively discussion."[42]

On another evening, the Podhoretzes came to Jackie's Fifth Avenue apartment for dinner. Jackie "ran her big eyes up and down from my head to my toes," Podhoretz recalled; "she smiled sweetly and said, 'Oh, so you scooted across the park in your little brown suit and your big brown shoes.' To which the Brooklyn boy still alive in me replied, 'Fuck you, Jackie.'" She liked the Brooklyn boy's retort, and they "became even faster friends than we already were." They would have tea alone together, she to retail the Washington political, he the New York literary "dirt." Once, as Willie Morris would remember, Podhoretz "noticed that the servants had been dismissed . . . and was tortured by the idea that she was soliciting an advance. 'I didn't know what to do,' he told us. 'You know if anything happened you could never *tell* anyone.'"[43]

In the last analysis she was merely using him, not just for Bobby's career but in order to play his acquaintance Styron off against his pal Mailer for the sake of exacting vengeance on the latter. Podhoretz had good reason to feel dished, especially when (to look ahead) the pal would tap his resentment in reviewing *Making It*, and when Jackie herself, not relishing that book's candor, would go on to have a reconciliation with the pal.

It was like the dance of courtiers around the throne of the Virgin Queen. Wilson's catty view was that the Upper West Side now contained "a whole . . . *Cultural Establishment*," with "Jackie Kennedy . . . somehow on the fringes" but exerting an influence befitting the center. "Cal [Robert] Lowell has been turning somersaults about her, and Norman Podhoretz has lunch with her so often that his wife is said to be annoyed. The Podhoretzes are part of the Establishment: the Jewish-intellectual department."[44] As it would turn out, lunch with Bobby in March 1965 was the climax of the Podhoretzes' relations with the clan – in part because Bobby's enemy, President Johnson, was also cultivating them.

Thus after the lunch with Bobby, Norman and Midge, trying to relax in their hotel room before dinner, were ordered by Goodwin to "get your asses over here!" – meaning to the White House, where Johnson "will say hello to you." It turned out to be more than hello. Upon arrival, as Midge related, we are rushed through the gate, pushed, by Goodwin, through the corridors and brought to the Oval [Office] – a sanctum sanctorum....

We shook Mr. Johnson's hand, and then, far from being hurried on, Mr. Johnson said to us, "Siddown, yo'all siddown. Le's have a cuppa coffee and set and talk a while." ... We sat down. And then I cannot tell exactly how it started, but the President sat with us and regaled us with stories for $3\frac{1}{2}$ hours.... This monologue was free, aimless, meandering and moved in incredible sequences from oratory about civil rights to reminiscences about his Daddy and the Texas State Legislature to stories about how FDR outsmarted him, [and] how he regularly outsmarted Richard Nixon.... He is the most incredibly vain, tough, brilliant, clever and appositely articulate man I know I've ever met and I think I ever want to meet. What was most astonishing was his speech itself.... N. will have to characterize it for you.... [45]

N.'s characterization of Johnson's speech and demeanor does him justice:

More often than not, he himself would break up at a punch line; once he laughed so hard the tears came rolling down his cheeks. The dignity of his presence is immense, but it is not a dignity that depends on stiffness of manner. There is no need for Lyndon Johnson to deny himself the pleasure of walking across his office to show a visitor exactly how Estes Kefauver used to enter a Senate committee hearing ("Here come old Estes, chargin' in like a b'ar"), or to feel inhibited about mimicking a woman's voice when telling a story, or to refrain from making wry comments about people who have criticized him, or to give vent to the slightest embarrassment in quoting those who have praised him ("Warn't that *nice* o' him to say that, warn't it?")....

The Johnson one sees on television, stiffly got up in his Sunday best, has little in common with the earthy, humorous, salty, sophisticated, expansive, complicated character one meets in the Oval Room of the White House.[46]

The year before, as we have seen, Podhoretz had suspected Johnson of cynically staging a crisis in the Gulf of Tonkin in order to show himself firm against the communist threat, but the man in person was compelling – not "in the mold of Prince Hal become Henry V," which Camelot devotees imagined for Kennedy, but in the mold of Henry VIII, "large, loud, full of gusto and appetite, and luxuriating in the freedom – a royal prerogative indeed – of uninhibited self-display."[47] If Johnson should "ever let loose" and show his real self in public, Podhoretz believed, "America would become a more interesting country to live in. Who knows? There could even be consequences for the history of the world."[48]

The epistolary exchanges between Midge Decter and Jacqueline Wheldon are an ongoing revelation of their respective domestic scenes. Referring both to Wynn's toilet rituals and to his fantasy life, Jacqueline confessed that it was "quite Turn of the Screwish round here sometimes,"[49] and Midge, claiming seniority as a mother, would assure her that everything was normal and that her own son was just such a *Where the Wild Things Are* creature – "demanding, arrogant, destructive, and immovable."

Each succeeding little one, I find, is forced to bring himself more and more dramatically to your consciousness as anything but a pure organic and sensual object. We turned around when it became unavoidable, and there he was. Boy, when you have a baby you are doing nothing less than setting a whole life, as big and immediate as your own to someone, in motion.[50]

Of course John was all of two. Coddled by his older sisters, he was resisted only by "Ruthie, poor dear," who had to represent the "reality principle in his life." As for the older girls, "Rachel wears my clothes already, and devours all the dirty books in the house, while Naomi looks on disdainfully, feeling herself the only true disciple of J. D. Salinger."[51]

How, between children and writerly ambitions, a woman was supposed to conduct her love life was a question for – well, for romantic fools, who were legion in the sixties, especially within the Family. Referring to some unnamed but apparently earthy female novelist, Midge told Jacqueline that

all she [properly] cares about is the reception of her books. She doesn't give a shit about sex, and if the truth be told, neither does any of us. That is what I want to say, and I am afraid. Afraid for one grisly afternoon years ago at the Trillings with the Marcuses when Steve and Diana were holding forth for what seemed like hours on the subject of "what we know" about the female orgasm. And finally, when I felt the blood rising above my temples, I burst out, "*Can't we change the subject?*" And instantly four pairs of pitying and all-knowing eyes were trained on me. Honestly, Jacq, I don't know where all this nonsense is going to end.[52]

Marcus shared the Trillings' commitment to Freud, and was working on *The Other Victorians: A Study of Sexuality and Pornography in Mid-Nineteenth-Century England*, which would come out in 1966. The book had shock value, but it was imprisoned within the psychoanalytic system, as, to Midge and Jacqueline, was its author. As Jacqueline once remarked: "If there's one thing in this world makes me sick it's the male gynecologist who doesn't know his place."[53] And then there was Diana Trilling, back from Lionel's year at Oxford, who was displaying herself as "the world's [latest] unsurpassed Anglophile. To wit, she now holds firmly to the conviction that what is wrong with American men, as compared with the men in Oxford, is that they are, as she puts it, 'not permitted' to undergo their youthful homosexual experience."[54]

Beyond gossip, the point in culling these remarks about Marcus or Diana is to indicate what, for Decter in particular, was becoming a new specialty. Increasingly, the male and female ideologues were trying to define female identity, sensibility, liberation, and responsibility in terms that didn't jibe with Decter's own, or many other women's, experience. The challenge would be to write a book-length rejoinder – and it would entail making a career change. After marrying Norman, she had worked briefly as Herman Kahn's assistant and then for a longer while at Columbia Records, editing its Legacy Series of books bundled with recordings on vinyl. "I make quite a lot of money for a girl," she told Jacqueline in 1964. But then Norman gave her "a long lecture (which he has since, in absolutely caddishly cowardly and disingenuous fashion, taken back)" about how she ought "to go back to writing," whether it be short pieces he would gladly publish in *Commentary* or what Jacqueline alluded to as "your proper work ... this book about women. Which in its time will be much more useful to your children than any extra dollars you make now and they wolf up without so much as a thought about where it came from."[55]

Having recovered from her stabbing, Adele Morales soon divorced Norman Mailer. He then married Lady Jeanne Campbell, not least, Podhoretz thought, because she was "the daughter of the Duke of Argyle, the granddaughter of Beaverbrook, the mistress of Henry Luce." She and Mailer fought constantly and soon divorced. Next came Beverly Bentley, a former model with aspirations to the stage, whom he met in P. J. Clarke's bar. He "walked in," as Decter recounted, and "there was this gorgeous blonde at the bar who said to him, 'Norman Mailer, motherfucker!' But she never struck me as a prima donna, she struck me as having a head full of quasi-mystical nonsense."[56]

Mailer's "foul-weather friend" is what Podhoretz would later claim to have been, and in those earlier years was sufficiently so that Mailer asked him "to be my literary executor if and when."[57] In the late fifties and early sixties, Trilling "dryly" spoke of the Norman Invasion, coupling Mailer and Podhoretz with Norman O. Brown.[58] Mailer's ambition was to write a "big book" of fiction, under the impression that a major postwar American novel had to rival Melville's *Moby-Dick* or perhaps Dreiser's *An American Tragedy*, big not just in size but in thematic purpose. Meanwhile he wrote smaller (and finally inconsequential) novels like *An American Dream* (1965) and *Why Are We in Vietnam?* (1967), the British edition of which was dedicated to Podhoretz. Then came that remarkable hybrid, the history-as-novel titled *The Armies of the Night* (1968), which is about the previous year's march on Washington in protest against the war in Vietnam. Large sections appeared in *Harper's*, with a postscript in *Commentary*.

Willie Morris and Decter – he was *Harper's* chief editor, she had become its executive editor – flew in a small plane up to Provincetown in the spring of 1968 to retrieve the manuscript from Mailer. Staying sober an entire month (and boring Beverly stiff), he had written not the expected 20,000 but 90,000 words. Reading it on the spot, Morris and Decter knew they had the best thing the man had ever written. He seemed to think so, too, though as he and Morris "cruis[ed] Provincetown in the snow, drinking [Wild Turkey] straight from the bottle," he finally had to say, "God dammit, Morris, stop telling me how good it is. You're like every southern boy I ever knew. You're too effusive in your compliments."[59]

Mailer had arrived at the radically antiwar politics of *Armies* in very rapid fashion. In 1965, the fall issue of *Partisan Review* had printed an open letter protesting the war, signed by Podhoretz, Howe, Kazin, Malamud, Marcus, Richard Poirier, and others, all careful not to appear pro-communist and all too "lukewarm" for Mailer the dormant Trotskyite. Their letter opened with "We do not think that the present or past policies of the United States are good ones," but after bemoaning military involvement, they admitted having no "alternative policy" for peace, freedom, and prosperity in Southeast Asia. *Partisan Review* published Mailer's response in the same issue: "Three cheers, lads. Your words read like they were written in milk of magnesia.... The editors ask for a counterpolicy. I offer it. It is to get out of Asia."

Like Goodman and Brown, Mailer believed sociopolitical problems were a manifestation of psychological ones. Therefore, if Americans really had a psychological need to fight, let them, he declared, buy a tract of land in South America and conduct live war games – a reprise of his serio-comic suggestion that juvenile delinquents conduct gladiatorial jousts in Central Park. It was a straight line from this to the Yippie threat to "levitate the Pentagon." Metaphors, expletives, street demonstrations, and balls-testing showboating were replacing reasoned argument – as when, at Truman Capote's black-and-white ball in November 1966, Mailer invited McGeorge Bundy, who had softly excused Mailer's bumptiousness about the war by saying "Well, of course, you don't really know much about it," to step outside.[60]

Mailer had what Podhoretz later called a "sissy problem." Therefore he "would spend the rest of his life overcoming the stigma of [his] reputation as a 'nice Jewish boy' by doing as an adult all the hooliganish things he had failed to do in childhood and adolescence." The boy Podhoretz, though also nice, Jewish, and from Brooklyn, had faced most of the street dangers, and been precociously beforehand in matters sexual, as the boy Mailer had not. One consequence was that the adult Podhoretz, while quite "as obsessed" with sex as Mailer was, never regarded it "as an *issue*." Mailer's fifties fiction, anticipating the monomaniacal focus on sex in the mid-sixties novels of Roth and Updike, was arrested in adolescence. "I was embarrassed on his behalf by the apocalyptic significance he attributed to sex in general and to kinky or perverted sex in particular," Podhoretz would write. "It struck me as callow of him to treat oral sex as such a big deal in *The Deer Park* or to attribute a veritably metaphysical significance to the act of heterosexual anal penetration in 'The Time of Her Time.'"[61]

The Podhoretz of the sixties was morally committed to the ideal, at least, of marital fidelity. Mailer, by contrast, offered no obeisance to such "establishment" notions, and demanded for himself unhindered probings "backward toward being," located, often as not, "three inches below and back of the Erogenous Zone Clitoric."[62] Not that his wildly promiscuous affairs were mechanical and empty. He loaded them with mystic significance, and urged Podhoretz to follow his lead – an impossible demand, even if Podhoretz had wanted to abandon the monogamous ideal.[63] Who after all could keep pace with Mailer? Despite his best-selling author's income, he was hard-pressed to pay all those alimonies, to say nothing of the constant meals and hotel rooms required by star-coupling women, sometimes more than one a day. The economical as well as virtuous thing, Podhoretz realized, was to grow up.

One more item for now about Mailer. From December 1962 to October 1963, *Commentary* published six "Responses & Reactions" by him to Martin Buber's *Tales of the Hasidim*. Podhoretz had offered him bimonthly space as a favor (Mailer had wanted to appear every month), making an exception to the magazine's scholarly standards so that his intellectually fecund friend could have a say about Judaism. It was a subject on which he was almost totally ignorant. So relentless had been his campaign to eradicate the "nice Jewish boy from Brooklyn" from his persona that he seemed entirely deracinated, almost surely to his detriment as a novelist. Hence Podhoretz's fascination with his *wanting* to do commentaries on Buber. Would an examination of his Jewish roots profit him as a man and as a writer?

The answer, briefly, was no, but thanks to Podhoretz he did at least see something of the living Hasidic community in Brooklyn. On the eve of Yom Kippur, the pair of them went to a Lubavitch service in Crown Heights, the room soon "as crowded as a subway at rush hour," and "the mob" parting like the Red Sea when the rebbe was announced. After "the opening prayer of *Kol Nidre*," however, "Mailer whispered that he had seen enough, and asked if we could leave. Once outside, he pronounced himself delighted by how 'mean and tough' the Hasidim were. Their attitude, he said (with considerable shrewdness), was 'Out of my way, motherfucker,' and he was all for it." Unfortunately, "Out of my way, motherfucker" doesn't get one very far with Buber, and after the six columns Mailer's series "was quietly dropped." As Podhoretz would write, "the whole episode left a bad taste in both our mouths – in mine because I had given in to his bullying, in his because I had been less than fully loyal to him."[64]

Mailer, Goodman, Brown, and Podhoretz were literary symptoms of the movement that would become the New Left. But Podhoretz, judging the concrete upshot of this or that radical idea, was finding himself obliged to draw lines – which is what Midge was doing as early as 1964, when she wrote to Jacqueline of the antipathy she was starting to feel toward people who were supposed to be her ideological kin:

I sometimes...feel inclined to support the Vietnam war – which on the whole I do not do – simply out of the huge well of contempt I feel for most of the people who oppose it. Do you know what I mean? Life is really quite frightening when things reach such a point. Things anyway seem at a very low ebb in what Jack Thompson calls "the U.S. and A.": everybody under 30 seems slumped beneath a cloud of marijuana; while everybody over 30 seems to find that this vast and hardy sanity of ours wants a bit of tinkering with and have taken to systematically inducing hallucinations in themselves, by L.S.D., which they then call "perception." Is this not the same in England? And do you understand what it is about, I mean really about?[65]

Was whatever was wrong with those people perhaps also wrong with their movement? Take Timothy Leary, who was facing a prison sentence for using, distributing, and promoting the legalization of marijuana and LSD. In 1966, along with Kenneth Koch, Sontag, Robert Creeley, Mailer, Epstein, and the usual suspects, Podhoretz signed an "appeal against American persecution of Dr. Timothy Leary" – or so claimed Allen Ginsberg, who didn't say what was "in" the appeal.[66] Anyway, Podhoretz was soon apologizing: "I still feel the sentence is monstrous, but having since learned a few things about Leary that I didn't know at the time, I now regret having allowed my name to be used in such a way as to give the impression that I support his crusade."[67] *Time* was then noticing Podhoretz and *Commentary*'s political disenchantment with the movement: "He believes that the New Left of the '60s is as misled about Communist totalitarianism as was the Old Left of the '30s. In turn, New Leftists pay him the compliment of calling him a 'fink.'"[68]

Radicals befogged and benumbed by drugs were looking suspiciously like Know-Nothing Bohemians, only more so. The tag that fit them best was a malapropism of Jimmy Breslin, the hot reporter for the *New York Daily News*. He had come to interview John P. Roche, Special Consultant to Johnson, who wrote Podhoretz: "Between us, I had never heard of Breslin when he turned up to talk to me. We chatted genially for an hour. He tootled off.... When I saw the 'interview,' I thought it was hilarious (Jacobins emerged as 'jackal-bins'!)."[69] "Jackal-bins" became code at *Commentary* for supporters and fellow travelers of the New Left, harbingers of political fecklessness to come.

In 1964, Farrar, Straus had brought out *Doings and Undoings*, a 371-page collection of Podhoretz's essays and reviews on American subjects, from his first pieces on Malamud and Bellow to "My Negro Problem." Rallied as a formidable "hanging judge" by Mailer and responsible for no few "undoings" of literary reputations, Podhoretz now dreaded being undone by other reviewers. Two are worth noting here.

Marvin Mudrick in the *Hudson Review*, coupling Podhoretz's book with Diana Trilling's *Claremont Essays*, showed what the intellectuals clustered around Columbia (the Trillings lived on Claremont Avenue), or the New York Family generally, looked like to a considerable number of people west of the Hudson. Mudrick taught at the University of California, Santa Barbara, and someone once called him the Mike Hammer of *belle lettres*. Why, he asked, were American "deep-think specialists" often as humorless as the sage of Columbia himself? He supposed it was because, "having without resistance yielded to the social sciences all the claims of literature in myth, psychology, history, morality, American writers have nothing to talk about but their own group superstitions." He conjured up a holy family "daguerreotype," Lionel holding his piece on Wordsworth and the rabbis and Diana her earnest introduction to Lawrence, while "Podhoretz – still muttering at the prospect of a mocha-colored grandchild – irritably straightens his crown of thorns."[70]

The other would-be undoer was a former "confederate," Amherst professor Benjamin DeMott, a lightweight compared with Mudrick but publishing in the more widely circulated *New York Review*. With a crudeness that exceeded even Mudrick's, he complained about Podhoretz's references to his own experience ("he has taught himself to emit – when his learning flags – a piquantly malodorous autobiographical smog") and about the "weary insiderism" of Family book-reviewing generally. While lovers of literature in Massachusetts pored over books in private, the New York critic seemed "to think of himself as inhabiting a world in which print is but a beginning, a preliminary to the refining and close-tuning that will be undertaken later in conversation" – at all those Family lunches and parties.[71]

Podhoretz discounted Mudrick altogether, but was troubled by hints of anti-Semitism in DeMott, about which Lichtheim offered some cool counsel. "There seems to be an undercurrent of irritation with the Big City on the part of academia.... If you want further consolation, Marx was called an 'impudent Jew-boy' by an eminent German academician with whom he had quarreled. It didn't do any permanent damage."[72] Nor would insinuations like DeMott's. In any event, positive reviews canceled out the negative ones, and Podhoretz's value on what he called the New York "stock-market report on reputation" "eventually leveled off at a new high."[73]

Another rub occasioned by *Doings and Undoings* was Trilling's demurrer about Podhoretz's characterization of him in the book's introduction. There Podhoretz explains that he has addressed himself to contemporary fiction because it offers a way – one way among several – to understand the culture's present condition. No one (other than Leavis perhaps) would argue with that. But then he sticks his chin out by distinguishing his recent "moral response" to Cold War challenges from that of "the revisionist liberalism of the 50's – which is associated with names like Lionel Trilling, Sidney Hook, Daniel Bell, and Richard Hofstadter, and which exerted a considerable influence on the earliest pieces in this collection."[74]

Trilling was not pleased. Grouping him with Hook, Bell, and Hofstadter, he told Podhoretz, "constitutes, as you must surely be aware, what in Stalinist days used to be called an amalgam, a polemical device" whereby "the faults or deficiencies of the views of any one... are imputed to all." Naturally he respected these other intellectuals, but he didn't feel at one with them on many points. In any case, and more centrally:

Your ambivalence toward my work is by now an old matter, taken for granted between us. I have hitherto been able to suppose that it was as strong in its positive as in its negative feelings, and I have been able to regard it as a natural and useful element in the development of your thought and even to take a kind of pleasure in it, as making between us an interesting dialectic. The terms which you choose to set it forth on this occasion are, to put it minimally, a surprise to me.

And there was something else. At the beginning of his introduction, Podhoretz took pains to indicate he was no art-for-art's-sake critic: "Almost always it was the issues rather than the book itself that I really cared about. Is that a damaging admission for a literary critic to make? I suppose in a way it is. A literary critic ought – or so they tell me – to regard literature as an end in itself; otherwise he has no business being a literary critic." Trilling was very sensitive on this point. After quoting the passage above, he continued: "Who, I must ask, are 'they' who sought to impose [an art-for-art's sake 'doctrine'] on you? Surely not your teachers either at Columbia College or at Cambridge. I should say that they proposed quite the contrary doctrine to you."[75]

"Maybe I'm being an oversensitive author to have detected pique in your note about my book," Podhoretz replied. "I suppose you may have just been teasing me. In any case, I don't understand in what sense it is a 'fantasy' to associate you (but not, God forbid, completely and utterly) with the revisionist liberalism of the 50's. Is it a fantasy that you once wrote an enormously influential book called *The Liberal Imagination?*" That, of course, hadn't been Trilling's point. He was hurt that Podhoretz seemed to be dumping his ideas wholesale for the sake of the new radicalism.

In fact, he wasn't.

8

One Shoe Drops

Trilling and Podhoretz were exactly a quarter century apart – the one's 1935 was the other's 1960 – and the younger critic was naturally struck by the differences as well as the similarities between their eras. A partner in his revision of "revisionist liberalism" (to stick with Podhoretz's somewhat vague label) was Willie Morris (1934–1999), whom we have already met. A Mississippian, a Rhodes Scholar, a star editor for the crusading *Texas Observer* in Austin, and then an associate editor at *Harper's*, Morris in 1967 was named editor-in-chief of that "bastion of middlebrow gentility." Like Podhoretz at *Commentary* seven years before, he turned *Harper's* into a hot book by chasing and defining the emerging *Zeitgeist*.

When his appointment was made public, Podhoretz telephoned with good wishes and a caution: "They all love you now. Just wait." Editorial honeymoons are brutish and brief, and Morris was fortunate to have designated Decter, then forty-one, as his executive editor.

Morris was fond of his bottle, and, like Podhoretz, who he remembered could down thirteen martinis at a sitting, he considered it a point of literary pride to drink like a Russian – which is to say like a Southern novelist, citing Faulkner's cracker-Dionysian remark that "There's a lot of nourishment in an acre of corn." At the huge parties Norman and Midge threw in the mid-sixties, Morris would be among the company who "had a habit of passing out peacefully sometime in the early morning hours and then being awakened and taken home by his wife or a friend as the last guests were leaving" – or emerging on Sunday afternoon from the maid's room, politely wondering whether the party was "over already."[1]

Morris would write that, "for a while" in the late sixties, "the Pod" was "my best friend . . . irreverent, amusing, bawdy, and confident." He stood "not much more than five and a half feet, and stocky, with very blue eyes, boyish and balding."

FIGURE 13. Norman Podhoretz (far left) with (left to right) writer Jay Milner, writer and *Harper's* editor Willie Morris, and Texas state senator Don Kennard in Fort Worth, Texas, May 1968.

[M]any was the late afternoon I would meet Pod . . . after work for magazine conversation and gossip. He would usually hurry in a few minutes late and sit down and order a drink and start talking, for there was a breathless quality about him, a not unattractive air of rush, a sense of movement and accomplishment and briskness trailed in his wake, and he was never for a moment banal or boring. . . . Here we were . . . , the young Dixie WASP and the young Brooklyn Jew, joined by literature and America and mutual friends and liberal politics and magazines.

They were publishing, and Podhoretz was writing, some of the best essays of the decade, and doubtless their affection for each other was heightened by "the hot bosky bit of Tennessee summertime" (Walker Percy's phrase) in their glasses.

That the bosky bit made Morris smarmy, however, is obvious. Many years later, he would languorously ask whether he and Podhoretz "ever [did] really have much in common at all? Perhaps this, too, is an American question." But he accurately as well as fondly understood how "the intellectual parties at [Norman] and Midge's huge apartment on West End Avenue . . . [were] so removed in tone and mood from the ones, say, at George Plimpton's flat on the East River with their athletes and *Playboy* bunnies and disarranged writers of fiction and spiffy songs on the piano as to seem a different American setting altogether" – namely, the Family versus the jet-set.[2]

The most memorable adventure Podhoretz had with Morris was a trip to the Mississippi Delta. Its ostensible purpose was to give Morris courage: he was booked to give a speech to the students at his old high school in Yazoo City. But Podhoretz's purpose was to see a different America. The "lush" Mississippi springtime "odors of perfumed air and growing things" were so rich that, as they deplaned in Jackson, he asked: "What's that I smell? A chocolate factory?" To show him "cotton growing," Morris took him to a plantation where Podhoretz "began talking to an old black sharecropper. The poor old fellow was straight out of [Edwin] Markham's [revolution-portending poem] 'The Man with the Hoe,'" and someone utterly dissimilar to any problematic "Negro" back in Brooklyn. They "could have been talking different tongues, for each barely comprehended a word the other said."[3]

They visited the local cemetery with Morris's grandmother. Gazing at the tombs of the Confederate dead, the men asked if these boys had died in vain. Her curt reply: "They'd have been dead by now anyway." They had had their cause. Morris's cause was racial justice, and he believed that, thanks to its bloody history, the South had the "tragic" wisdom needed to achieve it.[4] For him, it was cause enough. Trying also to tackle the problem of left-wing totalitarianism, which then entailed military resistance to its attack on the government of South Vietnam, was too much. His Yazoo City neighbors seemed to agree, being less "for" the war than, like Decter, "against the kind of people who were against it."[5]

Morris would soon publish *North Towards Home*, which tells a story similar to Podhoretz's in *Making It*, only with something crucial missing. He never mentions the "dirty little secret" of ambition that, for Podhoretz, was central to any candid account of a writer's rise in contemporary America. Morris's persona was that of the Oxford-educated lover of "fine writing," more interested in style than in ideas. He had the deepest of southern accents "and a 'shit-kicking' country-boy manner to go with it," but he also had used that Oxford degree as a catapult for his career in the Big Apple, landing in the editor's chair at *Harper's* at a younger age than anyone before him.

In 1971, having put the magazine on the verge of insolvency and posing as (in Decter's phrase) "a martyr to Lit-er-a-toor" succumbing to the Mammonism of the business office, Morris resigned before he could be fired.[6] That was the sort of "fecklessness" he was candid about in his writing, as he was about the anomie of New York, the "Big Cave" as he called it, in contrast to the homey Delta. But about ambition, "the determining force in his life," he never spoke or wrote.[7]

In his later memoir, Morris would alternate between expressions of distress over his old friend's perceived political shift to the right – something a man "literary to a fault" was unable to understand – and expressions of affection: "I granted [Podhoretz] his politics, but was nonetheless strangely saddened. I loved the guy, and still in old memory do, and choose to recall those youthful

early evenings . . . with the world alight and all its rewards and risks and cir-
cuities before us. As Oscar Levant said of Doris Day, 'I knew her before she
was a virgin.'"[8]

Doings and Undoings had been a collection Podhoretz was compelled to offer
the publisher Roger Straus in lieu of the book on postwar writers that he found
wasn't "in" him after all. What was authentically "in" him, it had turned out,
was "My Negro Problem," the coda to *Doings*. It was a harbinger of the mix
of memoir, description, and analysis he would offer in his next book, *Making
It*. He got under way with it almost at once, Decter writing the Wheldons in
August 1964 that he was laboring three weeks each month to put an issue of
Commentary together, then taking a week to write in seclusion up at Yaddo,
the 400-acre writer-and-artist colony in Saratoga Springs, New York. He was
working not from notes but from inspiration: "What he has been doing is
extremely slow and painful and – the most difficult of all for him – quite out
of control, so that he can't plan or manipulate what emerges. He just has to
accept what is offered up to him by himself – at least so far." The two chapters
he had written were "really marvelous and, to me, humbling. . . . But he doesn't
know it yet, and can't be sure where it's going."[9]

He pushed steadily on, and in 1966 could still complain to Moynihan that
"Progress on the book is slow and unbelievably painful, but I suppose I deserve
that for being such an arrogant bastard."[10] He was writing *Making It* both to
deprecate and to account for his arrogance, success, and ambition and to reveal
the insecurities and fears that underlay them. Also, he aimed to put forward
his story as representative of those of "young men from the provinces" in
general, and of sons of immigrant Jews from Brooklyn, intellectuals in an "age
of criticism," and "the young generation" in postwar America in particular.
And so it would eventually be understood: as an adaptation of "the traditional
Bildungsroman," or novel about growing up, "to a new constituency," and also
"a hard book to put down once you've started reading it." Thus in 1984 the
poet David Lehman, who goes on to cite Mark Schechner in the *Harvard Guide
to Contemporary American Writing*: "Ostensibly just a memoir, *Making It* is,
in its way, a novel as well, the imagination of a life in terms of a significant
moral pattern. . . . [It] remains the only Jewish novel after the war . . . whose
hero is allowed to achieve social success without paying a moral price."[11]
However, these recognitions would require more than a decade, and the rise of
a new generation, to materialize, and by then Podhoretz had gone on to other
things.

At the time, naturally, he also hoped the book would bring in some much
needed money. He and Midge were sending the four children to the Dalton
School on East 89th Street, which in 1966 was costing them $6,094 for tuition
and $540 for transportation (now $42,245 altogether). This, as he told the
headmaster, totaled "almost *twenty-five percent* of my present salary as editor
of *Commentary*." Midge's salary at *Harper's* covered the tuition, but not the
cost of the maid who looked after the kids in her absence.[12]

Through his agent, Lynn Nesbit, Podhoretz was asking Straus for a $25,000 advance, which from the latter's point of view would necessitate selling 50,000 copies just to break even. That is, it would have to be a major work. Podhoretz had gone through enough fertile if interrupted periods of inspiration at Yaddo to believe it would be. Here, in part, is the outline he gave Nesbit:

My contention is that it is impossible to grow up in America ... without believing that the goal of life is to be a Success. But it's also impossible to grow up in America without believing that Success requires, and bespeaks, a radical corruption of the spirit. Where did this contradiction come from? What does it mean? How does it work itself out in the life of an ambitious kid? What sort of attitudes, overt and covert, does it foster? How does it color friendships, careers, love affairs?

These are the questions I want to explore, alternating between the theoretical-descriptive and the autobiographical-anecdotal modes.[13]

He ended up combining the chronological and the thematic, the confessional and the analytical.

He was also trying out his subject in public forums. On WNBC-TV's "Open Mind," for instance, he argued that there is no "inexorable law of history that artists should be totally alienated ... and struggling and starving in garrets." How could the serious contemporary artist "entertain" an audience wide enough to sustain him – buy his books, his paintings, or whatever – and intelligent enough to profit by his insights? For most highbrows, it almost went without saying that if an artist was popular he must be no good. Podhoretz wanted to reopen the question.

However enthusiastic Straus may have been about a book analyzing modern American intellectuals' love–hate relations with ambition and success, including their own, he was alarmed by what Podhoretz actually gave him. Granted, the thesis was at least plausible, and the auto-case history more than fascinating. But his sketches of important living people – Family demigods like Rahv, Arendt, McCarthy, Sontag, the Greenbergs (whom everyone would recognize behind his constant "The Boss") – or his revelations of Baldwin playing the race card or Leavis sounding paranoid, if they didn't usher in an eternity of libel suits, would surely doom the book in the eyes of those same people. And it was those people who dictated the tenor of reviews, which in turn dictated sales. Straus therefore backed out, as did Nesbit. But another agent, Candida Donadio, recognized the book as "a valuable document of historical significance which had to be published" and eagerly agreed to represent it. She soon aroused the interest of James Silberman at Random House, who passed it up to board chairman Bennett Cerf.

"I'm crazy about it," Cerf said. "It talks about all the smart young people in the intellectual establishment, and I think it's going to be a great success."[14] To Edmund Wilson, this sounded like the kiss of death. He hadn't read the typescript but lapped up the gossip, telling his diary:

Everyone I saw who had read it thought that it was awful. It purported to be a success story.... It told how Norman had now no accent, had been accepted, entertained, toasted and feted by all the élite of New York – who were Lillian, ourselves, Jackie Kennedy and everybody that everybody saw without anybody else's regarding it as a sign of having made it.... Jason, who disliked it more than anybody, was obliged, as an old friend of Norman's, to allow Random House to take it.[15]

Today, one reads *Making It* wondering what the fuss was about. As Daphne Merkin would write in 1999, the book "seems positively prescient about both the acquisitive egotism of the eighties and the wave of literary confessionalism which began in that decade"[16] – just as, that same year, Richard Poirier, a critic of American literature at Rutgers, affirmed that the book's argument about intellectuals wanting the kinds of success traditionally reserved for "the high rollers in business, investment and entertainment" "has since been accepted as pretty close to the truth."[17]

What did critics not see in 1968 that Merkin and Poirier could see thirty years on? Trilling, to start with a still almost entirely friendly adviser, urged Podhoretz not to publish the book at all. That cannot have been because he disliked the thesis about ambition and success, since he had all along encouraged his student frankly to embrace the desirability of "power." What moved Trilling – and what moved his wife Diana to appeal to Decter to intervene[18] – was simple anxiety about the consequences of candor. Literary intellectuals, Family or otherwise, didn't want to hear about their "dirty little secret," least of all from someone as envied as Podhoretz.

The author himself was anxious. Writing to Frank Kermode, he freely referred to his "suicidal book." And when the New York gossip became "even more vicious than I had imagined in my most paranoid moments," he determined to "cultivate a kind of Lichtheimian attitude to defend myself against the slings and arrows of an outrageous family."[19] He wouldn't have enough of that attitude. No one, as Dan Jacobson told him, ever does: "The thing to do is simply to give up the hope of *ever* reaching a stage where one is genuinely indifferent to attack.... The part of oneself which cares, cares – that's all there is to it.... Which is cold comfort, I admit."[20]

Friends like Jacobson recognized the value of *Making It* at once. Glazer gave Random House's publicists a blurb that carried authority: "an original and brilliant analysis of the classic motivations of fame, power, and money, how they went underground in his world, because they were considered impure, but continued to work nevertheless in surprising ways." Here at last was a book demonstrating that "power, fame, and money" could "be more interesting than sex."[21] Jack Thompson, reading the typescript, had a private revelation: "Everything you said seemed to be news, brand-new news, and yet news of a world that is so familiar I never dreamed I didn't really understand it.... At the end I felt violently in the presence of a dirty little secret which wasn't little anymore."[22] Podhoretz's Newport Reading Club friend understood that a lot of the perks of "making it" were both finally specious and alluring just the same. If the other club member, Jason Epstein, was very unhappy, perhaps that was because he didn't want anyone to notice how frankly he enjoyed such perks. "Balzac should have written [the book]," Epstein allegedly said, "about somebody else."[23]

Making It came out in January 1968. If the gossip had been discouraging, the reviews were poisonous. The writer Joseph Epstein (no relation to Jason) would recall the atmosphere of "envy and *Schadenfreude*" that had been festering for a decade: "Here was Norman P., this still young man, the favorite of the famous teachers of the time, writing for the *New Yorker* and most anywhere else he chose, editor of *Commentary* at 30, making his way in the world at a much quicker rate than anyone else, and extremely brash." Someone had told Podhoretz that "You're the new Clifton Fadiman," which, Epstein said, "was really a kind of anti-Semitic code for saying 'You're the new Sammy Glick' – a hustler, an operator. So when he wrote *Making It*, saying all the things that one wasn't supposed to say in that day, everyone saw the chance to kick him in the pants, fore and aft."[24]

Kick him they did, some after having first told him to his face that they liked the book and were looking forward to saying so in print. Others simply went for the jugular. Silvers at the *New York Review* asked Hilton Kramer to do the book. "It was an example of the sort of preening ego-trip that I most disliked about the New York intellectual scene," Kramer later said. "And while trying to be respectful I ended up writing a review that I and several of my friends thought was pretty harsh. When I sent it on to the *New York Review* I was told that the *New York Review* wasn't interested in publishing a 'valentine' to Norman Podhoretz!"[25]

Wanting something harsher still, Silvers got it from Edgar Z. Friedenberg, a sociologist who specialized in the study of American youth and education and whom Podhoretz had discovered for *Commentary* back in 1960. He had written sixteen pieces for the magazine through 1966, but his mood apparently had gone sour. Allowing that an up-from-Brownsville tale might confirm "the American promise of opportunity to the industrious and gifted," he hastened to pronounce that *Making It* didn't deliver. Why? Because Podhoretz suffered from "acrophilia," a love of heights or celebrity-mongering. When he went to Family parties it wasn't to observe society, as Proust did, but to check his price in that "stock-market report on reputations." As for the wonderful sections devoted to "Mrs. K.," from which we have amply drawn, the tin-eared Friedenberg declared them motivated by "frozen hatred."[26]

Wilfrid Sheed, a novelist who happens to be Catholic, reviewed *Making It* in *Atlantic Monthly*. This was an exceptionally nasty piece of work, with sneers in every paragraph and a negativity so determined that even the unwary would have to notice:

The real point of the book is not to describe a scene or even himself, but to rationalize and justify his own living standard. It is as if he wanted the reader to say, it's OK, you can keep the money. He is demanding, through bluster and wheedle, some kind of open-ended absolution. The words we might use to condemn him have all lost their jurisdiction overnight: from arriviste to apple polisher to sellout.

And so on. Sheed acknowledged that Podhoretz has occasionally tried "to cover himself" by "put[ting] a tiny twist in his voice," but he was deaf to the irony a more dispassionate reader would hear in nearly every place it is called for. Grossly imputing that Podhoretz was now a man of opulence – this of a middle-class husband and father straining to make ends meet – Sheed seemed almost to resent how easy life had been for this upstart. For him, the tale ought to have been told in the mode of Fitzgerald's *Crack-up*, fraught with worry about whether the writer had lived up to his potential. In sum, having set out to explode the favored myth of the intelligentsia – that success corrupts the spirit – Podhoretz had unwittingly confirmed it.[27]

If Sheed's was "easily the most vicious" review,[28] the most painful was Mailer's. What he published in *Partisan Review* was a signal event in Podhoretz's life, remembered, analyzed, agonized over as though it were an act of fratricide.

When, out in Provincetown, Mailer read the galleys, he had enthusiastically declared it "a marvelous book. I learned more about American sociology from it than anything I've read in a long time. But I think you're too nice to people." Podhoretz remembered those words. Mailer had also said that he "couldn't understand what everybody was carrying on about" back in New York. Then, four months later, Podhoretz saw the galleys of Mailer's review, "Up the Family Tree," and was "flabbergasted."

Mailer's explanation, on the phone, was "I reread it and changed my mind, so I had to say so." In that case, Podhoretz later realized he ought to have replied, "you shouldn't have written about it." If his pal couldn't help him when he was "down," he should at least refrain from "giving me another kick in the ribs."[29]

What does "Up the Family Tree" – twenty-six pages in *Partisan Review* – argue? Mailer begins by decrying the brutal hazing the "Inner Clan" gave Podhoretz through its notices of *Making It* and, worse, through its wicked prepublication gossip about him personally. New York was filled with writers who wanted to see the editor of *Commentary* fail, who envied his rapid rise and his apparently effortless possession of (in Mailer's words) "wisdom and worldliness." Here was "my old dear great and good friend Norman Podhoretz who brings the mind of a major engineer to elucidating the character of complex literary structures" and who in "the innocence of his good heart" had sought "to climb the Matterhorn on ice skates." Which he hadn't quite done. Instead of "a great or major book," he had written "a minor work of much excellence, seriously flawed," and flawed not by "ten or twelve isolated phrases, sentences, and paragraphs so unhappy, ill-chosen, and aggressively flatulent that no reviewer with an eye to the cruel could fail to notice" but by something else – which turns out to be remissness in treating the Family the way Mailer himself would have treated it.

Mailer pauses to discover the motive, deeper than envy and resentment, for "the exceptional hostility" *Making It* had evoked. Put simply, most critics hadn't understood that, in writing a midcareer autobiography, Podhoretz had chosen to cast his story in a form resembling fiction. He presented himself as "a *literary* character," just as, though Mailer doesn't say this, he himself had done in *Armies of the Night* (whose loopy subtitle is *History as a Novel, the*

Novel as History). Mailer then passes on to evaluate this "autobiography as fiction" as, presumably, he would any novel.

Making It offers us "Podhoretz" as a sort of Stendhal or Balzac hero, writes Mailer, "the young man from the provinces who moves to the city and succeeds." The entire first half of the book soundly analyzes the young man, his progress, and the metropolitan site of his success. Podhoretz treats the Family circles "as if they were the equivalent to him of Versailles for Saint-Simon." But here, alas, "the novel begins, most subtly, to falter," and this because Podhoretz has succumbed to "the one weakness which is fatal to the young novelist: flattery."

Critical toward the "Podhoretz" character all the way through, *Making It*, charges Mailer, fails to be equally critical toward the Family,

that peculiar colony, aviary, and zoo of the most ferocious, idealistic, egotistic, narcissistic, cultivated, constipated, brilliant, sensitive, brutally insensitive, half-productive, and near-sterile gang of the best and worst literary court ever to rise right out of the immigrant ranks of a nation. The comic and tragic aspects of that gang take one's novelistic breath away – the satiric possibilities put it back.

And so, having written no satire, Podhoretz has also written no novel. His autobiography-as-fiction becomes a too forgiving "memoir," dwindling to a close in "sketchy anecdotes, abortive essays, isolated insights."

But if Podhoretz was "too nice" not to forgive the Family, why then did the Family refuse to forgive *him*? Mailer doesn't think it has anything to do with spilling the beans about ambition and success. It is because inwardly the New York Intellectuals *know* they are weak – what with their political vacillations and their consequent failure to produce a single major critic, poet, or novelist. Who *are* these intellectuals anyway? "Put-on" artists is what they are – offering no ideas, only the posture of being intellectuals. Why do they spin their brilliant analyses? Not for any moral or political principles. They don't *have* any. Ergo, Podhoretz's unforgivable sin is to have had "the idiocy or the suicidal strength to move to the center of the stage, open his box, exhibit his tricks" – and thus reveal the hollowness of all the other Family acts, too.[30]

If "Up the Family Tree" was a crucial event in Podhoretz's life, it was not just because it raised the question of whether his book would be relegated to honorable "minor" status. It was crucial because of the challenge Mailer laid down at the end. Forget about the Family, that bunch of put-ons. They don't stand for anything real – no substance, no principle. Mailer himself was, in his own terms, trying *to* stand for something real (hipsterism straining to become a revolution in narcotic and sexual gratification, and getting America "out of Asia"). What would Podhoretz try to stand for?

Podhoretz would always remember "Up the Family Tree" as harsher than it was. Mailer had found the first half if not two-thirds of *Making It* to be remarkable, its world presented and analyzed with "the quiet authority of good art," and he had plausibly explained the Family savagery as an indignant reaction to the exposure of their intellectual act as a form of charlatanry.

Nonetheless, Podhoretz may have been accurate in his conviction that Mailer hadn't so much changed his mind as "simply lost his nerve." That is, the novelist caved in to the Family pressure to join in the hounding of a scion who, politically, wasn't after all the good New Leftist everyone had thought he was – as Mailer noted accurately, the book takes a "relatively benign view of middle-class American values" – and who, morally, was guilty of a kind of treason in denying "that intellectuals... represented a true or superior alternative" to those values.

Podhoretz believed that Mailer lost his nerve in another sense as well. Not so much in the review, where he bracingly challenged the *New York Review* coterie to stop attitudinizing and do something that might get them arrested, but in life itself. He might have been able to get himself arrested, but at the end of the day his role was that of jester to the literary establishment, licensed to say outrageously critical things, including about *it*, but also obliged to observe an uncrossable line. In a prose sometimes "so baroque that it became the rhetorical equivalent of the cap and bells," Mailer, Podhoretz would aver, first criticized the radical feminists in *The Prisoner of Sex* (1971); then, discovering that Women's Lib "was becoming a real force on the radical scene," he "began to cajole and flatter it." He was *the* put-on artist, and one who couldn't finally sever his relationship with the mandarin Left.[31]

Mailer himself, looking back, posited a compound theory about the tone of "Up the Family Tree." On the one hand, it was an act of petty payback for Podhoretz's having acceded to Jackie Kennedy's stipulation that, for her New York party, he be excluded from the invitees: "Maybe it was my way of saying, 'Fuck you back.'" On the other hand, Mailer was persuaded that he had a disinterested critical point to make: "I felt he'd injured a promising book," he said, though adding, "I probably... crossed the line from objective criticism to self-serving criticism in that I began to enjoy pointing out what the faults were."[32]

Finally, Mailer may have believed that the time had come to shiver the Norman Invasion. One of his biographers, Mary V. Dearborn, argues that if Podhoretz really couldn't bring himself to split from the Family of put-ons, then his friend would blacken them all with the same brush: What use were *any* of them "in a world in a state of grim moral emergency"? Dearborn suggests that "With Norman P. attempting to claim pride of place with the family, Norman M. had to set him straight about who the family's real darling was, while undermining the whole idea of the family. In this high-flown version of a Brooklyn street fight, Mailer set his principles aside."[33]

Far from the Brooklyn street, an older and wiser writer in England reported her astonishment. Reviewing the book in the London *Sunday Telegraph*, Rebecca West, the novelist and critic, evoked a sentimental British painting that shows "a solemn big dog sitting on a doorstep beside a bouncy small dog." The big dog can signify the American literary establishment, the little one the up-from-nowhere Podhoretz. The little dog has revealed things about dogs in general that the big one doesn't like. Hence the baying of reviewers.

"This is a pity," West said. "*Making It* is luminously written, it is not only humourous but good-humoured, and it shows a real reverence for the things of the mind." The big-dog dignitaries were obliged to pretend that their saintly literary aim was always to write something "as good as the Book of Job or the Gospel of St. John," while the impudent little dog has yipped that, truth be told, "all of us would settle to write like Balzac, who was frankly greedy for money and whose greed was linked with his genius."

On the subject of money and virtue, West alluded to the passing of the old Calvinist conviction "that the good are industrious as part of their goodness, and so . . . owe their riches to their virtuous industry." Nowadays, the "sophisticated" who make money spend it "with an air of nausea, claiming that the stuff smells and is loaded with germs, and suggesting that someone ought to take it away."

West was thinking specifically of the hypocritical fastidiousness of the New Left intellectuals and their academic sympathizers, whose "brainless denigration of the [American] social system" had contributed so grievously to the creation of the "hippies and dropouts" now so numerous as "to make it doubtful whether the United States can in the near future find enough personnel to run the essential social services." Indeed, she concludes, "The only terrifying thing about this book are the references to politics. Neither [Podhoretz] nor his adversaries have a clue"[34] – by which she seems to mean they don't realize just how destructive New Left antinomianism is. (As we know, Podhoretz was fast finding out.)

West's review was comforting, as were private communications from Lichtheim, who, also in London, could ridicule the back-stabbing proclivities of New Yorkers, or from Arnold Beichman, who was not only in Podhoretz's corner, toweling him off and offering him a bottle, but also spot-on about what was happening in the center of the ring.

I've just finished reading IT. I'm filled with amazement – what's all the screaming and jeering about? I'm not talking about whether it's a good book – it is – or whether I enjoyed reading it – I did, very much – or whether it's an important book – yes, most assuredly – I just don't know why the violent reaction among your friends and mine, why so splenetic and vicious (as I heard with my own ears the other night), so personal, so unforgiving.

Beichman also reminded Podhoretz of Oliver Wendell Holmes's remark: "It is sometimes more important to emphasize the obvious than to elucidate the obscure." The Family – and "Some 'family'!" it was – couldn't abide anyone emphasizing the obvious fact that its members were all ambitiously on the make.[35]

Robert Graves had been through a similar hazing after the publication of his memoir *Good-Bye to All That* in 1929, and from Mallorca he dropped Podhoretz a gratifying line: "I am now off to London to get another gold medal from the Queen in private audience. This is all very odd, and results from going my own way; *as you also seem to do*" (emphasis added).[36] Out of the blue there also came a passionately appreciative, hand-written letter from

Ernest Lehman, author of the novella *The Sweet Smell of Success* and (with Clifford Odets) the movie's screenplay, plus screenplays for *Sabrina, The King and I, North by Northwest, West Side Story, Sound of Music, Who's Afraid of Virginia Woolf?*, and *Hello, Dolly!* Having grown up on Long Island during the Depression and then studied at City College of New York (CCNY), Lehman recounted how he used his "slick" qualities to "make it" in magazine writing in New York and then in Hollywood – until he suffered a nervous breakdown. The letter was a deeply plaintive cry from one whose own "dirty little secret" was that his brand of success was merely middlebrow, and that he yearned for the highbrow success Podhoretz had attained.[37]

Nice, but Podhoretz's spirits were so low that he put out feelers for academic gigs. A desperate idea, but who could blame him? His and Midge's exhaustingly busy social calendar went suddenly blank in mid-February 1968. He began to drink, if not more than before, then sadly alone. When Jacobson's wife, Margaret, asked Podhoretz why he was drinking so much, he answered, "To cure a diseased will" – "a striking phrase," Jacobson would recall. "It was obviously something he'd thought about."[38] His stepdaughter Rachel would remember poignantly how he would "drink most of a fifth of Jack Daniels every night – this wasn't at parties, this was just at home. I said to him, 'Why are you drinking so much? You're drunk.' He said to me, 'I drink to be sociable.' And I said, 'Well, you're not *being* very sociable.'"[39]

Thinking about Vietnam, Podhoretz was in the uncomfortable middle. Feeling that all credible positions should be heard, he published the pro-war, anti-communist essays of Oscar Gass, but worried that, in its liberal-democratic fervor, America might be overextending itself in Southeast Asia. Hence he also gave space to Robert Heilbroner's "Counterrevolutionary America," which argued that (in Podhoretz's synopsis) "Communism has been and can be a more effective agent of modernization in underdeveloped countries than other social systems which may be less murderous." To be sure, Heilbroner couldn't "come anywhere near proving" such a claim, and therefore had to offer up his intellect in an "ecstatic surrender to historical inevitability" – just the kind of sacrifice Podhoretz himself rejected. Cutting between Gass and Heilbroner, he was "coming more and more to believe that the U.S. is miserably equipped for playing an imperial role, even one guided by benevolent intent, and that we probably would do well to keep our noses out of the Third World altogether."[40] This was what Decter had come to think. It was the right war, insofar as it was benevolently intended, but at the wrong time and in the wrong place.[41]

The key phrase was "imperial role," which Lichtheim had the historical perspective to see clearly. In 1967, he was ready to prophesy that in three years Vietnam would be partitioned like the two Koreas, with the South becoming an American protectorate. "Will you forgive me if an old British imperialist like myself splits his sides as the Americans go over all that old ground?" Since the end of World War II, America had "everywhere stepped into Britain's shoes," and its citizens had roughly the same policy options British citizens once had.

With regard to Vietnam, America could take a moralizing position, siding either with the Maoists and working for the North's military victory or with the pacifists, which meant renouncing the violence on all sides. Or America could embrace a nonmoralizing realism, recognizing "that the US has unfortunately become a great imperial power, and that there is *nothing* the radical-democratic movement at home can do about it, except deplore it [and] wait for the day when the empire will dissolve, as empires have a way of doing."

Lichtheim advised Podhoretz to bracket moral arguments: "Keep away from conscience, and say you are worried about the probability of war with China." Such "Gaullist" realism was admittedly "a European privilege," but one *Commentary* should strive to claim for itself: "You have to steer your editorial boat between the Scylla of the official liberal imperialism and [the Charybdis of] the New Left. I can quite see that it isn't easy, especially since the moralists (including the phonies like Staughton Lynd) are making such a clatter."[42]

This was cogent, but Podhoretz couldn't leave conscience out of his analysis. Supposing that America was Britain's imperial successor – a role, again, for which it was spiritually and intellectually unprepared – the question remained: "Imperialism to what purpose?"[43] If a plausible moral justification could be adduced – say, that the United States was in Vietnam not merely to protect its commercial interests (in fact there were none) but to defend a nation from the evils of totalitarianism – then one also had to ask whether the country had the power and the will to do the job.

Finally, there was the hard task of distinguishing the right from the wrong place and time for intervention. Was Vietnam the wrong place, Eugene V. Rostow, a professor of law at Yale, challenged Podhoretz? If so, how did it differ from Korea – a war that nearly every liberal had approved of? Podhoretz took Rostow's point. He was worried about a resurgent isolationism: the Cold War, which his conscience knew was a just war, demanded America's continuing commitment. So perhaps Vietnam, a right war, *was* in a right place. Maybe it was simply the wrong time.

In 1968 there was a presidential race. Lichtheim again took a *Realpolitik* long view:

[T]he thing to do this year is to vote for Nixon, and hope that Humphrey will not only lose the election, but every single state in the Union. Then after having been thoroughly smashed and reorganized, the Democrats can come back in 1972 with Teddy [Kennedy]. The only cure lies in complete collapse.... Four years of Nixon will do no harm, and on Israel he is preferable to all the others.

But Podhoretz wasn't so sure. If a Republican administration turned out to be as repressive as some of the speeches of Nixon's vice-presidential pick Spiro Agnew were suggesting, the experience "would not only be terrible in itself, but would have the even more terrible consequence of forcing me into defending all those people on the Left whom I detest."[44]

Beyond the student protesters who had been busy that year trashing college campuses, the detestables included members of the Family who were turning hard left; Jason Epstein, for instance. In 1958, he had, like the rest of the Family, believed that the United States was fighting the Cold War to defeat "an enemy as evil and as dangerous as Nazi Germany," and if he had known that the CIA was funding anticommunist committees like the Congress for Cultural Freedom and magazines like *Encounter*, he probably "would have been titillated to find himself connected with an undercover operation."[45] A decade later, he was equating the Nazis not with the Soviets but with America. He told Diana Trilling that while he was glad America had given him the chance to acquire money and power, he required that it "not embarrass me by killing people against whom I have no grievance." As to the current "mad exploit to create a liberal anti-Communist government out of a pack of Mandarin thieves in Saigon," the real problem, he averred, was "that it has become increasingly hard for Americans to distinguish themselves, unless they are grossly insensitive to murder, from those Germans who didn't notice the smell of burning flesh from the chimneys at the end of the road."[46] It was such talk, as we have seen, that led to the terminal rupture of the old Epstein-Podhoretz friendship.

In 1968, from the New Hampshire primary on, Podhoretz supported the candidacy of Eugene McCarthy and stuck firm, instead of later jumping to Bobby Kennedy the way many intellectuals did. Well before the primaries, McCarthy had had lunch with Podhoretz in New York, arriving at the restaurant carrying a volume of Lowell's poems. The senator from Minnesota had made speeches against the war, but now, he said, it was time to do more. It was hopeless to think the cautious Kennedy would take the initiative and run against LBJ.

Compared with the "brilliantly witty" and erudite McCarthy, Kennedy seemed to Podhoretz altogether slow – "earnest and plodding and unimaginative." If he "had any interest at all in 'ideas' that were not immediately translatable into a ten-point program, it could only have been as an additional luxury of the rich and the powerful or as a means of self-improvement."[47] But now Kennedy was seriously absorbing "ideas" from Goodwin, who was forsaking the liberalism to which he had been so faithful a servant and becoming a New Leftist, citing Mailer on the "plague" of American civilization and looking to what he called "radical changes in ideology – and consequently in action." When McCarthy's victory in New Hampshire suggested that radicalism might really be the ticket, the Goodwinized Kennedy quickly announced his own candidacy.

If Podhoretz, having encouraged McCarthy to run, remained an ally, it was with increasingly faint hopes for him, Kennedy, or the Democratic Party itself.[48]

The wounds from the nasty reviews of *Making It* were still smarting in 1969, but Podhoretz was determined to show that he hadn't been thrown off his game. His first plan was to pursue a book about the thirties that he had begun to conceive before *Making It* was in press. He would profile "people (not necessarily all famous) from a variety of areas" – John L. Lewis, Louis B. Mayer, Harry Hopkins, Robert Sherwood, John Dos Passos, Father Coughlin,

Ben Shahn, Joseph Freeman, Aaron Copland, and so on – treating each in a "Stracheyesque" manner, "by which I mean that I would write about them judgmentally, sometimes with ridicule, sometimes with admiration, and never with academic neutrality."[49]

When this book didn't gel, his second plan was to write one about the sixties that would focus on the war, the young, and the blacks. We have been seeing what he might have said about the war, and we can guess what he might have said about the Know-Nothing young. But we can determine exactly what he wanted to say about the blacks, for it is the one section he managed to finish, though not right away.

His ideas about the blacks were formed in dialogue with Baldwin, "My Negro Problem" having been a rejoinder to *The Fire Next Time*, and the section in the projected book beginning as a rejoinder (he finally judged it too inchoate to publish) to Baldwin's 1967 essay in the *New York Times Magazine* "Negroes Are Anti-Semitic Because They're Anti-White." Baldwin accused Jews of "shamelessly" appealing to the Holocaust "in the hope of not being held responsible for their [own] bigotry." Blacks weren't fooled, however. Jews certainly had suffered, but blacks had suffered more. Besides, Jews in America had succeeded because they had white skins, and could feel proud of their suffering. Blacks, by contrast, had failed because of their skin color, and had "been taught to be ashamed of everything, especially their suffering." Then there was the issue of violence: "The Jew is a white man, and when white men rise up against oppression [as in the Warsaw ghetto], they are heroes: when black men rise [as in Watts and Harlem], they have reverted to their native savagery."

Not that Baldwin's real villain was the white race or its Judeo-Christianity; it was the rich in general, who in America usually happened to be white Christians or Jews but whose wickedness stemmed mainly from their privileges as a class. "The crisis taking place in the world, and in the minds and hearts of black men everywhere," Baldwin concluded, "is not produced by the star of David, but by the old, rugged Roman cross on which Christendom's most celebrated Jew was murdered. And not by Jews." It was, he implies, the Roman rich of the day who killed the revolutionary Jesus.[50]

Directly, Podhoretz began to draft an "Open Letter to James Baldwin," writing as friend to friend:

I have to tell you that your article made me nervous....I know that you are not an anti-Semite, but if I had not been intimately familiar with your work and your opinions, I would have taken the author of that article for a dangerous anti-Semite – and all the more dangerous for being clever enough to condemn anti-Semitism in the abstract while peddling insinuations with an unmistakably anti-Semitic resonance.

He cited some of the passages just quoted, but then stopped.[51] The letter was never finished and never sent. Podhoretz soon had other race-related issues to grapple with.

He was noticing that the supposed double-thinking that Baldwin decried among whites – violence was good in the cause of the liberation of Jews, say, but evil in that of blacks – was also becoming common among blacks, but in the reverse. Following an exchange of views with Ralph Ellison, Podhoretz wondered, "Why is it that when Ralph Ellison uses ad-hominem arguments (like saying that Nat Glazer puts on black face), he is exercising his 'right to as many styles and ways of responding as he feels he needs,' whereas when I make a deliberately similar crack against him, I'm a 'white man trying to keep the Negro in his place'?"[52]

Ellison counted as a moderate. What about the racial essentialists – those who maintained that how one thinks, feels, writes, and views the world is a function of biological characteristics, and who were to be found both on the extreme Right and the extreme Left? Their position was expressed by Eldridge Cleaver, whose *Soul on Ice* (1968) was making a huge impression on the young. It projected, Podhoretz said, "a cold, heartless, cruel white society, encumbered with a total guilt and total power, facing a Negro population marked only by helplessness, innocence, and nobility of spirit."

The objective critical question was whether Cleaver was "a good or a lousy writer," but it was increasingly difficult if not impossible to declare for either "good" or "lousy" apart from an author's skin color, sex, social class, nationality, age, or religion. In this case, Cleaver was supposed to be "good," like blacks in general, merely because of his race. Black supremacism was mirroring white supremacism. American culture, Podhoretz could see, was being hit by "a shit storm of simplistic thinking, double standards of moral and ethical judgment, and an ethos which patronizes the Negro out of his humanity instead of persecuting him out of it. If those of us who care about these things refuse to stand up forthrightly against them, we will all surely be drowned."[53]

"Black fascism" is what Howe, sotto voce, called this simplism. Writing Podhoretz from Stanford, where he was spending the year, he noticed how the storm was coming to a head in New York. In the fall of 1968, the unionized and striking public-school teachers, many of them Jewish and led by union president Albert Shanker, were pitted against black community groups that wanted to control the schools in mostly black districts and had gained funding from the patrician likes of the Ford Foundation. Howe observed that:

Affluent "radical" intellectuals are making alliances with black "militants." They line up against the plebeian and lower-middle-class whites. The results could be frightening. Whatever one thinks of Shanker's strategies, and I have criticisms, there is something disingenuous in intellectuals who abandoned the public schools for their own children a decade ago now to become righteous against the teachers and "for" the public schools. I think you might have someone write on this (I mean to, for *Dissent*); but it has obvious implications for the Jews.[54]

Lichtheim, still in London, noted that "the Negro anti-Jewish thing has finally burst into the open. . . . I trust the next stage will be for someone to pluck up enough courage to point out that 'fascist pig' is probably a better description of Stokely [Carmichael] than of some dumb policeman who never even heard of fascism."[55]

Podhoretz replied that "fascism" was now on everyone's lips but still had the power to shock. Martin Mayer, who had given him such good editorial counsel in 1960,

> was up at the Ford Foundation the other day and told a few of the top executives there that when he was a boy, there was a name for the alliance between the very rich and the lumpenproletariat. "What word is that?" they asked him politely. "Fascism" he said, at which point they all nearly fainted like a bunch of consumptive Victorian ladies. The alliance has in fact been made (and it naturally has its corps of unpaid propagandists in the person of some of our Jewish Quisling friends around the *New York Review*).[56]

It made a difference, Baldwin had noted in his *New York Times Magazine* article, that while American Jews could look to Israel to defend Jewish interests everywhere in the world, American blacks could look nowhere. Black nationalism was "nationalism without a nation," Theodore Draper wrote in *Commentary*, and therefore a "fantasy."[57] Hence, however, the impulse among many blacks to identify with Israel's Arab enemies (the Palestinians, too, had no nation) – as though it were a way of knocking down the Jewish landlords in Harlem or the Jewish teachers in Bedford-Stuyvesant.

We can see fears and fantasies astir around the Six-Day War of June 1967. With Egypt's president Gamal Abdel Nasser blocking Israeli shipping through the Straits of Tiran, Egyptian troops deploying across the border in the Sinai ready to drive the Jews "into the sea," and President Johnson showing no sign of honoring the commitments made to Israel by the Eisenhower administration after the 1956 Suez crisis, the Israeli government launched preemptive and simultaneous strikes. Its forces drove Egypt out of the Sinai while defending and extending its northern border against Syria and its eastern one against Jordan. After six days, Israel had gained control of the Gaza Strip, the Sinai Peninsula, the West Bank, and the Golan Heights.

It was a fretful week, during which Podhoretz's correspondents anticipated the Western powers' abandonment of the Jewish state. After its deliverance and victory, Podhoretz's Cambridge friend Aaron Klug wrote of the "nearly three weeks of sickening disgust" watching Arab television footage of "effigies of Jews (with traditional hooked noses and thin rimmed spectacles) hanging from lampposts or slung between the street buildings" or hearing "the deference some [Western] commentators... extend to the great, wise statesman Nasser (and the King of Serenity Feisal [in Saudi Arabia])." How quickly, Klug lamented, people will forget "the horror of Israel's encirclement by her enemies who planned *physical* destruction of the Jews (*extermination* is what Feisal said on BBC and had to be retracted the next day to 'termination') and Israel's vulnerability on the weekend of May 26." Klug implored Podhoretz "to exert whatever influence you can" to persuade Johnson of Israel's ongoing vulnerability and the Arabs' reflex merely to lie and repeat "the constant refrain that Israel is the source of their troubles."[58]

What Podhoretz could do was, for the August *Commentary*, line up a kind of "white paper" on the Six-Day War with pieces by frequent contributors Theodore Draper and Walter Laqueur, plus the Israeli journalist Amos Elon and the American rabbi and historian Arthur Hertzberg, and help organize a pro-Israel statement for the newspapers bearing the signatures of these and other intellectuals. Not that of Robert Lowell, however. The poet told Podhoretz that:

A thousand years of Egypt blockading the Gulf of Tiran would be less costly than a war. I think, of course that we must secure Israel's borders, and do what we can to finagle the blockade away.... I've just been reading again about the opening of our Civil War, how the whole useless, monstrous thing happened because neither side could back down from its stances of honor. I wish I could appeal to you to see this crisis with more gentleness and complexity.[59]

"Useless" was a curious word for the war that ended slavery in the United States, especially from the author of "For the Union Dead." In reply, Podhoretz merely iterated "that the very existence of Israel is at stake in this matter and that a strong stand by the United States is the only thing short of war that can help."[60]

Along with anxiety about Israel's survival, the state's lightning victory in the Six-Day War sparked a surge in Jewish confidence – which, however, made some American Jewish liberals uncomfortable. David Riesman suggested that Podhoretz get Erich Fromm, the moralizing Frankfurt School psychoanalyst, to write on the distinction between Jewish martyrs and Jewish heroes – in the hope of not letting the latter obscure the glorious tradition of the former. Podhoretz was sure Fromm would get the distinction wrong and use the occasion to attack "what I would guess he considers an outburst of Jewish 'chauvinism.'" Besides, martyrdom was a role Jews had played too often in the past, "when in their total powerlessness" they had no other choice. Having power and using it effectively: *that* would take some getting used to.[61]

In their subsequent correspondence, Fromm remonstrated that the "new admiration for the 'hero' (we Jews have shown that we are not cowards, etc.)" shouldn't be allowed to depreciate the value of martyrdom – especially since "it happens that the Jews[,] like the Christians and the Buddhists, put the martyr in the highest place."[62] Podhoretz replied: "If the term martyrdom signifies a voluntary death for the sake of a religious conviction, the Jews who died in Auschwitz cannot be considered martyrs"; they were, instead, "*powerless* objects of a murderous program." What had "moved so many Jews outside Israel" during the Six-Day War was the Israeli demonstration "that Jews need not always be powerless before the murderous intentions of their enemies." There was nothing worrisomely "militarist or chauvinist" about it.[63] It simply meant, as Emil Frackenheim would write the following year, that Hitler must not be granted any posthumous victories.[64]

While Jewish intellectuals were debating the proper ratio between assertiveness and conciliation in Israel's relations with its Arab enemies, black intellectuals, almost all of whom were on the Left, seemed of one mind. Their assumptions about Israel's culpability and Arab-Muslim benignity were shared by New Left sympathizers like Andrew Kopkind at the *New Republic* – to whom Lichtheim would have wished to point out, as he wrote to Podhoretz, that:

(a) The Arabs practically invented the African slave trade, and are hated by African Negroes, but no one has told the American Blacks the truth about that.
(b) The only powers currently engaged in mass murder of African Blacks are the Moslem governments of Nigeria and the Sudan.
(c) Egyptian pilots drop bombs on Biafra, the while Stokely Carmichael fraternizes with Nasser.
(d) It may be natural for US Negroes to dislike Jews, but that doesn't explain why CORE and SNCC ideologists have publicly deplored that Hitler didn't kill more Jews.[65]

These points became axiomatic for Podhoretz as well.

In the winter of 1969, Podhoretz gave an interview to Beverly Kempton and David Gelman for the *Manhattan Tribune*. It provides an occasion to gauge his end-of-the-decade mood. A year's reflection had taught him that the "unjust" response to *Making It* was in large part "theological." "The book was a polemic against a certain set of values about which most educated Americans are extremely pious, and so it was treated as a kind of blasphemy." And the theological impinged on the political. Although indeed critical of American society, the book also "assumes, in fact it argues, that it is possible to live a reasonably decent life and maintain one's moral, intellectual and spiritual integrity without becoming a revolutionary," which also, among right-thinking intellectuals, now counted as "a kind of blasphemy." If you didn't condemn the whole American show from top to bottom, you must be a reactionary.

Such either/or thinking was conspicuous in the conflict over "community control" of schools. When left-wing intellectuals demanded to know "Are you for or against black radicalism?" they effectually "preempt[ed] the moral ground," implying that anyone who wasn't radical must be "against the blacks." In "My Negro Problem," Podhoretz had doubted that integration would work, for which he was called a "bigot." Now, dubious about decentralization and community control, which would do nothing toward fixing "the relatively high degree of retardation in reading-grade level among Negro children," he was being called a "racist." Debate about a "gimmick" like decentralization had "merely helped define the lower middle class as the main enemy of the poor." It must make "the right wing and the rich . . . very happy to see the have-littles and the have-nots at each other's throats" in the inner cities, leaving *them* undisturbed with their private schools or in the comfortable suburbs.

Podhoretz at the time continued to reject the label of "conservative": "I regard myself... as a left-wing liberal." But all these tussles with his fellow intellectuals were teaching him a crucial lesson. It was, in words he would naturally have remembered from T. S. Eliot, a lesson in how "to care and not to care" about politics.

There's a great truth in what Dr. Johnson said: "How small of all that human hearts endure, / That part which laws or kings can cause or cure." To look to politics for too much, for salvation, which is the kind of thing that happens in a highly politicized period, is dangerous. The only political systems that have ever really presumed to offer the hope of salvation are the totalitarian systems. There's more than a little totalitarian emotion in the air around us these days, and not enough dissent from it.[66]

In the winter of 1969–70, registering his own dissent against totalitarian emotion, Podhoretz would go back to the artists' colony Yaddo to work on that book about the sixties. He would confront not just the idea behind Johnson's couplet but the *reality* of the idea, and thereby attempt to square his identity with whatever he truly thought about and expected from politics.

9

Dropping the Other Shoe

Yaddo's director was the *Saturday Review* critic Granville Hicks, who with his wife, Dorothy, would host a cocktail party before every supper. The writers-and-artists colony was openly awash in booze and, as guests visited one another after-hours, was also reputed to be awash in sex. The booze was the only distraction Podhoretz wanted, mainly in the desperate hope that it might help him finish his large tome about the sixties.

Donadio had sold it to Simon & Schuster, which had given Podhoretz a $35,000 (now $186,000) advance. He had used nearly half of the money to buy a country place near the Moynihans' up in Delaware County. Having driven three and a half hours to take a look, Podhoretz got out of his car and asked his friend to orientate him. "Right," said Pat, "well, over there are the Catskill Mountains." "Funny," said Podhoretz after a pregnant pause, "they don't *look* Jewish."[1] It was the first real estate the Podhoretzes would own (they were renting their West Side apartment and the Fire Island cottage): twenty-eight acres, an old farmhouse, and, at Moynihan's insistence, a one-room schoolhouse, all for "practically nothing" – $15,000 (about $92,650 today).

From 1967 to 1973, it was to be the pastorally happy scene of many a school-year weekend, or many a summer week, with the Moynihans. "Those were wonderful times," Podhoretz would remember, including a New Year's Eve they spent together. Moynihan had procured some saucer sleds, "almost hubcaps," and laid out a run down a hillside going from station to station "where he had planted bottles of champagne." Once Podhoretz's parents came to visit, and though his father wasn't feeling well, the Moynihans "invited us over, and Pat treated my parents beautifully.... Most of my friends were rotten to their own parents, let alone anybody else's. But that was Pat, a wonderful man."[2]

To keep the "farm," however, Podhoretz needed to deliver the book. The first part was about the counterculture, a subject he had already astutely treated in "The Know-Nothing Bohemians," and neither he nor Decter was satisfied with what he was saying now. That was the blocked condition he took to Yaddo in February 1970. He drank heavily throughout the day, and at night would sit in his cabin feeling increasingly depressed. One evening, during cocktails, Kenneth Burke, thirty-three years Podhoretz's senior and an indomitable literary critic, gave the younger man "the evil eye," telling him in effect that his approach was unworkable. "So," Podhoretz would relate, "the next day, in my cups, drunk but still able to keep going, I packed up my stuff and without telling anyone I got into my car – it was snowing – and drove along two-lane country roads for over a hundred miles: it was a miracle I made it, no snow tires." Arriving at his farmhouse late at night, he felt tremendously relieved "to have escaped not just from Burke's evil eye but also from the prying gaze of all the other wonderfully productive painters, composers, and writers at Yaddo."

Although he had driven through a late winter blizzard, the next day he could sense that "spring was on the way," and all at once he realized how his book needed to be organized: one hundred pages each on the blacks, the young, and the war. He was able to write again, working for hours every day in the schoolhouse an eighth of a mile down the road. He drafted the section on the blacks – as we have noted – but "then the ax came down" and, standing soberly aside, he judged that what he had written wasn't good enough. Despairing, he struggled with the sections on the young and the war, but without success.

"I later realized what was wrong: I had not yet dropped the other shoe. I was still writing from the inside" – trying, like Howe, Kazin, and others, to hold on to his left-wing credentials. "What I actually wanted to do, but wasn't aware of it, was to say goodbye to all that. I wasn't quite ready; I was at a [political] way station, among the crowd of social democrats. And therefore I couldn't write."

If this was a way station, where was the terminus? Podhoretz had turned forty in January, an apt midlife moment for clarification and, in his case, for a new direction. Alone on his upstate property, he had a variety of religious experience, the epiphany that would be the turning point of his life. He never was able to publish anything about it, but he has eloquently spoken:

I was walking along this little road, in front of my house, that went through the fields and the farms, a little country lane. My house was situated up a slope, and as you faced it there was to the left a gully, a little rivulet as the snow was beginning to melt. It was a sunny day, in the afternoon, very pretty. I was finished working and was carrying a martini with me. There I was, walking on this beautiful, chilly, early spring day and the sun hitting the snow. I was feeling very content, benign, the writing had gone well, I had an excellent drink, and all of a sudden I had a vision.

The renewal of earth and the renewal of the writer walking up and down a stretch of Delaware County road happened to coincide. The martini doesn't exactly fit – a prop left over from the city or from the cocktail hour at

Yaddo – but it was emblematic of what he needed to leave behind, a vanity for a coming bonfire.

> I saw Eternity the other night
> Like a great Ring of pure and endless light
>   All calm as it was bright;
> And round beneath it, Time, in hours, days, years,
>   Driven by the spheres,
> Like a vast shadow moved, in which the world
>   And all her train were hurled.

Thus the English poet Henry Vaughan begins "The World" (1650) in a rapture Podhoretz has compared to his own, though "what I saw was not eternity or a great whatever of light: I saw physically, in the sky, though it was obviously in my head, a kind of diagram that resembled a family tree. And it was instantly clear to me that this diagram contained the secret of life and existence and knowledge: that you start with this, and you follow to that. It all had a logic of interconnectedness."

This visionary experience was the terminus of his sixties journey. His own account of it starts with the family tree, which is the tree of life, an organism that grows not higgledy-piggledy but by natural law:

All modalities of human existence were subject to this law. All knowledge was subject to this law, which meant there was nothing esoteric: everyone was speaking the same things in different languages. Poems, pieces of music, paintings – they were all saying the same kind of things at given moments in history. Just using different accents.

So when, for example, all the Romantic poets and painters began to sing together, affirming certain "natural supernaturalist" convictions of the late eighteenth and early nineteenth centuries, it was no accident. They were in their variegated voices expressing their understanding of the laws of life, which held human and nonhuman nature together. And so with all the Classical, Gothic, Neoclassical, and Modernist artists, in their several modes, at their historical moments, sensing the sense of things.

To be sure, some modes are better than others, and art itself does not hold all the answers. What Podhoretz also realized, in those thirty luminous seconds, "was that Judaism was true." A hard saying, even for Jews – for, he said, "the Judaism that was true was the Judaism of the Bible, not of the Talmud," the major source of "Judaism as we know it" today. The "hermeneutics," or method of interpretation, employed by the rabbis of the Talmud "allowed them all kinds of stuff, which cannot be found in the Bible – most importantly, an afterlife." Podhoretz went back to the mythic beginning. Before the law was revealed to Moses on Sinai, there was the Garden with our original, mortal parents. "Man and woman created He them," Podhoretz said. "From that union came life. That's it. You're born, and you'll die. Period. All my views of gay marriage and cloning come from this." The law of God, according to

Genesis, dictates that there be the two sexes, meant for one another in marriage, the primary purpose of which is procreation.

And God is law first, love only second. Christianity argues the other way around, not, for Podhoretz, because of Jesus' sayings but because of Paul's: "When St. Paul decided that God was love, he was rebelling against the law. The law was death, and 'who shall deliver me from the body of this death?' The body of this death not only meant this corrupt, this 'dying animal' (as Yeats called the body); it also meant that which shall die – the law itself." Paul felt that "it's the law that kills you." Why? "Because," he thought, "the law is impossibly hard to obey: the flesh is so weak that people are *bound* to fall into sin," and that seemed unjust.

We may want to obey, but we can't. Yet if Paul had put his question to Judaism itself, the answers would be (a) that no one will deliver you from the body of this death, and (b) yes you *can* obey the law. I've placed it (said God) not in the heavens above: I've created you such that you can, if you will, follow My law.

That is where God's love comes in. He doesn't say, "Poor baby, it's okay that you can't obey." He says, "My love consists of enabling you to live in such a way as to have the fullest life possible on earth. You can choose *not* to obey, but you can also choose *to* obey. It's not difficult: it's not a matter of hidden gnostic knowledge. It's right in front of you – the chance to have all the life there is to live."

This was a promise, a covenant, to be grateful for. Hence the rabbis insisted that "you should say a blessing for practically everything" and should "'seize the day.' You are commanded, in the words of the Shulhan Arukh [a sixteenth-century codification of the Law], 'to rise like a lion to do the bidding of your God.' By placing yourself in a state of such exquisite conscious gratitude, you get not only all the life there is to live, you get almost too much." Thus no complaints "about not having enough."

This wasn't craziness, this rush of elaboration on the envisaged diagram. "I'd never been more lucid," Podhoretz said, and not only about the "ghastly" sinfulness of suicide ("I'd had some suicidal impulses, especially when I suffered from blocks"). He was lucid also in his resolve to live as a "good biblical Jew, a Karaite" – "*kara*" being the root form of one of the words for scripture, the written law, and the historical Karaites a sect rejecting the authority of the Talmud, the oral law.

Podhoretz would tell people "jokingly" that he was a Karaite: "It was not necessary for me to go to services, eat kosher, all that stuff – as long as I obeyed the law. Because I knew what the law meant. I was arrogant and in a way wrong, but I did manage to live this way for several months." To live, that is, with energy, gratitude, and self-acceptance: "Your limits should be embraced rather than resisted. Your limits are good not bad. They are actually liberating rather than restricting, if properly observed."

He was taking his stand on the side of benign legalism against antinomianism – of duty and responsibility against rights and entitlements. It was a clarification palpably liberating for Podhoretz when, never returning to Yaddo, he got back to Manhattan. He soon "stopped drinking – not because drinking was bad or sinful, but because it hindered my ability to live according to the law. It was an evasion." Further, he "developed not the evil but a benevolent eye," therapeutically "aware of everything" and able to "see into people's souls. This sounds cuckoo, but over and over again, I was like a fortune-teller. I could talk to you, look at you, and tell what was bothering you and what you should do about it." This mattered for Rachel and Naomi, as their stepfather began discerning what was at the root of their adolescent rebellion and helping them channel it into creative, not destructive, activity. (Podhoretz noted: "I couldn't do that now, by the way. I realized that that was what it must have meant to be a saint or a prophet: someone who never lost the capacity to see into people's souls.")

Podhoretz "went around confronting, encountering everyone." What is it that troubles you? he might have asked. "'Well, my mother's sick and I don't have any money.' It's always one thing, which the other things grow out of. The one thing is always related to the fear of death, ultimately, in the sense that it touches most closely on our limitations – our mortality. Everybody tries to evade confrontation with that." He would diagnose the condition and prescribe the spiritual cure. "What scared" people, he observed, "was that I was like some sort of magician."[3] Jack Thompson was scared enough to declare, in a frantic phone call to Midge, that her husband had gone mad: "I recognize it from Cal [the poet Robert Lowell]," he said. "Cal was like that, he got manic, and pretty soon Norman's going to start hitting you."[4] An alcoholic, Thompson may have been alarmed because Podhoretz told him what *he* was using booze to escape from (death was only two years off for Thompson).

Podhoretz's son, John, was too young to grasp what was happening to his father at the time, but he could "appreciate how he was a very unhappy and depressed guy." Looking back, he surmised that

when a man systematically alienates everyone in his circle, gets into fights with them and yells at them, it's not beyond the bounds of reason to think there's something going on – something destructive. . . . If you are morally uncompromising and are doing yourself harm, then from the point of view of a psychiatrist you'd wonder to what extent you're saying things because you're brave, and to what extent you're being self-destructive. Though in the end I think my father was being brave, Jack Thompson's presumption that he was being self-destructive was not irrational,[5]

One can understand the head-tapping reaction to Podhoretz's half-earnest, half-ironic references to his tree-of-life "vision" up in Delaware County. People didn't look at him the way a William James or a Bernard Shaw looked at, say, the vision-seeing Joan of Arc. They just assumed that he had hallucinated, which by definition meant he had either perceived something that wasn't there at all or had distorted something that was. As Podhoretz himself remarked, however, the diagram he saw was "obviously" in his mind, an imaginative externalization of what was otherwise internal. In any event, he discovered that clairvoyance – fronting existential dread, holding fast to the physical and moral laws of life, intervening with solicitude in the lives of friends and family – was too exhausting.

As though wanting to fix this defining experience and then move on, he wrote to Jacqueline Wheldon in late summer 1970:

Alas, so sunk in sin am I that I can scarcely even remember "it" any longer. That, too, was part of the discovery – that as soon as the truth is revealed it is forgotten, which is why Jews are commanded to *daven* (usually translated as "pray," but meaning in my view something closer to "recite" or "rehearse" or "remind" than to supplication and praise). I quote from memory from the Bible: "Thou shalt teach them [the commandments] to thy sons and thou shalt speak of them as thou liest down and as thou risest up and as thou goest forth on the road." This is to make sure that the revelation of how one is to live . . . won't slip away as it constantly threatens to do. It slips away leaving the mind utterly blank; at other times it slips away into over-complication and the falsities of the abstruse. Why does it slip away? Because to know it, to remember it, to hold onto it firmly (one is told to hold onto the Torah, the law, the commandments, as to the Tree of Life) is to hold on firmly to the awareness of one's own mortality, the fear of which, the refusal to accept and acknowledge which, is what leads to (or perhaps even itself constitutes) the pact with the Devil who promises (in the words of the Serpent to Eve) "*Lo mot t'motoon*" or (as *I* would translate it and more accurately than it is usually translated) "Thou shalt not surely die dead." Not only is Satan incapable of delivering on this promise; he delivers only the opposite, robbing (as it were) the salt of its savor, the days of their length. . . . A being in league with the devil is a being in league with the forces conducive to its own destruction.[6]

"Move on" is perhaps the wrong phrase. Podhoretz would, as he told Jacqueline, strive to "remember 'it'" by reciting and rehearsing its meaning – holding "firmly to the awareness of one's own mortality," which entailed the refusal of any devilish temptation to grasp at an impossible *im*mortality and obeying the Torah's commandments, the essence of which was, until one actually died, to "choose life" – a ramifying imperative we will return to.

The book on the sixties, meanwhile, wasn't abandoned all at once. Podhoretz believed he could write its three sections from the perspective his vision had led him to. But in the immediate term, from June 1970 to April 1973, his efforts bore literary fruit only in short *Commentary* editorials under the rubric of "Issues." In May 1973, he decided that he wouldn't be able to finish the book – a decision that not only signaled the utter loss, or so it seemed, of more than four years of work, but also required the return of his $35,000 advance to Simon & Schuster, which in turn required the selling of the farm. It wasn't until 1979, with *Breaking Ranks*, that most of the cultural, political, and personal implications of his vision came together in a long account. The religious implications wouldn't be given large treatment until 2002, when he published *The Prophets: Who They Were, What They Are*, and 2009, when *Why Are Jews Liberals?* would offer a kind of coda.

Podhoretz did, in the summer and fall of 1970, remember his day job. It was time to effect an editorial revolution.

Harvard-educated Neal Kozodoy, who had joined the staff in the fall of 1966, had been running *Commentary* during Podhoretz's absence at Yaddo. He now thought he should finish his interrupted doctoral program in comparative literature at Columbia. (The academic job market hadn't yet shown signs of the severe contraction that would soon set in.) Podhoretz granted Kozodoy leave, holding his job open while he retreated with his wife and baby girl to the house in western Massachusetts he had bought in 1967 with his fee for ghosting Abba Eban's *My People*. He passed his qualifying exams, quit smoking, and started a dissertation on medieval Hebrew and Provençal love lyrics. He would publish one chapter, devoted to secular Hebrew poetry, but when the year's leave was up in September 1971 he returned to *Commentary*. His vocation, like Podhoretz's, wasn't academic but high journalistic.

In taking a year off, Kozodoy missed some of the opening salvos of the war Podhoretz was declaring on the countercultural and political Left. Having come "down from the mountain-top" and "loaded for bear for the first time in years,"[7] Podhoretz had told his assembled staff that *Commentary* was going "on the offensive." It was an aggressive move that, as he wrote to Jacobson, was "life-giving for me to a degree that temporizing and trimming could never match."[8] Starting in June, he would write the aforementioned "Issues" columns; they would redesign the magazine's cover and layout; and they had already commissioned pieces – like Samuel McCracken's "Quackery in the Classroom," about "the new breed of romantic educational reformers," and Renee Winegarten's "Literary Revolutionism," a survey of political illusions from Byron and Shelley to Sartre and Beauvoir – that would be more than an annunciatory whiff of grapeshot. Soon enough, the magazine had begun, as Kozodoy later said, "to *count*" in the way it had in the early sixties. The "training period" was over, "new fronts could be opened," and, as Charles Krauthammer would later remark, "The shofar was now blasting."[9]

Liebe Klug, Aaron's wife, spoke for many readers when she rejoiced in *Commentary*'s attacks on "our enemies, blow by blow – the New Left, the radicalised professor, the generation gap, the Black Panthers, the clercs, the WASP 'patriciate,' the antisemites and Israel haters, and now the type strain of them all, the *New York Review*," "that pernicious journal."[10] For there was plainly a contest between that journal, with its nearly 100,000 claimed subscribers, and *Commentary*, with its then roughly 30,000, to see which would turn the heads of the makers, consumers, and critics of the nation's higher culture.

Like *Partisan Review*, *Dissent*, and *Commentary*, the *New York Review* was dismissive both of mainstream or "middlebrow" writers and the counter-culture's Kurt Vonnegut, Ken Kesey, and crew. It would publish a review of the latest biography of Ivan Turgenev or a new introduction to Henry James's *The Golden Bowl*, but always from a left-wing point of view, which usually strove to mark the book's "relevance" to the problems of the day – racism, the war in Vietnam, environmental pollution, the sexual revolution, feminism, and so on. The *New York Review* made *Dissent* look moderate, and *Partisan Review* or *Commentary* positively conservative. Podhoretz wasn't thinking in terms of conservative versus liberal, however. As we have seen, he still regarded himself as a left-liberal, intent on rescuing the tradition from its distorters on the extreme Left. That is why he ran Dennis Wrong's "The Case of the *New York Review*" in November 1970.

It was at once a surgical strike and, should anyone have doubted the severity of the breach, a cutting of diplomatic relations. Wrong traces the *New York Review*'s evolution from its inception in February 1963, when it seemed to one wag to be "*Partisan Review* on butcher paper," to something initially more like the *Times Literary Supplement* but finally more like the *New Statesman* under Kingsley Martin, whose politics, when not communist-sympathizing, were democratic-socialist. This slide into "*haut* New Leftism" generated contradictions that most *New York Review* readers, forty percent of whom were professors or graduate students, either embraced or merely became inured to, but that couldn't hold up under examination. That is, one couldn't advertise a commitment to high cultural standards and then remain silent when student radicals destroyed property and curricula at Columbia or Wisconsin, Cornell or Harvard. Nor could one parade a dedication to refined literary sensibility and then give a pass to "the more idiotic slogans" offered in justification of such destruction as harmless "expressions of a new 'life style' not to be taken too literally."

But that was exactly what the *New York Review* was doing. Wrong cites Jason Epstein's radical hyperboles about American society; Kempton's "typical mixture of *Weltschmerz*, heavy irony, and the arrogance of proclaimed humility"; and the August 24, 1967, issue with a Molotov cocktail on the cover and, inside, Kopkind's crying up of Black Power revolution: "Morality, like politics, starts at the barrel of a gun."

Undisciplined though they were, the New Left revolutionaries – the more desperate of whom had by 1970 gone into the Weatherman underground – thought they understood the world and were determined to change it. Either, their reasoning went, revolution would lead "to the emergence of an unspecified 'better society,' or, in a more openly catastrophist version, the triumph of reaction ('fascism')" would be but "a prelude to the successful revolt of vastly expanded numbers of the oppressed and victimized."[11] This "worse is better" supposition was something Podhoretz often drew attention to in his editorials. What Wrong's analysis showed in particular, Podhoretz wrote heatedly in the same issue, was that over the past half-decade the *New York Review* had contributed to the manufacturing of an atmosphere of crisis – a "*trahison* [treachery] . . . against the defining values of the intellectual life" that was "more complacent, more arrogant, and if not actually more philistine then at least more insidiously so than any the world has ever seen before."[12]

Negative reactions to Wrong's essay and Podhoretz's editorial weren't slow in coming, particularly from the people they had named. Kempton claimed incredulity at Wrong's language of "original insult" and wondered whether Podhoretz had a hand in it: "Measuring your skills against his, I feel cause to suspect that the phrase about 'the arrogance of proclaimed humility,' having some grace as it does, is more likely yours than his."[13] (Podhoretz replied that the phrase was Wrong's, and that his own tone in addressing Kempton had been marked by "civility and affection."[14]) Lillian Hellman, who had "her (personal, not political) gripes against the *New York Review*," as Podhoretz told Wrong, was nevertheless concerned "that the Powers of Repression," namely the Nixon administration, "would only be encouraged" by this intramural fight between liberal and radical intellectuals, especially when the former imputed "disloyalty" to the latter.[15] His Columbia friend John Hollander, then teaching at Hunter College, wondered whether Podhoretz wasn't becoming an objective Nixonite:

If I didn't love you, and if I didn't know as well as you how hard times really are, I couldn't have resisted the temptation to [decry] . . . the new *Commentary* policy of not only assuring one's hard-headedness by donning a hard hat, but also by butting the enemy in the tummy with it, and if you happen to hit someone else, well you can't break eggs without claiming there's an omelet cooking, etc.

"What the hell kind of cheap trick is that to pull," Podhoretz asked in answer, "saying that if you didn't love me you would say nasty things to me that you then go on to say? It's a ploy worthy of Alfred Kazin himself."[16] The Trillings, too, had been "scolding Norman," as Midge wrote Jacqueline, "for being too hard on the *young radicals!!!*" Lionel "not long ago . . . went so far as to say – all full of love, of course – that he felt more inclined to write for Mr. Silvers's paper than for *Commentary* because he wanted posterity to understand him as a *complicated* person."[17]

Hellman, Hollander, and the Trillings' reactions were shared by a contingent of workaday subscribers to *Commentary*. A woman from the Boston area wrote to Podhoretz, describing herself and her husband, in their forties, as products of Madison and Berkeley, where they had been "activist, pro-labor, YPSL [Young People's Socialist League]" radicals. She deplored the way *Commentary* was turning Jewish liberals into "upper-middle class Jewish hard hats." Small wonder that students she knew at Harvard, caught up in an "exciting search and revival of Jewish consciousness," were simply "repelled and turned off by *Commentary*." She supposed that Podhoretz's own "success, personal and corporate," had rendered him "uninterested and insensitive to their *concern for failure*."[18]

Such admonitions did make an impression. As Podhoretz confided to Theodore Draper: "I've been trying, partly in response to a continual stream of pressure from 'well-wishers,' to ease off a bit on the revolutionary Left."[19]

It could not last. Jason Epstein again gave him occasion by attacking Tom Wolfe's essay "Radical Chic," which had appeared in *New York* and became an instant classic. It was a send-up of Leonard and Felicia Bernstein's gathering of friends on Park Avenue in support of the Black Panthers. Epstein claimed that what Wolfe missed, "in his cruel and shallow way," was that "Radical Chic is . . . only the unhappy residue of the broken promises and defeated politics of the Kennedys, the still flickering desire of an impotent and aristocratic liberalism to restore citizenship to the poor."[20]

Joseph Epstein, in reviewing a Wolfe collection that included "Radical Chic," understood the nostalgia for Kennedyite idealism but was alarmed at the form it was taking not just at the Bernsteins' but at the *New York Review*. That form, in Wolfe's felicitous phrase, was the *nostalgie de la boue* (literally, "nostalgia for the mud"), observable all too recently in the Germany of the thirties with its alliance between the "idiot rich" and the "lumpen-revolutionaries" – the one delighting as the other destroyed both the Christian and the Jewish bulwarks of respectability.[21] The parallel was all the more eerie insofar as the Black Panthers were, under the guise of anti-Zionism, patently anti-Semitic, their diatribes against "robber" Israel melding into diatribes, per Wolfe's quotation, against "the robber barons that exploit us in the garment industry and the bandit merchants and greedy slumlords that operate in our communities."

These black–Jewish tensions had boiled to the surface during the debate about "local control" of New York City schools. To review: in the fall of 1968, the United Federation of Teachers (UFT) went out on strike in protest against the efforts of the Board of Education, starting in the Ocean Hill-Brownsville neighborhood of Brooklyn, to promote black teachers even though they lacked the seniority called for in the contract between the union and the city; to "decentralize" the administrative bureaucracy; and to give control of neighborhood schools to the local board. If the effort, backed by Mayor John Lindsay, were to prevail, the black and Puerto Rican militants in Ocean Hill-Brownsville would run the show, and the current cohort of administrators and teachers – seventy-five percent white, more than half of these Jewish – would have to go. The UFT had an impeccable record in supporting programs to improve the education of black children, but when several of its members were discharged without due process, and to the accompaniment of anti-Semitic rhetoric, it had to act.

From Jason Epstein's point of view, the UFT was, first, exaggerating the manifestations of black anti-Semitism "in a way that suggests that the Nuremberg Rallies are about to be resumed in [Harlem's] Abyssinian Baptist Church" and, second, refusing to admit "the inadequacy of [its own] instructional programs."[22] Podhoretz, on the contrary, felt "a certain anxiety" that, whatever the UFT's alleged amplifications, black anti-Semitism was indeed growing and "the city's Jews" had reason to be wary. Besides, decentralization would do nothing to remedy the poor performance of black and Puerto Rican students. It would simply mean that the bulk of administrative or teaching jobs would go to blacks and Puerto Ricans, whether qualified or not, while pedagogic methods remained as inadequate as ever.

Why, Podhoretz asked, were John Lindsay and the Ford Foundation, a major enabler of the effort, keen to fund minority programs that would "purchase civil peace in the United States – I do not say social justice – at the direct expense of the Jews"? Why was black anti-Semitism "understood" and tolerated, and almost never "forthrightly and straightforwardly condemned"? Were the Jews going to serve as scapegoats in America just as they had immemorially done in Europe? If so, how prescient of Orwell to have written "that the greatest danger to liberal democracy would come from 'An army of unemployed led by millionaires preaching the Sermon on the Mount.'"

Martin Mayer was right to tell the Ford Foundation directors that this was what in Europe had been called fascism. What needed reaffirmation was the liberal-democratic principle that "treated all persons on the basis of their merits as individuals regardless of 'race, color, creed, or place of national origin.'" That principle was beginning to sound "quaintly archaic" to many American liberals because it hadn't yielded equal outcomes. Such equal outcomes, they believed, would therefore have to be engineered by, for instance, a policy of proportional representation in university admissions. But should universities truly pursue such a policy, it would mean that Jews, who were a mere three percent of the American population, "would be driven out" in order that blacks and other minorities could be let in. "To put the matter brutally, but with no touch whatever of distortion or exaggeration," Podhoretz wrote, "in the name of justice to blacks, discriminatory measures were to be instituted once more against the Jews."

Under these circumstances there was nothing paranoid in feeling anxious about "Jewish vulnerability" or in puzzling over the motives of the numerous Jewish intellectuals bent on exacerbating it. Those intellectuals had "insultingly" lectured their fellow Jews "on the virtues of universalism... draw[ing] from a debased and discredited tradition of 19th-century Jewish thought" that emphasized the wolf-lies-down-with-the-lamb rhapsodics of Isaiah over the more realistic political analyses of most of the other biblical prophets. But, Podhoretz continued, historical debate misses the central point: defending Jews in America is inseparable from defending America itself as a liberal democracy, where individuals are free to display their merit without regard to race, creed, ethnicity, and so on, and where the equality guaranteed by the Constitution is the equality not of outcome but of opportunity.[23]

These are themes – central to Podhoretz's contribution to post-sixties America's debate about its own ideals – that would still be dominating his thought thirty years later, when he published *My Love Affair with America*, *The Prophets*, and *Why Are Jews Liberals?*

Proponents of proportional representation or affirmative action, as it would soon be (mis)called, often took pains to deny that favoring blacks or Latinos in university admissions, for instance, entailed disfavoring Jews. But that it *would* disfavor Jews was something Moynihan had predicted in a commencement speech at the New School for Social Research in 1968: "Formal... quotas *for* this or that group... are instantly translated into quotas *against*" (emphases added).[24] That was Dorothy Rabinowitz's thesis in "Are Jewish Students Different?" (*Change*, Summer 1971), in which she implied that, by encouraging applications from students of color, Harvard was willy-nilly bound to reduce the number of its Jewish students.

Harvard faculty and staff, including Jews such as Nathan Glazer and Seymour Martin Lipset, wrote the editor of *Change* to deny the rumor "that Harvard is discriminating against Jews in admissions" and to posit a distinction between recruiting and selecting. Widening the applicant pool was one thing, selecting only "the most promising and best suited for Harvard" was another. "As a result there are no racial quotas at Harvard," they said, "and there will be none." They did acknowledge that "middle-class students [in general] will probably find fewer places at Harvard," but there was no "intention to reduce the substantial number of Jewish students" in particular, only "to increase representation of students from poor backgrounds and from ethnic and social groups which at present contribute relatively few students to Harvard."[25]

Noting that Glazer, Lipset, and their colleagues said nothing about academic qualifications, Podhoretz was not reassured. He was convinced that an applicant's academic qualifications, which Jews often had in abundance, would be trumped by his or her membership in a social, sexual, or racial category. It was all too reminiscent of the institution of Jewish quotas back in the twenties.[26] Chase M. Peterson, an acquaintance who was Dean of Admissions at Harvard, offered to comfort Podhoretz with the information that the percentage of Jewish students, which he guessed to be between "25 to 45 per cent" (with such wide parameters, he implied, his office was obviously not counting), had remained fairly constant. Rather, "of the two large old constituencies, the New England Yankee WASP appears to have given up far more spaces than have east coast Jews."

Apropos of another theme in Podhoretz's "A Certain Anxiety," Peterson observed that minority students "in city colleges" do probably bring their New Left, "third-world" militant views with them, but that at Harvard "we find we have brought in very conservative, hardworking, scholastically oriented students of an old and very precious mold." "Ironically," the New Left element at Harvard consisted largely of "WASP students" who are "guilt ridden from an affluence they don't understand and guilt ridden because fate denied them the persecution which goes with another color of skin and so set about to make their penitence in college."[27]

These amiable exchanges didn't alter Podhoretz's view about admissions policy. Nor was his apprehension limited to the likely results for Jews alone. A "very powerful case," he wrote Peterson,

can be made out against the idea that proportional representation according to group or sex – under whatever euphemisms or under whatever numerical formula such an idea may be advanced – would lead to damaging consequences in the quality of American life and would do more harm than good, even in the short run, to the groups it is presumably intended to benefit.[28]

Peterson invited Podhoretz to come up to Cambridge so that the admissions office could, as Podhoretz would remember, "persuade me that Harvard had no intention of doing what both of us knew it was in fact already doing"; that is, instituting the double-standards policy that writer Kenneth Rexroth wittily called "Crow-Jimism." Podhoretz did meet with Peterson's plainly hostile staff, "and when I finished the questions were so charged with hatred that I found myself wondering whether even a public reading from *Mein Kampf* could have elicited greater outrage."[29]

American life would flourish best, Podhoretz implied in a letter to an academic who had wondered whether he now considered himself a "conservative," if each group just backed its own in the meritocratic scuffle. "I certainly do agree that self-interest is a more reliable guide to decent political behavior than abstract ideals, at least in most social situations. Why do you call that belief a conservative teaching? Surely it is an essential element of classic liberal political theory."[30] The self-interest of intellectuals, for example, ought to galvanize them in support of meritocracy. Places in freshman classes, or jobs in whatever profession or company, oughtn't go to a Gentile if a Jewish candidate's credentials were better – just as no Jewish candidate should be preferred over a Gentile whose credentials were better. Justice means treating equals equally.

These meritocratic criteria operated with tolerable purity in sports, about which Podhoretz had always cared. In the fall of 1972, he was on a Yale panel, "Sports in America – Larger than Life," where he remarked that Americans were increasingly preoccupied by sports because they "remain one of the few areas of our national life and culture relatively uncontaminated by the erosion of standards." Furthermore, everyone agrees that "the better the person or team does something, the more honor and . . . greater riches are likely to accrue to them. We want that kind of world, [and] we see it in less and less pure form in other areas of our national life."

True, these "greater riches" are generated by market capitalism, not the state, and therefore players and teams move around. Podhoretz confessed that like everyone in Brooklyn he was sad (not to say angry) when Walter O'Malley made the business decision to move the Dodgers to Los Angeles in 1958. Consumers adjust, however, and to an "extraordinary . . . degree . . . local loyalties seem to remain intact. The Dodgers went away and the Mets were created." The fans at Shea Stadium in Queens were transplants from Ebbets Field in Brooklyn: "They have the same loser-loving psychology."

And speaking of loving losers, "I don't suppose I'll ever be so much in love with anyone or anything," Podhoretz said, "as I was at the age of twelve with Pete Reiser, who then ruined himself by crashing into the center field wall of Ebbets Field a few times and was subsequently beaned." And it wasn't only baseball. Podhoretz had recently "come to adore professional basketball," particularly the hometown Knicks (who had won the NBA title in 1970 and would do so again in 1973): "The energy, the grace, the tactical brilliance and the precision that these huge creatures can command[,] and in the case of my team, the New York Knicks, the capacity for selfless teamwork[,] does present a spectacle that I find beautiful, exciting . . . and, if I may be pompous, spiritually exhilarating."[31] It was an exhilaration going all the way back to Brownsville, where, a demi-jock among future college athletes, he had been sports editor of the Boys High newspaper.

Behind Podhoretz's "Issues" editorials about race relations lay the ninety pages he had written in the spring of 1970. They amounted to a sustained history of the Civil Rights Movement from what Bayard Rustin, the Gandhi-tutored black leader, called the "heroic period" at the beginning of the sixties to, at the end, the divisive arguments among Black Power separatists, resentful working-class ethnics, affirmative-action liberals like the Dean of Admissions at Harvard, and integrationists holding onto the principle of individual merit, like Podhoretz himself.

The heroic period was crowned by the Civil Rights Acts of 1964–65 and by the famous march on the nation's capital, when, as Podhoretz wrote, "the future looked so lovely and when black and white together sang 'We Shall Overcome.'"[32] The march was the "first ecumenical event in living political memory" and "more theatrically effective than the producer of any melodrama would ever have dared to hope," with Martin Luther King, Jr. "the newest American saint, [and] Bull Connor . . . the newest villain." Once the Civil Rights Acts had been made law, what remained was "the issue of enforcement" and the adjustment of attitudes: for blacks, exorcising the sense of inferiority internalized during the long centuries of white racism, and for whites, Podhoretz implied, dropping the fantasy of their innate superiority.

Hence the focus on the classroom, the key public site for everyone's attitudinal transformation. In 1954 the psychologist Kenneth Clark told the Supreme Court that black children performed badly because "they were afflicted with the disease of self-hate." End de jure segregation and you will end self-hatred. The Supreme Court agreed, declaring the South's de jure segregation illegal; the Civil Rights Acts then finished the task. In the North, ending de jure segregation hadn't been necessary for it didn't exist. What did exist, "de facto segregation," sounded bad, but it was really a misnomer for a voluntary "separation of the races," which in itself was "not really an evil whose abolition could contribute significantly to the breaking of the circle of self-contempt" blacks were caught in. Such separation just meant people living in their own neighborhoods – a pattern they liked because, as in the Brooklyn of Podhoretz's childhood, it was comparatively comfortable.

The pace at which "deserving Negroes" were being absorbed into the middle class, in any case, was slow indeed. Therefore came the last-ditch "advocacy of 'preferential treatment' or 'benign quotas'" to achieve normalized distribution, meaning that blacks would be distributed in the same proportions as any other group along the curve of income and status, a result that "the mere abolition of discrimination" and improved facilities and instruction "would obviously never bring about unaided." Initially, liberals weren't comfortable with oxymoronic phrases like "benevolent discrimination and benign quotas." But the experiment "was nevertheless successfully sold" to the majority of them, with the threat that people would otherwise stop calling them liberals.

What were Podhoretz and Moynihan, his chief ally in the analysis of race and ethnicity, missing? To their minds, nothing. For more than two centuries, American law, and the culture that stood behind it, had progressively treated the individual *as* an individual, not as a member of a category based on sex, race, or class. The ideal of social justice was that rewards should be distributed according to personal merit. What the law guaranteed wasn't equal outcomes, to say nothing of equal incomes. What the law guaranteed was equal *opportunity*. Some, with a combination of innate talent and energy, acquired knowledge and skills, and some lucky breaks, would cull more prizes. Those with combinations less impressive would cull fewer prizes. But it was also in the American grain that relative losers should be cared for by private and public charities. No one should be left unaccommodated, starving or homeless.[33] Much, too, ought to be done to enable the less successful, and especially their children, to compete more successfully in the next go.

In sum, New Deal capitalism, having put safety nets beneath those truly incapable of helping themselves, had enabled nearly everyone to rise into what, in any earlier epoch, would have been regarded as the middle class. But the New Left pooh-poohed this accomplishment, first because it disapproved of the material trappings of "the middle-class way of life" and second (somewhat inconsistently) because there were entire categories of people that hadn't achieved those trappings. Ergo, the "exploiters and oppressors" would have to be expropriated in favor of their "victims" – people of the "wrong" sex, race, or class.

In this kind of analysis, which would dominate the academy and the Democratic Party for the rest of the century and beyond, individual trees, as it were, didn't matter. What mattered were whole forests. Consider the reception of Moynihan's 1965 report, "The Negro Family: The Case for National Action," written while he was working as Assistant Secretary of Labor. He had insisted that facts must be faced: the crumbling of the black family structure – absent fathers, single mothers – would hamstring blacks' economic progress, which in turn would slow their accession to political power. He was accused of having "blamed the victim," although in fact he had attributed the dissolution of the black family not to personal turpitude but to (a) the slavery and discrimination of the past and (b) the perverse welfare system that effectually encouraged black fathers to abandon their families so that mothers could collect Aid to Dependent Children. Moynihan had expressly called for a reform of that system but, in the new climate, he found it difficult to get a hearing. The black family dysfunctional? No way. Blacks should be praised, cried the New Left, for their creative response to slavery and discrimination: "The 'fatherless' family became," Podhoretz wrote, "a family with surrogate fathers, or a family whose children, far from being neglected (as the 'white' perspective seemed to imply), were lovingly and responsibly tended by mothers, grandmothers, aunts, sisters, siblings."[34]

That would be fine if black children were growing up healthy, wealthy, and wise. But they weren't. Young males too often had no at-home models of manly responsibility – working hard at one's job, staying faithful to one's wife – and therefore, as Podhoretz put it, "Many more of them than anyone wanted to admit were heroin addicts... listless, apathetic, gone-to-seed, past caring." To offer such people "a multiplication of opportunities of which they were already incapable of taking advantage" would just "make things worse," leaving them without anyone "to blame... but themselves" – which wasn't to say that they or their leaders would stop blaming whites.

The whites who took the brunt of this blame weren't the well-to-do but the working-class "ethnics" – the very groups in the North whom the well-to-do equated with the rednecks in the South. Liberal integrationists were "ramming Negroes down [the ethnics'] protesting throats: by locating public-housing projects in *their* neighborhoods, busing Negro children into *their* schools, forcing Negro workers into *their* unions." More than capable of seeing that liberals had inoculated themselves against any serious inconvenience or danger, a working-class white could only "cackle" at their unbelievable gall in telling him that the advancement of blacks, just now occurring at his expense, would in the long run greatly benefit him as well.[35]

The liberal integrationists had miscalculated not just the degree of ethnic resentment but also "the perversely stubborn truth... that the Negroes *were* different – from the Jews, from the Italians, from the Irish, from the Poles, from the Wasps, and from every other group of whites in America, just as every one of these groups was different from all the others." To ask the blacks to be, in effect, like the Jews was to ask them "to play from their weaknesses instead of from their strengths," just as it would be to ask the Italians, say, to be like the Poles. What was needed was a new metaphor for America: not the melting pot, which reduced the several colors to one, off-white, but what Canadians called the cultural mosaic, which contained diverse elements that kept their distinctive qualities. In the eighties and nineties, Podhoretz would remind these diverse elements of all they had in common, especially the secular faith in America's liberal democracy. But in the late sixties and early seventies he underlined cultural distinctiveness – and he saluted America's genius for permitting, encouraging, and refereeing the peaceable competition among its many cultural communities. The miscellany that would result, neighborhood by neighborhood, could then go on making America the most fascinating, multipartite country in the world.

Yes, blacks had been admitted in large numbers to colleges and universities, once admissions criteria were bent to permit nonacademic experiences to substitute for "presumably 'culture-bound' tests," or transcripts. But "it soon became an open secret that vast numbers of black students were only passing by virtue of the charitable or guilty refusal of their teachers to give them failing grades." Besides, the "relevant" courses they demanded – for instance, "separate instruction in the black heritage" – in practice "turned out to be a self-abasing confession of their inability to compete on an equal footing with whites, while the demand for separate residential and social facilities expressed the shame and humiliation they felt at their failure and the need to hide it from the prying eyes of the world." None of this would have happened if black leaders had urged the mass of their people to concentrate on what, for generations, they had proved they could do well – "popular music and athletics," for starters. Baldwin says somewhere that "All whitey ever gave us was basketballs." From the perspective Podhoretz was developing, those basketballs were a more beneficent contribution than a shelf of works by classic Western writers. A Baldwin or an Ellison, having as it were no gift for basketball, *would* find a way to get at those writers, and, with the aid of a truly benign educational system, break the mold.

At the end of these ninety pages, which (again) were too inconclusive for him to publish as a whole, Podhoretz both empathizes with blacks' frustration and reminds them that despair is a sin. Frustration and despair stemmed from the feeling "that the evil they wished to undo [was] entirely beyond the reach of ordinary political action," and that the only recourse was vengeance – "to bring America down" with violence.

That was the message of the Black Panthers. One of the strongest pieces *Commentary* ran in the early seventies was "A Perspective on the Panthers," by a precocious YPSL member, Tom Milstein. He rightly saw the Panthers' "world" as a collage "constructed by Kurt Vonnegut out of bits and pieces of Dostoevsky," with an internal governance entirely totalitarian ("The only form of criticism permitted is [individual] self-criticism"). The Great Society programs of the mid-sixties were worth pursuing, Milstein felt, but not through the Panthers' advocacy of "economic separatism" and their corollary insistence that people "pick up the gun" in order to defend "the community," usually by "offing the pig." Having begun as a "self-defense" militia shooting it out with the Oakland police, the Panthers had willed their own destruction – for the obvious reason that the police could always outgun them.

The harm done by the Panthers was compounded by supporters like William Kunstler, who had also headed the defense team in the Chicago Conspiracy Trial (the seven defendants were charged with having incited people to riot during the 1968 Democratic national convention). Kunstler was telling "huge student audiences" that they "must learn to fight in the streets, learn to revolt, learn to shoot guns. We will learn to do all the things property owners fear.... You may ultimately be bathed in blood. So will others. But you will have to do it."[36]

Jason Epstein's *The Great Conspiracy Trial*, a book about Kunstler's defense of the Chicago Seven before Judge Julius Hoffman, looked upon violence as a hygienic imperative. Reviewing the book in *Commentary*, Alexander M. Bickel, professor at Yale Law School, understood the abyss toward which such radical reportage was headed: "American society is so immeasurably culpable," the abyss-lovers were declaring, "that random murders of any of its white members can be perceived as just." From Bickel's point of view, the government's case in prosecuting the seven for conspiracy was "plausible." Judge Hoffman may have erred here and there during the trial, but Kunstler's behavior was worse, being "more interested in the verdict of the streets and of the press than in the verdict of the jury."[37]

Podhoretz thought he knew where Huey Newton, Bobby Seale, and the other Black Panthers were going with their calls to violence. As "revolutionists of an ecumenically 'Marxist-Leninist' stripe," they had a problem: the country wasn't *in* a "revolutionary situation." The vast majority of citizens agreed with Bickel that, yes, there were social ills, but they were being remedied. The Panthers and the Weathermen were therefore doing the classic and diabolical thing: they were trying, in what Wrong called the "catastrophist" option, to *create* a revolutionary situation – by bidding chaos come again.[38]

The tensions between Jews and blacks were concentrated on the differences between a generally successful minority and a minority still educationally, economically, and politically in arrears. Why should these domestic tensions have been aggravated by events in the faraway Middle East? As we have noted, blacks in America, especially educated blacks, were increasingly identifying with the Arabs, not on account of race but on account, as they imagined, of their both being oppressed, or dispossessed, by Jews. The logic of "my enemy's enemy is my friend," here couched in the rhetoric of Third-World, wretched-of-the-earth brotherhood, gave black anti-Semitism a revolutionary caché that proved irresistible to many white intellectuals, no few of them Jewish. White or black, these intellectuals didn't consider themselves anti-Semitic. No, they were simply anti-Zionist, deploring the way in which Israel had been created at the expense of the Palestinians in 1948 and had been so maintained in the decades since.

The *New York Review* gave full-throated expression to black anti-Semitism, though never admitted as such, during the UFT strike and in its general coverage of "urban problems." During the late sixties and early seventies, however, the magazine shied away from the topic of the Middle East. A notable exception was a piece by I. F. Stone reviewing a collection of writings by Jewish and Arab hands in Sartre's Paris journal, *Les Temps Modernes*, directly on the heels of the Six-Day War.

Coming before the more distinctly partisan arguments of Noam Chomsky and Edward Said, who would dominate much of the *New York Review* discourse in the decades that followed, Stone's "Holy War" admits that the Jewish and Arab "tribal" projects in Palestine are "incommensurable": the Jews bring to the struggle the knowledge of the Holocaust, while the Arabs bring the knowledge of the successful Algerian fight for independence. The Holocaust notwithstanding, the Palestinian Arabs believed their rights had been violated, their property stolen. Stone summarizes their credo:

that Israel is a colonialist implantation in the Middle East, supported from the beginning by imperialist powers; that it is an enemy of Arab union and progress; that the sufferings of the Jews in the West were the consequence of an anti-Semitism the Arabs have never shared; and that there is no reason why the Arabs of Palestine should be displaced from their homes in recompense for wrongs committed by Hitler's Germany.

Stone sympathizes. The Jews themselves, he implies, ought to have objected to the whole Zionist enterprise. For Stone, a lifelong socialist (indeed, a fellow-traveling communist in the forties if not an actual agent),[39] it was simple: the Israeli (the bad Jew) was "concerned only with his own tribe's welfare," while the "mission" of the good Jew was to be "a Witness" to socialism "in the human wilderness." Between now and the millennium, the "ideal solution" would therefore be for Jews in all countries to make their contributions *to* those countries, "while Israel finds acceptance as a Jewish State in a renascent Arab civilization" – a province, one supposes, in some Middle Eastern federation.[40]

Stone's survey of Israel's dilemma was representative of the New Left's view of what was at stake for Jews and Arabs. How, as a centrist liberal, did Podhoretz reply? In summary, he conceded, explicitly or implicitly, that the early Zionist leaders were either ignorant of or economical with the truth about the existence of Arabs in Palestine; that the Western and Eastern powers did dump the consequences of their own anti-Semitism into the lap of the Arabs; and that "the ideal solution" would involve on all sides a transcendence of ethnocentrism – the lamb, as it were, lying down with the lamb. But because the disease of anti-Semitism erupted in the twentieth century with unprecedented virulence, the Jews *had* to protect themselves, and for this purpose they needed a homeland. The only one genuinely on offer was in Palestine, and there, after Hitler's war, many of them went. When in 1948 the seven Arab nations attacked the new state, populations were inevitably shuffled: Jews were exiled from Arab countries and embraced by Israel, and Arabs were displaced in Israel and – embraced by no one – settled into refugee camps. They and their fellow Arabs across the narrow borders called for Israel to be destroyed and the Jews driven into the sea. Jews had faced eliminationists before, and six million of them had been killed. They weren't going to let that happen again.

Stone deplored Israeli self-defense as tribalism, but to Podhoretz it was common-sense statecraft – and when faced with implacable and aggressive hatred, the only real alternative to suicide. As for anti-Zionism, in practice it was inseparable from anti-Semitism. Indeed, hatred of Jews occasionally unified Arab peoples who, given the thugs who led them, would otherwise have been at daggers drawn with one another. Moreover, if Jews could be targeted in Israel, then Jews elsewhere, including those in America, "would be next." And why not, if "there was indeed a malevolent will at work . . . to make the entire world *Judenrein*? And if such a will existed, with Hitler as its servant formerly in Europe and with the Arabs and the Russians as its servants now in the Middle East, would it not find suitable and equally surprising servants" – not the implausible American Nazi Party but the all-too-plausible Black Panthers – "to carry the work still further even in the old *goldene medineh* of the East European immigrants, even in the 'golden land,' even in America itself?"

The one big ray of light, or so the Six-Day War strongly suggested, shone in the fighting spirit of the Jews themselves. There had been, Podhoretz felt, a "recovery, after a long and uncertain convalescence, of the Jewish remnant from the grievous and so nearly fatal psychic and spiritual wounds it suffered at the hands of the Nazis." Now there was "resistance" in place of "submission." "The Jews, who had so often violated the commandment to choose life, now obeyed that commandment and chose life. It was a thing to celebrate."[41]

These, then, were some of the applications of Podhoretz's springtime epiphany of 1970. His vision had told him that "Judaism was true"; i.e., that there were moral as well as physical laws governing life, and that people who knew what was good for them didn't violate those laws. It was, for example, a moral imperative to respect the humanity of every person, whatever his race. Discrimination was a sin – and so was reverse discrimination. This respect for other groups entailed respect for one's own. Self-hatred in a Jew was just as immoral as self-hatred in a black or Arab, and Jews were obligated to aid their kin, especially the beleaguered mass in Israel, from those who would kill them.

10

Liberalism Lost

The antinomianism Podhoretz would so forcefully oppose throughout the seventies had, in the prior decade, no more spectacular manifestation than the German Peter Weiss's play *Marat/Sade* (1963). Opening in New York at the very end of 1965, it was a carnivalesque fusion of Brechtian "demonstration" (ideas spelled out through dialogue, signs, can't-miss symbols, etc.) and Artaudian "cruelty" (a sometimes-bloody breaking of conventions for the sake of heightened perception). In January 1966, with the director Peter Brook, Leslie Fiedler, and others, Podhoretz participated in a forum devoted to the play. He confined himself to a few common-sense remarks about Weiss's "unresolved" opposition of classical radicalism and Sadean nihilism.

Fiedler, for his part, rapturously declared that the play's purpose was "to remind us that the sky might fall on our heads at any moment," and this because, in the mid-sixties, American culture was at sixes and sevens. Witness the Road Vultures, a motorcycle gang in Buffalo that decorated its clubhouse with "pictures of Hitler and the killers of all the American presidents," covered its tables with "Communist and Maoist literature," and wrote on the wall "Death to the fascist fuzz." This congeries of artifacts was, for Fiedler, analogous to the effect of *Marat/Sade*: "a refreshing and terrifying... confusion of the classical Right and the classical Left." The difference between Fiedler and the Vultures, apparently, lay in his resemblance to Weiss's Sade, who "stands outside of his own madness instead of twitching with it."

Podhoretz was having none of it. "I don't take the madness of the play that seriously," he said. "The play is largely about politics," the revolutionist's "dark night of the soul.... The arguments about terror... are clearly related to present-day events. It's not a question of sanity or madness, but of whether or not you believe in this kind of terror based on ideology, whether you think it can clean up the world."[1] He was implicitly reminding Fiedler of the liberal anticommunist tenets that Fiedler himself had so intelligently defended in the fifties – tenets that many of the young radicals seemed never to have understood or even heard of.

In this contest, at least, Saul Bellow was entirely in Podhoretz's corner. His *Mr. Sammler's Planet* (1970) was strongly critical of New Left posturings, and if it provoked resentment among "The Young," so be it. Podhoretz was increasingly convinced "that no deals are possible any longer and that the hardening of attitudes . . . might be best for everyone."[2] Bellow thought so, too, telling Podhoretz in a letter (they were briefly on speaking terms) that though he had "never wanted to become an infighter," he was discovering himself to "have a feeling for polemics" after all. "When I was in Paris," he continued, "I was told that Mary McCarthy was screaming for my blood. Then, at nightfall, in London, who should turn up at a bus stop but Leslie Fiedler, his beard looking rather plucked about the chin. He was very friendly and proposed that we should have a friendly conversation next day. But I said No . . . I can never understand why revolutionaries try to hold on to liberal friendly relations with me."[3]

"Kid"-worshipping, revolutionary intellectuals were suddenly everywhere. At a conference once, Fiedler offered an "emotional affirmation . . . that he would never, never betray the child in himself!" Dan Jacobson's reply – "But one can betray the adult in oneself as well"[4] – was apt, even if it didn't altogether register with Fiedler, or with reluctant grown-ups generally. It was against these enthusiasts of "Consciousness III," in the terminology coined by the fellow-traveling academic Charles Reich, that Podhoretz was pitching his magazine, trying to persuade them not to betray their adult commitments.

Returning to literary criticism after nearly a decade's furlough, Podhoretz in 1974 published "The Literary Light as Eternal Flame" in the *Saturday Review*. It was a sortie against the scribbling counterculture. The early-seventies market was hyping the Bohemian Know-Nothingism Podhoretz had attacked in the late fifties; indeed, many of the books left-leaning college students had in the intervening years been choosing for themselves – flippant or portentous novels by Joseph Heller and Herman Hesse, turgid tracts by Herbert Marcuse and Norman O. Brown, guides for the very perplexed like the *I Ching* and the *Kama Sutra* – encouraged the rejection of language itself. Why read, write, or discuss when there is a world out there to *feel*? That at least was what one heard from the students who were stoned. The conscious and politically active sympathized with a different claim: that "good writing" was itself reactionary. Caught up in the beauties of art, the worry was, readers would lose their outrage over social evils.

Podhoretz reminds the radical theorists that the good writing of Dickens, for example, had aroused, not numbed, readers' outrage, and that good books have more often than not enabled readers to behold and criticize the world afresh. But he also admits that both the politicos and the mystics have a point: like any great art, literature "is most often anti-political in its influence, a dampener of activist ardors, a chastener of utopian greeds." This is because truly great literature insists on our grasping, and finally accepting, the world as it is. "No wonder then," Podhoretz said, "that radicals who seek as earnestly to transform themselves as to transform society have generally been hostile to literature."

In support of this attitude of mature acceptance of the world as it is, Podhoretz cites a distinction of T. S. Eliot that goes to the heart of his own sensibility: "In criticism you are responsible only for what you want, [but] in creation you are responsible for what you can do with material which you must simply accept."[5] Critics who believe that opinion and idea are decisive in literature are finally like the Marxists who regard art as a weapon in the class war. Podhoretz thought such politicization as bad as its opposite, art-for-art's-sake aestheticism. The crucial principle is the criticism of literature *as* literature, as a work independent of the person who wrote it. But there is an important qualification in cases where a disposition *for* this or *against* that idea permeates an author's work. That does indeed affect our criticism of his work, and should. Thus, if anti-Semitism, conscious or not, is a pervading aspect of (say) T. S. Eliot's writing, then the critic, if he is like Podhoretz, will rank him lower, for all his formal genius, than a writer possessed of equivalent formal genius but also deeper moral self-awareness.

It follows that, if he is to be helpful, a critic must be willing to stick his neck out – something Podhoretz had, from the beginning of his career, the special courage to do. Often it meant hurting people's feelings, and being hurt in return. As he wrote to Clive James, just then starting what would be a notable career as a man of letters, it was a pleasure to see his poem about the contemporary cultural scene, "Peregrine Prykke," in the *New Republic*: "My only criticism, really, is that your inclusion of friends forces you to be good-natured too much of the time; as with Byron (and I don't drop his name lightly) the malicious parts are better than the humorous ones." One notes the congruence between this don't-be-too-nice counsel and Mailer's criticism of *Making It*. Having learned the hard way that his own friends weren't afraid of being "malicious," Podhoretz was passing the lesson on to James. And for the highest reason: a critic mustn't be afraid of opposing "the prevailing political winds in the literary-intellectual world," whoever might be blowing in them, as vigorously as he opposes "their strictly literary counterparts."[6]

The courage to oppose was what a good editor also needed. Podhoretz was as shrewd at finding bold writers when *Commentary* went on the counter-countercultural offensive as he had been when jump-starting the counterculture itself at the beginning of his tenure – or as he had been in discovering Philip Roth in 1957, when he plucked Roth's "You Can't Tell a Man by the Song He Sings" from the slush pile at *Commentary* and insisted that the Greenbergs publish it. Any journalistic movement, or happy "find," occurs amid a magazine's daily round, which Podhoretz described, in a 1965 article for *Harper's*, in frank but elevated terms. Elevated in that the top editors were said to labor in service of the English language itself – and of the wider culture that depended on it. Because the specialized journals had become unreadable for the laity, the general-audience magazine editor had to find the scholars, or the amateurs familiar with them, who could explain their ideas in accessible prose.[7]

The back and forth between editor and contributor is usually a matter of line-by-line phrasing, ordering statements, catching an audience's attention at the start, and bringing everything together at the close. Occasionally, though, an editor will put his finger on a spot in a writer's manuscript in such a way as to turn a bright piece into something brilliant. This happened famously on the occasion of Cynthia Ozick's novella "Envy; or, Yiddish in America," which appeared in *Commentary* in November 1969.

When Podhoretz read the story in draft, he wrote Ozick: "I think – and everyone at *Commentary* agrees – that you let a masterpiece, one of the potentially great stories of our time, get away from you somewhere" toward the final quarter – a long, disorienting vision in which her protagonist Edelshtein, a sixty-seven-year-old Yiddish poet, imagines himself educating his young American translator "by letting the deathcamp cinders cover her like a black snow."[8] Initially reluctant about revising an ending that seemed so right – "I can't *visualize* this story without the procession of its last twenty pages: without the disorientation, the madness, the fury, the pity" – Ozick came to see, after talking with Podhoretz, how revision was nevertheless a step toward perfection. Revise, therefore, she did.

Podhoretz's verdict was highly commendatory, as was that of Roth, who wrote her that "*Envy* is a marvelous story, and it makes me envious. . . . You've written the story that I have been waiting for years to see."[9] Speaking thirty-five years later of Podhoretz's suggestions, Ozick averred that what made them "the most valuable I've ever gotten from any editor was that he said 'If you won't do it or can't do it, I'll publish this story anyway.'" She hadn't at first seen the wisdom of calling it "Envy" – her own title had been simply "Yiddish in America" – "but of course he was right." His "publication of 'Envy' opened up the world to me, and on the dedication page of *Pagan Rabbi* I referred to him as *ba'al hanifla'ot*, which means 'master of miracles.'" Publication in *Commentary*, to her the most magnificent of magazines, gave her the recognition without which, she believed, her literary career would never have gotten off the ground.[10]

As we know, the master of miracles was just then, in the fall of 1969, still smarting from the effects of another "envy." No wonder he grasped what the main title of Ozick's tale should be. When in the spring of 1970 he had his great epiphany – "Judaism is true" – it may in part have been because of how Ozick's tale had underlined that claim. She had insisted, first, on remembrance: Yiddish must be kept alive because it was the tongue of generations of middle-European Jews, most of whom were murdered by the Nazis. She had insisted, second – the implication is strong – on solidarity and survival: Jews must stick together for their own sake, not just out of narrow self-regard (though that is itself a tonic instinct) but also out of concern for every one of God's children. The Chosen People are chosen, after all, not just to receive and obey the law but also to bear witness to it. God commands *all* human beings to choose life.

If Ozick gave Podhoretz reinforcement of his own Jewish wisdom, he gave her fortitude, even temerity – and a bit of argumentative street smarts. As she wrote him, "in intellectual life in this country *Commentary*'s been the indispensable starter." She was adept at taking long views of "Jewish fate in the twentieth century," but she felt herself "unequipped" to duke it out in everyday political debate.[11] For that – the ideas and the will – she relied on Podhoretz and his magazine.

He in turn understood how to get the best from her. Hence her precious acknowledgment: "I think you know what praise from you means to me. When at the gates of the World-to-Come they ask me to tell my merits, I'll be able to say: Norman Podhoretz liked something I wrote."[12] Also, as we have noted, he told her how, with her convictions and intelligence, she was bound to have "many Moral (or Immoral) Adventures," and therefore to make enemies. It was important to make enemies, for how else would one know that one had stood for something?[13]

In the late sixties and early seventies, Podhoretz and allies like Kristol, Glazer, and Moynihan weren't altogether sure what to call themselves. As Democrats, they regarded their core beliefs as liberal, in a tradition stretching back to Johnson, Kennedy, Truman, and Franklin Roosevelt: equal-opportunity promotion of civil rights, provision of a social safety net, antitotalitarian foreign policy, and, in cultural matters, an insistence on high ethical and aesthetic standards. But New Left intellectuals had so influenced discussion on these subjects that many mainstream Democrats, attracted by the youth and numbers of the movement, had begun to cozy up to them.

If, for instance, the radicals called for confiscatory redistribution of capital resources or the sponsorship of communist revolution in the third world, then mainstream Democrats, as though meeting them halfway, offered quotas and neutralist isolationism. In demurring, Podhoretz and his allies found themselves in an unaccustomed place for supporters of the FDR-to-LBJ heritage. They were to the right of a shifted center.

Did that mean "conservative," with or without quotation marks? Podhoretz wished that Robert L. Bartley, in his *Wall Street Journal* column about the "new" *Commentary*, hadn't used the word: "Those who are friendly to the kind of thing I have been doing lately fear that it will be discredited by being characterized as conservative; those who are hostile can point . . . in triumph at this apparent exposure of my secret and sinister political designs."[14] Plainly, however, the "liberal" label was becoming otiose. As Kristol told a correspondent, anyone who realizes, as Glazer did, "that social reform is a long, difficult, complex and, at best, imperfect affair" – and not an instant and self-generating paradise – "cannot be a man of the left." Descriptive compounds like "conservative liberal" or "liberal conservative" would be fair, if it weren't that "American liberalism, as presently constituted," rejected the adjective in any combination. Thus the dilemma faced by Kristol, Glazer, Podhoretz, and the others.

Kristol's brother-in-law, Milton Himmelfarb, sent Podhoretz an apt remark from the nineteenth-century Christian socialist F. D. Maurice: "I knew... that I was in danger of attaching myself to a party which should inscribe 'No Party' on its flag. Many had fallen into that snare."[15] The editors of *National Review*, those "scrambled eggheads on the right," as Dwight Macdonald had once called them,[16] now offered to unscramble the New York eggheads. The magazine's egg count was fairly accurate: from the liberal anticommunist consensus of the fifties, there had emerged in the sixties

(1) radicals born during the Depression (Sontag, Chomsky, Jason Epstein, Podhoretz) who became convinced that anticommunism had gone too far; and

(2) radicals who had been young in the thirties, "erstwhile anti-Stalinists" and therefore usually Trotskyists (Fiedler, Riesman, Rahv, Macdonald, McCarthy, Dupee), who now were being re-radicalized.

In addition, there were the young radicals, if not always the "red-diaper" children of Old Left parents, then certainly children of liberal parents. While hardly ever pro-Soviet, these mixed-generation radicals were titillated to identify with Ho Chi Minh or Castro – "Bohemian and, somehow, the Artist" – as opposed to the squares, careerists, and sinister power brokers who ran the American political parties.

So why, suddenly, had some of these left-leaning intellectuals – Podhoretz, Kristol, Glazer, Moynihan, et al. – begun to split from the sexy boho Family? Because, said *National Review*, many of them were Jews, and the emergence of anti-Semitism in reaction to the UFT strike and to Israel's victory in the Six-Day War made them feel that Jews were in danger. Moreover, the student rebellions that had trashed campuses from Columbia to Berkeley made them feel threatened simply as intellectuals. What troubled *National Review*, in turn, was that "these wanderings into and out of radicalism" seemed "matters of mood and accident, traceable to, at best, fortuitous occurrences in the objective world. They are insufficiently rooted in serious political realities, in general principle, or coherent intellectual tradition."[17]

This last was a sound objection. One task these particular New York Intellectuals took up in the seventies was, in fact, to assimilate their reactive concerns into the extant "conservative liberal" or "liberal conservative" tradition. For Podhoretz, the goal was to strike a proper balance between hoping too little and hoping too much from New-Deal-to-Great-Society programs. His immediate worry, given the New Left's seizure of the political spotlight, was about the "havoc... wreaked" by hoping too much. Blaming "society" for all ills, the radicals expected the state to remedy them. Intellectuals like Glazer, Moynihan, and Podhoretz were taking up the thankless job of reminding their peers that while some ills might be remedied by local government initiatives and private charities, many were simply endemic to existence itself. There were "large areas of human experience" in which "the surly tyranny of the activist temper" could do no good, though by meddling it could do harm.[18]

If *National Review* welcomed these cautions against hoping too much, the leftist *Nation* felt obliged to say the ex-radicals were guilty of hoping too little. In "The Deradicalized Intellectuals," Eugene Goodheart, a literary critic at Brandeis, while granting "there is nothing intrinsically dishonorable in the conservative idea," warned that it led to complacency. "There *are* limits to what politics can accomplish.... But to turn this truth into an occasion for avoiding the political failure of America to stop its criminal war in Vietnam by taking the long view of the killing, as Podhoretz does now (in the long run we'll all be dead), is inexcusable." The noble thing, Goodheart asserted, was to try democratic socialism again and again until we got it right, and meanwhile to accuse the deradicalized of being unconscionably evasive.[19]

Joseph Epstein's "The New Conservatism: Intellectuals in Retreat," in Howe's *Dissent*, was a more inward critique. He sent Podhoretz a forewarning: "You have never been other than gracious and helpful to me, both personally and professionally. I disagree with the turn your politics have taken, but I hardly think of you as an enemy. Nor do I ever expect to do so."[20] Through most of the nineteenth century, Epstein observed in his essay, conservatives were derided as the stupid party, their position based on class or temperament, not ideas. During the Cold War, F. A. Hayck, Milton Friedman, Hook, Buckley, and others had shown that conservatives were hardly stupid: their ideas were in an honorable line stretching back to Burke and Coleridge. But the conservatives now writing about domestic policy for Kristol's *Public Interest* or about foreign policy for Podhoretz's *Commentary* were something novel – an epiphenomenon of the New Left. They weren't alone in being repulsed by that movement's violence, anti-intellectualism, and sheer Stalinism. Howe had also been repulsed, and his response had been to shore up the real Left: democratic socialism. But Podhoretz and his allies had separated from the Left altogether, as became evident when in 1972, in "a starkly symbolic act" of disenchantment, they took out an ad in the *New York Times* to announce their intention of voting for Nixon and Agnew. Epstein could understand the disenchantment, but was aghast at any move rightward toward Nixon. Politics may be a choice between evils, but why choose the greater one?[21]

The blurred boundaries between socialist and liberal, liberal and conservative, paleo- and neoconservative, can appear to defy political cartographers – to the point where one wants simply to repeat Glazer's definition of a neoconservative as "someone who [in the old days] wasn't a conservative" and leave it at that. But, roughly, one can say that in domestic policy neoconservatives stood for equality of opportunity, period. They defended this position against the Left, which wanted equality of results at whatever cost in social engineering, and against the Right, which believed the leveling principle of equality, even equality of opportunity, could only do mischief. In foreign policy, the neoconservatives combated communism because it denied freedom. They defended this position against the Left, which softly regarded communism as democratic socialism gone (perhaps) too far, and against the Right, which hated communism because it was atheistic, but which also tended to leave commissars and slaves alike to discover their own salvation. Totalitarianism was *their* problem, not ours. The Right, in other words, was isolationist: a good Christian nation like America, guarded by two oceans, could safely mind its own business.

In short, paleoconservatives rejected liberalism in all its manifestations, secular and egalitarian. Neoconservatives, by contrast, were faithful to the liberalism that had guided the activist, Democratic presidents of their youth – Roosevelt, Truman, Kennedy – who had been progressivist at home and anti-totalitarian abroad. As Dan Himmelfarb, in 1988 on the staff of the *Public Interest*, would say with refreshing clarity:

[N]eoconservatives belong to the tradition of liberal-democratic modernity, the tradition of Montesquieu, Madison, and Tocqueville; paleoconservatives are the heirs to the Christian and aristocratic Middle Ages, to Augustine, Aquinas, and Hooker. The principles of neoconservatism are individual liberty, self-government, and equality of opportunity; those of paleoconservatism are religious – particularly Christian – belief, hierarchy, and prescription.

While the paleoconservatives, under the pressures of the discontents of the sixties and seventies, had moved further right, and the McGovernite new liberals further left, the neoconservatives were old liberals who "stayed put." This, Himmelfarb declared, is why "'neoconservatism' is probably a misnomer – and doubly so: it is not particularly new, and it is not necessarily conservative (at least not in the classical or medieval sense). Perhaps 'paleoliberalism' would be a better term."[22]

Paleoliberalism, understood in Dan Himmelfarb's fashion, would indeed have been a better term, but it never caught on. The new conservatives eventually embraced the label of neoconservatives, and it stuck.

The year 1972, it goes without saying, was not a politically good year for them. George McGovern, the Democratic presidential candidate, represented the New Leftish drift the party had experienced since 1968, when the centrist liberal Hubert Humphrey lost to Nixon. If Podhoretz was now going to vote for Nixon, it was simply in order not to vote for McGovern.[23] He couldn't bring himself to sign the *Times* ad Epstein referred to, and once the electoral landslide had settled, he was in the vanguard of intellectuals still hoping to reclaim the Democratic Party.

McGovern's rallying cry of "Come Home, America!" had implied retreat not only from Vietnam but from any line of confrontation with the Soviets in Europe. Calling themselves the Coalition for a Democratic Majority (CDM), a somewhat different group of neoconservatives announced, in another *Times* ad immediately after the election, that it was the Democrats who needed to "come home" – that is, to return to their roots. The formation of the CDM had, as Jeane Kirkpatrick later recalled, a distinctly Russian-anarchist feel. Contacting one another separately, the conspirators discovered their unanimity "about the nature of the illness" and thought "that if only we could get together to discuss it we might even come up with an appropriate and effective remedy. And so there came a day, as the lawyers say, or a night, that we agreed to meet at a particular bar in a particular hotel. No one knew who else would be there until we arrived."[24]

Podhoretz became part of the CDM because, in domestic policy, he still believed in the FDR-to-LBJ case for government programs. Take the speech he had given to the convention of the Socialist Party USA in June 1970, at the beginning of *Commentary*'s "offensive" against the New Left and the counterculture. These radicals were manifesting a hatred of America "not for its failures... but precisely for the degree of success to which this country has been realizing some of its more classical objectives – which I would define as the universal embourgeoisement of the population." If that goal, raising everyone to the level of middle-class prosperity, was to be reached, it would never be in an alliance with people who regarded America as a force for "political, social, and spiritual evil in the world at large." Social democrats had to separate themselves from, if they couldn't convert, such malcontents; they had to defend the country's free democratic institutions, "precious," "fragile," and "imperfect" as they might be.[25] At that point they might be in a position to contend with "the vicious right" – the Nixonites on the East Coast, the Reaganites on the West, who now controlled the Republican Party.

There were exceptionally smart social democrats, one-time members of the Young People's Socialist League, who stepped forward with Podhoretz in this campaign. They included Tom Milstein, Penn Kemble, and Carl Gershman, plus Joshua Muravchik, who ghosted for Bayard Rustin, and Tom Kahn, who worked for the AFL-CIO. Initially at least, these "socialists" were – a fact almost entirely forgotten – pro-Vietnam War for the reasons that George Meany, head of the AFL-CIO, was pro-Vietnam War: because it was an anti-communist fight. Communism was a bad deal for workers. If they came to favor American withdrawal from the war, it was for Podhoretz's reasons: we weren't going to do what would be necessary in order to win, and it made no sense to shed American blood, as we had in Korea, for a mere return to the *status quo ante* (a country divided between north and south).[26]

As the 1972 election drew near, Podhoretz predicted that if McGovern lost, the Democrats, like the Republicans after Goldwater's catastrophic defeat in 1964, would move back to the center, "politely overriding their now discredited and demoralized insurgents." If by some miracle of coalition-building McGovern actually won, then a massive realignment would occur, "with a sizable number of Jews and other former Democrats" turning to the Republican Party to reconstitute a center for the nation.[27] This was remarkably prescient. McGovern did lose – only Massachusetts, the District of Columbia, and thirty-seven-and-a-half percent of the popular vote were his – and lifelong Democrats like Podhoretz and Decter did hope the CDM could help the party tack to starboard. When in time that failed – Jimmy Carter's administration (1977–80) demonstrating that the McGovernite New Class now *was* the party – "a sizable number of Jews and other former Democrats" did turn to the Republican Party to reconstitute a political center. The glorious thing about the center, as Decter would later say, was that most of the time one couldn't tell the difference between Democrat and Republican – simply "because everybody was rooting for the country."[28]

First, however, came the effort to get the Democrats back on track. Podhoretz may have climbed out of his parents' social class, but his moral bearings still pointed to its interests. What America had meant and still should mean for the working poor was at the top of the six-point CDM manifesto "Come Home, Democrats," written by Podhoretz and Decter and mailed to prospective contributors and members. America meant (1) "an ever expanding opportunity for individuals without regard to race, class, sex, or ethnic origin" and (2) "an ever fairer distribution of the fruits of the country's vast wealth and productivity." From (1) and (2) followed the idea implied in (3): If a quota system was the wrong way to achieve "fairer distribution" (compensating "those who have by birth and background been disadvantaged"), the right way was to give them "a full opportunity to compete as equals," presumably through enlightened programs in early education. To protect democratic institutions, what was needed was (4): "a sober but spirited assumption of America's share of responsibility for the establishment of a more secure international community." That is, a foreign policy not of a feckless "Coming Home" but of a canny defending of democracy against totalitarianism.

At home, there must be (5): "a knowledge that without democratic order there can be no justice and without justice there can be no democratic order." This was an effort to emphasize the issue of effective police and courts, which the Republicans had cleverly cornered. Finally, at the root of all, was the required insight into human nature that the Founders had taken for granted but that some Democrats had forgotten, namely (6): "a belief that democracy works and that it works because American voters are wisely and prudently aware of their own self-interest."

The New Politics had "derided the organized labor movement"; "sneered at the greatness of America"; "dismissed as morally unworthy the long-range values and daily concerns of tens of millions of ordinary people"; and finally "allowed the Republican Party – a party so long and so accurately known as the party of privilege – to represent itself for the first time as the champion of such values and concerns." Therefore, concluded the manifesto, trust the people who voted with the majority:

We believe that in repudiating the Democratic/"New Politics" presidential candidacy in this election while re-electing a Democratic Congress, the voters were speaking with precision and sophistication. What they said was that American society should continue on in that very Democratic tradition which, abandoned by the forces temporarily in control of the national Democratic Party in 1972, was usurped in some measure by the Republicans.

The statement carried the signatures of its authors, plus Beichman, Glazer, Rustin, Kemble, Kahn, Kirkpatrick, Daniel and Pearl Bell, Zbigniew

Brzezinski, James T. Farrell, Seymour Martin Lipset, Michael Novak, Richard Pipes, A. Philip Randolph, Eugene Rostow, Albert Shanker, Adam Ulam, Frederick Morgan, John P. Roche, Ben Wattenberg, Congressmen Richard Bolling, Thomas S. Foley, James G. O'Hara, and others.[29]

These were intellectuals and politicians who during the primaries had supported either Hubert Humphrey or Henry "Scoop" Jackson, senator from Washington. Whatever their small differences, both Humphrey and Jackson continued to believe, a dozen years on, in Kennedy's "Let's get the country moving again," which meant generating productivity, projecting American power abroad, and righting economic and social wrongs through better-administered Great Society programs. Nothing "material," however, compelled Podhoretz or anyone else to hold firm to these traditional Democratic ideas in 1972.[30] His "No!" to the New Politics was strictly "spiritual," a result of moral logic, not economic conditions.

And in many if not most of its particulars, this moral logic was that of most of the nation's people. By 1978, for example, a Gallup poll showed eighty-three percent against quotas and reverse discrimination, an opposition joined by fifty-one percent of blacks. Never had there been so large a majority on any issue Gallup had surveyed, suggesting that affirmative action was not progressive at all but, as Podhoretz would later write, "profoundly reactionary and illiberal."[31]

For a few years, the CDM gave its members a feeling that there was *something*, with a letterhead and a few dollars, to rely on. Kemble was named director, but he and the other young activists who worked for Humphrey, Jackson, or Meany were hobbled by their YPSL experience of "hole-in-the-wall" marginality. "There was a banquet every year for about three or four years," Decter later said, "but that was it: nothing ever happened. Nothing. So that was the end of CDM" – the organization, not the ideas.

In any case it quickly became evident that there was no hope the Democrat apparatchiks – the party chairmen, the candidates, and their supporters – themselves would return to their roots. The neoconservative writers paid no attention to Reagan when he ran for the Republican nomination in 1976, but the disillusioning Carter years would prompt them to look around. What they would discover was that the former governor of California was a neoconservative, too. Like them, he had begun his political career on the Left (indeed, as "a Stalinoid liberal") and then, at age fifty-one, moved somewhere right of center. He became "our man," said Decter, a more effectual counter to the New Politics than either Humphrey, Jackson, or certainly Carter had ever been.[32]

Lionel Trilling was feeling tired, even passé. Turning down William Phillips's invitation to participate in a *Partisan Review* symposium on "the New Cultural Conservatism," he said he didn't care much for "the new" anything, which was getting too warm a reception all around: "Everybody is very nice and kind to

the new and hopes it succeeds and secretly wishes it weren't so ghastly boring."
He would wager Phillips

that you can't name me one book in the last five years that has meant something to you,
personally, ... *meant* in the way ... *The Waste Land* did, or *A Portrait of the Artist* (I
don't demand *Ulysses*), and so on. The new is weekly celebrated in the *Times Book
Review*, or at least *received*, but the terms of the welcome by its partisans give the show
away: such dull hurrahs.[33]

Trilling's discouragement had been aggravated when, in 1968, Mark Rudd
and other student radicals took over the campus of Columbia. Figuring that
these students' minds had to some degree been formed in classrooms like his
own, Trilling felt responsible for their bad behavior. In "On the Teaching of
Modern Literature" and "The Two Environments: Reflections on the Study
of English," he had earlier in the decade come to the rather belated recognition that, ever since the Romantics, great imaginative writers had usually been
opposed to mainstream society. That opposition had been ramped up considerably in the early twentieth century and now, in the late sixties, he imagined
he saw the students taking "modernism" into the streets. They weren't waving
copies of *Women in Love* or *The Waste Land*, however; they were screaming
"Shut the motherfucker down!" and scrawling "Off the Pigs" on the walls of
Butler Library.

Trilling did protest intellectually, as in his letter to Podhoretz about Mailer's
hipsterism: what was needed was not more appetitive subjectivity but rational, even scientific, objectivity. Yet when faced with the radicals' *putsch* at
Columbia – the riots reminding Pearl Bell (Daniel's spouse and Kazin's sister)
of scenes from *Marat/Sade*[34] – Trilling temporized. Publicly, he said "that,
contrary to his first expectations, he had 'great respect' for 'the relatively moderate but still militant students' and that their 'demands' made sense to him."
Privately, he said "that he could not simply oppose them because they were,
after all, his own students."[35] To some Columbia faculty and administrators,
such talk, especially from Trilling, represented a liberal cave-in. It was a signal
to find jobs elsewhere.

To be sure, Trilling was exaggerating the impact of his courses in Romanticism and modernism. He had what the critic Frederick Crews, writing to
Podhoretz from Berkeley, called "a teacher's illusion":

Of all the silly things that were said in the sixties – 90% of them on the left, *bien
entendu* – the silliest of all was the claim that unruly radicals were taking their cues
from Nietzsche and Artaud. People don't simultaneously read books and throw rocks;
the rock-throwers weren't there in class to hear the lecture on existential nihilism or
whatever.[36]

The violence in the streets, as Alvin Kernan has suggested, may have reminded
Trilling of the violence that he had seen in the thirties, and it frightened him.[37]
His first impulse was to do battle with the knaves and fools on the New Left, as
he had once done with the Stalinists on the Old. So when Podhoretz committed

Commentary to "an all-out offensive against the Movement," Trilling seemed to wake up. Podhoretz would recall the occasion:

"I see," he said, "that it isn't all over yet."
"Will you help me then?" I asked. "I need you."
"You shall have me," he replied.
But I never did.

Podhoretz never did because, he came to believe, Trilling was afraid to breast the current in any way that would be publicly conspicuous. Better, and safer, to hide his counter-countercultural sentiments behind the velleities and convolutions of his last book of literary criticism, *Sincerity and Authenticity*, or the inaugural Thomas Jefferson Lecture, "Mind in the Modern World" (both 1972).[38] He was against the right things – the insanity defense for "geniuses," quota systems in admissions – but few could tell, and almost no one cared.

During a symposium, "Culture and the Present Moment," sponsored by *Commentary* and the Rockefeller Foundation in December 1974 (less than a year before Trilling's death), Podhoretz observed that if intellectuals didn't speak up in defense of their own values *as* intellectuals, they shouldn't be surprised if no one else did. Why, from the late sixties on, this "failure of nerve"? For him, the answer was moral: "There was an epidemic of cowardice, together with an enormous panic to get on the right side of what looked like a triumphant revolution." Podhoretz was speaking broadly, but Trilling evidently took the remark as referring to himself. "There is a reason to say cowardice in individual cases," he said, "but as a general explanation of the situation Norman Podhoretz refers to I think the word 'cowardice' might lead us astray." Better words were "fatigue" and "alienation": issues had been "presented in a way that made one's spirits fail. It wasn't that one was afraid to go into it, or afraid of being in opposition – I suppose I am speaking personally – but rather that in looking at the matter one's reaction was likely to be a despairing shrug."

The discussion turned to the subject of the middle class, which for years had heard nothing but indictments of its imputed racism, imperialism, materialism, and so on, and thus had not been able, as Hilton Kramer put it, "to generate any compelling romance about itself that has not involved the repudiation of its own mode of life." Podhoretz remarked: "This is the only ruling class in history" – taking the middle class as "ruling" because it constituted the electoral majority – "that has been unable to co-opt the 'poets,' that has not been celebrated by its artists," but that instead has "subsidize[d] a class of artists who are not only hostile to it but evidently hostile to the death. There has been a war between the life of the middle class and the culture of the middle class," and the upshot has been "a complete undermining of society's sense of itself."

Those passionate words moved Trilling to interject, in what must have been a thin sepulchral voice: "one of the most fascinating occurrences, I think, in the history of the world." But this was too "fatigued," too detached for Podhoretz, who said that

if someone declares war on you and says you are evil, you can either say yes, you're right, do with me what you will, or you can say, maybe I'm not perfect but I'm not going to offer my throat to your knife. You needn't be in possession of an absolute truth in order to defend yourself against assault, especially a murderous assault.[39]

Trilling may have had reasons for feeling that he had outlived his time, but Podhoretz and Kramer still felt very much *in* their time and were eager to carry on the fight.[40] Podhoretz especially would do so in what he understood to be Trilling's own liberal anticommunist shadow. What his teacher had said in the fifties was that America was, in the main, all right. It was a message that needed to be resuscitated following the patch during which the New Left had endeavored to replace reform with revolution. Trilling may have agreed, theoretically, but he disliked the bare-knuckled way Podhoretz waged the battle in the early seventies. With "unmistakable coldness," the latter would recall, "Lionel told me one evening (using the Yiddish word for soiled or besmirched) that Sidney Hook had '*beschmutzed*' his own name by going too far to the Right in his recoil from Communism and that I was in danger of doing the same to myself in my war against the New Left."

A decade before, when Podhoretz was publishing Goodman, Hughes, Lynd, and Riesman, Trilling's worry was that he was "going too far" left.[41] No wonder it proved so difficult for the two men to keep their friendship. But the effort, on both sides, did bear fruit. When Trilling lay dying in the fall of 1975, his conversations with Podhoretz were less about the politics and literature of the present than about those of the past. Podhoretz had been rereading Thomas Mann's *Doctor Faustus*, which he thought superb. Back in the late forties and early fifties, Trilling had downgraded Mann for his too-sympathetic views of communist East Germany. But if, in spite of this, Podhoretz now said Mann might turn out to be the century's greatest novelist, then he would have to reconsider. After Trilling's death, Diana sent his personal copy of Wordsworth's *Lyrical Ballads* to Podhoretz, with "hope [that] it will give you pleasure as a remembrance of your days as a student of Lionel's."[42]

A kind gesture, but her management of her husband's funeral produced a sharp disappointment for Podhoretz. Trilling had all his life been uneasy about his Jewishness. He had been tutored for his bar mitzvah, but he and Diana, who had been given no Jewish education whatsoever, brought up their only child James in a strictly secular fashion. After all, Trilling had declared in the forties that Judaism had never done anything to enrich his own sensibility, or that of any modern writer he could think of. "Once," Podhoretz recalled, "he challenged me to name anything good that had come out of the culture of the eastern European Jewish world. 'You,' I shot back, at which he had the good grace to laugh, if not to be convinced."

This made it all the more poignant that, as the end drew near, Diana asked Podhoretz to instruct James in the recital of the Kaddish, the mourner's prayer.

Podhoretz eagerly agreed – so eagerly that, he realized, Diana in her Freudian way had been quite right to say her husband had been "a surrogate father to me." Just as James was ready to deliver a perfect Kaddish, however, Diana altered course. There was to be nothing Jewish about her husband's funeral, which was held in the Episcopal chapel on the Columbia campus, with Martin Luther's "A Mighty Fortress Is Our God" as the recessional hymn and with no eulogies. Only God, as the Kaddish insists, is above or beyond eulogizing, and though keeping the thought to himself, Podhoretz believed there was something "impious or even blasphemous" in presuming that a literary critic, however eminent, could be beyond or above the Kaddish itself.[43]

George Lichtheim, Pat Moynihan, and a Lecture Tour

Late in 1971, Podhoretz's father died, "expectedly," as he told Jacobson, "in the sense that he had been an invalid from emphysema for a long time, but unexpectedly in the sense that the end came very suddenly of a massive coronary."[1] During all these years he, Midge, and the children had visited his parents in Brooklyn on an almost weekly basis and, with his mother now a widow, such occasions, and often daily phone calls, became even more important.

The older girls, Rachel and Naomi, who were called Decter after their biological father but in every other way were Podhoretz's children, were now young adults. They had reached that stage more or less sound in mind and body because, as they both later admitted, he took his stepfatherly duties seriously. Midge said he "saved" them, indeed, for when countercultural temptations presented themselves – the usual drugs, sex, dropping out – she had initially been inclined to let nature take its course, while he understood that nature sometimes requires resistance and direction. Therefore he set limits, whether with regard to the hour at which the girls were to be back home or with regard to their need to finish homework before going out at all. As Rachel remarked, "They were liberal parents until I started doing certain things, at which point they discovered that they actually *weren't* liberal parents, and didn't want to be."[2]

Neither one, as Naomi remembered, ever got down on the floor to play with the kids; instead, they read them poems and told them stories. They weren't involved in the children's homework, which at the ultraliberal Dalton School lacked rigor anyway, but they somehow managed to teach them all they knew. Having gone through the usual battles with these morally and culturally conservative parents, Rachel and Naomi discovered, in turn, that their moral and cultural instincts were conservative, too. Thus they never, during their adolescent years, did anything remotely as outrageous as what many of their Dalton classmates were doing in the way of promiscuity and self-destruction. The parental resistance produced lots of raised-voice arguments that weren't necessarily followed up by reconciliations and apologies but were informed by lots of love and support. Once Naomi said something like "fuck you" to her mother, who slapped her face. But it stopped there.[3]

Professionally, one of the strongest relationships Podhoretz had through the sixties and into the early seventies was with George Lichtheim. He wasn't a friend the way his coevals Mailer, Morris, Jason Epstein, Thompson, and Moynihan were. Nor was he, like Trilling, a surrogate father and teacher or, like Warshow, an in-the-office elder brother, but he combined their roles. For a short period in the late fifties, when *Commentary* was being jointly edited by Martin Greenberg, Podhoretz, and Lichtheim, the latter passed on a good deal of Warshow-like know-how to his young colleague. From then on, having more worldly experience than Trilling ever did, Lichtheim became, mostly through letters, not a fatherly but an avuncular figure.

He had been born into a well-to-do, thoroughly assimilated Jewish family in Berlin in 1912. His father, Richard, an important Zionist leader, was instrumental during World War I in keeping Turkey from expelling Jews from Palestine, and during World War II, when he worked for the Jewish Agency in Geneva, in apprising the Allies of the Final Solution under way in the Reich. He was also a Kantian antisocialist. George's filial rebellion took the form of embracing a Hegelian-tinted (that is, nonvulgar) Marxist socialism and, what chimed with socialist orthodoxy in his youth, an indifference toward Zionism. The age of nationalisms, after all, was supposed to be over.

But his anti-Zionism was never doctrinaire. Living in Jerusalem in the thirties and working for the *Palestine* (now *Jerusalem*) *Post*, he felt nothing but sympathy for the Jewish settlers trying to make a life in "Palestine as it then was" (later his habitual way of referring to Israel). After World War II, Lichtheim settled in London, where, under the pseudonym of "G. L. Arnold," he made a strong impression as a witty and skeptical political commentator. Thanks to an English governess, his "English was perfect," Podhoretz would recall, "though it was not his native language." "Always depressed" and frequently "abrasive in social situations," he was difficult for many people to like, but Podhoretz and he "got along very well," not just in the late fifties but after.[4]

Lichtheim was convinced that a form of democratic socialism was possible in the United States – its dawn always about a decade distant – and as late as 1972 Podhoretz shared his friend's hopes, though doubting the chances of their ever being realized. It wouldn't have bothered Lichtheim to learn that his divinations were inaccurate. Democratic socialism was, for him, a Hegelian ideal, always worthy of contemplation even when material conditions didn't favor its realization – which they never did.

In the late sixties, Lichtheim resumed an affair with a woman he had known in his youthful Berlin days, but when she died of cancer in 1970, he could think of little besides suicide. Moreover, the economic pressure was so great that he proposed writing a textbook on political theory for Viking, which he hoped would sell 100,000 copies. "I *must* have 12,000 dollars in the next two years," he told Podhoretz, "or I shall have to take the short way out and quit the scene." He also wanted to arrange an intelligently favorable reviewer for his *Europe in the Twentieth Century*, which Praeger had just brought out. The crucial thing was to keep the book out of the hands of "that accursed witch Hannah Arendt, who hates me."[5]

His letters became more desperate: "My insomnia has taken a sudden drastic turn for the worse, so that even with the maximum permissible intake of drugs and alcohol I can only sleep 3–4 hours a night." Then came his first suicide attempt, followed by hospitalization. Podhoretz pleaded with him: "I know that you've been in despair, but I beg you to give the doctors a chance and to give yourself a chance. *Please* hang on for the sake of all of us who love you and need you."[6] During the winter of 1973 he did progress with his history of political thought. But the wolf was at the door, and *Commentary* and Viking combined couldn't provide him with the necessary margin. Returning to London after a visit in Germany with the renowned leftist intellectual Jürgen Habermas – perhaps not the occasion for cheering up – he had reached the end of his tether. "This time it's final," he wrote Podhoretz. "Sorry to have let you down, but the fact is I have written myself out and can do no more. Thank you for all you have [done] for me."[7] John Gross remembered that it was "a totally secular funeral. Nobody said anything. Very eerie feeling: we just hung around, silent, and then drifted away. No discharge of feeling."[8]

Just before Lichtheim's crisis began looming, Podhoretz had been thinking skeptically about the thesis of Alfred Alvarez's *The Savage God*, a study of literary suicides like the poet Sylvia Plath's, which he wanted the British critic Renee Winegarten to review: it was "an opportunity to discuss the question of whether and to what extent the modernist movement in the arts really has been dominated by a suicidal spirit, and if so, whether one ought to take as sympathetic an attitude toward it, and indeed toward suicide itself, as Alvarez does (he evidently sees nothing wrong with suicide and considers opposition to it unenlightened)."[9] Podhoretz knew from experience – and not just from his vision in the spring of 1970 – that there was nothing "enlightened" about self-slaughter. Quite the reverse: it was a terrible sin against the commandment to "choose life," which must simply have added to the sorrow he felt for the brilliant Lichtheim.

Maturing in these years, too, was a friendship, even more personal than professional, with Daniel Patrick Moynihan (1927–2003). Three years older than Podhoretz, the future senator was born in Oklahoma but, from the age of six, had been raised poor in New York City. After serving in the navy (1944–47), he went to Tufts, where he eventually earned five degrees, and to the London School of Economics, where he had a Fulbright.

Leonard Garment, who worked as Nixon's attorney during the Watergate affair and later with Moynihan at the United Nations, has given these dry facts a tang: the Irish boy's East Harlem, he said, wasn't quite as impoverished as Podhoretz's Brownsville, which was a "rag-picker neighborhood," but it was poor enough. Moynihan's father, a journalist, was a "boozer" who simply absconded, but he and his brother had the protection of their mother, "a strong woman." He grew up fast in an Irish neighborhood – "they got the language, they got the songs, a bardic family, steeped in politics, and he's picking up politics the way Gershwin picked up music on the street." This smart, determined, eventually six-foot-five young American was "a stammerer" who, in England, "figures out – because he's so smart – that he's kind of beautiful. He loves language and he's Irish, he has a sense of theater, so he imitates the upper classes, and converts a stammer into a style." This, incidentally, has been said of Henry James, another Irish-American who imitated the English upper classes and had a sense of theater. Moynihan's theater would be political. It didn't "happen overnight," but he became, in Garment's words, "kind of the American Parnell," managing his own "entrances" and "exits."[10]

There were several academic gigs along the way, but the political ones included the jobs of secretary to New York Governor Averell Harriman in the mid-fifties and Assistant Secretary of Labor to Kennedy and Johnson, helping formulate policy in the latter's war on poverty (we have noted how the New Left willfully misrepresented his report on the black family); an unsuccessful run for the presidency of the New York City Council; and by 1968 a post as Nixon's adviser on urban affairs. His memo indicating that in racial matters the country could use some cooling off, what he called "a period of benign neglect," gave the language an enduring phrase and the Left another idea to misconstrue. He didn't mean that the government should ignore the problems of the blacks; he meant that some of Nixon's positions, against busing for example, were playing into the hands of New Politics demagogues, and for a time, therefore, it might be better to emphasize other problems, other programs.

When Moynihan first read Podhoretz's "My Negro Problem" – "it is to your honor that you wrote that article" – he recognized a deep affinity: "I did not quite grow up in the same neighborhood as you, but I went to school in one such – East Harlem. I have a headful of scars to prove it."[11] The two soon became bantering drinking buddies. Aside from that, Moynihan was contributing to Podhoretz's magazine, his earliest pieces revealing the ways ethnicity affected politics in New York City. He went on to study the workings of ethnicity throughout America and, years later, in the Soviet Union. As Glazer would observe, Moynihan was one of the few intellectuals in the West to foresee ethnicity's role in the breakup of that empire.[12]

The ethnic differences between Podhoretz and Moynihan dwindled to nothing compared with their affinities of class and temperament. Their families would spend weeks with each other during summers in Delaware County, the teenage Rachel nannying Pat and Liz's children. In the public world, Moynihan's attempts to defend traditional liberalism were likewise in harmony with Podhoretz's. First he was reminding the heads of Tufts and Harvard that their mission ought to remain that of disinterested inquiry, not of partisan shutdown of debate;[13] then he was reminding academic intellectuals generally that the real world was a complicated place. Those intellectuals, he wrote Podhoretz, were "quite right that Glazer and I have been in government and nothing is more obvious than that they have not. They have a conspiracy theory of the national government which sometimes precludes serious discussion. They are in Plato's cave"[14] – that is, under the illusion that, for example, a society could go directly from the wish to have blacks enter the American mainstream to its realization. The only way would be by zig and zag, three steps forward and two back, not least because different groups with different resources and different aptitudes and interests were intensely competing with one another.

In the spring of 1973, Moynihan was in New Delhi as American ambassador to India, whence he wrote Ben Wattenberg that should "the Big Fellow," Podhoretz, "ever [have] a mind to visit... an elephant awaits him. This is nothing symbolic, merely a matter of logistics. If you come, there will be a donkey on hand" – Wattenberg having voted for McGovern.[15] The Big Fellow would soon have to sell his Delaware County farm, and from India Moynihan's response was splendidly light-of-touch and, with its offer of "'our place' for the summer," warmly generous.[16]

Intuitively, Moynihan knew "exactly what you did and why you did it" – the dropping of the book on the sixties, the return of the publisher's advance, and so on. "It seemed to me the pressures on your thinking were fierce to the point of being intolerable, and in opposing directions. The brain, if you will, was working too well. And so on to something else" – the "Issues" editorials had been a good start, and perhaps another kind of book would occur to him by and by. "In the meantime you have helped to raise the price of land in Delaware County by an order of magnitude, a science way of saying times ten. You may be sure this will be taken into account," he went on with patent irony, "when you next come up looking for a bit of choice acreage, of which, as you know, I have an ample supply."

In New Delhi, far away from a Washington administration that, in its Watergate paranoia, seemed "[t]he obverse, if you will, of our fancy friends who blow up university laboratories because the government is fascist and bombs Vietnam,"[17] Moynihan rejoiced to learn that Podhoretz would soon be visiting. The United States Information Agency (USIA) was sending him on a circuit of Asian and Australian cities to talk about the conditions of American culture. His official profile quoted the *Times Book Review*'s characterization of him as "the intellectual's intellectual... who not only helped to put Jewish writing squarely on the map of American literature, but also, for a season or more, threatened to push almost everything else off it."[18] New Delhi would indeed have to bring out an elephant or two. "We would adore to see you," Moynihan wrote. Besides, "It is America time out here... and relations with the United States are noticeably on the mend."[19]

The gist of Podhoretz's USIA talk, as he told Moynihan, was "that the governing elites of the country, both liberal and conservative, are... in deep trouble, but that the American people are in most essential respects in a stronger and healthier condition than they were in the early 60's." This analysis was in line with the CDM platform and the "Issues" pieces he had been writing. "I then conclude by blaming the crisis of the elites on their insufficient regard for the wishes and feelings of the people they presume to lead." Though the State Department had invited Decter to accompany her husband, she, for job and family reasons, was staying home. This would disappoint the Moynihans, but something else would tickle their spirits: Podhoretz announced, with all insouciance, that he had given up trying to conceal his baldness. "The thought of traveling to the Far East with a hair dryer and a month's supply of Alberto VO-5 hair spray was too much to bear. . . . There are, inevitably, those who say that I now look like John Ehrlichman, but that, believe me, is a small enough price to pay for a true liberation."[20]

The USIA trip, lasting roughly five weeks from late August to early October, freed him from the desk at *Commentary*, from New York, and from the United States itself, and introduced him to subcontinental and Pacific Rim countries he had never seen before. Also, it gave him occasion, for the only time in his life, to keep a diary. Written in the form of letters to Midge, it provides an invaluable account of his quotidian impressions and reflections. What follows are a few highlights.

Briefed in Washington before the trip, Podhoretz was struck by the unexpectedly "sharp youngish types" at the State Department, intelligent but somehow inbred. There was a certain pathos in a foreign service career, rather like in the universities. Decline of empire was the cause. Podhoretz had given his roadshow talk the sensational title "Is America Falling Apart?"[21] The State Department officers were "all nervous about the country. 'Is it falling apart?' they ask, pretending to be joking. They aren't joking."

Seeing the Wheldons very briefly in London, Podhoretz blessed Huw for persuading him to "leave a suitcase there and consolidate my stuff into 2 bags after having seen me struggle like a comic figure through London airport trying to manage 3 bags and a briefcase."[22] Then, on the plane to New Delhi, he scribbled away:

Doze, keep to myself, aggressively avoiding conversation with an American Turk drumming his fingers all the way. (What is he doing in first class?) Read Gandhi's Autobiography, unable finally to prevent myself from skipping, partly because it's dull and partly because I have decided irrevocably to finish before arriving in India. The book – or rather Gandhi – isn't as loathsome to me as I had expected it and him to be. In my present mood, in fact, there is a secret appeal – not so secret really – in the idea of renunciation. . . . Mostly I find Gandhi tiresome and I am mystified by his – what? – charisma, his success in moving multitudes. He is so unappetizing, so un-humble . . . so *Victorian* in the worst sense.

Upon landing, he was met by Moynihan himself on the tarmac, without the "40 elephants" that Kozodoy had wryly fancied but with a cohort of officials and, for protection against Arab terrorists, a bodyguard.

Moynihan's mood was "decidedly choleric, with a touch of melancholy mixed in," Podhoretz wrote, but the ambassadorial residence was all "grandeur . . . pomp and *rank*," which would once "have filled me with wonder"

but now "I'm too old, I've been around too much...and anyway Pat's attitude won't permit gushing." The gloom of Watergate was affecting everyone,
including the Glazers, who happened to be visiting, and Podhoretz was beginning "to wonder whether I was after all a fool for coming on this trip: who
needed to be unhappy someplace else, *with* someone else?"[23] The cure was
talk, which flowed from him as it "almost always do[es] in Pat's presence."
At this point he candidly stepped back: "Is it this I've been missing and being
depressed as a result – an admiring audience for my performances? Is that *really*
why I gave up the ['Issues'] column – because it wasn't being admired enough?
I fear it may be so."

In the city's teeming marketplace, all the squalor that distressed him in
Mexico or Puerto Rico suddenly seemed attractive –

the real thing somehow. What did God have in mind? What *does* God have in mind?
The same question that used to pop into my head in seeing nature films or Africa films.
All those species – what are they there for? All these people – what are [they] there
for? How do they stand it and why?...What goes on behind those mysterious faces
which are so much more various than I had imagined Indians to be: there are, it seems,
a hundred different races here and colors as well as creeds. I begin, reluctantly, and
with great surprise, to feel the pull of this place, including (or especially?) the pull of its
horror.

He had a similar reaction to Calcutta, for which he felt

love...almost at first sight....[T]his is what 18th-century or 19th-century London
must have been like, down to and including the poverty and the filth, and like Johnson's
or Dickens's London it speaks not of death but of life....It teaches that so much of
what horrifies me – disease and starvation and extreme discomfort – and terrifies me is
endurable, possibly even by me, "no more than e'en a man."

He gave the "Is America Falling Apart?" lecture to resident journalists,
academics, bureaucrats, and students. In Delhi, he had a standing-room-only
audience of more than three hundred and was elated by Liz Moynihan's saying

that I'm not only the smartest guy around but the most confident....It goes very
well indeed, including many laughs from my interpolations. I have them, it's a triumph....Thank God!...I am wet when it's over but glowing as I always do when
I'm a hit. Indians present me with thanks and with books....A lady has written a
novel – she is Jewish (B'nai Israel). She will send me the manuscript. Why not? Sure. I
am all smiles and willingness and benignity.

The Delhi audience "asked me to talk about minorities in [the] US and then
asked me a lot of questions about 'Zionist' influence on US policy in 'West
Asia,' as they call it. The questions were all hostile to Israel, but they listened
very courteously to my answers."

On to Australia, where it was gratifying to discover that "I'm a
celebrity...no doubt about it....But I'm not altogether pleased at being in
the hands of this crowd." About his going-native enthusiasm for Calcutta,
his hosts "respond with bewilderment or they think it's a put-on or they are

offended. [A] bossy kike lawyer even told me that I ought to take this problem to my psychiatrist." But neither are the local intellectuals enamored of
their own country. "Much Australian self-hatred in evidence here – to speak
of Australian politics, everyone says, is to 'descend into buffoonery.'"

It was pleasant for Podhoretz to discover that he could still dazzle, but he
was a writer, not a dinner-party raconteur. The strain of lecturing, discussing,
convivializing, and sheer moving around was starting to tell. "I *like* being busy
and in demand; it pleases me (the great executive fantasy), but I may have to
slow down if I don't want to get sick or something. (Please God, don't let me
get sick.) . . . I have just to my utter astonishment burst into tears. Why am I so
keyed up? I can't even sit still this morning, let alone rest."

One reason for this friable state of mind was the anxiety he felt about
Maxwell Newton, his randy, Esau-like friend from Cambridge days who had
gone into economics. "Is he all right?" When Podhoretz asked about him at
parties, people gave him cold if polite stares. Finally, Sam Lipski, a reporter
and editor in Melbourne, called to explain, reassuringly, that people disliked
Newton because "he's . . . a wild man. Also he's now publishing a Sunday 'tits
and bottom paper' which is doing well financially. Also he has called the new
Labor Government the 'Black Panther government.'" At this last, Podhoretz
felt "much relieved and delighted."

Podhoretz had no difficulty, during questions after his Sydney lecture,
responding to "a hippie girl who wants to know about Angela Davis and
black political prisoners, and a middle-aged Jewish (naturally) Stalinist who
delivers himself of an incoherent diatribe against America and against me and
gets some applause." But next morning he was vexed that the *Australian* didn't
cover the lecture, while the *Australian Jewish Times* called for an interview. He
hadn't come to this country just to discuss Jewish concerns. But the dynamic
was inescapable: the Jews paid attention to him, and he returned the favor. At
a dinner party *chez* Lipski, he was

struck, even flabbergasted, once again by how much the children of East European
Jews resemble one another no matter what country they grew up in. Just as [the South
Africans] Aaron [Klug] and Dan [Jacobson] seemed mysteriously kin to me 20 years ago
in Cambridge, these two Melbourne Jews do (they even read *Partisan Review* when they
were younger!). There is no theory of culture that accounts satisfactorily for this. . . . O
the Jews, what is one to do with them, everywhere the same.

At last he met with Newton. Alcoholic and overweight, "almost gross,"
divorced and living with a younger woman, he was a cautionary figure. Two
weeks before, after a bender, "he made a suicide attempt" and did it, Podhoretz realized with a shock, in the very hotel room in which he was then
staying. Reciting the Alcoholics Anonymous rhetoric Newton had been hearing – "You're a coward" not to face life's problems one at a time; you're trying
to escape through booze; "For you, it's either AA or amen" – Podhoretz admitted to himself that it sounded familiar. "Am *I* an alcoholic?" he wondered.
He had been on the wagon for more than three years, ever since the epiphanic
vernal solstice of 1970. But so what if Newton was an alcoholic?

Sitting listening to Newton, Podhoretz said, "my love for him comes back." It was clear, however, that abstaining from drink would for Newton be only a first step, for inside all was dark. His "tits and bottom paper" was, he confessed, vulgar, but he rationalized it by declaring that "serious papers are dead, and the only thing left is the newspaper and entertainment." Podhoretz couldn't help wondering if "the whole enterprise isn't an expression of self-hatred. After all, a few years ago, he was an influence in Australian politics and something of a power in the land."

What would it be like *truly* to be a power in the land? The question wasn't far from the reading Podhoretz did on the plane – Gandhi's *Autobiography* on the way to India, and now, between Sydney and Bali, André Malraux's *Anti-Memoirs*. Apropos of Malraux meeting Nehru in Delhi, where they had talked of their respective prison experiences, Podhoretz ruminated: "Nehru spent *13* years in jail! They deserve their majesty, these revolutionary leaders, having purchased it with so much suffering. Malraux says that the French ambassador, listening to their private reminiscences, began to feel ashamed that he had never even been taken to a police station. Me too, I'm afraid."

Podhoretz's mind was never far from relations with position-taking friends and ex-friends back home. Kozodoy had sent a clipping about Hellman, and

earlier in the day, swimming, I think of Lillian and Mailer . . . they so often go together as symbols of my self-pitying lot (come to think of it, I first met Mailer in Lillian's house). Am I turning into a disappointed man? Once Lillian called Louis Kronenberger that, and the sound of it chilled my blood. With good reason, I see all too clearly now. I reflect (still swimming in the buoyant water) that the lust for association with celebrities is still powerfully present in me and I wish I could overcome it. I have bad values, stemming from impure hungers. If Gandhi is to be believed, renunciation is the way to overcome such values and such hungers, but I think he was wrong. Malraux writes about his own contact with the great in a tone I would give anything to command; but then he is himself great and the great men he meets acknowledge him as their peer. ("So, you're a minister now," Nehru says to him in Delhi, having last seen him in Paris 20 years earlier.) I think of Pat in this connection and the thought is both comforting and disturbing. What *am* I [to] do with this business?

These are revealing statements. A man of extraordinary talent naturally wants to associate with and measure himself against other people of extraordinary talent, but the first desire is "impure" and the second ultimately frustrating – for who is to certify the *most* extraordinary talent? "Am I turning into a disappointed man?" To avoid that "chilling" fate, Podhoretz could, Gandhi-like, renounce hopes and projects altogether. But of course Gandhi himself had done no such thing. Malraux had the right idea: it was to use his talent in a way that would fulfill him.

Not by becoming a minister, however: Moynihan was the man for that sort of role. Could Podhoretz's vocation, not for the absorption of reflected glory but for the advancement of liberal democracy, be to use his pen to further his friend's career? That, mutatis mutandis, would be to play Malraux – "I am still impressed with him" – to Moynihan's de Gaulle. Few people figure out their vocation in the blink of an eye. Even Podhoretz's epiphany hadn't told him what exactly to *do*. But during this vacation from business, "still swimming in the buoyant water," he was understanding, not for the first time but more deeply, his calling.

In Jakarta, Indonesia, Podhoretz had the opportunity to see the effects of a moderately repressive dictatorship on intellectual life. Since Suharto's coup in 1967, it had been illegal to teach Marxism in the universities. Predictably, that ideology now had an exotic appeal: "I even give myself a *frisson* when I casually mention the Leninist theory of imperialism. Some of these kids may never, for all I know, have even *heard* of Lenin, or may know of him as a dim and distant figure of evil (like St. Paul, say, to me when I was a kid)." Press freedoms were also restricted, "but the editors to whom I talk seem quite cheerful about it. They even joke about spies in their midst. I find myself unable to imagine what their situation is really like – partly because this place doesn't have the *feel* of political fear about it. But then again, how would I know, knowing only the 'fear' caused by an Agnew (!) at first hand?"

At lunch in the embassy he was refreshed to meet a "Chinese lady sociologist [who] expresses indignation when I tell the ambassador that a lunch like this – men without their wives – could no longer be held in New York. 'That's regression, not progress,' she says, 'Why should the wives wish to be invited if they have no connection with the event? They should have more self-respect than that if they wish to be liberated.' No wonder she admires Midge" about whom he later cracked: "I agree with my wife about everything; that's how liberated *I* am."

Mainly, however, Podhoretz felt he was part of a beleaguered minority, even east of Suez. Lunching with half a dozen members of the English department at Singapore University, he found "all of them *very* au courant with everything lit'ry, and all of them nice. But . . . I keep encountering *resistance* in this place from liberal elitists when I would have thought the opposite would be the case." More of the same followed his lecture, "this time from a professor (also educated in America) who 'without offense' compares my ideas to George Wallace. I might just as well have stood in New York."

Meeting with students, professors, and journalists in Singapore and Kuala Lumpur and reading Barbara Tuchman's *Stilwell and the American Experience in China*, he found himself "wondering how anyone can now look with equanimity at the situation in Asia, with Japan moving toward the realization of a 'Co-Prosperity Sphere' after all – not through the sword but through the Sony – and with China and North Vietnam looming up there, biding their time (and in the case of Hanoi not biding their time at all, but being rather aggressive)." The American influence that was getting through to the Malaysians was the wrong kind. The student leaders he met with in Penang

turn out to be the local variant of SDS, complete with Angela Davis posters, YSA [Young Socialist Alliance] publications, and admiring talk about Jane Fonda. But thanks to repression, they are much more mannerly and nicer than their American counterparts used to be (and in addition to repression, backwardness also helps). They call themselves socialists and even (very quietly) revolutionaries, but actually they have the air of mischievous, naughty children.

Most of the naughty children "take my teasing good-naturedly, if with a certain puzzlement (as when I tell them, drinking coke, that the universal popularity of Coca-Cola is a definitive refutation of the theory of cultural relativism). They don't quite know what to make of me. I know what to make of *them*, however: they are sad and sweet and pathetic – so far." The worry was that they might become adult Pol Pots.

There was a brief stop in Hong Kong, where he met Liz Moynihan and her son John. Pat was being offered the job of Assistant Secretary of State, which to Podhoretz's relief he decided not to take, conceivably because he had no need of closer affiliation with the Nixon White House. Podhoretz went on to Tokyo, where he was met by Midge. She thought the Japanese were "empty inside, without an inhibiting culture (unlike the Chinese): their famous culture is, she says, willed." How "inhibiting," how self-regulating, was American culture? In that time of Watergate and the slow dissolve of the war in Vietnam, it was a central question.

Everything was put on hold, however, by the news that broke while Podhoretz was in Seoul on October 7th: war had again erupted in the Middle East. He wanted to go home at once, "But I am trapped and all I can do is have a good cry in the shower. . . . I am beginning to get headaches again: nerves, fatigue, irritability nerves. Home is very far away." Reliable news about the Yom Kippur War was hard to come by, but Podhoretz could already sense from early reports that Israeli casualties were frighteningly high.[24] "I want to get home, quite as though the war were in N.Y. and I a potential soldier." As the return was only days away, he read through the newest *Commentary*, realizing once more that "*My line from now on must be elitist in culture, anti-elitist in politics.*"

The issue included Walter Berns's remarkable "Thinking about the City," which touched on "the cultural price to be paid for democracy." It had been a theme of Podhoretz's talks during this USIA tour, when, as he summarized in his diary, he had argued

that our political, social, and economic systems were rare and precious historical achievements, but that our culture was shallow. This used to be understood about America in the 19th century, but lately the country has been attacked most ferociously on its strongest points rather than on its weakest – no doubt because to attack the culture is to attack those who *make* the culture – i.e. the intellectuals. And so we come back again to the *Commentary-New York Review* split: they concentrating their fire on the polity, we on the culture, including of course its political ideas and pretensions.[25]

If Podhoretz couldn't personally fight in Israel's war against its invading Arab neighbors, he could fight in what amounted to a culture-and-politics war in America.

Domesticities, Lillian Hellman, and the Question of America's Nerve

Starting in what Decter called "the blue period" following the slamming of *Making It*, Podhoretz turned listening to music into a daily meditative ritual, a means both of learning the classical tradition and of settling his soul.[1] In 1974, he offered Rachel and Naomi, who were in Israel, a facetious depiction of his audiophilia. He had a new stereo system,

which, I need hardly say, was both chosen and hooked up by Neal [Kozodoy] It's literally like an addiction: [the record store] Sam Goody, the connection, feeds my habit and I use the needle for a fix every morning and then late into the night. . . . I am slowly driving everyone crazy, especially John, who wonders and wails about: 1) when he's going to get his father back; 2) when he'll ever get to watch the color television set again; 3) whether I will ever go to the movies with him again. Little does he know how much I am suffering, caught helplessly in a compulsion, a gluttony no less ferocious (indeed more ferocious) for being spiritual.

With an ironic shrug, he added that the girls' mother would pass along "news concerning trivial matters like births and deaths."[2]

We get another view of the Podhoretz apartment that autumn. Kozodoy had installed speakers in the bedroom so that Norman, as Midge wrote the Wheldons, could listen to his "infernal Mahler and Bruckner and Wagner" without disturbing the rest of the family. This speaker system was to be thanked for getting him through Midge's widowed father's wedding, the ceremony being held "in a small Manhattan synagogue" and followed by a breakfast at home. Her father showed the family "the disarming discourtesy of being most boyishly happy and silly," while "Norman, who cannot abide my father but has in the past few years learned to make zombie-like gestures of filial dutifulness toward him, turned up the volume of his stereophonic speakers and sailed through, pausing now and then to bestow tender smiles and administer stern and helpful scoldings to his irrational wife." This wedding evidently also sent Podhoretz's own mother, "who has lately been secretly – it is anyway a secret from her – much agitated over the whole question of remarriage, . . . into a great slump."

As for the children, John was in one of those "only in America" high-school courses on film as history, which meant he could go to the movies "proclaiming in tones of odious self-righteousness that he is *doing his homework*." He was eager to take over Ruthie's room when, the next year, she would go off at seventeen to the University of Chicago. Naomi was home from Israel, looking for a job – she soon found one in the letters-from-readers department at *Newsweek* – and prepared to move out when she could, while Rachel, still playing "Mother Earth on her kibbutz," had a certifiably serious beau whom she had met there, a "swarthy Tunisian" (as Podhoretz said) whose name was Moshe Mark.

In the summer of 1975, she brought the young man to New York as her fiancé. As Midge wrote to Jacqueline, he was determined "to support Rachel in her own country," but his credentials as "a skilled citrus farmer, cotton grower, and tankist" weren't likely to put him "at the head of the line of essential manpower in N.Y.C." He was "beautiful and charming – in fact, delicious – also stubborn, determined, manly, and intelligent.... Norman is more or less edgy and suspicious, but I do believe that I'm the only one who sees it. He has even fooled beady-eyed Rachel into imagining that his attitude is actually welcoming."[3]

The wedding took place on Labor Day in the Podhoretz apartment before some sixty or seventy guests. The couple were happy, though unsure where they would live or how they would earn a living. As for Norman, he was, Midge wrote, "suffering from a certain mysterious malaise to which he can affix neither name nor explanation"[4] – though we can guess it was along the lines of wondering what this girl, for all intents his daughter, thought she was *doing*.

The Wheldons were, as always, sympathetic correspondents. In August 1974, Jacqueline wrote Midge of Moynihan's having visited them in London, their talk all "about America and the Podhoretzes and *Commentary*." Now done with his ambassadorial stint in India and heading back to Harvard, Moynihan admitted "that he did not 'relish teaching the American young for the next twenty years.'" Podhoretz and *Commentary*, on the other hand, represented a reason for hope. "Pat once said that Norman had single-handed effected a change in America's political consciousness," and Dan Jacobson, whom by chance the Wheldons had recently met while touring North Wales, "elaborated on the absolutely heroic qualities that had gone into this . . . and spoke of the cost paid up in all those things that you and Norman hold dear in life – friendship and sociability."

Jacqueline was concerned for Huw, however. What was he "going to do when he retires in two years time"?[5] It seemed too early for any of these people to be looking past their middle, and possibly most productive, years. But then the radical children Decter wrote about – "the Youngs" – were perhaps making the middle-aged feel old, as when the Wheldons had a nephew descend upon them, fresh with "a new set of values" after three years in Australia and "with someone's wife (aged 19) and someone's baby (Violet)" to boot.[6]

Jacqueline's second, impossible novel had grown to two volumes. Sent sections to read, Podhoretz initially was "overwhelmed by the *seriousness* of this work, the depths out of which it comes, the resonances it strikes, its incandescent language, the patience and faith implicit in its pacing and (yes) in its length, the sheer Godliness of it all." But the incandescence lay in particular passages, and though she was stitching them together, the whole simply didn't cohere. While he tried to explain this to her, the "angelic" Decter encouraged her to keep at it – the thing could be cut and compressed when it had to be[7] – but alas the monster opus would never be finished. Nor, after Jacqueline's death, could its parts be melded by Jacobson or others who sympathetically tried to do so.

None of this meant that she wasn't a remarkably effective mother for her girls, Sian and Megan, or for Wynn, whom she was coaching through school. "Jay is doing chemistry," Huw wrote Norman. "It would be far better if Wynn did it, seeing that it is he who is said to be poor at it."[8] Meanwhile, John Podhoretz, a ninth-grader, rather wished Jacqueline were nearby to help with *his* homework (the bits outside the movie theater anyway). He had a crush on her, "the most warmhearted, tender and loving person I know,"[9] and he read *Mrs. Bratbe's August Picnic* with an enthusiasm he had earlier felt only for *Jane Eyre* or for his own mother's works. "*Liberal Parents, Radical Children* is the most painful book!" he told Jacqueline. "Twice, at the end of 'The Dropout' [section], and at the end of 'A Letter to the Young,' I have broken out into tears. May God In Heaven prevent the 60s phenomena from coming back again!"[10] He couldn't wait for November, when the Wheldons would be visiting: "We are so unfortunate all the time when you aren't here, and that can be a drag...so come more often! Live here, even."[11]

Huw would be eager to leave England for a spell, what with the new distractions of a television-and-book collaboration with J. H. Plumb about the Royal art collections[12] and his duties as Chairman of the London School of Economics. He wrote Midge about accommodations:

If you and Norman are away we shall stay in some stately hotel and put eau de cologne on our ear-lobes before eating breakfast in the crisp November sunshine. If, however, you are about, could we perhaps stay at least part of the time with you? We are both of us very much against turfing poor Johnny out of his room once more. How about one of the bathrooms? Jay is forever talking about camping.[13]

The camping seems to have gone off swimmingly, and the next month Jacqueline sent the Podhoretzes Christmas gifts, which, being Jewish, they "won't of course like," and "to increase your distaste it comes with LOVE and DEVOTION." For Norman, she had chosen a "plaid" vest – "the Podhoretz-clan tartan" – which, she teased, would "look so very svelte" on him.[14]

He could directly tease her back, for she was now Lady Wheldon. At the beginning of 1976, Huw became Sir Huw, knighted for his services to British broadcasting and culture. Jacqueline's vulgar expressions of "love and devotion" attached to the Christmas present, Podhoretz mock-archly wrote, merely confirm one's suspicions that your presently high station has been reached only after an unimaginably strenuous climb from the nether regions of Fulham, or some such place. This suspicion is further strengthened by your evident belief that a person of my sober and exquisitely muted tastes would so far forget himself as to be seen in public in a luridly embroidered garment fit only for the ostentatious likes of Sir Huw, or even of Ambassador Moynihan.[15]

Later that year, though, the time for jokes was over. In the summer, Huw had an "infected wound," which began to manifest the cancer that would eventually kill him. "Apart from the pain," Jacqueline wrote, there was "deep in him, I know, . . . fear and a great bundle of grief. It's nothing to do with losing courage or patience, it's far deeper and primeval." Jacqueline herself was devastated, unable to distinguish the big shocks from the "small ones – they are getting to be all the same enormous size." As her husband's appearance became, in the hospital, "terrible . . . more and more unrecognisable," she seemed to grow "dumb, sitting about trying to remind him gently by simply being there that there is this other world" made up of people who weren't on the ward.[16] "Undoubtedly," she added, "it is Norman he will need at the point where he has to, and is able to, express what has happened to him and he is going to get to terms with the next great hurdle. How he is going to live."

Though his final decline had begun, Huw would live on for another ten years, and by October, ready for discharge, he could devote himself to worrying about Jacqueline. On a weekend visit to the hospital, he told Norman, she "convalesced while I walked about like an energetic peacock." By November, Huw was home and back at work, though still unable to confront the "podhorean analysis of how and why it was that the devil made entry upon me" – doubtless an application of the "clairvoyant" analysis that Podhoretz still had a knack for.[17]

For Lillian Hellman (1905–84), an important figure for a period of Podhoretz's life, a condensed summary must suffice. He met her at a Trilling party in 1957. Since the Trillings were well known for their anticommunism and disdain for middlebrow culture, Hellman's presence – she was an unreconstructed Stalinist and the author of middlebrow plays – was unexpected. As Diana explained to Podhoretz the next day, the overture had come from Hellman, who seemed to want to resume an acquaintanceship going back to the twenties.

Friendship between her and the Trillings was out of the question, but not between her and Podhoretz. He was too young to mind her being a Stalinist, a term that by the late fifties designated not so much an actual follower of the murderous dictator who after Lenin's death in 1924 took over the leadership of the communist movement as any sort of Communist Party member or fellow-traveling true believer. In the Brownsville of Podhoretz's childhood, "Uncle Joe" Stalin had been "our dear ally" in the war against Nazism, and the boy hadn't thought twice when a leftist teacher urged him to submit his "epic poem" on Stalingrad to the magazine published by the American Youth for Democracy, the newly coined name for the Young Communist League. By the time

Podhoretz was lecturing his fellow soldiers in Germany on the background to the Cold War, however, he had become a liberal anticommunist like his teachers at Columbia. He knew about the ruthless suppression in 1921 of the anti-Bolshevik, pro-democracy revolt of sailors and soldiers in the Baltic seaport of Kronstadt; about Stalin's murder of millions of peasants who opposed collectivization of farms in the early thirties; about the show trials of the mid-thirties; about the pact with Hitler from summer 1939 to summer 1941; and about the subversion of East European governments by Moscow's agents on the heels of the conquering Red Army.

But after Khrushchev's 1956 speech admitting Stalin's crimes and the appearance of a "thaw" in the Cold War, to which we have earlier alluded, friendships with people like Hellman, who were now calling themselves "radicals" or "socialists," seemed morally defensible after all.

Besides, she knew how to work on the twenty-seven-year-old Podhoretz's writerly susceptibilities, telling him how struck she was by his *New Yorker* piece on her old friend Nathanael West – "Pep" as she called him – who as the night manager of his father's hotel used to give free rooms to "Dash" Hammett (the detective novelist with whom she would have a decades-long affair), "Sid" Perelman, "Dottie" Parker, and "Bunny" Wilson. As Podhoretz had hoped, she soon invited him and Midge to dinner, which produced the effect of Rahv's party in 1953 all over again, except that Hellman had earned so much money, more in the theater than in Hollywood, that she was able to live in an opulence beyond the dreams of Greenwich Villagers.

From the late fifties through the sixties, Podhoretz found it all "heady . . . exciting . . . fun. But the most fun of all – playful, mischievous, bitchy, earthy, and always up for a laugh – was Lillian herself." She didn't ordinarily like men's wives, but she liked Midge, and they would drop in on each other's apartments for drinks or go to movies together. One Saturday night, after dinner, she brought the director William Wyler over to the Podhoretzes' apartment. Norman and Midge had been "chatting with an obscure young professor of political science from Syracuse," namely "the awestruck" Moynihan, who later exclaimed, "Is *this* how you live in New York?"

But the glamour came with a price. On the one hand, Hellman appeared to regard Podhoretz as a sort of *cavalier servente*, available at all hours "to chaperone her" – and, as he put it, "she managed somehow to let me know that she considered it tacky to plead the feelings or wishes of my wife (in spite of being relatively fond of her) or the needs of my children (whose existence she resolutely ignored) as an excuse for begging off." On the other hand, he had to hide his own demurrers about her literary work – first the well-made plays that never rose above the level of the very "Broadway intellectuals" she enjoyed putting down and then her books of memoirs, *An Unfinished Woman* (1969), *Pentimento* (1973), and *Scoundrel Time* (1976). Her "posturing" prose style – "an imitation of Hammett's imitation of Hemingway, and already so corrupted by affectation and falsity in the original that only a miracle could have rendered it capable of anything genuine at this third remove"[18] – was bad enough, but her "self-serving" accounts of her political activity put Podhoretz in an impossible position.

If he didn't "pretend to admire" the whole show, he risked losing her friendship. And since he wasn't ready for that, he "lied" about the draft of *Unfinished Woman* she had shown him "and told her how good it was." Soon after, when she wanted his reassurance about working up "a certain incident in her life," he urged her to go ahead. The story became "Julia" in *Pentimento*, and she had had reason to hesitate: it transpired that the events hadn't happened to her at all. Muriel Gardiner, a New York psychiatrist, demonstrated that she was "Julia" and that Hellman, whom she never knew, had without attribution appropriated material from her own unpublished memoirs.[19]

Though Mary McCarthy's charge, on the Dick Cavett Show, that "every word [Hellman] writes is a lie, including 'and' and 'the,'" went too far – litigation in Hellman's libel suit for $2.5 million was still going on when she died in 1984 at age seventy-nine – the record shows that in her writing about political matters fiction trumped fact again and again. One source of the problem may have been her willful denial not of her Jewish descent but of the spiritual and cultural connections it ought to have entailed. Her communism required her to rise above ethnic or national particularism, but to Podhoretz it seemed more like an intellectual rationalization of "Jewish anti-Semitism."

Nor, as she placed her faith in the moral purity of radicalism, was this her only form of denial. In *Scoundrel Time*, recalling her testimony before the House Committee on Un-American Activities (popularly scrambled as the House Un-American Activities Committee, or HUAC), she denied, or explained away, the crimes of Lenin, Stalin, and their successors. The "scoundrels" to her certainly weren't the communists who, like her, had gone on defending Stalin, whatever his crimes. Nor, on the other hand, were they even the congressional members of HUAC or McCarthyites generally. Instead, they were ex-communists like the film director Elia Kazan who, sick of Stalin's crimes, gave testimony about party members – "naming names" of former "comrades" – and endeavored to inform the public about the party's dangerous ways and means.

As William Phillips remarked, some of those so-called comrades "*were* Communists and what one was being asked to do was to defend their right to lie about it." It was necessary to say this because, as Glazer noted in his review of *Scoundrel Time* in *Commentary*, younger scholars seemed nearly unanimous in adopting Hellman's line that "cold-war anti-Communism" had led to the double disaster of the war in Vietnam and the election of Nixon, while she, Hammett, and others had been martyred for preferring humanity to anything so narrow as country. That same mind-set dictated Hellman's facile and, to Podhoretz, blasphemous comparison of the long imprisonments, harsh tortures, and bullets in the back of the head suffered by East European dissidents to the "six months Dashiell Hammett spent in jail cleaning bathrooms" or to her own exile from Hollywood spent in good houses on the Upper East Side and Martha's Vineyard.

What she got away with included, during her lifetime, keeping mum about having been a Communist Party member between 1938 and 1940, as she admitted in a posthumously published letter to one of her lawyers.[20] In Podhoretz's opinion, her commitment to communism arose more from "loyalty to Hammett" than from loyalty to the Soviet Union. In any event, like Hammett, she was almost universally absolved of her activities. In 1977, a film was made of "Julia," with Hammett and Hellman played by Jason Robards and Jane Fonda, "the First Lady of the Hollywood radicalism of the sixties." When Hellman was called onstage at the Academy Awards celebration, with fifty million Americans watching, she "received a protracted standing ovation." Her "sins" were washed away "by her sufferings at the hands of the McCarthyite inquisitors" – and so, by extension, Stalin's sins were if not forgiven then that much more forgotten.

Besides, by the eighties, as Podhoretz records, the traditional distinctions between truth and falsehood, fact and fiction, had become passé. Thus,

in a culture in which the old distinction between highbrow and middlebrow hardly retained even a vestigial existence and which was less and less capable of distinguishing between attitudinizing and genuine feeling, her counterfeit writings were accepted as real and valued far beyond their true literary worth; and in an age when the very concept of truth was being deconstructed by jesting critical Pilates and philosophical relativists alike, the self-aggrandizing lies she told about herself and her life were either dismissed as unimportant or justified on grounds of artistic license.

Back in the early seventies, Hellman and Podhoretz had discussed their political disagreements over a roast goose dinner she had prepared in her "grand Park Avenue apartment," but neither could persuade the other. In 1974, he wrote warning her of Edward Grossman's forthcoming review of *Pentimento*: "Things have been awkward enough between us without an unfavorable review of your book appearing in *Commentary*, but there was simply no honorable way for me to reject this piece. Still, I'd rather you got a copy of it directly from me instead of hearing about it from someone else."[21] She replied:

Yes, things are awkward between us. But I want you and Midge to know that I am sorry about that and miss both of you very much. I think maybe you both care more than I do about the awkwardness. Maybe time or any or all of us will change.[22]

That kindly note adds poignancy to Podhoretz's memory of seeing her for the last time, shortly before her death. She was

being carried in the arms of a young man into her building on Park Avenue from a car. The pity of it hit me hard, and I had a powerful impulse to run over and plant a kiss on her forehead. By this point, however, we had become not just estranged friends who retained a lingering fondness for each other but passionate and bitter enemies, and I had long since forfeited the right to make any such tender or affectionate gesture. Besides, I was pretty sure that if I were foolish enough to try, she would have summoned enough strength, even in the moribund condition she was clearly in, to tell me to go fuck myself.[23]

With the winding down of the war in Vietnam, the likeliest flashpoint between democracy and communism seemed to be the Middle East, where in October

1973 Israel had eked out a victory in the Yom Kippur War and where, then and later, the Arab members of the Organization of Petroleum Exporting Countries were using the "oil weapon." Though the Arab states ended the embargo on shipments to America in March 1974, OPEC as a whole quadrupled the price of oil, setting off a panic in the industrialized nations.

In January 1975, Robert W. Tucker, professor of international relations at Johns Hopkins, turned to *Commentary* to put forward a case for American military intervention in the Persian Gulf. His essay jibed with and to some extent reflected Podhoretz's own thinking. Stating a theme that would become commonplace over the next quarter century, Tucker looked to an energy-independent future but insisted that meanwhile America needed to figure out a response to the OPEC stranglehold. Formerly, big states would deploy force when little states threatened their vital interests. Gerald Ford's administration, by contrast, had done nothing except lecture the OPEC countries about destabilizing world markets and propose the sale of arms to Iran and Saudi Arabia for the protection of their "vast underground treasure." Protection against the Western democracies, no less.

Like the Vietnam-weary general public, Tucker observed, the foreign policy establishment wanted to believe there had been "a revolutionary change in the very nature of international society," whereby military force was no longer necessary or even thinkable. An OPEC-precipitated economic depression was making it thinkable, however, and quite possibly necessary. America mustn't follow the European example of "substituting philosophy for policy," telling itself that the West was justly being dished after a "century or more" of exploiting the Middle East. That way lay "quietism" and self-flagellation. It was in the West's vital strategic interest to have access to affordable oil, both in order that existing democracies could remain democratic – by remaining economically productive – and in order that developing countries might *become* democratic and not the helots of Arab rulers.[24]

But, Tucker wrote, the perception of interests and the capacity for winning, though necessary, were not sufficient. A nation had to have the political *will* to win – a will America ultimately lacked in Vietnam. The question, therefore, was whether that lugubrious failure had unmanned the country indefinitely or whether the OPEC crisis, or some other, would prompt the United States to bestir itself.

While it soon became clear that the United States wasn't about to invade the Gulf states, the oil crisis was precipitating some soul-searching among American intellectuals. One indication thereof was "A Failure of Nerve?," the pointed title of a symposium *Commentary* sponsored in the spring of 1975.

Podhoretz's own view was plain: political, cultural, and even business leaders who, with the ascension of John F. Kennedy, had routinely praised America as "on the whole a good society and a desirable model for others to follow" were now inclined not just to bemoan the country's failings but also "to question the legitimacy" of the "industrialized liberal" democratic project in toto. Did this portend, he asked in the editorial introduction, "an adjustment to hopeful new international realities like détente and interdependence; or are we . . . witnessing a resurgence of 'the spirit of Munich'?" Was it a sign, at long last, of American "maturity" or of "a failure of nerve and a loss of political will?"

The sheer variety among the twenty-some participants proves that the magazine could not fairly be charged with suppressing or ignoring dissenting voices. On the left was, for example, the journalist Ronald Steel, with his snide "Relax, *Commentary*. Just because the United States has not bombed or invaded anyone this week does not mean that Western civilization is tottering on the brink of ruin." On the right was the philosophical critic William Barrett, with his image "of the monolith of the Communist states as a single glacier pressing on the West." In the center was the political scientist Stanley Hoffmann, with his image of America, in a complex and multipolar world, like "Gulliver tied, or the biggest fly on the flypaper." For Hoffman there was no choice but to be "a state skillfully maneuvering with other states . . . disconnecting dominoes, discriminating among challenges, and allying ourselves with rather than opposing, defusing rather than defying, foreign nationalisms."

Podhoretz's own position was closest to Barrett's, but the strongest expression of it may have come from Sidney Hook. Whatever the imprudence of the war in Vietnam, and whatever the scurrying of formerly nonaligned countries to "seek some accommodation with the Soviet Union whose tenacity of purpose they do not doubt," we must, said Hook, reject the Munich-style illusions about appeasement bringing "peace in our time." The truth today is what it was in 1938: "Only the will to use American power in defense of freedom can preserve peace." That entailed making it unmistakably evident to the Soviets that containment meant containment.[25]

And that, for Podhoretz, meant a campaign to keep American statesmanship from subsiding into quietism – or what others were calling détente.

"I consider myself a centrist liberal," Podhoretz replied to a correspondent who wondered if he was now "on the Right," "and since I used to be associated with the radical Left, I suppose I *have* moved to the Right as compared with where I once stood. But I wouldn't say that I'm *on* the Right."[26] It was all relative. On the issue of communism, for instance, when in 1976 Podhoretz wrote "Making the World Safe for Communism," his purpose was to remind the post-Vietnam pessimists of the practical differences between liberal democracy and left-wing totalitarianism and to gird their loins in defense of the one against the other. He may not have imagined himself changing the minds of liberal intellectuals (or, for that matter, the minds of many of the liberal leaders of *Commentary*'s sponsoring organization, the American Jewish Committee), but he did hope to make them less complacent.

Other important contributions to this ongoing argument included Moynihan's defense of Woodrow Wilson's pro-democracy foreign policy, titled "Was Woodrow Wilson Right?," and in the following year his application of Wilsonian principles to dealing with a markedly anti-American United Nations ("The United States in Opposition"). Both of these essays, but especially the second, which Podhoretz carved out of a "long and unwieldy" typescript,[27] had an impact beyond the usual circle of academic and public intellectuals.

Most of the intellectuals who had planned and pushed the war in Vietnam, Moynihan wrote in "Was Woodrow Wilson Right?," were now declaring their erstwhile "Wilsonian idealism" to be "synonymous with dangerous nonsense: the prattle of soft and privileged people in a hard and threatening world." As realists like Secretary of State Henry Kissinger disparaged Wilsonianism "for enthusiasm," amoralism was becoming the motif of American foreign policy. We could do better than that. What foreign policy in a hard world needs, Moynihan said, is hard moralizing – i.e., ideals backed by strength, prudently deployed to protect those whose freedom is threatened and to liberate those whose freedom has already been denied. This was a cause that idealists and realists alike should take up: America standing "for liberty, for the expansion of liberty. Anything less risks the contraction of liberty: our own included."[28]

This analysis led directly to "The United States in Opposition," the first essay *Commentary* ever introduced at a press conference. Moynihan's criticism here is directed against his country's "repeated plea of *nolo contendere*" whenever the third world–dominated U.N. General Assembly leveled an indictment against it. The indictment might focus on our environmental and economic sins, on our defense of Israel, or on our "exploitation" of less developed countries (LDCs) generally. The common demands were for self-abasement, which American ambassadors and conference representatives gladly displayed, and a redistribution, if not yet a "looting," of our "vast stores of unethically accumulated wealth," which our too-polite ambassadors and representatives were treating not as a mugging but as a justifiable stipulation.

Instead of supinely allowing themselves to be called cannibals, guilty of figuratively eating "the little children of the Sahel, of Ethiopia, and of Bangladesh," American diplomats, Moynihan stated, should go "*into opposition.*" And, since their accusers invariably wielded the cudgel of a socialist-inspired egalitarianism in cataloging our alleged sins against human decency, American diplomats could begin by stating, as forcefully as necessary, the facts of economic life: (a) that free markets have enabled the capitalist goose to lay a great many golden eggs; (b) that citizens in democratic countries have been able to consume and reinvest those eggs within a system that guarantees the other essential freedoms to think, speak, publish, gather, and worship as they choose; and (c) that those freedoms, material and spiritual, are indivisible.

After all, "nations which have put liberty ahead of equality have ended up doing better by equality than those with the reverse priority." This historical verity should "be shouted to the heavens in the years now upon us. *This is our case. We are* of the liberty party, and it might surprise us what energies might be released were we to unfurl those banners."[29]

Reading this essay in England, Jacqueline Wheldon directly wrote to the Podhoretzes about its "breakthrough" impact: "I was stunned by it. I thought it was breathtaking. It makes things so extraordinarily *clear* – what's happening here, as well as internationally.... It's the kind of thing, you can't help believing, 'something will come of.'"[30]

The something would in fact be Moynihan's appointment as U.S. ambassador to the United Nations.

13

Moynihan, Podhoretz, and "the Party of Liberty"

The offer of the job at the U.N. came from Kissinger. The secretary of state had found Moynihan's *Commentary* article so "staggeringly good" that he "suddenly . . . understood what was going on out there." For a while, at least, Moynihan's thesis galvanized the State Department: instead of "interminably" maundering on "about 'damage limitation,'" it could, like *Commentary*, go on the attack.

Moynihan didn't altogether trust Kissinger. But Kissinger "needed – we needed – some successes," Moynihan would write, and "The United States in Opposition" indicated a strategy for success.[1] Moynihan took the U.N. job in large part because of the urgings of his friends, James Q. Wilson, Kristol, Bell, Podhoretz, and above all Leonard Garment. A partner in the New York law firm Nixon had joined in 1963, Garment (though a Democrat) had worked on his campaign in 1968 and ended up as White House counsel, replacing John Dean, through the Watergate crisis.

Moynihan's "closest friend" during his two years in Washington, Garment was in 1975 back in New York, "saddened but not diminished." Watergate aside, the sadness stemmed from feeling out of place in his old firm and from the agony of his wife's mental breakdown (she finally committed suicide). Offering him a job on staff at the U.N. was Moynihan's way of bringing "Leopold Bloom" – his Joycean nickname for Garment, a Jew who was also, at least in spirit, Irish – back into the political game.[2] In addition, Moynihan would have the aid of Suzanne Weaver, his former teaching assistant at Harvard, who had gone on to teach political science at Yale. She and Garment would later marry.

Our attention to Moynihan may seem out of place in a biography of Norman Podhoretz, but it isn't – for in 1975–76 their personal friendship grew into an intellectual symbiosis of major public import. Liz Moynihan told Garment that, along with Jim Wilson, her husband's colleague at Harvard, Podhoretz was the man he trusted without reservation. In him, Moynihan had found a friend who could edit both the scripts of his essays and the script of his career. They were a stunningly balanced "yin and yang" pair, Garment said, the tall "American Parnell" complemented by the short-in-stature, tough-at-heart "fighter extraordinaire, kid in opposition, the battler compelled by an ambition formed by spirituality – diffuse, Jewish, something – a spectacle very beautiful," going at "orbital speed" and doing "what he had to do. He would have died if he didn't do what he had to do."[3]

In February 1975, at a dinner at the Century Club to mark Podhoretz's fifteenth year as editor, Moynihan himself would recall how he and Podhoretz "had made our way together" since 1961, when Podhoretz published his precocious piece on the Democrats in New York. It had been so remarkable a run that *Commentary* was now, as the *Economist* had said "with just the prudent hedging of a question mark, 'The world's best magazine?'"[4]

The editor of the "world's best magazine" would long afterward refer to Moynihan as his "tiger," who he hoped would rise to offices yet higher than those in Turtle Bay. A tiger among turtles is indeed what Moynihan was during his eight months as ambassador. Podhoretz was the primary source for his maiden speech on September 2, 1975 (the day after Rachel's wedding to Moshe Mark). The ideas were in the vein of "The United States in Opposition." Kissinger had announced America's readiness to build a world "from which starvation would be eliminated and in which everyone would be assured a basic minimum of economic sustenance." But, as Podhoretz wrote to Moynihan, America's readiness didn't derive from a guilty conscience, or a desire to do penance. "We repudiate the charge that we have exploited or plundered other countries, or that our own prosperity has ever rested on any such relation. We are prosperous because we are an energetic and productive people who have lived under a system which has encouraged the development of our productive capacities and energies." And since "we have been reasonably helpful and generous in our economic dealings with other countries," we won't tolerate talk about "reparations," or the "romantic illusion" concerning "poor power." The positive message was that of Wilsonian humanitarianism: "We wish to take whatever effective measures we can to alleviate suffering that can be alleviated and to eliminate such causes of suffering as can be eliminated" (the operative word is "can").

Podhoretz also wanted Moynihan to remind the world that our liberal-democratic principles were grounded in the classics of nineteenth-century English writers like Arnold, Dickens, and Mill. American capitalists "tend to think that they don't have ideas, they are practical men getting on with business, or (when they move into politics) they're pragmatists who take each problem as it comes and deal with it on its individual merits." But, whether they know it or not, our economic system, like our political one, is founded on ideas – better ones than those on offer from the communist and socialist nations. We can win the philosophical war if we stop crying *peccavi* and if, like a certain magazine, we play a little rough.

Podhoretz admitted that his way of putting the case was "too sermonic and hortatory," not to say literary, but he trusted Moynihan's "Irish Catholic conditioning" to find the properly earthy mode of expression.[5] He did find it – and not just in his maiden speech. When an Indian diplomat asked a member of the American delegation if India was being threatened, Moynihan instructed his colleague "to tell the Indian 'Yes.'" Did the Tanzanian government, for its part, regard the American warning as "rude and intimidatory"? Moynihan again said yes: "Let the Tanzanians get their aid from the same capitals from which they got their politics," while the friendly Ivory Coast continued to get its aid from America.[6]

This was to apply ward-heeling political tactics – nakedly using money to influence people's behavior – to foreign affairs. The use of such leverage, instantly comprehensible to other governments, was infinitely healthier than actually joining the LDC and communist war dances against American interests.

On July 9, 1975, Barbara M. White cabled the American Mission a euphoric report on the U.N.-sponsored International Women's Year Conference in Mexico City. Moynihan's initial reaction was happy: the United States could at last get on the side of the LDCs and, under the banner of feminism, pull some of them away from the Soviet lodestone. There were poisoned dregs at the bottom of the cup, however. With Israel and America voting no, the Conference had also called for the "elimination of . . . Zionism, apartheid, [and] racial discrimination." It was what Garment later named "the thing from 20,000 Leagues Below the Sea." He and Weaver told Moynihan that "'this is trouble, Zionism as a form of racism.' And Pat, leaning in, said, 'Well, *isn't* it?'" Knowing next to nothing about the origins of Zionism or the subtler permutations of anti-Semitism, Moynihan didn't, Garment remembered, think it "unreasonable for an ethicist to say that this is a Jewish people just taking the land from Palestinian people and declaring '*you're* not going to come here, *we're* here.'"[7]

Bringing Moynihan up to speed, Garment and Weaver called on their "biggest gun," Podhoretz, more knowledgeable and more intimate with Moynihan than they were, to conduct dinner-table seminars. Podhoretz himself had learned a great deal about the history of the Zionism-as-racism calumny from the English-born Princeton scholar Bernard Lewis and got Moynihan to read him, too. Garment, "though Jewish, was only just getting interested" in Israel, Podhoretz recalled: "What Pat and Len together didn't know could, as the cliché goes, fill an encyclopedia." But they soon caught on, Moynihan in particular being "a quick study, as intelligent a person as you could ever meet in higher walks of life, and he rigorously cross-examined me." He also invited Podhoretz to compose most of the speech, especially the first paragraph, that he would give in the General Assembly when a U.N. resolution defining and denouncing Zionism as "a form of racism and racial discrimination" came up for a vote – and passed.

Giving urgency to these seminars was the pace of events. Idi Amin, the Ugandan president, spoke on October 1 before the Thirtieth General Assembly about Africans' gratitude to the communist countries for assistance in their struggle "to free themselves from the bondage of imperialism, racism and *apartheid*." And just as South Africa had been colonized by the Dutch and the English, he added, so Palestine had been colonized by Jews, the same people who in America "own virtually all the banking institutions, the major manufacturing and processing industries and the major means of communication," and who in support of "the atrocious Zionist movement... have turned the CIA into a murder squad to eliminate any form of just resistance anywhere in the world." He therefore formally demanded "the expulsion of Israel from the United Nations and the extinction of Israel as a State." He was applauded throughout, especially by the forty-six African nations. On the following night, he was honored at a party given by the U.N. Secretary-General Kurt Waldheim, one-time officer in the SA serving in the Balkans, whose wartime record would come under investigation in 1985.[8]

It was a classic gambit: in order to shift attention from his own genocidal campaigns against ethnic minorities in Uganda – the 1974 International Commission of Jurists reported that, since he came to power in 1971, somewhere between 25,000 and 250,000 had been murdered – Amin told reporters that bankruptcy was looming over New York City because the United States was spending a fortune to "send arms to Israel to murder the Arabs." The State Department said nothing. Moynihan, heading for an AFL-CIO conference in San Francisco, decided "It was time to create a crisis."

Labor leaders would see directly how the Soviet Union was once again using the non-aligned countries to target the United States by targeting Israel. He wrote his AFL-CIO speech on the plane, with maximal candor and minimal "diplomacy." The left-wing totalitarian and old- and new-style despotic regimes in the U.N., he observed, outnumbered the democracies five to one, and their persistent attacks on the most powerful democracy, the United States, were motivated by the zero-sum "conviction that their success ultimately depends on our failure." America had to fight back, broadly by supporting trade unions everywhere (the unions having been far more stable and reliable over the past three generations than governments) and narrowly by opposing the call of Idi Amin, "this 'racist murderer'" as a *New York Times* editorial identified him, for the "extinction of Israel as a state."

The tempest Moynihan's speech aroused, notably in its use of the "racist murderer" epithet, was fiercest among African nations. At the U.S. Mission in New York, "career officers" began trying to placate them by separating Amin's "morally offensive" remarks to the General Assembly from those that had "earned wide approval." Moynihan had to tell those officers "that not one goddam thing Amin had said won my 'wide approval.'" Happily, President Ford and the *Times* fully agreed with what Moynihan had said in San Francisco, though this only intensified the African nations' delusion that "Zionists" controlled the big American institutions.

As a refugee from the Nazis' war on the Jews, Kissinger certainly understood that, when it came to attacks on the Jewish state, the very existence of his own people was at risk. Nevertheless, because he had to do the statesman's work of seeking reconcilement between Israel and its Arab enemies, he had compelled himself to see both sides of the dispute. "He *became* neutral," at least intellectually. So wrote Moynihan, who for his part could claim neutrality toward Israel from the very start: "Israel was not *my* religion." And as for Zionism, he "took it to be a kind of Jewish *risorgimento*," an attempt by a people who had lost their original language, as the Irish had lost Gaelic, and had lost control over their original territory, as the Bretons had lost Brittany, to reclaim both. But Moynihan also felt sure that dispossession of Palestinian Arabs had never been part of the Zionist plan.[9]

What the forty Islamic countries now claimed was that Palestine had been "colonized" by European Jews. In addition, the Zionist colonizers had tried to create a state exclusively for the Jewish "race," disadvantaging and often dispossessing the people of other "races" who happened to be around. These charges and others would be incorporated in Resolution 3379, scheduled for discussion and a vote on November 10. In chiseled phrases, Podhoretz formulated Moynihan's rebuttal.[10]

First, Zionism had nothing to do with a "belief in the inherent or natural biological superiority of [their] own racial group to all others," if only because Jews never considered themselves a "race" at all. The notion of the Jews as a race was the invention of nineteenth-century anti-Semites like Houston Stewart Chamberlain (1855–1927), the theorist of the "Aryan" race, and Edouard Drumont (1844–1917), the virulent anti-Dreyfusard – both of whom, in a post-religious age, justified "excluding and persecuting Jews" on eugenic grounds. This secularized anti-Semitism made no sense to Jews for the simple reason that "any person of any racial stock" – think of Ethiopian Jews, for instance – "can be or become a Jew merely by converting to the Jewish religion."

Second, modern Zionism was a *political* movement born in the late nineteenth century, analogous with the German or Italian nationalist movements after 1848, and seeking "self-determination for the Jewish people." Since the founding of the Jewish state in 1948, its courts had consistently addressed the question of "Who Is a Jew?" by referring to religion, not race, and those citizens who weren't Jewish suffered no civil disabilities. It was true that only Jews were conscripted to serve in the armed forces and also that only Jews were privileged under the so-called Law of Return, whereby "any person born of a Jewish mother or [who has] converted to Judaism" possesses "an automatic right to settle in Israel as a citizen." Non-Jews, by contrast, were required to "obtain visas and undergo naturalization," but through a process "about as liberal as those of most Western countries, and considerably more liberal than some (e.g., Switzerland)." The stipulations about the Law of Return needfully "guarantee[d] that the Jewish State would always serve as a refuge for Jews fleeing from anti-Semitic persecution in other countries."

Third, in the Middle East it was the Arabs, not the Jews, who were racist. "In accusing Israel of racism, [the sponsors of the resolution] are utilizing the technique of the Big Lie in the sense of imputing their own sins to an innocent party. In Israel diversity of every kind – religious, ethnic, racial, political – is tolerated and sometimes even encouraged."

Finally, there was something odd about African nations, Muslim or otherwise, imagining the Arabs to be their natural allies. As Lichtheim had pointed out, it was "the Arabs who first introduced African slavery to the world on a large scale beginning in the 7th century." Moreover, "the Arabs evidently considered black Africans as especially fit for slavery, so much so that the Arabic word for slave, *abd*, to this day is used in many Arabic dialects to mean black man." Racist in their view of blacks, Arabs were also racist in their view of Jews – for instance, Egypt under Nasser in 1960 disseminating *The Protocols of the Elders of Zion*, the notoriously anti-Semitic product of Czarist fabricators purporting a Jewish conspiracy to dominate the world; and under Sadat in 1973 "reviv[ing] the medieval blood libel according to which Jews murder Christian children and use their blood in the Passover observances."[11]

These motifs of Arab anti-Semitism would become wearisomely familiar over the ensuing decades. In 1975, however, they were shockingly fresh – ancient but resuscitated – and the Israelis themselves, according to Chaim Herzog, their U.N. ambassador, were unprepared. After all, a nation "born in bloody struggle and surviving by virtue of intense, unceasing vigilance" always had other threats to worry about. As Moynihan would write, Israel "lived like an aircraft carrier in a hostile sea, ready to fight on six or seven minutes' notice," yet here were these torpedoes homing in – not just the Zionism-as-racism resolution but the stand-offishness of the United States, Europe, and Japan, all anxious about their oil supplies and thus reluctant to counter the Arabs' diplomatic maneuvers.[12]

The vote in the General Assembly was as foreseen – seventy in favor, twenty-nine against, with twenty-seven abstentions – after which, in Herzog's words, "the Arabs broke into long and mocking applause; indeed, they seemed on the verge of a war dance." Podhoretz, who was present, would recall how most of the delegates voting *against* the resolution cravenly apologized for doing so. "One after another they marched to the platform to declare that they yielded to no one in their detestation of Israel's crimes"; they were voting against the resolution because it made no practical contribution toward "a 'just' solution," meaning a Palestinian state; they uttered not one "word of moral criticism, let alone censure, of the monstrous lie that was being propagated before their very eyes."[13]

Herzog had instructed his delegation "to show no signs of emotion," but Moynihan was under no such orders. "As our delegation gathered up its papers," Herzog wrote, "Pat Moynihan got up, the blood rushing to his face. He straightened his tie and buttoned his jacket. As he came toward me, I rose to greet him. He took my hand, pulled me to him, and embraced me in front of the entire hall. His gut reaction spoke more than anything else. I was very moved indeed."[14] For what Moynihan said, loud enough for those close by to hear, was pugnaciously succinct: "Fuck 'em!"[15]

Moynihan's own speech began with Podhoretz's ringing sentence, building on the rhetoric of Franklin Roosevelt and Lincoln's most famous orations:

As this day will live in infamy, it behooves those who sought to avert it to declare their thoughts so that historians will know that we fought here, that we were not small in number – not this time – and that while we lost, we fought with full knowledge of what indeed would *be* lost.

And in patent Podhoretzian vein, Moynihan repeated Orwell's lesson in "Politics and the English Language":

The harm will arise first because it will strip from racism the precise and abhorrent meaning that it still precariously holds today. How will the peoples of the world feel about racism, and about the need to struggle against it, when they are told that it is an idea so broad as to include the Jewish national liberation movement?

"Racism" rendered meaningless today, the language of "human rights" rendered meaningless tomorrow.[16]

During these eight months at the U.N., Moynihan's oppositional speeches, let alone his manly demeanor, were stunning. "Nothing like so sustained, and sophisticated, a celebration of America had been heard for years," Podhoretz would remark, "and it elicited a wildly enthusiastic response" – both in the writings of editorialists and columnists and more feelingly in the cheers of cab drivers or the standing applause of diners when Moynihan would enter restaurants throughout the city. Once, "we went to a concert in Carnegie Hall together," Podhoretz recalled, "and the whole place stood up and gave him an ovation." Podhoretz then began to realize "that the long era of self-flagellation and self-hatred through which we had lived since the mid-1960s was finally reaching its end." The huge crowds celebrating the nation's bicentennial offered another sign of remoralization: as the tall ships sailed into the harbor, even liberal New Yorkers "cheered and many wept," such that one seemed to be "witnessing a Freudian 'return of the repressed' that was all the more explosive for having been kept down for so long."[17]

Cooling signs from a less emotional State Department and the far-seeing Kissinger were unmistakable, however, and Moynihan started to feel like Adlai Stevenson in 1962, when the Kennedy White House maneuvered him into resigning as ambassador to the U.N. Not Ford but Kissinger, publicly supporting but privately undermining, was pushing him in the same way. The secretary of state didn't have to *intend* such a maneuver. It was, thought Moynihan, in his boss's "nature" to eliminate rivals – just as in Aesop it is in the nature of the scorpion, in midriver, to sting the frog who, after no-sting assurances, promised to ferry him over.[18] He couldn't help it.

In late January 1976, Moynihan resigned his post at the U.N. It was an election year, and Ben Wattenberg, Scoop Jackson, and others besides Podhoretz began urging Moynihan to run for the United States Senate. As Podhoretz would recollect, Moynihan insisted "no, he didn't want to," but "with his own complicated psychology, he was only pretending that he needed to be talked into it. Partly so that he could blame someone else if he were defeated."[19] Moynihan and all his urgers in any case agreed about the main issue: Would the New York Democrats nominate a candidate who would reprise the McGovernite themes of 1972, or would they once more take up John Kennedy's call of "pay any price, bear any burden, meet any hardship ... to assure the survival and the success of liberty"?

In "Making the World Safe for Communism" (April 1976), Podhoretz articulated the foreign-policy stakes in the coming election. While Democrats, he said, had throughout the twentieth century been the more interventionist of America's two dominant parties, taking the country into both world wars plus Korea and Vietnam, they were now on the cusp of becoming the party of isolationism. That had been a dirty word since the discrediting of Charles Lindbergh and other stay-home-America spokesmen in the Nazi-threatened thirties, but it was the right word for "the proposition that the United States should never go to war for any purpose other than the defense of its own territory against attack."

Even Kissinger spoke much about managing the realignment of forces in the world as the Soviets' influence grew and America's shrank. We could protect ourselves with our "invulnerable arsenal of nuclear missiles capable of destroying the Soviet Union many times over," and naturally we wished our West European and Israeli allies well in their independent endeavors to resist Soviet domination. If they should falter, however, the logic of Kissinger's position seemed to dictate that (in Podhoretz's paraphrase) "we could do business with a Finlandized Europe or a Sovietized Middle East" and, in the spirit of détente, with the Soviet Union itself.

From any conscientious point of view, Podhoretz declared, this was an impossible position. Were we to do business with a totalitarian empire good at nothing but "producing nuclear bombs and missiles"? With an empire that after sixty years was "still unable to feed itself despite vast expanses of fertile land" and that eradicated "liberty and humane culture wherever [its] writ extends"? Kissinger needed no lessons in morality, of course. That was why he "often sounds like Churchill" when defending liberal democracy. But then again he "just as often acts like Chamberlain" – and sounded like him, too, for instance asking "American critics of the SALT agreements" (apparently in a moment of petulance), "What in the name of God is strategic superiority? What do you do with it?" Podhoretz suggested he ask "the Russians, who seem to know very well both what it is and what you do with it.... What you do with it is intimidate other nuclear powers who might wish to stand in your way when you start to move ahead."[20]

There wasn't, in Glazer's words, "the slightest possibility that even the most minimal degree of civil or political liberty will ever be allowed under Communism."[21] As for those countries outside the Iron Curtain, Podhoretz went on, it might be bad to be externally Finlandized, having one's domestic and foreign policies dictated by the Soviets. But it could be worse to be Finlandized (as Laqueur put it) "from within." This was happening, Podhoretz could see, among West European and North American intellectuals who, forgetting the most fundamental moral distinctions, had taken to declaring that, while the Soviets were no better than the Americans, they were also no worse: "They have their problems, we have ours." Here at home, where Moynihan had called upon Americans to rally to the banner of liberty, our liberal intellectuals, instead of rallying, were refusing to "condemn [the Soviets'] crimes against political liberty," and, in terms "drearily familiar" from left-wing polemics of the past, were claiming that *we* hadn't been fighting for liberty at all. How could we have been, allied as we were with "certain authoritarian regimes and right-wing dictatorships"?

Such objections may have been drearily familiar, but Podhoretz summoned the required patience. In a very imperfect world, he explained, foreign alliances must always be measured by degree, and those with authoritarian dictators were "an unfortunate political and military necessity" – better than surrendering those corrupt regimes to still more corrupt totalitarians. Even dictatorships like those in Spain, Portugal, South Korea, or South Vietnam afforded "a greater degree of freedom than the Communist countries." And such regimes – consider, since World War II, the history of West Germany, Austria, Italy, Japan, and recently Greece – were also far more likely than communist ones eventually to yield to democratic governments.

Our policy in Vietnam, as Podhoretz was among the first to protest, had been most imprudent. But we had to draw the proper lesson from it – not that we must fly from engaging any enemies at all but that we must engage them wisely.[22] It was the principle affirmed in the sixties disarmament debate: we ought not to take our deterrent off the table just because the Soviets were rattling theirs. Rather, we should, just a little, rattle ours, and meanwhile seek other, conventional means to defeat them and what they stood for. If we retreated into isolation, then we could be sure the Soviets, bold to intervene themselves, would prevail. If we projected our power firmly and shrewdly, the Soviets would lose, and we, Moynihan's "party of liberty," would win. The vast majority of the Soviet people themselves, and peoples elsewhere, would then rejoice.

Late in the spring of 1976, Moynihan launched his campaign for the New York Democratic Party's nomination for the Senate. He had run for office once before – a bid for the presidency of the City Council of New York in the Democratic primary of 1965. He lost badly, and Podhoretz remembered being amazed at how "humiliated" Moynihan had felt. In this primary, the serious competition was Congresswoman Bella Abzug, a Stalinoid leftist and – with her big hat, big mouth, and viraginous flamboyance – a feminist caricature. Blacks were in her corner, thanks to the stigma Moynihan still bore from having authored that report for Johnson and from having advised Nixon to give race matters a period of "benign neglect."

As at the U.N., Moynihan's team of advisers included Podhoretz, Garment, and Weaver. The problem for them was to get Moynihan to *close* with Abzug.

FIGURE 14. Standing, from left to right, are Leonard Garment, agent Harry Walker, Pat Moynihan, Maura Moynihan, and Norman Podhoretz, circa 1976.

Podhoretz recalled that with only three weeks to go Moynihan had lost his seventeen-point lead in the polls. "It was very unclear what he was calling for," and the "reason was that he was afraid of provoking" Abzug into highlighting his service under Nixon – something "that Liz, who by then was half-running the campaign, was terrified of." With the polls dead even, Moynihan met with Podhoretz over drinks:

"What do you think?"
"I think you're going to lose."
"What should I do?"

"I think you have to attack her," Podhoretz said, "be more clear and ringing" on the issues of foreign policy, defense policy, domestic affairs, and Israel. So Moynihan "put it in my hands, and for the first and last time in my life I wrote four speeches on those areas. We picked locations that were dramatic for delivering them. And the speeches got condensed to be run in ads," which, under Weaver's direction, were a collage of Podhoretz's phrasings.

What about the hustings? There, too, Moynihan should attack, and head-on. But head-on wasn't Moynihan's style, "even when he was feeling aggressive," and, Podhoretz recalled, "Liz violently objected to my advice. *Violently.*" So the intellectual aggressiveness in the campaign was confined almost entirely to Podhoretz's speech- and ad-writing, particularly on the subject of Israel. Abzug had "voted against every bill for military aid to Israel," always with the excuse that such aid was "attached to some larger defense-spending bill that she had to vote against. . . . She claimed to be pro-Israel, but in practical terms she was against it." The flyer on this subject that the campaign distributed throughout heavily Jewish neighborhoods like Co-op City in the Bronx and Brighton Beach, where Podhoretz's mother then lived, "made a huge impact"[23] – possibly huger than the key endorsement of Moynihan by the *New York Times*.

Elliott Abrams, who had been Glazer's protégé at Harvard and more recently Jackson's campaign manager in the early presidential primaries, was now working for Moynihan. Since Abzug would try to stereotype him "as a Nixon Republican and as an effete intellectual snob from Harvard," Abrams encouraged him to "stress your service with President Kennedy, and your background in New York. I believe that the more clearly you are perceived as an Irish Catholic boy who worked his way up from Hell's Kitchen, the more votes you will get; it is the next best thing to a log cabin."[24] (Abrams, then twenty-eight, would become Moynihan's administrative assistant when he went to the Senate, and in 1980 would become Podhoretz's son-in-law, marrying Rachel after her divorce from Moshe Mark.)

The primary race with Abzug was a close call: Moynihan won by only 10,000 votes, less than one percent of the electorate. But the final contest against the Republicans' James Buckley was much easier. New York was solidly Democratic, and besides, young and not so young, Moynihan's team had put together a substantive platform. Huw Wheldon, looking on from London, where he was recuperating from his operation, noticed Podhoretz's "unchallengeably brilliant" writing: the campaign materials were "not propaganda, but (give or take one or two understandable if immodest claims on the candidate's behalf) an extremely elegant, spare, truthful, and precise statement of a real political position. . . . It is curious how pressure serves in this way to squeeze into being what could not be conceived in a more calm and relaxed atmosphere."[25]

Moynihan's election to the Senate, a triumph for the Jackson wing of the Democratic Party, was worth savoring – as, over dinner with the new senator at the Carlyle Hotel, on the night after the election, Podhoretz did. "We were celebrating, very happy and tired," he recalled. He liked to imagine Moynihan going on to become president one day. That night, though, all his friend said was: "Look, I want you to make me a promise. If you think I'm fucking up, I need you to tell me." And, Podhoretz remembered, "I was stupid enough to take that straight – to believe that was what he actually wanted."[26]

Not that he or any of the Jacksonites had any illusions about Moynihan being their puppet. He had his own antecedents, and it wasn't surprising that his edges should occasionally bump against those of other sorts of people. It was disturbing, early on, when he waffled on President Carter's nomination of Paul Warnke, a well-connected Washington liberal, as head of the Arms Control and Disarmament Agency and therefore as chief negotiator on those subjects with the Soviets. Warnke had contended that the United States and the Soviet Union were, as Podhoretz quoted, like "apes on a treadmill, chasing each other endlessly in an arms race." This, Podhoretz pursued, was "exactly the opposite to what we believed, which was that the Soviets were not aping us, they were outdistancing us. The idea that Pat should vote to confirm Warnke was unthinkable." Moynihan ended up facing both ways: yes on Warnke's nomination to the Arms Control Agency, no on his nomination as negotiator. Podhoretz said: "The whole episode worried me. Oh-oh, I thought, here we go."

In "another bad choice," Carter nominated Theodore C. Sorensen to be director of the CIA. Podhoretz had given a talk to a group of Democrats that was the germ of "Making the World Safe for Communism," and Sorensen, whom he had known during the Kennedy years, had as much difficulty sympathizing with the argument as did nearly everyone else in the room. Podhoretz remarked: "Ted, I don't know exactly what you're complaining about. I'm saying that the Democratic Party should return to the position you guys held in the Kennedy years. . . . This is the old time religion I'm preaching." But Sorensen and most of the other ex-New Frontiersmen had deconverted. Moynihan hadn't – but that didn't keep him from introducing his fellow New Yorker to the intelligence committee in the most needlessly "flowery terms." As it turned out, Sorensen wasn't confirmed, but Podhoretz remained anxious.[27]

The good news was that Moynihan didn't waver in his own anticommunism. When Senator Frank Church of Idaho reproved him for speaking as though the Soviet leaders were irrational, he answered that he didn't regard them as "mad" at all: "I think them to be evil and sane," and therefore very dangerous – only not as dangerous as the Jacksonites believed. Hence his low-profile ambivalence toward the Warnke hearings or Carter's nomination of the détente-favoring Cyrus Vance for secretary of state. "The papers have been full of more 'bad' news every day," Kozodoy wrote Podhoretz, who was in London; "we're back in interesting times."[28]

The Jacksonites were probably expecting too much too soon from Moynihan. After all, he was new to the Senate chamber, and he was also forming the opinion – thanks to his access to classified material as a member of the intelligence committee – that the Soviet Union was an exhausted power, terminally decadent, and likely, as he would later write in *Newsweek*, to implode before the century was out. Ethnic tensions, he presciently said, would be the agent.[29]

But as Moynihan later told his biographer, "The people who got me this job, wonderful people" – Podhoretz first among them – "weren't much interested in what government could do." That is, what it could do practically. They were preoccupied by the Soviet threat, by Israel imperiled, and by "black anti-Semitism in the United States." And about these government could do only so much.[30] That, of course, had been a crucial neoconservative insight, especially with regard to domestic problems. Nevertheless, Moynihan's record on domestic policy in the Senate was, in Podhoretz's opinion, largely indistinguishable from what Abzug's had been in the House. Most big government programs weren't effective but, to please liberal New Yorkers, he kept voting to fund them.

Faithful to his promise, Podhoretz tried "to tell him when he was fucking up." Moynihan would answer, "You've got to let me cover my ass." On domestic issues, Podhoretz thought that was fair. In foreign policy – where the neoconservatives also understood that government couldn't solve *all* the problems – Podhoretz was convinced that it could do much more than Moynihan, now that he was in office, seemed to believe. "Once he got into the Senate," Podhoretz stated, "he took a look around and decided there was no future in Scoop Jackson's point of view. If he wanted to stay there, which he did, then he was going to have to accommodate himself. Not losing was more important than being right." Moynihan's wobbling on defense spending and détente was a disappointment for people whose hearts had been lifted up by those eight months at the U.N., and at some level he may have been disappointed in himself.

At home on one St. Patrick's Day – Podhoretz couldn't remember the year – "the buzzer rang from downstairs and the awestruck doorman said 'Senator Moynihan is here to see you.'" The New York parade had ended on 86th Street, only a few blocks north. "He came up alone, in his cups – he was never as much of a drunk as people thought: he drank a lot, but he was not that bad – and he wanted to defend himself." Essentially Jacksonite in "his political conscience," Moynihan had fashioned himself into something else on the Senate floor. When Jackson phoned to say "Listen, can you do something about that friend of yours, he's acting like a flake," Podhoretz had to confess himself powerless. Moynihan clearly felt he had to "conduct himself so as to avoid a primary challenge from the Left when he was up for reelection." But Podhoretz thought he was misreading his robust popularity in New York. If he had only "picked up that [party of liberty] banner," he could have led his electors, and his fellow senators, back to the liberal center. But he didn't.

In 1982, Podhoretz agreed to appear on a Georgetown University–sponsored television program, "American Interests," to debate about arms control with Moynihan and Eric Breindel, a *Commentary* writer and a young staffer on the senator's intelligence committee. Podhoretz's thesis was that SALT-II, the second phase of the Strategic Arms Limitation Talks, which would supposedly ensure peace by reducing nuclear warheads on both sides, was a big mistake. At one point Moynihan "was asked what the alternative to SALT-II was, and he said 'Well, the alternative is nuclear war.'" As Podhoretz remembered with a laugh, "I couldn't believe my ears: that such words should come out of the mouth of Pat Moynihan – I would have bet the ranch and everything else I owned against such a possibility."

What Moynihan more elaborately said was that "co-existence with the Soviet Union" wasn't a choice but a "necessity. Absent that, you have Armageddon." Moreover, to distance himself from Podhoretz, he declared himself no neoconservative but "just a Kennedy Democrat."[31] Of course, he had to know that Podhoretz and the other neoconservatives were by and large

Jack Kennedy Democrats, too, "loyal to those basic principles that used to be associated with liberalism and that now are associated with conservatism." As Podhoretz had said on a recent occasion, the neoconservatives had stayed on center, while the New Politics Democrats, including many of the senators with whom Moynihan now had to cooperate, had moved left.[32] He also had to know, very well, that the likeliest way to trigger nuclear war was for the Soviets to gain superiority, which the SALT-II proposals all but guaranteed.

But "Pat's way of dealing with me then and subsequently," Podhoretz noted, "was not to fight – like a boxer who would not engage." The Georgetown debate over, they repaired to a bar and until midnight had something more like a real exchange. Moynihan "did argue but not very well," Podhoretz said, largely "because his case was weak, and anyway I don't think he believed it." Podhoretz actually lost his voice, "talking so passionately, so vehemently, so long, pleading with Pat, begging him to mend his ways." On another occasion, at the Council on Foreign Relations later in the Reagan years, Podhoretz again found himself jabbing and punching while Moynihan backed and dodged. The topic was international law. Citing Churchill's dictum about fighting a totalitarian enemy like Hitler, Podhoretz asserted that appealing to international law is "a form of unilateral disarmament": the democracies would obey it and the totalitarians wouldn't.

All of this Moynihan had said in public many times. As Podhoretz later remarked, echoing F. Scott Fitzgerald's words that "In the deep dark night of the soul it's always three o'clock in the morning," he had spent "many three o'clock in the morning times with Pat Moynihan. And in the deep dark night of his soul he was to the right of *me!*" That may be why "he was made uncomfortable by me.... When we stopped seeing each other – he stopped seeing me, though we never had a fight – I said I don't really blame him."

Nevertheless, in 1979 Podhoretz wrote and spoke on behalf of a Moynihan campaign for the presidency. It was an anti-Carter move, with Moynihan potentially running as Jackson's heir. He declined to enter the race, however, even when it became clear that Ted Kennedy's challenge to Carter was a squib. Moynihan probably saw that competing for the presidency as a Democrat in 1980 would be hopeless. The party was incapable of returning to "the old-time religion." This was why, as Podhoretz would write, it took Ronald Reagan, who had himself been a Democrat until age fifty-one, to come, "out of nowhere as it seemed," "flying by on his mount" to snatch up "this tattered ensign, and [wave] it proudly in the air."[33]

That is to get too far ahead of the story politically. But it is an apt moment to start drawing the curtain on Podhoretz's friendship with Moynihan. Jim Wilson, though entirely at one with Podhoretz intellectually, also managed "to remain on cordial and intimate terms" with Moynihan, as did both Glazer, who soon moved "way to the left of Pat," and Kristol, who moved further right. "I don't know," Podhoretz remarked, "maybe there was something wrong with me, but I just wasn't able to remain intimate." Moynihan found that life in the Senate was good, and "for all the wrong reasons" he kept getting reelected as "a more and more revered character." Podhoretz once said to him, "'Look, no matter what you do they're never going to forgive you,' meaning the blacks, the Left." But, he acknowledged, "I was wrong: they did forgive him. All he had to do was basically come over to their side," even as, in his three o'clock in the morning soul, he remained true to himself in certain speeches and in articles like "Defining Deviancy Down."

When, to look far ahead, Podhoretz retired from the editorship at *Commentary* in 1995, there was a major banquet. Writing congratulations from Washington, where he claimed he was needed on the Senate floor for an important vote, Moynihan, quoting John Podhoretz's declaration, "It's been a helluva ride," confirmed his love and added, "I've gone with you. Almost all the way." Podhoretz reciprocated the love, but plainly was hurt that Moynihan didn't come in person to deliver one of the formal toasts as scheduled. "As Len Garment used to say [with a drawl], whenever you wanted a senator the excuse was always 'The senator is on the floor.' Anyway, he did not show up. 'The pity of it, Iago, the pity of it.'"

Moynihan's image – what he symbolized to others – was more riven than that of most politicians. The left-leaning Democrats sometimes didn't know what to do with his Jacksonite notions, and the Jacksonites didn't know why he thought he had to pay homage to the McGovernite camp. Since, prior to his election to the Senate, he had served Republican as well as Democratic administrations, he was a riddle to the party-machine imagination. For the memorial service that followed some time after his death in 2003, his wife, Liz, and daughter Maura "prepared a very elaborate brochure – pictures, big detailed biography – and the Nixon connection was eliminated: there was no mention," Podhoretz recalled. "It was like something out of Soviet media: they air-brushed out the Nixon connection."[34]

14

Breaking and Closing Ranks

Back in 1976, the battle over Abzug's record on Israel could not help being informed by the fact that, instead of Moynihan at the U.N., America now had William Scranton, former governor of Pennsylvania. For Podhoretz, as for many Jewish voters, the defense of the Jewish state and the defense of America were twinned. It was a personal matter, but it was also a matter of principle: both Israel and the United States were democracies threatened by the left-wing totalitarianism of the Soviets or their clients in the Arab world. It was particularly worrisome, therefore, that Scranton seemed gulled by the Arab diplomats who asserted that Zionists had tricked America into World War I, that *The Diary of Anne Frank* was a forgery, or that the Holocaust was a myth. Scranton's gullibility only went along with the tenor of administration policy since the Yom Kippur War: Ford and Kissinger had pressured Israel to evacuate the occupied territories while asking the Arabs to do precisely nothing in return. The hope, apparently, was both to guarantee access to the Arabs' oil and to avoid confrontation with their superpower ally, the Soviet Union.

Did this mean, as the title of Podhoretz's July 1976 essay put it, "The Abandonment of Israel"? For nearly thirty years, with the Holocaust vivid in people's memory, anti-Zionist passions had been restrained. But now, for younger Europeans and Americans, the Holocaust was either a fading memory or not a memory at all – it was a botheration, possibly even a figment out of their parents' past. How else could one explain the success of the latest inversions portraying the Israelis as the new Nazis and the Palestinians as the new Jews – or the Israelis as white imperialists and the Palestinians as dark-skinned natives seeking natural rights?

No state, Podhoretz asserted, has ever conformed "in every detail to the dictates of the contemporary liberal conscience," and no state ever can. More than anti-Zionist, it was anti-Semitic to single out Israel as the state that should do so. "All other peoples are entitled to national self-determination," he wrote; "when the Jews exercise this right, they are committing the crimes of racism and imperialism. All other nations are entitled to defend themselves against armed attack; when a Jewish nation defends itself, it is committing the crime of aggression." Yes, there were "three-quarters of a million [Palestinians] displaced in the Jewish war of national liberation," but that was a small number compared with "the estimated thirty-five million refugees who have been displaced by war and other calamities since 1945 alone." Those other refugees were responsibly absorbed by other countries, while the Arab countries, with the partial exception of Jordan, had deliberately left the Palestinians in their camps to be a thorn in Israel's side. Why should Israel alone be required to repatriate refugees created by its war of independence? Or why, as Senator William Fulbright asked after the Six-Day War, has no other "modern military victor" seriously been asked to return conquered territory? Certainly no permanent member of the U.N. Security Council had ever been asked to do so.

For the Arabs, indeed, the core issue wasn't Israel's niggled-over gains of the Six-Day War. It was the idea of Israel's very existence, which the Arabs had opposed since well before 1948. Under the Ottoman Empire, to go no further back, Palestine had been ruled by the Sultan, and Jews, there or anywhere in the Middle East, had been a subject minority. What was a subject minority now doing in the saddle? The Arabs weren't going to pull back when, thanks to the oil weapon, they sensed a good chance of getting back into the saddle themselves. And they might well be right, given the trend of American policy, the logic of which was "as inexorable as it is terrible": we needed Arab oil, and therefore we implicitly sided with the Arabs against Israel. The diplomatic process strikingly resembled the one leading up to Munich in 1938. Then, the Western powers convinced themselves that Czechoslovakia was an artificial creation, that the Sudeten Germans were a persecuted minority, and that the Czechs were being intransigent. Likewise with Israel now.

But unlike the Czechs in 1938, or for that matter the South Vietnamese in 1975, the Israelis weren't going to allow themselves to be destroyed without a fight. It was a fight they would wage at first conventionally but at the last, if need be, with nuclear weapons. Would that be a revival of the "Masada complex," as in the collective suicide, in 73 C.E., of some thousand holdouts from the Roman destruction of Jerusalem who, their fortress overcome, preferred death to servitude? No. If the Israelis became suicidal, it would be in the tradition of Samson, who brought the roof down on the Philistines as well as himself. That was what a nuclear weapon would do anywhere in or around their tiny country. And that was the Samson-like corner into which the United States was pushing its traditional ally.[1]

English writer John Wain understood at once the significance of "The Abandonment of Israel," an article he called "important, true, and crucial":

God knows what can actually be done about that situation; as soon as the screw of oil supplies began to be tightened, it became clear that Israel's friends would begin to desert her and go on until she was left to her fate. . . . But to have the issues stated so clearly, the choice so unequivocally laid before the remaining democracies of the world, as in your article – that is important and everyone who values freedom and intellectual honesty must be grateful.[2]

A central statement, "The Abandonment of Israel" looked back to pieces written in the aftermath of the Six-Day War and forward to ones written during the war in Lebanon in the early eighties, the first Intifada in the late eighties, or the Oslo Peace Accords of the early nineties.

As for the Soviet Union, the Jackson Democrats didn't want to "play ball" with it; they wanted to contrive its dissolution. In voting for Carter in 1976, Podhoretz had had high hopes that the country would be led by a governor-from-Georgia version of the senator from Washington State. An Annapolis graduate who knew what the inside of a submarine looked like, Carter surely would promote a strong defense policy.

Disillusionment came quickly. Carter positively welcomed the War Powers Resolution of 1973, which required the president to consult with Congress before starting to deploy forces abroad and to withdraw those forces if after sixty days Congress hadn't either declared war or officially authorized the use of force. The exercise of executive power, in the new president's view, had committed America to the foolish war in Vietnam, and a reduction of that power was therefore entirely "appropriate." The really welcome news, Carter concluded, was that the mandated consultations with Congress would "minimize greatly the chances that we will get involved in combat anywhere in the world."[3] With the "lessons of Vietnam" thus skewed left, it was as though McGovern had won after all.

For Israel, between the Soviets and their Egyptian clients on one side and the supportive but desperate for Arab oil Americans on the other, the late seventies seemed a period of strangulation. In 1979, Hillel Halkin, author and distinguished translator from Hebrew, wrote Kozodoy that "the country is in for a big crash, political and economic, and the only question is how long it can be staved off. My guess is about three years – long enough for the Egyptians and Americans to get us out of Sinai and into their little Palestinian squeeze play. What a miserable world. If there is a Jewish God, He's a loser for sure; it was a mistake to have ever gotten involved with Him."[4]

Dark metaphysical thoughts were occurring to Podhoretz as well. As he told the *Jerusalem Post*, the freedom from anti-Semitism that he had enjoyed as a boy and as a young man was turning out to be exceptional, for the ancient prejudice was clearly making a comeback:

I have an almost mystical belief that if another major Jewish community [Israel] were destroyed in this century, after European Jewry [was] permitted to be wiped out, it would prove that there was a will at work to wipe the Jews off the face of the earth entirely, to make the whole world "Judenrein" as the Nazis used to say, and that this will would be powerful enough to work its way in America, with the next major Jewish community.

Still, if the Jews' powers of resistance were being tested, then resist they must. They must not assume their destruction – or their survival – to be inevitable. They could, and they must, choose life – not go on "collaborating with their enemies" to destroy Jewry itself as, out of a desire to please their protector, the United States, many were unintentionally doing.[5]

The great protector's current leaders seemed ignorant of what was at stake. Early in the Carter administration, Zbigniew Brzezinski, the National Security Adviser, had warned that America had to exert itself to prevent friendly Arab governments from allying themselves with the Soviets; otherwise, America and the West European democracies would "suffer and ultimately Israel will perish." As Beichman asked Podhoretz, "about what other country in the world could a national security adviser to the President use the verb, 'perish'? Chad, Liberia, Taiwan, Monaco?"[6] Then came an apparent reprieve in the form of the Camp David Accords of September 1978 and the Israel–Egypt Treaty of March 1979.[7]

That treaty, the first between Israel and an Arab state, at least had the merit of leaving the Soviets out of the loop – Carter, to Egyptian President Anwar Sadat's astonished distress, having initially wanted them *in*. Israel was required to evacuate the Sinai Peninsula, which it had conquered during the Yom Kippur War; Egypt in return agreed to a cease fire along a mutually recognized border. But although the Israeli people went on to honor the spirit as well as the letter of the treaty, the Egyptian people, on the whole, didn't. They would think of the treaty as the child of Sadat's brain, softened by Israeli Prime Minister Menachem Begin and Carter.

This was what Podhoretz had foreseen, keeping his eye less on what the Egyptians, the Arabs, and particularly the Palestinians said than on what they *did*. Addressing a 1979 conference organized in Jerusalem by the thirty-year-old Benjamin Netanyahu – whose brother had led and been killed in the rescue of hostages held by Palestinian terrorists with the support of Idi Amin's soldiers at Entebbe Airport in Uganda – Podhoretz asked why terrorists did such horrible things. It could not any longer be for attention since Yasser Arafat, the head of the Palestine Liberation Organization (PLO), commanded more television time than Kissinger. Their purpose rather was to manipulate the media and thereby determine public discourse. They had succeeded, Podhoretz said, to the point that people have "become morally numb" to the bloody acts – "accept[ing] the presence of the terrorists at the table, and consider[ing] their demands discussable." Since discussion inevitably started with the "social causes" behind terrorism, the media exculpated the killers in the same way they had exculpated campus rioters in the sixties, wondering solicitously "what these students 'were trying to tell us.'"

Podhoretz urged the democracies to cut to the chase: "the cause of terrorism is terrorists," not "social" conditions. Media manipulation aside, what allowed these terrorists to operate effectively was the "financial support and sanctuary" granted by states that desired the destruction, or at least the crippling, of the terrorists' target. In the case of the PLO, support, sanctuary, and training

FIGURE 15. At the book party for *Breaking Ranks* (1979) are Norman Podhoretz with Midge Decter and the publisher, Erwin Glikes.

had come "in our day from the Soviet Union, its agents and Arab allies." Accordingly, Israel, the United States, and the other liberal democracies needed to adopt a policy "that would indeed lead to the caging of these beasts" and to the checking of their Soviet enablers.[8]

The year 1979 also saw the publication of *Breaking Ranks*, the "political memoir" Podhoretz had begun under the title *A Traitor to My Class*. It is an account, indispensable not just as autobiography but as cultural history, that we have drawn on repeatedly in these pages. The preface is a fourteen-page letter to his son, John, who "The other day . . . asked me with astonishment in [his] voice whether I had ever really believed 'all that stuff'" – namely, sixties radicalism. The body of the book would gauge the depth of his original belief, trace the divagations of his ambivalence, and mark at last his renunciation. Writing with speed in the summer and fall of 1977, he was finished in a little less than five months.

The freedom to present himself once again as a representative figure was something he owed to the realignment of his own social relationships since the savaging of *Making It* and the epiphanic clarification that followed. Of whom did Podhoretz imagine himself to be representative? Broadly, of people who had begun their adult lives on the Left and who, having been "mugged by reality" (as Kristol famously said), moved to the Right – or who, as we have suggested, by finally staying true to the liberalism of their youth (the pre-New

Left period), found themselves to the right of the new center. In acceptance of this gravitational shift, they came to embrace the neoconservative label.

Beyond these sympathetic readers, Podhoretz was reaching out to ones on the Left – the democratic socialists, for instance – asking them to recognize their shared anticommunism and to reconsider their own strategies for blocking the spread of Marxism–Leninism in Europe, Africa, Asia, or Latin America. Further, he wanted readers on the old Right – the intellectuals around Buckley's *National Review*, say – to recognize their common defense of liberal democracy and to see that support of Israel was integral to it. This was an issue that would come to the fore in the eighties.[9]

Jacqueline Wheldon saw directly what her friend had accomplished in *Breaking Ranks*. Its exposition is so "refreshingly *clear*," she wrote Decter, and "so extraordinarily *readable*" that "no critic will be able to match" it. His "plain words," she told Podhoretz himself, do "make you vulnerable"; he hadn't hidden behind the standard obfuscations. Reviewers would naturally attack, but they wouldn't be capable of refuting the logic of his political development.[10] Kristol agreed: "I am not suggesting for a moment that you will get many *friendly* reviews! But because the book is serious and *argued* in a way that *Making It* was not, my guess is that the hostile critics are more likely to be dismissive than vitriolic."[11]

In the *Washington Post*, George F. Will put a very favorable case for the book, saying that under Podhoretz's editorship *Commentary* had become "America's most consequential journal of ideas" and that his writings were "a scourge of intellectual foolishness, his own emphatically included." Did it matter "that Susan Sontag said 'the white race is the cancer of human history' and that Norman Mailer called Castro 'the first and greatest hero' since World War II?" It did matter, Will tacitly conceded, for it demonstrated how the celebrated sixties radicals were indulging a form of hysteria, while "the general populace...preserved its sanity."[12] *Breaking Ranks* certified Podhoretz's status as a leading spokesman for that general populace.

Joseph Epstein also praised the book, having been assigned by the *New York Times Book Review* no less. ("They never made that mistake again," he would say.)[13] *Breaking Ranks* was "more candid, more confident, written with a better humor and a larger heart" than *Making It*, he declared, and like that book it possessed "considerable documentary value" as a guide to the Family's intellectual and social life.

Epstein did wish Podhoretz had a thicker skin. Podhoretz treated the assaults on *Making It* as politically motivated, when, to Epstein's thinking, they had been simply visceral – the roughing-up, however "sickening," of a brashly successful young man. This insistence on translating the personal into the political then made it easier for Podhoretz's enemies – like Joseph Heller in his novel *Good as Gold* – to insinuate that he had taken *Commentary* to the Right because the Left had spat on him. What, Epstein wondered, was *with* these people? They were scapegoating a writer whose only "crime" was to have "perceived that the assumptions upon which he [like most of them] had been educated were half-cocked, intellectually bankrupt and – as put into action between 1965 and 1975 – finally pernicious."[14]

Noel Annan reviewed *Breaking Ranks* for the *Times Literary Supplement* in England. The "intelligentsia" there, he noted, had by and large not relished *Making It*'s "cock-a-hoop delight in getting on in the world." Those arriviste sins were now compounded, with Podhoretz coming across as "altogether too vulgar, too ludicrous in imagining that the petty squabbles between intellectuals in New York had any significance in American or in world politics," and "too irresponsible in exculpating serious moral outrages perpetrated in the name of America in Cambodia or . . . during the Watergate scandal." This, Annan observed, was entirely unfair. If there were sins in the right-hand column of America's ledger – and *Breaking Ranks* passed harsh judgment on them – there were also sins in the left-hand column. "What wounds have those who espoused the cause of Black Power, Women's Lib, permissiveness, the emasculation of America as a world power, inflicted upon their society?" Better Podhoretz's serious reformism than their revolutionary posturing.[15]

It was a long drop from *TLS* to the *Village Voice*, but its columnist Ellen Willis did at least strive to distance herself from the vituperations of the radical right-wing Murray N. Rothbard in *Inquiry* ("a dumb book, a stupid book" written by "a plodding boob")[16] or his sidewalk counterparts on the radical Left ("*That* asshole! I can't take him seriously!"). Slurs like these, Willis said, suggested Podhoretz was touching a nerve. She tried to take him seriously, though her project wasn't helped by her editors' placing a moronic "comic-book version" of *Making It* adjacent to her review. The first panel showed the "aging editor of a Jewish intellectual magazine" "making it" with "his friend, the Bitch Goddess," the Slut of Success; half-under the sheets, she rides Podhoretz, who must find it hard to breathe between her breasts. "Do you know Mailer?" he asks in the second panel. "*Do I!*" she says in the third. In the final panel, Podhoretz, looking tiny between Manhattan buildings, still envies his old pal: "I bet Mailer gets to make it with the *Gentile* Bitch Goddess!" Willis compared her quarrel with Podhoretz with the one she had with her father, who had recently retired from the New York City Police Department. The quarrel, in short, was generational: Podhoretz "was born too early" to be an effective leader of the sixties movement, though he gave it a try during his Paul Goodman phase, and he was too much the young fogey to see that growing up didn't necessarily entail settling down.[17]

A few members of Podhoretz's own faction – he now had one, whereas in 1968 he had scarcely seemed to – sent a telegram from Washington. The crew of young staffers in Moynihan's office – Abrams, Judy Bardacke, Chester Finn, Charles Horner, and Tim Russert – had to miss the publisher's party for *Breaking Ranks* in New York but promised to have one of their own in the Senate Office Building. "We congratulate you," they said with amiable hyperbole, "on giving us a book which will establish you, along with St. Augustine, Jean-Jacques Rousseau, Henry Adams, and Daniel P. Moynihan, as a master creator of confessional literature. Be assured that whatever the condition of our Manhattan comrades, we are closing ranks behind you here in the nation's capital."[18]

The bicentennial celebrations of 1976 had been reassuring to many Americans: the war in Vietnam was over, our losses cut, and (as many were pleased to think) the rotters in Saigon had been left to their own devices. Plus, the scandal of Watergate had been constitutionally resolved. Was America "back to normal again"? Podhoretz had thought not. In "The Culture of Appeasement," which appeared in *Harper's* the next year, he held that the country's Vietnam experience had introduced cultural and political abnormalities of an extremely dangerous kind.

The post-Vietnam symptoms were threefold. First, the war was regarded as unredeemable, and arming for a new struggle – *any* new struggle – was denounced as not merely futile but unconscionable. Second, "native anti-Americanism," the mainstreaming of New Left slogans of the sixties, so preoccupied our elite that they couldn't be bothered by warnings against Soviet subterfuges. Third, opposition to the spread of left-wing totalitarianism, the cause for which we committed troops to Vietnam, was now interpreted as a baleful enchantment – Carter himself speaking of our "inordinate fear of Communism," at last happily exorcised. Members of the Committee on the Present Danger (CPD) – a group of Jackson Democrats, including Podhoretz, who had come together after Carter's election – sounded an alarm, but they were "rewarded for their pains with accusations of hysteria, paranoia, servility toward the Pentagon, and worse." It was all too predictable, given that Soviet missiles weren't yet raining down on American cities – just as, in the thirties, Nazi bombs hadn't yet been raining down on London.

Podhoretz compared the relatively familiar story of England in the thirties with the unfolding story of American demoralization in the seventies. "Nothing good could be said about war," most British intellectuals averred in the thirties: "It was wanton carnage pure and simple. Nor was it ever justified." Thus thousands of British undergraduates took the "Oxford Pledge never to fight 'for King and country.'" Both on the Right and on the Left, writers concurred that parliamentary democracy was boring and the dominant culture hopelessly philistine. As Rebecca West remarked, patriotism between the wars "had 'something dowdy about it,'" while "treason" – affiliation with antidemocratic fascism or communism – "had 'a certain style, a sort of elegance.'"

In post-Vietnam America, Podhoretz contended, similar attitudes were being voiced by writers like Ginsberg, Baldwin, and Vidal, plus "a host of less distinguished publicists," some of them homosexual. They exhibited a "combination of pacifism . . . hostility to one's own country and its putatively dreary middle-class way of life, and derision of the idea that it stands for anything worth defending or that it is threatened by anything but its own stupidity and wickedness." Orwell's denunciation of "so-called artists who spend on sodomy what they have gained by sponging" (his words) – artists who, with their "sluttish antinomianism," fed "the paralysis of British will in the face of an ever-growing Nazi threat" (Podhoretz's words) – meshed with another remark Podhoretz would quote often in years to come: "The fact to which we have got to cling, as to a life-belt," Orwell wrote, "is that it *is* possible to be a normal decent person and yet to be fully alive."[19]

Podhoretz's task was to make the present danger so "clear" that even those "in denial" – some of them anyway – would have to accept the implications and ready themselves for necessary action. Not that there was any hope of bringing along the *Village Voice-* or *Nation-*reading Left. But what about Carter? By the spring of 1978, uneasy about the Soviets' arms buildup and interventions in Angola and the horn of Africa, the president had begun to suggest that the powers of his office had perhaps been *too* diminished. Still, he was loath to consult his military advisers, hoping rather that, as Podhoretz wrote, "the negative effects of Soviet racism and atheism will lead of their own unaided weight to a Russian defeat."[20] Nor was Carter's posture as a champion of human rights directed at Moscow so much as at "small powerless right-wing countries like Uruguay and Chile." In the arms race, he had cancelled or deferred "the B-1 bomber, the cruise missile, the neutron bomb... with no more than a pious wish that the Russians would follow suit."

Were Carter more like Churchill than Chamberlain, he might have led the country toward a new, antitotalitarian consensus. But he was what he was – "content to go on representing a perfect embodiment of the stalemate in the general climate of opinion." Therefore, prospects for his administration's succumbing in 1980, "possibly to a challenge from within the Democratic Party, possibly to a Republican opponent," were growing by the month.[21]

Yet, as the next election approached, lifelong Democrats like Podhoretz, Decter, Kirkpatrick, Wattenberg, Elliott Abrams, and others active in the CDM and CPD – people who had voted for Nixon against McGovern in 1972 but who in 1976 had hoped that Carter would stand in for Jackson – still wondered (hope against hope) whether he might yet do so. After all, the Soviet invasion of Afghanistan, which began on Christmas 1979, had ended the president's delusions about détente – so he said – and he invited a group of Jackson Democrats to meet with him about foreign policy. At the start of the meeting in the cabinet room, Vice President Walter Mondale gave a "terrific speech," as Abrams would later recall, "the perfect pitch for an audience" wanting to be "wooed back." But when Carter spoke it was "testily" to deny that the Soviet invasion of Afghanistan had seriously changed his foreign policy. And so, having made "the perfect pitch in the wrong way," he left the room in high dudgeon.[22]

As the Jacksonites took their leave of the White House, reporters approached them on the lawn. Kirkpatrick ended whatever suspense might be in the air by announcing that she, for one, couldn't endorse Carter for reelection. She was putting her oar in for Ronald Reagan. All the others, Wattenberg perhaps excepted, were doing the same.

As the election neared, Podhoretz's principal contribution, and it was tremendous, was a 109-page book called *The Present Danger*. It would by

FIGURE 16. Norman Podhoretz at his desk in the *Commentary* office in 1980, the year he published *The Present Danger*.

itself justify the historian Richard Gid Powers's assertion that "during those bleakest winter days of American anticommunism" it was Podhoretz alone who seemed able to call up "the will, the strength and the imagination to commence the giant task of rebuilding" the movement.[23] Drawing on "The Culture of Appeasement," "Making the World Safe for Communism," and other pieces, *The Present Danger*, in effect an extended pamphlet, was published in August 1980, in good time to impact the November balloting.

Hailing it as a "critically important book," Reagan shared Podhoretz's ideas about defending democracy against left-wing totalitarianism. In office, he would restart the weapons programs Carter had suspended and go on to guide America and the liberal democracies toward what, soon after the close of his second term, became victory in the Cold War. What Joseph Epstein had said a few years earlier was proving prophetic: the Republicans, so long called (like the Tories in nineteenth-century England) "the stupid party," were becoming the party of ideas. Indeed the Reagan presidency was to be the neoconservative version of Kennedy's Camelot, as upward of sixty veterans of the CPD were recruited to work for the new administration. Some of them (Paul Wolfowitz and Richard Perle, for example) would reappear as important players in the second Bush era.[24]

Meanwhile, back at the apartment, the Podhoretzes' family life entered the empty-nest phase. It was a new apartment. When Midge and John looked out the window of their Upper West Side place during a power-failure blackout in July 1977 and saw the looters at their mischief, she thought the time to move had come. Norman *knew* it had come. Though John was most unhappy to leave his childhood home, the family decamped to the Upper East Side in the fall of 1978. In the summer of 1977 they had also made another move, buying a "shack" in East Hampton (on the eastern tip of Long Island) that, Decter would remember, "cost nothing – and we had nothing, which was perfect." It would become their getaway, a replacement for the old Fire Island cottage and Delaware County farmhouse.[25]

By the fall of 1978, in any case, John was a freshman at the University of Chicago, where Ruthie had also studied. The family's only boy, he had grown up in what he gradually realized were circumstances different from his schoolfellows'. He particularly recollected how, around age twelve or thirteen, he brought a friend home for dinner:

Ruthie brings up the subject of homosexuality: "I don't *understand* it," she said. My dad began to expound on what homosexuality is, and this little boy sat there with a look of absolute horror on his face. He was some sweet kid, and his family talked about whatever people talk about at dinner table – what they did that day, sports, shopping, whatever and this was an alarming experience for him. He went home, and after that we weren't friends anymore.

From his third until about his fourteenth year, his mother having gone back to work, John (like Ruthie) was cared for each day by a nanny from Belize named Imelda. However wonderful, she couldn't see to all of the kids' needs. John didn't go to a dentist until he chipped a tooth at age ten; he may have needed glasses for a couple of years before his parents noticed that he couldn't read a traffic sign.

In 1972, a guest speaker at his middle school took a straw poll for the presidential election; he was the only kid to stand up for Nixon. No doubt appalled at the boy's politics, the headmaster nonetheless praised his bravery. The sixties had been bewildering enough for Rachel and Naomi: they were, as John remembered, having problems with their biological father, Moshe Decter, whom they almost never saw, and the moneyed Dalton scene bristled with drugs and promiscuity. Rachel had managed to gain admission to St. John's College, and Naomi went to Brandeis but in her third year transferred to Hebrew University in Jerusalem. For John in the mid-seventies, Dalton was similarly discombobulating. "People complain about how bad things in high schools are now," he later said. "They have no *clue*."[26]

With faculty including Allan Bloom, Milton Friedman, Saul Bellow, Leon Kass, and Wayne Booth, Chicago was a good place for a young counter-countercultural mind. And John discovered a significant minority of like-minded students with whom he could discuss books, write and produce plays, and start a magazine. By the end of his first quarter, he was entirely in the swim, "having a fantastic time," he told Jacqueline Wheldon, with "many friends... and what is most important, command[ing] a lot of respect, some-thing which I really haven't done before." One reason for the respect was that the future film critic had co-written a twenty-minute musical comedy, *The Tribulations of Harry Murray*, about the sole remaining Chicago professor who hadn't won a Nobel Prize.[27]

In October 1978, Ruthie imitated Naomi in decamping for Hebrew University in Jerusalem. She had been at Chicago for two years, following many expensive years at Dalton and a few decidedly precocious years at the Bronx High School of Science. At home, she had been in the middle of a great deal of intellectual back and forth and, as her father was amused to learn from the papers she wrote for school, had developed her own, often outrageous, ideas. In one, she had set out to defend King George III and oppose the American Revolutionists, those "ingrates." In another she questioned the need for the First or Fifth Amendment and deemed it "ridiculous that the police should need search warrants or that there should be inadmissible evidence." It was her way of being like her parents, only more so.

In high school, Ruthie got into the standard sorts of trouble – drinking, taking drugs, running with boys – and if her parents were often too busy to monitor her behavior, they ultimately were there to lay down the truly requisite pro-hibitions and provide an irreplaceable model of intellectual concentration and professional productivity. They seemed to Ruthie the connubial ideal, which both inspired and daunted their children. How in the world could one ever be like them? Discouraging, too, was their appearing not to "need" their children: "they had each other," and they stuck together. Nor did the parents make the expected distinctions between Rachel and Naomi Decter and Ruthie and John Podhoretz. John felt that if anything his father was "a saint" for hav-ing adopted Midge's daughters in the first place. They may have called him "Norman" or "Normie," but they knew him to be their functional father.[28] Ruthie felt that with his Decter daughters her father could be loving but detached and even handed, while with his own children came "anxiety." Midge was somehow able to regard all four children as "separate entities," not exten-sions of herself.[29]

When Ruthie left Chicago for Israel, it was for the sake of a young Israeli boyfriend who disappeared as soon as she arrived. Momentarily stunned, she quickly went to work finishing her bachelor's degree. In July 1981 she married an Israeli lawyer named Nadav Blum, with whom she would have four children, and eventually became a writer for the *Jerusalem Post*, Israel's English-language newspaper. For years, Ruthie Blum was a sort of Dear Abby columnist, and more recently has been both a writer of piquant profiles of character types within her country's divided society and an incomparable interviewer.

Back around 1980, it seems, the romantic lives of the two older children were complicated. Having divorced Moshe Mark, Rachel would marry Elliott Abrams in March 1980. Naomi would in September marry Steven Munson – "formerly of the *American Spectator*, now of the *New York Times Magazine*," as Norman informed a correspondent.[30] Munson, whose politics were as conservative as Naomi's, was not born Jewish but converted before the marriage.[31]

And marriage was the right goal: all three girls agreed with their mother on that. As she had recently told Megan Rosenfeld at the *Washington Post*:

I have daughters in their late 20s and I think relations between men and women at that age are absolutely ghastly. There's a kind of miserable, joyless falling into bed, the men feel downgraded and sapped and rendered impotent by the women.... Young women today are suffering very much from the absence of men who have faith in themselves.

Faith, that is, not just in their sexual potency but in their ability to "protect and defend" the members of their family. Their lack of such faith, Decter believed, was the consequence of the women's movement's having declared men the enemy. For their part, men without the responsibilities of true partnership – supporting a family, being a father – were adrift: "neurasthenic, narcissistic, they're running all the time and greasing their bodies and doing this, that and the other thing to go through substitute motions of manliness."[32]

Both Midge and Norman understood their "gender" roles in what academics call "essentialist" terms. "I think there is such a thing as the nature of man and the nature of woman," Podhoretz told another interviewer. "In relation to children," he and Midge "have *performed* different functions.... Midge was the one who took care of them, comforted, consoled, disciplined them in day-to-day life. I think mothers are by nature the ones who do that. But they depended on me to set moral standards for them" – for example, stressing the importance of "try[ing] to do well in school." To him, Midge was a feminist "in the classical sense," believing that a woman could have a career apart from her work as a wife and mother.

Some young women, Decter remarked in the same interview, "think that looking after little children is nothing but changing diapers." They didn't know, and no one seemed to write about, "how much fun" looking after children was. "Anybody who has spent time with a two-year-old knows that it's both a terrific pain in the neck, a big worry, and a sensual and social pleasure of the extremest kind."

She had a friend whose husband, like her own, did little to help with the housework. "Taking out the garbage," Norman said, "is about the only household chore I do." The friend was asked how, with her own career to pursue, she managed to stay married. Her reply, Midge remembered, was that her husband "*amuses* me! Which is the most important thing in a marriage." Midge believed the success of Norman's and her marriage derived from "the fact that we are awfully good friends. That means we are on one another's side.... Once when I was being light-handed on the subject of feminine and masculine roles – when I was opposing the women's liberation movement – my formulation was: I bring him coffee and he gives me courage."[33]

However Norman and Midge may have divided their disciplinary tasks, they made no appeals to religion. They gave the children "an entirely nonreligious upbringing," though early on they would join the Brownsville Podhoretzes for Passover and ultimately hold seders at their own apartment. But there was no Sunday school or Hebrew school. Perhaps it was in reaction to JTS, where both parents had gone, Midge adding that she indeed "lived there, took meals there and got to know all of these people – and I said I'm not sending my children to them." Hence there was no bat mitzvah ceremony for the girls, "but John *had* to be bar mitzvahed – there's no choice about that – though he now complains about how awful the tutor was" and about his lack of formal training in Judaism generally. Still, "when the day came he was perfect, absolutely perfect."[34]

15

Present Dangers

The title piece for *The Present Danger* had appeared in the February 1980 issue of *Commentary*. If the United States is to survive as a free society, Podhoretz argued, it must reaffirm the Truman Doctrine of 1947, which pledged, in that president's words, "to support free peoples who are resisting attempted subjugation by armed minorities or by outside pressure" and thereby to "contain" the spread of left-wing totalitarianism. The Truman Doctrine had been most eloquently articulated by George F. Kennan in "The Sources of Soviet Conduct" (*Foreign Affairs*, July 1947). Soviet expansionism was something that, Kennan said, "can be contained by the adroit and vigilant application of counterforce at a series of constantly shifting geographical and political points, corresponding to the shifts and maneuvers of Soviet policy, but which cannot be charmed or talked out of existence."

Counterforce had a military as well as political dimension, as was demonstrated by what Podhoretz called our "unremarkable" decisions to intervene in Korea and Vietnam. Our goal, in either instance, wasn't to roll back communism, as the doctrine's more hawkish right-wing critics wanted to do, but, by reestablishing recognized borders between north and south, at least halt it. And why was this *America's* job? Kennan's peroration was squarely within the tradition of the country's exceptionalism:

The thoughtful observer of Russian-American relations will find no cause for complaint in the Kremlin's challenge to American society. He will rather experience a certain gratitude for a Providence which, by providing the American people with this implacable challenge, has made their entire security as a nation dependent on their pulling themselves together and accepting the responsibilities of moral and political leadership that history plainly intended them to bear.[1]

Eisenhower, Kennedy, and Johnson had all subscribed to the Cold War consensus, behind which lay the Wilsonian worldview we have seen Moynihan trying to revive in the mid-seventies. The reason it needed reviving was that Nixon, in 1969, had substituted his own doctrine for Truman's. In his earlier days, Nixon had if anything been an advocate of rollback, but as president he recognized how deeply the experience of Vietnam had soured the American public on the idea of a providential mission to defend liberty in faraway places. With the help of Kissinger, he therefore inaugurated the era of détente. The Soviets were in an imperially expansionist phase of development; they might very well win in the end. But America could delay that bleak day through intelligent diplomacy – which meant, for example, cooperating with the Soviets in peaceful projects in return for their quiescence in Europe, Africa, or Asia.

Détente's record, as Podhoretz recounted, hadn't been good. Peoples who with American arms had tried to resist communist or other illiberal rebellions had failed – the South Vietnamese, the supporters of the Shah in Iran – and the regimes that succeeded were repressively cousin to Stalinism. The Nixon Doctrine, in a word, had proved empty; America lost, and the Soviets and their communist system won. Moreover, as one domino fell, others followed – first South Vietnam, then Cambodia, Laos, Ethiopia, Mozambique, and Afghanistan.[2]

Then came Carter, who concocted his own doctrine. This was premised on the assumption that the East–West contest of ideology had been superseded by a contest of economics: rich North versus poor South, or the "one-third rich" versus the "two-thirds hungry." A humanitarian America should be feeding those hungry sheep. To Podhoretz, though, it was apparent that the Soviets were more intent on fleecing – not just those hungry sheep of the South but the well-fed flocks of the North as well. What was the invasion of Afghanistan if not a step toward controlling the Middle East's oil fields? What about the fall of the Shah in Iran, the elevation of the Ayatollah Khomeini, and the taking of hostages in the American embassy? One couldn't prove it, but America's failure to seize the oil fields in the Gulf States in 1974, when "the very lifeblood of its civilization" had been threatened, surely "emboldened" the Iranian revolutionaries in 1979.[3]

Podhoretz was composing another variation on a central theme: the late seventies were mirroring the late thirties. Just as pacific voices then urged "mature restraint" in the face of Hitler's provocations, so now a Carter or a Ted Kennedy was assuring us that a combination of Muslim loathing of Soviet atheism and fierce nationalist independence would turn Afghanistan into Moscow's Vietnam. No need to put our own soldiers in the field. Besides, our nuclear deterrent would stay the Soviets' hand. "*Would* it?" Podhoretz asked. Not if they felt they could get away with a first strike, which, with Carter's cancellation of the MX and ABM missile programs designed to protect our Minuteman force, they well might. The wise thing would be to return to the early sixties development of "flexible response" through conventional or counterinsurgent forces. If we didn't, Podhoretz wrote, then "the President of the United States, whoever he might be, would have to choose between nuclear war or Soviet control over the oil supply of the West. By then the vulnerability of our missiles to a Soviet first strike would automatically dictate surrender – checkmate by telephone."[4]

With the Soviets' control of the oil fields of the Middle East giving them the leverage to reduce the liberal democracies to vassalage, Podhoretz believed, the consequent Finlandization of America would be bloodless. Americans would undergo a subtle transformation, politicians and intellectuals clapping their hands over "a new era of 'peace' and 'friendship' and 'cooperation' between the Soviet Union and the United States," while objectors to this Orwellian Newspeak "would be castigated as warmongers" and pressured into silence. The original cold warrior Kennan was already toeing the new green line: "If the Persian Gulf is really vital to our security, it is surely we who, by our unrestrained greed for oil, have made it so."[5]

Was liberal democracy worth fighting, and dying, for? Having read their *Catch-22* and *Slaughterhouse-Five*, and having heard many of their elders declare that *we* were a graver threat to world peace than the Soviets, many young people seemed inclined to say no – or to say they weren't going to bleed for Exxon. But the issue, for Podhoretz, wasn't Exxon or our dependence on oil. The issue was the fullness of life under liberal democracy as opposed to the emptiness – the poverty, the repression, the pervasive inequality – of life under communism. Communism was the "missing term" in the debate.

President-elect Reagan couldn't have said it better himself, and his blurb urging "all Americans to read this critically important book," emblazoned on a red-and-white "bellyband" wrapped around the blue-jacketed *The Present Danger*, following the November election, was joined by others from Jackson, Rostow, and Moynihan. Kissinger said the book focused "attention on what is in fact the central challenge of our time"; William Safire in the *Times* called it "the 'little red book' of Reagan men."[6]

As for the reviews of *The Present Danger*, they followed the predictable paths. In one sector of the Right, *Business Week* stressed the desirability of commerce with communist states: "the Chinese hate the Russians and are allied to the U.S.," while "the Vietnamese hate the Chinese and are allied with the Russians," and none of it has "to do with ideology."[7] On the Far Left, there was Erik Bert in the *Daily World*: Podhoretz isn't only like Goebbels in his fanatic anti-Sovietism, he is "like Solzhenitsyn," preferring a "Russia 'still being ruled by the czars.'"[8] Seeking a middle ground, perhaps, the *New Republic*'s Ronald Steel offered to arrest the public "panic" occasioned by all the voguish talk about a "present danger": "The real-life fact [is] that communism has hardly spread anywhere, and that the term itself – as a description of a nation's economic or foreign policy – has become largely meaningless," Steel adding that this hadn't "diminish[ed] the urgent breathlessness of [Podhoretz's] argument, for the argument is one that rests on faith, and on fear."[9]

Michael Novak, the theologian and cultural critic, protested against Steel's "innuendo and character assassination."[10] Moynihan also protested, wondering about Steel's "intellectual integrity, or it may be, his capacity." The editorial of the very issue of the *New Republic* containing Steel's review concurred with Podhoretz's thesis that America's "leadership role in the world" was now in question because politicians, including some Republicans, were "seeking every avenue of retreat from both power and responsibility." Podhoretz's view therefore shouldn't be "misrepresented," Moynihan admonished, for "you might say he said it first."[11]

During the election campaign, Reagan repeatedly declared that "we're in greater danger today than we were the day after Pearl Harbor." Such talk wasn't meant to spread panic, as Steel alleged, but to wake Americans from the delusion that the Soviet Union was a normal country that merely wanted its "place in the sun." The Soviets, Podhoretz insisted, were an "expansionist" and "revolutionary" power, as the Nazis had been. They couldn't be appeased. The choice was between surrender and resistance, the latter of which might well work. Much would depend on how faithfully Reagan followed through on his campaign rhetoric. Getting into high office can change a man, as it changed Nixon from "the staunch anti-Communist" to the inventor of détente. Meanwhile, Podhoretz was simply grateful to have an attentive reader in high office. "The new leader of the free world," the journalist Michael Kramer noted, "isn't plugging anyone else's book."[12]

Liberal critics might have agreed that democracy was preferable to totalitarianism, and a few might even have admitted the greater productivity and efficiency of free markets. But they commonly balked at the way our competition with the Soviet Union sent us into bed with right-wing dictators like Anastasio Somoza in Nicaragua or Mohammad Reza Pahlavi in Iran. With characteristically American fastidiousness, Carter's administration had left those rulers to look out for themselves.

The definitive critique of such fastidiousness, Jeane Kirkpatrick's "Dictatorships and Double Standards," had appeared in *Commentary* in November 1979. Like Moynihan's "The United States in Opposition," it turned out to be a work that would bring its author the job of United States ambassador to the United Nations. "What you gave me to read was extraordinary!" then-candidate Reagan told his foreign policy adviser Richard V. Allen. "Who is this guy Jeane Kirkpatrick?" *She* was nervous about meeting the Republican presidential contender, telling Allen: "I am an AFL-CIO Democrat and I am quite concerned that my meeting Ronald Reagan on any basis will be misunderstood." Allen assured her that Reagan, long a species of AFL-CIO Democrat himself, wasn't seeking an endorsement (though she would of course endorse him). After several meetings and the landslide election, in any event, the new president was ready to send her into that peculiar snake pit, the U.N. General Assembly, where the discomfited would sometimes call her "the ambassador from *Commentary*."[13]

A professor of political science at Georgetown, Kirkpatrick had written an enormous draft of her argument in the house in the south of France where she and her husband "Kirk" (Evron Maurice Kirkpatrick)[14] spent each summer. Podhoretz and Kozodoy trimmed and reworked it into the classic it instantly became. Like Podhoretz's own "My Negro Problem," "Dictatorships" was momentous for Kirkpatrick not only because she wrote it entirely from her own inspiration – the culmination of a deal of brave talk on the lawn in France – but also because it declared her independence from the shop mentality of most of her academic colleagues. "Maliciously" misunderstanding her essay, they made her pay, socially and professionally, and when as ambassador she delivered guest lectures at Berkeley, Minnesota, the University of Washington, etc., crowds of protesters jeered and hooted. "Not just extremely unpleasant, but painful experiences," she would recall.[15]

But that would be later. In her 1979 essay, she begins by observing how liberals commonly deplore our giving aid to right-wing dictators. What is wrong with their critique is its ignorance of history – an ignorance that makes it, ethically, nearly useless. Democracy has always been based on "disciplines and habits" that are the products of "decades, if not centuries" of experience – as in England, France, or America. How can countries that aren't now democratic get there? Not by way of totalitarian government. Totalitarian rulers lock down every aspect – the totality – of life, and suppress even the least interesting forms of free thought or action. History does, however, show instances of right-wing dictatorships evolving into democracies – Spain and Brazil most recently. How on earth does that happen?

One needs to grasp the distinction between totalitarian and authoritarian regimes. Politicians like Carter would prefer to regard communists as kin to socialists, and socialists as kin to liberals – merely liberals "in a hurry." After all, Kirkpatrick writes, socialists "speak our language," professing "universalistic norms" based on "reason, science, education, and progress." Thus, when "left-wing revolutionaries invoke the symbols and values of democracy," they are romanticized as disciples of the signers of the Declaration of Independence, only wearing jungle fatigues. When they turn out to be totalitarians, the "duped" liberals call for patience, assured that Americans are finally once again on the right side of history.

But are they? If democracy is the desired end, then the smarter bet, historically, is with "traditional authoritarian governments," even when run, as in Nicaragua, by a Somoza. Because they "are less repressive than revolutionary autocracies," they "are more susceptible of liberalization." When one considers how Red China is worse than Taiwan, North Korea worse than South Korea, and the Soviet Union much worse than Czarist Russia, one begins to suspect that the right side of history is, in fact, the Right (Not, of course, the totalitarian Right, as in Nazi Germany.)

Kirkpatrick sweeps nothing under the carpet. Traditional societies are "less developed," with their "masses in poverty," their "miseries" and "untouchables." But while a trickle of enterprising people may emigrate from them, there have been no waves of refugees. Communist regimes, by contrast, actually "create refugees," for by "claim[ing] jurisdiction over the whole life of the society," they "so violate internalized values and habits that inhabitants flee by the tens of thousands." It isn't a fairy-tale conflict of absolute good versus evil but an analysis of comparative better and worse.

Looking closely at Carter's foreign policy, Kirkpatrick can only conclude that "Something very odd is going on here." The United States is on record as a supporter of liberal democracy in *all* places, but because it ignores the antidemocratic abuses of totalitarian regimes while obsessing about the antidemocratic abuses of authoritarian regimes, it is actually supporting democracy only in *some* places. That is why it is guilty of deploying "a double standard." The moral cure would be a single standard. It would enable us to discriminate between what makes for democracy in those countries that lack it and what doesn't. What doesn't is totalitarianism. What does is authoritarian dictatorship.

As for the United States itself, Kirkpatrick's plea was what Moynihan's had been: "The United States is not in fact a racist, colonial power, it does not practice genocide, it does not threaten world peace with expansionist activities," and it has "moved further, faster, in eliminating domestic racism than any multiracial society in the world."[16] Taking her ambassadorial place at the U.N., she would speak truths like these to the majority in the General Assembly. And she wouldn't lack occasion, for the majority's impulse at every crisis – whether it was the Khmer Rouge's murder of almost half of their fellow Cambodians or the Soviets' invasion of Afghanistan – was, as she said, to "blame America first."[17]

Kirkpatrick was a charter member of the Committee for a Free World, which Decter, leaving her editor's job at Basic Books, had formed in the summer of 1980. She was granted $100,000 from the Mellon-based Carthage Foundation.[18] Its roster of Americans (Barrett, Bellow, Kozodoy, Kramer, Kristol, Seymour Martin Lipset, Carl Gershman, Edward Shils, George Will) to some extent overlapped with that of the Committee on the Present Danger, which it more or less replaced, and it added an international group of intellectuals (Raymond Aron, Luigi Barzini, Alain Besançon, Paul Johnson, Melvin Lasky, Golo Mann, Hugh Seton-Watson, Leopold Labedz, Jacqueline Wheldon) concerned about the spread of totalitarian doctrines. The committee's function was in some measure social since Decter, "a kind of motherly figure," as the critic Ruth Wisse said,[19] helped these disparate and geographically scattered people feel part of a new family. It wasn't the old Family, which had the advantages as well as disadvantages of shared metropolitan turf. But they were at least connected.

Decter conceived the committee as heir to the postwar (and, as it turned out, CIA-funded) Congress for Cultural Freedom, which had been concerned with communist subversion. The new threat was, externally, Soviet missiles and, internally, self-Finlandization.[20] A year into Reagan's presidency, the CFW was starting to wonder when he would get around to the serious buildup of American arms that would neutralize the Soviet missiles and again give the West a more than Finnish belief in itself. "Carterism without Carter" is what Tucker called the first year's shilly-shallying.[21]

In May 1982, Podhoretz put the discontent into an essay for the *New York Times Magazine* that attracted nationwide attention, and a long phone call from Reagan himself. This, by the way, was the only time Reagan actually consulted with Podhoretz about foreign policy, despite the insistent rumors that the author of *The Present Danger* "really was calling the shots from behind the scenes."[22] The White House couldn't ignore "The Neo-Conservative Anguish Over Reagan's Foreign Policy," as the title ran, because the anguish referred to the very rationale for the neoconservatives' support for their fellow former Democrat in 1980 – his pledge to reassert the country's military and political power.

Reagan had begun a program of rearmament, but his administration seemed uncertain about what the arms were *for*. Presumably, Podhoretz said, to persuade the Soviets to stop their imperial "fishing in troubled waters." Yet in the Middle East we were selling the Saudis our AWACS (Airborne Warning and Control System) planes – ostensibly so that the advanced radar could detect a Soviet air attack but more likely an Israeli one. Why this undermining of Israel's deterrent? And why, in another instance, had Reagan instructed Kirkpatrick to join the vote condemning Israel's preemptive strike against Saddam Hussein's nuclear facility at Osirak in 1981 (a strike the world later had reason to be grateful for)?

And what about Lech Walesa's Solidarity movement in Poland, which wanted to throw off, for the sake of all Poles, the puppet regime of Jaruzelski? When the Polish workers rose up in 1981, Reagan could simply have withdrawn the business the Soviets had come to rely on by "cutting off credits and other forms of economic aid, making an all-out effort to halt the construction of the natural-gas pipeline from Siberia to West Europe and possibly reinstating an embargo on grain and technology," which even Carter had had the gumption to impose after the invasion of Afghanistan. Was George Will right in remarking that this Republican administration "loves commerce more than it loathes Communism"? "Is it too late for the President to put a classically Reaganite stamp on the foreign policy of his own administration?" Podhoretz asked. "I do not think it is, but I do think that time is running out."[23]

The administration didn't immediately change direction, but the president reacted personally to Podhoretz's concern. The latter wrote Beichman that, "As you might have heard, Reagan called me himself, and he was also asked about me at his last press conference. There have been several swipes at the piece – by Tony Lewis, Flora Lewis, Philip Geyelin, Joseph Harsch, and Jimmy Wechsler – but mostly in the context of praise for Reagan for having finally come to see the light as they all see it."[24] They were praising Reagan, that is, for *giving* the neoconservatives all that anguish. In his phone call, Reagan thrice assured Podhoretz that he didn't believe in détente. But each time he said it, Podhoretz, "honored but not reassured," felt his "heart [sink] a bit, since it was clear ... that he *did* believe in something that I *would* call détente."

There were some positive signs, to be sure. Certainly Podhoretz had overcome his first impression of Reagan during a meeting with neoconservative intellectuals in 1979: good-looking, uncommonly jaunty, but obtuse. It was clear that he was no "amiable dunce" (Clark Clifford's put-down), nor any kind of hypocrite (tough talk, wimpish action). He was smart enough to grasp that the "evil" Soviet empire could collapse. "The people over there," he told Podhoretz, "were reduced to eating dog food" – a fancifully phrased but proper assessment of the economic ineptitude that, when he later announced his strategic missile defense initiative, kept the Soviets from competing.[25] In October 1982, Podhoretz could say that Reagan's policy "*has* changed somewhat for the better."[26] Actions were beginning to match words, and some of the words – to the British Parliament at Westminster in June 1982, for instance – were matchless.

The clarity of Reagan's high rhetoric at Westminster – with its certainty that, if we were willing to stand by the liberal democracy we say we love, then communist totalitarianism would end up on the ash heap of history – was one thing. But politics is for the most part about choosing lesser evils. To imagine otherwise, as Sidney Hook noted, was the fatal mistake of the "ritualistic liberals" in Weimar Germany who couldn't stomach allying themselves with the Social Democrats, a lesser evil, and so ended up helpless in the face of a greater evil, the National Socialists. Likewise today liberals "demand that our foreign policy be based on the Declaration of Independence," seemingly "unaware that if we took its words literally we would be actually engaged in trying to overthrow totalitarian communist regimes."[27]

What may have been in the back of Hook's mind was the report on the CFW's February conference at the Plaza Hotel that Alfred Kazin wrote for the *New York Review*. It was rife with snide remarks about the neoconservative "vision of America resembl[ing] that of a defense contractor" or the conferees' needless gloom about "anti-Americanism," homosexuals, or an alleged "'radical whirlwind' in Mrs. Thatcher's England and Mr. Reagan's America." Podhoretz himself wasn't "gloomy," Kazin stated; rather, he "radiated confidence," proclaiming "the neoconservative cause" now to be "the dominant faction within the world of ideas." Kazin

wondered what had led this ambitious man to such delusion about his importance, to so much paranoia about the "liberal enemy," to so much heartlessness in a world where the evidence of wretchedness on the streets of New York north and west of the Plaza would once have been enough to jar someone who had grown up in the Brownsville section of Brooklyn.

Kazin ended by ridiculing Podhoretz's thesis that "if George Orwell were alive today he would be a neoconservative." Weren't neoconservatives "against" the working classes and wasn't Orwell "for" them? And what about Orwell's love of "neutrality and objective truth" and hatred of Newspeak's

FIGURE 17. Norman Podhoretz speaking at the Conference of the Committee for the Free World, held at the Plaza Hotel in New York, 1984. (Copyright Rebecca Hammel. All rights reserved.)

distortions of everything past and present? It was Podhoretz and his crowd who were the real distorters.[28]

Podhoretz's "If Orwell Were Alive Today" in *Harper's* (January 1983), a run-up to 1984 itself, did indeed stir a tempest. Reading through the four volumes of Orwell's essays and reviews, Podhoretz had been "struck by the uncanny resemblances between the debates of the 30's, 40's and those of the present. The world goes on changing, the arguments remain the same."[29] Orwell died of tuberculosis in 1950 when only forty-seven years old. Where would his arguments have pointed today? It wasn't an easy question, given the way he kept changing his mind on big as well as little issues. While calling himself a socialist, he was nonetheless a severe critic of socialist ideology and its followers. A species of "Tory anarchist" in the early thirties and semi-Trotskyist in the late thirties, he discovered during the war that at a deeper level he was simply a patriot – "My Country, Right or Left." After the defeat of right-wing totalitarianism in that war, he began to worry about the left-wing version; hence *Animal Farm* and *Nineteen Eighty-Four*.

To be sure, though these books were openly anticommunist, Orwell denied that they were antisocialist. But he failed to indicate how, in Podhoretz's words, "a socialist revolution could be accomplished without a betrayal of the ideals of liberty and equality to whose full realization socialism was in theory committed." Because there was no foreseeable end to this debate, however, Podhoretz cut through the theorizing by appealing to what Burke would have called Orwell's prejudices.

Orwell understood the obnoxious arrogance of the left-wing intellectuals with whom he worked, finding "more saving political and moral wisdom in the instincts and mores of 'ordinary' people." He was also sharply critical of writers who thought Nazism, or later communism, could be defeated with pacifism. As he said in 1945, "One has to belong to the intelligentsia to believe things like that; no ordinary man could be such a fool." The ordinary man thinks as Orwell himself did in 1938: "If someone drops a bomb on your mother, go and drop two bombs on his mother. The only apparent alternatives are to smash dwelling houses to powder, blow out human entrails and burn holes in children with lumps of thermite" – Orwell believed it essential to say concretely what was involved – "or be enslaved by people who are more ready to do these things than you are yourself; as yet no one has suggested a practical way out."

The conclusion? Maybe, like most literary intellectuals, Orwell, had he lived into the 1980s, would have continued as a nominal socialist. All in all, though, Podhoretz couldn't imagine it.[30]

Orwell had said of Dickens that he was so capacious and many-sided that everyone from Christians to communists wanted to claim him as an ally. Something similar was true of Orwell himself.[31] The battle in the letters column of *Harper's* occasioned by Podhoretz's essay, especially the exchange between him and Christopher Hitchens, went on for an extraordinary three months and left scars that neither would forgive.[32] Many of its points were repeated in a debate Podhoretz and Irving Howe would have about Orwell as 1984 approached.

Both critics identified with Orwell, but especially Podhoretz. As he told John Rodden in 1986, "Orwell snuffed out the 'smelly little orthodoxies' of the London Left; I tried to expose the 'dirty little secret' of my New York world." "I don't think it's necessary or proper to look for ancestors who aren't your ancestors," he continued, "and if I believed that Orwell were not what I've portrayed him – anti-pacifist, anti-neutralist, and on American's side in the Cold War – I'd give him up. But Orwell *is* an ancestor on the issues that concern me: democracy versus totalitarianism."[33]

There was no need to draft Kissinger as a neoconservative ally for he had already volunteered. In occasional writings during the Carter years, taking advantage of the freedom of being out of office, he pressed the administration to fulfill the West's obligation to contain Soviet expansionism. The memoirs Kissinger meant for posterity – *White House Years* (1979) and *Years of Upheaval* (1982), later to be completed by *Years of Renewal* (1999) – defended his and Nixon's policy of détente, described his own diplomatic shuttling, and gave a vivid account of personalities met along the way. After reading the first volume, Podhoretz wrote him to say that, aside from "overwhelmingly" winning the "debate with the Left" though not the "debate with the critics of détente," the book as a whole possessed such "immense literary and intellectual distinction... [that] it will stand the test of time better than some of the policies it describes and defends so brilliantly."³⁴

Publication of the second volume gave Podhoretz the opportunity, in a full-dress review, to place Kissinger's accomplishments. The memoirs, he believed, weren't merely among the highest examples of political autobiography, where the competition would include Churchill and Charles de Gaulle; they were among the great books of our era, period. This was because Kissinger offered "writing that is equally at ease in portraiture and abstract analysis; that can shape a narrative as skillfully as it can paint a scene; that can achieve marvels of compression while moving at an expansive and leisurely pace." The volumes' characterizations, even in thumbnail, were often unforgettable, not least those of Nixon, who "never learned where his home was," and Kissinger himself, who, though born in Germany, always knew where his center was – in undivided allegiance to America and to the Jewish people.

Podhoretz's rejection of the Nixon–Kissinger policy of détente stemmed from his assessment of the communist leaders. Like their fellow totalitarian Hitler, they played for all or nothing. The democracies could ensure that the totalitarian states would *get* nothing, but typically only after being galvanized by events like the invasion of Poland in 1939 or Afghanistan in 1979, when "the nature of the enemy revealed itself unambiguously in action." Americans were slow to pull themselves together thanks to their tendency toward isolationism, which Kissinger, so perceptive about other peoples' national traits, never quite understood. Americans didn't like to go to war for "merely geopolitical reasons"; they wanted a Wilsonian ideal to fight for. The failure to articulate, forcefully and consistently, such an ideal was but one of the prudential mistakes American presidents and other politicians had been guilty of during the war in Vietnam.

Podhoretz felt an absence of such an ideal in Kissinger's efforts to ally the United States with China against the Soviets – an absence resulting, ultimately, from the statesman's belief "that he could negotiate *anything*." There was always the "*breakthrough*" ahead: the Paris peace accord ending the war in Vietnam, the 1972 agreement on the structure of détente, the prospect of an enduring rapprochement between Israel and its Arab neighbors. This last, Podhoretz feared, was as much a mirage as the other two for, like the communists, the Arabs sought victory, while the Israelis sought peaceful accommodation.

Still, what Podhoretz didn't doubt was the sheer immensity of the difficulties that troubled any diplomat, even one as brilliant as Kissinger, as he worked in the dark, without knowledge of the future and often without adequate information about what was going on in the present. If Kissinger made conceptual and tactical mistakes, who, reading his memoirs, could finally blame him?³⁵

Kissinger at once responded: "Contrary to your expectation, I was very pleased with your review.... You stated no disagreement with which I was not familiar from talking with you. Besides, I got the best of both worlds because now both your admirers and detractors can buy the book with a clear conscience." He raised a single "substantive point" about the cease-fire negotiations in 1973 between Israel and Egypt. "There is no military solution for three million against 120 million that can last for eternity," he wrote, implying that the Sisyphean struggle for a diplomatic solution must continue.[36]

There were two other illuminating exchanges at the time between Kissinger and Podhoretz, who in the coming years would grow to be exceptionally close friends. One was over Charles Horner's *Commentary* review of Nixon's *The Real War*.[37] Kissinger sent Podhoretz a "not for publication" letter complaining how those anticommunists who opposed our Vietnam policy as being not tough enough "prefer to forget" the complications of the period – "the domestic turmoil, and Congress's massive assaults on the defense budget and the national rebellion against executive authority." The fact is "that if one wanted to resist Communism, one could not collapse ignominiously in Vietnam. Nixon surely deserves credit for understanding this central point, especially since events after 1975 have proved him right." Were the issue

only the injustice of being attacked by the left for being too tough and by the new right for being too conciliatory, it would be easy to let history clean up the record. But the problem is more complex. The new revisionism seems designed to deprive America of any memory.... Surely it can be in nobody's interest to create the myth that those who manned the barricades in a tragic period were really no different than their opponents.[38]

The second exchange was occasioned by another *Commentary* review, also by Horner, of the British journalist William Shawcross's *Sideshow: Kissinger, Nixon, and the Destruction of Cambodia* (1979). While "grateful for the conclusion that Nixon and I were not quite as bad as Pol Pot," Kissinger was nevertheless dismayed at Horner's acceptance of "Shawcross's misleading and cynical version of the facts" and at the implied endorsement of Shawcross's view of the supposedly "corrupt, deceitful" practices marking the "secret" war in Cambodia. "What exactly did the Administration I served do to justify such charges?" Kissinger asked.

We inherited a war involving over 500,000 Americans and millions of Vietnamese and Laotians. We thought we had an obligation to those around the world whose freedom and security depended on us to end it in a controlled manner. We did not think it right simply to turn over whole populations to totalitarian rule – the only alternative ever offered to us – especially when so many of them had linked their fate to ours in reliance on our predecessors' promises.... History will have to judge – if it has not already – who represented the moral side in this debate over the fate of Indochina.[39]

After receiving such missives from Kissinger, Podhoretz may well have felt that a new and different book about the war needed to come out. That, decidedly, had been the message from Norman B. Hannah at *National Review*, who after the publication of *The Present Danger* stressed to Podhoretz the desirability of "a simple exposition to the common man of how the tragedy of Vietnam resulted from the misconceptions and indecision of a few men – not from original sin."[40] Eugene Rostow agreed. He had been part of the team that planned American strategy in Vietnam. Given the subsequent "shock and setback" of that war, it wasn't surprising that residual isolationism should become prominent once more. "We were not 'defeated' in Vietnam," wrote Rostow. "We got tired of it and pulled out, which is different."[41]

Podhoretz took these several comments to heart. The United States couldn't go forward with the Trumanesque foreign policy reaffirmed in *The Present Danger* until it came to terms with the most depressing reversal such policy had suffered. *Why Are We in Vietnam?* was the interrogative title of Mailer's 1969 novel, dedicated to (among others) Podhoretz. Mailer's answer had been that Americans suffered from a congenital psychological deficit – like Hannah's reference to "original sin" – which they were forever trying to work through in heart-of-darkness places like the jungles of Southeast Asia. The title of Podhoretz's book would be *Why We Were in Vietnam*, pointing not to some amoral instinct but to a thoroughly moral idea.

Proposing the book to Erwin A. Glikes at Simon & Schuster, Podhoretz said it would "be done from the point of view of a writer who participated actively, and from the beginning, in making the case against American intervention into the Vietnam war, but who now believes that, far from being a criminal act, it was a morally sound though recklessly imprudent use of American power." He would be reopening the debate "to help restore the repute of the political strategy of which Vietnam was a mistaken tactical application."[42] If in some sick way America *had* gone into Vietnam in order to get the kicks of domination, then, as he would have no trouble revealing, it had been sorely disappointed. In fact, our inability to dominate anyone in Vietnam, at least within our self-imposed rules of engagement, was undermining our present confidence about doing anything, anywhere, for our allies.

In very compressed mode, Podhoretz's analysis is as follows. We were in Vietnam not to rape and pillage, nor to assert and extend the white man's hegemony over Southeast Asia, but, like traditional Wilsonian idealists, to protect the South against the totalitarian regime of the North and its Vietcong allies. Eisenhower's advisers had been reluctant but, as the Pentagon Papers showed, Kennedy was eager to intervene. There was nothing inadvertent about it. However, Kennedy committed himself to "slow and small" operations, hoping to achieve his objectives "on the cheap": "he willed the end but not the means – just as he had done before with the Bay of Pigs."[43] Johnson escalated our military effort, but *his* on the cheap approach was political, refraining from any effort to persuade the public that our reasons for defending the government of South Vietnam against communist totalitarianism were noble. By concentrating on a realistic, power-politics *raison de guerre* – we were holding a line in Vietnam in order to contain China, etc. – Johnson and his advisers allowed the New Left to dictate the terms of the moral argument and thus dishearten those, including the leading media, who until 1967 had supported the war.

After the 1968 election, Nixon took the on-the-cheap *strategic* approach of gradual, not precipitate, withdrawal. Needless to say, he and Kissinger weren't surrendering. The idea was that the South Vietnamese would assume responsibility for their own defense. But the majority of American citizens wanted an end to what they had been persuaded to think was an immoral war, and when their representatives in Congress cut off funding, it was only a matter of time before the helicopters would be extricating the last Americans and as many of their endangered Vietnamese associates as possible.

An immoral war? Podhoretz, in his final chapter, titled "Whose Immorality?," doesn't think so. The young protesters on the campuses may have had some excuse for not knowing about the wars of the past, but their older professors and the politicians in Washington had none. They knew what World War II or Korea had been for, and they understood the brutal nature of modern combat. The doves' denunciations of our methods of killing the enemy (and, collaterally, civilians) were so shrill as to make America seem, to the unhistorical American imagination, like Nazi Germany, and our Marines like the SS.[44] But there were no more "war crimes" committed by our troops in Vietnam than by our troops in World War II. The atrocity at My Lai, as even Daniel Ellsberg admitted, was an exception. In Korea, up to seventy percent of people killed had been civilians, while in Vietnam the figure was at most forty-five percent, approximately the figure for World War II; and in any event a substantial portion of these deaths, especially after 1969, were caused by the Vietcong and the North Vietnamese. The war protesters engaged in doublethink: violence committed by American troops and their allies, like their alleged violations of international law, was always evil, whereas violence committed by communist troops, like their real violations of international law, was always good.

In the end, Podhoretz concedes, the "effort to save Vietnam from Communism was indeed beyond [America's] intellectual and moral capabilities." But, Carter notwithstanding, there was nothing morally impoverished about our effort. However imprudent it may have been, it was, as Reagan rightly said, "noble."

Commentary's own pioneering coverage of the war, dating as we have seen from pieces by Joseph J. Zasloff and Hans Morgenthau in 1961–62, hadn't called the effort noble. The nobility of fighting against leftist totalitarianism was simply assumed. What Zasloff and Morgenthau contended was that under the circumstances America couldn't "win such a war in such a place at acceptable cost."[45] By 1969, Podhoretz himself believed "that the war was lost, that a negotiated settlement was impossible, and that an immediate American withdrawal, although undesirable, was the least bad of the alternatives now before us."[46] He would later accuse himself of having been "facile in failing to take the full measure of what an American defeat would cost," most grievously in the resurgence of American isolationism. One way or another, he came to realize, "all of us" who called for withdrawal from Vietnam had, "explicitly or implicitly, favored" America's "defeat." He had written *Why We Were in Vietnam* to identify the proper lessons, separating, if he could, the things that had been "right" and the things that had been "wrong, horribly wrong," both in the government's policy and in the ideas of its critics (his own included).

Podhoretz's thesis that American policy was nobly intended but imprudently carried out, like his corollary that the imprudence never produced systematically "immoral" fighting tactics, was lost on critics unwilling, or unable, to countenance even such minimal complexities. Following Theodore Draper's lead, reviewers (as Podhoretz later wrote) "accused me of trying to keep it 'a secret from the reader' that I too had been an opponent of the war." By thus "smearing the character of the author," they hoped "to discredit [his] argument."[47]

Draper's torpedoing was not only hysterical but, by any reputable journalistic standards, unconscionable. A long-time contributor to *Commentary* – his acerbic critiques of détente in the seventies were as sharp as his attacks on American involvement in Vietnam had been in the sixties – Draper now took to the pages of the *New Republic*, where Martin Peretz was editor, to claim that the neoconservatives were launching "a corrosive campaign to reopen the wounds of the war and envenom America political life once again." In pointing out the moral justifications of the war, Podhoretz gave credence to the domino theory: if South Vietnam were toppled, it could start a chain reaction all the way to Australia or Indonesia. Draper jeered at such unrealism: Podhoretz's war "exists in an ideal realm of anti-Communism, no matter where, by what means, at what price, or against whom."[48]

Draper's review came out a full three weeks before *Why We Were in Vietnam*'s release date. What Peretz had unleashed, as Glikes said to Robert Bartley at the *Wall Street Journal*, was a "preemptive strike."[49] That was one aspect of Draper's unconscionability. Another was his distortion of the record not only of Podhoretz's writing but of his magazine. Marion Magid at *Commentary* wrote the *New Republic* editors to remind them that, "even at the height of their opposition to the war," *Commentary*'s authors, including Draper himself, always "took care . . . to dissociate their position from those who wanted North Vietnam to win, and from those (not always distinguishable) who believed that the so called Communist threat in Vietnam was a delusion." When *Commentary* criticized the war, it was "chiefly on political rather than moral grounds. If Mr. Draper now thinks this distinction is unimportant – or for that matter that the domino theory has been discredited – he should ask the boat people."[50]

The question of why, in going after *Why We Were in Vietnam*, Draper went out of his way to go after its author cannot be answered with certainty. He had been Podhoretz's friend as well as literary colleague. As Christopher Lehmann-Haupt wrote in his obituary for Draper in 2006, the *New Republic* review "left Mr. Podhoretz bewildered":

When approached by a reporter for an interview about his life, [Draper] declined and offered instead to write a statement to be sent in a sealed envelope and not opened until his death. In it, he said of his review of *Why We Were in Vietnam*: "I broke with Podhoretz when he changed the political line of *Commentary*."[51]

But of course the magazine had changed a dozen years before, in no small part through Draper's own anti-détente pieces.

Podhoretz would later say he didn't "think there was anything personal in Ted Draper's betrayal of me. The main point is that it was a betrayal, and the virulence with which he attacked me (not the substance of the attack) suggests that down deep he knew it." Once "a devoted Communist" and then "an equally devoted anti-Communist," Draper was "determined never to cross the shifting red line that defined the boundaries of a permissible rightward move. It was," Podhoretz continued, "because I went too far in that sense that they [not just Draper, but Bell and Glazer] all felt it necessary to break with me and, as an additional precaution, to make their dissociation clear to the world."[52]

The other prominently corrosive review was by Arthur Schlesinger in *Harper's*. Quite aside from implying that Podhoretz was a supporter of the war rather than, like himself "at least from 1965 on," an opponent, Schlesinger failed to grasp his method. Throughout *Why We Were in Vietnam*, Podhoretz had argued that both idealism and realism must be at work in American foreign policy, but Schlesinger, the biographer of and counselor to all the Kennedys, labeled him a mere idealist, a "West Side mini-Spengler," a doomsaying prophet "dumb" and "giddy," whose attempts to exculpate America for its "immoral war" were "as moralistic and sentimental as the New Left blather he so righteously condemns."[53]

Other reviews – several exceptionally positive, most viciously negative – came in, and at the end of the summer Beichman summarized them in *National Review*: "It wasn't just that the book itself was gassed, shrapneled, bayoneted, strafed, bombed, and nuked: the author, in turn, was made out to be an amalgam of Strangelove, Hitler, Pegler, and Pecksniff." Even though Podhoretz wasn't claiming that the war was "wonderful," "winnable," or "desirable," unrepentant New Leftists and McGovernites apparently saw "democratic civilization as being served better by Marxist guerrillas in Latin America or Africa" than by their anticommunist opponents. Since they were "moving toward unilateral disarmament," they found Podhoretz's "defense of the war in Vietnam... *their* present danger. And they will not let up on Podhoretz until, somehow, he is silenced."[54]

Many veterans' groups wrote in praise of Podhoretz's study of the war, as, from Paris, did Jean-François Revel, who after "breathlessly" reading "the first 80 pages" said: "It is one of your most perfect books, written both with the accuracy of a scientific demonstration and with the inspired style of a modern Demosthenes."[55] As the *Wall Street Journal* editorialized, below the personal conflicts between Podhoretz and his critics lay something deeper – the Democratic Party's "objection to *any*... challenge to the established literary wisdom that the problem in Vietnam was American immorality, military incompetence, and government duplicity."[56]

While the fracas over *Why We Were in Vietnam* was under way, Podhoretz was busy writing one of his more controversial essays, "J'Accuse." The title echoes that of Émile Zola's famous 1898 pamphlet on behalf of Alfred Dreyfus, the French army officer who was the victim of anti-Semitism. Podhoretz's piece was about the widespread "liberal" reaction to Israel's incursion into Lebanon in 1982 – a reaction he considered a new outbreak of anti-Semitism.

On June 6, Menachem Begin's government ordered troops into southern Lebanon to stop PLO shelling of towns in northern Israel. The plan was to create a twenty-five-mile-deep buffer zone, but Defense Minister Ariel Sharon, hoping to extirpate the PLO altogether, pushed all the way to Beirut. Protest demonstrations were organized in Israel by a new group, Peace Now, which believed these military actions unjustified because no "immediate threat to Israel's existence" had been made. (The shellings of northern towns were supposedly mere harassment.) In mid-August, the PLO, boxed in but still firing, agreed to submit to an American plan: it would leave Beirut by sea and establish its headquarters in Tunis.

On September 14, Lebanon's president-elect, Bashir Gemayel, a Maronite Christian, was assassinated. Palestinians claimed responsibility, and the Maronite Phalange party swore vengeance. Israeli forces were caught in between. On September 17, Phalangist soldiers entered the two Palestinian refugee camps of Sabra and Shatilla, nominally under the protection of the Israelis, and killed 2,300 people – a few hundred PLO combatants but mostly civilians, including women and children. A Peace Now demonstration in Tel Aviv on September 25 involved 400,000 people, a tenth of the population of the Jewish state. By then, the Israeli government had already begun its withdrawal into the narrow zone of southern Lebanon where, in future years, skirmishes with Hezbollah, the Iran supported "Party of God," would be ongoing.[57]

As Podhoretz argued in the *New York Times*, Israel's incursion to defeat both the PLO and the Syrians was an opportunity: first, to restore Lebanon's democracy, and second, to renew the peace process begun by Carter, Begin, and Sadat at Camp David.[58] What troubled him, as the summer wore on, wasn't the usual criticism of Israel's actions from left-wing writers like Alexander Cockburn or Nicholas von Hoffman in the *Nation* or the *Village Voice*. It was that centrist liberal organs – *Harper's,* the *New York Times*, the *International Herald Tribune* – were publishing writers who routinely compared the Israeli Defense Forces to the Nazis. And these were the professed friends of Israel. The professed enemies could only be emboldened to speak of Israel's "apocalyptic logic of exterminism," as Edward Said wrote. "Hitler's work goes on," thundered William Pfaff, while, to John Le Carré, "too many Israelis," having "persuaded themselves that every Palestinian man and woman and child is by definition a military target," are "inflicting upon another people the disgraceful criteria once inflicted upon themselves."

Israel like Nazi Germany? In "J'Accuse," Podhoretz hammered home a few elementary facts: the Nazis set out to murder every Jew on earth, while the Israelis, far from purposing any such bloody design on the Palestinians under Israel's sovereignty, had provided them "a degree of civil and political liberty, not to mention prosperity, unknown to Arabs living in any country under Arab sovereignty." The Israeli occupation of Gaza and the West Bank like the Nazi occupation of Eastern Europe? "The Nazis in less than six years managed to kill more than five million Jews in occupied territory. How many Palestinian Arabs have been killed by the Israelis in fifteen years? A hundred? And if even that many, has a single civilian been killed as a matter of policy?"

In short, any analogy "between the way Israel has treated the Palestinians and the way the Nazis dealt with the Jews is . . . disproportionate to a monstrous degree." Having no rational relation to fact, the analogy "must be driven by some other impulse." This other impulse is anti-Semitism. And what exactly was that? Not, Podhoretz explained, a mere "dislike of Jews":

Historically anti-Semitism has taken the form of labeling certain vices and failings as specifically Jewish when they are in fact common to all humanity: Jews are greedy, Jews are tricky, Jews are ambitious, Jews are clannish – as though Jews were uniquely or disproportionately guilty of all those sins. Correlatively, Jews are condemned when they claim or exercise the right to do things that all other people are accorded an unchallengeable right to do.

That is, anti-Semites employ a double standard: it is all right for other people to do "x" but it is wrong for Jews. Nor was it any less anti-Semitic when the double standard was applied by Jews themselves – like Anthony Lewis, who in an "endless series of columns" for the *Times* alternated between calling Israel a "fascist" state and demanding that it become Isaiah's holy "light among the nations."

Then came the deeper insight. In 1982, the anti-Semitism manifesting itself among Western liberals had little if anything to do with the ancient Christian hatred of Jews for having "killed Christ" or, as in the Dreyfus persecution, the bourgeois establishment's distrust of allegedly socialist Jewish intellectuals, and so on. The new anti-Semitism derived from something else – the humiliation felt when beholding, in contrast to Western nations' "sickly, sallow, even decadent" condition, the toughness of Israel:

[T]he fierceness of its will to live is what has made it a scandal and a reproach to its fellow democracies in the Western world. . . . We in the West confront in the Soviet Union a deadly enemy sworn to our destruction, just as Israel does in the Arab world. But whereas the Israelis have faced the reality of their peril and have willingly borne the sacrifices essential to coping with it, we in the West have increasingly fallen into the habit of denial, and we have shown ourselves reluctant to do what the survival of our civilization requires.

Something like a general rule suggested itself:

In the past, anti-Semitism has been a barometer of the health of democratic societies, rising in times of social or national despair, falling in periods of self-confidence. It is the same today with attitudes toward Israel. Hostility toward Israel is a sure sign of failing faith in and support for the virtues and values of Western civilization in general and of America in particular.

This meant that the sin of anti-Semitism had been subsumed within "the broader sin of faithlessness to the interests of the United States and indeed to the values of Western civilization as a whole."[59] There was a lot at stake here.

Podhoretz received dozens of letters on "J'Accuse," including one from Reagan saying he had "read it with great interest and, while at times I thought Israel overreacted to PLO forays in West Beirut, like you I was amazed at the one-sided reporting, particularly on television. No attempt was made to differentiate between civilian casualties and those that were PLO fighters. Your article will do much to straighten the record."[60] Reagan presumably understood Podhoretz's careful qualification: there was a resurgence of anti-Semitism, but not *all* critics of Israel's campaign against the PLO in Lebanon were anti-Semites. The anti-Semitic critics were the ones who, like the PLO itself, simply denied the Jewish state's right to defend itself militarily. Not too arcane a distinction, surely, but Podhoretz's use of the term "anti-Semitism" threw off some people – even, as we will see, some of his conservative allies.

In the early eighties, Podhoretz also wrote an extraordinary number of essays in literary criticism – on Camus, Henry Adams, Milan Kundera, and (as noted) on Orwell. Many were published in the *New Criterion*, which Hilton Kramer had established in 1982 as a counterpoise to what was starting to be called the "politically correct" (i.e., left-wing) mainstream. The essay that surely had the strongest personal charge was the one Podhoretz did on Leavis, his mentor at Cambridge, who well before his death in 1978 had been marginalized by that mainstream.

The reasons had something to do with politics. Leavis after all had rarely compromised his dedication to strictly literary values – the best words in the best order, and for the sake of an "enacted" (not simply preached) moral vision of life – while other critics were casually hailing this or that new writer, usually a representative of some oppressed group, as a major talent. Leavis had spoken for a twentieth-century revolution in taste parallel to the one Samuel Johnson had spoken for in the eighteenth century. "Taste taken seriously has a logic of its own," Podhoretz wrote, "and to this logic Leavis was relentlessly true." For Leavis, the works of George Eliot or James, Shakespeare or Lawrence, were a substitute for the Bible of his Huguenot ancestors, and criticism was "a substitute for devotional meditation and scriptural exegesis."[61]

Dan Jacobson hailed the Leavis essay not just for its affectionate "warmth" but also for its remembrance of "a time when the politics of culture seemed to matter more than the culture of politics – if that distinction makes any sense to you."[62] It did make sense – which may be why on a long flight to Australia to address audiences mostly of business people and politicians about the "New Defenders of Capitalism," Podhoretz found himself reading William Empson's *New York Review* essay on the poet John Donne. It was "a ridiculously internal piece," he wrote in his trip journal, but one "that nevertheless makes me feel envious somehow, of him *and* of the *NYR*. (Am I *really* pining for literature?)"[63] Although literary critics weren't an especially gentle species, even in England, the literary life would be easier, Podhoretz mused, and it attracted him, as an escape, in ways only a few of his intimates understood. Beichman was one who did. Podhoretz wrote to him: "The usual response from friends and acquaintances to attacks on me is to say things like: 'That kind of thing really doesn't bother you, does it?'; or 'What else do you expect?'; or 'You're tough – you can take it.' The very fact that you recognize how bad these things are, and how hard they are to take, is in itself an act of imagination and generosity for which I am grateful."[64]

As his son, John, would later say, "The interesting psychological aspect of his life is that being praised always meant a great deal to him," and yet he so often "put himself in a position where he was no longer praised" but damned, and not just damned but defamed. One such defamer was Cockburn, first in his media-criticism column in the *Village Voice* and later at the *Nation*, where he referred to Podhoretz as "a mass murderer every time he sits down to type or stands up to speak." To make matters worse, Cockburn was also a regular op-ed contributor for the *Wall Street Journal*. "My father couldn't laugh it off," John remarked. "Every time was like being stabbed in the back."[65]

But the imperatives of battle trumped the desire for peace and praise. As he got off that plane to Australia, he left the Empson essay behind.

16

"The Great Satan of the American Romantic Left"

With the Soviets bogged down in Afghanistan, the cold warriors' attention in the early eighties shifted to Latin America, where left wing insurgencies were rising against right-wing authoritarian rulers. In Nicaragua, the deed was already done, the Somoza regime having yielded to the Sandinista movement in July 1979. Toward El Salvador, Reagan, like Carter, cast a wary eye. He was reluctant to send troops, yet unwilling to see the country fall to Marxist guerrillas. As Podhoretz jotted privately to himself: "If they prevail we're *finished* (our backyard). Will they?"[1] Not if the United States stepped in to "help create a democratic Center as an alternative both to the Communist-dominated guerrillas (who are *not* supported by the people of El Salvador, as they showed in the last election) and to the extreme Right."[2] To create such a democratic center, the United States would doubtless have to act alone. Its intervention in Grenada in October 1983, both in reaction to a Soviet–Cuban expansion of an airfield that could be used for military purposes and out of concern for American medical students who might be held hostage by the new revolutionary government, had been condemned in the U.N. General Assembly by an overwhelming margin.

Why was the Grenada intervention right and the Soviet invasion of Afghanistan wrong? It was, as Raymond Aron had said, "a question of what the invading army is bringing with it."[3] Podhoretz agreed with Beichman, who argued that American support for anticommunists in Latin America, the Caribbean, or elsewhere was like Roosevelt's support of Lend-Lease in 1940, which helped Great Britain in its lone stand against Nazism. Of course the policy was imperfect, and people were killed, some of them innocent. But Roosevelt's program was the lesser evil – preferable to the victory of right-wing totalitarianism. So now with America's struggle against left-wing totalitarianism.[4]

The dominoes in Latin America were certainly teetering. The government under severest stress, that of El Salvador, couldn't seriously heed the cries of North American or West European liberals that it negotiate with local

guerrillas to form a "popular front" administration. As Kristol explained in
the *Wall Street Journal*, guerrillas weren't interested in sharing power, or in
elections (they had boycotted the most recent one). Give a country stability –
by preventing "a Castro-type insurrection" that would shut down all hope of
democratic development – and at least it had a chance of flourishing economically. Although the Democrats in Congress believed that the United States
ought to support this or that scheme for "a presumptive... egalitarianism,"
Americans, Kristol asserted, needed to check the mental disorientation that set
in whenever the Left pushed its "social justice" button. "The inadequacies [of
the existing regime] are real enough, as are the sins," yet those of revolutionary
left-wing regimes were invariably worse.[5]

The task of persuading the general public of this thesis, an application of
Kirkpatrick's "Dictatorships and Double Standards," was taken up by neoconservatives like Podhoretz's son-in-law Elliott Abrams, who for a time served
as Reagan's Assistant Secretary of State for Human Rights and Humanitarian
Affairs and in April 1985 was named Assistant Secretary for Inter-American
Affairs, thus becoming the youngest assistant secretary in the State Department's history. The Left questioned Reagan's commitment to "human rights";
Abrams replied that anticommunism was by definition a commitment to human
rights.[6] The problem was that stopping guerrillas from shooting people who
wanted to vote required shooting guerrillas – just as stopping Nazis from
engulfing the world had required shooting Nazis.

Roman Catholics had centuries of experience wrestling with the problem
of social justice, and in the early eighties their own Left and Right went to
the mat once more. Bishops in the United States, typically more liberal than
the majority of their congregants, were often disposed toward the claims of
"liberation theology," a mostly Latin American movement that yoked Marxism
together with the so-called social gospel. What made people poor, supposedly,
was capitalism; let the revolutionary state abolish private property, divvy up
the pot, and so end poverty. This, for Abrams, wasn't merely the pursuit of
a will-o'-the-wisp, it was idolatry – the worship of the false god of politics,
which presumes the city of man can become the city of God. The history
of Eastern Europe, which had "witnessed the transformation of theoretical
Utopias into real Gulags time after time," showed that what Latin America
had to resist wasn't America and capitalism but Marxist guerrillas.[7] In his
State Department positions, Abrams was echoing the specifically theological
arguments of conservative Catholics like Michael Novak, George Weigel, and
Richard Neuhaus (a convert in 1990, he would regard his earlier Lutheranism
as proto-Catholic).

Podhoretz counted on Pat Moynihan to support aid both to the Salvadoran
government and to the Contras in Nicaragua. The Boland Amendment, which
was passed in the House without opposition and signed into law by Reagan in
December 1982, forbade direct American assistance to the Contras' drive to
overthrow the Sandinista government. "Why in the name of God," Podhoretz

wrote Moynihan in April 1983, "should the United States Congress provide special protection to the Sandinistas?" Replying that the Boland Amendment "came about well past the mid-point of my efforts" and now had "to be upheld," Moynihan offered friendly counsel: "Don't despair. Worry less." Podhoretz wasn't to be put off: "You're right to counsel me against despair. Despair is a sin. As such it pertains, strictly speaking, only to individuals. But the Boland Amendment, especially taken in conjunction with the cutback of military aid to El Salvador, emerges (to put the best possible face on it and to interpret it charitably) out of national or collective despair. And that too is sin of a kind."[8]

Two years on, Congress did vote to approve $100 million in direct aid to the Contras. Moynihan, though, voted against it. He would have preferred, it seems, to send in the Marines, devoting taxpayer dollars to *them* and not to surrogates:

How would you like the proposition that the decline of America came on the day the best equipped most looked after and cared for Army in the world (for which read [Marine] Corps) decided it would not go down to Nicaragua for the umpteenth time to straighten out matters but would leave the job to a rag tag group of ex guardsmen, social democrats and children.... Pay others to get shot at. You might be surprised how strong this sense is in the Congress.[9]

Podhoretz replied: "Well, yes, you can describe the Contras in that way. But I daresay they aren't any more ragtag than any other guerrilla army known to history, and there are a lot more of them than most such armies, including a few that succeeded, were able to recruit." As for the implied alternative: "If you really think the only way to solve it is by sending in the Marines, I wish you would say so in public." If, however, we *weren't* going to send in the Marines, "why in God's name shouldn't we give the Nicaraguans themselves a chance to do the job?"[10]

Podhoretz began to write a weekly column for the *New York Post* in March 1985, continuing until February 1989. The columns appeared not just in the *New York Post* but throughout the syndicate of newspapers owned by Rupert Murdoch. The Australian – "he's not at all ['the monster'] people imagine," Podhoretz said – had been at Oxford when Podhoretz was at Cambridge. Meeting through Maxwell Newton, they had known each other socially in America, but the inspiration for a Podhoretz column came from *New York Post* editors John O'Sullivan and Roger Wood, who wanted him to substitute for Pat Buchanan, soon to become White House Communications Director. Over dinner, Wood suggested three columns a week. Knowing his own exacting standards of craftsmanship, Podhoretz said one a week would suffice. Aware also that a George Will or Robert Novak made something in the "high six figures" annually for their weekly efforts, "I demanded more money than I thought the *Post* would agree to, but they did agree to it and I was stuck." The compensation would be $50,000 (currently about $100,000) a year, which was "a big incentive" – "No man but a blockhead ever wrote, except for money," as Samuel Johnson famously observed. Persuasive, too, was the prospect of being featured in the *Washington Post*. Meg Greenfield, its editorial page editor, bought rights to the column before it even started.

Greenfield's purchase of syndication rights, however, didn't oblige her to print a given week's column. She was more desirous of his pieces on cultural and literary issues – Heller's *Catch-22*, Philip Roth, Gore Vidal, manners and morals – than those on politics. This added anxiety to the burden of laboring three days over each weekly piece (as opposed to the thirty minutes William Safire admitted devoting to certain columns). Podhoretz's conscientiousness paid off, literarily. The columns were always exquisitely formed: a clearly presented question, a consideration of alternatives, evidence adduced for preferring one to another, and all in language that was forceful and often felicitous. Some were gems.

To many people, the gems were frequently obscured by the "trash" that was the *New York Post*'s most prominent topographic feature. Who would expect journalistic excellence amid girlie photos and shock accounts of celebrity life? In years past, the *New York Post* had been very liberal. Murdoch was not only a conservative but had hired editors who turned the paper into a look-alike of the British tabloids, a species so low, as Podhoretz later said, that they "make American tabloids seem like the London *Times* of the 19th century." In England, a John Gross or a Paul Johnson wrote brilliantly for tabloids and no one raised an eyebrow. In America, all that Podhoretz's intellectual peers claimed to see was the *New York Post*'s vulgarity and its open political partisanship. "Now," he has said, "everyone recognizes that the *New York Times* or the *Washington Post* is just as partisan, if in the other direction," but those papers "hypocritically" claim to be objective. The *New York Post* was at least honest in its profession of partisanship.[11]

The perdurable partisan issue in the mid-eighties was the Cold War, and Podhoretz continued to give the business to the spirit of appeasement. In the fall of 1984, that spirit manifested itself in a piece co-authored by McGeorge Bundy, Kennan, Robert McNamara, and Gerard Smith, which *Foreign Affairs* published as "A Portentous Year." Bundy & Co. endorsed a pledge of no first use of nuclear weapons, which they supposed (in Podhoretz's paraphrase) would "*strengthen* the American commitment to the defense of Western Europe." Yet this hypothesis had been refuted by a bipartisan group of West German intellectuals: "Not only would renunciation of first use fail to contribute to the 'internal health of the Western Alliance itself,' but it would have the opposite effect of increasing insecurity and fear." Why? Because NATO's nuclear weapons were the *only* credible defense against a Soviet attack with "*conventional* forces. . . . Therefore to renounce first use means renouncing deterrence of a conventional war; it is also to counsel surrender in the face of an inevitable defeat by decisively superior forces."

Predictably, the neoconservative case for hardening America's moral and military position was taken by the liberals of the day not as war-deterring but as war-mongering. Flora Lewis, columnist in the *New York Times*, alleged that some opponents of arms reductions were guided by the "ugly" belief "that war is inevitable, and the United States must prepare to 'prevail.' Norman Podhoretz, for example, veils this reasoning with analogies to the thirties appeasement of Nazi Germany and Japan."[12] "Did she have it right?" asked a *Commentary* reader. Podhoretz said no, she had been "not only inaccurate but defamatory. I have never said, and I do not believe, that nuclear war is inevitable. Nor have I ever spoken of a need 'to prevail.' What I have said, and what I do believe, is that policies of appeasing the Soviets such as Flora Lewis advocates will either lead to a Soviet dominated world or a nuclear war or both."[13]

At the time, the most inspiring figure in the anticommunist struggle was Aleksandr Solzhenitsyn (1919–2008). The Russian novelist had lived in the belly of the leviathan itself during the eight years (1945–53) he spent in the prison camps of the Gulag and the more than three years he spent afterward in internal exile. His three-volume study of those camps, written between 1958 and 1968 under excruciatingly difficult conditions, bore the rhyming title *Arkhipelag GULAg* ("GULAg" is the acronym for the Russian "Chief Administration for Corrective Labor Camps"). The metaphoric comparison of a chain of camps and a chain of islands was hauntingly right. Only the totalitarian bureaucrats, and often not even they, knew which prisoners were on which "island" and why. Relying on the testimony of 227 former prisoners and his own findings about the evolution of the Soviet penal system, Solzhenitsyn managed to memorialize what may have been as many as thirty million political prisoners, a third of whom perished. Like Russia itself, they were victims of Marxist–Leninist ideology. Solzhenitsyn's volumes were smuggled out in manuscript and published in the West in 1973. He was deported the next year.

The Gulag Archipelago's impact on the West was immense. Four years after its appearance, the writer Tom Wolfe told Podhoretz: "That book has absolutely altered the terms of the debate over communism and socialism, no matter who is doing the debating.... Without *The Gulag Archipelago* Jimmy Carter could not have opened his mouth about human rights." As Podhoretz was to note in an essay on Solzhenitsyn in 1985, in some measure stimulated by Wolfe, the Soviet authorities were found to be right after all: the author of the *Gulag* was indeed a traitor to the Kremlin. Not that such a charge hurt him in the minds of Western liberals, who in their morally equivalent fashion approved dissent whatever its direction: "Angela Davis here," as Podhoretz paraphrased the mood, "Solzhenitsyn there: it was all the same." Except that, once Solzhenitsyn was "here," it wasn't the same: for it turned out he was also anti-liberal and anti-détente, castigating the West for its failure of nerve in the face of the communist threat.

The West's custody fight over Solzhenitsyn – was he more useful to the Left or Right? – was similar to the one waged over Orwell, only the Russian

was still very much alive. Wolfe's letter indicates some of the issues in the
fray:

I notice that the smears are becoming part of the ordinary chatter of Journalism/Lit
folk who have never read a page of his. He is a Christian zealot, a fascist, he wants
to bring back the Tsar, he's an egotistical boor with a martyr complex, etc. More
recently one hears: He's a dreadful writer, the Russian Upton Sinclair, an utter bore –
this from the likes of Gore Vidal and Anthony Burgess (and many others). In my
opinion there is not a novelist writing in English who is his match in terms of technique
(and especially the creation of character) and breadth of theme and vision.... I go on
a bit about Solzhenitsyn's novelistic talents only because his literary reputation was
essential to the tremendous effect that *The Gulag* – not a great piece of literature by
any means, in terms of technique – was to have. It gave him a religious eminence, so
to speak. Hence the practical connection between the political and literary denunciations.[14]

Podhoretz's own position would be somewhat different. He had read
Solzhenitsyn's breakthrough novel, *One Day in the Life of Ivan Denisovich*
(1962, in English 1963), with the widely shared conviction that Russian literature had been reborn. *One Day*, published with Khrushchev's blessing, was a
truthful account, told from an ordinary prisoner's point of view, of an experience common to many Russians – that of being utterly at the mercy not so much
of ideologues as of "gangsters," who at a whim could release a prisoner or add
ten years to his sentence.[15] This is why thousands of former prisoners (*zeks*) sent
letters of thanks to Solzhenitsyn. But Podhoretz couldn't share Wolfe's enthusiasm for the literary qualities of *The First Circle* or *Cancer Ward* (published
in the West in 1968, and not at all in the Soviet Union), or for *August 1914*
and the later installments of *The Red Wheel* cycle, an epic about the Russian
Revolution meant to parallel Tolstoy's epic about the Napoleonic invasion.
And even *One Day*, Podhoretz realized going back, was severely limited by
the very triumph of its aesthetic form – Solzhenitsyn's confining himself, à la
Dostoevsky in *The House of the Dead*, to the limits of an uneducated peasant's
consciousness. We participate in his suffering, but we don't necessarily grasp
its full meaning.

The critic Clive James put his finger on one aspect of that meaning: "It isn't
Solzhenitsyn who can't create rounded characters – it's Stalin who destroyed
the possibility of them."[16] Be that as it may, Podhoretz believed that readers
could best apprehend the political meaning of *One Day* through Solzhenitsyn's
nonfiction, notably *The Gulag* and the autobiographical *The Oak and the Calf*
(1980), both of which displayed a verve, animation, sarcasm, and irony so
great as to almost overwhelm their subjects. But it wasn't only the style, it was
the man: these two books were "majestic achievements" because Solzhenitsyn
believed himself to be "an instrument of the will of God," appointed to remember the millions who suffered in the Gulag. And "whether or not one believes
in God, and whether or not one believes that Solzhenitsyn is an instrument of
the divine will, *his* belief has produced those 'clear effects' to which William
James pointed as the 'pragmatic' test of a genuine religious experience."

What Solzhenitsyn's words revealed, and what the victims of the Gulag hadn't the opportunity to say, was

that Communism is irredeemable, that there exist no "better" variants of Communism; that it is incapable of growing "kinder," that it cannot survive as an ideology without using terror, and that, consequently, to coexist with Communism on the same planet is impossible. Either it will spread, cancer-like, to destroy mankind, or else mankind will have to rid itself of Communism (and even then face lengthy treatment for secondary tumors).

This hard truth-telling was the main reason for Solzhenitsyn's unpopularity in the West. The charge that Solzhenitsyn's work showed signs of anti-Semitism, which Podhoretz found negligible, was a diversion from the central challenge, namely the call for Western resistance to communist totalitarianism. "Solzhenitsyn's terrible and terrifying question to us is this: is it possible that courage like his own is all that we require to escape from the fate he has come to warn us against?"[17]

In December 1984, Elliott Abrams attended a U.N. seminar in Geneva on "The Encouragement of Understanding, Tolerance and Respect in matters relating to freedom of religion or belief." The "moderate" Saudi delegate spoke of how "the Jews had created anti-Semitism" and how "the Talmud requires Jews to drink Christian blood every year."[18] This, another day in the life of the U.N., was also another signal for Jews in and outside Israel to recognize, as Podhoretz would later tell the Jerusalem *Post*, that their very preservation required a general manning of "the ramparts." And not least by intellectuals, who must correct the impression conveyed by the media, even in Israel itself, that the Jewish state was "the worst country in the world."[19]

Worst, best – try normal. That was Podhoretz's consistent theme. Normal countries didn't have to apologize for their existence, as Israel was so often obliged to do. True, its own factions attacked each other without letup; usually, however, the unhappiest of Israeli skeptics kept their suicidal impulses in check. The Israeli Left had no love for Menachem Begin, who came to power in 1977 as the country's first right-wing president, but it shared his determination to deny Hitler any "posthumous victories." If only the Diaspora Left, whose lives weren't immediately on the line, would catch up with their Israeli counterparts. And it couldn't happen soon enough, as Podhoretz argued in "The State of World Jewry" (December 1983), for it was on the survival of the Jewish state that the entire Jewish heritage depended.[20]

The struggle to keep not just Jewish but Gentile intellectuals focused on the full story of the conflict in the Middle East was never-ending. One instructive approach was to connect PLO terrorists with their cousins – the Irish Republican Army, the Basque separatists, or the Red Brigades in Italy – and demonstrate how terrorism and the media had become symbiotically linked. Since the late sixties, one had seen the emergence of what columnist Charles Krauthammer called "media terrorism": targeted killing had become "a form of political advertising," wherein reporters, drawn to the carnage, obligingly interviewed terrorist representatives for a lecture about "root causes" – poverty, oppression, dispossession, and so on – quite oblivious to the fact that, as Podhoretz tirelessly insisted, the immediate cause of terrorism was terrorists.

In 1984, Krauthammer, Podhoretz, and others joined in a *Harper's* roundtable on the subject. A telling point was made by John O'Sullivan, then working at the London *Daily Telegraph*. The popular press, he maintained, was better than the quality press at covering terrorist acts. "The assumption of the popular press is that terrorists are important for what they *do*" – i.e., kill innocents. "The assumption of the quality press is that terrorists are important for what they *say*" – i.e., that they are calling attention to legitimate grievances. Krauthammer agreed, and proposed a rule of thumb: "In covering terrorist events, reporters ought to concentrate on who, what, where, and when. They should leave the question of why to the historians and the psychiatrists."

Bob Woodward immediately objected that no "journalist would want to eliminate the 'whys' from any story," but for George Will, Krauthammer, O'Sullivan, and of course Podhoretz the problem was that the terrorists' "why" was indefensible. As the French intellectual Alain Besançon remarked, "The ideology of most terrorist groups holds that capitalist society is doomed and does not deserve to be defended, [and] that from its destruction something more worthwhile will emerge." It was an ideology, dating back at least to the Russian 1880s, that boasted of literary sympathizers like Tolstoy and Sartre and, in part for that reason, deeply colored the education of the university graduates who went on to become journalists.[21]

It was remarkable but true, as Jean-François Revel noticed, that "democratic civilization is the first in history to blame itself because another power is working to destroy it." Only yesterday, it seemed, there had been a liberal anticommunist consensus in the West. Was it simply that Vietnam, race riots, persistent pockets of poverty, and so forth had made that consensus untenable? This, to Podhoretz, didn't seem an adequate explanation. There was something about the Western psyche that needed to believe in the possibility of paradise on earth – "Communism with a human face" – and that no amount of negative evidence from the Soviet Union, China, North Korea, Vietnam, Cuba, or Nicaragua could finally dissuade. "To the liberal culture of the democracies," Podhoretz wrote, "built as they are on the idea of human perfectibility, the utopian vision...is a standing temptation." If it can't find an objective correlative in any "worker's paradise" on the ground, it seeks the psychological compensation of loathing the non-utopian competition, namely America.

What does one do with people who hate their own country? Give them a proper object for their love – to wit, their own country rightly understood, not as the agent of "capitalist encirclement" but as the blessed upholder of "the virtues and values of democratic civilization."[22] Better journalism – along the spectrum reaching from the *New York Post* to *Commentary* – had an educational, indeed a patriotic, mission.

When it came to justly praising, criticizing, and challenging America, "this almost chosen people," Reagan had few compeers. What, however, was the leader of the free world doing, in May 1985, laying a wreath with West German Chancellor Kohl at a military cemetery near Bitburg, Germany, where Waffen SS were buried? The presence of SS graves was a surprise – they had been covered by snow when Reagan's aides first made inspection – and many groups, including Jews and American war veterans, pleaded with Reagan to find some other spot to meet Kohl. But Reagan went ahead. He had agreed to the ceremony both because he thought that after forty years it was time for reconciliation between former foes and because he wanted to repay Kohl for his support in basing Pershing II missiles in Europe. He then used the occasion to speak about how young Germans (most of these dead SS had been between seventeen and twenty years old) were victimized by Nazism as much as those who perished in the Bergen-Belsen concentration camp, which he and Kohl also visited.

Podhoretz shared the protesters' dismay at Reagan's equating German soldiers and Jews as "victims of Nazism": presumably the soldiers had at least some freedom to resist, though it might have cost them their lives, while the Jews had virtually none. More profoundly, however, he understood that a well-meaning gesture might undermine a major premise of Reagan's own foreign policy. This, as Kirkpatrick had reminded people, was that "there is something special, something unique, about totalitarian states." For Reagan "to lay a wreath at a military cemetery in which Nazi stormtroopers lie buried . . . is for all practical purposes" to affirm that Nazi Germany was "just one ordinary nation at war with other ordinary nations" and therefore to give "aid and comfort" to those who regarded the Soviet Union as an ordinary nation, too.[23] No wreaths for Nazis, no wreaths for communists.

George Will wondered what was wrong with observing that "there were thousands of soldiers to whom Nazism meant no more than a brutal end to a short life" or that "we can mourn the German war dead as human beings crushed by a vicious ideology." Leon Wieseltier replied that "Strictly speaking, nothing is wrong" – except "the emphasis," which insinuated a "moral equivalence" between these dead and those. Podhoretz, Wieseltier affirmed, had gotten it right: "The stake in the Bitburg visit was finally the proper interpretation of totalitarianism."[24]

This high ground – the proper interpretation of totalitarianism – was clarifying, but it wasn't where debate about Bitburg was commonly focused. It was focused instead on the alleged touchiness of Jews, including some Jewish intellectuals, when it came to such issues as Israel or the uniqueness of the Nazis' war against the Jewish people. A year after Bitburg, for instance, Joseph Sobran, an editor at *National Review*, insinuated that by ordering attacks on Libya (in response to its government's complicity in a terrorist bombing of a Berlin discotheque that killed two American servicemen), Reagan had been acting more in Israel's than in America's interest; that the *New York Times* had for once supported such military action because the paper was owned by Jews; and that Reagan had done the right thing at Bitburg. Decter wrote Sobran a scathing letter, with copies to mutual friends like William F. Buckley, Novak, Neuhaus, and R. Emmett Tyrrell in hopes that they would "share in my contempt for what you [Sobran] have permitted yourself to become," namely, "a crude and naked anti-Semite."[25]

Buckley both regretted her tone and denied that Sobran was the ogre she claimed: "Joe . . . is not a naked anti-Semite, nor, in my opinion, a crypto or even a latent anti-Semite." Buckley did concede, however, that Sobran needed to learn "that certain immunities *properly* attach to pro-Israel sentiment for historical reasons." He had already told Sobran "that his columns were provocative in the unseemly sense: that they stir up, not the kind of thought associated with Joe's ironic inquiries into establishmentarian paradoxes, but rather the kind of anti-Israeli Know-Nothingism which, were he to see it flower, he would oppose vigorously."[26] Decter didn't withdraw her criticisms, though she repented of having addressed herself to Sobran's person, not just his words.

While Buckley thenceforth proscribed Sobran's writing in *National Review* on Jews, Judaism, or Israel, Decter and Podhoretz still believed there was something about Jews and anti-Semitism that Buckley "just didn't get."[27] Why otherwise would he have insisted, in early 1987, that if Sobran was his problem as a Catholic, then "Marty" Peretz, who at the *New Republic* was exceptionally "outrageous" in criticisms of *National Review*, was Podhoretz's problem as a Jew?[28] Podhoretz asked: "What *can* you mean by saying that Marty Peretz is my problem? That he and I are both Jewish? Why on earth should I apologize for him?"[29] After a while, this tiff was forgotten. But the question of whether *National Review*, or even Buckley himself, was or wasn't free of the taint of anti-Semitism would come up again.

Podhoretz had quite enough vilification to worry about among discomfited Jews. As usual, debates about ideas passed into clashes of personality – who said what about whom – and not least among intellectuals who might, from an outsider's viewpoint, appear to be allies. Not a whole lot, on a good day, separated Podhoretz and Peretz's political positions – both were strongly anti-totalitarian, pro-Israel, old-style liberals. But good days in the Reagan years were few and far between, and Peretz's magazine seemed sometimes to get away from him. As an illustrative example, because *Contentions*, the CFW publication Decter edited, had quizzed the thinking of *New Republic* contributor Michael Walzer, that magazine struck back in an editorial. Podhoretz then complained to Peretz: "Hard on the heels of giving Diana Trilling space to compare me and my friends to Stalinists and to call me a liar, you accuse Midge of 'ugly sectarianism.'" Further, "What does it smack of when Wieseltier in his *New Republic* essay [on nuclear weapons] accuses *Commentary* writers of being a 'war party'? Do you seriously believe that making such a charge is legitimate, but that answering it is sectarian? What the hell is the matter with you anyway?"[30]

Behind Podhoretz's anger, surely, was undiminished resentment at Peretz's having commissioned Draper's preemptive strike against *Why We Were in Vietnam* two years before. As on the streets of Brownsville, one didn't forget – and hardly felt called on to forgive – having been punched in the stomach by people who, if they hadn't ever been friends, one had at least respected. In the end, there was nothing to do but either go silent as a writer or carry on in defiance. Let Jules Feiffer, in a *Village Voice* comic strip, present a talk show on which someone called "Norman Podfurious," editor of "Hortatory," says, "It is an egregious misunderstanding of power for the President *not* to go to war in Central America, *not* to strike back in the Middle East, *not* to stand tall and bring down the Soviet Union," to which the talk-show hostess replies: "Dear me! *Wherever* do you get your ideas, Mr. Podfurious?" His answer: "In literature, Lionel Trilling. In diplomacy, Al Capp" – Capp being the creator of the "Li'l Abner" comic strip and a scold of the sixties counterculture.[31] Old friends might hoot along with Feiffer, but that wasn't the same as engaging Podhoretz intellectually.[32]

By not equivocating – by insisting on the principles that guided his judgments – Podhoretz may well have made left-wingers uncomfortable. What was it, after all, that gave their clique coherence, aside from the conviction of being fashionably for peace and social justice? How did they intend to preserve the one and achieve the other? Through hope and handouts?

"I try to exercise influence through my writing, not through friendship," Podhoretz told Lehman. That sounds like a lonely remark as well as a brave one. But friendship was a pleasure not entirely confined to the years just before and after his appointment as editor of *Commentary* in 1960. In January 1985, the twenty-fifth anniversary of that career-changing elevation, Podhoretz was feted in the RCA Building's Rainbow Room by a new and, with regard to his moral character, a better discerning group of friends. There were distinguished politicians in the company as well as men of letters like Kramer, Kristol, Joseph Epstein, and John Gross, who were seated together. (Looking around at the potentates, Kramer got a laugh by telling his tablemates, "Well, I see we've been assigned to the kiddie table.")

At the podium, Kissinger jocularly allowed that "It is a special privilege to pay tribute to Norman Podhoretz who, I understand, objected to moving [Reagan's second] Inauguration indoors as an unnecessary appeasement to the weather." He then went on to make the serious point that America could ill afford to do without this unappeasable writer:

What is an intellectual to do in a society which thinks that "peace" is a subject to be studied, which thinks stability is the normal condition, which has no experience with evil, which has never known irremediable disaster? . . . In an environment in which all of these problems are treated as merely tactical in nature, it is hard to convince people that parties or nations may disagree, occasionally or frequently, not because they misunderstand each other but because they understand each other only too well.

For all these reasons, it is right and proper and crucial for all of us that Norman is an implacable nag, that he will not make any compromises. I, myself, substantially agree with his analysis of international affairs. At the same time, he and I have argued forever, because he looks at policy from the perspective of a prophet and I look at policy from the perspective of a policy-maker. He insists the truth is absolute. He is right. I believe that it has to be reached in imperfect stages.

FIGURE 18. Norman Podhoretz with art critic and editor Hilton Kramer, 1998. (Photo by William Baker.)

The prophetic writer and the policy-maker served the truth – in this case, the primacy of fostering peace not war, liberal democracy not totalitarianism, and the right of a Jewish state to exist in Israel – in different but complementary ways. The tensions between them were often fruitful. One could discover such tensions, Moynihan implied in his own remarks, even within Podhoretz himself. In the first issues of *Commentary* he edited, in 1960, he advocated the vatic utopianism of Paul Goodman; but he also insisted, with statesman-like realism, that the fifties had demonstrated the staying power of "the Protestant-liberal-bourgeois synthesis." This meant, in Moynihan's words, that "our ['capitalist'] civilization was in fact proving itself capable of adapting to new circumstances without losing form or identity" and could prevail in the struggle against what the young editor called "an old and monstrous tyranny," the Soviet Union.

Further praise came from Kramer: "I think it was William Dean Howells who once said that making enemies is easy – keeping them is difficult. It can be said of Norman that that difficulty, like many others, is one he has triumphantly surmounted" – not least because many of them were "the right enemies" to keep. This, as Michael Novak succinctly put it, was why Podhoretz had the high honor of being "perhaps the most hated editor in America today": simply for having the courage "to take up the unpalatable arguments neglected by others, and to face exactly those issues which other intellectuals of the age refuse to face."

Podhoretz's reply began deftly:

I saw Henry Kissinger a few weeks ago at breakfast. We have breakfast from time to time, to argue, over his poached egg and my black coffee, about the role of ideology in foreign policy. I mentioned to Henry that George Shultz was planning to be here this evening. He raised his eyebrows slightly. I went on, "Incidentally, there is some difficulty deciding what protocol requires. Does the Secretary of State speak first, or does he speak last?" Henry said, "Why don't you ask him?" "Well," I said, "you were the Secretary of State, so I'm asking you." And Henry said, "Yes, but when I was the Secretary of State, I wouldn't have come to a dinner in your honor" [laughter]....

I'm very grateful that my mother was able to be here tonight [applause]. My mother hasn't heard so many nice things said about me since my graduation from Junior High School. Lyndon Johnson – this is a story I learned from Pat Moynihan – is reputed to have said on the occasion of a dinner in his honor that he was very sorry his parents weren't there. His father, he said, would have enjoyed all the things said about him, and his mother would have believed them [laughter]. I daresay my mother has believed a few of the things said tonight.

As indeed she did, though they came close to exceeding even her capacity for belief. Cynthia Ozick overheard a pert exchange toward the end of the evening: "Person being introduced to Norman's mother: 'But you must have expected this from the time Norman was very little.' Norman's mother: 'Oh, I expected *some*thing, but *royalty* I didn't expect!'"[33]

Podhoretz's serious remarks were so cogent a statement of what he had striven for as an editor and writer that he would later cite them as a personal touchstone:

I am also proud that I have been able, in and through *Commentary*, to defend my own my own country and the values and institutions for which it stands; my own people and the religious and cultural heritage by which we have been shaped. Like so many of us, I was educated to believe that the *last* thing one ought to be defending was one's own, that it was more honorable and nobler to turn one's back on one's own and fight for others and for other things in which one had no personal stake or interest. This has been a very hard lesson to unlearn, and I am proud to have unlearned it.

Commentary has defended America at a time when America has been under moral and ideological attack. *Commentary* has defended the Jewish people and the Jewish state when they too, and for many of the same reasons, have been subjected to a relentless assault on their legitimacy and even their very existence. For me there has been no conflict or contradiction involved in defending this dual heritage by which I have been formed. As an American and as a Jew, I have seen that distinctive new species of tyranny, totalitarianism – and especially in our day its Communist variant – as the main threat to the values and institutions of liberty. I am proud to have devoted myself so fully to the fight against that threat and the correlative fight for the survival of liberty.

He admitted, after twenty-five years, to being "a little tired," yet the Cold War wasn't over and he had, "as they used to say in World War II, enlisted for the duration." Thus "I am resolved to continue in this intolerable wrestle with words and meanings and in this dangerous and difficult struggle to preserve and protect the blessings of liberty, as the Founding Fathers enjoined us to do, for ourselves and our posterity."[34] Allusions both to T. S. Eliot's poem "East Coker" and to the preamble to the Constitution were apt for someone whose sense of literature and sense of country were unitary.

Reagan's recent reelection may have contributed to the impression that Podhoretz and his fellow neoconservatives had reached the apogee of their influence. The heirs of New Left politics now seemed confined to academia – radical historians and literary critics dazzling (and bamboozling) the young with the deconstruction of *epistemes* and paradigms, while teaching them to loathe Western civilization's shortcomings and, often, to ignore its achievements. Everyday politics was now dominated by wonkish intellectuals in neoconservative magazines – or so, as James Atlas said in a *New York Times Magazine* piece, one would suppose. But Podhoretz disabused him of that notion: "Have you ever met anyone who was against a nuclear freeze?" It was like the film critic Pauline Kael, in 1972, wondering how Nixon could possibly have been elected when all the people she knew had voted for McGovern. The metropolitan culture remained dominantly left-liberal, its favorite magazine the *New York Review*, and its "celebrity intellectual" Susan Sontag, whom Kramer called "La Pasionaria" of the "new, pleasure-seeking revolution in sensibility" that lit its sparklers in the sixties.[35]

Atlas maintained that, in general, fewer people were paying attention to intellectuals than had been the case when Podhoretz, Sontag, Kramer, and the rest were starting out in the fifties. This made their writings not less but more valuable, indeed indispensable, given that most people were simply tuning in to the electronic media, which dumbed down the important religious and moral ideas. In any case, Atlas observed, their magazines, especially Podhoretz's *Commentary*, still possessed an influence in political circles that *Partisan Review* or Cohen's *Commentary* in pre- and postwar years would have found unimaginable. Hadn't *Commentary* in a fashion "made" two U.N. ambassadors, Moynihan and Kirkpatrick? Weren't its contents passed around, in samizdat, from dissident to dissident inside the Soviet empire? Informed readers, not surprisingly, still cared about politics, even if, to Atlas's sorrow, they didn't seem to care as much about art and literature.[36]

Partisan Review, like *Dissent*, now believed in a Left that would be both democratic and anticommunist, able to balance freedom and equality while upholding high culture. This, to Podhoretz, was utopian – a word that literally meant *nowhere*. As he argued in what would be his last piece in Phillips's magazine, Americans should be cherishing, defending, and, as best they could, reforming the society they actually had. *Partisan Review's* early fifties pro-American phase had never really taken root. "As Hilton Kramer has so devastatingly put it: as between Auschwitz and the Gulag, on the whole most *PR* intellectuals preferred New York" – New York, that is, instead of America. New York may have been a good place for left-utopian dreams but, as represented in the pages of the magazine, those dreams had bred a waking "neutralism no less dangerous and immoral today than its counterpart was in the late thirties."[37]

The refusal of neutralism was what Podhoretz called on the Czech novelist Milan Kundera to undertake in an "open letter" that same autumn (1984). Unlike the bulk of left-leaning writers, Kundera had identified himself, as Orwell did, with ordinary people and their workaday lives, setting out, in his fiction, to discover "the *terra* previously *incognita* of the everyday." But when they weren't congratulating themselves on supporting another dissident behind the Iron Curtain, liberal Western intellectuals were falsifying Kundera's achievement. They insisted that his novels were about memory and laughter, sex and love, being and nonbeing – all depoliticized topics. In fact, they were about an overarching political topic, life under communist totalitarianism. Podhoretz wanted Kundera to repossess his own writing, first by explicitly connecting the quality of personal relationships with the quality of public relationships and second by realizing that the precious literature and music of the West could, in the end, be defended only by identifying with the West's liberal democracy. After all, it was the philosophy of liberty that enabled people of genius to *produce* that literature and music.[38]

The Kundera article, along with ones on Camus, Orwell, Leavis, Kissinger, Solzhenitsyn, and Henry Adams, were collected as *The Bloody Crossroads* in spring 1986. It was an opportunity to remind the public of Podhoretz's core training as a literary critic and of his engagements at the Trillingesque crossroads where poems and stories meet ideas and ideologies. In his review, published in the *New York Times*, John Gross understood what was at issue in such meetings during the twentieth century, when writers had frequently been not only victims but also inciters of political oppression. Too often they had neglected their primary responsibility, which was to tell truths both pleasant and unpleasant, in favor of promoting some sacred or secular program. Anyone impolitic enough to name and indict such sellouts – as Camus, Orwell, Leavis, and Podhoretz himself had done – received the inevitable tribute of sneers, "inspired by the grand old principle once enunciated by a Victorian lawyer: 'No case – abuse plaintiff's attorney.'"[39]

Such no-case abuse came from the journalist (and later adviser to President Clinton) Sidney Blumenthal, who in the *Washington Post* charged Podhoretz with having "reproduced, down to the most exact nuances, the faded American Stalinist aesthetic" – insinuating that for the neoconservative as for the Stalinist, the ultimate test was simply "Which side are you on?"[40] Redress came from Ozick in the *Times Book Review*. She noted that though, with relative shyness, Podhoretz had always confined himself to "the quiet clamor of print," this hadn't kept him from becoming "the Great Satan of the American Romantic Left." And all because he had shown how its utopianism "leads," in her phrase, "as ineluctably to the gulag as Nazism led ineluctably to the death camps." She also understood what Blumenthal didn't: that Podhoretz's sensibility was above all *literary*. He could admit, for instance, that Solzhenitsyn's fiction was mostly dead on the page in spite of his sound ideas. He might have cut Kissinger too much slack – the memoirs were "good personal journalism," not "masterwork[s]" – but his essays as a whole rested squarely in the tradition of Trilling, who refused to be "hypnotized by totalitarian poesy."[41]

Podhoretz had wished for louder, unstinting plaudits, for he knew that the tenor of most of the reviews would follow not Gross but Blumenthal. Ozick supposed that her friend and mentor was unhappy with her disagreement about Kissinger, who lacked that "inclination toward the introspective" that any "literary masterwork" must contain. But that wasn't the rub. Podhoretz wanted an ally's review to match the throw-weight of the enemy's. Ozick had reason, for her part, to feel she had done her combat rotation. Not only had some "*copy* editor" at the *Times* presumed to tell her that he thought Allen Ginsberg was right in dubbing Podhoretz the representative of a "protopolice surveillance movement" but she also had received hate mail "condemning me for praising your book" and felt rather bold in the face of "normal" liberals' lurking irrationality:

It turns out (when you press) that they never read *Commentary*; they attack it without knowing what's in it; they've not read your books; it isn't issues they're concerned with. It's something else, something psychological, they're after, something almost occult; I wasn't exaggerating when I came up with the phrase Great Satan.[42]

The liberal critics continued to pile on, the last on the heap being the Irish writer Conor Cruise O'Brien in "Trop de Zèle," itself an overzealous exercise in character assassination in the *New York Review*. Graced with a David Levine caricature of Podhoretz as a Contra with a grenade clipped to his shoulder and a rifle in his hands, O'Brien's piece offered to put Podhoretz away – forever: "In general, the essays in this collection seem to be the work of a writer who knows quite a lot about literature, without any longer being much interested in the subject – and who is passionately interested in politics, without knowing much about them." While he "writes competently . . . Mr. Podhoretz is neither Henry Kissinger nor Henry Adams. And he is not so much an authority on 'the bloody crossroads' as another of the romantic and power-infatuated victims with whom that crossroads is bestrewn."[43] Literary road kill.

Hoping to console, Laqueur wrote Podhoretz that O'Brien's piece had in fact been "far too laudatory for [the *New York Review*'s] purposes. . . . [A]ll in all this was a very temperate piece considering the place where it appeared." To which Podhoretz replied:

I wonder if you would think a piece like Conor Cruise O'Brien's were laudatory or even temperate if it were about you. Apart from everything else, it is written in very bad faith and is also completely wrong about my own ambitions [to be either a Henry Kissinger or a Henry Adams]. On the other hand, publication of the review does mark the end of the *New York Review*'s boycott (I use the word advisedly) of me. This is the first notice they have taken of my work since *Making It*.[44]

Nasty notice was better than no notice at all.

Regulated Hatreds

The fact that Huw Wheldon had so recently died, at home in London attended by Jacqueline and their children, must have exacerbated Podhoretz's feelings of lonely beleagueredness. His final letter to the man who had married his dearest female friend save Midge, and become his best male friend, is poignant:

When I said to you the other day on the phone that you are constantly in my thoughts – and you are, you are – you replied "I'm not worth it." Now *those* words keep ringing in my head. I keep wondering: Does he feel that way because [in Yeats's phrase] he's fastened to a dying animal? Does he feel that way because he is withdrawing from life, the better to leave it? If so, writing this letter may be a cruel thing to do. I don't know; I truly don't; and I don't have you, whom I would turn to for advice if it were anyone else, to consult. And so I am taking the risk, all on my own, of saying this to you while I still have the chance: *Worth it??* Knowing you all these years has been for me so great a privilege that I am now torn between gratitude at having been granted such a friendship and self-pity at being untimely robbed of so much joy, so much delight, so much *light,* so much laughter, so much wit, so much fun, so much comfort, so much love. *Ich* habe *nicht* genug von Wheldon.[1]

Publicly, Podhoretz paid tribute in his *New York Post* column. He felt awed by Wheldon's resistance to death, obedient to his fellow Welshman Dylan Thomas's commandment:

Do not go gentle into that good night,
Old age should burn and rave at close of day;
Rage, rage against the dying of the light.

Wheldon had come to Podhoretz's twenty-fifth anniversary celebration. "I could see," Podhoretz would write, "that he was in spiritual torment over his inability to resign himself, to make his peace with death." Wheldon's Presbyterian religious resources were similar to his own Jewish ones: "My friend would never have said flatly, 'There is no God' – he would have thought it brazen and crass – but if he ever had, he would certainly have added [in George Santayana's vein], 'and the Bible is His word.'"

That is, he held to the essential truth of Christianity and Judaism, "the idea that the reason we are here on earth is to serve God and to praise Him." Praise came in the form of affirming life, a daily "readiness to enjoy what there was to be enjoyed, . . . to savor what there was to be savored, and most especially to accept every invitation to a good laugh that the world had to offer." That was a species of holy living.

Holy dying, welcoming the *release* from earthly sufferings, was harder. Why?

He hinted at the answer in telling me that one day, when his physical pain was at its most unbearable, he turned in a desperate search for help to a cantata about dying by Johann Sebastian Bach, *Ich habe genug* – "I have had enough." And he asked himself: "If Bach can say it, why can't I?" He meant that if Bach, in his eyes perhaps the greatest of all men, was permitted to yearn for death as an escape from the awful miseries of this life, why should he, an ordinary mortal, be required to go on raging?

But of course he knew why. Bach, who believed in an afterlife, was permitted to serve God and praise Him by welcoming death as a deliverance into the arms of his savior. My friend could only serve God and praise Him by cherishing life on this earth to the very end and by refusing to curse it.

And so even, or rather especially, in the extremity of his suffering, he did not curse life – neither with the words of his mouth nor, I feel sure, in the meditations of his heart. Least of all did he curse it as so many do nowadays when they declare that life is worth having only when it is good and, worse yet, when they act on that satanic idea.

This then is what Podhoretz meant when he wrote his friend that "*Ich* habe *nicht* genug von Wheldon." Raging is different from cursing, from damning and therefore rejecting life, for within life's contract is the clause saying it must sooner or later end – the clause that in fact enhances and refines the pleasure of the moments given. Raging is also different from committing suicide, or asking to be euthanized, surely the "satanic idea" Podhoretz alludes to. Wheldon had taught him "how, in what he himself called these spiritually illiterate times, when it is so hard to die with the peaceful resignation of a true believer, it is still possible to live a truly godly life."[2]

Later that summer, Midge wrote Jacqueline urging her to take her time grieving, to postpone making decisions about the future, and simply to come to New York and stay with them. "When you announced to Norman that you were marrying Huw, you wrote a sentence I've never forgotten. . . . 'There is all the difference in the world,' you wrote, 'between wanting to marry and feeling you ought to marry.'"[3] Marrying is another praise and affirmation of life, and none of these four ever praised or savored anything because they felt obliged to. They did it out of the desire and the will to live.

Not accidentally, this brings us to the question of homosexuality. Was *that* a denial, even a cursing, of life? These days the question is all but impermissible, but in the eighties, when the AIDS epidemic was first manifesting itself, some writers did try to work it through. On one side, to put the matter very simply, were those who insisted that homosexuality wasn't a chosen but an inherited mode of sexuality; on the other side were those who held that, if in a small number of cases it was inherited, in a far greater number it was chosen. And chosen, many conservatives said, for bad reasons – summed up in the narcissism of people who refuse to take their place in the adult world. Becoming an adult, these conservatives maintained, commonly entails breeding and the raising of children, and then gradually giving way to a subsequent generation. It is a process that may end in raging against death but that affirms rather than curses the cycles of life.

The best essay along these lines is Decter's "The Boys on the Beach," which in 1980 raised a storm that didn't soon subside. Though AIDS wouldn't be identified until the following year, she had reasons to be worried about the condition of the homosexual community, whose culture had so changed from what she remembered at Fire Island Pines, the south shore Long Island beach community where she, Podhoretz, and their children had vacationed during the mid-sixties. The homosexuals who then had been conspicuous for their gentle "attention to the youth and beauty of their bodies" were now "'out' with a mighty and terrible bang." Feeling obliged to be politically aggressive, "they have lost their lightness of touch, and with it, whatever lightness of heart it made possible." Gay? Not much evidence of that – what with the drugs tossed in with the booze of earlier days and with apparently "ubiquitous" sadomasochistic practices like fisting.

Escapism was the leitmotif of the homosexual culture Decter had earlier observed. If more "tender" than the recent leather-jacket-and-crew-cut style, it was also "vain, pouting, girlish," the latter word implying not effeminacy exactly but immaturity – for example, a flirting that reminds one of "the anxious air of a high-school prom, in which everyone must either be a winner or a loser." What is such "girlishness" protracted beyond high school? It is flight from womanhood and from marriage, with its responsibilities of reproduction and nurture and, profoundly, its intimations of mortality. It is adult females "who principally teach the lesson that to be human is to be born, to grow old, and to die. And men who seek to appropriate the advantages of girlishness – i.e., homosexuals – are most of all expressing their refusal to receive that message."

Denial of death's inevitability – and of "the displacement of oneself by others" – is finally what "sent those Fire Island homosexuals into the arms of other men." And this denial entailed, Decter remembered, a hostility toward heterosexual women like herself. What, to homosexuals, were heterosexual women with children but reminders of "the human condition which necessitates a division into two sexes" and of the day when the illusion of an eternal "tender adolescence" must be given up? And what, to homosexuals, were heterosexual men but reminders of their own fathers, mere breeders and nurturers? If heterosexual women, even the "fag hags" among them, inevitably "feel devalued and sexually rejected" in homosexual company, heterosexual men

feel mocked in their unending thralldom to the female body and thus their unending dependence on those who possess it. . . .

They feel mocked most of all for having become, in style as well as in substance, family men, caught up in getting and begetting, thinking of mortgages, schools, and the affordable, marking the passage of years in obedience to all the grubby imperatives that heterosexual manhood seems to impose.

Decter was describing, among others, her own husband, who in marrying her, adopting Rachel and Naomi, and fathering Ruthie and John had accepted the role that the human condition had scripted for adult males and respected its terms.[4]

The letters to the editor about "The Boys on the Beach" were what one might expect: agreement expressed in terms brief and thankful, disagreement prolix and bitter – and often in *ad feminam* mode. Typical was this from a law student at Berkeley:

Miss Decter's feelings of sexual rejection by, and corresponding resentment of, gay men characterize the mentality of the young girl socialized into the belief that her self-worth depends upon her physical attractiveness to men. It is the essence of our sexist society ... [and] it all flows naturally from Miss Decter's notion that a man's failure to sleep with women should be construed as rejection of, "flight from," and an immature refusal to be "domesticated" by them. This can only make sense to one who accepts the premise that woman's domestication of man and man's provision for woman are the bases of human relations.

Decter replied that she was indeed "one who accepts the premise that woman's domestication of man and man's provision for woman are the bases of human relations," and who believed that the movement for gay rights, like the one for women's liberation, "offers not 'love, choice, and identity' but a hatred of life the way it is."

To be sure, nothing was more anathematized in those years, or since, than appealing to the way life is according to nature as opposed to the dogma that the modalities of human life are just conventions or "constructs." Like most of his professors, the Berkeley law student was simply attempting to shut down further discussion. So, at least, Decter thought: "I am to be considered a bigot simply for having written an essay on the subject of homosexuals in any terms except those authorized by the Gay Rights movement." It was a "silencing" tactic she has seen before, as from black or feminist "militants" on the subject of affirmative action.[5]

There was nothing in his wife's meditations on homosexuality that Podhoretz didn't endorse. He had, as we have seen, had his own youthful exposures to homosexuals, his reaction evolving from incredulity and indifference to surprise and civil rejection. Not only was homosexuality not in his own nature, it didn't square with "the law" set forth in the Hebrew Bible that, in 1970, he had seen was true. People were commanded by God to "choose life"; men who preferred the anus to the vagina, the conduit for feces to the conduit for babies, were "doing dirt" on life and, in effect, choosing death. Podhoretz had written plenty about this central topic of choosing life but had kept his feelings and thoughts about homosexuality mostly to himself.

That returns us to Allen Ginsberg (1926–1997), whom Podhoretz had known during those Columbia days when the older student, editor of the literary magazine, had so pleased the younger by accepting a long, callow poem titled "Jeremiah." We have already marked the later "war," as Podhoretz would call it, between himself and Ginsberg over "The Know-Nothing Bohemians." There were several choice episodes to come.

In 1980, Ginsberg wrote an author's note for a reprinting of his 1961 essay "When the Mode of the Music Changes, the Walls of the City Shake." Podhoretz's "The Know-Nothing Bohemians" and other "amazing attack[s]" on the Beats' poetics and prejudices, Ginsberg now claimed, had failed. Even then he had been confident that

the poetics would be triumphant, the texts permanent, my complaints exemplary – to set example to future generations what depression and inertia and hostility we had to plough through to instruct, cajole, admonish, plead with for possession of America's heart. Why? So as to leave a record of combat against native fascist militarization of U.S. soul. It seemed to me that . . . political liberty . . . could only be defended by undaunted, free, bold humorous imagination, open field mentality, open field poetics, open field democracy.[6]

Of course, what Ginsberg called "native fascist militarization" was what Podhoretz and many other critics called liberal democracy defended by arms against totalitarianism, just as they called Ginsberg's "open field democracy" antinomian anarchy. Ginsberg was right to believe that changing the music could shake the city. The question was what kind of music, and what sort of city.

When Podhoretz visited Václav Havel in Prague in 1988, he remembered that "the first thing that hit my eye upon entering his apartment was a huge poster of John Lennon hanging on the wall. Disconcerted, I tried to persuade Havel that the counterculture in the West was no friend of anti-Communists like himself," yet to no avail.[7] The same went for Ginsberg. If, like Lennon, he was lionized by dissidents within the communist empire, it was probably because the bosses in Havana and Prague had expelled him "for various forms of homosexual exhibitionism." But Ginsberg's ethos was blithely libertarian. He had none of the active discipline necessary, within a liberal democracy, to protect political, economic, and personal freedoms – to say nothing of the submissive discipline mandated by totalitarianism.

"Good old Norman Podhoretz," the poet related in 1987:

If he weren't there like a wall I could butt my head against, I wouldn't have anybody to hate. And why hate him? He's part of my world, and he's sort of like the character, Mr. Meany or the Bluenose or Blue Meany. At the same time, he has some sense in him. And the poor guy is dying, like all of us. So, how could I pile my hatred on him any more? Or did I ever really hate him or was I just sort of fascinated by him?

Podhoretz was, Ginsberg confessed, "a sort of sacred personage in my life . . . whose vision is so opposite from mine that it's provocative and interesting. . . . In fact, maybe he's more honest than I am because he attacks me openly."[8]

Not hatred but fascination, not the Bluenose but a sacred personage? Podhoretz evidently represented to Ginsberg something like the voice of conscience – a representative of the judgment his family and particularly his father, had he lived, would no doubt have passed on his errancies; his quasi-criminal pranks as an undergraduate, for instance. Columbia had suspended him for a year not just because he had etched "Butler has no balls" (referring to the university's president) and "Fuck the Jews" into the grime on his dorm window. It was also because he and Kerouac were caught in bed together, where they pleaded that they "hadn't done anything." Readmitted, Ginsberg was caught transporting stolen goods, which put him "in serious danger of going to jail" until, after the intervention of Trilling, Van Doren, and other professors, he was sent for eight months to a psychiatric hospital. William Burroughs thought that there was a Trilling inside Ginsberg, and that the latter may have regarded Podhoretz as their professor's surrogate.

Those eight months in the hospital gave the "mad" Ginsberg material for "Howl," the poem that made him famous, just as his mother's own madness informed the portrait he did of her in "Kaddish." But Ginsberg, like Mailer in a different way, came close to *recommending* psychiatric disorder: since American culture is insane, sensitive people ought to drop out and, through a sort of higher insanity, find an alternative reality. One was supposed to cleanse those Blakean "doors of perception," lose oneself, and be reborn outside the boundaries of "national or class or race chauvinist identity." This, Podhoretz remarked,

was heartless nonsense. Far from being in touch with a higher reality, the crazy people I had known – and I had known a few – were cut off in the most frightening ways from themselves and the world around them. There was something cruel about drafting such pitiable characters into the service of an ideological aggression against the kind of normal life to which they would have given everything to return. And it was all the more heartless for parading itself as compassion.

If Ginsberg was heartlessly nonsensical about drugs and insanity, he was predatorily so about homosexuality. It was one thing to be "tempted" by Ginsberg's "world of complete freedom . . . a world that promised endless erotic possibility," especially if one was, like Podhoretz, married at twenty-six, with two adopted kids at home and two of one's own on the way. But the homosexuality depicted in Ginsberg's poems repelled Podhoretz. Like Sartre canonizing the French homosexual writer Jean Genet as "Saint Genet," Ginsberg tried to "beatify" the homosexuals "who," as he rhapsodized, "let themselves be fucked in the ass by saintly motorcyclists, and screamed with joy," etc. In 1972, Ginsberg himself wondered about these lines:

[W]ho wants to be queer? Who wants the pain of being fucked in the ass at times when it is painful, which it occasionally is. That's part of the scene, too. . . .
    And again I have a line like: "who blew and were blown by those human seraphim, the sailors, caresses of Atlantic and Caribbean love," referring to Hart Crane, actually. It was an acknowledgment of the basic reality of homosexual joy. That was a breakthrough in the sense of a public statement of feelings and emotions and attitudes that I would not have wanted my father or my family to see, and I even hesitated to make public.[9]

The ambivalence here, the obvious shame before parents and family, is worth noting. To Podhoretz, such indications, along with Ginsberg's overprotestations "that the perverse was infinitely superior to the normal," confirmed a suspicion that he had "become a homosexual not out of erotic compulsion but by an act of will and as another way of expressing his contempt for normal life." Might Ginsberg have "converted" to homosexuality, perhaps in the hope that it would make him a better poet? If so, he was mistaken, but it must have brought him other pleasures since he "remained an active and enthusiastic homosexual once he had given up his youthful struggles against it and stopped sleeping with girls." Only, his conscience wasn't absolutely clear about his activity. Having dropped the hallucinogenic drink yaga "in Peru in the early 60's, he had a vision in which it came to him that his 'queer isolation' was the price he was paying for his flight from women, which was itself tied 'to my lack of ... contact with birth – my fear to be and to die – to bear life.'" Exactly Decter's diagnosis of the boys on the beach she had known.

In 1997, when Ginsberg died, the obituarists, with the exception of George Will and an editorialist in the *New Criterion*, outbid one another in lauding the Whitman of Our Age. Not a word, Podhoretz would recall, about "the encouragement he gave to drugs and sexual licentiousness of every kind," save for its being

breezily treated as a charming foible or as an expression of ideas that might have seemed a bit extreme in 1956 when (to paraphrase one elegist) "repression and conformity, and not the Russians and the Chinese, were the true enemies of America" but that were in the end revealed (in the words of another elegist) as "the beginning of a renewal of American values."

Nor was there any mention of the AIDS epidemic spread by "the rampant homosexual promiscuity" Ginsberg promoted – Podhoretz cites some nauseating passages – or his "active sponsorship of the abominable North American Man Boy Love Alliance (NAMBLA), an organization devoted to the legalization of homosexual pedophilia. 'I don't know exactly how to define what's underage,' [Ginsberg] once explained, quickly adding that he himself had 'never made it with anyone under fifteen.'"

The legalization of pedophilia: Podhoretz saw something like this coming as far back as the late fifties, when certain writers began speaking about the "natural rights" of homosexuality. He remembered telling Midge that this "wave of the future" would move on to encompass incest, polygamy, pedophilia – "you name it" – as "benign forms of love." As long as these forms were deemed "natural" – in this context the cultural Left liked the word – who was to say no?[10]

Ginsberg, an encourager of pedophilia, may toward the end of his life have forgiven Podhoretz, the "sacred personage" who at some level seems to have stood in for his moral sense. But people's lives were at stake, and Podhoretz "could not bring myself to forgive *him*, not even now that he was dead."

The tension between Podhoretz and Gore Vidal was of a different order. Though from the mid-fifties through the sixties they were on amicable enough terms – as late as 1970, Vidal had published "Literary Gangsters" in *Commentary* – they rarely saw one another and weren't really friends. Vidal was in any case a *New York Review* and *Nation* author, and Podhoretz had no desire to seek the work of someone who looked askance at what Truman Capote once called the "Jewish Mafia in American letters."

Like Capote, Vidal may have thought himself "an O.K. goy" in the eyes of this imagined mafia, but no truly critical mind, Jewish or otherwise, could have a high opinion of his best-selling middlebrow novels or screenplays. His literary standing depended on his essays. There he was lucid, witty, and urbane, not least because of the confidence he felt as a scion of a family deeply rooted in America (grandson of Senator Thomas Gore from Oklahoma, son of the co-founder of three airlines and then FDR's director of Air Commerce, connected through his divorced mother's subsequent marriage to Hugh D. Auchincloss, who was the eventual stepfather of Jacqueline Bouvier Kennedy, and so on). As an open homosexual – his early novels caused a stir on that account – he enjoyed the role of acerbic left-wing gadfly to the political muckamucks.

To Vidal, it was no coincidence that Reagan's ascendancy would be marked by an essay like Decter's "The Boys on the Beach," which Barbara Epstein at the *New York Review* had brought to his attention. He placed it in an allegedly homophobic line begun, for present purposes, by Joseph Epstein's "Homo/Hetero" in *Harper's* ten years earlier. That article had provoked a protest by homosexuals at the magazine's office. Didn't *Harper's* realize, they demanded, that this essay would drive still more homosexuals to commit suicide? It was a stunning accusation, the full import of which Decter didn't at the time understand.

Epstein had admitted feeling an "irretrievably square" physical repulsion toward "the brutally simple fact that two men make love to each other." He couldn't get over that or the feeling that homosexuals "are different from the rest of us" in a way that is "fundamental. Cursed without clear cause, afflicted without apparent cure, they are an affront to our rationality, living evidence of our despair of ever finding a sensible, an explainable, design to the world." He declared that, "If I had the power to do so, I would wish homosexuality off the face of this earth."[11] And now came Decter announcing, to Vidal's ear, that Epstein could relax: nobody would have to push a button to eliminate the homosexuals from "the face of the earth," for they seemed to be doing the job themselves.

Vidal's own notion was that the wish to eliminate homosexuals was like the wish to eliminate Jews. The threatened groups really should be allies – and Jewish liberals should denounce the likes of Epstein, Decter, and of course her husband. This idea was too much even for the *New York Review*, which objected to the trivialization of the Holocaust implied by Vidal's comparison. The *Nation*, however, was glad to print his essay, whose title, "Pink Triangle and Yellow Star," was a reminder that in the concentration camps the Nazis forced homosexuals to wear the triangle and Jews to wear the star – tags to differentiate their degeneracies and facilitate their liquidation.[12]

Apropos of Decter's "The Boys on the Beach," Vidal wondered what this "New York Jewish publicist" was doing: Didn't she realize that if the homosexuals went, she and her kind would go next? Here "in these last days of empire," wasn't it obvious that capitalist America, like the communist East, was preparing to eliminate its Jews, "fags," and blacks?[13] Not, apparently, to certain Jews, whom Vidal tried to wave away with ridicule. Decter had recalled how lesbians on Fire Island possessed "a marked tendency to hang out in the company of large and ferocious dogs." "Well," said Vidal, "if I were a dyke and a pair of Podhoretzes came waddling toward me on the beach, copies of Leviticus and Freud in hand, I'd get in touch with the nearest Alsatian dealer pronto."

Decter's "most unusual thesis" – that homosexuals were so riddled with self-hatred that they were seeking to kill themselves, either directly or roundaboutly through hundreds of anonymous bath-house buggerings and blow jobs – wasn't, for Vidal, morally serious. Self-hatred? "Not even the authors of *The Protocols of the Elders of Zion* ever suggested that the Jews, who were so hateful to them, were also hateful to themselves. So Decter has managed to go one step further than the *Protocols*' authors; she is indeed a virtuoso of hate, and thus do pogroms begin."[14]

That was the end of round one. Round two, shifting from sexual to foreign relations, came five years later with Vidal's even haughtier "The Empire Lovers Strike Back," also in the *Nation*. Here Decter was "Midge," Podhoretz "Poddy," a dismissive nickname of Vidal's own invention. The two together, an "Israeli Fifth Column Division," "are now, in their old age [their mid-50's], more and more like refugees from a Woody Allen film: *The Purple Prose of West End Avenue*." Why did they go on so about the evil Soviet empire? In order, Vidal charged, to plump the defense budget, a goodly chunk of which went to "the support of Israel in its never-ending wars against just about everyone." Apparently, Podhoretz and Decter hadn't learned from all those historical romances Vidal himself had been spinning for the "American public," which drew the parallels between America's shame and Israel's: "We stole other people's land. We murdered the inhabitants. We imposed our religion – and rule – on the survivors." Some great Americans (like Vidal himself) were "ashamed" of their country's imperialism. But Decter wasn't ashamed "because in the Middle East another predatory people is busy stealing other people's land in the name of an alien theocracy. She is a propagandist for these predators (paid for?), and that is what all this nonsense is about."

In *Contentions*, Decter had charged Vidal with not liking his country. "Poor Midge. Of course I like my country. After all, I'm its current biographer. But now that we're really leveling with each other, I've got to tell you I don't much like your country, which is Israel."[15]

Joseph Epstein characterized "The Empire Lovers Strike Back" as "one of the nastiest [pieces] I have ever read. I am surprised even at [Victor] Navasky [the *Nation*'s editor] for publishing it."[16] Writer Jeffrey Hart, coining the nickname Gore "Abu" Vidal, would later call him "straight-forwardly evil . . . a monster of cold cynicism and vanity" who was bitter because "America has not rewarded him to the unlimited extent of his self-perceived merit."[17]

His venom had been injected in the *Nation*'s 120th-anniversary issue, which listed the magazine's prominent "friends." Marion Magid at *Commentary* forthwith sent a letter to those friends – Bella Abzug, Leonard Bernstein, Norman Birnbaum, Bill Bradley, Frances Fitzgerald, Fred Friendly, Seymour Hersh, Peter Jennings, Edward Kennedy, Edward Koch, Eugene McCarthy, Robert Silvers, Gloria Steinem, Tom Wicker, et al. – challenging them to protest Vidal's anti-Semitism. Most didn't reply, perhaps because they felt that if he was guilty of anything, it was merely of "literary anti-Semitism." Elie Wiesel agreed with Podhoretz, however: it wasn't "literary anti-Semitism," it was "crude anti-Semitism." "Incredible. How does one answer ugliness?"[18]

How, specifically, did one answer the charge of dual loyalty, which was sharpened in June 1986 by the Jonathan Pollard case (a U.S. naval intelligence analyst, Pollard confessed to having acted as a spy for Israel)? What Podhoretz argued, patiently and repeatedly, was that allegiance to America and support of Israel went hand-in-glove. Both were based on a dedication to liberal democracy. Should either government ever become undemocratically authoritarian, he would make every attempt to restore its lost tradition. Should either government ever collapse into totalitarianism, one could count on his joining the dissident underground.

But these were unworldly hypotheticals. On the ground, there was no possibility of America or Israel collapsing into anything resembling authoritarianism or totalitarianism. Both countries, however, were *in danger*, insofar as their democratic debates were being skewed by irrational voices speaking what Podhoretz called "the hate that dare not speak its name." The intended irony of this phrase, the title of a 1986 essay in *Commentary*, depends on one's knowing Lord Alfred Douglas's coinage – "I am the Love that dare not speak its name" – in reference to homosexuality, which was a criminal offense in his and Oscar Wilde's England. The concealed offense of Vidal was no longer homosexuality; it was anti-Semitism, which since the Holocaust was supposed to have been cast beyond the pale among respectable people. Yet here was America's "current biographer" reviving the highbrow anti-Semitism of, for example, Henry Adams or his brother, the historian Brooks Adams, who grumbled: "I tell you Rome was a blessed garden paradise beside the rotten, unsexed, swindling, lying Jews, represented by Pierpont Morgan and the gang who have been manipulating the country for the last few years." (As though J. P. Morgan were Jewish or any more representative of Jews in general than was his Jewish contemporary Mayer Rothschild.)

The *New Republic* ran an editorial denouncing Vidal's article as anti-Semitic, but the *Nation* remained unrepentant, Vidal saying that "the Podhoretzes are doing more to arouse the essential anti-Semitism of the American people than anyone since Father Coughlin" and Navasky saying that "Vidal should be acclaimed for his courage in 'violating the taboo that forbids the discussion of the relationship of the American Jewish community to the state of Israel.'"

Surprisingly, it was the *Village Voice*, in the person of Paul Berman, who sprang to Podhoretz's defense. He had no choice, Berman said, when his "right-minded" but "discombobulated friends at the *Nation*" had "so bol-lix[ed] things. . . . [Navasky] had no business publishing Gore Vidal's spleen." The anti-Semitic attacks from the Right, which we have surveyed in the Sobran affair, were comparatively harmless, Berman added: Buckley had done the nec-essary "housecleaning." It was a new thing, this anti-Semitism coming from the Left, with Navasky and his fellow editors not even knowing which closet the broom was in.[19]

Actually, some of the intellectuals on the Right were losing their grip on the broom. The Rockford Institute, a paleoconservative organization founded in 1976 with offices in Rockford, Illinois, published *Chronicles of Culture* (now simply *Chronicles*), which claimed a circulation of some 17,000. Its editor, Thomas Fleming, wrote a lead editorial in the March 1989 issue titled "The Real American Dilemma," in which he worried that immigration from devel-oping countries was becoming a flood threatening the Eurocentric tradition of America. "One doesn't wish to be unkind," he said, "but cultural pluralism is not the most attractive legacy we can leave to our children."

These remarks alarmed Richard Neuhaus, still a Lutheran pastor and the head of Rockford East in New York, where he edited the institute's serious journal, *This World*. As he wrote his boss Allan Carlson back in Illinois, Fleming's editorial culminated a trend: "In issue after issue, the emphasis upon cultural rootedness has assumed the nature of a running polemic against those whom the reader is invited to view as rootless, deracinated, and cosmopolitan elites." Constant mention of "New York" or "the 'more recent immigrants' who have dominated 'the business of literature' since the 30's," Neuhaus said, left "no doubt in a reasonable person's mind that the reference is negative and the reference is to Jews."

Damning Fleming's "nativist bigotry," Podhoretz had told Neuhaus how alarmed he was by two other articles in the same issue, virtual

hymns of praise to Gore Vidal. He is celebrated as a great conservative (*sic*) and his critics – specifically those who have protested against his anti-Semitic attack on me – are dismissed as carping pygmies. As for his violent opposition to what one of these encomiasts refers to with some embarrassment as "er, family values," it is not allowed to stand in the way of his elevation to the pantheon of great conservative thinkers and as a defender of (*sic* again, and sick again too) "civilization."

"In any case," Podhoretz told Neuhaus, "I know an enemy when I see one, and *Chronicles* has become just that so far as I personally am concerned – and, I would hope, so far as any decent conservative of any stripe is concerned as well."[20]

One consequence of these protests by Podhoretz and Neuhaus was Rock-ford's decision simply to close the New York office. In May 1989, five heavies from Illinois, including three board members, turned Neuhaus and his small staff out onto the sidewalk.[21] It was just as well. Besides converting to Catholicism, Neuhaus went on to found the Institute of Religion, Culture, and Public Life and to publish *First Things*, successor to *This World* but with a broader and more cosmopolitan mandate. Decter would eventually work at *First Things*, and Neuhaus, like Weigel, Novak, and of course Buckley, would as Catholics be important allies in the culture wars of the nineties.

Nativists were on the fringe. Humane Catholic and Protestant conservatives, a mix of neo- and paleo-, never wavered in their support of the Jewish state's right to defend itself against its enemies. In 1987, in what was called an Intifada, or uprising, those enemies were presenting themselves in the persons of Palestinian teenagers and even children who threw rocks and bottles at Israeli police and soldiers. These outbursts seemed initially spontaneous, set off now by a traffic accident, then by a Muslim cleric's denunciation of Israel's occupation of Gaza or the West Bank. But soon the PLO or rival terrorist groups like Hamas or the Palestinian Islamic Jihad were deliberately exploiting the rock-throwers in order to provoke Israeli retaliation – rubber bullets, tear gas, live ammunition fired over their heads – which would occasionally injure or kill some Palestinians, which in turn would become the focus of media coverage.

For Podhoretz, the Intifada had to be understood as a phase in the war between Israel and its Arab foes that had been going on since the U.N. partition of Palestine. Whatever the Israeli Defense Forces (IDF) did in response to the rock throwers, he said, they "bring condemnation down on their heads." Israel's position was "impossibly difficult, not because the Israelis are brutal but precisely because the Israelis are restrained" – in comparison with the treatment Palestinians had received from the Syrians and Jordanians and in stark contrast to the PLO itself. Egypt and Jordan, meanwhile, cruelly disoriented the Palestinians by giving their children schoolbooks with maps of the region on which the name of Israel never appeared. In this they were like many Western intellectuals who, carrying Israel-free maps of the Middle East in their heads, at the same time blamed Israel for whatever went wrong.[22]

Because so many parties wanted it dead, Israel simply couldn't accept a Palestinian state on the West Bank. Even if, for tactical reasons, the PLO were to drop the articles in its Charter rejecting Israel's right to exist and calling for its elimination, odds were that an independent Palestinian state would mean not peace but war – first, as Podhoretz projected, a civil war among Palestinian factions in which Damascus would at some point intervene, then a war between Israel and the Palestinians and Syrians simultaneously. Israel would probably win, but, in the words of one IDF analyst, "the price of victory would be at least 100,000 Israeli casualties."

Surrendering the West Bank and Gaza in order to inaugurate a Palestinian state would thus simply bring Israel back full circle – once again occupying the territories, but at a terrible cost in lives.[23]

In 1985, Mikhail Sergeyevich Gorbachev became General Secretary of the Communist Party in the Soviet Union. His efforts to reform the decrepit system through *glasnost* (political "openness"), *perestroika* (organizational "restructuring"), and *uskoreniye* (economic "acceleration") were all the news, as Khrushchev's de-Stalinization program had been thirty years before. Communist fellow travelers were given fresh hope that the totalitarian machine could, as they said, be given "a human face." Even some neoconservatives – Irving Kristol, for instance – were for the moment convinced that Gorbachev was rejigging the machine to serve less a war economy than a peacetime one. Those who thought otherwise, Kristol said, were "mired in the 1950s." Other anticommunists – Beichman, for instance, who confessed himself "mired in the 1920s because that's really when it all began"[24] – believed the machine *could* not be transformed.

In his second term, Reagan began to sound positively Carterite about relations with Gorbachev's regime. Ever since he had spoken with his younger counterpart at the November 1985 summit in Geneva, Reagan seemed persuaded that the Soviets were no longer bent on world domination and that the United States should directly and drastically reduce its military expenditures. Reagan likened Gorbachev to Lenin, somehow a more saintly version of Marxist than Stalin and the rest had been. This prompted Podhoretz to write to Moynihan that, on the scale of phoniness, he "regard[ed] Ronald Reagan's newfound admiration for Lenin as a fair trade for Mikhail Gorbachev's conversion to Jeffersonianism."[25]

Looking back on the Reagan presidency a decade later, Podhoretz could recognize his own contradictions. He wanted very much to believe that in combating the evil empire Reagan knew all along what he was doing, but he also had to admit that in his second term the president was showing signs of the Alzheimer's to which he finally succumbed. Take his apparent obliviousness to the arms-for-hostages deal that, on his orders, his subordinates had closed. Or take his proposing to Gorbachev at Reykjavik in 1986 (the two leaders were holding the second of four summits) that the superpowers abolish all nuclear weapons – a proposal not just unviable, since such weapons could always be produced anew, but also undesirable, since abolition would have left the Soviets with conventional superiority. These episodes were strong indicators that the president did *not* know what he was doing. He was saved from folly at Reykjavik by Gorbachev himself, who insisted that America's strategic defense initiative (SDI) be abolished, too.

SDI was, Podhoretz felt, an original idea, motivated by the desire "to rectify a situation in which the United States remained – by a deliberate choice arrived at through the mercifully forgotten dogmas of the arms-control theologians – completely defenseless against a missile attack."[26] Reagan's many critics may have ridiculed the cost and feasibility of SDI, but he believed in it and so, fatefully, did the Soviets. Foreseeing the time when such a missile defense "would render their entire nuclear arsenal obsolete," Gorbachev instituted the reforms he hoped would generate the money and the technology that could keep his country in the game. It was those reforms, most analysts agree, that "blew their whole system apart."[27] In any event, when the abolitionist proposal

FIGURE 19. Norman Podhoretz with President Ronald Reagan, Heritage Foundation head Edwin Feulner, and Feulner's wife, Linda, circa 1986. (Photo by Charles Geer.)

at Reykjavik fell through, spending on missiles and missile defense proceeded apace, and the Soviets were bankrupted. Earlier, they had been able to make tanks but not toasters. In the end, they couldn't even make tanks.[28]

In the summer of 1989, Podhoretz published a piece in *Geopolitique* wondering how it was "that what no Soviet leader from Stalin to Brezhnev managed to achieve by means of the scowl is precisely what Gorbachev is accomplishing by means of the smile."[29] As if to find out, he visited the Soviet Union, taking part in a conference of a group of American intellectuals and more than 200 scholars at the Kinocenter in Moscow. They could, he told the Russians, rejoice in the policy of *glasnost* that made such a meeting possible: "I have friends who spent many years in the gulag for saying a lot less than what we're saying today." And one of the things he wanted to help the Soviets say was that their government, not his, had been responsible for starting and intensifying the Cold War. "I gave not an inch," Podhoretz recalled: Soviet citizens had been "aggressively lied to"; communism was "absolutely evil"; Lenin, Gorbachev notwithstanding, was no democrat; and, notwithstanding a proud gray-haired veteran who intervened from the floor, the Soviet Army's invasion of Czechoslovakia in 1968 was not that nation's "shortcut to democracy."[30]

Though the Soviets treated Podhoretz to every luxury – "more royally than I've ever been treated in any country before" – the atmosphere was shudderingly totalitarian, and, as he later told Robert Conquest, he "hated the place."[31] Nevertheless, he appreciated how the Moscow students heaped encomiums on him, or how, on another occasion, the cellist and dissident émigré Mstislav Rostropovich, "a very demonstrative guy, threw his arms around me and said 'Ohhhhh, the hero!'"[32]

Would neoconservatism have any relevance after the Cold War was over, as indeed it soon would be? By 1992, Francis Fukuyama would be wondering whether history itself had effectively ended, now that the dramatic conflict between left-wing totalitarianism and liberal, capitalist democracy had been resolved.[33] Podhoretz was pretty sure history would go on, and so would the struggle to prevent the too-contented peoples of the West, suddenly lacking an external enemy, from turning against the very peace, prosperity, and democracy their own contentment depended on. To begin with, Podhoretz pointed out, neoconservatives needed to challenge those social democrats who didn't yet grasp why the success of *capitalism*, "this almost universally despised system," was essential to the failure of communism, not to mention its role both as a form of freedom in its own right and as a necessary (though not sufficient) condition of freedom in the political realm. Beyond this economic salient, there was the ongoing culture war on behalf "of the traditional moral values which had been condemned by the counterculture as instruments of oppression" but in fact "were not only more conducive to personal health and happiness than any alternative 'life styles' but were also the indispensable foundation of a prosperous society."

"Far from being played out and ready to die," therefore, neoconservatism was "being given a whole new set of jobs to do and a whole new lease on life."[34] And that wasn't the half of it.

18

Culture Wars

In 1990, Paul Ferris, an Englishman who had written biographies of poet Dylan Thomas and actor Richard Burton, published one of another Welshman, the late Huw Wheldon. Novelist Kingsley Amis, a family friend, had recommended Ferris to Jacqueline Wheldon. Clearly, someone needed to tell the story of the BBC's liveliest, most intelligent impresario during what, it was already plain, had been television's golden age. In the United States as in the United Kingdom, millions had seen Alistair Cooke's *America*, Kenneth Clark's *Civilisation*, and Jacob Bronowski's *The Ascent of Man*, all Wheldon projects.

Regrettably, Ferris's method was to look down at Wheldon, offering nothing but pop-psychological commonplaces about adolescent anxieties over sex, peeks at pornography, and fumbling love affairs before meeting Jacqueline. Although Wheldon and Podhoretz didn't talk much about politics, Ferris assumed they had. He wrote insinuatingly to Podhoretz: "One encounters occasional left-of-centre friends and acquaintances of Huw who...use his friendship with you to suggest that in later years he changed colour politically and (in their opinion) for the worse." To which Podhoretz replied: "Contrary to what you have been told, [Wheldon's political] views never changed. He was, and always remained, a liberal in the old and best sense of that currently much misused word."[1]

In a review of the book, Brian Wenham wondered whether Ferris hadn't displayed "what is meant by bias against understanding." In private life Wheldon may have been an everyman, but in public life, making "the popular good and the good popular," he was larger than anyone else in "his time or since. A truer Life would have revealed this."[2,3]

That is what Jacqueline felt, though for her the objections were deeply personal. She had turned her husband's papers over to Ferris trustingly. Now, reading the galleys, she was appalled at the "amateur Freudianism – the original tidings were that Huw had a 'florid father fixation,'" from which Ferris construed "the Oedipus Complex; and impotence?!"[4] Small wonder that the book party hosted by Brenda Maddox was a bust, with the Wheldons, like the senior BBC executives, conspicuously absent and Amis feigning laryngitis.[5] As Wynn Wheldon recalled, his mother felt that, by not having sorted through the letters and papers she gave Ferris, "she was the real sinner, that she had betrayed her husband ('inexcusable treachery' was the term she used), and by this her fragile morale was destroyed." She tried "to write her own memoir of her husband, but characteristically found that her need to know everything bogged her down." Isolated by increasing deafness and by obsession with the novel she couldn't complete, she was to die of cancer in June 1993.[6]

Friends less intimate but still deeply important – professional colleagues for many years – were dying nearer home. Lucy Dawidowicz (b. 1915) died in December 1990, coinciding with the publication in *Commentary* of her final essay, "How They Teach the Holocaust." Her classic *The War Against the Jews, 1933–1945* (1975) had been a thorough indictment not just of ordinary Germans who were aware of and assisted the Nazis but of German culture itself, rife with *Judenhass* since its Christianization. At the funeral, Podhoretz's eulogy began by recalling her sardonic quip that, since she was dying just as the December issue was coming out, "At least now I won't have to answer the *expletive deleted* letters on that article"! "All of us here," Podhoretz went on more earnestly, "will have to go on with lives diminished by the loss of a fierce and tough-minded and infinitely loving friend. But the world in general will be a little darker by the extinguishing of this candle, this American candle, this Jewish light unto the nations."[7]

Marion Magid died in 1993 at age sixty-one. Younger than Podhoretz by two years, she had worked at *Commentary* – "an ardent companion [as Kozodoy wrote], gallant, kind, and good . . . the permanent and irreplaceable darling of our hearts" – since 1963. She had then seemed to Podhoretz the very figure of the "cultural pluralism" she claimed to know nothing about – a feminine complement, in fact, of his own. "She looked," he said in eulogy,

like someone who had stepped directly out of Weimar Berlin: the raincoat, the hair, the slightly distracted raffish Bohemian air. . . . But of course it was the Bronx that Marion came out of, and beyond that the shtetl of Semyatich from which her parents had emigrated to America and to which she so often referred, and beyond that the world of East European Jewry in general: a world of which she was in the most profound sense a product and an ornament.

Brilliant, witty, and ironic in conversation, Magid suffered as a writer from "an especially ferocious block," which meant that most of her aperçus were reserved for her friends. One in particular stayed with Podhoretz as a key to the personal impact of the counterculture: "'Do you realize,' she asked me upon surveying a crowd of sorry-looking radicals who had assembled for a debate in a dingy union hall in the early 60's, 'do you realize that every person in this room is a tragedy to some family?'"[8]

Then, in December 1994, Samuel Lipman, younger than Podhoretz by four years, died at sixty. He had become *Commentary*'s music critic in 1975 and, with Kramer, founded the *New Criterion* in 1982. Eulogizing him, Podhoretz had to chuckle admiringly at his friend's pertinacious argufying. For years they had gone back and forth about the merits of Vladimir Horowitz (whom Lipman revered and Podhoretz didn't) or Richard Goode (Lipman thought Artur Schnabel the greater performer of Beethoven, while Podhoretz wasn't so sure). Even as Lipman lay dying in the hospital,

> hardly able to breathe and moving in and out of lucidity because of the medication they had fed him, he regaled me with the wonders, not this time of Horowitz but of his counterpart on the violin, Heifetz. He had been listening to the new set of Heifetz reissues on compact disc with the intention – still! – of writing a piece about them, and no more than a minute after I walked into the hospital room, he waved one of the discs at me and declared challengingly that Heifetz was "the greatest violinist who ever lived." "What about Szigeti?" I demurred, thinking he would be disappointed if I failed to put up at least a little resistance. In response, he smiled a sweet smile, and then went on to tell me again, as he had so often before but now for the very last time, how worried he was about the fate of our civilization.

It wasn't just that Lipman, like Dawidowicz, Magid, or either of the Wheldons, wouldn't go gentle into that good night; it was that his rage was directed at the declining health of the culture that his forebears had helped create, that he as musician and critic had helped sustain, and that his survivors needed to take responsibility for. They needed to do so, Podhoretz observed, in Lipman's own fashion, with attention to the details that, in sum, *are* our civilization.

> It always seemed to me that he wrote about music the way he had learned to perform it: by playing the notes, all the notes, as accurately as he could play them. There was no reaching above them or going around them: everything there was to say had to be said in and through the notes – everything, including or perhaps even especially the most transcendent truths, was rooted in those homely individual details, and had to be spelled out point by careful point.[9]

All of Podhoretz's eulogizing statements underline a central theme: death is not a bugaboo to frighten and paralyze us but part and parcel of life, its final moment. The business of the living is *to live* – in awareness of death to choose life and, by attending to the "homely individual details" of defending their freedom, enable them to pursue their different ways of being happy.

Defending freedom and making the pursuit of happiness possible was what Podhoretz's son-in-law and Rachel's husband, Elliott Abrams, knew he was doing while serving the Reagan administration. The Abramses and the Podhoretzes naturally saw one another at family gatherings for Seder or Thanksgiving, and the Munsons – Naomi and her husband, Steve – would be there, too. Podhoretz remembered Steve, "very hard-line and judgmental, and very envious of Elliott," baiting him about the gap between Reaganite principles and Reaganite practice, a gap that also troubled Podhoretz. Soon there would be a two-on-one fight, with "Elliott, the good soldier," explaining the compromises necessary as moral theory is translated into workable policy. "It was not pleasant."

Abrams's rise had been meteoric. "I was ten-thousand-percent behind him," Podhoretz would recall, "loving his brashness and candor. But in fact I was wrong." Wrong, that is, not to notice how the brashness and candor grated on Washington politicians, a species not famous for humility. "If he'd been more diplomatic with some of those senators, they might not have gone after him" the way they did during the Iran-Contra hearings. Abrams would later tell the tale on himself, joking to friends that "the only crime I probably committed was contempt of Congress," saying to a member of the Foreign Relations Committee, "Congressman, you're on the wrong committee, you ought to get yourself on the Intelligence Committee," or to John Kerry, "Listen to me, Senator; you're not listening."[10] Podhoretz used to remark that "Elliott Abrams was a young man on whose parade no rain had ever fallen. When the rain fell, however, it fell in cloudbursts."[11] We can mark for ourselves the parallel with Podhoretz's own career up to the publication of *Making It*, and the time of ashes that followed.

This isn't the place to pore over the details of the Iran-Contra hearings or, in 1991, the "undue process," as Abrams dubbed it, to which he was subjected by independent counsel Lawrence E. Walsh, an eighty-year-old judge charged by Reagan to investigate the affair. The background is this. When Congress cut off funds for military support of the Contras, Reagan's appointees began, on his instructions, to seek still legal private means of funding the Contras' nonmilitary needs (clothing, food, medicine). Abrams was directed to feel out the Sultan of Brunei, who, insisting on secrecy, pledged $10 million. Because of a clerical error (a mistyped Swiss account number), the money never did materialize, but Walsh was bothered by Abrams's failure, in 1986, to tell Congress everything he knew. "Was there foreign money?" He had said no, which was strictly true because the Sultan's money hadn't arrived. He omitted saying that the money was expected.[12] There were also, thanks to Oliver North's covert machinations, millions of Saudi dollars going to the Contras, but Abrams had been kept in the dark about that, as about the arms sales to Iran – no doubt because North knew that, if Abrams knew, he would tell Secretary of State George Shultz, who then would shut them down.[13] Walsh now argued that Abrams "should have known" both about North and about the activities of the CIA, whose human-rights abuses turned out, Abrams confessed, to be "worse than I had known. Much worse." Why hadn't he "insisted on knowing *everything* the Agency was up to?" He admits that, on this issue, Walsh was right: "I was supposed to be the point man, not the front man. I was supposed to be leading the NSC and the CIA efforts, not providing cover for them."[14]

These were serious mistakes, but they were mistakes in implementing pres-idential policy. The executive branch and its officers, for reasons of national security, have never told all they have known to the legislative branch: that practice had been understood for more than two hundred years. But in the polarized eighties and early nineties, with the Democrat-controlled Congress pitched increasingly against the Republican-controlled White House, tradition-ally understood practices were called into question. Walsh and his young staff believed they had a congressional mandate to go after North, John Poindexter, Robert McFarlane, and finally Abrams – surrogates, evidently, for the higher-up and well-insulated Shultz, George H. W. Bush, or Reagan himself. How ironic, thought Abrams, that he and the Reagan administration "used to be accused . . . of being 'ideological'!"[15]

Abrams's first instinct, passionately reinforced by his wife, Rachel, was to fight Walsh all the way. Let him bring an indictment: they would go to court and win acquittal, or if not go down with guns blazing. To go down meant going to prison, however, and Abrams finally decided, for Rachel and their children's sake, not to risk it. He therefore pleaded guilty to two misdemeanors related to withholding information from Congress. Chief Judge Aubrey Robinson, a black appointee of Lyndon Johnson, "imposed no fine . . . just the fifty-dollar court costs the law required," placed him on probation for two years, and assigned him one hundred hours of community service. This was a judicial way (1) of indicating that a momentary error of judgment shouldn't expunge twelve years of honorable service to the country and (2) telling the independent counsel to shut up shop.

After five years and $50 million, Walsh's office had achieved practically nothing. In the two cases brought to trial, North and Poindexter had ultimately won acquittal, while the plea cases, like Abrams's and McFarlane's, had ended with sentences so light as to amount to dismissals.[16] The lot of them had been scapegoated by a president – Reagan – who, instead of standing by his men, had "deserted" them, Abrams would write, flinging their lives "into the abyss." Nor did Reagan grant any executive pardons at the end of his second term: "He remained silent, and it was a sorry performance. Presidents must demand loyalty, but they must reward it and return it as well."[17] Of course Abrams himself had required no pardon at the end of Reagan's tenure. With a "criminal record," however, he did need one at the end of President George H. W. Bush's tenure, and, along with a number of other Iran-Contra defendants, he received it in late 1992.

Undue Process, the book Abrams wrote about this ordeal, makes it clear that his in-laws were thoroughly supportive throughout. He doesn't go into detail, but his attorneys' fees were nearly a million dollars. The Podhoretzes were ready from day one to pony up everything they had to fight the case, offering to mortgage their city apartment and their house in East Hampton and to turn all their assets over to Abrams's defense fund. They helped him write letters to people known to assist conservative causes. Podhoretz recalled that he "even wrote some columns defending him and attacking Lawrence Walsh. It wasn't just for Elliott's sake, it was for the sake of a cause I believed in. . . . In public Elliott carried all this off magnificently. Privately I know he suffered badly" – he lost weight, had a heart-attack scare – and "Rachel suffered something fierce. There were demonstrations in front of their house in Washington; the kids were subjected to this."

The most poignant passages in Abrams's book have to do with Rachel's abiding by him, and her murderous anger toward Walsh and his team. "I entered . . . this concrete-covered swamp" of Washington, she wrote her closest

FIGURE 20. Norman Podhoretz with then Vice-President George H. W. Bush and writer and editor R. Emmett ("Bob") Tyrrell, 1987. (Photo by Katherine Andriotis.)

friend, "almost twelve years ago, left New York and all behind me, brimming with hope. I was married to this golden man, my prize. And here I am, clenching, grinding, my teeth, wondering how to save him from, how to hurt, how to savage, how to kill, the people who have called him a criminal." It was a more intimate repetition of the care she had offered her wounded stepfather, her first golden man, more than twenty years before, when he fell into depression after people turned on him for writing *Making It*. And who were these persecutors? Politicians who had plotted with Sandinistas, leaked classified documents to reporters, and then written vicious and slanted stories about her husband: the "abominable, bloated, check-kiting, drunken, . . . whoring, xenophobic, yellow-bellied, zeros who populate the Congress."[18]

Frankly expecting the worst from Judge Robinson, Norman and Midge came to Washington for the day of the sentencing – she to stay with the grandchildren at home, he to accompany Elliott and Rachel to court. Reporters and photographers were waiting outside. Then, as proceedings got under way, it became clear that Robinson intended to deny the Walsh team the trophy they hungered for. He cut off their iteration of the charges – "All right, we know all that, just sit down, sit down!" – and didn't ask Abrams to express remorse or regale him with the customary allocution. Just the terse announcement of the fine, the suspended sentence, and the community service. "It was wonderful – [Robinson's] contempt for Walsh and his office, this black liberal judge saying in effect that he couldn't throw out the whole thing but he was going to show them he thought it ridiculous. Fantastic," Podhoretz remarked. "I get tears just thinking about it."[19]

Gerald Green, author of the fine populist novel *The Last Angry Man* and son (as it happened) of a Dr. Greenberg who once had pulled Norman out of a childhood illness, was no neoconservative, but he and Podhoretz shared a concern for the on-going danger of anti-Semitism. The right-wing origins of that disease were well-known to both, and Green acknowledged the left-wing outbreaks Podhoretz had recently identified, whether in Vidal's "unconscionable" attack in the *Nation* or, Green added, in the spleen vented by "Noam Chomsky, Jesse Jackson, and the *Village Voice* writers who continually bash Israel." Green's advice to Podhoretz was, while not giving the Left any free passes, to keep after the anti-Semites on the Right.[20]

Podhoretz didn't disagree. He pursued that mission when defending America's intervention in the Persian Gulf against critics like Patrick Buchanan, the former Nixon press secretary and current columnist and TV commentator, who was "dragging Israel and its 'amen corner' into the center of an issue to which they are at best marginal," and again in an open letter to Buckley after the publication of the latter's *In Search of Anti-Semitism*. What Podhoretz could applaud in Buckley's book was his recognition, after some waffling, that Buchanan's statements about Operation Desert Storm were symptomatic of an anti-Semitic bias in his writings generally.[21]

By formally putting the right-wing anti-Semites behind him, Buckley was in effect continuing the project he had begun, as a young editor in 1957, of dissociating *National Review* from them. He should go on, Podhoretz wrote, to address the story of the Church of Rome's anti-Semitism in the past and its residue in the present: "the Vatican still has no diplomatic relations with the state of Israel. If this is not a symptom of trouble with the Jewish problem, what is it?"[22]

Not that Podhoretz believed that Christian or indeed Jewish "obtuseness," including his own on occasion, should unsettle the burgeoning alliance among religiously informed conservatives against what both he and Buckley perceived to be an antireligious Left. For that group, open hostility toward practicing Jews was (most of the time) infra dig, but baiting practicing Catholics and Moral Majority Protestant fundamentalists still seemed as popular as it had been in H. L. Mencken's heyday. In 1991, for instance, KCET in Los Angeles produced a television program titled "Stop the Church," which was so toxically anti-Catholic that, out of 321 PBS affiliates, only those in Boston, New York, and San Francisco broadcast it. As Weigel pointed out in the *Los Angeles Times*, the film ridiculed pastoral practice and moral teaching "with such palpable rage and hatred" that one couldn't miss the desire "to cripple" the Church itself.[23] Neuhaus wondered whether Weigel's critique wasn't "a bit too forceful." "I told him he was mistaken," Weigel said to an applauding Podhoretz, who commissioned a fuller (and, as it turned out, extraordinarily forceful) article for *Commentary*.[24]

It was one thing to fall away from religion: deconversion had after all been a rite of passage for a large percentage of intellectuals since the beginning of the Enlightenment. What was troubling many conservatives during the eighties and early nineties was the absence of *any* religious training for many American children, leaving them oblivious of the history, rituals, and moral meaning of churches and synagogues altogether. The remedy had to lie in education.

This explains, back in 1987, Podhoretz's enthusiasm for Allan Bloom's *The Closing of the American Mind*, which, for all its philosophical difficulty, sold half a million copies in hardcover. The "closing of mind" Bloom's title referred to was the paradoxical consequence of the liberally open mind, which not only dismissed any attempts, such as those by Plato or the Hebrew prophets, to provide a rational basis for moral judgments but also scoffed at the battle between good and evil represented in traditional literature. Small wonder young people were bored by, as well as confused about, their education. As for the culture beyond the universities, liberals went on publicly blaming "Reagan's budget cuts" for "violent crime, pornography, drugs, teenage pregnancy and AIDS." Privately, however, "more and more liberals are apparently coming to understand that their inability or unwillingness to declare that some things are right and some things are wrong has exacted a terrible toll – in their own lives, in the lives of their children, and in the life of society as a whole."[25]

Bloom's notoriety, from 1987 until his death in 1992, mirrored that of Paul Goodman thirty years before. Both were University of Chicago mavericks declaring something rotten in the state of academia; both were homosexuals shy of, not to say disdainful toward, the vulgarities of the gay rights movement; both were at once culturally elitist and politically democratic; and both found a champion, at different phases of their careers, in Podhoretz. He understood completely their combination of cultural elitism and political democracy.

Bloom's cultural elitism, like Goodman's, was simply a function of recognizing that some writers and artists were better than others, now and in the past. The superiority of Plato, Aristotle, Locke, or Rousseau resided in the intrinsic qualities of their books and not, as the mind-closing liberal educators would argue, in extrinsic factors having to do with economic and political "power." The latter argument declared that Aristotle, say, was on school reading lists because rich and politically influential people thought his philosophy helped bolster their privileges. The supposed corrective was to replace Aristotle's *Politics* with something favoring revolution, say Franz Fanon's *The Wretched of the Earth*. The curricula of most American colleges now reflected this world-turned-upside-down revision of the canon.

There was an answer to this regnant pedagogy, as Bloom told a Harvard audience in a lecture published by Podhoretz. There was no need to deny that extrinsic power played its part in forming curricula – of course it did. Of greater importance, considered historically, were the "transcultural values," moral as well as aesthetic, that gave a work its universality, its ability to speak to audiences regardless of time and place, let alone the now holy trinity of gender, race, and class. As opposed to the black student at Stanford for whom "the implicit message of the Western civilization curriculum is 'nigger go home,'" Bloom set the early twentieth-century black historian W. E. B. Du Bois's assertion that "I sit with Shakespeare and he winces not. Across the color line I move arm and arm with Balzac and Dumas." That was the proven path to liberation.

Bloom assumed nearly everyone would agree that science was "somehow transcultural." He assumed, too, that most of his fellow intellectuals would agree that religion was culturally specific – Hinduism in India, Catholicism in Poland. The crucial question was whether philosophy and literature were to be treated like science, offering something true across all cultures, or like religion, "historicized" and relativized to the point of irrelevance. As for identifying the "something true" Bloom thought educators should promote, the short answer, joining his cultural elitism with his commitment to political democracy, was what Podhoretz and *Commentary* writers generally had been promoting since the mid-seventies: freedom.

Freedom, intellectual and political, was also what the student protesters in Tiananmen Square had been demanding in the summer of 1989. Yes, Bloom observed, they debated whether their Statue of Liberty "should be altered to have Chinese rather than *Eurocentric* features, [but] there was a consensus that it did not make any difference." It was a good thing they hadn't matriculated at Harvard or Stanford since all that "the dominant schools in American universities can tell the Chinese students... [is] that they should avoid Eurocentrism, that rationalism has failed, that they should study non-Western cultures, and that bourgeois liberalism is the most despicable of regimes" – a set of ideas quite the opposite of "what the Chinese need. They have Deng Xiaoping to deconstruct their Statue of Liberty. We owe them something much better."[26]

In 1991, Podhoretz reviewed Noel Annan's *Our Age: English Intellectuals between the World Wars*. Annan, as we have noted, would have directed Podhoretz's proposed Cambridge dissertation on Disraeli, and had written a friendly notice on *Breaking Ranks*. It was commendable of him, Podhoretz now said, to admit that the democratic socialist program his generation so civilly recommended between the wars, and so thoroughly implemented when Labour defeated Churchill in 1945, had led to a "whirlwind" of "crime, violence, drugs, and promiscuity" in the sixties and to economic lassitude prior to Mrs. Thatcher. Unfortunately, though, Annan didn't think democratic socialist theory was wrong: it simply needed to be adjusted. Thus he detested someone like Paul Johnson, a one-time democratic socialist and former editor of the *New Statesman*, who, along with other neoconservatives, had, as Podhoretz said, "the intellectual and moral courage to rethink [the theory's] assumptions in the light of their ugly practical consequences."[27]

Reading this review in her summer home in Provence, Jeane Kirkpatrick wrote Podhoretz in urgent puzzlement: Why should Annan, a man "tolerant to a fault," hate Paul Johnson? Indeed why generally "do *they* hate *us*?

Like you, I believe this to be a central – perhaps the central – question about
Western Culture in the last quarter of this century." She went on in an arresting
vein:

The devastation of the various totalitarianisms is the tragedy of the century. And the
attraction for intellectuals of communism was the central mystery of the first two thirds
or so of the century. The rage against neoconservatives is a central phenomenon of the
last quarter century.

I believe classical Freudian denial is the most plausible explanation of the latter, with
the effort to defend the denied fact consuming an ever larger portion of energy and
attention – and any threat to the denial provoking intense rage.

But what finally is being denied? Why is it so central?

And what is it that links attraction to totalitarianism and animosity to neoconservatives? What explains "liberals" ready to forgive treason and genocide but implacably
hostile to anti-communism?

It is not easy to understand this determination to be wrong about the most important
questions.

Obviously they hate traditional liberalism. They hate the skeptical habits of mind
and rejection of mystification, thus the special distaste so long reserved for Orwell. And
they hate a bourgeois insistence on individual responsibility.

Is it this rejection of personal responsibility (I suspect there is no other kind) that
links the rejection of capitalism with the rejection of religion and family, on the one
hand, to the rage against anti-communists on the other?

Can they accept *anyone* who insists that *even intellectuals* must assume moral responsibility for the consequences of their ideas? What could be more boorish than harping
on terror and genocide when these are the consequences of the clever ideas of clever
people?

I don't know.

But I do know that liberal rage against neo-cons is intense and unreasoning and
stands in the sharpest of contrast to the endless liberal tolerance of error and mayhem
on the left.

And it is apparently unaffected by the collapse of communism and the end of the
Cold War.[28]

Podhoretz's reply refines Kirkpatrick's analytical categories and adds a theological explanation to her psychological one:

Like you, I remain puzzled by the hatred they feel for us. Your speculation is plausible,
and probably contains at least a part of the answer, but it isn't fully satisfying. My own
guess is that it's our apostasy from what amounts to a religious creed (socialism, even in
its attenuated "liberal" mutation) that is the decisive element here. After all, even people
like Irving Howe hate us, not because we're anti-Communists (since they are too) but
because we no longer believe in socialism and because we have in effect converted to
the "church" of the ancestral enemy.[29]

The ancestral enemy was capitalism – not the oligarchical capitalism that
sympathized with the fascists back in the twenties and thirties but the democratic capitalism that Franklin Roosevelt had enabled America to preserve.

Democratic capitalism had defeated fascism first and now appeared to have all but finished off the other totalitarian power, communism. Democratic capitalism wasn't, however, to be confused with democratic socialism, which was Irving Howe's last best hope, for democratic socialism denied people economic liberty.

Podhoretz had repeatedly made this case during the eighties, but never better than in "The New Defenders of Capitalism" (1981), which we should belatedly glance at here. Economic liberty, he maintained, was itself a form of the liberty that, for centuries, liberals had bled for. Milton Friedman, Peter Berger, Novak, and Kristol were among those who defied the mass of their intellectual peers and dared to rally for the system Adam Smith believed produced "the wealth of nations." But it was William Barrett who, for Podhoretz, put the case with the most eloquent brevity:

How could we ever have believed that you could deprive human beings of the fundamental right to initiate and engage in their own economic activity without putting every other human right in jeopardy? And to pass from questions of rights to those of fact: everything we observe about the behavior of human beings in groups, everything we know about that behavior from history, should tell us that you cannot unite political and economic power in one center without opening the door to tyranny.

It wasn't, in short, only a matter of moral logic, but a matter of empirical test. Besides ensuring liberty, capitalism had done a better job than socialism in realizing equality. It did this not necessarily by reducing inequality among competing individuals, some of whom would, in the nature of things, always do work that was more valuable than others, but by improving "the lot of everyone. Rich and poor alike grow richer under capitalism," the proverbial "pie" expanding to a degree that "in capitalist societies the very idea of what constitutes poverty undergoes a change from absolute to relative deprivation." Ask the folks from places like Brownsville.

As for the longing for a meaning to life not encompassed by material goods – the longing that animated countercultural rebellions – Podhoretz approved of Barrett's cold-shower candor. Such "spiritual sickness... cannot be cured by any set of economic or political arrangements, and... a great virtue of capitalism is that it refuses even to try. It is thus a bulwark against totalitarianism, not only because it allows liberty but also because its claims are limited: 'we are not required to worship it.'"

In part because capitalism, like any other economic system, couldn't guarantee spiritual health or personal happiness, Kristol had titled a book *Two Cheers for Capitalism*, withholding the third cheer. Counting each of capitalism's virtues, however, Podhoretz did cheer three times: capitalism "is a necessary, if not a sufficient, condition of freedom;... it is both a necessary and a sufficient condition of wealth; and... it provides a better chance than any known alternative for the most widespread sharing in the wealth it produces."[30] Since such wider, more equal sharing made the greatest number of people happier, perhaps Kristol should, on classical utilitarian grounds, offer a third cheer after all.

Speaking of private enterprise, beginning in 1990, *Commentary*, which had been sponsored by the AJC for forty-five years, was told it needed to raise money on its own. The vehicle for doing so would be the Commentary Fund, and Podhoretz was surprised to discover how effective he could be in scaring up donations, not just from individuals but also from foundations, "most of which," he told Walter H. Annenberg, "incidentally are non-Jewish."[31]

In early 1995, Podhoretz's fund-raising letter to subscribers and potential donors began with an announcement that beginning in June Neal Kozodoy would be *Commentary*'s editor, while he would become editor-at-large. Podhoretz was retiring after thirty-five years at the helm and felt complete confidence in Kozodoy, "a brilliant editor, the best I have ever worked with." For perhaps the last ten years, the younger man had been assuming ever greater responsibility for getting the magazine out. Hence "he will bring to his new job a range of experience and a loyalty to the magazine's traditions that are impossible to match." While celebrating those traditions, Podhoretz also confessed he was worried about "Jewish continuity," not merely the survival of Israel but, in America, the bad news/good news conditions created by "the rising rate of intermarriage and the declining rate of [mainstream] anti-Semitism." He appealed to subscribers to help *Commentary* raise the wherewithal to carry on its advocacy for Western democracy and Jewish survival. This retirement letter and appeal, sent to 14,000 people, brought in $142,000 – a success that, as Podhoretz told Buckley, was "in no small part thanks to you since your own annual letters [on behalf of *National Review*] served as my model."[32]

As his retirement approached, Podhoretz received some exceptionally thoughtful letters summing up his work as writer and editor. One of the best had already come in from John Wain, the English poet, novelist, and critic, who had outgrown his affiliations with the Angry Young Men of the fifties:

[*Commentary*] has played a crucial role in my life in keeping me reasonably up to date with what is happening in the world. Of course it is Jewish and American, and I am neither, but both of those are advantages; America is such a cross-roads of power and influence in the world, and the Jews are such a vital nerve-centre within the American population, that I don't think I have ever, even once, had the sensation of listening in to a debate that didn't concern me. On the contrary, you have always kept the really central issues so much in the foreground: what makes for a healthful body politic? Where does vital experimentation end and cultural decline begin, riddled with kitsch and opportunism? How can the academy pay suitable attention to questions of the hour, and issues of the contemporary world, without being merely swamped by the propaganda of pressure groups and attention-seekers? In your pages I have always found these issues contemplated so steadily that it has actually buoyed me up, month by month, year by year. What I owe to *Commentary*, and to you for sending me *Commentary*, is almost beyond expression.[33]

When Podhoretz tried to imagine *Commentary*'s ideal reader, surely someone like Wain must have occurred to him.

But people directly in the limelight of political history figured, too. On the very eve of Podhoretz's retirement, Benjamin Netanyahu, who would become Israeli prime minister the next year, wrote a tribute: "Changing the course of a mighty river used to be considered a mythological feat, yet this is precisely what you have done in your long and remarkable career as the guiding intellectual light of American conservatism."[34] In sending his last-minute regrets that senatorial duties would keep him from attending the retirement banquet at the Hotel Pierre, Moynihan looked back on Podhoretz's thirty-five years and said with "your John... [that] it has been a hell of a ride. You know of my ever-growing gratitude for taking me along. Most of the way."[35] That "Most of the way" was frank; as we have seen, the compromises Moynihan had made in elected office since 1977 had put considerable daylight between the two men. But as he would affirm five years later, on the jacket of Podhoretz's *My Love Affair with America*: "It is America he loves, not ideology. Almost a half century ago he was chosen Soldier of the Month by his unit in Occupied Germany. Some would hold that in the wars of ideas that swept over us since, he has been Soldier of the Century."[36]

That was, ringingly, the spirit of recognition expressed in the toasts offered at the banquet. The event constituted, as *Jerusalem Post* editor David Bar-Illan quipped, a gathering of intellectuals whose "passport to respectability" was to be on the same "enemy lists" as the man they were honoring. How, Kristol asked, had Podhoretz made *Commentary* "the finest, most important, and most influential" Jewish magazine "ever published, anywhere, at any time," and "one of the two or three most influential" American "magazines of the past 35 years"? Kristol answered his own question with the authority of one who had edited magazines for almost half a century: Podhoretz had "the editorial imagination... the ability to look at a manuscript and see the article that it ought to be, and then to know how to make it into that article. It's like a sculptor looking at a slab of stone, and seeing the object of art that will emerge from inside it." This rare editorial ability was joined, Ozick remarked, with a writerly ability rare at any time, but not least in America during the highly polemicized postwar era.

Podhoretz's growing up in America, Ruth Wisse said, had made him love "freedom and democracy" and given him the confidence to fight for them against communism, the counterculture, and, "almost by accident," the enemies of "the House of Israel." He had found himself an aggressive "watchman" precisely because, collectively, Jews have so great a "stake in fantasies of tolerance" that they "have a hard time facing political reality." Given the deadly "aggression directed against us," Podhoretz knew there was no room for "deception, or self-deception," whatever the pity one felt "for the decimated Diaspora Jews or the war-weary Israelis."

Kozodoy spoke last, his remarks freighted with affection. Podhoretz had, early and late, borne "the cost" of standing by the truth as he saw it – the cost (though Kozodoy didn't stoop to analyze it) tallied in friendships broken, mud slung, and ostracism from the pages of intellectual magazines that, when he was a pace-setter on the Left, had often sought him out. "He bore that cost; we garnered the benefits." Remembering Decter's tart remark – "I bring him coffee; he brings me courage" – Kozodoy capped it: "Whatever we in our different ways have brought him, courage is what he brought us." Of course it would have been "*too* personal" to speak in concrete particulars of Podhoretz's love – for Midge, his children and grandchildren, or his friends – but Kozodoy did venture to declare that love to be "hugely spacious, indulgent, equable, unshakable, ardent, vivifying, expectant, and full of mirth: the low humor of Brownsville, the high laughter of the prophets," and above all "human" in the way music is human, "puls[ing] . . . through Creation."

Most people in that room, many famous for their hardheadedness, must have teared up at such encomiums, and inwardly Podhoretz was surely one of them. Outwardly, he knew how to strike the tonic chord:

Now they tell me.
    A few months ago, the *New York Times* ran a piece about my impending retirement that many people were surprised by: it seemed so relatively unhostile, even benign. Pat Moynihan was asked why he thought the piece was so friendly, and without missing a beat Pat said, "Well, he's *leaving!*"

Podhoretz then revisited the decades, centering on the crisis of the late sixties when he saw that the Left "was, to borrow one of its own favorite formulas, part of the problem rather than part of the solution." The people he had known "over there" were often so "dazzling" intellectually "that they blinded me temporarily to the foolishness and recklessness of their ideas." Combating foolishness and recklessness, as he set out to do, may be a noble sport, as Teddy Roosevelt believed, but

it is also . . . a very bloody one. And so, to my lasting regret, breaking with the Left cost me the friendship of most – well, not most, more like all – of these interesting and amusing people. Still, the rewards of that break were much greater than the price. In breaking ranks and becoming a critic of the Left, I forged new friendships and new associations with a much wider and more variegated circle of writers, many of whom, to my great delight and my great gratitude, are gathered here tonight

– and with whom he had collaborated in "repair[ing] at least some of the damage I had helped wreak as a partisan of the Left." The hero of what John Gross later called *The Podyssey* was ready to say goodbye.[37]
    Beichman can be forgiven a moment of euphoric histrionics when he dashed off a note to Podhoretz the following day:

I was reminded of that illustration in Barbara Tuchman's first book on World War I, the photograph of all the crowned heads of Europe, pre August 1, 1914, mounted on fiery steeds assembled at Buckingham Palace to celebrate some royal birthday. Never again in our lifetime would such an assemblage of lions be seen under one roof as we saw last night at the Pierre. And it could only have happened because of you – post hoc, propter hoc – not a logical fallacy but a hard fact.[38]

There is no such photograph in either Tuchman's *The Guns of August* or *The Proud Tower*, but the lions, nearly 400 of them if we count spouses and a few children, had certainly been assembled. In addition to names that have been mentioned throughout this book, one might note Robert Bork, David Brooks, Roger Hertog, Lane Kirkland, Edward Koch, Bernard Lewis, Frederick Morgan, Charles Murray, Richard Pipes, David Pryce-Jones, Dorothy Rabinowitz, Diane Ravitch, A. M. Rosenthal, Donald Rumsfeld, Ariel Sharon, Sam Tanenhaus, Terry Teachout, Elie Wiesel, and Tom Wolfe. The range of eminence – from politicians and public servants, to imaginative writers, historians, and highbrow journalists – fairly represents the *kind* of people who are *Commentary* readers. No country can have too many of them.

19

A Literary Indian Summer

The transition to editor-at-large was energizing. In the short run, Podhoretz produced a flush of essays under the rubrics of literary criticism, sexual politics, and the Middle East – each an expansion on themes he had been exploring since the fifties. In the long run, he published three books between 1999 and 2002: *Ex-Friends, My Love Affair with America,* and *The Prophets.* The first two brought his memoirist-cum-critic treatment of America's cultural politics up to the end of the century. The third brought the wisdom of classical Hebrew prophecy to bear on that politics while, as a bonus, providing a pedagogic introduction to the relevant books in the Bible.

To begin with literary criticism: after turning sixty, Podhoretz complained of failing concentration. Granted, he still read for hours a day at the office – the manuscripts needing to be shaped, the galley proofs, the competing magazines, the daily papers – but in the evening, for recreation, what? Light fiction (mysteries, romances) wouldn't do, though oddly its aesthetic equivalent on television or at the movies often seemed to satisfy him: he and Midge would "[while] away a restless evening" watching dramas that were often as good as they were because they had been written by Ph.D.s in English who had gone to work in Hollywood. But this wasn't *literature*, and literature was what Podhoretz loved. He was brought back to it by the Library of America series, the brainchild of Edmund Wilson and Jason Epstein back in the sixties that had come to fruition with seed money from the Ford Foundation – McGeorge Bundy finally did something right – and from the National Endowment for the Humanities. The volumes began appearing in 1982.

Recounting all this in "On Reading for Pleasure Again," Podhoretz was particularly glad to report on the exhilaration of seeing afresh, and defending, American authors whom he remembered Trilling had denigrated. The Theodore Dreiser of *Sister Carrie* and especially of *An American Tragedy*, for instance, "is in his own way as great a novelist" as Trilling's favorite, Henry James. Other "social realists," like Frank Norris, Jack London, and Sinclair Lewis, who for decades had been beneath the notice of English professors, had their claims, too. Take Lewis, who in *Main Street* and *Babbitt* portrayed American "society as vulgar, philistine, materialistic, and puritanical" but who also "retained a degree of respect, affection, and even love for" that society, which after all had been his home. How unlike his "contemporary spiritual descendants," by whom Podhoretz meant garden-variety academics and writers in magazines like the *New York Review*, the *Nation*, and the *New Yorker*, who continued damning the vulgarity and philistinism but showed none of Lewis's capacity for respect and affection.[1]

Podhoretz was also relishing a contemporary American classic, the novelist Philip Roth, who seemed to be reinventing himself. Long after the remarkable debut of *Goodbye, Columbus* (1959), the *succès du scandale* of *Portnoy's Complaint* (1969), and the Zuckerman trilogy of the eighties, it was clear in *Operation Shylock* (1993), *Sabbath's Theater* (1995), *American Pastoral* (1997), and *I Married a Communist* (1998) that Roth was making a bid for greatness. He had always written in an aesthetically pleasing way. Podhoretz saw that as early as 1957, when he may be said to have "discovered" Roth. Going through the "slush pile" as an assistant editor at *Commentary*, he came upon "You Can't Tell a Man by the Song He Sings," recognized its worth, and drew it to the attention of the Greenbergs, who liked it enough to publish it.

From the first it had been Roth's ambition "to take stock of the world in which he lived and," as Podhoretz said, "give it the business, as only someone with so wicked a pen and so unforgiving a mind as his could do." During the seventies and eighties, he had become the laureate of the New Class, the left-liberal intellectuals who regarded themselves as the nation's "conscience." Like them, he was anti-anticommunist (practically anti-American) in geopolitical matters and anti-Zionist (practically anti-Semitic) in matters pertaining to Israel and the Jews.

In *American Pastoral*, though, Roth suddenly appeared to be reevaluating some of those New Class assumptions. "Here, for once," Podhoretz noted, "it was the ordinary Jews of his childhood who were celebrated – for their decency, their sense of responsibility, their seriousness about their work, their patriotism – and here, for once, those who rejected and despised such virtues were shown to be either pathologically nihilistic or smug, self-righteous, and unimaginative." In brief, the novel evinced neoconservative ideas to a degree that would have embarrassed the National Book Award Committee had it really read the text.[2] Still, the committee needn't have worried. Roth's next books, *I Married a Communist*, which centered on the McCarthy hearings, and *The Human Stain* (2000), which centered on Clinton's troubles in the scandal involving the White House intern Monica Lewinsky, evinced Roth's dedication to the Left's world picture.

Roth had told an interviewer that what was going on in Washington reminded him of Hawthorne's *The Scarlet Letter*, which was to say that his America was identical to what Arthur Miller projected allegorically in his McCarthy-era melodrama *The Crucible* – a country forever possessed by the repressive, witch-hunting spirit of seventeenth-century Puritanism. As Podhoretz devastatingly remarked,

Such a statement would be breathtaking coming from anyone living at a time and in a place where sex in every shape and form is easily available, advocated, and even celebrated in every public forum and medium of entertainment, and where the only scarlet letters are pasted on those who offer so much as a smidgen of resistance to this tidal wave of erotomania. But issuing from the mouth of a man who has achieved fame, honor, and riches with books that would have served as the kindling for burning him alive in the world described by Hawthorne, the comparison between the America of today and the America of *The Scarlet Letter* is very nearly demented.

Podhoretz thought Bellow's *Ravelstein* (2000) a greater book than *The Human Stain*, though less as a "novel" than as a memoir or biography – Bellow having written a *roman à clef* about his friend Allan Bloom that was "all *clef* and no *roman.*" *Ravelstein* is greater because, while Roth's subsequent work disappointed "the tantalizing hopes held out by *An American Pastoral,*" Bellow had painted an "infinitely loving portrait" of the man who in *The Closing of the American Mind* worked to *open* the American mind to the best that had been thought and said, who got fabulously rich on the sales of that book, and who happened to be a homosexual. Some friends of Bloom had protested against Bellow's "out[ing]" him as both a homosexual and "a vulgar materialist," hooked on "Lalique crystal or Lanvin jackets." Podhoretz replied that everyone knew Bloom was a homosexual and that Bloom himself never made a big deal about it. Neither had Bellow. As for the crystal and the jackets, "Bloom loved luxury for its own sake – and why not?" Besides, there was "in Bellow's eyes a kind of greatness – as spiritual as it is material – in the extremity of Bloom's extravagance, no less than in his insatiable appetite for gossip, especially about the doings in high places, in his presumptuous meddling with the lives of his students, in his delight in dirty jokes."[3] Podhoretz himself, like any of the old Family, had an appetite for gossip, paid good money for high-end audio equipment, and could in season tell and laugh at a dirty joke. But beyond that, he relished how Bloom had "chosen life" in all its spiritual refinement and material grossness, and, for all their old differences, he applauded Bellow for choosing it, too.

Joseph Heller died in 1999 at age seventy-six. A World War II veteran, he had been a masters-degree student at Columbia during Podhoretz's time and owed the younger man a debt of gratitude for so favorably reviewing his novel *Catch-22* when it came out in 1961. Few other critics had paid it any attention, for in that year Americans largely supported Kennedy's "bear any burden, pay any price" commitment to defend democracy against left-wing totalitarianism and would merely have wondered at an author depicting the war against right-wing totalitarianism as insane. But *Catch-22*, Podhoretz had argued, was less about World War II than about fifties America – profit-mad, bureaucracy-ridden, careless of individual lives, and hard to distinguish from any totalitarian enemy. Hence the hero Yossarian's determination to save his own skin and bid the *dulce et decorum est pro patria mori* boys go hang.

Toward the end of the book, however, Heller had a minor character, Major Danby, tell Yossarian that if the fascists were to win, they would both be killed. This grain of truth, Podhoretz pointed out, unbalanced the whole novel: Heller had spent all his "joyful energy" showing up the war as "a fraud, having nothing whatever to do with ideals or values," and yet he had to concede that it was genuine after all. The antifascist cause *was* "worth laying down [one's] life for," and Yossarian in Sweden, if he ever got there, would feel the emptiness of lacking, not to mention the guilt of forsaking, such a cause.[4]

How had *Catch-22* worked upon young readers as the sixties unfolded? Most nefariously, Podhoretz thought as he looked back after Heller's death. In homage to Heller, James Webb, a decorated Vietnam veteran, former Secretary of the Navy, and future senator from Virginia, praised what he took to be *Catch-22*'s message: war dehumanizes all who participate. That was something Webb felt in Vietnam, and so did masses of Webb's generation who were persuaded, on Heller's cue, that America was "ruled by an 'establishment' made up of madmen and criminals." Podhoretz was willing to grant that a young Marine officer like Webb, fighting in a "mismanaged" war in 1969, could find solace in Heller's novel. But how could "a professional military man" worship a book that was "nihilistic" in its thinking not only about the effects of war (dehumanization of combatants and noncombatants alike, etc.) but also about war's causes – the reasons good people, however reluctantly, resort to it?

Podhoretz found some solace in noting how Tom Brokaw's book *The Greatest Generation* and Steven Spielberg's film *Saving Private Ryan* had recently stressed the good-war theme that Heller almost completely ignored. Still, the no-body-bags attitude toward conflict – this was one year prior to the al Qaeda attacks on the World Trade Center and the Pentagon – was, for Podhoretz, a troubling hold-over from the Vietnam-era pacifism Heller's comic gift had done so much to promote. What was it but a return of the cultural climate "prevalent after World War I," which maintained "that war is simply a means by which cynical people commit legalized murder in pursuit of power and profits; that patriotism is a fraud; and that nothing is worth dying for (this last sentiment, according to Nietzsche, being a mark of the slave)"?[5]

Then there was the black writer Ralph Ellison (1914–1994). The posthumous publication of his *Juneteenth* (1999), the semicoherent condensation of a truly incoherent 2,000-page typescript he had left upon his death, occasioned a searching retrospective by Podhoretz. Ralph *Waldo* Ellison, as many readers needed to be reminded, was proud of his American roots, which were as important to him as equally deep American roots were to Jewish writers like Bellow, Malamud, or Roth. Ellison refused to be ghettoized. Plainly he was a black writer, but he was also a pluralist who felt free to read and "own" any book on the shelf, whatever the author's skin color, and who, like the young Baldwin, recognized that *mere* "protest novels" were morally reductive.

The *artful* protest novel – Stendhal's *Red and Black*, Dickens's *Bleak House*, Twain's *Huckleberry Finn* – made its case while also complicating motives and consequences, which is what Ellison's own *Invisible Man* (1952) had done.

Ellison could never finish *Juneteenth* because he couldn't shake the voice of William Faulkner the way he had, in the earlier novel, shaken off the voice of Ernest Hemingway. By finding his own voice in *Invisible Man*, he had overcome what he called "The greatest difficulty for a Negro writer," namely that "of revealing what he really felt, rather than serving up what Negroes were supposed to feel, and were encouraged to feel." Even so, Podhoretz could now see, *Invisible Man* was too deliberately symbolist in method and too lacking in the profound universality that might have compensated for its patently "dated" theme. Dated because blacks were in fact no longer "invisible," thanks in part to a multiculturalist privileging that Ellison himself would have deplored, and dated in another sense because Ellison's fictional hustlers and pimps were benignly "represented [by him] as ingenious and admirably resourceful," whereas in recent decades what had most affected race relations in America was "black violence and criminality, the fear of which has spread even among the most sympathetic white liberals."[6]

Sexual politics had been Decter's subject for a quarter century. Then, in the early nineties, the radical feminist "discovery" of "date" or "acquaintance" rape – a kind of violation of women that had supposedly been there for millennia but only recognized "the day before yesterday" – brought Podhoretz himself into the fray.

He began by pointing out that, historically, there had never been a distinction between "stranger rape" and the date or acquaintance variety: in the Hebrew Bible, for instance, God's wrath comes down alike upon Amnon, the rapist of his half-sister Tamar, and upon Shechem, the Gentile rapist of Jacob's daughter Dinah. Both were acts of violence. The idea of date or acquaintance rape seemed to Podhoretz a "brazen" invention meant "to redefine seduction as a form of rape, and more slyly to identify practically all men as rapists" – as when Susan Brownmiller accounted rape as "nothing more or less than a conscious process of intimidation by which *all men* keep *all women* in a state of fear," or when Andrea Dworkin, not to be outdone, revalued heterosexual intercourse itself as rape, an act comparable to "wartime invasion and occupation." As Podhoretz remarked, "however great men's contempt for women may be, it could hardly match the contempt for women exemplified in" such radical feminist statements, which caricatured women "as timorous, cowering, helpless creatures who are at the mercy of any male they may be unfortunate enough to run into."

The background of this reinterpretation of the war between the sexes was the ballyhooed sexual revolution of the sixties. That revolution, Podhoretz declared, had been nothing less than a triumph for men, who were suddenly ceded what they had so long dreamt of – namely, promiscuous sex "with no conditions attached." But if the sexual revolution was merely a reassertion of male domination, radical feminism was a no less disastrous counterrevolution, the radical feminists concluding that heterosexuality itself, or simply nature, was to blame, and that the only way to break free "was to shun men altogether in favor either of abstinence" or lesbianism. But since these rallying cries would never appeal to large numbers of women, the feminists also put forth a minimal demand – for a "wholesale change in the relation between the sexes." Heterosexual intercourse, if it was still to go on, ought always to be at the woman's instigation.

The good news, to borrow from the ecologists' book of slogans, was that "nature bats last." The psychosocial norms of human behavior guarantee that "most young men and most young women will not be repelled or frightened off" by feminist "studies" but "will play their naturally ordained parts in the unending and inescapable war between the sexes, suffering the usual wounds, exulting in the usual victories, and even eventually arriving at that armistice known as marriage." They were the lucky ones, the majority. As for the unlucky minority, "too impressionable or too frightened or too weak to hold out against the imperatives of the new sexual dispensation," they could in no small measure thank the radical "anti-date-rape brigade" for their lives "of loneliness, frustration, resentment, and sterility."[7]

In particular, some unlucky young men victimized by the new sexual counterculture might feel themselves driven into its homosexual purlieus, where the danger of contracting AIDS was by the early nineties becoming palpable. As Podhoretz described in "How the Gay-Rights Movement Won" (1996), there was, on the issue of homosexuality, an evident split between the culture and the polity. By the culture, he meant the attitudes of leaders in the arts, religion, academia, and the media generally, most of whom not only went along with Disney World's Gay Days poster featuring "Mickey Mouse and Donald Duck as a hand-holding couple" but also regarded homosexuality as an innate condition like race, ethnicity, or gender. The courts, in their isolated and elitist fashion, were by and large reflecting these shifts in the culture.

By the polity, Podhoretz meant legislatures, which reflected the attitudes of ordinary people who were resisting the culture's pressure to regard same-sex couples as the legal equivalents to the traditional kind. The Defense of Marriage Act, for instance, passed by overwhelming majorities and signed into law by President Clinton, essentially declared that, even if one state should legalize same-sex marriage (as Massachusetts would do in 2004), no other states had to recognize that legality, and that the federal government *may* not recognize them – any more than it may recognize polygamous marriages – solely because marriage was by definition between "one man and one woman." These were legislative fingers in a very leaky dike, however, and Podhoretz was convinced that it was only a matter of time before "the gay-rights movement" would triumph in the polity as it had in the culture.

Podhoretz didn't try to confute what seemed unanswerable. He didn't doubt that genes determine sexual preference. But "it does not follow from this that homosexuality is healthy; after all, many disabilities, diseases, and self-destructive tendencies are genetically transmitted." Besides, individuals still have "free will, as witness the many people (including those with powerful homosexual inclinations) who have successfully struggled against inborn predispositions" – struggled, presumably, either to marry and have children or to be chaste. It wasn't the born homosexuals or the born heterosexuals whom Podhoretz worried about but the "waverers" who, for whatever reason, seemed "capable of going either way." These individuals did have a choice, and it mattered greatly what sort of encouragement they got. The particular peril for male waverers was that they might be "seduced" into homosexuality, especially "when feminism has made girls even more formidably intimidating than they have always been to young boys." To them, entanglements with women could seem "more frightening even than AIDS."

Instead of being helped "to overcome their fears of a normal [heterosexual] life," such boys were "being abandoned to the ministrations of a culture that not only legitimizes homosexuality but glorifies and glamorizes it, even to the point of representing those who die of AIDS as martyrs and heroes and even as angels" – an allusion to Tony Kushner's play, *Angels in America: A Gay Fantasia on National Themes* (1991). Podhoretz couldn't fantasize "homosexuals, not even those who fall victim to AIDS, as martyrs and heroes, let alone as angels. Nevertheless my heart goes out to all of them because I believe that – even aside from AIDS – the life they live is not as good as the life available to men who make their beds with women."

Wasn't all this *obvious*? Well, as Orwell said, sometimes it was necessary to restate the obvious, which Podhoretz accordingly did: "men using one another as women constitutes a perversion" if it is self-willed or, if it isn't, a hobble or handicap like being born with one leg shorter than the other. "To my unreconstructed mind," he concluded, "this is as true as ever; and so far as I am concerned, it would still be true even if gay sex no longer entailed the danger of infection and even if everything about it were legalized by all 50 states and ratified by all nine Justices of the Supreme Court."[8]

Podhoretz's 1997 essay "*Lolita*, My Mother-in-Law, the Marquis de Sade, and Larry Flynt" is one of his best. The pollution of our cultural environment, through pornography in this case, cried out for governmental regulation quite as much as did the pollution of our natural environment. Only, one couldn't imagine bureaucrats or judges capable of discriminating between misogynistic deviants like de Sade and Flynt (respectively, the eighteenth-century author of *Justine* and the twentieth-century publisher of *Hustler* magazine) and artists like D. H. Lawrence, who wrote *Lady Chatterley's Lover*, or Vladimir Nabokov, who wrote *Lolita*. In an earlier age of reticence, bureaucrats and judges had been inclined to lump the latter with the former, dirty minds all. Nowadays, they were likely to do the same in reverse. That was the premise of Milos Forman's *The People vs. Larry Flynt*, a film presenting "the People" as puritan troglodytes and Flynt as a sweet splicing of Huck Finn and Abbie Hoffman.

Things were more complicated than that. *Lolita* was an uncommonly artful novel. Still, by treating pedophilia so "beautifully," Nabokov had made it, if not beautiful in itself (he did regard it as a sickness), then less "unthinkable." Tolerance for it in the suave hero Humbert Humbert snuck in under the radar, so to speak, rather as moral equivocation and pacifism infiltrated *Catch-22* behind Heller's madcap comedy. To understand Humbert's disorder, as Trilling claimed the novel enabled him to do, was a major step toward forgiving and accepting it. From there it was a quick slide down the slippery slope to the "pornotopian" realm where *all* sex acts are equivalent and where "liberated" swingers are supposed to enjoy "unalloyed ecstasy." In the place where real people live, Podhoretz was bold to say, pornotopia and promiscuity bring nothing but "the unbearable lightness of being" that we in America face when, deviance having been defined downward, the Humbert of the hour has become someone like Woody Allen playing the fool with his lover Mia Farrow's Lolita-aged daughter.[9]

One couldn't reach a more squalidly intriguing nadir than the one briefly known as "Sexgate," involving President Clinton and Monica Lewinsky in 1998. Podhoretz had to wonder where the "sisterhood" of radical feminists, who had rallied to Anita Hill's side when she charged Supreme Court nominee Clarence Thomas with sexual harassment in 1991, were now. At the harasser's side was the answer, if not on their knees in front of him. Erica Jong, of *Fear of Flying* fame, showed herself more the *enfant terrible* than ever by swooning, "Oh, imagine swallowing the presidential come." The feminists were confessing their status as a mere subsidiary of the Democratic Party, which meant that if down-market singers like Gennifer Flowers, or Arkansas state employees who fixed their hair the wrong way like Paula Jones, had by the new radical definition been "raped," then tough luck. The roguish boy president mustn't fall victim to a vast right-wing conspiracy.

But this was an exceptional circumstance. In "'Sexgate,' the Sisterhood, and Mr. Bumble," Podhoretz argued that whatever feminists might say (or not say) in the case of Clinton, what had to be grasped was the extent to which the new theories about sexual harassment had indeed conquered the minds of cultural poohbahs both Left and Right, and had as well begun to affect legislatures and courts – giving more credence than ever to the declaration of the bailiff Mr. Bumble in Dickens's *Oliver Twist*: "The law is a ass – a idiot." The context of Bumble's "immortal outburst" was the suggestion that "the law supposes that your wife acts under your direction" when in reality Bumble was thoroughly henpecked. What current law "supposes" about sexual harassment was equally divorced from the way men and women have forever approached one another – a way far more complex, and far more interesting, than the critical legal theorists conceived.

In losing one another's erotic company, men and women were losing something more: the "manners and morals and informal codes of socially approved or sanctioned behavior" that had hitherto governed their interactions. Manners, morals, and codes were what great imaginative writers have always depicted; they were what parents passed on to their children; and they were what conservatives, Podhoretz insisted, ought to reaffirm against the "noisy and noisome tribe" of feminists. Instead, most conservatives, "blinded by rage against Clinton and eager to take political advantage of his womanizing," had misguidedly taken up sexual harassment law themselves. No, Podhoretz said: Paula Jones's case against Clinton should be dismissed – not because he was innocent of what she charged but because the code of conduct he had violated was of the kind that was legally "unenforceable."

Was the fact that public opinion remained so favorable toward Clinton a sign, as cultural commentators like William Bennett said, that America's moral sense was in serious decline? Podhoretz didn't think so – not yet. In evidence, he adduced *An Officer and a Gentleman*, a film containing plenty of "obscene language and graphically depicted casual sex" but also having a traditional reform-the-rogue marriage plot: "One might say that the movie was using the lingo of the liberationist culture to reaffirm the values of the traditionalist culture and to make them more palatable to a hip contemporary audience." And so with television's *Ally McBeal*, about a feminist lawyer sowing wild oats before settling down to be a faithful wife and mother. As Huw Wheldon used to tell his BBC writers, "If they were to turn out successful dramatic shows, they needed to appreciate that 'the deep mores of a people change very slowly.'" A good thing – and if our culture was "really lucky," the mephitic influence of the feminist movement might soon begin to fade.[10]

Verdicts

We now turn from sexual politics to politics. After Saddam Hussein's forces invaded Kuwait in August 1990, the United States began working with U.N. coalition forces to reverse that act, whether through diplomacy and economic sanctions or, more likely, through arms. During the buildup of troops in Saudi Arabia, President George H. W. Bush enjoyed broad support from neoconservatives, needless to say, and from moderates across the spectrum. Surprisingly, he also at first enjoyed support from the Left – partly because he was working with the U.N. and partly because Saddam's claims to be another Castro or Mao fighting the capitalist West were plainly risible.

What about the paleoconservatives? Wanting to focus the debate on America's need for oil from the Middle East, William Buckley proposed "a 15-year treaty with Saudi Arabia" by which we would "guarantee [their] sovereignty" against the depredations of Saddam and they would "guarantee to sell us (and other signatories) oil at the price of oil in Galveston, Texas." What, though, about America's interest in "the defense of Israel," a country of which Saddam was a ferocious enemy? Did *that* question, Buckley wondered, portend "a genuine and long-term split within the conservative movement, separating neo-isolationists from internationalists?"[1]

It did. From the Far Right, Patrick Buchanan, equating neoconservatives with Jews, was (as we have seen) denouncing their foreign policy agenda as less pro-America than pro-Israel. Podhoretz's response was quick, cogent, and defiant. Yes, Saddam's missiles would, if he weren't toppled, soon be falling on Tel Aviv and Jerusalem. It was obvious that Israel would welcome an American effort to topple him. But protecting the Jewish state was only one reason among several for removing Saddam both from Kuwait City and from Baghdad. The other reasons had to do with preventing Kuwait's oil reserves "from falling into the hands of a ruthless aggressor," discouraging other rogue states from imitating his cross-border transgression, and thereby ensuring "a more peaceful order in the post-cold-war" Middle East. It was feckless to will these ends, as even the *New York Times* did, without willing the means – the threat, and in all probability the use, of deadly force. The waffling subsequent to those cries of we-must-do-something reminded Podhoretz all too much of the attitude of the *Times*, and of the American public generally, toward Vietnam in the sixties: we go in with nearly unanimous enthusiasm, casualties mount, noncombatants are killed, and, plaintively asking whether the price is too high, we get cold feet.[2]

By the end of 1990, on the eve (as it soon turned out) of Desert Storm, the neoisolationists on the Right were in bed with the never-use-arms Left, which had found its sixties voice again. Ramsay Clark and Jesse Jackson deemed Saddam a reasonable man to negotiate peace with, and former Carter officials declared that the cost of any measures beyond "sanctions-*cum*-diplomacy" would be unacceptable. Podhoretz reminded readers that *not* using our military to destroy Saddam's would exact a still higher cost. Having already used chemical weapons against the Kurds of his own country, Saddam manifestly wanted to be able to wage "nuclear and biological warfare," too. With a ruler like Saddam, appeasement (to say nothing of pacifism) was an *impossible* position.

But appeasement, predictably, was what was coming both from the American Catholic bishops and from the liberal Protestant "God box," the National Council of Churches in New York – the one group denying that the criteria for a "just war" were being met, the other collapsing into virtual pacifism. As for the virtual pacifists, what could Podhoretz recommend aside from a study of the history of the thirties? As for the bishops, he cited Weigel's demonstration that the criteria for a just war *were* being met: "the elimination of a clear evil threatening many other countries in addition to our own, and the opportunity to prevent something worse in the future."

But the justice of this war depended on going all the way to Baghdad. To achieve Augustine's stipulated "tranquillity of order" after the fighting, Weigel maintained (in necessary disagreement with the bishops of his own church), Saddam's "chemical weapons, his nascent nuclear-weapons capability, his missiles, and the bulk of his armor" must be taken out: "Anything short of that simply guarantees that a more horrible war will ensue down the line." The coalition forces would naturally be morally responsible "for their actions: which will, tragically but certainly, include the killing of innocents." This was bad, although "it should also be understood that those who reject the use of military force... have not been absolved from moral responsibility for what follows: which will, certainly, include [Saddam's] killing of innocents, and in large numbers." This was *worse*. Innocents would die if the American-led coalition went into Kuwait and Iraq; more would die if it didn't.[3]

In January and February 1991, we liberated Kuwait. We didn't, however, drive to Baghdad to remove Saddam, and therefore Weigel's requirements for a just outcome were not met. Saddam remained in power, able to rebuild his armaments and turn them on his enemies inside as well as outside his borders, thus guaranteeing "that a more horrible war," the one that began in March 2003, would "ensue down the line."

To be sure, the first Gulf War was horrible enough, and not least for Israel, where, from January 13 to 23, Podhoretz and Decter were visiting their daughter Ruthie and her family in Jerusalem. Decter had scheduled her own visit months before, and Podhoretz decided to accompany her in large part "to put my body where my mouth is." He felt "a sweet sense of relief" making this decision: war would put the Jewish state in great danger, and should the worst come to pass he would be there to suffer the consequences along with Ruthie; her husband, Nadav Blum; and their four children (Noam, eight; Alon, five; and the one-year-old twins Boaz and Avital). Since Washington had insisted that Israel refrain from retaliating in the event of missile attack, those consequences could be dire.

Was there anything good that could come from Israel's experience of this war – the experience, for once, of being praised by the West for showing "restraint" and therefore appearing again as "passive victims to be wept over," as in pre-1948 days, rather "than as feisty warriors to be reckoned with"? Something good might emerge, Podhoretz thought, from the maps constantly being displayed on CNN during the days and nights of Saddam's blitz: looking at them, Americans would see just how tiny Israel was, "so small that you can hardly locate it in the vast ocean of surrounding Arab countries." Surely there was nothing "paranoid" about a country that said it needed weapons to defend itself from those antagonistic neighbors, who were as close as New Jersey (not New Mexico) was to New York. Plus, images of Palestinians allying themselves with Saddam against the United States, calling down poison gas attacks on Israel, and then brazenly asking the Israeli government for free gas masks for themselves would surely make the American public balk at supporting *their* demands for an independent state "only a stone's throw away from Tel Aviv and Jerusalem."

Or maybe not. Bush and his secretary of state, James Baker, quite apart from their desire to keep the Arab states inside the coalition, were eyeing "the postwar settlement." They imagined they could bring lasting peace to the Middle East by "forcing Israel into withdrawing from the territories in favor of a Palestinian state." Hence their pressure to keep Israeli planes on the ground and to insist on strictly American crews to work the Patriot antimissile missiles – one of which actually struck one of Saddam's Scud missiles on the morning of Podhoretz's return to New York.[4]

After negotiations ended the Gulf War, attention in the Middle East shifted to the "peace process" between Israel and the Palestinians. The collapse of the Soviet Union had changed the equation: the Palestinians no longer had a superpower to bankroll them, and they were being stiffed by the major Arab countries for having allied themselves with Saddam. Maybe the PLO would now be flexible, abandoning terrorism and granting Israel's right to exist. Maybe Israel, for its part, would then be willing to withdraw its forces from sections of the Gaza Strip and the West Bank, grant a measure of Palestinian self-government under the newly created Palestinian Authority, and eventually (through "phases") work out an agreement on independent Palestinian statehood.

The process, begun under American constraint at an international conference in Madrid in 1991,[5] would eventuate in the accords signed in Oslo in August 1993, which were officially signalized the next month in Washington with the famous photos of President Clinton blessing the handshake between Israel's prime minister Yitzhak Rabin and PLO chairman Yasser Arafat.[6]

Podhoretz's statements leading up to Oslo reveal why the accords couldn't hold. To begin with, which Palestinian politicians could Israel talk to? Obviously not Hamas, the "Islamic Resistance Movement" founded in 1987 as the Gaza wing of the Muslim Brotherhood – if only because it regarded communication with Israel as "high treason" and had, by 1993, killed more of Arafat's Fatah faction within the PLO than had the Israeli Defense Forces. But Fatah itself was almost as bad, sponsoring the murder of other "Palestinians for 'collaboration' with Israel" and disguising its own rejection of the latter's right to exist behind diplomatic double-talk. Rabin seemed to think he could halt the process at Palestinian "autonomy," but Podhoretz believed he was "fooling himself." Arafat had made it clear that autonomy was nothing more than the Palestinians' "right to collect their own garbage" and that he regarded it as only "a temporary way station on the road to statehood."

It was predictable that many Israeli voters, demoralized by the "loss" of "the war known as the *intifada*" and by America's having prevented them from retaliating against Saddam's Scud attacks, were clutching at the idea that peace might be at hand.[7] Expecting no thanks, Podhoretz reminded the Labor majority that they were following a descendant of the false prophets whom Jeremiah had denounced for crying "'Peace, peace,' when there is no peace." A consoling slogan, but as misleading in the present as it was in the past.[8]

The Rabin government was so distressed by Podhoretz's challenge that it instructed the Israeli embassy in Washington to reply. Was Podhoretz part of a conspiracy "to cut American aid" and bring down the Labor government? Hardly, but Podhoretz felt bound to remind Rabin and his cabinet of what they already knew – that, for example, "Syria has thus far offered *nothing* beyond a declaration of nonbelligerence in exchange for *complete* Israeli withdrawal from the Golan Heights," or that negotiating with such you-give-we-take parties, like the "peace accords" with Nazis in the thirties or Vietnamese communists in the seventies, could only bring disaster. There was nothing for it but to hang around, "stalling as much as possible" and enduring the status quo. The alternative scenario – "a Lebanonized Palestinian state . . . a civil war between the PLO and Hamas, followed by Syrian intervention, followed by another Arab–Israeli war – would be far, far worse."[9]

During the 1992 election campaign in Israel, Rabin had dined with Podhoretz in New York, assuring him that he, too, was anxious about his party's land-for-peace left wing. He told Podhoretz "that he could handle those people, and that he 'hated' them – that was his exact word – even more than I did. He never said anything quite that blunt to the Israeli voters, but they got the idea anyway." That was why they "became very bitter" at his Oslo bargaining.[10] Very likely the real mover, however, wasn't Rabin but his foreign minister, Shimon Peres, who "envisages a Middle East in which peace will serve as the foundation of a regional prosperity rivaling that of East Asia." Israel would be "separated from a restive Palestinian population it is neither willing nor able to control, and at peace with all the surrounding Arab states." Not that it really mattered who the principal dreamer was. All the doves in the dovecote couldn't compel the PLO to fulfill its end of the deal.[11]

Expanding these commentaries on the peace process was Podhoretz's "In Israel – With Grandchildren," which mixed caustic criticism of the Labor government with warm expressions of affection for the people, beginning with Ruthie and her children, who lived under it. War-weariness, as Podhoretz had noticed before, seemed to have led Israelis to the counterfactual assumption that their country was weak and the Palestinians strong. The mood of defeatist pacifism reminded him of the self-loathing many American intellectuals felt during and after the Vietnam War, but Labor seemed eager to go the doves in America one better. Very few of *them* were ever "going to be driven by [their] ideas into actually giving the country back to the Indians, [whereas] Israeli politicians like Rabin and Peres were about to turn over a large swath of territory to the Palestinians."

Neoconservatives had managed, in the wake of our defeat in Vietnam, to remind people that countries normally defend themselves against their enemies and that our chief enemy was the Soviet Union. Its invasion of Afghanistan had made that clear even to Carter. What crisis would concentrate Israelis' minds? Unfortunately, it would have to be Palestinian terrorist attacks, and possibly a wider war, which would show that the Palestinian leadership had no intention of settling for a state comprising the West Bank and Gaza but wanted instead to eradicate the Jewish state itself. At the end of his visit, Podhoretz wept to think that his Israeli grandchildren were growing up in a country whose peril, acute enough already, was being increased by a government that thought it was living in fairyland.[12]

Peres had assumed the prime ministry after Rabin's assassination in November 1995, but in May 1996 he lost to the Likud challenger Benjamin "Bibi" Netanyahu, whose view of the peace process was as skeptical as Podhoretz's. In some ways, Podhoretz almost wished Peres had won, for then the peace process would have been brought to its predetermined conclusion and everyone would see how deluded the suppositions behind it had been. Arafat, in the meantime, seemed bent on getting his favorite dupe, Peres, back in office, or at least on forcing Netanyahu to accept Peres as a partner in a national-unity government.[13]

Podhoretz's "Israel and the United States: A Complex History" (1998) was an irreplaceable *summa* of the whole topic, organized around three ideas.

First, he offered a plausible speculation about why Rabin endorsed Oslo's land-for-peace provisions: he must have talked himself into believing that the Palestinians and the Syrians weren't "existential" threats to Israel because he needed to keep the United States at his side when the *real* existential threats, Iran and Iraq, launched their missiles. A similar necessity was bearing down on Netanyahu, whose job it was to keep America sympathetic to the Israeli version of the conflict.

Second, America should *commit* itself to the Israeli version. The Palestinian terrorists and their Arab sponsors refused to accept Israel's right to exist and had no intention of living peaceably beside it. To imagine otherwise did great, if "unwitting," harm. America had to recognize "that the only true hope of peace lies in the modernization and democratization of the Arab world."

That was the third idea, encouraging "modernizing and democratizing forces in the Middle East," just as, during and following the collapse of communism, we had encouraged such forces in Eastern Europe. Such a policy would be "entirely consistent with and congenial to the American spirit." As with Kirkpatrick's plea for a single standard in foreign policy in the late seventies, Podhoretz was wondering why we so rarely "talk[ed] about human rights in Saudi Arabia or complain[ed] about the suppression of political liberty everywhere else in the region, including even countries like Syria where there is no oil to worry about."[14] It was, we can now see, an anticipation of the neoconservative campaign to introduce modernity and democracy to Afghanistan and Iraq following September 11, 2001.

Beyond Israel, the defeat of Saddam – expelling him from Kuwait and bottling him up between no-fly zones in Iraq – looked like something to cheer about. Maybe now he would behave and the United States could go home and stay. That sentiment was strong in Patrick Buchanan, who in 1992 ran against the incumbent Bush for the Republican nomination for president. Conservatives of varying stripes were unhappy with Bush for other reasons, mainly his raising of taxes and his signing of a civil rights bill that tended toward affirmative action quotas. The editors at *National Review*, Buckley and John O'Sullivan, wanted William Bennett or Jack Kemp to lead the insurgency, but when each of them declined, the magazine offered its "tactical" support to Buchanan: perhaps in the New Hampshire primary he could do to Bush what Eugene McCarthy had in 1968 done to Johnson, after which, like Robert Kennedy, Bennett or Kemp might enter the race.

This, Podhoretz held, was an utterly deluded scenario. Why should Buckley and O'Sullivan put themselves in a position of having to apologize for Buchanan's anti-Semitism in private while hailing him as the *echt*-Reaganite, the un-Bush, in public? It was as embarrassingly awkward as liberal Democrats in 1988 having to accommodate the extremism of Jesse Jackson, and it helped sustain Jewish voters' inveterate impression that the more dangerous anti-Semitism still came from the Right.[15]

In the end, Buchanan's rebellion succumbed to the centrist power of Bush's supporters. "Fuck the Jews, they don't vote for us anyway," Secretary of State James Baker had reportedly told Bush. It wasn't true – 35 percent of Jews had voted for "us" in 1988 – but this time around Clinton won with 80% Jewish support. Podhoretz didn't vote at all.[16]

Though Clinton had offered himself as a Democratic Leadership Council (DLC)–style centrist, he was, Podhoretz averred, just pretending for the sake of winning. Once in the White House, he "blithely stripped off the centrist mask and revealed the face of the old Adam living on below (with an even more fervent McGovernite Eve standing beside him in the shape of Hillary Rodham Clinton)." Hence the DLC's resentment: "like so many of the many women in Clinton's life," it had been "seduced, used, and then abandoned." Newt Gingrich, the new majority leader in the House, dubbed Clinton a "counter-culture McGovernik," a judgment more sympathetically echoed in the *Village Voice* by Ellen Willis, who referred to the first couple as "inescapably 60's figures. Their history, their body language, their visceral response to social issues carries the imprint of sex, drugs, rock and roll, Vietnam protest, and feminism."

Not all would be ill, however. Podhoretz went on to credit Clinton with steering his party back to the center at home and abroad, following the lead of his second secretary of state, Madeline Albright. In an almost "reckless Wilsonian" style, she urged the president to use American warplanes to enforce the no-fly zone imposed on Saddam Hussein, to intervene in Somalia, to send American troops into Bosnia, and most notably (in conjunction with NATO) to save the Kosovar Albanians from the depredations of Slobodan Milosevic by dropping bombs on Belgrade. That campaign was "stupidly executed" – like every president since Truman, Clinton adhered to a strict doctrine of minimal American casualties, and not "victory" but "restoration of the *status quo ante*" but at least he had launched the planes.

Would a Democratic president continue along this de-McGovernized path that Clinton had opened up?[17] That turned out to be a hypothetical question, for it was George W. Bush, winner of the next two elections, who would pursue Clinton's rediscovered centrism in foreign policy, while Democratic congressmen, as well as presidential hopefuls, reverted to a never-use-force, never-suffer-casualties brand of isolationism.

Podhoretz and his friends couldn't discuss foreign policy apart from morals, or morals apart from religion. And, in the nineties, discussion about the place of religion in public life couldn't ignore Pat Robertson, the most prominent leader of the Gingrich party at prayer. His television network, and books such as *The New World Order* (1991), gave him immense influence over Christians generally, not just Protestant fundamentalists. The question about him in 1995 was, for Podhoretz, what it had been in 1992 about Buchanan: was he an anti-Semite?

Liberal journalists, happy to undercut any member of the conservative coalition, said yes, adducing "crackpot" passages in *The New World Order* about, say, a plot by nineteenth-century Jewish bankers "to take over the world" that sounded like something out of *The Protocols of the Elders of Zion*. Robertson's protestations of innocence were so obviously sincere, however, that Podhoretz took him to be the preacherly equivalent to Truman Capote thirty years back – entirely unaware of the provenance of the anti-Semitic ideas he was entertaining. Buchanan, on the other hand, seemed more like Gore Vidal – not only aware of the anti-Semitic tradition but for political and possibly personal reasons believing in it.

What mattered with Robertson was what mattered with Solzhenitsyn when the question of *his* attitudes toward Jews arose in the eighties. Podhoretz acquitted the Russian writer of anti-Semitism because he had consistently befriended Israel. So what if Protestant fundamentalists were basing their support for Israel on prophecies that Christ's second coming would coincide with the return of Jews to their homeland and their eventual conversion to Christianity?[18] If and when the Messiah comes, Jews could consider their options. Podhoretz meanwhile offered tactical support to Robertson in his battle against liberal Jews, who, when they weren't anti-Zionist, were so fervently antireligious as to make one "think that the only commandments Moses brought down from Sinai were 'Thou shalt not oppose abortion' and 'Thou shalt not oppose gay rights.'"[19]

What about abortion? It had long troubled conservative Catholics like Weigel that *Commentary* so rarely addressed the subject. Podhoretz, a "choose life" Jew if there ever was one, never tried to promote abortion. He simply understood that in some situations it was a lesser evil, and that attempts to make all or most abortion procedures illegal would only put an unenforceable law onto the books and send the practice into a yet more dangerous-to-life back alley.[20]

Neuhaus and others at *First Things* disagreed. In 1996, that magazine published a symposium, "The End of Democracy?," denouncing court decisions like *Roe v. Wade* that had legalized abortion, declaring the current "regime" in Washington "illegitimate," and calling for acts of opposition "ranging from non-compliance to resistance to civil disobedience to morally justified revolution." This rhetorical echo of the New Left's attacks on America in the sixties so appalled Podhoretz that he protested to Neuhaus: "I did not become a conservative in order to become a radical, let alone to support the preaching of revolution against this country" or to countenance language comparing the war against the unborn to the Nazis' war against the Jews.

Not that Podhoretz was against "the attack on judicial imperialism" – he had once called the Supreme Court "a lawless institution" for alchemizing the Civil Rights Act of 1964 into a warrant for "quotas and reverse discrimination" – but he counseled patient reliance on constitutional process. Whenever one branch of the federal government went too far, the other two branches could be counted on, sooner or later, to assert themselves and rein it back in. By contrast, the religious conservatives who were tormented by images of unborn fetuses were like the Weathermen in the sixties tormented by images of napalmed Vietnamese children. As the Weathermen went after the military-industrial complex, so the "right-to-lifers . . . bombed abortion clinics or murdered doctors who worked in them." Were they to receive *First Things'* sanction?

Fortunately, Neuhaus ultimately disavowed his symposiasts' more extreme views – or claimed that they had been misconstrued. Tempers, including Podhoretz's, cooled.[21] But one mustn't lose sight of the Burkean point Podhoretz had made: the country's Constitution is its most precious possession. Reform is possible within the law. Powers are separated, and the vagaries of one can be corrected by the good sense of the others. Violent revolution, and even the kind of civil disobedience that is tantamount to violence, cannot be tolerated – for the simple reason that both would destroy the Constitution and replace it with a blunt and brutal instrument.

Another leader of the religious Right, Paul Weyrich, one of the founders of the Heritage Foundation, was advising Christian conservatives "to 'secede' from the mainstream of American society and retreat into enclaves of their own" – the inner-exilic equivalent to, say, the Mormons betaking themselves, more than 150 years ago, to the Great Basin. Podhoretz could hardly encourage this, not least because it would mean reversing the very process of politicizing those conservatives that Weyrich "himself had done much to get going in the first place."

Neuhaus, too, distanced himself from Weyrich's secessionism. He would "go on fighting," on all the constitutionally protected platforms, "for the right of religion to make itself heard without apology in American political discourse."[22] Podhoretz, who at the height of the *First Things* altercation had despaired that he was about to make himself a "new set of ex-friends," was greatly relieved.

It is hard to overstate the importance of friends to Podhoretz, from school days on. He cherished them, and he suffered greatly if he lost them, as he did in spades when he broke ranks with the radical Left. *Ex-Friends*, the 1999 memoir we have often consulted in these pages, opened with a chapter describing the breakup of "Our 'Family'" and ended with a "Requiem" for its "Lost World."

What had kept the members of the Family together? It was, on the one hand, "a similar set of standards in the arts," and, on the other, "a common disdain . . . for the middle-class or 'bourgeois' civilization" that didn't seem to care about the arts at all and sometimes mocked the mollycoddles who did. But devotion to high standards, and disdain for middling ones, can make people very narrow. One reason Podhoretz turned away from the Family, he explained, was that he didn't sympathize with the arrogance of a Harold Rosenberg or Paul Goodman, who could never suffer the obtuseness of their good editors, let alone their philistine readers.[23]

Even if the Family had been made up of ego-effacing lovers of the common people, it would not have survived the dispersals that began in the early seventies, if not before. Many New York Intellectuals capitalized on the prestige won in the pages of *Partisan Review*, *Commentary*, *Dissent*, the *New Republic*, and "slicks" like the *New Yorker* to get light-load, high-pay academic jobs at

Brandeis, Bard, Stanford, and so on. This scattering meant no more interesting lunches and parties where personalities, affairs, and most importantly ideas could be picked over. Besides, the wars of the sixties had opened fissures among Family members that proved to be irreparable, neither *Commentary* nor the *New York Review* being able to create anything more than a "virtual" new family – a subscription list, letters to the editor, the occasional fund-raiser – to replace the old one.

Then, too, the new intellectuals, the smartest products of the graduate programs, were usually "policy wonks" – Podhoretz's own variegated stable of Moynihan, Kirkpatrick, Jim Wilson, Leon Kass, Joshua Muravchik, Edward Luttwak, Glazer, Kristol, Himmelfarb, Draper, Laqueur, Novak, and Weigel standing among the best of them. Superbly trained in economics, history, sociology, political science, or religion, many of them lacked the broad literary and artistic sensibility of Trilling, Rahv, Phillips, Macdonald, Mary McCarthy, Arendt, Baldwin, Hellman, Howe, Goodman, and Mailer. That sensibility had given their utterances about politics and society a weight, if not a validity, similar to that possessed by their utterances on culture, traditionally understood.

The old Family broke up, but Podhoretz and his neoconservative allies, whether wonkish or in some cases literary, had waged a counter-countercultural campaign that could be summed up as follows. America, for all its miscalculations in Vietnam, could and should continue the war against left-wing totalitarianism. Individual merit, not sex, race, or ethnicity, should be decisive in questions about who gets into a school, who gets a job, or who gets a raise. Aesthetic excellence, not the biological or sociological categories an artist falls into, should determine the status of his work. Above all, the freedom of the individual, whether artist, merchant, teacher, machinist, physician, or whatever, to offer his services or sell his goods in the open market was inseparable from political freedom as such – the freedom to publish, to assemble, or to send representatives into government.

These, Podhoretz insisted, were important advances, for the old Family had never fully understood that the Stalinism they set out to oppose was less "a betrayal of the socialist dreams of the Russian Revolution" than "their logical fulfillment." Because it couldn't "overcome its ancestral antipathy to capitalism, the Family helped keep the false promises of socialism alive, and out of this . . . emerged many of the social programs that did more harm to the poor (and to the country as a whole) than good." For Podhoretz to have said good-bye to socialism, Great Society programs, and the antinomian counterculture, had meant saying good-bye to the friends who continued to cling to them. While "In all truth, I much prefer who I am to who I was," he wrote,

I cannot help feeling nostalgic about the "old days" when I was, in Norman Mailer's authoritative estimation, so much "merrier" than I am now, and I cannot help missing the people I admired, liked, enjoyed, and even (in a few cases) loved when I was young and they, though not so young, were all at their best and still in their prime.[24]

A plangent confession of mixed feelings.

The reviewers of *Ex-Friends* heard the note of loneliness, and even John Leonard in the *Nation* managed, while withholding approval, a bit of empathy:

It's an old story, and even my own.... Once upon a time you were a *Wunderkind*, and now, oh so suddenly, you're an old fart. And it turns out that a lot of people you thought were your friends really just wanted you to write something for them, or publish something they had written, or get them a foundation grant, and now they've gone to some other party for Susan Sontag.[25]

Podhoretz's book betrayed rancor on occasion, as Daphne Merkin acknowledged in the *New Yorker*, but little if any rage. She noticed how the portraits were "touched by a crusty, almost resisted tenderness," and this for Family members "not one of whom, you can be sure, was a picnic." She observed how "readable," "even charming in places," the book was, Podhoretz writing "a virile, offhand prose that moves easily between novelistic scene-setting... and savvy exposition." He was never falsely modest about the rightness of his turn to the Right, and if self-knowledge was sometimes indistinguishable from self-praise, that was "undoubtedly part of Podhoretz's peacockish allure." Podhoretz's self-confidence actually "makes for a kind of strong-arming seduction; half of him is the class showoff, and the other half is reminiscent of Sally Field at the Academy Awards, exclaiming wonderingly, 'You like me, you really like me!'"[26]

Critic Marcus Klein was perceptive about Podhoretz's tone throughout his memoirs, starting with *Making It*. That book, like Abraham Cahan's *The Rise of David Levinsky*, should be read as an "immigrant" novel, "crowing and vulgar and convincing (moving, even) in the claim of its hero to pride of achievement" *and* in its hero's feelings of "guilt about the past he had left behind." No doubt the fact that, thirty years on, most of the New York Intellectuals were dying off meant that, with *Ex-Friends*, the "still quarreling" Podhoretz was getting kinder reviews all around. A younger set of readers could recognize that, as Klein put it, for a "jittery" outsider from Brownsville what was "quick and alive" was necessarily compounded with what was "presuming... belligerent... lofty, defensive, [and] challenging."[27]

But, to return to Merkin, she cared about Podhoretz's grief for the lost world of the Family, even as she conceded that there was nothing intrinsically wrong with forsaking Henry James for Henry Kissinger. Ever since the early seventies, after all, it had been hard to take literary intellectuals at their own valuation:

[T]he glitz has gone out of critical discourse. No one seriously cares what one writer has to say about another writer's book; such exchanges no longer send out ripples, no longer provoke the "unique excitement" that Podhoretz attributed to the highbrow writing of the fifties. For him, as for the world at large, the clinking change of reality – tomorrow's news – has replaced the currency of ideas.

Merkin's point was similar to James Atlas's in commenting (as we have seen) on the passing of the New York Intellectuals. It wasn't quite right, but it was close. Certainly Lionel Trilling would never have been invited to any of the

Washington parties *Ex-Friends* passingly refers to, and, for their part, many of
the "conservative policy wonks" at the American Enterprise Institute wouldn't
"know Thomas Mann from Clarence Thomas."[28] But Merkin would have
been surprised at how many of them *did* know Mann, and she ought to have
recognized how, throughout Podhoretz's writing, the currency of ideas – the
philosophical concepts underpinning everything – had at every point informed
his journalistic attention to the clinking change of reality.

On the last day of 1999, which was the last day of the millennium, Podhoretz's
Wall Street Journal article explained why, in all those centuries, "Science Hasn't
Killed God." Briefly sketching the battles between faith and reason, he made
the familiar point that science has dazzled us with its theories about "how"
things happen but has been necessarily mum about "why" they happen. The
ninety-five percent of Americans who profess a belief in God therefore have
their excuses. Conflict between faith and reason may nevertheless break out
again, this time over the pretensions of ethicists such as Peter Singer, who
would euthanize defective infants, or bio-engineers such as Francis Crick and
James D. Watson, who would custom-design human beings. These brilliant
people were in effect offering to replace the God who, if He wasn't killed by
the earlier rationalists, has seemed to absent Himself.

But only seemed. Podhoretz believed God is and always has been present in
creation. Present in the form of law, both the physical laws that govern organic
and inorganic material goings-on and in the moral law that governs specifically
human behavior. Of course there have always been several systems of moral
law, but the law disclosed in the Hebrew Bible has proved foundational. It is
the best we have – which is why it has always made sense to call the Jews to
whom it was decreed (or by whom it was articulated) the "chosen people."[29]

In December 1999, Podhoretz published an essay under the piquant title
"Was Bach Jewish?," a *jeu d'esprit* contrasting the felt spirit of Bach's music
(earth-bound, law-abiding, accepting of the mortal human condition) with
that of Beethoven's (mystical, antinomian, defiant toward death). The one was
essentially Old Testament, the other New Testament.

Now, Bach was Lutheran, and Luther had been particularly offended by
works-based religion, whether in its Jewish or its Catholic form. Lutheranism
was faith-based, so what could possibly be Jewish about Bach?

It is, wrote Podhoretz, his devotion to law – explicitly musical law but
implicitly the moral law as well. The Old Testament isn't concerned with the
next life (Podhoretz thought it all but rules the possibility out); it is concerned
with this life, and with the moral law that, if followed, rewards people with
prosperity and length of days. Bach's music doesn't sweep doubt away, but "it
shows that remaining within the finite limits of the Law is the way to infinite
riches," material and spiritual. Here is God's plenty – all of human experience –
in music.

As for the theology behind the music, Podhoretz recurred to the history of
Jesus and Paul. The first had no intention of forming a new religion: he wanted

to fulfill the Law, not destroy it. Paul, by contrast, wanted to abrogate the Law altogether, which he couldn't obey, he cried, because he was corrupted by original sin, and so was everyone else. Therefore God, he argued, had through the sacrifice of Jesus overcome the Law and its foundation, death itself. Believers in Jesus were spared worry about the Law: they needed only to trust in him to inherit eternal life.

Taken literally, this for Podhoretz is antinomianism. It is the mystic message we can hear in Beethoven – a Pauline desire to transcend all law, which in the musical arena the composer rebelliously tried to do, especially in the late quartets and sonatas. The polarity of Bach and Beethoven, in brief, is analogous to that between Judaism and Christianity. Some people want to accept life on earth and enjoy it; others, in an impossibilist vein, want to transcend life on earth for the sake of a better world elsewhere.[30] Podhoretz, it goes without saying, wasn't one of them.

"Was Bach Jewish?" was as close as he had come to saying in public what, in his epiphany in spring 1970, he had *seen*. He would reveal more in *The Prophets*, a book already under way as the new century began.

New Wars for a New Century

Manifest throughout Podhoretz's *My Love Affair with America: The Cautionary Tale of a Cheerful Conservative* (2000) is an acceptance of his country as neither a hell nor a heaven but as the sort of place human beings have always inhabited – only, thanks to its natural resources and even more to its political system, a place much better than most.

In the eighteenth century, Samuel Johnson called patriotism – "vigorous support for one's country" (*Oxford English Dictionary*) – "the last refuge of a scoundrel." So it has sometimes been. But it has also been a noble emotion, especially when the country in question has stood for liberty. What Bertrand Russell said of his country – "Love of England is very nearly the strongest emotion I possess" – Podhoretz wished to say about his: love of it had been strong since he was a boy, when our men fought overseas to save other nations from the tyrannies of fascism and Kate Smith sang "God Bless America" every week on the radio.

Not that a New York writer starting out in the fifties was often called on to express patriotic sentiments. Expression became urgent, for Podhoretz, only in the late sixties, when his reaction to the hostility of the New Left and its fellow travelers was largely defensive. But soon after his epiphany in 1970, he went on the offensive, and now, nearer the end than the beginning of his life, he wanted to finish the job – to glorify America "with a full throat and a whole heart."

Episodes in *My Love Affair with America* having contributed to many scenes in the present book, it is enough here to mark the final chapter, "*Dayyenu* American Style." *Dayyenu* is Hebrew for what Podhoretz roughly translates as "That alone would have been enough for us." It is the refrain of a hymn from the *Haggadah* listing all the historical blessings that, at Passover, celebrants are thankful for, saying, after each, "*dayyenu*" – the idea being that God might well have been content to stop at one.[1] So, among the blessings that had come to Podhoretz because he was an American, it would have been enough to be free from persecution, but on top of that came the freedom to study at a great university, and on top of that the freedom to pursue a career in letters, and on top of that the freedom to support, while often dissenting from, the country's government.

There are many good reasons to love America, then, but how did its civilization stack up against other great ones, like Periclean Athens, Elizabethan England, Victorian England, or Czarist Russia? By our modern criteria, there was much amiss in each of these, but all made undeniably major advances in the sundry arts. America is on the list of greats because of its high development of political art and because of its not inconsiderable achievements in the pictorial and literary arts. In any case, different epochs within a civilization are called to do different things. Podhoretz quotes a letter from one of the Founders, John Adams:

I must study politics and war that my sons may have liberty to study mathematics and philosophy. My sons ought to study mathematics and philosophy, geography, natural history, naval architecture, navigation, commerce, and agriculture, in order to give their children a right to study painting, poetry, music, architecture, statuary, tapestry, and porcelain.[2]

These stages – traceable, for instance, from John Adams to John Quincy Adams to Henry Adams – have to be gone through again and again, family by family, immigrant group by immigrant group, especially in a country as socially fluid as ours.

In the frame of Podhoretz's career, the fifties were a time mostly for consolidating the gains of modernism in the arts and liberalism in politics, the sixties a time for challenging and nearly destroying those gains, the seventies a time for a successful conservative counterchallenge, and the eighties a time for shoring up the (all too temporary) conservative victories. With all these overlapping regressions and progressions, America by the mid-twentieth century, if not before, had become the most interesting country in the world.

One could argue that, since 1948, the world's second most interesting country, and not just in the pages of *Commentary*, had been Israel, and in this new century Podhoretz continued to reflect on its situation. Things stayed the same even as they changed. In 1999, Labor's Ehud Barak became prime minister, and, under the auspices of Clinton at Camp David, put the hitherto unthinkable on the table: withdrawing Israeli troops from the security zone in southern Lebanon, returning the Golan Heights to Syria, and granting the creation of an independent Palestinian state. Even more radically, he offered to set aside districts of East Jerusalem as the Palestinian capital, to put the city's holy places under international supervision, and, as Podhoretz recounted, to grant "the 'right of return' to some 100,000 Palestinian refugees," compensating the rest "with money that Clinton (a little too confidently) assured him would be forthcoming from America." To this bonanza, Arafat said, flatly, no.[3]

Then came the outbreak of Intifada II. What Arafat plainly hoped was that the violence would precipitate a major war, with the chief Arab powers joining him in a *jihad* for a Jew-free Palestine.

All of Israel's options were bad: it had to choose a policy "less bad than others." Denunciations of Israeli "intransigence" and demands for a revived "peace process" would of course continue, but the fact remained that the process was dead because of *Palestinian* intransigence.[4] What was needed under these suboptimal conditions, when the Arab threat seemed on hair-trigger, was a credible Israeli deterrence.

This ought to have been all the more obvious during the series of suicide bombings that, in Intifada II, the Palestinian Authority (PA) and their Arab supporters were promoting. To Podhoretz, this horrible reinstitution of child sacrifice was "a striking case of religion's being conscripted into the service of political ends, traditional Islamic conceptions of martyrdom [being] invoked to recruit suicide bombers in their teens and early twenties ... and to ensure the approval even of the parents of the young Palestinian corpses thus created."[5] Perhaps, one thinks, this is how the Japanese kamikaze pilots, or the soldiers who refused to surrender on Okinawa, were conditioned. But Tokyo didn't send children into combat.

While Arafat kept Palestinian passions astir, Podhoretz repeated his stern counsel: Israel has no viable choice but "to hold tight, to keep its powder dry, to refine the anti-terrorist techniques it has already developed, to ensure the credibility of its military power as a deterrent against larger-scale attack, and to use that power if and when the Arabs force it to." That was not to rule out the possibility that peaceful co-existence might "yet come" – and perhaps even "sooner than people like me expect, just as the collapse of the Soviet Union" came sooner. "But deluding oneself into thinking that it has already come – which is what the architects of Oslo did – can," he concluded, "do Israel no good."[6]

Podhoretz's *The Prophets: Who They Were, What They Are* (2002) was the elaborate sequel, so to speak, to "Was Bach Jewish?" The author was resuming, half a century on, the study of Hebrew literature he had begun with Heschel and others at the Jewish Theological Seminary. The book is divided into three parts: "Clouds of Ancestral Glory," on Moses, Joshua, Samuel, Elijah, and others; "Eruption," the wide middle of the book, on the classical prophets Amos, Hosea, Micah, First and Second Isaiah, Jeremiah, Ezekiel, and others; and "Aftershocks," treating the "what they are" question – the prophets' relevance to our country and our culture.

Liberal interpreters of the Bible have, broadly speaking, tried to salvage a universal ethical core from the Old and New Testaments alike, a sort of residue after siphoning off legendary or mythical materials – from the miraculous (healings, resurrections, theophanies) to the presumptuous (divine covenants with a chosen people, divine incarnation in a messiah). The liberal emphasis

FIGURE 21 Norman Podhoretz and Midge Decter at the Heritage Foundation, 2005. (Photo by Charles Geer.)

is on morals: what the Hebrews' religious experience revealed was that proper conduct paid and improper conduct didn't. And when enough people conduct themselves properly, the world will enjoy the everlasting peace prefigured by Micah and First Isaiah: nations "shall beat their swords into plowshares, and their spears into pruning hooks: nation shall not lift up a sword against nation, neither shall they learn war any more."

For Podhoretz, however, to foreground such end-of-days passages over other parts of the Bible – to regard them as the enlightened evolutionary goal toward which the more bellicose, ritualistic, "primitive," and politically realistic passages have been tending – is not only to remove the idealistic "uplift" from its context but also to diminish the Bible as a whole. If we read *all* of the Bible, we get both the lamb lying down with the wolf and David lying down with Bathsheba, the wife of Uriah the Hittite. We get God punishing him for that and then rewarding him for slaughtering the Amalekites. We get God's law thundered down from Sinai, Abraham arguing with Him about the justice of destroying all the people of Sodom and Gomorrah, or Jeremiah and Job contending with Him over why He permits the wicked to prosper while the innocent go to the wall.

Consider the story of God's instruction to Abraham to bind and sacrifice his son Isaac as an offering to Himself. The old man proceeds unblinkingly to do as he is bid until, at the last moment, an angel orders him to stop. There is a ram behind him caught in a thicket, which he substitutes for Isaac. For Christians, Abraham is the Father of Faith. For Jews, Podhoretz argues, he is the Father of Obedience – obedience, that is, to God's will, which in Moses becomes explicitly His law, a law that emphatically rules out child sacrifice. The Ten Commandments are slightly more concerned with social interactions than with rituals like remembering the sabbath, but Moses regarded the whole series organically, and so did the prophets who succeeded him: right conduct and right ritual went together. If the children of Israel worshipped God properly, they then had a good chance of treating one another decently and thus (as was part of God's plan) providing a happy model for neighboring peoples.

We can differentiate the prophets' secondary themes – Ezekiel stressing individual responsibility, Amos social justice, Hosea sexual propriety – but what ought to be unmistakable is their primary theme: a unanimous opposition to idolatry, whether it be the outright denial of the God of Abraham or the syncretistic diminishment of Him as but one deity among many. The Bible's theology is monotheistic, and its central imperative, "the elusive 'essence of Judaism,'" as Podhoretz calls it, is in Deuteronomy 30:11–14, 19:

For this commandment which I command thee this day, it is not hidden from thee, neither is it far off. It is not in heaven.... Neither is it beyond the sea.... But the word is very nigh unto thee, in thy mouth, and in thy heart, that thou mayest do it.... I call heaven and earth to record this day against you, that I have set before you life and death, blessing and cursing: therefore choose life, that both thou and thy seed may live.

This moral command – to which we have earlier referred – is always coupled with ritual commands having to do with sabbath observance, diet, hygiene, and so forth. Liberals want to uncouple the two sorts of commands. Podhoretz thinks that a mistake. The ethic and the ritual go together – at least for Jews. The ritual is a sign of their chosenness.

Liberal interpreters have felt uneasy about what the great nineteenth-century German theologian Friedrich Schleiermacher called the "scandal of particularity" in God's choosing a single people to do this moral modeling. Why not start by putting all the nations on the same ethical page and at the same time? In *The Prophets*, Podhoretz neatly answers this shocked question. As the biblical writers make clear, God had – at least He chose – to start *some*where, as opposed to *every*where, persuaded that the moral laws of life could be realized only through trial-and-error experiments.

Of course that is not the end of it. In a lecture given in Jerusalem in 2007, Podhoretz would pursue the theme of particularity to what one might call its final redoubt – the Jewish claim on Jerusalem not just as the capital of ancient Judah after the division of David and Solomon's kingdom (in the tenth century B.C.E.) but of Judaism itself. In so doing, Podhoretz again faced the deep discomfort of many, including many Jews, with the idea of a chosen people. Some of these skeptics (Podhoretz's friend Dan Jacobson, for instance, whose

The Story of the Stories is a remarkably eloquent attack on theological particularism)[7] point out that it is through the conceit of chosenness "that the evil of
racism came into the world – the very evil which ultimately mutated into the
claim of the Nazis that they were a master race, and of which, by a tremendously tragic irony, the Jews themselves would become the major victim."
Others, even if they believe in God, make the liberal argument that chosenness
is "a primitive tribal superstition" that enlightened folk have "outgrown."

That is the program both of Reform Judaism, which favors the universalism of God's moral law over the particularism of ritual, and Reconstructionist
Judaism, which goes "so far as to purge from the liturgy any and all references to the doctrine of chosenness." To Podhoretz, however, the Reform and
Reconstructionist objections, to say nothing of the agnostic or atheist ones,
don't really stick, because the universalism they are based on is a pipe dream.

Not that universal truths don't exist. Clearly, for someone who believes in
God and in His commandment to choose life, universal truths do exist. Only,
as the poet and painter William Blake said, such truths "cannot exist but in
minutely organized particulars." That was an artist's way of affirming that
God's law is apprehensible only through history – disclosed in this particular
time, in that particular place, through these particular individuals, and in the
subsequent stories told about them. Also, Podhoretz maintains, the particularity of Judaism itself, the notion that this people was chosen by God to manifest
His law, seems empirically verifiable, for see how all the empires of the antique
world are now dust, but the Jews have survived. This is in spite of persecutions,
even Hitler's "final solution," which eliminated a third of the eighteen million
Jews then living in the world, and in spite of Stalin, too.

If those monsters failed to kill all the Jews, then, Podhoretz concludes, the
Arabs and Persians (Iranians) will fail as well. As Mark Twain observed in
1899, "The Jews constitute but one-quarter of one percent of the human race.
It suggests a nebulous, dim puff of stardust lost in the blaze of the Milky
Way. Properly, the Jew ought hardly to be heard of; but he is heard of, has
always been heard of" – in the arts and sciences, in finance and philosophy.
"All things are mortal but the Jew; all other forces pass, but he remains. What
is the secret of his immortality?" Charles Murray, a secular non-Jew, would
ask the same question in 2007, and after reviewing the data would come up,
somewhat "playfully," with the mystically improbable answer that, to coin a
phrase, "The Jews are God's chosen people."[8,9]

What current lessons does Podhoretz draw from the classical prophets not
just for Jews but for everyone, especially Americans? It is evident, to begin
with, that the prophets' political counsels, addressed "to a tiny and weak
country caught between rival empires," can have almost nothing to say to a
superpower like the United States. We mustn't pretend to be weak; we must
learn to use our strength for our own and others' good. Still, it is evident
that the prophets' lessons about human frailty say something crucial to us.
Even the strongest people – kings, priests, or prophets themselves – cannot

create a utopia: "*only God can bring about the messianic era.*" The best, as the saying goes, is often enemy to the good. Twentieth-century revolutionaries have "felt justified in constructing totalitarian regimes and murdering as many millions as they thought it would take to create such a [best] world." They have been wrong, and the classical prophets, if on the spot, would have told them why.

So much for what the Protestant theologian Reinhold Niebuhr called "immoral society." What about "moral man"? Absent any likelihood of a personal afterlife – Podhoretz insists that the Hebrew Bible as a whole offers at most the hope of a people's generation-to-generation perpetuity – it has always been difficult for Jews to remain faithful to a God who, His own promises notwithstanding, has often allowed the wicked to get away with their wickedness. In an afterlife, such as the one Christianity looks to, the books could be balanced. Therefore it isn't surprising that, when they had a choice, some Jews converted. Or, despairing of the God of their fathers, they turned to paganism, with its pleasuring of the senses, or to other sorts of idolatry. That once meant serving this or that tinhorn Near Eastern deity. Now – for Jews as for backsliding Christians, Muslims, or other apostates from monotheism – it essentially means serving the tinhorn self: a summary term for such contemporary works of our own hands as money, power, celebrity, or status.

What Podhoretz believes we know in our hearts, for all the liberated talk about taking control of our reproductive destinies, and so forth, is that there is an opposition between the good biblical imperatives to "be fruitful and multiply" or to "choose life" and the evil, unfruitful practices of abortion, same-sex sex, or (with regard to nurturing the children we do bring into the world) parenting through surrogates, neglecting our schools, or implicitly telling our children, when they come to important decisions, that they are on their own. Being on their own amounts to either narcissistic hedonism ("What's in it for *me*?") or identity politics ("What's in it for *us*?").[10]

Podhoretz's Jewish particularism can appear to be a form of identity politics, too. But he is also an American, pinning his faith on the principles of liberal democracy, which in social terms best embody the moral law that Jews, to say nothing of Christians and Muslims, have learned from the Hebrew Bible. Practically, therefore, any Christian, Muslim, or Jew, fervent or lapsed, who does what he can to promote life instead of death is at minimum an honorary member of God's "chosen." To invert Blake's comment about Milton, such people are of God's party without knowing it.[11]

Podhoretz would round off his contemplations on the chosen people almost a decade later in *Why Are Jews Liberals?* (2009). The historical answer to the title question is easy: during the many centuries when the Left seemed their only ally against persecution from the Right, of course Jews were liberals. But why do they – and others – remain committed to liberalism in an era when both their own best interests and the interests of America and the West generally are under attack from the international Left?

FIGURE 22. Norman Podhoretz speaking at the Heritage Foundation, 2005. (Photo by Charles Geer.)

Surveying over three hundred years of Jewish history, Podhoretz attempts to answer that great puzzle by focusing first on the paradoxical fact that the Jews' friends on the Left have often been of dubious mettle. That is, they have liked Jews well enough, but only so long as they were willing not to be Jewish.

Take the Jews' embrace of those Enlightenment *philosophes* who strove to emancipate them from civil disabilities and shield them from the tortures of the Inquisition. It seemed an obvious step forward, and yet the most famous of the *philosophes*, Voltaire, while agreeing that Jews ought not to be burned at the stake, argued that, like all supernaturalists, including Christians, they should abandon their archaic beliefs and take up the new Religion of Reason. This demand for apostasy was echoed by both the French Revolutionists and the reform-minded politicians in nineteenth-century countries like Germany, when they opposed the existence of "a nation within a nation." The European Left was prepared to tolerate Jews as individuals but not as a people. This only meant that the Left was less dangerous than the Right, which wouldn't hear of toleration for Jews even as individuals.

Of course it seemed reasonable that many secularizing Jewish intellectuals of the nineteenth and twentieth centuries should follow the liberals' lead into the arms of socialist and even Marxist ideology: the liberation of oppressed workers would necessarily entail the liberation of oppressed Jews. But in doing so these Jewish intellectuals had to blind themselves to the anti-Semitism of communist doctrine. Not only had Marx declared, in an extension of earlier Christian attacks on Jews as usurers, that under capitalism the deity of Christians and Jews alike was money: away with their god, and away with them! Marx had also envisaged a utopia, after the money-worshippers had been sent "away," wherein all differences among people – race, religion, and above all class – would disappear and everyone would be undifferentiatedly proletarian and happy. That was theory. In practice, Lenin and Stalin's Soviet Union turned this program of radical assimilation for Jews into one of radical elimination.

In short, the great puzzle remains. Sociological explanations for Jews' clinging to liberalism – whether as a consequence of their need to defend themselves against the Right, their descent from forebears pledged to socialism or communism, or their attendance at colleges and universities where liberalism is virtually the only "culture" on offer – don't suffice. Judaism, most Jews appear to believe, is simply synonymous with liberalism. Take, for instance, the Jewish pundit who in the 2008 presidential election insisted that since "It is fundamental to Judaism that those who are blessed with 'more' have an obligation – not a choice – to help those who have less," she could never cast her ballot for John McCain: as Senator he had "voted against the minimum wage at least ten times" and "believe[d] in the privatization of Social Security." To which Podhoretz replies that it is preposterous to think that the Torah endorses such specific policies and, as he maintained throughout *The Prophets*, equally preposterous to extrapolate liberalism from the Hebrew Bible as a whole.

No less preposterously, the journalist and rabbi Henry Siegman insists that "There is something decidedly '*goyish*' about a Darwinian marketplace in which only the fittest survive" and the social critic Michael Walzer announces that "The prophetic books reaffirm the values of the Exodus story: indeed, no other body of literature is so likely to press people who take it seriously toward an identification with the poor and oppressed." One might imagine that Siegman and Walzer were confusing Judaism with Christianity, except that the Christian tradition contains more complex moral and political thinking than the "liberation theology" they unwittingly echo.

The truth, Podhoretz claims, is that liberal Jews don't know – and don't want to know – their own religious tradition. The New Testament may appear to equate virtue with giving "all you have" to the poor or condemn the love of money as the root of all evil. But the Hebrew Bible, while hardly condoning cupidity, consistently sees riches as "a blessing," and when it speaks of charity, "the poor to whom Jews are commanded to do justice 'are primarily other Jews.'" When, finally, the Hebrew prophets envision "the ultimate salvation of the whole world," a theme of great importance to Christianity, they stipulate that "the redemption of the Children of Israel" is "the necessary precondition for this glorious future, which in any event will not be achieved until all nations cast away their idols and bow their knees to the one true God, the God of Israel."

Naturally, liberal Jews go on clinging to their version of religion, and with the fervor marking believers in all times and places. Just as Job said of the God who allowed Satan to torment him, "Though He slay me, yet will I trust in Him," so for many years did Jewish Marxists hold to their belief "in the glorious promise of socialism," however much it was refuted "by the horrors of 'actually existing socialism' in the Soviet Union and other countries living under communism." There is always a fallback position. Since the collapse of communism in the Soviet Union and Eastern Europe, erstwhile Jewish Marxists have become social democrats – their beliefs being as resistant to falsification by argument or data as they were before.

This stubbornness reminds Podhoretz of the "guns of Singapore" syndrome, after the shortsightedness of the British at the outbreak of World War II, when they pointed all their artillery in the direction from which "the island had last been invaded" and thus were helpless when the Japanese attacked from the other side. Just as generals tend to fight "the last war instead of the one that needs to be fought now," Jewish liberals keep their guns pointed against the threat of anti-Semitism on the Right – the last war – and are oblivious to the threat now on the Left.[12]

As we have suggested, Judaism and the Bible were already on Podhoretz's mind earlier in the new millennium, in part because they were coming under direct challenge by fundamentalist adherents of the Qur'an – Muslims determined to impose its laws not only on their lax co-religionists but also on "infidels." If World War III had been the Cold War against communism, then the war against Islamofascism, to call the enemy by a single name, should become known as World War IV. This coinage, popularized by Podhoretz, originally belonged to the defense analyst Eliot A. Cohen. In the wake of the attacks on 9/11, Cohen had pointed up the analogies: like World War III, the new one would be "global"; it would entail not just arms but also ideas and information; it might "go on for a long time"; and, most importantly, it had "ideological roots" – for it wasn't "the generalized abstraction 'terrorism,' but rather 'militant Islam'" that was the true enemy.

The West, as Podhoretz argued in "How to Win World War IV" (2002), had been here before: "Militant Islam today represents a revival of the expansionism by the sword that carried the new religion from its birthplace in Arabia in the 7th century C.E. through North Africa, the Balkans, Spain, and as far [North-] West as the gates of Vienna in the 1680's." There were distinctions to be drawn between Sunni and Shi'a, and between them and sectarian movements like the Wahabbi, but insofar as each was an orthodox branch of Islam – the word "Islam" itself meaning not "peace" but "submission" – its followers were bound to obey the Prophet's call "to wage holy war, or jihad, against 'infidels.'" That was what Osama bin Laden was doing when he directed his henchmen to attack targets on American soil.

On the morning of September 11th, Podhoretz had been downtown, on jury duty, when the hijacked planes hit the World Trade Center. He remembered that "we all poured into the street – just as the second tower collapsed. And this sight, as if it weren't impossible to believe in itself, was made all the more incredible by the perfection of the sky stretching so beautifully over it."[13] This literally and metaphorically "out of the blue" attack revealed just what America, the West, and Israel were up against.

From Cairo and Damascus to Baghdad and Tehran, Muslims danced in the streets as, in televised replay after replay, the twin towers crumbled. Was there any way, Podhoretz asked, to defeat a jihad so avidly supported? The answer was yes: take Osama bin Laden down, and Muslims would abandon his cause. As bin Laden himself remarked, "When people see a strong horse and a weak horse, by nature they will like the strong horse." And it wasn't just a matter of fear and hatred of the ruler; it was also, Podhoretz maintained, a matter of love for freedom. Witness "the outburst of relief and happiness that became so vivid among the people of Kabul after we had driven out their Taliban oppressors." If Afghanistan and other Middle Eastern nations could enjoy the modernization Kemal Atatürk brought to Turkey after World War I, then Islam could become in those nations what it had become in Turkey – a relatively tolerant religion separated from the state and acclimated to living in the world side by side with other faiths. No more conversion by the sword.

The power of American arms and example, Podhoretz understood, wouldn't establish liberal democracy in the Middle East just like that. In the West, it had taken centuries to create the impartial judiciary, the right to private property, or the separation of church and state on which democracy depends, but the timetable could be considerably shortened. Think, Podhoretz said, of the transformations of totalitarian regimes in Germany, Japan, and now Eastern Europe and the "evil" Soviet empire itself: these, in long historical view, seemed to occur "overnight." Political and cultural change must be organic, but the process could apparently be telescoped from centuries to decades.

It was a process recent American presidents had done little to move forward. Confronted with terrorist violence, they had practiced appeasement, evasion, and damage control. Their refusal to use American hard power against al Qaeda in particular persuaded bin Laden "that we were a nation on the way down." We seemed "so afraid to die that we lacked the will even to stand up for ourselves and defend our degenerate way of life." When the Twin Towers vaporized and part of the Pentagon lay smoldering, however, what bin Laden discovered wasn't American despair but "an outpouring of rage and an upsurge of patriotic sentiment such as younger Americans had never witnessed except in the movies, let alone experienced in their own souls and on their own flesh." The awakening was most evident in George W. Bush, who was modeling himself not after his father but after Reagan. The "evil empire" was now replaced by the "axis of evil," the Cold War by a hot one.[14]

Still, the struggle would not be easy, and there would be plenty of opposition to it here at home. When in 1941 Roosevelt called on Congress to declare war, there wasn't "a peep of protest" from the isolationists. If we studied the internal workings of Japan or Germany, it wasn't "in order to love and justify them but to learn better how to defeat them." Contrast the study, if that is the word, of Islam among American academics, who tendered a "selectively roseate" view of the religion. And while liberal intellectuals soft-pedaled or denied the genuinely fascistic side of Islamic fundamentalism, they loudly denounced the allegedly fascistic side of American politics and culture.

Sontag, for instance, had written a *New Yorker* piece blaming the September 11th attacks on "specific American alliances and actions" (presumably our support of Israel); Mailer wrote a *New York Review* fantasia "comparing the Twin Towers to 'two huge buck teeth,' and pronouncing the ruins at ground zero 'more beautiful than the buildings were.'" Would an elite intellectual minority turn public opinion against the war on Islamofascism as it once had done against the war on communism in Vietnam? George W. Bush, ridiculed like Reagan "as a simpleton and a 'cowboy,'" would need all the help he could get.[15]

"The biggest deal imaginable," Podhoretz told an interviewer in June 2004, not just "the most wonderful honor ever to come my way" but "the most wonderful honor I could ever imagine." He was referring to the Presidential Medal of Freedom, an award that had nothing to do with any personal relation with Bush, whom he had met only once (a simple shaking of hands). Nor, to Podhoretz's knowledge, had Elliott Abrams, who had become the National Security Council's Middle East adviser, lobbied for the choice. The Medal of Freedom, the highest honor given to a civilian, typically goes each year to some dozen individuals from diverse fields of achievement. In 2004, the honorees included Rita Moreno, the actress who portrayed Anita in *West Side Story*; Arnold Palmer, the golf champion; Gordon B. Hinkley, president of the Mormon church; and (in an unusual reaching out beyond our borders) Pope John Paul II, champion of freedom from communist tyranny. Besides Podhoretz, the only writer to be distinguished (posthumously) was his friend Robert L. Bartley, who had run the editorial page of the *Wall Street Journal* for many years.

Beichman wrote a congratulatory note, asking how one "horses around with the President," to which Podhoretz replied that "when Bush put the medal around my neck, I whispered to him, 'I wish I could give one of these to you.' To which he responded, 'Well, bless you for that.... I'm only gettin' started, you know.'" As the recipients lined up with the Bushes for a group photo, Podhoretz found himself standing next to the president. Wondering if he should move, he was told: "You stay right where you are. You feelin' the way you do about me, I'm not lettin' you go."[16]

At the end of the Clinton administration and the beginning of Bush's, a strong bipartisan consensus held that Saddam Hussein retained the biological and chemical weapons of mass destruction (WMDs) he had earlier used against Iran, with which he had warred between 1980 and 1988, and against the independence-minded Kurdish citizens of Iraq itself. A bipartisan consensus also held that he was developing the ultimate WMD, a nuclear bomb. It wasn't just the CIA, concerned over his acquisition of aluminum tubes intended for centrifuges. The intelligence agencies of Britain, Germany, Russia, China, Israel, and even France were similarly alarmed, as was U.N. weapons inspector Hans Blix. Like the Republicans, the leading Democrats – from Hillary Clinton

FIGURE 23. Norman Podhoretz receiving the Medal of Freedom from President George W. Bush, 2004. (Official White House photo.)

and John Kerry to Al Gore and Nancy Pelosi – called for the United States to stop Saddam and cut his ties with al Qaeda.

When the American-led coalition forces entered Iraq and failed to turn up stockpiles of WMDs, however, these Democrats changed their tune. Taking political advantage of Bush's embarrassment, they claimed that he had "lied" about the WMDs from the start. It was, as Podhoretz wrote, an inconceivable charge: Why in the world should Bush have said "x" if he thought "x" to be false? Knowledgeable people on all sides believed "x" to be true. If some of them were now internalizing the notion that Bush had lied about Saddam's WMDs, it was because they *wanted* to think he had. And they wanted to think so because it would reinforce the comforting illusion that September 11th hadn't changed anything: America and the West weren't really at war with Islamofascism. Those young men who attacked the Twin Towers and the Pentagon were merely criminals: "they do not constitute or control a state," *New Yorker* columnist Hendrik Hertzberg hastened to assert directly after the attacks, "and do not even appear to aspire to control one."[17] Al Qaeda was just a network the FBI and the international police could take care of.

In fact, Podhoretz stressed, Bush had never justified war on Saddam by referring to an "imminent" WMD threat. To wait for an imminent threat would be to wait too long. Instead, a strategy of preemption – striking Saddam before he could disastrously strike us, and before he had the nuclear capacity to deter our strike – was the sensible option. No deceit about that. Nor was there any deceit about the link, "cooperative, if informal," between Saddam and al Qaeda. That was the conclusion of both the bipartisan Senate Intelligence Committee and Lord Butler's bipartisan commission in Britain. Bush didn't make it up. Indeed, he would have deserved impeachment if, on the basis of this intelligence consensus, he hadn't acted to "preserve, protect, and defend" our country. Who was lying about Iraq? It wasn't Bush but his Democratic critics, the disloyal opposition playing in the political sandbox while America was at war.[18]

The book that Doubleday published on the sixth anniversary of September 11th, *World War IV: The Long Struggle Against Islamofascism*, did more than collect the best passages of Podhoretz's articles from 2002 to 2006. He rewove and refashioned them, with ample additions, into as vigorous and eloquent a defense of the Bush Doctrine as anyone had offered since the president began formulating it in late 2001.

The defense was necessary for many reasons, the most obvious of which was the inability of most of the doctrine's supporters or opponents to rise above the daily partisan bickering that preoccupied the media, and especially as, in the fall of 2007, the media focused obsessively on the next year's presidential campaign. Only the Republican frontrunners, John McCain and Rudy Guiliani, had pledged themselves to win the war against Islamofascism. All the Democratic contenders, from Hillary Clinton to Barack Obama, were under pressure to declare a deadline for admitting defeat, withdrawing American troops from Afghanistan and Iraq, and promising – in the spirit of McGovern some thirty-five years before – to let them not just come home but stay home. That would guarantee, Podhoretz was persuaded, not peace in our time but war, and war far closer to home.

We must, Podhoretz went on, concentrate our minds on the fact that the enemy wasn't a bunch of backstreet terrorists. The Islamofascism was supported by followers adept at building popular support among the poor and by a theology that appealed even to rich and educated Muslims. Its cadres were ready to die if it meant sending the Great and the Little Satans, America and Israel, to hell and themselves to heaven. Disturbingly, even if Islamofascists made up no more than "10 percent to 15 percent of the Muslim population worldwide," there were still some 125 to 200 million of them – more "than all the fascists and communists, combined, who ever lived."[19]

Thus, if Bush offered a foreign policy different from his predecessors', it was because the enemy was different – as intransigent as Stalin and as irrational as Hitler, and with irregular combatants obviously capable of penetrating our open borders. The president had in effect awakened from the dogmatic slumbers of the "liberal internationalism" and "realism" his predecessors had variously practiced. And what he saw, thus awakened, was the Wilsonian idealism that, in the mid-seventies, *Commentary* had promoted.

This Wilsonized Bush Doctrine, as Podhoretz summarized it, was going the Truman Doctrine one better: not containment – an impossibility against fanatics armed or soon to be armed with WMDs – but rollback. Not retaliation but preemption.

The Left's reaction to all this had been proceeding along lines rehearsed forty years earlier in the protests against the war in Vietnam, only worse, for, Podhoretz noted, the Left was now joined by "sectors of the American Right" and enjoyed cyberspace synergies undreamt of by SDS. Further, the domestic reaction was, if anything, surpassed by the reaction abroad. From the dancing in the Arab streets after the Twin Towers collapsed to the huge demonstrations in European capitals protesting the invasion of Iraq, anti-Americanism, in Podhoretz's view, "metastasized" like a cancer.

The European Left didn't use the mullahs' "Great Satan" language to refer to the United States, but it did insinuate that, with respect to September 11th, Americans were "asking for it" by being the world's "bullies." Thus the words of Dario Of, the Italian playwright who in 1997 won the Nobel Prize for Literature: "The great speculators wallow in an economy that every year kills tens of millions of people with poverty – so what is 20,000 [*sic*] dead in New York?" To which Podhoretz replied that whatever our sins (like any country, we were guilty of many), they weren't the sins the European Left charged us with:

[F]ar from being a nation of overbearing bullies, we were humbly begging for the support of tiny countries we could easily have pushed around. Far from being "unilateralists," we were busy soliciting the gratuitous permission and the dubious blessing of the Security Council before taking military action against Saddam Hussein. Far from "rushing into war," we were spending months dancing a diplomatic gavotte in the vain hope of enlisting the help of France, Germany, and Russia.

Naturally a war against Islamofascism would bring displacements, wounds, and deaths. Podhoretz lagged behind no one in giving these sufferings solemn recognition. But he urged readers to see them in historical perspective. When American deaths in Iraq reached the 2,000 mark, the media went into deep mourning, but it wasn't callous to point out that the 2,000 figure was small compared with our dead in past wars: 405,399 in World War II, 36,574 in Korea, 58,209 in Vietnam. Naturally, too, there were mistakes in tactics and strategy in Iraq, but mistakes were made in all wars, including many by the victorious allies in World War II – as in the failure to anticipate the Battle of the Bulge, the late 1944 German offensive through Belgium, in which, in only forty-four days, America took an astonishing 89,987 casualties.[20]

American forces eventually broke through the Bulge and went on to Berlin. The cost of victory was steep, but there was no alternative – not if we were to rid Europe of fascism. And now in the Middle East? America's volunteer forces, as was evident on a number of their blogs and in letters home, were making "amazing progress... even under the gun of Islamofascist terrorism, in building – from scratch – the political morale of a country ravaged by 'post-totalitarian stress disorder'" and in establishing the political and economic foundations of a free society. Why no mainstream media recognition of this progress? Because any signs of success in this reputedly new Vietnam might actually help Americans understand, in response to the facile "War Is Not the Answer" bumperstickers, that, in the last resort, war sometimes – as in the Union's fight against the Confederacy to end slavery, or the Allies' fight against fascism in World War II – *was* the answer.

So potent was Podhoretz's analysis of the conflict between liberal democracy and Islamofascism that Rudy Giuliani, then a candidate for the Republican presidential nomination, took notice. Giuliani's leadership in the New York mayor's office after the September 11th attacks had made him a national figure ("Churchill in a Yankees cap," as one observer called him) and, during the summer of 2007, the polls showed him to be the Republican favorite. In the spring, he asked Podhoretz for a thirty-minute briefing on the war that went on for two-and-a-half hours. It was, Podhoretz said, "my first extended exposure to him, and I came away very impressed with his intelligence, his quickness, his willingness to listen (unusual in pols) and his cheerfulness – very much the 'happy warrior.'" Giuliani's refusal "to envisage any alternative to victory" was reminiscent of Reagan, as was his optimistic *toujours attaquer* style.

When Giuliani later invited him to become a senior foreign policy adviser, Podhoretz remarked, "I unhesitatingly said yes." His role as adviser was to "comment on material they send me, make suggestions for his weekend reading list," and generally to support "his position on the war (which, truth be told, is all I care about)."[21] Of course the arrangement came under immediate fire – journalist-blogger Andrew Sullivan, for example, declaring "Yep. It's official. The bombing [of Iran, presumably] begins in five minutes."[22]

Podhoretz was serious about the bombing. He told Giuliani it would have been better if he, and not his Republican rival John McCain, had been the first to state "that the only thing worse than bombing Iran is allowing Iran to get the bomb." This lesser-evil counsel was the same Podhoretz had privately given Bush in the spring of 2007. Having requested a meeting while the president was in New York, he was granted "about thirty-five minutes, with only Karl Rove present to take notes." In stating his case, "I spoke – as I told him explicitly – first as an American and then as a Jew. Thanks to his manner and his warmth, which encouraged me to talk frankly and plainly, the meeting went well." Though naturally Bush "didn't tip his hand," Podhoretz thought that the president wouldn't "leave office with Iran in possession, or in imminent possession, of a nuclear capability."[23]

Podhoretz's "The Case for Bombing Iran" was originally a lecture given at a conference at the Center for Jewish Studies at Queens College titled "Is It 1938 Again?" Answer: it *was*. For just as the appeasing diplomats of that year wanted to do business with Hitler, their counterparts now wanted to "engage" Iran. Iranian President Mahmoud Ahmadinejad looked a lot like Hitler, not merely in his pledge to "wipe Israel off the map" but in his express ambition to dominate the Middle East, spread Islam into Europe, and finally realize "a world without America" – that is, a world in which America would have little or no influence in international affairs. But in an important way Ahmadinejad was also different from Hitler, for in and around 1938 many people believed that Hitler was telling the truth about how, after Munich, he would rest content. In 2007, "no one believes that Ahmadinejad is telling the truth when he says that Iran has no wish to develop a nuclear arsenal," and "virtually everyone agrees that it would be best if he were stopped, only not, God forbid, with military force – not now, and not ever."

Stopped how, then? The liberal internationalists' "diplomatic gavotte," like the minuet at Munich, was merely buying "the Iranians more time" for developing nuclear weapons. The same was true of sanctions, three years' worth of which hadn't achieved the desired result, and meanwhile the regime was getting closer to producing its mushroom cloud. That, Podhoretz concluded, was why "there is no alternative to the actual use of military force – any more than there was an alternative to force if Hitler was to be stopped in 1938." The force envisaged wasn't ground troops but air strikes off the three American carriers already in the Gulf. Even if American planes were not able to destroy all of Iran's nuclear facilities, dispersed as they were in many underground sites, bombing those sites would buy *America* time – as Israel's bombing of Saddam's nuclear reactor once bought time – and it might produce, better than tough sanctions could, "the overthrow of the mullahs."[24]

Such a visceral sense of endangerment – to return to *World War IV* – must have motivated American presidents, from Truman to Reagan, who knew evil when they saw it and remembered their responsibilities to preserve and protect. For Podhoretz, Bush was in that line, and for courageously taking his stand he had been "battered more mercilessly and with less justification than any other [president] in living memory." Yet nothing, "neither the polls nor the antiwar forces nor the conservative defeatists," had derailed him.[25] Whether he, or his successor, would be able to "carry the American people" to victory over Islamofascism, Podhoretz predicted, would depend on their capacity for patience – just as America's victories in World War II and World War III had depended on patience.

How would historians look back on our age and the struggle of the West, or rather of America on behalf of the West, against Islamofascism? Podhoretz admitted having underestimated, as Bush did, "the ferocity of the opposition to democratization" in Afghanistan and Iraq, but like Bush he believed defeat was not an option. Americans needed, as then Defense Secretary Donald Rumsfeld put it, to "stay the course as long as it takes and not a day longer," but also to understand that the course would have to be measured not in days but in years. If, after many years, America should then win, the result in the Middle East wouldn't be an ideal society. But conditions would be *better*, and the chances for prosperous liberal democracy greatly improved. Surely that was a cause as stirring, as worthy of sacrifice, as the causes motivating the "greatest generation" of World War II and the not-so-bad generations of World War III. However "bleak the prospects look, as of September 11, 2006," Podhoretz stubbornly believed that the current generation could and would rise to the occasion.[26]

World War IV sold better than any book Podhoretz had ever written, briefly rising to number fifteen on the *New York Times* best-seller list before dropping somewhere below number twenty. Making the list at all was a sign that a significant body of readers was ready to grasp the discomfiting truth that the United States was at war with Islamofascism. In February 2008, Power Line, an important conservative weblog, named *World War IV* its book of the year, and in its honor donated $25,000, the gift of an anonymous benefactor, to Soldiers' Angels, a group that supports members of the armed forces, with everything from care packages to family assistance, both during and after deployment to combat zones.[27] By that point, thanks to a successful new counterinsurgency strategy adopted the previous year, and to Bush's stubborn perseverance, the military situation in Iraq had turned around dramatically and both American and Iraqi casualties had dropped precipitously.

Neal Kozodoy had been with *Commentary* since 1966 and on the front line as its editor since Podhoretz's retirement in 1995. In 2006, fulfilling a long-nurtured hope, he, with the help of others, led negotiations that achieved an amicable separation from the American Jewish Committee, establishing a new independent organization, Commentary Inc., as the magazine's owner and publisher.

The transfer of ownership gave fresh impetus toward resolving another issue – editorial succession – that had vexed Kozodoy and that now engaged the attention of the new organization's board of directors. In the spring of 2007, a private search was set in motion, fortunately abbreviated by a chance telephone conversation with John Podhoretz, who against every expectation – at the age of forty-six, he had long since established himself in his own career as a writer – expressed to Kozodoy an interest in being considered for the position of *Commentary*'s next chief editor. In October, after three or four months of interviews and conversations with the board, it was announced that John would be joining the staff immediately as Editorial Director and in January 2009 would take the helm.

With William Kristol, John Podhoretz had cofounded the very successful *Weekly Standard*, for which he later served as the regular film reviewer. He had recently been editorial page editor of the *New York Post*, and though he no longer held that position, he remained the newspaper's principal political columnist. The titles of his three books – *Hell of a Ride: Backstage at the White House Follies 1989–1993*; *Bush Country: How George W. Bush Became the First Great Leader of the 21st Century – While Driving Liberals Insane*; and *Can She Be Stopped?: Hillary Clinton Will Be the Next President of the United States Unless . . .* – offered an insight into at least some of his interests, and indicated the forceful energy he brought to their discussion.

John's father, who hadn't been consulted about this appointment, heard about it only a day or two before the official announcement. Keeping him out of it was one way for John to show that he got the job on his own merits. Norman's response to the announcement was "amazement and joy, mixed with anxiety over the beating he'll take from our enemies who will scream nepotism."[28] And of course they did.[29] The challenge would be to retain the seriousness and edge that had, from 1960 on, made *Commentary* "a must-read" among thinking people of all persuasions – an act that would be staggeringly difficult for *anyone* to follow but that could only be eased by a lifetime's identification with that magazine's core ideas and purposes and a proven record of intellectual imagination and achievement.

Epilogue

So busy was Podhoretz's literary life after retiring from the editorship at *Commentary* – five books and, every year, four or five essays – that he might have seemed to lack the leisure for anything else. And it is true that, compared with the strenuous socializing and child-rearing of the early years, his and Midge's routine quieted down. The days of Family partying in New York were long over, their neoconservative friends were scattered around the country, and in any event the Podhoretzes were of an age when the occasional dinner party or conference gathering satisfied their gregarious appetite. They preferred the visits of Rachel, Naomi, and their families from Washington, Ruthie and her children from Israel, and John, now in his forties, happily married and with two children, from the Upper West Side.

Such visits typically occurred in East Hampton, where the Podhoretzes spent much of the summer and early fall. Not far away was Roger Hertog, an investment specialist whom Podhoretz had come to know when helping raise money for Moynihan's Senate campaigns in 1976 and 1982. Sometime around the latter year Podhoretz asked whether Hertog would be willing to manage the roughly $25,000 he had been able to set aside – not realizing that Hertog's firm, Sanford C. Bernstein & Co. (now AllianceBernstein), commonly took on portfolios starting at a quarter-million. "I told him I'd be honored," Hertog would remember, recognizing it as an opportunity to aid one of the most prominent literary intellectuals of his time. The firm insisted on *carte blanche*: the client gave it money to invest and meanwhile busied himself with other things. It was an arrangement that "relieved Norman of his anxiety," Hertog said, and "actually made him a considerable amount of money."[1] That nest egg, plus AJC retirement benefits, a consulting position as *Commentary*'s editor-at-large, and foundation grants administered by the Hudson Institute, enabled Podhoretz, during the years after he stopped drawing a salary, to concentrate not on monthly bills but on writing.

"If you hold out long enough," Huw Wheldon once told him, "you'll become venerable." And to Podhoretz's surprise it began to happen. Honors came to

FIGURE 24. Podhoretz family portrait, 2007. Front row: Joseph Abrams, Alon Blum, Midge Decter. Second row: John Podhoretz with Shiri Podhoretz on lap, Elliott Abrams, Sam Munson, Jacob Abrams, Zachary Munson, Norman Podhoretz. Third row: Ayala Podhoretz, Rachel Abrams, Sarah Abrams, Shayna Podhoretz, Leah Munson, Naomi Decter, Ruthie Blum Liebowitz. Missing are three of Ruthie's children – Noam, Avital, and Boaz. (Photo by Susie Drasnin.)

him – not just the Presidential Medal of Freedom but the American Enterprise Institute's Francis Boyer Award in 2002, the occasion for a standing ovation that lasted close to five minutes. Kozodoy reported that, during Podhoretz's ensuing lecture, "America at War: 'The One Thing Needful,'" Hertog had noticed Supreme Court Justice Clarence Thomas "sitting literally on the edge of his seat": "Even you [Podhoretz] must have sensed the same anticipation, excitement, and sheer concentration, that feeling of not wanting to lose a single word, all over the room."[2]

Such plaudits did not dampen the energies of his vilifiers, however, especially in the blogosphere, where he was regularly damned as "the not-so-secret head of the Jewish conspiracy and so on." But that, as Podhoretz knew, is what befalls intellectuals who, like Sidney Hook even in his nineties, never become *hors de combat*. The vilifiers seemed unaware of how Podhoretz needed to keep up a front of militant confidence to check his longing to be loved and cheered: "If other people had known," he said, "they'd *really* have gone after me."[3]

Besides the ritual attacks, these years brought the natural griefs. Shortly before his retirement in 1995, Podhoretz's mother died at ninety-two. Every week during her final decade, he and Midge had visited her in Brooklyn; he "telephoned twice a day, just to ask about her health"; and with his sister, Millie, he was often called on to deal with medical emergencies – the series of mini-strokes and then the aortal aneurism that led to the final crisis. In her last years, Decter would recall, there were "not many pleasures left to her. For instance, all the old men in her building were dead, and she was left to content herself with playing poker with the women, something that drove her crazy because they were so stupid and didn't know how to count the cards."[4] At the end, Norman sat at her bedside reading Psalms in Hebrew to her while Rachel leaned over to hear her last words.

Also, in summer 2001, Millie died of lung cancer. "I saw her in her coffin," Podhoretz said, "and kept thinking, 'What are you doing there?'"[5]

There were his own bouts with ill-health, too: in his seventies he had trouble with his prostate and later his heart. But these not uncommon ordeals, relieved by minimally invasive surgeries, didn't seriously impede his literary productivity. In 2008, working on *Why Are Jews Liberals?*, he experienced none of the writing blocks that had plagued him throughout his career.

Once, in the mid-nineties, a serious block had prompted him, for the first and only time in his life, to see a psychiatrist. It may seem remarkable that he had never done so before since, back in the fifties and sixties, nearly every member of the Freud-saturated Family had been in analysis, as Decter said specifically of the Trillings, "for a hundred years." Yet all that therapy seemed to have given the Family little "self knowledge"; if anything, Decter remarked, "they'd come out with negative self-knowledge."[6]

In the year after retiring, however, Podhoretz found himself too despondent to write the planned sequel to *Breaking Ranks* and reluctantly consulted a psychiatrist on the chance that medication might help. The doctor prescribed Zoloft, but it not only failed to work but had unpleasant side effects, and Podhoretz soon stopped taking it. For a long time, though, he stayed on another medication, what he called his "life of the party pill," since it slightly allayed his "social anxiety": "If I had a date to go somewhere on Friday, I would spend the whole week brooding about how I could get out of it.... What the pill did was cut down the number of days in which I'd scheme to get out of it to two rather than five. Which was a gain."

But he gradually swore off this pill, too – just as his psychiatrist, in a manner of speaking, swore off him. Having for several months pursued the usual all-listen, no-talk approach, this doctor finally broke out in an encomium to and scolding of his patient: "Why had I retired? What a terrible thing to have done to people like himself!" Turning out to be a great fan of Podhoretz's writing, the doctor accused him of having "in effect abandoned the field. No *wonder* I was depressed! I *deserved* to be depressed! So I told people later that I was perhaps the only patient ever to be fired by a shrink. He fired me, and then *he* retired. Hilarious in a way."[7]

If, over the decades, Podhoretz ever came close to the Slough of Despond, it was his wife who pulled him to safety, and not just once or twice. Ruth

Wisse contrasted the Podhoretzes' relationship with the Trillings'. The latter "did not work complementarily. Diana did not devote her life to the things that advanced Lionel, he did not devote his life to the things that enhanced her. The Podhoretzes in that sense have been blessed: intellectually, emotionally, politically, in every way they've been in synch with one another, and that has doubled their capacity."[8] This judgment was echoed by many of their neoconservative colleagues, who thought that only the marital partnership of Irving Kristol and Gertrude "Bea" Himmelfarb came anywhere close. Decter never regarded herself "as even within the same category as Norman, and I'm perfectly content not to be. In other ways we have a perfect peerdom. I have a different kind of mind than his, tending less to abstraction and more to chit-chat and [knocking on the table] to saying 'this is wood, this is a table, and it's brown.'"[9]

Far from competing with Podhoretz, she reinforced his sense of the world, his twofold identity as an American and a Jew. For her as well as for him, America "is the last best hope of mankind, and anything that conduces to its well-being or to its influence is to be supported. He has no doubts. He doesn't say 'Yes, the country is fine, but – .' There are no 'but's' about the United States of America." Not because a "but" is a concession that doesn't serve the argument but "because a 'but' is a tilt in the utopian direction – as in 'It's okay, but if only the poor were better off' or 'if only this or that.' You have to ask 'as compared with *what* in the history of mankind?'" To reach for something better would be to reach for the incomparable – a utopian urge that "ends up murderous."

Podhoretz's Jewishness, as we have seen from his epiphany in 1970 to his reading of the Hebrew prophets three decades later, was proof against utopianism. What it meant in terms of religious "observance" was nothing remarkable. He and Midge went to synagogue for the two days of Rosh Hashana, the Jewish new year, and ten days later for Yom Kippur, the day of atonement, when they observed the ritual sundown-to-sundown fast. They also celebrated Passover. "Other than that," Decter admitted, "we're really very bad. We don't keep kosher." Their sense of Jewishness was, instead, "mostly internal, sentimental, life would not be the same without it" – a sense that was

complicated because the status of Judaism is complicated. Is it a religion? Yes. Is it a nationality? Well, it's a people – whatever the hell that means. What is it? You're a Jew even if you don't 'do anything' from the day of your birth to the day of your death, and even if you pretend that you're not. You *are*. So it's something very deep, very hard to describe, but in Norman's case it's an absolutely firm loyalty.[10]

We have concentrated on the ideas that ensued from Podhoretz's acceptance of the truth of Judaism. It *is* a religion. But Decter's comments remind us of the temperamental aspect of her husband's identification with a difficult-to-define "people," and the unwaveringness of his loyalty to them.

Podhoretz himself was quick to qualify the nature of his devotion to Judaism. He liked to quote Wordsworth's remark – "I made no vows, but vows / Were then made for me"[11] – to indicate that his devotion was to the faith of the people to whom he belonged by birth and by education. At the same time, his devotion to Judaism wasn't quite like that of his Catholic friends to their religion, which depends finally on transpersonal, even institutional foundations. When speaking of the truth, not only of Judaism but of anything else, Podhoretz said, "I mean the truth *as I see it*":

[N]ow that's not exactly relativistic, but it's not exactly absolutistic either. It's that what I believe to be the truth is, as far as I'm concerned, the truth. It's to *that* that I'm loyal. And so the struggle becomes one of trying to figure out what *you* think, or maybe what you *know* to be true – and to remain loyal to that, come hell or high water. That I have done – and in the teeth of a lot of inner resistance.

It was either that, Podhoretz explained, or "go silent as a writer." And since a writer is what he *was*, and since he didn't want to end his life, silence wasn't an option, again when it came to Judaism or anything else. Thus "in a way you can't even praise me for it. I truly had no choice."

Nor was writing from the first-person point of view ("*as I see it*") an exercise in self-aggrandizement or narcissism. The ideas weren't "coming from God, or from culture, or civilization, or reason – though of course they're 'reasoned' – but they're coming from a particular mind and a particular heart That seems to me properly modest and at the same time properly bold." For the truth "*as I see it*" was not only his firm conviction but also an appeal to others, like the appeal ("This is so, is it not?") that Leavis had taught him was implicit in every serious critical assertion. And readers, even if their response was "Yes, but –," had "that feeling we all remember from when we were young: 'Oh my god, other people are like that too! I'm not alone.'"[12]

Joseph Epstein spoke of Podhoretz's "style" as a writer. When people mention "style" it is often in terms of technique: baroque or classical, flowery or straightforward, and so on. In this regard Epstein rightly declared that Podhoretz never had "a marked style." Beyond the common courtesies, he was intent on lucidity above all. As Orwell remarked of the Victorian writer Samuel Butler, measuring him against a contemporary like Robert Louis Stevenson, "one sees what a tremendous advantage is gained simply by not trying to be clever."[13] But for Epstein "style" had a deeper meaning: "it's a way of looking at the world. Thus [V. S.] Naipaul has a kind of style – as dark as possible," while Orwell's amounted to "no one's telling the truth, but now I'm going to tell it."[14]

For Podhoretz, surely, Judaism helped determine his way of looking at the world. It contributed to making his "opinions," which for many writers vary with the weather, cohere. Intellectual fashions changed, but his assessments of Bellow, Heller, Nabokov, Mailer, Roth, and others – from the early fifties to the late nineties – weren't prompted by fashion, or by pique. They were prompted by his sense of life "ruled" by law, as Judaism understood it, and therefore life as it is lived, in America and elsewhere, by "ordinary, middle-class people," the married-with-children people who want to answer to each other and to God, not to the state.

"In defending middle-class society," said Podhoretz, "I'm in part defending my own life against attacks from people like Allen Ginsberg and Jack Kerouac – attacks directed personally to me – and also from my own inner desires to stray and break free. That's the life I've chosen to live, and there's no discrepancy between the way I've lived and the things I've defended."[15] To recall his statement in 1985: "I was educated to believe that the *last* thing one ought to be defending was one's own, that it was more honorable and nobler to turn one's back on one's own and fight for others and for other things in which one had no personal stake or interest. This has been a very hard lesson to unlearn, and I am proud to have unlearned it."[16]

No doubt his certitude about such things could seem cocksure to other people, and not just on first acquaintance. His confidence in himself, to quote Daphne Merkin once more, was "undoubtedly part of Podhoretz's peacockish allure," matched as it was "only by his wish for everyone else to share this confidence."[17] To the less sympathetic, Podhoretz's confidence could seem "aggressive, difficult, sometimes solipsistic" – altogether a figure who, as Epstein remarked, was "every anti-Semite's idea of a good time."[18]

Actually, even an anti-Semite wouldn't have found confrontation with Podhoretz a good time. While utterly tender with family and friends and gentlemanly with casually met strangers, he was redoubtable in public exchange. When she first knew him, Ruth Wisse wished he would do more to soften up his audience. But she soon realized that his direct, cogent, and brave approach was best: "What you don't want to do is feel you have to prove your bona fides, to make it clear what a good person you are and all the rest of it. If you have to do *that*, it weakens the force of your argument. It already suggests there's something suspect about your position. So, no apologies. It was very liberating for me."[19]

It was liberating for the *Wall Street Journal*'s Dorothy Rabinowitz, too. Podhoretz taught her that, while she needn't be "caustic or ferocious," she must in her prose show "no yielding. No 'on the other hand's' to concede a point. That was polemic – polemic that wasn't boring. It sounds very grand to say it, but underneath I did feel that there was a kind of war, that a certain kind of ammunition was needed, and that we had to tell the truth."[20]

Rabinowitz was referring to the culture war of the sixties and seventies, which never really ended, especially for intellectuals like Podhoretz. Age, as the ethicist and biblical scholar Leon Kass remarked, never essentially changed him. Kass remembered the moving ovation at the presentation of the Boyer Award, but "to sound perhaps churlish, there was a feeling that in his address he was still settling old scores," notably against Sontag, Mailer, and Noam Chomsky, who had said some outrageous things about the September 11th attacks. "We have very different temperaments," Kass continued. "Norman takes personally the stupidities and outrages of intellectuals. He thinks it would be a sign of personal dishonor to remain silent in the face of it. I have more reservation about it. Stupidity: you have to say to yourself that there's so much error and so little time – it's hopeless to try to fight *all* the idiots."[21]

Always the boy who in Brooklyn learned that backing down meant disaster, Podhoretz never submitted, though the polls and surveys might have said the cause was lost. Even after he left the editor's chair at *Commentary*, he never hung up his sword – as Richard Neuhaus revealed in a story about a book party he gave upon publication of William Buckley's *Nearer My God* (1997). Wilfred Sheed showed up, said Neuhaus, "now badly crippled and on crutches."

Norman walked in with Midge, and Sheed – a very engaging person – leaning on a crutch with one hand, offered him the other with "Oh, Norman!" And Norman looked right at him and said, "The statute of limitations has not run out yet." [This was thirty years after Sheed's withering review of *Making It*.] Now that says something about Norman. There aren't many people who would do that. Some would say it's the unattractive side to what, on the flipside, is a virtue – his belief that words are actions, and that there is such a thing as treason of ideas. From this point of view Wilfred Sheed was not just an ex-friend or an enemy, he was a traitor – to truth. And you don't shake hands with traitors, even thirty years later. Norman gives new meaning to the word "intense." There's *nothing* that doesn't matter.[22]

To give a last example, Podhoretz's son, John, observed that he got from his parents "the general sense that if you held views that were going to get you into social trouble, you had an obligation to argue them *in spite* of the pain it would cause you." It seemed to him a perverse, "almost masochistic compulsion." If he himself was "at a dinner party with some moron socialite who started saying stupid stuff," he didn't feel "obliged to get into a political argument with her. She didn't know what she was talking about, her views had no saliency, so the wise thing was to be patronizing and just skip over it." His father's idea, on the other hand, was that

if you remain silent you are acquiescing in a moral crime. His capacity for moral outrage is undiminished: he can't let things slide. My own "Why bother with the moron socialite?" position is actually very patronizing (who the hell *is* she?). But my father treats her just as he would Anthony Lewis: he draws no distinction. She is a person who is saying something he cannot abide, or something he can. It is very ingenuous[23]

– ingenuous in the sense not just of "candid" but perhaps also of "naive" and "noble."

British intellectuals like John Gross, Paul Johnson, and David Pryce-Jones would note how different social relations were in their country between writers on the Left and those on the Right. They might biff each other in the press, yet they not only mixed at dinner parties but were often fast friends. As Gross speculated, American intellectuals weren't like that because of the split between the cultural and the political capitals, New York and Washington. If the capitals were merged, as they are in London, then, Gross imagined, "an intellectual at the end of a day's work might hob-nob with a politician, and vice versa." In New York, he was convinced, the "political theology – the pure theory – was removed from practical politics," as manifest in the dogmatism and hair-splitting of a lot of Family writing.

Gross could recall a colloquium, "the twentieth anniversary of something," which was much more high-powered than any such British gathering would be. Sidney Hook, who was making some shrewd remarks about American culture, was sarcastically put down with "Oh, Sidney, spare us the Fourth of July rhetoric!" and Gross "noted the absolutely minute memories of what so-and-so had said in the pages of *Partisan Review* in Summer of 1941 about such-and-such. Maybe Americans are more serious – American editing certainly is." Still, it was a pity that the country lacked the British sense of all parties belonging to the same "organic community," for in England one would hardly ever encounter the appalling "automatic hatred" Gross discovered Podhoretz's name aroused in America:

I was once in a magazine office in New York, and the secretary called across the room, "John, there's a Mr. Podhoretz on the phone for you," and I felt every pair of eyes drilling into me, as though she'd said "There's a Mr. Himmler on the phone for you." As an Englishman I've often liked to lunch with the hare and dine with the hounds. But many dinner parties in America couldn't begin without a kind of ritual cursing of Norman and Midge.[24]

But, as Henry James's characters tiresomely say, there we are. Americans may sigh, envying the British their metropolitan bonhomie, but the split between our political and cultural capitals, and between our left- and right-wing intellectuals, only makes Podhoretz's achievement the more admirable. For in the face of sometimes outrageous animosity, he has persevered in the defense not just of serious literature but of ordinary people's freedom and aspirations; not just of American democracy but of Judaism and the Jewish state; not just of salutary ambition but of submission to the divine commandment to choose life – and this last with regard to relations between the sexes as well as relations among countries. Because he has done so in what Ozick calls "some of the finest and cleanest and most persuasive prose of our time," one is tempted to declare the quarrels among his attackers and defenders "a mere matter of the moment." He will, one thinks in echo of the poet John Keats, be among the American writers after his death.[25]

As for his life, Leonard Garment once asked Podhoretz what he regretted about it. "I regret," he answered, "the price I've had to pay to do the things I felt I had to do," meaning, Garment quoted, "the friendships I might have had, the pleasures I might have had, and [though here Garment couldn't recall the exact words] the going into ripe years covered with garlands – not just of praise, but of affection." By affection he meant not of family or the friends he made after breaking ranks – he had that in spades – but the affection still of those who had been his friends on the Left, whose lost friendship he regretted,

Garment felt, even while he knew that having "garlands heaped on him by the *New York Review of Books* crowd would be a sign of failure."[26]

To the permanent benefit not only of his own soul but of his country, his people, and the values they exemplify and share, for Podhoretz this sort of failure has never been in the cards.

Notes

Prologue

1. "Since Podhoretz, himself a bookish man, can never be a *Shtarker* [a tough-minded guy who 'doesn't give a damn about anyone or anything'], his government [and Israel] must fill that role," Ian Buruma has said. See his "His Toughness Problem – and Ours," review of *World War IV* by Norman Podhoretz, *New York Review of Books*, September 27, 2007. http://o-www.nybooks.com.articles/20590.
2. Daniel P. Moynihan and Suzanne Weaver, *A Dangerous Place* (Boston: Little, Brown, 1978), 48–49.
3. James Q. Wilson, interview with the author, March 21, 2005.
4. George Weigel, interview with the author, June 24, 2004.
5. Cynthia Ozick, interview with the author, June 17, 2004.
6. John Gross, interview with the author, April 27, 2004.
7. Thomas L. Jeffers, "Norman Podhoretz's Discourses on America," *Hudson Review*, 54 (Summer 2001): 202–28.

Chapter 1. Brownsville

1. Midge Decter, interview with the author, February 2004.
2. Norman Podhoretz, *My Love Affair with America: The Cautionary Tale of a Cheerful Conservative* (New York: Free Press, 2000), 17.
3. "Podhoretz" is Ukrainian. Many other immigrants so-named anglicized it to Podhurst or (in literal translation) Underhill. The Russian version is "Podgorny," the Polish "Podgorze," the German "Unterberg," and the Italian "Piedmont."
4. Podhoretz, *My Love Affair with America*, 15–16.
5. Ibid., 18.
6. Ibid., 95–96.
7. Ibid., 29.
8. Ibid., 23–24.
9. Decter interview, February 2004.
10. Norman Podhoretz, interview with the author, February 4, 2004.
11. Norman Podhoretz, *Making It* (New York: Random House, 1967), 200.

12. Decter interview, February 2004.
13. Podhoretz interview, February 4, 2004.
14. Midge Decter, interview with the author, May 6, 2005.
15. Podhoretz interview, February 4, 2004.
16. Sidney Hook, *Out of Step: An Unquiet Life in the 20th Century* (New York: Harper & Row, 1987), 7–8.
17. Frank Deford, "The Boxer and the Blonde," reprinted from *Sports Illustrated: The Best American Sports Writing of the Century*, ed. David Halberstam (Boston: Houghton Mifflin, 1999), 506.
18. Norman Podhoretz, interview with the author, May 5, 2005.
19. In 1944, she would in fact marry one of her bosses, a lawyer named Solomon Zuckerman, and went on working as a secretary for him and his partner. Later, after their two children, Alan and Evan, were well launched on their own careers, she was the very able secretary for a succession of presidents of the New York City Council. She died in 2002 at the age of seventy-eight, her husband having died three years earlier.
20. Podhoretz, *My Love Affair with America*, 38, 35–36.
21. Ibid., 41.
22. Ibid., 42–43.
23. Prior to Podhoretz's time, it had graduated film producer Irving Thalberg, composer Aaron Copland, and writers such as Sidney Hook, Isaac Asimov, Theodore Draper, Irving Kristol, and Norman Mailer, plus many who would go on to illustrious careers in medicine, business, and law. Closed as a school in the early seventies, the building now serves other municipal purposes.
24. Decter interview, May 6, 2005.
25. Podhoretz interview, February 4, 2004.
26. Podhoretz, *Making It*, 31.
27. Podhoretz interview, February 4, 2004.
28. Podhoretz, *Making It*, 13–14.
29. Ibid., 9.
30. Podhoretz, *My Love Affair with America*, 44.
31. Podhoretz interview, February 4, 2004.
32. Ibid.
33. Podhoretz, *Making It*, 18.
34. Ibid., 20–21.
35. Ibid., 25.
36. Ibid., 27.

Chapter 2. Columbia

1. Jacqueline Clarke Wheldon and Huw Wheldon, *Wheldon Letters*, by permission of Wynn Wheldon. Podhoretz to Jacqueline Clarke Wheldon, August 17, 1971.
2. Midge Decter would draw a distinction between Rabbinical School stars like Sidney Morgenbesser, Isaiah (Izzy) Scheffler, Harold (Red) Weisberg, and a few others who went on to academic careers, and the majority, who, though taking "courses at Columbia with a fantasy of escape," landed "in the rabbinate, out of cowardice, or out of being unable to make it academically, or out of discomfort with the big world." See Midge Decter, "An Activist Critic on the Upper West Side," in *Creators and Disturbers: Reminiscences by Jewish Intellectuals of New York*, ed. Bernard

Rosenberg and Ernest Goldstein (New York: Columbia University Press, 1982), 354.

3. Podhoretz, *Making It*, 30.
4. Ibid., 45–46; see also Norman Podhoretz, *Doings and Undoings: The Fifties and After in American Writing* (New York: Farrar, Straus & Giroux, 1964), 118.
5. Norman Podhoretz, interview with the author, February 7, 2004.
6. Ibid.
7. John Hollander, interview with the author, May 2004.
8. Podhoretz, *Making It*, 34–36. The "young man from the provinces" phrase, applied to novels like Stendhal's and Balzac's, was Trilling's.
9. Philip French, *Three Honest Men: Edmund Wilson, F. R. Leavis, Lionel Trilling: A Critical Mosaic* (Manchester: Caracanet New Press, 1980), 82.
10. Diana Trilling, "Lionel Trilling: A Jew at Columbia," in *Speaking of Literature and Society*, ed. Diana Trilling (New York: Harcourt Brace Jovanovich, 1980), 427. Reprinted from *Commentary*, March 1979, 40–46.
11. Podhoretz, *Making It*, 46–51.
12. Podhoretz, *My Love Affair with America*, 60.
13. Decter interview, February 2004.
14. Decter, "An Activist Critic," 352–54.
15. Midge Decter, *An Old Wife's Tale: My Seven Decades in Love and War* (New York: HarperCollins, Regan, 2001), 23–30.
16. He remarried, had another child, and soon became political editor of the Voice of America. Later in the fifties he worked as managing editor at the *New Leader*, a socialist anti-communist magazine, and eventually made his mark as an advocate for Soviet Jews. See Douglas Martin, "Moshe Decter, 85, Advocate for Soviet Jews, Dies." *New York Times*, July 5, 2007:B7.
17. Decter interview, February 2004.
18. Herb London, interview with the author, February 2004.
19. *Commentary* Archive, July 12, 1985. Stacy went on to teach English at the University of Hartford.
20. Podhoretz, *Making It*, 61.

Chapter 3. Cambridge

1. Unlike Isaiah, Podhoretz told his campers, Jeremiah suffered because he preferred poetry to prophecy. "I presented this agonized religious genius as a sort of Hebraic prototype of the Artist persecuted by a Hebraic prototype of bourgeois society – a Flaubert among the Jewish philistines.... The novelty of this approach was not lost even on fifteen-year-olds" (Podhoretz, *Doings and Undoings*, 120).
2. Norman Podhoretz, "Eulogy for Gerson Cohen," *Podhoretz Papers*, Library of Congress, 1991.
3. Podhoretz, *Making It*, 64; Podhoretz, *My Love Affair with America*, 100.
4. John Northam, interview with the author, April 30, 2004.
5. Podhoretz, *Podhoretz Papers*.
6. Ibid.
7. Podhoretz, *My Love Affair with America*, 112–14.
8. Norman Podhoretz and Lionel Trilling, *Trilling Papers*, Butler Library, Columbia University, 1950.
9. *Commentary* Archive, Podhoretz to John Carey, October 14, 1982.

10. See Denys Thompson, ed., *The Leavises: Recollections & Impressions* (Cambridge: Cambridge University Press, 1984); and Ian MacKillop, *F.R. Leavis: A Life in Criticism* (London: Allen Lane (Penguin), 1995). Both are critically sympathetic. For a sharply dissident view of Leavis and his followers, see George Watson, "The Messiah of Modernism: F. R. Leavis (1895–1978)," *Hudson Review*, 50 (Summer 1997): 227–41.

11. Norman Podhoretz, *Ex-Friends: Falling Out with Allen Ginsberg, Lionel & Diana Trilling, Lillian Hellman, Hannah Arendt, and Norman Mailer* (New York: Free Press, 1999), 64–65.

12. Podhoretz, *Making It*, 79–80.

13. Norman Podhoretz, interview with the author, April 12–13, 2004.

14. Norman Podhoretz, "The Arnoldian Function in American Criticism," review of *The Liberal Imagination* by Lionel Trilling, *Scrutiny*, 18 (June 1951): 59–65. *The Liberal Imagination* did indeed prove to be a classic, selling 100,000 copies in the Anchor paperback edition that Jason Epstein brought out in the mid-fifties. See Mark Krupnick, *Lionel Trilling and the Fate of Cultural Criticism* (Evanston, Ill.: Northwestern University Press, 1986), 102.

15. Podhoretz and Trilling, *Trilling Papers*, November 23, 1951.

16. Other "provincials" at Cambridge, especially Australians like Newton and South Africans like Aaron Klug and Dan Jacobson, were fascinated by Americans on the scene. Podhoretz and Steve Marcus in particular had a "great glamour," Jacobson would remember, "because in South Africa we 'knew' more about Americans than we'd 'seen' – and then Jewishness had started to become fashionable, especially in New York, where *Partisan Review* was edited by Jews: Norman seemed like a representative from that milieu" (Dan Jacobson, interview with the author, April 26, 2004).

17. Podhoretz, *Making It*, 83–86; Podhoretz, *My Love Affair with America*, 102–3.

18. Wynn Wheldon, interview with the author, April 26, 2004.

19. Wynn Wheldon, "Jacqueline Mary Wheldon, 1924–1993." Biographical sketch, 2007.

20. Podhoretz and Trilling, *Trilling Papers*, November 23, 1951.

21. In that same letter (December 3, 1951), Trilling also recommended Steven Marcus: "unusually gifted … very quick, keen, and accurate. … He talks well, writes less well – he needs training and breaking in," "a real intellectual, with *ambitions* in that line – what a relief!" (Podhoretz, *Podhoretz Papers*). Throughout the book, emphasis is in the original unless indicated otherwise.

22. Podhoretz, *Podhoretz Papers*, January 3, 1952.

23. Podhoretz, *Making It*, 95–98.

24. Ibid., 99–102.

25. Podhoretz interview, April 12–13, 2004.

26. Podhoretz, *Podhoretz Papers*.

27. The grounds? Grilled by the famous Dickensian Humphry House, Marcus didn't know, among other things, which group of soldiers had carried out the so-called Peterloo Massacre in 1819 (John Gross, interview with the author, April 27, 2004).

28. Podhoretz and Trilling, *Trilling Papers*, February 25, 1953.

29. Podhoretz interview, April 12–13, 2004.

30. Podhoretz and Trilling, *Trilling Papers*, June 5, 1953.

31. Ibid., June 15, 1953.

32. Podhoretz, *Podhoretz Papers*, June 6, 1953.
33. Later, when the Leavises publicly distanced themselves from him, even to the point of denying their one-time fondness, he was astonished. Had he not once been sick in bed, and had not Leavis himself stopped, gotten off his bicycle, and knocked on the door to deliver a get-well gift of jam that Queenie had made at home? Leavis denied it. Podhoretz's definitive response to this complicated and self-centered man was more than generous: see his "F. R. Leavis: A Revaluation," in Norman Podhoretz, *The Bloody Crossroads: Where Literature and Politics Meet* (New York: Simon & Schuster, 1986), 71–93.
34. Podhoretz, *Making It*, 92.
35. Podhoretz interview, April 12–13, 2004.
36. Podhoretz, *Making It*, 95.
37. Podhoretz interview, April 12–13, 2004. Apropos of Jacqueline's converting, he wrote her on November 26, 1953: "The Jews have a prayer which ends: 'Next year in Jerusalem.' From now on, I'm praying, 'Next Easter (no! *Passover*) in London with my darling.' You pray too. I love you" (Wheldon and Wheldon, *Wheldon Letters*).

Chapter 4. The Family and the Army

1. Podhoretz, *Making It*, 123–24.
2. Norman Podhoretz, *Breaking Ranks: A Political Memoir* (New York: Harper & Row, 1979), 16.
3. Podhoretz, *Ex-Friends*, 77.
4. Wheldon and Wheldon, *Wheldon Letters*, November 24, 1953.
5. See Mary McCarthy, "America the Beautiful," *Commentary*, September 1947: 201–7.
6. See Podhoretz, *Making It*, 116–30.
7. Ibid., 117–18.
8. The article appeared in *Commentary* (December 1953) and was reprinted as "The World of TV Drama" in Podhoretz, *Doings and Undoings*, 269–82. Like Warshow's classic essays on movies, it is better than its own subject.
9. Wheldon and Wheldon, *Wheldon Letters*, October 26, 1953.
10. Ibid.
11. Podhoretz, *Doings and Undoings*, 274–75.
12. Wheldon and Wheldon, *Wheldon Letters*, October 30, 1953.
13. The review was folded into the longer "Adventures of Saul Bellow" in Podhoretz, *Doings and Undoings*, 205–27, reprinted in *The Norman Podhoretz Reader: A Selection of His Writings from the 1950s through the 1990s*, ed. Thomas L. Jeffers (New York: Free Press, 2004), 7–23.
14. For all its dozen or more copies, this letter seems to have disappeared, along with nearly all the fifties correspondence in the *Commentary* Archive, which was destroyed by a disgruntled assistant when at the end of the decade the magazine moved to its present location on East 56th Street.
15. That Bellow never forgave Podhoretz's review of *Augie* became evident (if evidence were lacking) a quarter century later when John Podhoretz, a freshman at the University of Chicago, interviewed him for a student magazine:

    When, after two weeks of wrangling, I was finally allowed in to see the Great Man, who is by now quite old and surprisingly jowly, he said to me, "Are you one of the New York

Podhoretzes?" I replied in the affirmative, to which he said, "I've known your mother for many years – she is Midge isn't she? – yes, many years; oh but I don't know your father very well," he added, in *sotto voce*, and then repeated it a few times during the course of our fifteen minute conversation. . . . It is amazing that after twenty-five years, such a man could hold such a grudge, amazing. (Wheldon and Wheldon, *Wheldon Letters*, to Jacqueline, March 8, 1979)

The writer Ruth Wisse adds: "Saul always felt *Commentary* had been against him, and no matter how I tried to persuade him otherwise with the evidence of many positive reviews, he continued to think so. I think that he wanted unstinting and enthusiastic praise for his work with absolutely no reservations. Argument on every subject – yes. Criticism of his work – no. He remembered Norman's criticism and it smarted" (e-mail to the author, December 20, 2005).

16. Podhoretz, *Making It*, 155–59, 142.
17. Ibid., 150–51.
18. Wheldon and Wheldon, *Wheldon Letters*, November 9, 1953.
19. Ibid., December 2, 5, and 7, 1953.
20. Berryman, too, had gone to Columbia and been a Kellett at Clare in the thirties. "Somebody ought to tell him that he and I have more in common than [do] he and Bellow," Podhoretz wrote Jacqueline (ibid., November 24, 1953).
21. Ibid., December 20, 1953.
22. Podhoretz and Trilling, *Trilling Papers*, May 20, 1954.
23. Ibid.
24. See Podhoretz, *My Love Affair with America*, 119.
25. Wheldon and Wheldon, *Wheldon Letters*, May 20, 1954.
26. Podhoretz interview, April 12–13, 2004.
27. Podhoretz and Trilling, *Trillling Papers*, November 26, 1954.
28. Podhoretz interview, April 12–13, 2004.
29. See Podhoretz, *Ex-Friends*, 112–14.
30. Podhoretz interview, April 12–13, 2004.

Chapter 5. The Practicing Critic

1. Wheldon interview.
2. Decter, *An Old Wife's Tale*, 30–38.
3. Ibid., 43–44.
4. Wheldon and Wheldon, *Wheldon Letters*, March 20, 1955.
5. Podhoretz and Trilling, *Trilling Papers*, April 1, 1955.
6. Ibid., April 17, 1955.
7. Ibid., February 3, 1955.
8. Podhoretz, *Making It*, 198–99.
9. Going through a divorce, Clem had in 1955 suffered a nervous breakdown of his own, though nothing like Cohen's. Sherry Abel recalled the strain between them: while Cohen was keen on treating with like seriousness Casey Stengel, Henry James, and Norman Rockwell, Clem thought, in strict *Partisan Review* mode, that Stengel and Rockwell belonged in the *Saturday Evening Post*. It was a question of breadth of interests and level of tone. "Whenever they would have these editorial meetings," Abel recalled, "Clem never participated. . . . He just would sit apart from the others, scowling and acting superior. . . . He stayed on but he disapproved and never let anyone forget it." See Florence Rubenfeld, *Clement Greenberg: A Life* (New York: Scribner, 1997), 205.

10. Wheldon and Wheldon, *Wheldon Letters*, May 28, 1956.

11. Podhoretz, *Making It*, 201–4. The remark about powerlessness is from an interview, May 5, 2005.

12. Podhoretz, *Making It*, 207–10. The piece on Spinoza was by Felix Weltsch, "The Perennial Spinoza," *Commentary*, May 1956:448–53.

13. It was at 315 West 106th Street. In April 1961, they moved to 924 West End Avenue, on the corner of 105th, near tiny Strauss Park and a block east of Riverside Drive. "The building is so grand that now it would cost three million to buy the gigantic apartment we lived in: it had a huge living room with glass doors opening onto a large dining room – a perfect space for parties and we had a lot of them," Midge would remark. Luckily, it was rent-controlled: they began by paying $200-something a month, and fifteen years on were paying $300-something – at which point they bought the apartment for $5,000, "an unbelievable price" (Decter interview, February 2004). It was Murray Kempton, as John Podhoretz would later remark, who "cracked that only my father would think that 'making it' meant having an apartment on 105th and West End – because Murray Kempton lived on 103rd and West End" (John Podhoretz, interview with the author, April 14, 2004).

14. Norman Podhoretz and Midge Decter, "Two on an Island," interview with Jan Cherubin, *New York Daily News*, November 20, 1980.

15. Wheldon and Wheldon, *Wheldon Letters*, October 17, 1956.

16. Allen Barra, "Toots Shor's Sweet Sanctuary," review of the documentary film "Toots," *Wall Street Journal*, September 13, 2007:D7.

17. Podhoretz, *Making It*, 226–30.

18. Norman Podhoretz, interview with the author, April 17, 2004.

19. Podhoretz, *Making It*, 233. See Hannah Arendt, Mary McCarthy, and Carol Brightman, *Between Friends: The Correspondence of Hannah Arendt and Mary McCarthy, 1949–1975*, ed. Carol Brightman (New York: Harcourt Brace, 1995), 50; and Elisabeth Young-Bruehl, *Hannah Arendt: For Love of the World* (New Haven, Conn.: Yale University Press, 1982), 314.

20. Podhoretz, *Making It*, 235.

21. Podhoretz, "The Know-Nothing Bohemians," in *Doings and Undoings*, 143–58, reprinted in Jeffers, *The Norman Podhoretz Reader*, 29–40.

22. *Commentary* Archive, May 6, 1958.

23. Podhoretz, *Ex-Friends*, 32, quoting Allen Ginsberg, Barry Miles, and Carl Solomon, *Howl: Original Draft Facsimile, Transcript & Variant Versions, Fully Annotated by Author, with Contemporaneous Correspondence, Account of First Public Reading, Legal Skirmishes, Precursor Texts & Bibliography*, ed. Barry Miles (New York: Harper & Row, 1986).

24. Allen Ginsberg, Václav Havel, and David Carter, *Spontaneous Mind: Selected Interviews, 1958–1996*, ed. David Carter (New York: HarperCollins, 2001), 515–16.

25. See Podhoretz, *Ex-Friends*, 22–48.

26. Ginsberg, Havel, and Carter, *Spontaneous Mind*, 5.

27. Carl E. Rollyson, *The Lives of Norman Mailer: A Biography* (New York: Paragon House, 1991), 127–28.

28. Peter Manso, *Mailer, His Life and Times* (New York: Simon & Schuster, 1985), 264–65.

29. Wheldon and Wheldon, *Wheldon Letters*, February 9, 1959.

30. Podhoretz, *Doings and Undoings*, 187–204.
31. Manso, *Mailer*, 266.
32. Podhoretz, *Breaking Ranks*, 56–57.
33. Podhoretz and Trilling, *Trilling Papers*, August 22, 1959.
34. Hilary Mills, *Mailer, a Biography* (New York: Empire Books, Harper & Row, 1982), 187.
35. Manso, *Mailer*, 266.
36. Hilton Kramer, interview with the author, June 14, 2004.
37. Wheldon and Wheldon, *Wheldon Letters*, October 8, 1958.
38. Podhoretz, *My Love Affair with America*, 137.
39. Podhoretz, *Making It*, 250–52.
40. As Philip Roth wrote at the time, with such "theatrical *amor-vincit-omnia* boys," fifties novels were "like 'Dover Beach' ending happily for Matthew Arnold, and for us, because the poet is standing at the window with a woman who understands him." See Philip Roth, "Writing American Fiction," in *The Commentary Reader: Two Decades of Articles and Stories*, ed. Norman Podhoretz with an introduction by Alfred Kazin (New York: Atheneum, 1966), 595–609 at 599. Reprinted from *Commentary*, March 1961, 223–33. See also Thomas L. Jeffers, "What They Talked About When They Talked About Literature: *Commentary* in Its First Three Decades," in *Commentary in American Life*, ed. Murray Friedman (Philadelphia: Temple University Press, 2005), 99–126.
41. This comes from notes on Mailer's *Barbary Shore*, marked for "A chapter on Popular Culture, incorporating the TV piece and also using [David] Riesman or someone to show that the C-W [Cold War] feeling was a contraction. Each writer then becomes an example of someone resisting" (Podhoretz, *Podhoretz Papers*, n.d.).
42. Wheldon and Wheldon, *Wheldon Letters*, February 9, 1959.
43. Podhoretz, *Making It*, 270–72.
44. Arnold Beichman would recall how word of the suicide spread and people went to Cohen's apartment. "Shocked by the sight of the body," which was lying on the kitchen floor and couldn't be moved until the coroner arrived, Cohen's friends started "pouring themselves cocktails, and even bringing in roast beef sandwiches. At first, the conversation was about Cohen, but then it drifted to so and so's review of such and such, and so and so's essay about this and that" (David Brooks, "The Happy Cold Warrior: The First 90 Years of Arnold Beichman," *The Weekly Standard*, May 19, 2003:29).
45. Quoted in Rubenfeld, *Clement Greenberg*, 208–9. Clem later told the historian Alexander Bloom that he and Martin may have been "disgusted" with Podhoretz, who they thought lacked "convictions," but that "Norman happens to be a superb editor; he's done with *Commentary* what neither of us could have done – or would have done: in some part because we don't have his sheer ability, in other part because we didn't see magazine-editing as a career." See Alexander Bloom, *Prodigal Sons: The New York Intellectuals and Their World* (New York: Oxford University Press, 1986), 319.
46. Wheldon and Wheldon, *Wheldon Letters*, n.d. 1959.

Chapter 6. Boss

1. Mark Royden Winchell, *"Too Good to be True": The Life and Work of Leslie Fiedler* (Columbia: University of Missouri Press, 2002), 156–57.
2. *Commentary* Archive, letter to Richard Crossman, September 7, 1962.

3. Decter interview, May 6, 2005.
4. Kristol: "I told him 'Don't take it.' I remember it very well. He came in and said he had been offered the post, which didn't surprise me. But I wanted him to write directly for the *Reporter*, a regular column that would have paid him enough, a minimal salary anyhow. And I said 'Norman' – I was wrong about this, I swear, in all sorts of ways – 'The Jews as a subject are not so interesting anymore. The Holocaust is over, Israel is over – it's founded. You're better off writing as an intellectual on politics and literature for magazines and books. Then I think you could be the Edmund Wilson of your generation.' And he nodded solemnly, went out, and of course paid no attention" (Irving Kristol, interview with the author, May 19, 2003).
5. Podhoretz, *Making It*, 275–79.
6. Ibid., 288–89.
7. Ibid., 291–93. See also Bertram D. Wolfe, "Stalinism Versus Stalin," *Commentary*, June 1956:522–31; and his "The Durability of Soviet Despotism," *Commentary*, August 1957:93–104. That Wolfe, whose authority had been established in 1948 when he published the still-classic *Three Who Made a Revolution*, was correct in all essentials is confirmed by later histories that have had access to Soviet archives: see, for instance, Robert Service, *A History of Twentieth-Century Russia* (Cambridge, Mass.: Harvard University Press, 1998), 338–42.
8. Podhoretz, *Making It*, 294–95.
9. Podhoretz, interview with the author, June 15, 2004.
10. "Nobby" Brown's *Life Against Death* had sold perhaps 500 copies in its Wesleyan University Press edition. Epstein had glanced at the book and given it to Podhoretz, who read it with excitement and passed it along to Trilling. Struck by its radical (not to say fanciful) reinterpretation of Freud, Trilling wrote a long introduction to the reprinting Epstein brought out at Random House, and the book, like Goodman's, became in the sixties a countercultural vade mecum.
11. Podhoretz interview, June 13–15, 2004.
12. See Podhoretz, *Breaking Ranks*, 171.
13. See Norman Podhoretz, "The Issue," *Commentary*, February 1960:184.
14. Podhoretz, *Doings and Undoings*, 107–11.
15. Podhoretz interview, May 5, 2005.
16. Podhoretz, *Breaking Ranks*, 30; Podhoretz interview, June 15, 2004.
17. D. W. Brogan, "Unmanned Americans," *Guardian*, March 3, 1961.
18. Podhoretz, *Podhoretz Papers*, March 8, 1960 (carbons of letters between Mayer, Kristol, and Epstein).
19. *Commentary* Archive, March 26, 1960.
20. Ibid., June 10, 1960.
21. Podhoretz, *Making It*, 313.
22. Podhoretz, *Breaking Ranks*, 111.
23. Oscar Gass, "The New Frontier Fulfilled," *Commentary*, December 1961:467.
24. Podhoretz, *Podhoretz Papers*, January 7, 1964.
25. Wheldon and Wheldon, *Wheldon Letters*, May 21, 1964.
26. Podhoretz, *Podhoretz Papers*, June 5, 1964.
27. *Commentary* Archive, July 15, 1964.
28. Ibid., August 31, 1964.
29. Ibid., June 13, 1960.
30. Jason Epstein, "Living in New York," *New York Review of Books*, January 6, 1966. http://www.nybooks.com/articles/12623.

31. Decter, interview with the author, April 11, 2004.
32. Podhoretz interview, April 17, 2004. Columbia published Thompson's *The Founding of English Metre* in 1961; a volume of poems, *The Talking Girl*, came out from a small press in Cambridge in 1968.
33. *Commentary* Archive, December 21, 1960.
34. Wheldon and Wheldon, *Wheldon Letters*, February 24, 1961.
35. Ibid., April 27, 1961.
36. Ibid., October 21, 1961.
37. *Commentary* Archive, November 9, 1961.
38. Staughton Lynd, "How the Cold War Began," *Commentary*, November 1960:379–89.
39. Podhoretz, *Breaking Ranks*, 189. Lynd soon enough brought his allegiances into the open, asking in 1965 why anyone should consider it "immoral to desire a Vietcong victory." Weren't the Vietcong like America's Founders in wanting "literally, liberty or death"? In fact, as Irving Howe pointed out, the Lynd-Vietcong concept of liberty was antithetical to that of the Founders. See Staughton Lynd and Irving Howe, "An Exchange on Vietnam," *New York Review of Books*, December 23, 1965. http://www.nybooks.com/articles/12642.
40. H. Stuart Hughes, "The Strategy of Deterrence," *Commentary*, March 1961:185–92.
41. Sidney H. Hook, Stuart Hughes, Hans J. Morgenthau, and C. P. Snow, "Western Values and Total War," *Commentary*, October 1961:277–304.
42. Podhoretz, *Podhoretz Papers*, to Robert M. Wool, editor at *Show*, June 11, 1962.
43. Podhoretz, interview with the author, June 15, 2004.
44. See C. H. Rolph, ed., *The Trial of Lady Chatterley: Regina v. Penguin Books Limited: The Transcript of the Trial*, with a new foreword for this thirtieth anniversary edition by Geoffrey Robertson, with illustrations by Paul Hogarth and a selection of cartoons (London: Penguin Books, 1961); and, for a critical assessment, F. R. Leavis, "The Orthodoxy of Enlightenment," in *Anna Karenina and Other Essays* (New York: Simon & Schuster, 1969), 235–41. Reprint of "The New Orthodoxy," *Spectator*, February 1961:229–30.
45. Podhoretz and Trilling, *Trilling Papers*, December 30, 1950.
46. Paul Goodman, "Pornography, Art, and Censorship," *Commentary*, March 1961:203–12.
47. This eighteen-page typescript (n.d., probably 1961), which he never published, is among the *Podhoretz Papers*.
48. Wheldon and Wheldon, *Wheldon Letters*, September 12, 1964.
49. Ted Solotaroff, *First Loves: A Memoir* (New York: Seven Stories Press, 2003), 257–59.
50. Ibid., 260–61.
51. Ibid., 279–80.
52. Wheldon and Wheldon, *Wheldon Letters*, December 1, 1962.
53. Wheldon and Wheldon, *Wheldon Letters*, November 1962.
54. Podhoretz, *Making It*, 337.
55. Tom Hayden, "The Project Begins (from *Revolution in Mississippi*)," in *Reporting Civil Rights*, Vol. 1 (New York: Library of America, 2003), 619–26. Originally appeared in 1962.
56. Podhoretz interview, June 15, 2004. See also Podhoretz, *Breaking Ranks*, 198.

57. Tom Hayden to *Commentary* editors, *Commentary* Archive (n.d. [August 1961]).
58. See Tom Hayden, "Who Are the Student Boat-Rockers?" *Mademoiselle*, August 1961:236–39, 333–37.
59. *Commentary* Archive, August 24, 1961.
60. Dennis H. Wrong, "The American Left and Cuba," *Commentary*, February 1962:100–2.
61. Podhoretz, *Breaking Ranks*, 199–201.
62. Nathan Glazer, "The New Left and Its Limits," *Commentary*, July 1968:31–39.
63. See Lionel Trilling, "On the Teaching of Modern Literature," in *Beyond Culture: Essays on Literature and Learning* (New York: Harcourt Brace Jovanovich, 1978), 3–27. Originally appeared in 1961.
64. Fred Kaplan, *Gore Vidal: A Biography* (New York: Doubleday, 1999), 522.
65. Podhoretz interview, April 17, 2004. See Podhoretz, *Breaking Ranks*, 204.
66. *Commentary* Archive, August 10, 1962.
67. Podhoretz, *Podhoretz Papers*. The interview, intended for *The Writer Speaks* series, doesn't appear to have been published.
68. Podhoretz, *Making It*, 318. This gave Glazer the title for his 1970 book *Remembering the Answers: Essays on the American Student Revolt*.
69. *Commentary* Archive, November 17, 1960.
70. Michael Schumacher, *Dharma Lion: A Critical Biography of Allen Ginsberg* (New York: St. Martin's Press, 1992), 341–42.
71. Decter observed that Mailer "invents a lady character and then marries someone who has to play this role. Adele was cast as the primitive Indian [like Elena Esposito in *The Deer Park*] when in fact she was actually a girl from Brooklyn who wanted to be a painter" (quoted in Rollyson, *The Lives of Norman Mailer*, 141).
72. Ibid., 137.
73. Ibid., 136–41.
74. Quoted phrases from ibid., 168–69.
75. Podhoretz, *Ex-Friends*, 201, quoting Diana Trilling in reference to Lionel.
76. *Commentary* Archive, November 23, 1960.
77. Ibid., November 26, 1960.
78. Wheldon and Wheldon, *Wheldon Letters*, February 24, 1961. As Joseph Epstein would remark, it was nice that Mailer came around to accepting "responsibility" for stabbing his wife, or later for praising the writing of a criminal, Jack Henry Abbott, who upon release from prison in 1981 killed a man. "Responsibility?" Epstein said. "What about *blame*?" (Joseph Epstein, interview with the author, September 17, 2004).

Chapter 7. "This Was Bigger than Both of Us"

1. *Commentary* Archive, July 14, 1961.
2. Ibid., July 18, 22, 26, 1961.
3. Ibid., September 12, 1961. See Dan Jacobson, "James Baldwin as Spokesman," *Commentary*, December 1961:497–502; and, much earlier, his wonderful "A White Liberal Trapped by His Prejudices," *Commentary*, May 1953:454–59.
4. William J. Weatherby, *James Baldwin, Artist on Fire: A Portrait* (New York: D. I. Fine, 1989), 204, 209; and James Campbell, *Talking at the Gates: A Life of James Baldwin* (New York: Viking, 1991), 225.

5. Podhoretz, *Making It*, 339–42.
6. James Baldwin, "The Fire Next Time: Down at the Cross: Letter from a Region in My Mind," in *Reporting Civil Rights*, Vol. 1 (New York: Library of America, 2003), 710–61. Originally appeared in 1962.
7. *Commentary* Archive, December 9, 1962.
8. Podhoretz, *Making It*, 339–43.
9. Wheldon and Wheldon, *Wheldon Letters*, December 1, 1962.
10. Norman Podhoretz, "Postscript to the Touchstone Edition," in *Why We Were in Vietnam* (New York: Simon & Schuster, Touchstone, 1982), 92–96.
11. Alexis de Tocqueville, *Democracy in America*, trans. Arthur Goldhammer (New York: Library of America, 2004), 411–12.
12. Norman Podhoretz, "My Negro Problem – and Ours," in *Doings and Undoings*, 354–71, reprinted in *The Norman Podhoretz Reader*, 53–65.
13. James Baldwin, Fred L. Standley, and Louis H. Pratt, "Disturber of the Peace: James Baldwin, an Interview," interviewers Eve and Nancy Lynch Auchincloss, in *Conversations with James Baldwin*, ed. Fred L. Standley, Literary Conversations Series (Jackson: University Press of Mississippi, 1989), 66. Originally appeared in 1969.
14. Podhoretz and Trilling, *Trilling Papers*, January 5, 1963.
15. *Commentary* Archive, January 16, 25, 31, 1963.
16. Paul Goodman, "Letters from Readers, 'My Negro Problem' – I." *Commentary*, April 1963:343.
17. Burton Raffel, "Letters from Readers, 'My Negro Problem' – I." *Commentary*, April 1963:346.
18. Norman Podhoretz, "Postscript to 'My Negro Problem – and Ours,'" in *Blacks and Jews: Alliances and Arguments*, ed. by Paul Berman (New York: Delacourt, 1993), 96.
19. Lorraine Hansberry, "Letters from Readers, 'My Negro Problem' – II." *Commentary*, May 1963:430.
20. Podhoretz, *Breaking Ranks*, 141–43. It hadn't been long since the Podhoretzes and Carmichael were on friendly terms: Israeli writer Hanoch Bartov recalled being told by Decter that "they gave Stokely one of their cradles for his new baby" (Hanoch Bartov, interview with the author, April 22, 2004).
21. *Commentary* Archive, March 7, 1963.
22. Ibid., March 18, 1963.
23. Irving Howe, "Black Boys and Native Sons," *Dissent*, Autumn 1963: 353–68, reprinted with afterwords in Irving Howe, *Selected Writings, 1950–1990* (San Diego: Harcourt Brace Jovanovich, 1990), 119–39.
24. *Commentary* Archive, November 4 and 16, 1964.
25. Edmund Wilson, *The Sixties: The Last Journal, 1960–1972*, ed. and introduction by Lewis M. Dabney (New York: Farrar, Straus & Giroux, 1993), 205–6.
26. Podhoretz, *Podhoretz Papers*, July 6, 1964.
27. *Commentary* Archive, February 18, 1963.
28. Podhoretz, *Making It*, 346.
29. Hannah Arendt, *Eichmann in Jerusalem: A Report on the Banality of Evil*, revised and enlarged edition (New York: Viking, 1965), 123, 125. Originally published in 1963.
30. Podhoretz, *Podhoretz Papers*, September 8, 1958.
31. *Commentary* Archive, March 19, April 3, August 31, 1963.
32. Ibid., July 9, 1963.

33. Norman Podhoretz, "Hannah Arendt on Eichmann: A Study in the Perversity of Brilliance," in *Doings and Undoings*, 335–53, reprinted as "Hannah Arendt on Eichmann" in *The Norman Podhoretz Reader*, 66–79.

34. *Commentary* Archive, September 5 and 10, 1963.

35. Ibid., September 6, 1963. For an attempt at mediation between Arendt and her critics, see Dwight Macdonald's *Partisan Review* piece, "Hannah Arendt and the Jewish Establishment" (Spring 1964), reprinted in Dwight Macdonald, *Discriminations: Essays & Afterthoughts, 1938–1974* (New York: Grossman, 1974), 308–17. Though announcing that he was neither German nor Jewish but disinterested, Macdonald was decidedly friendly toward Arendt.

36. Podhoretz, *Ex-Friends*, 172; Podhoretz, *Breaking Ranks*, 163.

37. *Commentary* Archive, November 23, 1963.

38. Podhoretz, *Podhoretz Papers*, December 11, 1963, in response to a query from the Department of Cultural Affairs at the Organization of American States.

39. Ibid., December 21, 1964.

40. Podhoretz, *Podhoretz Papers*, February 16, 1965.

41. Wheldon and Wheldon, *Wheldon Letters*, March 9, 1965.

42. Podhoretz, *Podhoretz Papers*, March 1, 1965.

43. Willie Morris, *New York Days* (Boston: Little, Brown and Co., 1993), 193.

44. Wilson, *The Sixties*, 497–98.

45. Wheldon and Wheldon, *Wheldon Letters*, n. d. (April 1965).

46. Podhoretz, *Podhoretz Papers*, n.d. (1965).

47. Podhoretz, *Breaking Ranks*, 243–44.

48. Podhoretz, *Podhoretz Papers*, n.d. (1965).

49. Wheldon and Wheldon, *Wheldon Letters*, November 29, 1960.

50. Ibid., June 25, 1963.

51. Ibid., September 12, 1964.

52. Ibid.

53. Ibid., n.d. (1963?).

54. Ibid., August 5 (1965).

55. Ibid., September 13–14, 1965.

56. Manso, *Mailer*, 431.

57. Podhoretz, *Podhoretz Papers*, April 12, 1963.

58. Podhoretz, *Breaking Ranks*, 49.

59. Mills, *Mailer*, 321.

60. Ibid., 223–24.

61. Podhoretz, *Ex-Friends*, 196.

62. Norman Mailer, *The Armies of the Night* (New York: New American Library, 1968), 113.

63. See Podhoretz, *Ex-Friends*, 195–200.

64. Ibid., 204–6.

65. Wheldon and Wheldon, *Wheldon Letters*, August 5, 1964.

66. Allen Ginsberg and Bill Morgan, *Deliberate Prose: Selected Essays, 1952–1995*, ed. Bill Morgan (New York: HarperCollins, 2000), 114–15.

67. Podhoretz, *Podhoretz Papers*, June 3, 1966, writing to Elliot Charney.

68. "The Press." *Time*, May 20, 1966:58.

69. *Commentary* Archive, December 1, 1966. Breslin said the typesetter had made a mistake, but Podhoretz "always suspected that the typesetter was being blamed for Breslin's ignorance in transcribing a word he had never heard before" (Podhoretz, *Breaking Ranks*, 232).

70. Marvin Mudrick, _On Culture and Literature_ (New York: Horizon Press, 1970), 270–71.
71. Benjamin DeMott, "City Light," review of _Doings and Undoings_ by Norman Podhoretz, _New York Review of Books_, April 30, 1964. Nybooks.com/articles/13374.
72. _Commentary_ Archive, May 5, 1964.
73. Podhoretz, _Making It_, 350–51. Of the positive reviews of _Doings_, the most intelligent was by Ihab Hassan in the _Virginia Quarterly_ 40 (Summer 1964), 494, with an apt collocation of adjectives (shrewd, effortless, noisy, honest, undaunted, cantankerous, cerebral, charming, self-ironic) and a recognition that Podhoretz's eye was focused not on apocalypse but on the "life of reason in society." See also Frank Kermode in _Book Week_ (March 29, 1964), 3, in praise of Podhoretz's "humanely intelligent personality"; David Daiches in the _Times Book Review_ (March 29, 1964), 5, welcoming a mind "honest without any trace of exhibitionism, nourished by three pasts (the American, the European and the Jewish) and critically yet positively responsive to all the disturbing variety of the present." A mixed review came from Renata Adler in the _New Yorker_ (July 4, 1964), 60, disparaging, like Mudrick and DeMott, the "everyone I know" insider tone of the New York critics generally yet lauding Podhoretz as "a young man more interested in interpreting books than in pitting himself against them."
74. Podhoretz, _Doings and Undoings_, 6–8. "There are a lot of people you have to kill when you are young and you've made your mark early," Arnold Beichman told Alexander Bloom, adding that Podhoretz's hit-list included "Trilling, Hook, Bell, and Elliot Cohen." Bloom retails Daniel Bell's story that, during a dinner party in the early sixties, Podhoretz challenged Sidney Hook with "You call yourself a Socialist?" in such an abusive tone that Trilling walked out of the room. (Podhoretz denied the occurrence of such an incident.) On another occasion, Diana Trilling recalled, "I could see that it was taking a great effort for Lionel to keep himself under control, but he spoke very quietly to Norman and said he was sure they could find some basic premise in common and start off from there. To this Norman replied very violently that they had nothing in common!" (see Bloom, _Prodigal Sons_, 323). Bell's reminiscences are repeated and embellished in Sidney Blumenthal, _The Rise of the Counter-Establishment: From Conservative Ideology to Political Power_ (New York: Times Books, 1986), 133–47, an envenomed treatment. A similarly Freudian family romance has been sketched by Jacob Heilbrunn, who asserts that by taking _Commentary_ to the left Podhoretz was rebelling against both Trilling and the "editorial tyrant" Elliot Cohen. See Jacob Heilbrunn, _They Knew They Were Right: The Rise of the Neocons_ (New York: Doubleday, 2008), 78.
75. Podhoretz and Trilling, _Trilling Papers_, February 15, 1964. Trilling had reason to believe the "revisionist liberalism" label would send a possibly harmful hum along the wires. Beichman, while hardly defending Trilling, Bell, and Hofstadter, would call it a "quasi-Marxist epithet" redolent of "passé sectarianism," and would challenge Podhoretz to produce his own ideology. See Arnold Beichman, "Critic in Search of His Credo," review of _Doings and Undoings_ by Norman Podhoretz, _Christian Science Monitor_, April 23, 1964:11.

Chapter 8. One Shoe Drops

1. Morris, _New York Days_, 104; Podhoretz, _Breaking Ranks_, 152.
2. Morris, _New York Days_, 192.

3. Ibid.
4. Podhoretz, *Breaking Ranks*, 160, 148.
5. Ibid., 232–33.
6. Wheldon and Wheldon, *Wheldon Letters*, March 29, 1971.
7. Podhoretz, *Breaking Ranks*, 153; Podhoretz interview, June 5, 2004.
8. Morris, *New York Days*, 194.
9. Wheldon and Wheldon, *Wheldon Letters*, August 5, 1964.
10. *Commentary* Archive, August 15, 1966.
11. David Lehman, "Norman Podhoretz at 55: He'd Rather be Right," *Columbia College Today*, Winter 1985:16.
12. Podhoretz, *Podhoretz Papers*, January 25, 1966, writing to request scholarship aid from the school.
13. Ibid., n.d.
14. Ibid., February 24, 1967.
15. Wilson, *The Sixties*, 568.
16. Daphne Merkin, "Getting Even," review of *Ex-Friends* by Norman Podhoretz, *New Yorker*, March 22, 1999:167.
17. Richard Poirier, "Big Pod," review of *Ex-Friends* by Norman Podhoretz, *London Review of Books*, September 2, 1999:22.
18. Decter saying that she "never interfere[d] with these things," Diana "then turned to Norman and asked him what in the world other than something wrong with the book itself would make three such totally different people as Roger Straus, Jason Epstein, and Lionel Trilling all agree that the book shouldn't be published. To this Podhoretz answered without hesitation, 'Oh, I've thought about that – Class!' It was surely the only time Lionel was ever put in the same economic class with Roger Straus!" (Diana Trilling, quoted in Bloom, *Prodigal Sons*, 361; also see 363). What Podhoretz was probably thinking about was something else: how the benign "young man from the provinces" suddenly becomes the counter-jumping arriviste when he starts revealing the darker goings-on of the metropolis. The punishment is to demote him back to the class he came from.
19. *Commentary* Archive, November 30, August 30, December 7, 1967.
20. Ibid., March 28, 1967.
21. Podhoretz, *Podhoretz Papers*, October 1, 1967.
22. Ibid., January 16, 1967.
23. Merle Miller, "Why Norman and Jason Aren't Talking," *New York Times Magazine*, March 26, 1972:109.
24. Joseph Epstein, e-mail to the author, June 10, 2006, and interview, September 17, 2004.
25. Hilton Kramer, interview, June 14, 2004.
26. Edgar Z. Friedenberg, "Du Côté de Chez Podhoretz," review of *Making It* by Norman Podhoretz, *New York Review of Books*, February 1, 1968. Nybooks.com/articles/11810.
27. Wilfrid Sheed, "*Making It* in the Big City," review of *Making It* by Norman Podhoretz, *Atlantic Monthly*, April 1968:97–102.
28. Podhoretz to Beichman, *Commentary* Archive, February 19, 1975.
29. Manso, *Mailer*, 472.
30. Norman Mailer, *Existential Errands* (Boston: Little, Brown, 1972), 171–97.
31. Podhoretz, *Breaking Ranks*, 263–67. This is reprised in Podhoretz, *Ex-Friends*, 218–20.

32. Manso, *Mailer*, 474–75.
33. Mary V. Dearborn, *Mailer, a Biography* (Boston: Houghton Mifflin, 1999), 250.
34. Rebecca West, "Oh Why Is Success a Dirty Word?" review of *Making It* by Norman Podhoretz, *Sunday Telegraph*, September 1, 1968.
35. *Commentary* Archive, February 6, 1968. The reminder of Holmes's dictum was recalled by Beichman in an interview (Arnold Beichman, interview with the author, February 12, 2004).
36. *Commentary* Archive, November 29, 1968.
37. Podhoretz, *Podhoretz Papers*, February 2, 1968.
38. Jacobson interview.
39. Rachel Abrams, interview with the author, May 21, 2003.
40. *Commentary* Archive, to Ronnie Dugger, April 19, 1967.
41. See three earlier pieces he had published on Vietnam: Hans J. Morgenthau, "Asia: The American Algeria," *Commentary*, July 1961:43–47; Joseph J. Zasloff, "The Problem of South Viet Nam," *Commentary*, February 1962:126–35; and Hans J. Morgenthau, "Vietnam – Another Korea?" *Commentary*, May 1962:369–74.
42. *Commentary* Archive, April 21, 1967.
43. Ibid., May 3, 1967.
44. Ibid., September 7 and 11, 1968.
45. Podhoretz, *Breaking Ranks*, 35.
46. Podhoretz, *Podhoretz Papers*, April 21 and May 1, 1967 (carbons of these letters were sent to him).
47. Podhoretz, *Breaking Ranks*, 256–57.
48. See ibid., 262–63.
49. Podhoretz, *Podhoretz Papers*, to his agent, Candida Donadio, September 21, 1969.
50. James Baldwin, *Collected Essays* (New York: Library of America, 1998), 739–48.
51. Podhoretz, *Podhoretz Papers*, April 1967.
52. *Commentary* Archive, to Robert Blauner, a sociologist at Berkeley, August 14, 1967.
53. Ibid., to Jervis Anderson, August 22, 1968.
54. Ibid., November 14 and 15, 1968. See respectively Earl Raab, "The Black Revolution and the Jewish Question"; Maurice J. Goldbloom, "The New York School Crisis"; and Murray Friedman, "Is White Racism the Problem?" in *Commentary*, January 1969:23–33, 43–58, 61–65.
55. *Commentary* Archive, January 28, 1969.
56. Ibid., February 13, 1969.
57. Theodore Draper, "The Fantasy of Black Nationalism," *Commentary*, September 1969:27–54.
58. *Commentary* Archive, June 7, 1967.
59. Ibid., June 30, 1967. On a more practical level, Podhoretz had mentioned to Lichtheim that since the start of the war American Jews had raised "something like a quarter of a billion dollars . . . and an ultimate, and no doubt attainable, goal of a billion" (ibid., June 20, 1967).
60. Ibid., July 2, 1967.
61. Ibid., August 9, 1967.
62. Ibid., October 2, 1967.
63. Ibid., October 17, 1967.
64. Emil L. Fackenheim, "Jewish Faith and the Holocaust: A Fragment," *Commentary*, August 1968:32–33.
65. *Commentary* Archive, February 7, 1969.

66. Beverly Kempton and David Gelman, "Podhoretz on Intellectuals," Interview, *Manhattan Tribune*, February 1, 1969:4–5.

Chapter 9. Dropping the Other Shoe

1. Wilson interview.
2. Podhoretz interview, July 15–16, 2004.
3. Podhoretz interview, June 13–15, 2004.
4. Decter interview, April 11, 2004.
5. John Podhoretz, interview with the author, April 14, 2004.
6. Wheldon and Wheldon, *Wheldon Letters*, August 3, 1970.
7. *Commentary* Archive, to David Bazelon, May 13, 1970.
8. Ibid., December 16, 1970.
9. Neal Kozodoy, interview with the author, May 19, 2005.
10. *Commentary* Archive, December 28, 1970.
11. Dennis H. Wrong, "The Case of the 'New York Review,'" *Commentary*, November 1970:49–63.
12. Norman Podhoretz, "The Idea of Crisis," *Commentary*, November 1970: 4; Peter Coleman, "Right Turn: Norman Podhoretz and Neo-Conservatism," review of *Breaking Ranks* by Norman Podhoretz, *Quadrant*, June 1980:44–46.
13. *Commentary* Archive, October 22, 1970.
14. Ibid., October 27, 1970.
15. Ibid., December 3, 1970.
16. Ibid., n.d. [January] and January 19, 1971.
17. Wheldon and Wheldon, *Wheldon Letters*, March 29, 1971.
18. *Commentary* Archive, March 12, 1971.
19. Ibid., March 26, 1971.
20. Jason Epstein, "Journal Du Voyeur," review of *Radical Chic and Mau-Mauing the Flak Catchers* by Tom Wolfe, *New York Review of Books*, December 17, 1970. http://www.nybooks.com/articles/10715.
21. Joseph Epstein, "The Party's Over," review of *Radical Chic and Mau-Mauing the Flak Catchers* by Tom Wolfe, *Commentary*, March 1971:102.
22. Jason Epstein, "The Issue at Ocean Hill," *New York Review of Books*, November 21, 1968. http://www.nybooks.com/articles/11494.
23. Norman Podhoretz, "A Certain Anxiety," *Commentary*, August 1971:8.
24. Peter Kihss, "Moynihan Scores Ethnic Quota Idea," *New York Times*, June 5, 1968:29.
25. *Commentary* Archive (copy), August 18, 1971.
26. Stephen Steinberg, "How Jewish Quotas Began," *Commentary*, September 1971: 67–76.
27. *Commentary* Archive, September 13 and 15, 1971. Peterson's observation about the WASP-ish New Left would be part of Decter's contention in *Liberal Parents, Radical Children* (New York: Coward, McCann & Geoghegan, 1975).
28. *Commentary* Archive, October 8, 1971.
29. Podhoretz, *Breaking Ranks*, 302. For Rexroth, see 143.
30. *Commentary* Archive, to Paul McGouldrick at SUNY-Binghamton, October 8, 1971.
31. Norman Podhoretz, Thomas Bergin, and Red Smith, "Sports in America – Larger Than Life," *Yale Reports*, November 26, 1972:3.

32. Podhoretz, *Podhoretz Papers*, "Unpublished and Uncompleted Early Draft of Book on 60's." Subsequent quotations in this section, unless otherwise indicated, are from this typescript.
33. See Podhoretz, *Breaking Ranks*, 293–94.
34. See Ibid., 135–36.
35. Cf. ibid., 164–65.
36. Tom Milstein, "A Perspective on the Panthers," *Commentary*, September 1970:35–43.
37. Alexander M. Bickel, "Judging the Chicago Trial," *Commentary*, January 1971:31–40.
38. Norman Podhoretz, "Revolutionary Suicide," *Commentary*, September 1970:23.
39. John Earl Haynes, Alexander Vassiliev, and Harvey Klehr, "I. F. Stone, Soviet Agent–Case Closed," *Commentary*, May 2009:40–44.
40. I. F. Stone, "Holy War," *New York Review of Books*, August 3, 1967. http://www.nybooks.com/articles/12009.
41. Podhoretz, "A Certain Anxiety," 4.

Chapter 10. Liberalism Lost

1. Richard Schechner, ed., "*Marat/Sade* Forum," [Peter Brook, Geraldine Lust, Leslie Fiedler, and Norman Podhoretz], *Tulane Drama Review*, Summer 1966:217–23.
2. *Commentary* Archive, to Edward Grossman, September 2, 1970.
3. Ibid., March 11, 1971.
4. Ibid., November 4 and 25, 1970.
5. Norman Podhoretz, "The Literary Light as Eternal Flame," *Saturday Review*, August 24, 1974:90–98.
6. *Commentary* Archive, December 26, 1974.
7. Norman Podhoretz, "In Defense of Editing," *Harper's*, October 1965:143–47.
8. *Commentary* Archive (copies), September 4 and 8, 1969.
9. Ibid., November 8, 1969. Ozick sent a copy to Podhoretz, who told her "Phil Roth . . . isn't normally so generous" (ibid., December 10, 1969).
10. Ozick interview.
11. *Commentary* Archive, March 31, 1976.
12. Ibid., October 19, 1976.
13. Ibid., August 9, 1977.
14. Ibid., December 9, 1970.
15. Ibid., October 18, 1971. See Nathan Glazer, "On Being Deradicalized," *Commentary*, October 1970:74–80.
16. See Dwight Macdonald, "Scrambled Eggheads on the Right," *Commentary*, April 1956:367–73. The delightful title was Podhoretz's idea.
17. "Split in the Family?" *National Review*, December 15, 1970:1335.
18. Norman Podhoretz, "Laws, Kings, and Cures," *Commentary*, October 1970:31.
19. Eugene Goodheart, "The Deradicalized Intellectuals," *Nation*, February 8, 1971:177–80.
20. *Commentary* Archive, February 14, 1973.
21. Joseph Epstein, "The New Conservatism: Intellectuals in Retreat," *Dissent*, Spring 1973:151–62.
22. Dan Himmelfarb, "Conservative Splits," *Commentary*, May 1988:56, 58. Dan Himmelfarb was the son of Milton Himmelfarb; Irving Kristol was his uncle,

Gertrude Himmelfarb his aunt. On the period of label anxiety, and on the emergence of neoconservatives out of liberalism's war with the New Left, see also John Ehrman, *The Rise of Neoconservatism: Intellectuals and Foreign Affairs, 1945–1994* (New Haven, Conn.: Yale University Press, 1995), especially 33–62; and Mark Gerson, *The Neoconservative Vision: From the Cold War to the Culture Wars* (Lanham, Md.: Madison Books, 1996), 1–29.

23. *Commentary* Archive, to Beichman, August 2, 1972.
24. Donald M. Blinken et al., "Proceedings of the Dinner in Honor of Norman Podhoretz on His Twenty-Fifth Anniversary as Editor of *Commentary*," privately published for the occasion (New York: American Jewish Committee, 1985).
25. Norman Podhoretz, "Speech at Socialist Party USA Convention," *Podhoretz Papers*, 1970.
26. Decter interview, April 4, 2004.
27. Norman Podhoretz, "Between Nixon and the New Politics," *Commentary*, September 1972:8.
28. Decter interview, April 11, 2004.
29. *Commentary* Archive, November 1972.
30. See Podhoretz, *Breaking Ranks*, 291.
31. Norman Podhoretz, "Old-Fashioned Values Are Coming Back," *U.S. News & World Report*, December 24, 1979:58.
32. Decter interview, April 11, 2004.
33. Podhoretz and Trilling, *Trilling Papers*, December 14, 1971.
34. *Commentary* Archive, Beichman to Diana Trilling, May 14, 1979.
35. Podhoretz, *Breaking Ranks*, 297.
36. *Commentary* Archive, November 18, 1978.
37. Alvin B. Kernan, *The Death of Literature* (New Haven, Conn.: Yale University Press, 1990), 63.
38. Podhoretz, *Breaking Ranks*, 297, 303, 300.
39. Edward Grossman et al., "Culture and the Present Moment," *Commentary*, December 1974:45–46.
40. See Krupnick, *Lionel Trilling*, 156, 149.
41. Podhoretz, *Ex-Friends*, 90.
42. *Commentary* Archive, January 12, 1976.
43. Podhoretz, *Ex-Friends*, 92–102.

Chapter 11. George Lichtheim, Pat Moynihan, and a Lecture Tour

1. *Commentary* Archive, January 11, 1972.
2. Rachel Abrams interview.
3. Naomi Munson, interview with the author, May 20, 2003.
4. Podhoretz interview, April 17, 2004.
5. *Commentary* Archive, November 10, 1972.
6. Ibid., January 3, 1973.
7. Ibid., April 21, 1973.
8. Gross interview. These paragraphs rely also on Walter Laqueur, "George Lichtheim, 1912–1973," *Commentary*, August 1973:45–52.
9. *Commentary* Archive, March 2, 1972.
10. Leonard Garment, interview with the author, February 8, 2004.
11. *Commentary* Archive, February 21, 1963.

12. Nathan Glazer, "Daniel P. Moynihan on Ethnicity," in *Daniel Patrick Moynihan: The Intellectual in Public Life*, ed. Robert A. Katzmann (Washington, D.C./Baltimore: Woodrow Wilson Center Press/Johns Hopkins University Press, 1998), 15–16.

13. Especially good is Daniel P. Moynihan, "An Address to the Entering Class at Harvard College, 1972," *Commentary*, December 1972:55–60.

14. Podhoretz, *Podhoretz Papers*, August 26, 1972.

15. *Commentary* Archive, April 4, 1973.

16. Ibid., April 13, 1973.

17. Ibid., May 14, 1973.

18. Podhoretz, *Podhoretz Papers*.

19. Ibid., July 9 and 20, 1973.

20. Ibid., August 22 and July 30, 1973.

21. Later published as "Is America Falling Apart?" in the Australian journal *Quadrant*, December 1973:11–17.

22. Here conflating the diary and a letter to Decter (September 4, 1973).

23. As Glazer would later recall, the Moynihans "were mostly ensconced in the embassy – though Liz later developed an interest in Indian artists and architects. All their food was American, brought from the PX." Glazer and his wife, Logi, who is Indian, "were shocked, startled. They did put on a dinner for Logi's father, who had been involved in the freedom movement, and many of his friends, and it was the first time they let Indians into the embassy while they were there" (Nathan Glazer, interview with the author, March 3, 2004).

24. In the first two days alone, 2,000 Israeli soldiers were killed and 340 captured, forty-nine planes shot down, and 500 tanks destroyed. Hence the urgent calls from Jerusalem to Washington for emergency supplies, which, after Nixon swept aside bureaucratic obstacles, were airlifted by the Pentagon. See Norman Podhoretz, "Israel and the United States: A Complex History," *Commentary*, May 1998:34.

25. This and all the preceding quotations from the USIA trip journal are from the *Podhoretz Papers*.

Chapter 12. Domesticities, Lillian Hellman, and the Question of America's Nerve

1. Decter interview, February 2004.

2. Wheldon and Wheldon, *Wheldon Letters*, April 12, 1974.

3. Ibid., July 12, 1975.

4. Ibid., August 21, 1975.

5. Ibid., August 7, 1974.

6. Ibid., September 7, 1974.

7. Ibid., October 21, 1975.

8. Ibid., January 21, 1974.

9. Ibid., May 21, 1975.

10. Ibid., May 31, 1975.

11. Ibid., n.d. [1975].

12. See J. H. Plumb and Huw P. Wheldon, *Royal Heritage: The Treasures of the British Crown* (New York: Harcourt Brace Jovanovich, 1977).

13. Wheldon and Wheldon, *Wheldon Letters*, September 3, 1975.

14. Ibid., December 20, 1975.

15. Ibid., February 12, 1976.

16. Ibid., n.d. [August? 1976].

17. Ibid., October 5, 1976.

18. Podhoretz, *Breaking Ranks*, 317.

19. See Samuel McCracken, "'Julia' and Other Fictions by Lillian Hellman," *Commentary*, June 1984:35–43.

20. See William Wright, *Lillian Hellman: The Image, the Woman* (New York: Simon & Schuster, 1986), 365.

21. *Commentary* Archive, January 21, 1974.

22. Ibid., n.d.

23. Quotations in this section are, unless otherwise indicated, from Podhoretz, *Ex-Friends*, 103–38.

24. Robert W. Tucker, "Oil: The Issue of American Intervention," *Commentary*, January 1975:21–31.

25. Josiah Lee Auspitz et al., "America Now: A Failure of Nerve?" *Commentary*, July 1975:16–87.

26. *Commentary* Archive, to John Mack, February 26, 1976.

27. Podhoretz interview, July 15–16, 2004.

28. Daniel P. Moynihan, "Was Woodrow Wilson Right?" *Commentary*, May 1974: 25–31.

29. Daniel P. Moynihan, "The United States in Opposition," *Commentary*, March 1975:31–44.

30. Wheldon and Wheldon, *Wheldon Letters*, April 5, 1975.

Chapter 13. Moynihan, Podhoretz, and "the Party of Liberty"

1. Moynihan and Weaver, *Dangerous Place*, 49–50, 59.

2. Garment interview; Moynihan and Weaver, *Dangerous Place*, 60, 72. On these and other topics, see Leonard Garment, *Crazy Rhythm: My Journey from Brooklyn, Jazz, and Wall Street to Nixon's White House, Watergate, and Beyond* (Cambridge, Mass.: Da Capo Press, 2001). Originally published in 1997.

3. Garment interview.

4. Moynihan and Weaver, *Dangerous Place*, 48–49.

5. *Commentary* Archive, September 2, 1975.

6. Godfrey Hodgson, *The Gentleman from New York: Daniel Patrick Moynihan, a Biography* (Boston: Houghton Mifflin, 2000), 238.

7. Garment interview.

8. Moynihan and Weaver, *Dangerous Place*, 153–54. For Waldheim, see Simon Wiesenthal, *Justice, not Vengeance*, translated from the German by Ewald Osers (New York: Grove Weidenfeld, 1989); and Eli M. Rosenbaum and William Hoffer, *Betrayal: The Untold Story of the Kurt Waldheim Investigation and Cover-Up* (New York: St. Martin's Press, 1993).

9. Historians, revisionist or otherwise, usually offer more complicated and sometimes less forgiving accounts, but this is not the moment for summarizing them. See the above section on I. F. Stone; Paul Johnson, *A History of the Jews* (New York: Harper & Row, 1987), 433–47 (particularly the discussion of Vladimir Jabotinsky); Benny Morris, *The Birth of the Palestinian Refugee Problem Revisited,* Cambridge Middle East Studies (Cambridge: Cambridge University Press, 2004); or Benny Morris, *Righteous Victims: A History of the Zionist-Arab Conflict, 1881–2001* (New York: Vintage, 2001).

10. Only a few years before his death in 2003, while addressing a conference on accuracy in Middle East reporting, Moynihan granted, as Podhoretz related, "that his speech was indeed a great one, and *should* have been 'because Norman Podhoretz wrote it.' It's impossible to think of any other politician who'd make such an acknowledgement. An amazing gesture" (Podhoretz interview, July 15–16, 2004).

11. *Commentary* Archive, to Moynihan, November 6, 1975.

12. Moynihan and Weaver, *Dangerous Place*, 177.

13. Podhoretz, "Israel and the United States: A Complex History," 30.

14. Chaim Herzog, *Living History: A Memoir* (New York: Pantheon Books, 1996), 197–98.

15. Moynihan and Weaver, *Dangerous Place*, 184–85. Hodgson notes that sixteen years later the General Assembly would finally disembarrass itself, on this issue at least. President George H. W. Bush, with support from the European Community and even from the about-to-dissolve Soviet Union, called for a repeal of the infamous resolution. American diplomats actually twisted arms, telling their host governments that failure to vote for repeal would damage relations with the United States. And so, "On December 16, 1991, without fanfare, the General Assembly of the United Nations, by virtue of Resolution 4686, 'decides to revoke the determination contained in its Resolution 3379 of 10 November 1975'" (*Gentleman from New York*, 258).

    The U.N. might momentarily be disembarrassed, but the Left would continue to hawk the equation of Zionism and racism. See, for example, the stones of "apartheid," "racism," "colonialism," "victimizing," "ethnic cleansing," and "Judeo-Nazi" cast by contributors in Eugene L. Rogan and Avi Shlaim, eds., *The War for Palestine: Rewriting the History of 1948* (Cambridge: Cambridge University Press, 2001); and, from the Jewish Left in particular, pieces in *Wrestling with Zion: Progressive Jewish-American Responses to the Israeli-Palestinian Conflict*, edited and with an introduction by Tony Kushner and Alisa Solomon (New York: Grove Press, 2003).

16. Moynihan and Weaver, *Dangerous Place*, 188–89, 198–99.

17. Podhoretz interview, July 15–16, 2004; Podhoretz, *My Love Affair with America*, 182.

18. See Moynihan and Weaver, *Dangerous Place*, 213, 216–17, and Hodgson, *Gentleman from New York*, 225–26, 249, 251, for specific events leading up to Moynihan's resignation and Kissinger's role, or lack thereof, in them.

19. Podhoretz interview, July 15–16, 2004.

20. Norman Podhoretz, "Making the World Safe for Communism," *Commentary*, April 1976:35–38.

21. Nathan Glazer, "American Values & American Foreign Policy," *Commentary*, July 1976:34.

22. Podhoretz, "Making the World Safe for Communism," 39–41.

23. Podhoretz interview, July 15–16, 2004.

24. *Commentary* Archive, Abrams to Moynihan, June 30, 1976.

25. Wheldon and Wheldon, *Wheldon Letters*, September 28, 1976.

26. Podhoretz interview, July 15–16, 2004.

27. Ibid.

28. *Commentary* Archive, February 11, 1977.

29. Hodgson, *Gentleman from New York*, 282–83. Actually, Charles Horner, a Podhoretz protégé, wrote the *Newsweek* piece, "Will Russia Blow Up?" (November 19, 1979), 144, 147, building on Moynihan's analysis.

30. Hodgson, *Gentleman from New York*, 282.
31. "American Interests," Program 206 (December 14, 1982), Jefferson Communications, hosted by Peter F. Krogh and featuring Moynihan and Podhoretz (transcript in Podhoretz, *Podhoretz Papers*).
32. "Dialogue Forum Series," Center for Jewish History, featuring Podhoretz and moderated by William Berkowitz, October 25, 1982 (Podhoretz, *Podhoretz Papers*).
33. Norman Podhoretz, "Life of His Party," *National Review*, September 13, 1999: 50.
34. Podhoretz interview, July 15–16, 2004.

Chapter 14. Breaking and Closing Ranks

1. Norman Podhoretz, "The Abandonment of Israel," *Commentary*, July 1976:23–31.
2. *Commentary* Archive, September 1, 1976.
3. Quotations from Jimmy Carter, "Curb on Power to Make War," *New York Times*, March 6, 1977:30. Transcript of reply to question from phone caller No. 40.
4. *Commentary* Archive, July 30, 1979.
5. Norman Podhoretz, "Israel in Danger," interview with David Avidan, *Jerusalem Post* (Independence Day Supplement), April 20, 1977:11–13.
6. *Commentary* Archive, March 17, 1978. Beichman was quoting Brzezinski in an interview by Bernard Gwertzman in the *Times*, March 10, 1978.
7. *Commentary* Archive, March 23, 1978.
8. Norman Podhoretz, "The Subtle Collusion," transcript of contribution to Jerusalem Conference on International Terrorism, July 2–5, 1979, in *Terrorism and the Media: Abdication of Responsibility* (Jerusalem: Jonathan Institute, 1979), 22–27.
9. *Breaking Ranks* tells the story, from the inside, that writers like Peter Steinfels were beginning to understand had relevance to an entire generation of American intellectuals. See Peter Steinfels, *The Neoconservatives: The Men Who Are Changing America's Politics* (New York: Simon & Schuster, 1979).
10. Wheldon and Wheldon, *Wheldon Letters*, March 1 and April 6, 1979.
11. Podhoretz, *Podhoretz Papers*, July 5, 1979.
12. George F. Will, "Review of *Breaking Ranks*, by Norman Podhoretz," *Washington Post*, October 28, 1979:B7.
13. Joseph Epstein interview.
14. Joseph Epstein, "Remaking It," review of *Breaking Ranks* by Norman Podhoretz, *New York Times Book Review*, October 21, 1979:3ff.
15. Noel Annan, "An Editor and His Odyssey," review of *Breaking Ranks* by Norman Podhoretz, *Times Literary Supplement*, April 25, 1980:473.
16. Murray N. Rothbard, "The Evil of Banality," review of *Breaking Ranks* by Norman Podhoretz, *Inquiry*, December 10, 1979:26–28.
17. Ellen Willis, "My Podhoretz Problem – and His," review of *Breaking Ranks* by Norman Podhoretz, *The Village Voice*, December 3, 1979:1ff.
18. Podhoretz, *Podhoretz Papers*, October 24, 1979.
19. Orwell's comments were occasioned by Cyril Connolly's first novel, *The Rock Pool* (1936), whose hero, living a life of would-be "*escape*" among bohemians in France, is on the last page "left gazing at the world through a mist of Pernod but dimly feeling that his present degradation is better than respectable life in England." See George Orwell, Sonia Orwell, and Ian Angus, *The Collected Essays*,

Journalism and Letters of George Orwell, ed. Sonia Orwell (New York: Harcourt Brace Jovanovich, 1968), Vol. 1, 226.

20. Norman Podhoretz, "Countering Soviet Imperialism," Op-ed column, *New York Times*, May 31, 1978:A23.

21. Norman Podhoretz, "The Carter Stalemate," Op-ed column, *New York Times*, July 9, 1978:E17.

22. Elliott Abrams, interview with the author, March 7, 2004.

23. Richard Gid Powers, *Not Without Honor: The History of American Anticommunism* (New Haven, Conn.: Yale University Press, 1998), 340–41. Originally published in 1995.

24. Murray Friedman, *The Neoconservative Revolution: Jewish Intellectuals and the Shaping of Public Policy* (Cambridge: Cambridge University Press, 2005), 152.

25. When grandchildren came along in the eighties, the Podhoretzes, deciding it was time to "live in a grown-up house," built a two-story place on an East Hampton lot, which with a later addition was able to accommodate all the grandchildren and their parents (Decter interview, February 2004).

26. John Podhoretz interview.

27. Wheldon and Wheldon, *Wheldon Letters*, April 11, 1978.

28. They saw less and less of their biological father as the years passed, and though for a period Moshe Decter and Rachel's family were both living in Washington, they "never laid eyes on each other." He never saw the girls' children – his grandchildren (Decter interview, February 2004).

29. Ruthie Blum Liebowitz, interview with the author, April 19, 2004.

30. *Commentary* Archive, to Paul Warshow, May 2, 1980.

31. Naomi Munson interview.

32. Megan Rosenfeld, "Midge Decter and the Crisis of Feminism," *Washington Post*, July 31, 1979:B-1.

33. Podhoretz and Decter, "Two on an Island."

34. Decter interview, February 2004.

Chapter 15. Present Dangers

1. Norman Podhoretz, *The Present Danger: "Do We Have the Will to Reverse the Decline of American Power?"* (New York: Simon & Schuster, 1980), 22.

2. Ibid., 38.

3. Ibid., 45, 74.

4. Ibid., 57.

5. Ibid., 59, 74.

6. Full texts of these remarks are in Podhoretz, *Podhoretz Papers*.

7. Bruce Nussbaum, "Review of *The Present Danger* by Norman Podhoretz," *Business Week*, August 18, 1980:14.

8. Erik Bert, "An Advocate of Nuclear Madness," review of *The Present Danger* by Norman Podhoretz, *Daily World*, October 23, 1980.

9. Ronald Steel, "The Absent Danger," review of *The Present Danger* by Norman Podhoretz, *New Republic*, August 16, 1980:21–22.

10. Michael Novak, "Hammering Steel," Letter to the editors, *New Republic*, September 6, 1980:7.

11. Daniel Patrick Moynihan, "Reds Under the Bed," Letter to the editors, *New Republic*, September 20, 1980:7.

12. Michael Kramer, "The Book Reagan Wants You to Read," *New York*, December 1, 1980:23–26.
13. Richard V. Allen, "Jeane Kirkpatrick and the Great Democratic Defection," *New York Times*, December 16, 2006:A17; and Jay Winik, *On the Brink: The Dramatic, Behind-the-Scenes Saga of the Reagan Era and the Men and Women Who Won the Cold War* (New York: Simon & Schuster, 1996), 117. Kirkpatrick (1926–2006) was eulogized by Podhoretz in "A True American Hero," *Weekly Standard*, December 18, 2006:12.
14. Born in 1911, he was fifteen years her senior and her mentor. He had served in the Office of Strategic Services during World War II, was an expert in communist propaganda activities, and was the longtime executive director of the American Political Science Association. He died in 1995.
15. Jeane Kirkpatrick, interview with the author January 20, 2004.
16. Jeane Kirkpatrick, "Dictatorships and Double Standards," *Commentary*, November 1979:34–45.
17. Jeane Kirkpatrick, *The Reagan Phenomenon, and Other Speeches on Foreign Policy* (Washington, D.C.: American Enterprise Institute, 1983).
18. Alfred Kazin, "Saving My Soul at the Plaza," *New York Review of Books*, March 31, 1983. Nybooks.com/articles/6273.
19. Ruth Wisse, interview with the author, March 4, 2004.
20. Decter, *An Old Wife's Tale*, 127.
21. Robert W. Tucker, "The Middle East: Carterism Without Carter," *Commentary*, September 1981:27–36.
22. Norman Podhoretz, "The Riddle of Ronald Reagan," *Weekly Standard*, November 9, 1998:25.
23. Norman Podhoretz, "The Neo-Conservative Anguish Over Reagan's Foreign Policy," *New York Times Magazine*, May 2, 1982:30ff.
24. *Commentary* Archive, May 19, 1982.
25. Podhoretz, "The Riddle of Ronald Reagan," 26.
26. Norman Podhoretz, "Remarks," moderated by William Berkowitz, Dialogue Forum Series [lectures and discussions sponsored by Rabbi Berkowitz in New York City], 1982 (transcript in Podhoretz, *Podhoretz Papers*).
27. Podhoretz, *Podhoretz Papers*, July 18, 1983.
28. Kazin, "Saving My Soul." This piece brought Kazin the most fan mail he had ever received, including a note from a cultural critic at the *New York Times*, Herbert Mitgang, rejoicing at how "You hung [the neocons] by their own cut balls, laughingly, beautifully," and a note from Philip Roth declaring that his opening paragraph would "live forever in the annals of mockery." As Peter Steinfels had observed, "Political opponents are honorable men; former allies are something else. Anger clouds judgment; embitterment destroys reflection." All of these quotations are in Richard M. Cook, *Alfred Kazin: A Biography* (New Haven, Conn.: Yale University Press, 2007), 364. Kazin elaborated his dismay in his notebooks, portions of which blamed the "murderous" rhetoric of Gore Vidal and Alexander Cockburn on the "murderous" rhetoric of their favorite target, "the Podhoretz family": Norman, Midge, and son-in-law Elliott Abrams. See Alfred Kazin, "They Made It! From the Notebooks of a New Yorker," *Dissent*, Fall 1987:615–16.
    Podhoretz would later tell Cook that, "I thought sometimes that Alfred was 'crazy' – even thought that I had driven him crazy." Cook added that, "Demented or principled (or both), Kazin did come to view both Podhoretz and Irving Kristol

with a kind of moral loathing." Had they not forgotten where they came from? "Having grown up among the poor and the weak, they had, in his view, decided that their real interests lay with the rich and the powerful, and, unforgivably, against the poor and the weak" (Cook, *Alfred Kazin*, 367).

Other scholars worried, like Kazin, that neoconservative critics (Podhoretz, Joseph Epstein, Kenneth S. Lynn, Hilton Kramer) were winning the attention of the common reader, if only because academic criticism, befogged by deconstructionism, offered no competition. Sanford Pinsker, for one, was near despair: (a) Hemingway had said that "Fascism is made by disappointed people"; (b) the neoconservatives "are *disappointed*, imagining that the worst excesses of the sixties are alive and boogeying, and that America is going to hell in a unionmade handbasket"; (c) should, then, "the neoconservative critics get a taste of *real* power," watch out for fascism in America. See Sanford Pinsker, "Revisionism with Rancor: The Threat of the Neoconservative Critics," *Georgia Review*, Summer 1984:261.

29. Podhoretz, *Podhoretz Papers*, to Sidney Hook, October 1, 1982.
30. Norman Podhoretz, "If Orwell Were Alive Today," reprinted in *The Bloody Crossroads*, 50–68, and in *The Norman Podhoretz Reader*, 215–27. As Mark Royden Winchell has written, "To steal the Orwell of *Nineteen Eighty-Four* away from the anti-Communists would be akin to making Harriet Beecher Stowe into an apologist for antebellum slavery." See Mark Royden Winchell, *Neoconservative Criticism: Norman Podhoretz, Kenneth S. Lynn, and Joseph Epstein* (Boston: Twayne, 1991), 47.
31. See particularly Irving Howe, ed., *1984 Revisited: Totalitarianism in Our Century* (New York: Harper & Row, 1983); and John Rodden, *The Politics of Literary Reputation: The Making and Claiming of "St. George" Orwell* (New York: Oxford University Press, 1989).
32. Christopher Hitchens and Norman Podhoretz, "An Exchange on Orwell," *Harper's*, February 1983:56–58.
33. Rodden, *Politics of Literary Reputation*, 353–62.
34. *Commentary* Archive, January 2, 1980. Laqueur wrote a favorable review for *Commentary*, quoting the English writer Michael Howard: "One can but remark with some amazement on the amount of obloquy the American liberals have heaped on the man who eventually got them out of Vietnam compared with their sympathetic attitude toward those who got them in." See Walter Laqueur, "Kissinger and His Critics," *Commentary*, February 1980:57.
35. Norman Podhoretz, "Kissinger Reconsidered," *Commentary*, June 1982:19–28. Having in effect said that Kissinger had written a great book, one better than the policies it defended, Podhoretz would later marvel at the statesman's having anything to complain of. "If somebody had said that about me – that I'd written a great book – I wouldn't care if they compared me to Hitler," he said. But then Kissinger was not a "word" but an "idea" man: "As a diplomat, what he cares about is power," compared to which writing "a great book" may be "nice" but is "really of no great consequence" (Podhoretz interview, May 5, 2005).
36. *Commentary* Archive, May 26, 1982.
37. Charles Horner, "Hindsight," review of *The Real War* by Richard M. Nixon, *Commentary*, August 1980:64–65.
38. *Commentary* Archive, August 12, 1980.
39. Ibid., August 1, 1979.
40. Ibid., March 11, 1980.
41. Ibid., March 12, 1980.

42. Podhoretz, *Podhoretz Papers*, March 18, 1981.
43. Norman Podhoretz, *Why We Were in Vietnam* (New York: Simon & Schuster, 1982), 58.
44. Ibid., 193.
45. Ibid., 210.
46. Norman Podhoretz, "Postscript to the Touchstone Edition," in *Why We Were in Vietnam* (New York: Simon & Schuster, Touchstone, 1982), 214.
47. Ibid., 218–19.
48. Theodore Draper, *Present History* (New York: Random House, 1983), 353–60.
49. Podhoretz, *Podhoretz Papers*, March 31, 1982.
50. Marion Magid, "A Family Feud," Letter to the editors, *New Republic*, April 7, 1982:6.
51. Christopher Lehmann-Haupt, "Theodore Draper, Freelance Historian, is Dead at 93," Obituary, *New York Times*, February 22, 2006:A17.
52. Podhoretz, e-mails to the author, February 12–13, 2007.
53. Arthur Schlesinger, Jr., "Make War Not It," review of *Why We Were in Vietnam* by Norman Podhoretz, *Harper's*, March 1982:71–73.
54. Arnold Beichman, "Their Present Danger," *National Review*, September 3, 1982:1088–89.
55. Podhoretz, *Podhoretz Papers*, March 19, 1982.
56. Editorial, *Wall Street Journal*, April 1, 1982.
57. Martin Gilbert, *A History of the Twentieth Century*, Vol. 3 (New York: Harper-Collins, 1999), 589–93.
58. Norman Podhoretz, "Our Aims and Israel's," *New York Times*, June 15, 1982:A29.
59. Norman Podhoretz, "J'Accuse," *Commentary*, September 1982:21–31.
60. *Commentary* Archive, September 14, 1982.
61. Podhoretz, *The Bloody Crossroads*, 84–92.
62. *Commentary* Archive, November 16, 1982.
63. Podhoretz, *Podhoretz Papers*, November 16, 1981. Podhoretz's "internal" means something like "addressed strictly to fellow experts" rather than *Commentary*'s "common reader."
64. *Commentary* Archive, August 10, 1981.
65. John Podhoretz interview.

Chapter 16. "The Great Satan of the American Romantic Left"

1. Podhoretz, *Podhoretz Papers*, n.d. (1985).
2. Ibid., to Alastair G. M. Graham in Worcester, England, March 8, 1984.
3. *Commentary* Archive, to Richard N. Gardner at Columbia Law School, March 14, 1984 (quoting Aron).
4. Arnold Beichman, "Where's His Proof?" response to CNN Moscow bureau chief Stuart H. Loory, *Washington Times*, February 7, 1986.
5. Irving Kristol, "What Choice Is There in Salvador?" *Wall Street Journal*, April 4, 1983:16.
6. See Heilbrunn, *They Knew They Were Right*, 178.
7. Elliott Abrams, "Before the Christian Rescue Effort for the Emancipation of Dissidents," speech at Truro Episcopal Church, Fairfax, VA (in *Commentary* Archive), 1984.
8. Podhoretz, *Podhoretz Papers*, April 8, 14, 18, 1983.

9. Ibid., March 29, 1986.
10. Ibid., June 3, 1986.
11. Norman Podhoretz, interview, 2004.
12. Flora Lewis, "Offense and Defense," *New York Times*, January 29, 1985:A27.
13. *Commentary* Archive, to Meyer Schwartz in Newton Center, Mass., February 22, 1985.
14. Ibid., May 1977.
15. John Bayley, "Introduction," in Aleksandr Isaevich Solzhenitsyn, *One Day in the Life of Ivan Denisovich*, trans. H. T. Willetts (New York: Knopf, Everyman's Library, 1995), xii.
16. *Commentary* Archive, August 7, 1974.
17. Norman Podhoretz, "The Terrible Question of Aleksandr Solzhenitsyn," *Commentary*, February 1985:17–24.
18. *Commentary* Archive, January 3, 1985.
19. Moshe Kohn, "On Manning the Ramparts," interview with Norman Podhoretz, *Jerusalem Post*, January 22, 1986:6.
20. Norman Podhoretz, "The State of World Jewry," originated as fourth annual State of World Jewry Address at the 92nd Street Y, *Commentary*, December 1983:37–45.
21. Norman Podhoretz et al. "Terrorism and the Media: A Discussion," *Harper's*, October 1984:47–58.
22. Norman Podhoretz, "The Dialectic of Blame: Some Reflections on Anti-Americanism," *Encounter*, July–August 1985:8.
23. Norman Podhoretz, "The Worst Effect of Bitburg Visit," *New York Post*, April 23, 1985.
24. Leon Wieseltier, "Washington Diary," *New Republic*, May 27, 1985:43.
25. *Commentary* Archive, May 19, 1986.
26. Ibid., May 27, 1986.
27. Norman Podhoretz, "What Is Anti-Semitism? An Open Letter to William F. Buckley, Jr.," *Commentary*, February 1992:15–20, at 15–16.
28. *Commentary* Archive, February 26, 1987.
29. Ibid., both letters, March 2, 1987.
30. Ibid., February 9, 1984.
31. Jules Feiffer, "Podhoretz Cartoon," *Village Voice*, August 20, 1985:4.
32. Norman Podhoretz, "Politics and Culture in Modern America: An Interview with Norman Podhoretz," with Catherine Melchoir, *Issues*, October 1984:7–9.
33. Podhoretz, *Podhoretz Papers*, January 30, 1985.
34. See Blinken et al., "Proceedings."
35. La Pasionaria ("the passion flower") was the nickname of Dolores Ibárruri Gómez (1895–1989), a Communist Party leader in Spain. A then up-to-date chronicle of Sontag's ideological divagations may be found in Richard Grenier, "The Conversion of Susan Sontag," *New Republic*, April 14, 1982:15–19.
36. James Atlas, "The Changing World of New York Intellectuals," *New York Times Magazine*, August 23, 1985:22ff.
37. Norman Podhoretz, "The Future of America," *Partisan Review*, 51(4)/52(1) (Anniversary Double Issue) (1984): 864–68.
38. Norman Podhoretz, "An Open Letter to Milan Kundera," *Commentary*, October 1984:34–39.
39. John Gross, "Books of the Times," review of *The Bloody Crossroads* by Norman Podhoretz, *New York Times*, May 9, 1986:C33.

40. See Sidney Blumenthal, "Norman Podhoretz and the Right Stuff," review of *The Bloody Crossroads* by Norman Podhoretz, *Washington Post Book World*, May 18, 1986:11.
41. Cynthia Ozick, "'Hypnotized by Totalitarian Poesy,'" review of *The Bloody Crossroads* by Norman Podhoretz, *New York Times Book Review*, May 18, 1986:11–12.
42. *Commentary* Archive, June 5 and 17, 1986.
43. Conor Cruise O'Brien, "Trop de Zèle," review of *The Bloody Crossroads* by Norman Podhoretz, *New York Review of Books*, October 9, 1986:11–14. http://www.nybooks.com/articles/5011.
44. *Commentary* Archive, n.d. and October 9, 1986.

Chapter 17. Regulated Hatreds

1. Wheldon and Wheldon, *Wheldon Letters*, March 4, 1986.
2. Norman Podhoretz, "Do Not Go Gentle Into the Night," *New York Post*, March 18, 1986.
3. Wheldon and Wheldon, *Wheldon Letters*, July 14, 1986.
4. Midge Decter, "The Boys on the Beach," *Commentary*, September 1980:35–48.
5. Midge Decter et al., "Letters from Readers," *Commentary*, December 1980:14–15, 19–20.
6. Ginsberg and Morgan, *Deliberate Prose*, 253.
7. Quotations here and throughout this Ginsberg section are, unless otherwise indicated, from Podhoretz, *Ex-Friends*, 22–56.
8. Allen Ginsberg, "Sacred Speech: A Conversation with Allen Ginsberg," interviewers Robert Presson and Rebekah Steward, *New Letters*, Winter 1988:73–74; Allen Ginsberg, "I Sing of Norman P.," excerpt from "Sacred Speech," *Harper's*, July 1988:28.
9. Ginsberg, Havel, and Carter, *Spontaneous Mind*, 312–13.
10. Norman Podhoretz, interview with the author, June 13–15, 2004.
11. Joseph Epstein, "Homo/Hetero: The Struggle for Sexual Identity," *Harper's*, September 1970:50–51.
12. See Kaplan, *Gore Vidal*, 724–28.
13. Vidal's use of proscribed terms like "fags," "dykes," "queers," "fairies," "kike," etc. was, as his biographer notes, meant to be taken ironically. He wanted "both to shock and to call attention to the reality and complexity of American attitudes toward minority groups" (Kaplan, *Gore Vidal*, 729) – a technique that on the whole misfires.
14. Gore Vidal, "Pink Triangle and Yellow Star," in *United States: Essays 1952–1992* (New York: Random House, 1993), 595–611 (reprinted from the *Nation*, November 14, 1981).
15. Gore Vidal, "A Cheerful Response," in *United States*, 1017–20 (reprint of "The Empire Lovers Strike Back," *Nation*, March 22, 1986).
16. Podhoretz, *Podhoretz Papers*, March 31, 1986.
17. *Commentary* Archive, copy of letter to Leon Wieseltier, March 21, 1988.
18. Ibid., May 5, 1986.
19. Norman Podhoretz, "The Hate That Dare not Speak Its Name," *Commentary*, November 1986:21–32.
20. *Commentary* Archive, Neuhaus to Carlson, February 27, 1989; Podhoretz to Neuhaus, February 15, 1989.

21. Richard Bernstein, "Magazine Dispute Reflects Rift on U.S. Right," *New York Times*, May 16, 1989:A1, A20.
22. Norman Podhoretz, "Israel: Bully or Victim?" Speech in New York City, 1988, in *Podhoretz Papers*.
23. Norman Podhoretz, "An Interview with Norman Podhoretz," with Thomas Gross, *The Windmill* (Oxford University–Israel Society) (1987).
24. *Commentary* Archive, to Podhoretz, April 29, 1988.
25. Ibid., March 2, 1988.
26. Podhoretz, "The Riddle of Ronald Reagan," 27.
27. Norman Podhoretz, "Strange Bedfellows: A Guide to the New Foreign-Policy Debates," *Commentary*, December 1999:22.
28. Cf. Podhoretz, *Ex-Friends*, 227.
29. Norman Podhoretz, "Behind the Smile of Gorbachev," *Geopolitique*, Summer 1989:70–71.
30. Francis X. Clines, "Neo-Conservatives Taunt 'Evil' in Soviet Habitat," *New York Times*, June 21, 1989:A3.
31. *Commentary* Archive, August 23, 1990.
32. Podhoretz interview, January 5, 2005.
33. Francis Fukuyama, *The End of History and the Last Man* (New York: Free Press, 1992), 330.
34. Norman Podhoretz, "New Vistas for Neoconservatives," *Conservative Digest*, January–February 1989:57.

Chapter 18. Culture Wars

1. *Commentary* Archive, April 13, 1989. In Britain the reference is not to the Labour but to the Liberal Party, Wheldon's father having been an associate of David Lloyd-George. As for the Tories or Conservatives, Wheldon voted that way only twice: for Churchill in 1945 and for Margaret Thatcher in 1979 (Wynn Wheldon interview).
2. Brian Wenham, "Review of *Sir Huge: The Life of Huw Wheldon*, by Paul Ferris," *Financial Times*, 1990.
3. Byron Rogers, "Review of *Sir Huge: The Life of Huw Wheldon*, by Paul Ferris," *London Times*, 1990.
4. Wheldon and Wheldon, *Wheldon Letters*, March 8, 1990.
5. Ibid., June 29, 1990.
6. Wynn Wheldon, "Jacqueline Mary Wheldon, 1924–1993." As Wynn would recall, when his mother died, "all I wanted was Midge. And she came [to London]. A wonderful person" (Wynn Wheldon interview).
7. The eulogy is in Podhoretz, *Podhoretz Papers*. See also Neal Kozodoy, "In Memoriam: Lucy S. Dawidowicz," *Commentary*, May 1992:35–40.
8. Podhoretz, *Podhoretz Papers*, n.d. (1993).
9. Ibid., December 22, 1994.
10. Elliott Abrams, *Undue Process: A Story of How Political Differences Are Turned Into Crimes* (New York: Free Press, 1993), 89–90.
11. Podhoretz interview, October 24, 2004.
12. Abrams, *Undue Process*, 89–90.
13. Ibid., 57–58.
14. Ibid., 103.
15. Ibid., 140–41.

16. Ibid., 205–6.
17. Ibid., 227, 229.
18. Ibid., 100, 175, 177.
19. Podhoretz interview, October 24, 2004.
20. *Commentary* Archive, October 13, 17, and 21, 1990.
21. Buckley had been tutored by Joshua Muravchik, "Patrick J. Buchanan and the Jews," *Commentary*, January 1991:29–37.
22. Podhoretz, "What Is Anti-Semitism?"
23. George Weigel, "KCET's Action: The Antithesis of Freedom," *Los Angeles Times*, September 17, 1991.
24. George Weigel, "The New Anti-Catholicism," *Commentary*, July 1992:25–31.
25. Norman Podhoretz, "Conservative Book Becomes a Best-Seller," review of *The Closing of the American Mind* by Allan Bloom, *Human Events*, July 11, 1987:5–6.
26. Allan Bloom, "Western Civ – and Me: An Address at Harvard University," *Commentary*, August 1990:15–21.
27. Norman Podhoretz, "Portrait of a Generation," review of *Our Age* by Noel Annan, *The New Criterion*, January 1991:70–72.
28. *Commentary* Archive, June 27, 1991.
29. Ibid., July 12, 1991.
30. Norman Podhoretz, "The New Defenders of Capitalism," *Harvard Business Review*, March–April 1981:96–106.
31. *Commentary* Archive, December 23, 1991.
32. Ibid., October 19, 1995.
33. Ibid., June 24, 1991.
34. Ibid., May 2, 1995.
35. Ibid.
36. The daylight between Moynihan and Podhoretz needn't, from Jim Wilson's point of view, have been so great: "Pat just didn't harbor dislike. And he came in contact with a great many dislikable people. He would only talk about Norman with a certain degree of sadness – the feeling that Norman," in his passionate or (for Wilson) "hot-headed" way, "had deserted him" (Wilson interview).
37. Neal Kozodoy, ed., David Bar-Illan et al. speakers, "Proceedings of the Dinner in Honor of Norman Podhoretz Upon the Occasion of His Retirement After Thirty-Five Years as Editor-in-Chief of *Commentary*" (New York: Privately published for *Commentary*, 1995). Podhoretz's statement appeared in slightly different form as Norman Podhoretz, "Editing *Commentary*: A Valedictory," *Commentary*, June 1995:19–20.
38. *Commentary* Archive, May 3, 1995

Chapter 19. A Literary Indian Summer

1. Norman Podhoretz, "On Reading for Pleasure Again: A Tribute to the Library of America," *Commentary*, December 1992:37–42.
2. Norman Podhoretz, "The Adventures of Philip Roth," *Commentary*, October 1998:25–36.
3. Norman Podhoretz, "Bellow at 85, Roth at 67," *Commentary*, July–August 2000: 35–43.
4. See Podhoretz, "The Best Catch There Is," in *Doings and Undoings*, 228–35.

5. Norman Podhoretz, "Looking Back at 'Catch-22,'" *Commentary*, February 2000:32–37; Christopher Hitchens, "Unmaking Friends," review of *Ex-Friends* by Norman Podhoretz, *Harper's*, June 1999:74.
6. Norman Podhoretz, "What Happened to Ralph Ellison," *Commentary*, July–August 1999:46–58, reprinted in *The Norman Podhoretz Reader*, 349–72.
7. Norman Podhoretz, "Rape in Feminist Eyes," *Commentary*, October 1991:29–35.
8. Norman Podhoretz, "How the Gay-Rights Movement Won," *Commentary*, November 1996:32–41.
9. Norman Podhoretz, "*Lolita*, My Mother-in-Law, the Marquis de Sade, and Larry Flynt," *Commentary*, April 1997:23–35.
10. Norman Podhoretz, "'Sexgate,' the Sisterhood, and Mr. Bumble," *Commentary*, June 1998:23–36.

Chapter 20. Verdicts

1. *Commentary* Archive, September 4, 1990.
2. Norman Podhoretz, "A Statement on the Persian Gulf Crisis," *Commentary*, November 1990:17–20.
3. Norman Podhoretz, "Enter the Peace Party," *Commentary*, January 1991:17–21.
4. Ibid., 26.
5. See Norman Podhoretz, "America and Israel: An Ominous Change," *Commentary*, January 1992:21–25.
6. One might ask why George H. W. Bush or Clinton should have believed that an agreement between Israel and the Palestinians was a key to peace in the Middle East, given that from 1948 to 1991 at least nineteen wars, small and large, had broken out, none of them having to do with Israel or the Palestinians. The wars include the one between Iran and Iraq, Iraq's invasion of Kuwait, Desert Storm, the five-year (1962–67) clash between Egypt and Yemen, the civil wars in Lebanon, and Syrian attacks on that country and Jordan. See Norman Podhoretz, *Why Are Jews Liberals?* (New York: Doubleday, 2009), 222.
7. See Podhoretz, "Israel and the United States: A Complex History," 40.
8. Norman Podhoretz, "A Statement on the Peace Process," *Commentary*, April 1993:19–23.
9. Norman Podhoretz, "Another Statement on the Peace Process," *Commentary*, June 1993:25–30.
10. Podhoretz, "Israel and the United States: A Complex History," 39, n. 8.
11. Norman Podhoretz, "The Peace Process So Far," *Commentary*, December 1994:21–25.
12. Norman Podhoretz, "Israel – with Grandchildren," *Commentary*, December 1995:38–46.
13. Norman Podhoretz, "The Tragic Predicament of Benjamin Netanyahu," *Commentary*, December 1996:30–40.
14. Podhoretz, "Israel and the United States: A Complex History," 28–43.
15. Norman Podhoretz, "Buchanan and the Conservative Crackup," *Commentary*, May 1992:30–34.
16. Podhoretz, *Why Are Jews Liberals?* 223, 234.
17. Podhoretz, "Life of His Party," 52–56.
18. These Christians are "dispensationalists," as opposed to "supersessionists." The latter hold that since the Jews have rejected Jesus as the Messiah, they are in effect

no longer "the Jews," i.e., God's chosen people, but have been "superseded" by Christians, the "New Jews." The dispensationalists, on the other hand, argue that the Christian Church is a "parenthesis" in God's dealings with the Jews. He still cares for them, as will be shown after the "dispensation" called the Church Age, when the Jews will be restored to their land and will accept Jesus as their Messiah. Dispensationalists are therefore often called "Christian Zionists," emphasizing the New Testament's organic connection with the Old and foreseeing a "last days" emergence of a Hebraic form of Christianity. The Jews remain God's "chosen people," like the Christians, only on a different track.

19. Norman Podhoretz, "In the Matter of Pat Robertson," *Commentary*, August 1995:27–32.

20. A penetratingly conservative Jewish statement on the morality of abortion may be found in Hadley Arkes, "A Decorous Judaism," in *The Chosen People in an Almost Chosen Nation: Jews and Judaism in America*, ed. Richard John Neuhaus (Grand Rapids, Mich.: Eerdmans, 2002), 191–95, reprinted from *First Things*, March 1991:31–33.

21. Podhoretz, *My Love Affair with America*, 204–9. Neuhaus himself, looking back, couldn't quite accept the reasons for Podhoretz's opposition, or for the resignation of Gertrude Himmelfarb and Peter Berger from the editorial board of *First Things*, "simply because we were intellectually entertaining what happens when one arrives at the conclusion that this regime, this form of government, is no longer legitimate. That was simply a *verboten* question from their point of view" (Richard Neuhaus, interview with the author, June 2004). In this context, Neuhaus believed the "sacredness" of the Bible trumped the sacredness of the Constitution. An account of this episode may be found in Damon Linker, *The Theocons: Secular America under Siege* (New York: Doubleday, 2006), 94–110.

22. Podhoretz, *My Love Affair with America*, 212–14.

23. Podhoretz, *Ex-Friends*, 15, 20.

24. Ibid., 229, 233.

25. John Leonard, "A Partisan's View," review of *Ex-Friends* by Norman Podhoretz, *Nation*, March 22, 1999:29.

26. Merkin, "Getting Even," 170.

27. Marcus Klein, "A Jittery Outsidedness," review of *Ex-Friends* by Norman Podhoretz, *New Leader*, December 14–28, 1998:20–22.

28. Merkin, "Getting Even," 171.

29. Norman Podhoretz, "Science Hasn't Killed God," *Wall Street Journal*, December 30, 1999:A12.

30. Norman Podhoretz, "Was Bach Jewish?" *Prospect*, December 1999:21–24.

Chapter 21. New Wars for a New Century

1. Podhoretz, *My Love Affair with America*, 232.

2. Ibid., 228–29.

3. Norman Podhoretz, "Intifada II: Death of an Illusion?" *Commentary*, December 2000:33.

4. Ibid., 38.

5. Norman Podhoretz, "Oslo: The Peacemongers Return," *Commentary*, October 2001:21–23.

6. Ibid., 32.

7. Dan Jacobson, *The Story of the Stories: The Chosen People and Its God* (New York: Harper & Row, 1982).

8. Charles Murray, "Jewish Genius," *Commentary*, April 2007:35.

9. Norman Podhoretz, "Jerusalem: The Scandal of Particularity," *Commentary*, July–August 2007:34–40; Mark Twain, *Collected Tales, Sketches, Speeches & Essays, 1891–1910* (New York: Library of America, 1992), 369–70.

10. Fuller treatment of *The Prophets* may be found in Thomas L. Jeffers's essay-review "The Hebrew Prophets, Then and Now," *Yale Review*, 91 (Summer 2003): 151–61.

11. In thus interpreting the prophets, Podhoretz may strike some readers as sounding rather like a prophet himself – which for Jacob Heilbrunn is exactly right. He regards the neoconservatives' odyssey as a recapitulation of the biblical Jews', from the exodus under the leadership of Trotsky ("their Moses, you might say"), to the postwar wilderness years of liberal anticommunism, to the redemptive Reagan victories, and finally to "exile, where they belong – and where they are, in some respects, most content," since they are "less intellectuals than [uncompromising] prophets" (*They Knew They Were Right*, 12–13).

12. Podhoretz, *Why Are Jews Liberals?* 39–51, 61–66, 269, 276–81.

13. Norman Podhoretz, *World War IV: The Long Struggle Against Islamofascism* (New York: Doubleday, 2007), 17.

14. Norman Podhoretz, "How to Win World War IV," *Commentary*, February 2002:19–29.

15. Norman Podhoretz, "The Return of the 'Jackal Bins,'" *Commentary*, April 2002:29–36.

16. Podhoretz to Beichman, and e-mail to the author, June 24, 2004.

17. Hendrik Hertzberg, "Tuesday, and After," *New Yorker*, September 24, 2001:28.

18. Norman Podhoretz, "Who Is Lying About Iraq?" *Commentary*, December 2005:27–33. Podhoretz took special pleasure in defending the Bush Doctrine not just because he believed in it but because the president's speeches were truly eloquent. See Norman Podhoretz, "A Masterpiece of American Oratory," *American Spectator*, November 2006:32–39.

19. Podhoretz, *World War IV*, 14, quoting Daniel Pipes.

20. Ibid., 201. See also Victor Davis Hanson, "Dispatches from the Front," *Hoover Digest*, Winter 2008:9–24; and his "Nothing Succeeds Like Success," *Commentary*, April 2008:19–23.

21. Podhoretz, e-mail to the author, August 27, 2007. See also Norman Podhoretz, "A Real Neocon Speaks," interview with Kathryn Jean Lopez, *National Review On-Line*, September 11, 2007.

22. Peter J. Boyer, "Mayberry Man," *New Yorker*, August 20, 2007:60.

23. Podhoretz, e-mail to the author, April 26, 2007.

24. Norman Podhoretz, "The Case for Bombing Iran," *Commentary*, June 2007:17–23.

25. Podhoretz, *World War IV*, 197.

26. Ibid., 200–17. Early reviews fell into predictable patterns. The *Wall Street Journal* was laudatory, giving serious attention to Podhoretz's argument. See Christopher Willcox, "Why We Still Must Fight," review of *World War IV* by Norman Podhoretz, *Wall Street Journal*, September 11, 2007:D6. The *New York Times* was

dismissive, indeed derisory, Peter Beinart literalizing the figurative for the sake of getting a laugh:

"In its own way," Podhoretz declares, "this war of ideas [at home] is no less bloody than the one being fought by our troops in the Middle East." No less bloody? That's good to know. Next time I talk to my sister-in-law, an emergency medicine doctor serving at Camp Taji, north of Baghdad, I'll tell her we have it just as rough here at home. Norman Podhoretz is practically dodging I.E.D.'s on his way to Zabar's [a gourmet deli on the Upper West Side].

See Peter Beinart, "Enemies List," review of *World War IV* by Norman Podhoretz, and *The Iranian Time Bomb* by Michael A. Ledeen, *New York Times Book Review*, September 9, 2007:15. Also see Buruma, "His Toughness Problem – and Ours," which was pursuant to the reviewer's earlier quip that what "ties neoconservatives, Likudniks, and post-Cold War hawks together . . . is the conviction that liberalism is strictly for sissies."

27. Vintage Books brought out a paperback edition in September 2008 with a twenty-nine page postscript entitled "Spring 2008."
28. Podhoretz, e-mail to the author, October 14, 2008.
29. Patricia Cohen, "New Commentary Editor Denies Neo-Nepotism," *New York Times*, October 24, 2007: E1, E4.

Epilogue

1. Roger Hertog, interview with the author, April 14, 2004.
2. Podhoretz, *Podhoretz Papers*, February 14, 2002.
3. Podhoretz interview, May 5, 2005.
4. Podhoretz interview, January 7–9, 2005; Decter, e-mail to the author, October 27, 2008.
5. Podhoretz interview, January 7–9, 2005.
6. Decter interview, February 2004.
7. Podhoretz interview, January 7–9, 2005.
8. Ruth Wisse, interview with author, March 4, 2004.
9. Decter interview, February 2004.
10. Decter interview, May 6, 2005.
11. Wordsworth continues in terms Podhoretz would have found relevant: "bond unknown to me / Was given, that I should be, else sinning greatly, / A dedicated Spirit" (*The Prelude*, IV.335–37).
12. Podhoretz interview, May 5, 2005.
13. Orwell, *Collected Essays*, Vol. 1, 188.
14. Epstein interview.
15. Podhoretz interview, May 5, 2005.
16. Blinken et al., "Proceedings."
17. Merkin, "Getting Even," 170.
18. Epstein interview.
19. Wisse interview. The payoff of holding your ground, as Podhoretz soon understood, was not that you would "persuade" anyone: "Doesn't happen. But what can happen, if you plant that flag, make that case, without ambiguity and without defensiveness – 'There it is, I take my stand, I can do no other' – is that those who

feel like you will rally around. Others will just throw stones" (Podhoretz interview, January 7–9, 2005).

20. Dorothy Rabinowitz, interview with the author, July 15, 2004.

21. Leon Kass, interview with the author, June 21, 2004.

22. Richard Neuhaus, interview with the author, June 2004.

23. John Podhoretz interview.

24. Gross interview.

25. Ozick in Kozodoy et al., "Proceedings." As Keats wrote his brother and sister in October 1818 on the subject of positive and negative reviews: "This is a mere matter of the moment – I think I shall be among the English Poets after my death." See John Keats, *Letters of John Keats*, selected and prefaced by Frederick Page (London: Oxford University Press, 1954), 177.

26. Garment interview.

Bibliography

Abrams, Elliott. "Before the Christian Rescue Effort for the Emancipation of Dissidents." Speech at Truro Episcopal Church, Fairfax, VA (in *Commentary* Archive), 1984.
  Undue Process: A Story of How Political Differences Are Turned Into Crimes. New York: Free Press, 1993.
Adler, Renata. Review of *Doings and Undoings* by Norman Podhoretz. *New Yorker*, July 4, 1964:60–80.
Allen, Richard V. "Jeane Kirkpatrick and the Great Democratic Defection." *New York Times*, December 16, 2006:A17.
Annan, Noel. "An Editor and His Odyssey." Review of *Breaking Ranks* by Norman Podhoretz. *Times Literary Supplement*, April 25, 1980:473.
Anon. "The Press." *Time*, May 20, 1966:58.
Arendt, Hannah. *Eichmann in Jerusalem: A Report on the Banality of Evil*. New York: Viking, 1965. (Originally published in 1963.)
Arendt, Hannah, Mary McCarthy, and Carol Brightman. *Between Friends: The Correspondence of Hannah Arendt and Mary McCarthy, 1949–1975*, edited by Carol Brightman. New York: Harcourt Brace, 1995.
Arkes, Hadley. "A Decorous Judaism." In *The Chosen People in an Almost Chosen Nation: Jews and Judaism in America*, edited by Richard John Neuhaus, 191–95. Grand Rapids, Mich.: Eerdmans, 2002. Reprinted from *First Things*, March 1991:31–33.
Atlas, James. "The Changing World of New York Intellectuals." *New York Times Magazine*, August 23, 1985:22ff.
Auspitz, Josiah Lee, William Barrett, Peter L. Berger, and Norman Birnbaum. "America Now: A Failure of Nerve?" *Commentary*, July 1975:16–87.
Baldwin, James, Fred L. Standley, and Louis H. Pratt. "Disturber of the Peace: James Baldwin, an Interview," interviewers Eve and Nancy Lynch Auchincloss. In *Conversations with James Baldwin*, edited by Fred L. Standley, 199–216. Jackson: University Press of Mississippi, 1989. (Originally published in 1969.)
Baldwin, James. *Collected Essays*. New York: Library of America, 1998.

"The Fire Next Time: Down at the Cross: Letter from a Region in My Mind." In *Reporting Civil Rights*. New York: Library of America, 2003. (Originally published in 1962.)

Barra, Allen. "Toots Shor's Sweet Sanctuary." Review of the documentary film "Toots." *Wall Street Journal*, September 13, 2007:D7.

Bayley, John. "Introduction." In Aleksandr Isaevich Solzhenitsyn, *One Day in the Life of Ivan Denisovich*, translated by H. T. Willetts, vii–xvi. New York: Knopf, Everyman's Library, 1995.

Beichman, Arnold. "Critic in Search of His Credo." Review of *Doings and Undoings* by Norman Podhoretz. *Christian Science Monitor*, April 23, 1964:11.

"Their Present Danger." *National Review*, September 3, 1982:1088–89.

"Where's His Proof?" Response to CNN Moscow bureau chief Stuart H. Loory. *Washington Times*, February 7, 1986.

Beinart, Peter. "Enemies List." Review of *World War IV* by Norman Podhoretz and *The Iranian Time Bomb* by Michael A. Ledeen. *New York Times Book Review*, September 9, 2007:15.

Bernstein, Richard. "Magazine Dispute Reflects Rift on U.S. Right." *New York Times*, May 16, 1989:A1, A20.

Bert, Erik. "An Advocate of Nuclear Madness." Review of *The Present Danger* by Norman Podhoretz. *Daily World*, October 23, 1980.

Bickel, Alexander M. "Judging the Chicago Trial." *Commentary*, January 1971:31–40.

Blinken, Donald M., et al. "Proceedings of the Dinner in Honor of Norman Podhoretz on His Twenty-Fifth Anniversary as Editor of *Commentary*." Privately published for the occasion. New York: American Jewish Committee, January 29, 1985.

Bloom, Alexander. *Prodigal Sons: The New York Intellectuals and Their World*. New York: Oxford University Press, 1986.

Bloom, Allan. "Western Civ – and Me: An Address at Harvard University." *Commentary*, August 1990:15–21.

Blumenthal, Sidney. "Norman Podhoretz and the Right Stuff." Review of *The Bloody Crossroads* by Norman Podhoretz. *Washington Post Book World*, May 18, 1986:11.

The Rise of the Counter-Establishment: From Conservative Ideology to Political Power. New York: Times Books, 1986.

Boyer, Peter J. "Mayberry Man." *New Yorker*, August 20, 2007:44–61.

Brogan, D. W. "Unmanned Americans." *Guardian*, March 3, 1961.

Brooks, David. "The Happy Cold Warrior: The First 90 Years of Arnold Beichman." *Weekly Standard*, May 19, 2003:27–29.

Buruma, Ian. "His Toughness Problem – and Ours." Review of *World War IV* by Norman Podhoretz. *New York Review of Books*, September 27, 2007. http://o-www.nybooks.com.articles/20590.

Campbell, James. *Talking at the Gates: A Life of James Baldwin*. New York: Viking, 1991.

Carter, Jimmy. "Curb on Power to Make War." *New York Times*, March 6, 1977:30. Transcript of reply to question from phone caller No. 40.

Clines, Francis X. "Neo-Conservatives Taunt 'Evil' in Soviet Habitat." *New York Times*, June 21, 1989:A3.

Cohen, Patricia. "New Commentary Editor Denies Neo-Nepotism." *New York Times*, October 24, 2007:E1, E4.

Coleman, Peter. "Right Turn: Norman Podhoretz and Neo-Conservatism." Review of *Breaking Ranks* by Norman Podhoretz. *Quadrant*, June 1980:44–46.

Cook, Richard M. *Alfred Kazin: A Biography.* New Haven, Conn.: Yale University Press, 2007.

Daiches, David. Review of *Doings and Undoings* by Norman Podhoretz. *New York Times Book Review*, March 29, 1964:5.

Dearborn, Mary V. *Mailer, a Biography.* Boston: Houghton Mifflin, 1999.

Decter, Midge. "The Activist Critic on the Upper West Side." In Rosenberg, Bernard and Ernest Goldstein, eds. *Creators and Disturbers: Reminiscences by Jewish Intellectuals of New York.* New York: Columbia University Press, 1982. 351–67.

"The Boys on the Beach." *Commentary*, September 1980:35–48.

Liberal Parents, Radical Children. New York: Coward, McCann & Geoghegan, 1975.

An Old Wife's Tale: My Seven Decades in Love and War. New York: HarperCollins, Regan, 2001.

Decter, Midge, et al. "Letters from Readers." *Commentary*, December 1980:6–20.

Deford, Frank. "The Boxer and the Blonde." In *The Best American Sports Writing of the Century*, edited by David Halberstam, 499–524. Boston: Houghton Mifflin, 1999. Reprinted from *Sports Illustrated*, June 15, 1985.

DeMott, Benjamin. "City Light." Review of *Doings and Undoings* by Norman Podhoretz. *New York Review of Books*, April 30, 1964. Nybooks.com/articles/13374.

Draper, Theodore. *Present History.* New York: Random House, 1983.

"The Fantasy of Black Nationalism." *Commentary*, September 1969:27–54.

Ehrman, John. *The Rise of Neoconservatism: Intellectuals and Foreign Affairs, 1945–1994.* New Haven, Conn.: Yale University Press, 1995.

Epstein, Jason. "The Issue at Ocean Hill." *New York Review of Books*, November 21, 1968. http://www.nybooks.com/articles/11494.

"Journal Du Voyeur." Review of *Radical Chic and Mau-Mauing the Flak Catchers* by Tom Wolfe. *New York Review of Books*, December 17, 1970. http://www.nybooks.com/articles/10715.

"Living in New York." *New York Review of Books*, January 6, 1966. http://www.nybooks.com/articles/12623.

Epstein, Joseph. "Homo/Hetero: The Struggle for Sexual Identity." *Harper's*, September 1970:37–51.

"The New Conservatism: Intellectuals in Retreat." *Dissent*, Spring 1973:151–62.

"The Party's Over." Review of *Radical Chic and Mau-Mauing the Flak Catchers* by Tom Wolfe. *Commentary*, March 1971:98–102.

"Remaking It." Review of *Breaking Ranks* by Norman Podhoretz. *New York Times Book Review*, October 21, 1979:3ff.

Fackenheim, Emil L. "Jewish Faith and the Holocaust: A Fragment." *Commentary*, August 1968:30–36.

Feiffer, Jules. "Podhoretz Cartoon." *Village Voice*, August 20, 1985:4.

French, Philip. *Three Honest Men: Edmund Wilson, F. R. Leavis, Lionel Trilling: A Critical Mosaic.* Manchester: Caracanet New Press, 1980.

Friedenberg, Edgar Z. "Du Côté de Chez Podhoretz." Review of *Making It* by Norman Podhoretz. *New York Review of Books*, February 1, 1968. Nybooks.com/articles/11810.

Friedman, Murray. "Is White Racism the Problem?" *Commentary*, January 1969:61–
    65.
    *The Neoconservative Revolution: Jewish Intellectuals and the Shaping of Public Pol-
    icy*. Cambridge: Cambridge University Press, 2005.
Fukuyama, Francis. *The End of History and the Last Man*. New York: Free Press, 1992.
Garment, Leonard. *Crazy Rhythm: My Journey from Brooklyn, Jazz, and Wall Street
    to Nixon's White House, Watergate, and Beyond*. Cambridge, Mass.: Da Capo,
    2001. (Originally published in 1997.)
Gass, Oscar. "The New Frontier Fulfilled." *Commentary*, December 1961:461–73.
Gerson, Mark. *The Neoconservative Vision: From the Cold War to the Culture Wars*.
    Lanham, Md.: Madison Books, 1996.
Gilbert, Martin. *A History of the Twentieth Century*. New York: HarperCollins, 1997–
    99. 3 vols.
Ginsberg, Allen. "I Sing of Norman P." Excerpt from "Sacred Speech," interviewers
    Robert Presson and Rebekah Steward. *Harper's*, July 1988:28.
    "Sacred Speech: A Conversation with Allen Ginsberg," interviewers Robert Presson
    and Rebekah Steward. *New Letters*, Winter 1988:73ff.
Ginsberg, Allen, Václav Havel, and David Carter. *Spontaneous Mind: Selected Inter-
    views, 1958–1996*, edited by David Carter. New York: HarperCollins, 2001.
Ginsberg, Allen, Barry Miles, and Carl Solomon. *Howl: Original Draft Facsimile, Tran-
    script & Variant Versions, Fully Annotated by Author, with Contemporaneous
    Correspondence, Account of First Public Reading, Legal Skirmishes, Precursor
    Texts & Bibliography*, edited by Barry Miles. New York: Harper & Row, 1986.
Ginsberg, Allen and Bill Morgan. *Deliberate Prose: Selected Essays, 1952–1995*, edited
    by Bill Morgan. New York: HarperCollins, 2000.
Glazer, Nathan. "American Values & American Foreign Policy." *Commentary*, July
    1976:32–37.
    "Daniel P. Moynihan on Ethnicity." In *Daniel Patrick Moynihan: The Intellectual
    in Public Life*, edited by Robert A. Katzmann, 15–25. Washington, D.C. and
    Baltimore: Woodrow Wilson Center Press and Johns Hopkins University Press,
    1998.
    "The New Left and Its Limits." *Commentary*, July 1968:31–39.
    "On Being Deradicalized." *Commentary*, October 1970:74–80.
Goldbloom, Maurice J. "The New York School Crisis." *Commentary*, January
    1969:43–58.
Goodheart, Eugene. "The Deradicalized Intellectuals." *Nation*, February 8, 1971:177–
    80.
Goodman, Paul. "Letters from Readers, 'My Negro Problem' – I." *Commentary*, April
    1963:343.
    "Pornography, Art, and Censorship." *Commentary*, March 1961:203–12.
Grenier, Richard. "The Conversion of Susan Sontag." *New Republic*, April 14,
    1982:15–19.
Gross, John. "Books of the Times." Review of *The Bloody Crossroads* by Norman
    Podhoretz. *New York Times*, May 9, 1986:C33.
Grossman, Edward, Hilton Kramer, Michael Novak, and Cynthia Ozick. "Culture and
    the Present Moment." *Commentary*, December 1974:31–50.
Hansberry, Lorraine. "Letters from Readers, 'My Negro Problem' – II." *Commentary*,
    May 1963:430.
Hanson, Victor Davis. "Dispatches from the Front." *Hoover Digest*, Winter 2008:9–24.

"Nothing Succeeds Like Success." *Commentary*, April 2008:19–23.

Hassan, Ihab. Review of *Doings and Undoings* by Norman Podhoretz. *Virginia Quarterly Review*, 40 (Summer 1964): 494.

Hayden, Tom. "The Project Begins (from *Revolution in Mississippi*)." In *Reporting Civil Rights*, Volume 1, 619–26. New York: Library of America, 2003. (Originally published in 1962.)

"Who Are the Student Boat-Rockers?" *Mademoiselle*, August 1961:236–39, 333–37.

Haynes, John Earl, Alexander Vassiliev, and Harvey Klehr. "I. F. Stone, Soviet Agent – Case Closed." *Commentary*, May 2009:40–44.

Heilbrunn, Jacob. *They Knew They Were Right: The Rise of the Neocons*. New York: Doubleday, 2008.

Hertzberg, Hendrik. "Tuesday, and After." *New Yorker*, September 24, 2001:27–28.

Herzog, Chaim. *Living History, a Memoir*. New York: Pantheon Books, 1996.

Himmelfarb, Dan. "Conservative Splits." *Commentary*, May 1988:54–58.

Hitchens, Christopher. "Unmaking Friends." Review of *Ex-Friends* by Norman Podhoretz. *Harper's*, June 1999:73–76.

Hitchens, Christopher and Norman Podhoretz. "An Exchange on Orwell." *Harper's*, February 1983:56–58.

Hodgson, Godfrey. *The Gentleman from New York: Daniel Patrick Moynihan, a Biography*. Boston: Houghton Mifflin, 2000.

Hook, Sidney. *Out of Step: An Unquiet Life in the 20th Century*. New York: Harper & Row, 1987.

Hook, Sidney, H. Stuart Hughes, Hans J. Morgenthau, and C. P. Snow. "Western Values and Total War." *Commentary*, October 1961:277–304.

Horner, Charles. "Hindsight." Review of *The Real War* by Richard M. Nixon. *Commentary*, August 1980:64–65.

Howe, Irving. *Selected Writings, 1950–1990*. San Diego: Harcourt Brace Jovanovich, 1990.

ed. *1984 Revisited: Totalitarianism in Our Century*. New York: Harper & Row, 1983.

Hughes, H. Stuart. "The Strategy of Deterrence." *Commentary*, March 1961:185–92.

Jacobson, Dan. "James Baldwin as Spokesman." *Commentary*, December 1961:497–502.

The Story of the Stories: The Chosen People and Its God. New York: Harper & Row, 1982.

"A White Liberal Trapped by His Prejudices." *Commentary*, May 1953:454–59.

Jeffers, Thomas L. "The Hebrew Prophets, Then and Now." *Yale Review*, 91 (Summer 2003):151–61.

"Norman Podhoretz's Discourses on America." *Hudson Review*, 54 (Summer 2001): 202–28.

"What They Talked About When They Talked About Literature: *Commentary* in Its First Three Decades." In *Commentary in American Life*, edited by Murray Friedman, 99–126. Philadelphia: Temple University Press, 2005.

Johnson, Paul. *A History of the Jews*. New York: Harper & Row, 1987.

Kaplan, Fred. *Gore Vidal: A Biography*. New York: Doubleday, 1999.

Kazin, Alfred. "Saving My Soul at the Plaza." *New York Review of Books*, March 31, 1983. Nybooks.com/articles/6273.

"They Made It! From the Notebooks of a New Yorker." *Dissent*, Fall 1987:612–17.

Keats, John. *Letters of John Keats,* selected and prefaced by Frederick Page. London: Oxford University Press, 1954.

Kempton, Beverly and David Gelman. "Podhoretz on Intellectuals." Interview. *Manhattan Tribune,* February 1, 1969:4–5.

Kermode, Frank. Review of *Doings and Undoings* by Norman Podhoretz. *Book Week,* March 29, 1964:3.

Kernan, Alvin B. *The Death of Literature.* New Haven, Conn.: Yale University Press, 1990.

Kihss, Peter. "Moynihan Scores Ethnic Quota Idea." *New York Times,* June 5, 1968:29.

Kirkpatrick, Jeane J. "Dictatorships and Double Standards." *Commentary,* November 1979:34–45.
  The Reagan Phenomenon, and Other Speeches on Foreign Policy. Washington, D.C.: American Enterprise Institute, 1983.

Klein, Marcus. "A Jittery Outsidedness." Review of *Ex-Friends* by Norman Podhoretz. *New Leader,* December 14–28, 1998:20–22.

Kohn, Moshe. "On Manning the Ramparts." Interview with Norman Podhoretz. *Jerusalem Post,* January 22, 1986:6.

Kozodoy, Neal. "In Memoriam: Lucy S. Dawidowicz." *Commentary,* May 1992:35–40.
  ed. "Proceedings of the Dinner in Honor of Norman Podhoretz Upon the Occasion of His Retirement After Thirty-Five Years as Editor-in-Chief of *Commentary*." New York: Privately published for *Commentary,* 1995.

Kramer, Michael. "The Book Reagan Wants You to Read." *New York,* December 1, 1980:23–26.

Kristol, Irving. "What Choice Is There in Salvador?" *Wall Street Journal,* April 4, 1983:16.

Krupnick, Mark. *Lionel Trilling and the Fate of Cultural Criticism.* Evanston, Ill.: Northwestern University Press, 1986.

Kushner, Tony and Alisa Solomon, eds. *Wrestling with Zion: Progressive Jewish-American Responses to the Israeli-Palestinian Conflict.* New York: Grove Press, 2003.

Laqueur, Walter. "George Lichtheim, 1912–1973." *Commentary,* August 1973:45–52.
  "Kissinger and His Critics." *Commentary,* February 1980:57–61.

Leavis, F. R. "The Orthodoxy of Enlightenment." In *Anna Karenina and Other Essays,* 235–41. New York: Simon & Schuster, 1969. Reprint of "The New Orthodoxy," *Spectator,* February 1961:229–30.

Lehman, David. "Norman Podhoretz at 55: He'd Rather be Right." *Columbia College Today,* Winter 1985:15–18.

Lehmann-Haupt, Christopher. "Theodore Draper, Freelance Historian, is Dead at 93." *New York Times,* February 22, 2006:A17.

Leonard, John. "A Partisan's View." Review of *Ex-Friends* by Norman Podhoretz. *Nation,* March 22, 1999:25–29.

Lewis, Flora. "Offense and Defense." *New York Times,* January 29, 1985:A27.

Linker, Damon. *The Theocons: Secular America Under Siege.* New York: Doubleday, 2006.

Lynd, Staughton. "How the Cold War Began." *Commentary,* November 1960:379–89.

Lynd, Staughton and Irving Howe. "An Exchange on Vietnam." *New York Review of Books,* December 23, 1965. http://www.nybooks.com/articles/12642.

Macdonald, Dwight. *Discriminations: Essays & Afterthoughts, 1938–1974.* New York: Grossman, 1974.

"Scrambled Eggheads on the Right." *Commentary*, April 1956:367–73.

MacKillop, Ian. *F. R. Leavis: A Life in Criticism*. London: Allen Lane (Penguin), 1995.

Magid, Marion. "A Family Feud." Letter to the editors. *New Republic*, April 7, 1982:6.

Mailer, Norman. *The Armies of the Night*. New York: New American Library, 1968. *Existential Errands*. Boston: Little, Brown, 1972.

Manso, Peter. *Mailer, His Life and Times*. New York: Simon & Schuster, 1985.

Martin, Douglas. "Moshe Decter, 85, Advocate for Soviet Jews, Dies." *New York Times*, July 5, 2007:B7.

McCarthy, Mary. "America the Beautiful." *Commentary*, September 1947:201–7.

McCracken, Samuel. "'Julia' and Other Fictions by Lillian Hellman." *Commentary*, June 1984:35–43.

Merkin, Daphne. "Getting Even." Review of *Ex-Friends* by Norman Podhoretz. *New Yorker*, March 22, 1999:166–71.

Miller, Merle. "Why Norman and Jason Aren't Talking." *New York Times Magazine*, March 26, 1972:34–35, 104–11.

Mills, Hilary. *Mailer, a Biography*. New York: Empire Books, Harper & Row, 1982.

Milstein, Tom. "A Perspective on the Panthers." *Commentary*, September 1970:35–43.

Morgenthau, Hans J. "Asia: The American Algeria." *Commentary*, July 1961:43–47.

"Vietnam – Another Korea?" *Commentary*, May 1962:369–74.

Morris, Benny. *The Birth of the Palestinian Refugee Problem Revisited*. Cambridge Middle East Studies. Cambridge: Cambridge University Press, 2004. *Righteous Victims: A History of the Zionist-Arab Conflict, 1881–2001*. New York: Vintage, 2001.

Morris, Willie. *New York Days*. Boston: Little, Brown, 1993.

Moynihan, Daniel P. [and Charles Horner]. "Will Russia Blow Up?" *Newsweek*, November 19, 1979:144, 147.

Moynihan, Daniel P. and Suzanne Weaver. *A Dangerous Place*. Boston: Little, Brown, 1978.

Moynihan Daniel P. "An Address to the Entering Class at Harvard College, 1972." *Commentary*, December 1972:55–60.

"Reds Under the Bed." Letter to the editors. *New Republic*, September 20, 1980:7.

"The United States in Opposition." *Commentary*, March 1975:31–44.

"Was Woodrow Wilson Right?" *Commentary*, May 1974:25–31.

Mudrick, Marvin. *On Culture and Literature*. New York: Horizon Press, 1970.

Muravchik, Joshua. "Patrick J. Buchanan and the Jews." *Commentary*, January 1991:29–37.

Murray, Charles. "Jewish Genius." *Commentary*, April 2007:29–35.

Novak, Michael. "Hammering Steel." Letter to the editors. *New Republic*, September 6, 1980:7.

Nussbaum, Bruce. Review of *The Present Danger* by Norman Podhoretz. *Business Week*, August 18, 1980:14.

O'Brien, Conor Cruise. "Trop de Zèle." Review of *The Bloody Crossroads* by Norman Podhoretz. *New York Review of Books*, October 9, 1986:11–14. http://www.nybooks.com/articles/5011.

Orwell, George, Sonia Orwell, and Ian Angus. *The Collected Essays, Journalism and Letters of George Orwell*, edited by Sonia Orwell. New York: Harcourt Brace Jovanovich, 1968. 4 vols.

Ozick, Cynthia. "'Hypnotized by Totalitarian Poesy.'" Review of *The Bloody Crossroads* by Norman Podhoretz. *New York Times Book Review*, May 18, 1986:11–12.

Pinsker, Sanford. "Revisionism with Rancor: The Threat of the Neoconservative Critics." *Georgia Review*, Summer 1984:243–61.

Plumb, J. H. and Huw P. Wheldon. *Royal Heritage: The Treasures of the British Crown.* New York: Harcourt Brace Jovanovich, 1977.

Podhoretz, Norman. "The Abandonment of Israel." *Commentary*, July 1976:23–31.

"The Adventures of Philip Roth." *Commentary*, October 1998:25–36.

"America and Israel: An Ominous Change." *Commentary*, January 1992:21–25.

"Another Statement on the Peace Process." *Commentary*, June 1993:25–30.

"The Arnoldian Function in American Criticism." Review of *The Liberal Imagination* by Lionel Trilling. *Scrutiny*, 18 (June 1951): 59–65.

"Behind the Smile of Gorbachev." *Geopolitique*, Summer 1989:70–71.

"Bellow at 85, Roth at 67." *Commentary*, July–August 2000:35–43.

"Between Nixon and the New Politics." *Commentary*, September 1972:4–8.

The Bloody Crossroads: Where Literature and Politics Meet. New York: Simon & Schuster, 1986.

Breaking Ranks: A Political Memoir. New York: Harper & Row, 1979.

"Buchanan and the Conservative Crackup." *Commentary*, May 1992:30–34.

"The Carter Stalemate." Op-ed column. *New York Times*, July 9, 1978:E7.

"The Case for Bombing Iran." *Commentary*, June 2007:17–23.

"A Certain Anxiety." *Commentary*, August 1971:4–10.

"Conservative Book Becomes a Best-Seller." Review of *The Closing of the American Mind* by Allan Bloom. *Human Events*, July 11, 1987:5–6.

"Countering Soviet Imperialism." Op-ed column. *New York Times*, May 31, 1978:A23.

"The Dialectic of Blame: Some Reflections on Anti-Americanism." *Encounter*, July–August 1985:6–8.

"Do Not Go Gentle Into the Night." *New York Post*, March 18, 1986.

Doings and Undoings: The Fifties and After in American Writing. New York: Farrar, Straus & Giroux, 1964.

"Editing *Commentary*: A Valedictory." *Commentary*, June 1995:19–20.

"Enter the Peace Party." *Commentary*, January 1991:17–21.

"Eulogy for Gerson Cohen." *Podhoretz Papers*, Library of Congress, 1991.

Ex-Friends: Falling Out with Allen Ginsberg, Lionel & Diana Trilling, Lillian Hellman, Hannah Arendt, and Norman Mailer. New York: Free Press, 1999.

"The Future of America." *Partisan Review*, 51(4)/52(1) (Anniversary Double Issue) (1984):864–68.

"The Hate That Dare Not Speak Its Name." *Commentary*, November 1986:21–32.

"How the Gay-Rights Movement Won." *Commentary*, November 1996:32–41.

"How to Win World War IV." *Commentary*, February 2002:19–29.

"The Idea of Crisis." *Commentary*, November 1970:4.

"In Defense of Editing." *Harper's*, October 1965:143–47.

"In the Matter of Pat Robertson." *Commentary*, August 1995:27–32.

"An Interview with Norman Podhoretz," with Thomas Gross. *The Windmill* (Oxford University-Israel Society) (1987).

"Intifada II: Death of an Illusion?" *Commentary*, December 2000:27–38.

"Is America Falling Apart?" *Quadrant*, December 1973:11–17.

"Israel and the United States: A Complex History." *Commentary*, May 1998:28–43.

"Israel: Bully or Victim?" Speech in New York City, 1988. *Podhoretz Papers*.

"Israel in Danger," interview with David Avidan. *Jerusalem Post* (Independence Day Supplement), April 20, 1977:11–13.

"Israel – with Grandchildren." *Commentary*, December 1995:38–46.

"The Issue." *Commentary*, February 1960:184.

"J'Accuse." *Commentary*, September 1982:21–31.

"Jerusalem: The Scandal of Particularity." *Commentary*, July–August 2007:34–40.

"Kissinger Reconsidered." *Commentary*, June 1982:19–28.

"Laws, Kings, and Cures." *Commentary*, October 1970:30–31.

"Life of His Party." *National Review*, September 13, 1999:49–56.

"The Literary Light as Eternal Flame." *Saturday Review*, August 24, 1974:90–98.

"*Lolita*, My Mother-in-Law, the Marquis de Sade, and Larry Flynt." *Commentary*, April 1997:23–35.

"Looking Back at 'Catch-22.'" *Commentary*, February 2000:32–37.

Making It. New York: Random House, 1967.

"Making the World Safe for Communism." *Commentary*, April 1976:31–41.

"A Masterpiece of American Oratory." *American Spectator*, November 2006:32–39.

My Love Affair with America: The Cautionary Tale of a Cheerful Conservative. New York: Free Press, 2000.

"The Neo-Conservative Anguish Over Reagan's Foreign Policy." *New York Times Magazine*, May 2, 1982:30ff.

"The New Defenders of Capitalism." *Harvard Business Review*, March–April 1981:96 106.

"New Vistas for Neoconservatives." *Conservative Digest*, January–February 1989:56–57.

The Norman Podhoretz Reader: A Selection of His Writings from the 1950s through the 1990s, edited by Thomas L. Jeffers, introduction by Paul Johnson. New York: Free Press, 2004.

"Old-Fashioned Values Are Coming Back." *U.S. News & World Report*, December 24, 1979:58.

"On Reading for Pleasure Again: A Tribute to the Library of America." *Commentary*, December 1992:37–42.

"An Open Letter to Milan Kundera." *Commentary*, October 1984:34–39.

"Oslo: The Peacemongers Return." *Commentary*, October 2001:21–33.

"Our Aims and Israel's." *New York Times*, June 15, 1982:A29.

"The Peace Process So Far." *Commentary*, December 1994:21–25.

Podhoretz Papers, Library of Congress.

"Politics and Culture in Modern America: An Interview with Norman Podhoretz," with Catherine Melchoir. *Issues*, October 1984:7–9.

"Portrait of a Generation." Review of *Our Age* by Noel Annan. *New Criterion*, January 1991:70–72.

"Postscript to 'My Negro Problem – and Ours.'" In *Blacks and Jews: Alliances and Arguments*, edited by Paul Berman, 92–96. New York: Delacourt, 1993.

"Postscript to the Touchstone Edition." In *Why We Were in Vietnam*, 211–19. New York: Simon & Schuster, Touchstone, 1982.

The Present Danger: "Do We Have the Will to Reverse the Decline of American Power?" New York: Simon & Schuster, 1980.

"Rape in Feminist Eyes." *Commentary*, October 1991:29–35.

"A Real Neocon Speaks," interview with Kathryn Jean Lopez. *National Review On-Line*, September 11, 2007.

"Remarks," moderated by William Berkowitz. Dialogue Forum Series [lectures and discussions sponsored by Rabbi Berkowitz in New York City], 1982. Transcript in *Podhoretz Papers*.

"The Return of the 'Jackal Bins.'" *Commentary*, April 2002:29–36.

"Revolutionary Suicide." *Commentary*, September 1970:23.

"The Riddle of Ronald Reagan." *Weekly Standard*, November 9, 1998:22–29.

"Science Hasn't Killed God." *Wall Street Journal*, December 30, 1999:A12.

"'Sexgate,' the Sisterhood, and Mr. Bumble." *Commentary*, June 1998:23–36.

"Speech at Socialist Party USA Convention." *Podhoretz Papers*, 1970.

"The State of World Jewry." *Commentary*, December 1983:37–45. Originated as fourth annual State of World Jewry Address at the 92nd Street Y.

"A Statement on the Peace Process." *Commentary*, April 1993:19–23.

"A Statement on the Persian Gulf Crisis." *Commentary*, November 1990:17–20.

"Strange Bedfellows: A Guide to the New Foreign-Policy Debates." *Commentary*, December 1999:19–31.

"The Subtle Collusion." Transcript of contribution to Jerusalem Conference on International Terrorism, July 2–5, 1979. In *Terrorism and the Media: Abdication of Responsibility*, 22–27. Jerusalem: Jonathan Institute, 1979.

"The Terrible Question of Aleksandr Solzhenitsyn." *Commentary*, February 1985:17–24.

"The Tragic Predicament of Benjamin Netanyahu." *Commentary*, December 1996:30–40.

"A True American Hero [Jeane Kirkpatrick]." *Weekly Standard*, December 18, 2006:12.

"Was Bach Jewish?" *Prospect*, December 1999:21–24.

"What Happened to Ralph Ellison." *Commentary*, July–August 1999:46–58.

"What Is Anti-Semitism? An Open Letter to William F. Buckley, Jr." *Commentary*, February 1992:15–20.

"Who Is Lying About Iraq?" *Commentary*, December 2005:27–33.

Why Are Jews Liberals? New York: Doubleday, 2009.

Why We Were in Vietnam. New York: Simon & Schuster, 1982.

World War IV: The Long Struggle Against Islamofascism. New York: Doubleday, 2007.

"The Worst Effect of Bitburg Visit." *New York Post*, April 23, 1985.

Podhoretz, Norman, Thomas Bergin, and Red Smith. "Sports in America – Larger Than Life." *Yale Reports*, November 26, 1972:1–4.

Podhoretz, Norman and Midge Decter. "Two on an Island," interview with Jan Cherubin. *New York Daily News*, November 20, 1980.

Podhoretz, Norman, et al. "Terrorism and the Media: A Discussion." *Harper's*, October 1984:47–58.

Podhoretz, Norman and Lionel Trilling. *Trilling Papers*. Butler Library, Columbia University.

Poirier, Richard. "Big Pod." Review of *Ex-Friends* by Norman Podhoretz. *London Review of Books*, September 2, 1999:19–23.

Powers, Richard Gid. *Not Without Honor: The History of American Anticommunism*. New Haven, Conn.: Yale University Press, 1998. (Originally published in 1995.)

Raab, Earl. "The Black Revolution and the Jewish Question." *Commentary*, January 1969:23–33.

Raffel, Burton. "Letters from Readers, 'My Negro Problem' – I." *Commentary*, April 1963:346.

Rodden, John. *The Politics of Literary Reputation: The Making and Claiming of "St. George" Orwell*. New York: Oxford University Press, 1989.

Rogan, Eugene L. and Avi Shlaim, eds. *The War for Palestine: Rewriting the History of 1948*. Cambridge: Cambridge University Press, 2001.

Rogers, Byron. "Review of *Sir Huge: The Life of Huw Wheldon*, by Paul Ferris." *London Times* (1990).

Rollyson, Carl E. *The Lives of Norman Mailer: A Biography*. New York: Paragon House, 1991.

Rolph, C. H., ed. *The Trial of Lady Chatterley: Regina v. Penguin Books Limited: The Transcript of the Trial*. New York: Penguin, 1961.

Rosenbaum, Eli M. and William Hoffer. *Betrayal: The Untold Story of the Kurt Waldheim Investigation and Cover-Up*. New York: St. Martin's, 1993.

Rosenfeld, Megan. "Midge Decter and the Crisis of Feminism." *Washington Post*, July 31, 1979:B-1.

Roth, Philip. "Writing American Fiction." In *The Commentary Reader: Two Decades of Articles and Stories*, edited by Norman Podhoretz with an introduction by Alfred Kazin, 595–609. New York: Atheneum, 1966. Reprinted from *Commentary*, March 1961:223–33.

Rothbard, Murray N. "The Evil of Banality." Review of *Breaking Ranks* by Norman Podhoretz. *Inquiry*, December 10, 1979:26–28.

Rubenfeld, Florence. *Clement Greenberg: A Life*. New York: Scribner, 1997.

Schechner, Richard, ed. "*Marat/Sade* Forum." Peter Brook, Geraldine Lust, Leslie Fiedler, Norman Podhoretz. *Tulane Drama Review*, Summer 1966:214–37.

Schlesinger, Jr., Arthur. "Make War Not It." Review of *Why We Were in Vietnam* by Norman Podhoretz. *Harper's*, March 1982:71–73.

Schumacher, Michael. *Dharma Lion: A Critical Biography of Allen Ginsberg*. New York: St. Martin's, 1992.

Service, Robert. *A History of Twentieth Century Russia*. Cambridge, Mass.: Harvard University Press, 1998.

Sheed, Wilfrid. "Making It in the Big City." Review of *Making It* by Norman Podhoretz. *Atlantic Monthly*, April 1968:97–102.

Solotaroff, Ted. *First Loves: A Memoir*. New York: Seven Stories Press, 2003.

"Split in the Family?" *National Review*, December 15, 1970:1334–35.

Steel, Ronald. "The Absent Danger." Review of *The Present Danger* by Norman Podhoretz. *New Republic*, August 16, 1980:19–22.

Steinberg, Stephen. "How Jewish Quotas Began." *Commentary*, September 1971:67–76.

Steinfels, Peter. *The Neoconservatives: The Men Who Are Changing America's Politics*. New York: Simon & Schuster, 1979.

Stone, I. F. "Holy War." *New York Review of Books*, August 3, 1967. http://www.nybooks.com/articles/12009.

Thompson, Denys, ed. *The Leavises: Recollections & Impressions*. Cambridge: Cambridge University Press, 1984.

Tocqueville, Alexis de. *Democracy in America*, translated by Arthur Goldhammer. New York: Library of America, 2004.

Trilling, Diana. "Lionel Trilling: A Jew at Columbia." Appendix to Lionel Trilling, *Speaking of Literature and Society*, edited by Diana Trilling, 411–29. New York:

Harcourt Brace Jovanovich, 1980. Reprinted from *Commentary*, March 1979:40–
46.

Trilling, Lionel. "On the Teaching of Modern Literature." In *Beyond Culture: Essays
on Literature and Learning*, 3–27. New York: Harcourt Brace Jovanovich, 1978.
(Originally published in 1961.)

Tucker, Robert W. "The Middle East: Carterism Without Carter." *Commentary*,
September 1981:27–36.

"Oil: The Issue of American Intervention." *Commentary*, January 1975:21–31.

Twain, Mark. *Collected Tales, Sketches, Speeches & Essays, 1891–1910*. New York:
Library of America, 1992.

Vidal, Gore. "A Cheerful Response." In *United States: Essays, 1952–1992*, 1017–20.
New York: Random House, 1993. Reprint of "The Empire Lovers Strike Back,"
Nation, March 22, 1986:350–53.

"Pink Triangle and Yellow Star." In *United States: Essays, 1952–1992*, 595–611.
New York: Random House, 1993. Reprinted from the *Nation*, November 14,
1981:489–517.

Watson, George. "The Messiah of Modernism: F. R. Leavis (1895–1978)." *Hudson
Review*, 50 (Summer 1997):227–41.

Weatherby, William J. *James Baldwin, Artist on Fire: A Portrait*. New York: D. I. Fine,
1989.

Weigel, George. "KCET's Action: The Antithesis of Freedom." *Los Angeles Times*,
September 17, 1991.

"The New Anti-Catholicism." *Commentary*, July 1992:25–31.

Weltsch, Felix. "The Perennial Spinoza," *Commentary*, May 1956:448–53.

Wenham, Brian. Review of *Sir Huge: The Life of Huw Wheldon*, by Paul Ferris. *Financial Times* (1990).

West, Rebecca. "Oh Why Is Success a Dirty Word?" Review of *Making It* by Norman
Podhoretz. *Sunday Telegraph*, September 1, 1968.

Wheldon, Jacqueline Clarke and Huw Wheldon, *Wheldon Letters*. By permission of
Wynn Wheldon.

Wheldon, Wynn. "Jacqueline Mary Wheldon, 1924–1993." Biographical sketch, 2007
(unpublished).

Wieseltier, Leon. "Washington Diary." *New Republic*, May 27, 1985:43.

Wiesenthal, Simon. *Justice, not Vengeance*, translated from the German by Ewald Osers.
New York: Grove Weidenfeld, 1989.

Will, George F. Review of *Breaking Ranks*, by Norman Podhoretz. *Washington Post*,
October 28, 1979:B7.

Willcox, Christopher. "Why We Still Must Fight." Review of *World War IV* by Norman
Podhoretz. *Wall Street Journal*, September 11, 2007:D6.

Willis, Ellen. "My Podhoretz Problem – and His." Review of *Breaking Ranks* by
Norman Podhoretz. *The Village Voice*, December 3, 1979:1ff.

Wilson, Edmund. *The Sixties: The Last Journal, 1960–1972*, edited and with an introduction by Lewis M. Dabney. New York: Farrar, Straus & Giroux, 1993.

Winchell, Mark Royden. *Neoconservative Criticism: Norman Podhoretz, Kenneth S.
Lynn, and Joseph Epstein*. Boston: Twayne, 1991.

"*Too Good to Be True*": The Life and Work of Leslie Fiedler. Columbia: University
of Missouri Press, 2002.

Winik, Jay. *On the Brink: The Dramatic, Behind-the-Scenes Saga of the Reagan Era
and the Men and Women Who Won the Cold War*. New York: Simon & Schuster,
1996.

Wolfe, Bertram D. "Stalinism Versus Stalin." *Commentary*, June 1956:522–31.

"The Durability of Soviet Despotism." *Commentary*, August 1957:93–104.

Wright, William. *Lillian Hellman: The Image, the Woman*. New York: Simon & Schuster, 1986.

Wrong, Dennis H. "The American Left and Cuba." *Commentary*, February 1962:93–103.

"The Case of the 'New York Review.'" *Commentary*, November 1970:49–63.

Young-Bruehl, Elisabeth. *Hannah Arendt: For Love of the World*. New Haven, Conn.: Yale University Press, 1982.

Zasloff, Joseph J. "The Problem of South Viet Nam." *Commentary*, February 1962:126–35.

Interviews with the Author

Abrams, Elliott. March 7, 2004.

Abrams, Rachel. May 21, 2003.

Bartov, Hanoch. April 22, 2004.

Beichman, Arnold. February 12, 2004.

Decter, Midge. February 2004, April 4 and 11, 2004, May 6, 2005.

Epstein, Joseph. September 17, 2004.

Garment, Leonard. February 8, 2004.

Glazer, Nathan. March 3, 2004.

Gross, John. April 27, 2004.

Hertog, Roger. April 14, 2004.

Hollander, John. May 2004.

Jacobson, Dan. April 26, 2004.

Kass, Leon. June 21, 2004.

Kirkpatrick, Jeane. Janary 20, 2004.

Kozodoy, Neal. May 19, 2005.

Kramer, Hilton. June 14, 2004.

Kristol, Irving. May 19, 2003.

Liebowitz, Ruthie Blum. April 19, 2004.

London, Herb. February 2004.

Munson, Naomi. May 20, 2003.

Neuhaus, Richard. June 2004.

Northam, John. April 30, 2004.

Ozick, Cynthia. June 17, 2004.

Podhoretz, John. April 14, 2004.

Podhoretz, Norman. February 4, 7, April 12–13, 17, June 5, 13–15, July 15–16, October 24, 2004; January 7–9, May 5, 2005.

Rabinowitz, Dorothy. July 15, 2004.

Weigel, George. June 24, 2004.

Wheldon, Wynn. April 26, 2004.

Wilson, James Q. March 21, 2005.

Wisse, Ruth. March 4, 2004.

Index

Note: The abbreviation "NP" stands for Norman Podhoretz.